Immigration Law Library

1989 LEGALIZATION HANDBOOK

How to Obtain Lawful Residence Under the New Immigration Laws

by National Immigration Project of the National Lawyers Guild

Clark Boardman Company, Ltd.

Copyright 1989 by Clark Boardman Company, Ltd.

ISBN 0-87632-648-3

ACKNOWLEDGEMENTS

This revised edition of the Legalization Handbook would not have been possible without the assistance of many of my colleagues and friends whose expertise, time and support were invaluable in completing this book. In particular, I wish to express my grateful appreciation to Rhonda Berkower, who specializes in immigration law in Boston, Massachusetts, and who agreed to undertake the enormous task of researching and writing Chapter Five on Administrative Appeals, and to Dan Kanstroom, who teaches immigration law at Boston College School of Law, and who wrote Chapter Seven on Federal Court litigation and review. I also wish to express a very special thanks to Lory Rosenberg, who wrote major portions of the original text upon which this revised edition is based. Her invaluable ideas, suggestions and comments contributed substantially to the book as a whole.

The thoughtful comments and suggestions of several other immigration practitioners were indispensable in making this book a reality. Among them, special thanks go to Dan Kesselbrenner, Director of the National Immigration Project for his invaluable assistance; Attorney Peggy Gleason, United States Catholic Conference Migration and Refugee Services, and Larry Kleinman, Director of Pineros y Campesinos del Noroeste, who provided many helpful suggestions, comments and assistance.

In addition, I would like to thank law students Jane Kochman and Pam Kennedy, for their research, assistance, and friendship throughout the long process of revising the Handbook. I am especially grateful to Liz Facio, who put in many long hours and hard work in order to prepare the manuscript. Lastly, I would like to thank and dedicate this book to three wonderful people whose patience, understanding and support have enabled me to undertake the mammoth task of revising the Handbook, Adam Zipkin and my parents, Emma and Neil Reinhardt.

Sarah Reinhardt
Albuquerque, New Mexico

PREFACE

The National Immigration Project of the National Lawyer's Guild, Inc., is pleased to present the revised edition of the Legalization Handbook: Stage Two. This volume was developed and written by Project members Sarah Reinhardt, Rhonda Berkower and Dan Kanstroom.

The National Immigration Project is a non-profit organization of lawyers and community workers dedicated to the protection of the rights of the foreign born. Since its inception in 1971, the Project has focused its energies on the development of advocacy and defense skills, providing comprehensive practice manuals, offering substantive and technical skills seminars, and participating in litigation in the area of immigration law. Project members throughout the country provide legal counsel and representation to individuals, unions, congregations, and concerned community groups. The Project provides back-up support for educational and legal efforts, coordinates legal strategies, monitors and comments upon proposed legislation, and participates in litigation in the field.

The two main programs of the Immigration Reform and Control Act (IRCA)--the Legalization program and the Special Agricultural Worker (SAW) program--have officially concluded "Stage One" in which applications for temporary residence were accepted. However, numerous first stage issues are likely to remain with us for years to come as temporary resident applications continue to be adjudicated and denials of temporary resident status are appealed to the LAU or litigated in the courts. Frequent changes in the Stage One regulations and in internal INS procedures and policy guidelines, as well as the invalidation of certain restrictive regulations in the courts, resulted in additional groups of aliens being held eligible for temporary residence as the programs approached their close. Given the fact that many potential applicants had been told that they were ineligible for temporary resident status prior to these substantive changes, various courts have ordered the Immigration Service to accept applications after the programs' statutory filing deadlines had passed. These issues, and INS' challenge to the courts authority to extend a statutory deadline, are discussed in Chapters One and Five. The question of the ability of the courts or of the INS to extend a statutory deadline is expected to recur during Stage Two when aliens who achieve temporary residence after lengthy administrative delays seek to file permanent residence applications after the statutory deadline has passed.

Other problems are presented by the SAW program, which attracted far more applicants than initially expected. Despite its high turnout, only one quarter of all SAW applications had been approved as this book goes to press. Allegations of fraud in the SAW program have been widespread. The manner in which the INS plans to process pending SAW applications is uncertain and may be rendered more chaotic by the apparent eligibility of many pending SAW applicants for the Replenishment Agriculture Worker (RAW) Program. In 1989 the Replenishment Agricultural Worker's Provisions of IRCA will be implemented. If a shortage of agricultural workers is found, proposed regulations indicate that the INS intends to use the RAW program as a means of enabling those who were rejected under the SAW program to legalize their status.

The second stage of the legalization program, well under way as this book goes to press, began with the number of permanent residence applications received by the INS lagging far behind the number of aliens eligible to apply. To avoid a last minute crush, the INS has changed initial processing procedures to allow for the "advance filing" of applications by all temporary residents.

As the second stage unfolds, the "divided families" problem, i.e., where one or more family members did not qualify for temporary resident status, will grow. This problem has not been adequately addressed by the INS or by the Congress. Given the fact that 71% of all legalization applicants were from Mexico, a country whose second preference visa category is backlogged approximately 12 years, the pressure to find a solution will escalate. Various legislative proposals now pending before the Congress provide a partial solution to this problem.

This <u>Handbook</u> attempts to alert practitioners to these and other important issues at the initial application stages for both temporary and permanent residence and at the administrative appeal stage. Each of the various programs affording temporary and/or permanent resident status is dealt with separately in the <u>Handbook</u>, and the individual features, requirements and issues of each are identified and explored in detail. This volume provides both the experienced and the beginning practitioner with an in-depth discussion of the scope and the applicability of the various IRCA programs, including consideration of alternate remedies and benefits. It also provides practical advice on the preparation and filing of applications under the various programs.

Portions of the new second stage materials (included in Chapters 2, 3, and 4) are adapted or reprinted, with the permission of Federal Publications, Inc., from the author's article "Legalization, Second Stage: Adjustment Of Status to Permanent Residence," 9-4 <u>Immigration Briefings</u> (April 1989) which is copyright c by Federal Publications Inc."

TABLE OF CHAPTERS

1. Current Status of the Legalization Programs

2. Legalization: Stage Two--Substantive Requirements

3. Procedures for Applying for Adjustment to Permanent Resident Status

4. Permanent Residence for S.A.W.S Under INA §210

5. Legalization and SAW Appeals

6. Denials of Permanent Residence

7. Federal Court Litigation and Review

8. Termination of Temporary Residence

9. Replenishment Agricultural Workers Program

10. Legalization of Nationals From Countries Granted Extended Voluntary Departure: Poles, Ethiopians, Ugandans, and Afghans

11. Registry

12. Alternative Means of Obtaining Lawful Status

TABLE OF CONTENTS

CHAPTER ONE
CURRENT STATUS OF THE LEGALIZATION PROGRAMS

1.1	INTRODUCTION	1-5
1.2	THE LEGALIZATION PROGRAM, INA §245A	1-5
	1.2(a) Nonimmigrants: Unlawful Status in the United States Prior to January 1, 1982	1-6
	(1) Expiration of Authorized Stay; Duration of Status	1-7
	(2) Unlawful Status Known to the Government	1-8
	(3) Knowledge of Violation of Status by Government Agencies Other than the Immigration and Naturalization Service	1-16
	(4) Exchange Visitors	1-17
	(5) Unlawful Status Due to Fraud or Error in Visa Issuance	1-18
	(6) Other Qualifying Status Designations and Manners of Entry	1-20
	1.2(b) Continuous Unlawful Residence in the United States	1-22
	(1) Order of Deportation	1-24
	(2) Deportation Before January 1, 1982	1-27
	(3) Deportation After November 6, 1986	1-27
	1.2(c) Unlawful Status During Residence	1-28
	1.2(d) Continuous Physical Presence in the United States After May 1, 1987	1-29
	1.2(e) Statutory Bars Applicable to Legalization Applicants	1-31
	(1) In General	1-31
	(2) Misdemeanors and Felonies	1-31
	(3) Assisted in Persecution of Others	1-34
	(4) Selective Service Registration	1-34
	1.2(f) Burden of Proof: The Alien Must Establish Eligibility by a Preponderance of Credible and Verifiable Evidence	1-35
	(1) Preponderance of the Evidence	1-35
	(2) Proof of Identity	1-36
	(3) Proof of Residence and Physical Presence	1-36
	(4) Proof of Financial Responsibility	1-37
	(5) Other	1-38
	1.2(g) The Alien Must File the Application for Temporary Residence on Time	1-39
1.3	THE SPECIAL AGRICULTURAL WORKER (SAW) PROGRAM	1-42
	1.3(a) Ninety Days Employment in Seasonal Agricultural Services	1-43
	1.3(b) Fruits, Vegetables and Other Perishable Commodities	1-43
	(1) In General	1-43
	(2) Horticultural Specialties	1-47
	(i) Seasonal	1-48
	(ii) Critical and Unpredictable Labor Demands	1-48

i

		(3)	Grains	1-49
		(4)	Seed Crops	1-50
	1.3(c)	Field Work		1-51
		(1)	Duties Performed	1-51
		(2)	Location of Work Performed	1-52
		(3)	Nature of Employer's Business	1-53
	1.3(d)	Man-days		1-54
	1.3(e)	Physical Presence In and Entry To the United States		1-54
	1.3(f)	Residence in the United States		1-56
	1.3(g)	Additional Bars to Eligibility		1-57
	1.3(h)	Burden of Proof: Qualifying Employment Proven by a Preponderance of the Evidence		1-58
		(1)	In General	1-58
		(2)	INS' Burden to Disprove Eligibility	1-60
		(3)	Documentary Requirements	1-62
			(i) Proof of Identity	1-62
			(ii) Proof of Employment	1-63
			(iii) Proof of Fiscal Responsibility	1-68
	1.3(i)	Timely Filing of the Application		1-68
	1.3(j)	Overseas Processing		1-69
	1.3(k)	Temporary Admission at Designated Ports of Entry on the Southern Land Border		1-70
1.4	ADMISSIBILITY			1-71
	1.4(a)	Excludability for Criminal Conduct Under INA §§212(a)(9), (a)(10), and (a)(23)		1-71
		(1)	Definition of Conviction	1-74
		(2)	Offense Committed by an Alien Under Age 18	1-75
		(3)	Former Federal First Offender Act	1-76
		(4)	Foreign Convictions	1-77
		(5)	Crime of Moral Turpitude	1-77
		(6)	Petty Offenses	1-78
		(7)	Controlled Substance Offenses	1-79
		(8)	Post-Conviction Relief	1-80
	1.4(b)	Persons Likely to Become Public Charges, INA §212(a)(15)		1-82
		(1)	Determining Likelihood of Becoming a Public Charge	1-82
		(2)	Determining the Alternate Public Charge Inadmissibility Standard	1-86
		(3)	Public Cash Assistance	1-89
		(4)	Recipient of Public Cash Assistance	1-90
1.5	IMMIGRATION REFORM AND CONTROL ACT WAIVERS			1-92
	1.5(a)	Standard for IRCA Waivers		1-92
		(1)	Humanitarian Purposes	1-94
		(2)	Family Unity	1-95
		(3)	Public Interest	1-96
	1.5(b)	Procedures for Applying for a Waiver		1-98

	1.5(c) Waivers Under §212 of the INA	1-99
1.6	CONFIDENTIALITY, FRAUD AND RELATED CRIMINAL PENALTIES	1-105
	1.6(a) Confidentiality	1-105
	1.6(b) Fraud in the Making of a Application for Temporary Residence	1-107

CHAPTER TWO
LEGALIZATION: STAGE TWO--SUBSTANTIVE REQUIREMENTS

2.1	BASIC ELIGIBILITY REQUIREMENTS FOR ADJUSTMENT FROM TEMPORARY RESIDENT TO PERMANENT RESIDENT STATUS UNDER INA §245A	2-3
2.2	TEMPORARY RESIDENT STATUS UNDER INA §245A	2-5
2.3	CONTINUOUS RESIDENCE REQUIREMENT	2-5
2.4	PHYSICAL PRESENCE REQUIREMENT	2-10
2.5	ADMISSIBILITY REQUIREMENT	2-10
	2.5(a) General Requirements	2-10
	2.5(b) Medical and Mental Exclusion Grounds	2-12
	2.5(c) Economic Grounds	2-13
	2.5(d) Immigration and Documentary Grounds	2-15
	2.5(e) Criminal Grounds	2-16
	2.5(f) Other Exclusion Grounds	2-17
	2.5(g) Waivers of Excludability	2-18
2.6	ONE FELONY/3 MISDEMEANOR DISQUALIFICATION	2-20
2.7	BASIC CITIZENSHIP SKILLS REQUIREMENT	2-21
	2.7(a) General Requirements	2-21
	2.7(b) Exceptions	2-21
	2.7(c) Basic Citizenship Skills--The Examination Option	2-22
	(1) INS Examination	2-23
	(2) ETS Examination	2-23
	2.7(d) Basic Citizenship Skills--The Class Attendance Option	2-24
	2.7(e) Rejection of the Certificate of Satisfactory Pursuit	2-26
	2.7(f) Class Sponsorship Requirements	2-27
2.8	THE APPLICATION PERIOD	2-31
	2.8(a) Advance Filing	2-33
	2.8(b) Failure to File the Application on Time	2-34

2.9   DELAYED GRANTS OF TEMPORARY RESIDENT STATUS   2-35

CHAPTER THREE
PROCEDURES FOR APPLYING FOR ADJUSTMENT TO PERMANENT RESIDENT STATUS

3.1   SUMMARY OF SECOND STAGE PROCEDURES   3-3

3.2   THE APPLICATION FORM I-698   3-5
    3.2(a) Who Can Assist the Alien Applicant   3-5
    3.2(b) Completing the Application Form   3-6

3.3   DOCUMENTS SUBMITTED WITH THE APPLICATION   3-9
    3.3(a) Considerations Regarding the Submission of Documents   3-12
    3.3(b) HIV Serologic Test   3-13

3.4   FILING THE APPLICATION   3-14
    3.4(a) Calculating the Application Period   3-14
    3.4(b) Last-Minute Filings   3-15
    3.4(c) Where to File the Application   3-15

3.5   INS PROCESSING OF THE APPLICATION   3-17

3.6   THE INTERVIEW AND DECISION   3-18

3.7   REQUESTS FOR ADDITIONAL INFORMATION   3-21

3.8   POST-ADJUDICATION MATTERS   3-21

CHAPTER FOUR
PERMANENT RESIDENCE FOR S.A.W.S UNDER INA §210

4.1   INTRODUCTION   4-3

4.2   REQUIREMENTS FOR ADJUSTMENT OF STATUS TO PERMANENT
      RESIDENT STATUS UNDER INA §210   4-3
    4.2(a) Maintenance of Status as a Temporary Resident   4-3
    4.2(b) Deportable as Excludable at Entry   4-6

4.3   DATE OF ADJUSTMENT TO PERMANENT RESIDENCE STATUS   4-8

4.4	PROCEDURES FOR ADJUSTMENT TO PERMANENT RESIDENT STATUS		4-9
4.5	OTHER PROVISIONS RELATING TO SECOND STAGE SAWS		4-10
	4.5(a) Numerical Limitations		4-10
	4.5(b) Stay of Deportation and Employment Authorization		4-10
	4.5(c) Administrative and Judicial Review of Denials		4-10
	4.5(d) Permanent Resident Status		4-11

CHAPTER FIVE
LEGALIZATION AND SAW APPEALS

5.1	DENIAL OF TEMPORARY RESIDENCE		5-3
	5.1(a) Denial of the Application		5-3
	5.1(b) Notice of Denial and Right of Appeal		5-4
5.2	POST-DECISION MOTIONS AND CERTIFICATIONS		5-6
5.3	ADMINISTRATIVE APPEALS TO THE LEGALIZATION APPEALS UNIT		5-8
	5.3(a) Procedure and Preparation of the Appeal		5-9
	(1) Reviewing the Record of Proceedings		5-10
	(2) The Notice of Appeal and Appeal Brief		5-11
	5.3(b) Decision by the L.A.U.		5-14
5.4	SUBSTANTIVE AND PROCEDURAL GROUNDS OF APPEAL		5-15
	5.4(a) Grounds of Appeal in INA §245A Denials		5-17
	(1) Denials Based upon Failure to Establish Continuous Residence		5-17
	(A) Insufficient Documentation		5-17
	(B) Continuous Residence Broken by Absences in Excess of 45/180 Days		5-21
	(C) Denials Based upon Departure Caused by Deportation Order		5-25
	(2) Denials Based upon Failure to Establish Continuous Physical Presence		5-30
	(3) Denials Based upon Failure to Establish Unlawful Status		5-31
	(A) Expiration of Authorized Stay; Duration of Status		5-32
	(B) Unlawful Status "Known to the Government"		5-34
	(i) School Report of Violation of Nonimmigrant Status to the INS		5-37
	(C) Unlawful Status Due to Fraud		5-40
	(4) Denials Based upon Public Charge Grounds		5-40
	(5) Denials Based upon Criminal Grounds		5-48
	(A) The Finality of a Conviction		5-49

v

		(B)	The Effect of Post-Conviction Relief	5-51
		(C)	Denials Based upon the Unavailability of INA §212(h) Waivers	5-52
	(6)		Denials Based Upon Untimely Filing of the Application	5-56

5.4(b) Appeal of Denials of SAW Applications under INA §210   5-61
    (1) INS Suspicion of Fraud in SAW Program   5-61
    (2) Denials Based upon Insufficient Evidence or the Lack of Corroborative Documentation of Qualifying Employment   5-63
    (3) Denials Based upon Determination that Applicant did not Perform Ninety Days of Employment in Seasonal Agricultural Services   5-68
        (A) Denials Based upon Determination that Crop was not a Fruit, Vegetable or Other Perishable Commodity   5-68
            (i) Horticultural Specialties   5-72
            (ii) Grains and Seed Crops   5-73
        (B) Denials Based on a Finding that the Applicant did not Engage in Qualifying Field Work   5-75
    (4) Denials Based upon Grounds of Exclusion   5-77
        (A) Denials Based upon Public Charge Grounds   5-78
    (5) Denials Based upon Untimely Filing   5-79

5.5 APPEAL OF DENIAL OF WAIVER OF INELIGIBILITY   5-80

CHAPTER SIX
DENIALS OF PERMANENT RESIDENCE

6.1 APPEALS OF DENIALS OF PERMANENT RESIDENT STATUS   6-3

6.2 APPELLATE PROCEDURES   6-4

CHAPTER SEVEN
FEDERAL COURT LITIGATION AND REVIEW

7.1 DIRECT REVIEW OF ADMINISTRATIVE DENIALS   7-3
    7.1(a) Getting Into Deportation Proceedings   7-3
    7.1(b) Post-Deportation Procedures   7-7
        (1) Applicants with No Outstanding Orders of Deportation   7-7
        (2) Applicants Subject to Final Orders of Deportation   7-8

7.2 STRATEGIES FOR JUDICIAL REVIEW   7-9
    7.2(a) The Bitter With the Sweet?   7-9
    7.2(b) "Collateral" Judicial Review   7-12

CHAPTER EIGHT
TERMINATION OF TEMPORARY RESIDENCE

8.1	GROUNDS FOR TERMINATION OF TEMPORARY RESIDENT STATUS OBTAINED THROUGH THE LEGALIZATION PROGRAM, INA §245A	8-3
	8.1(a) Waiver of Excludability Grounds	8-4
	8.1(b) Procedure for Termination of Temporary Resident Status	8-5
	8.1(c) Effect of Termination of Lawful Temporary Resident Status	8-8
8.2	REVOCATION OF TEMPORARY RESIDENCE - SAWS	8-9
	8.2(a) Grounds for Termination of Temporary Resident Status Obtained through the SAW program, INA §210	8-9
	8.2(b) Grounds of Deportation	8-10

CHAPTER NINE
REPLENISHMENT AGRICULTURAL WORKERS PROGRAM

9.1	GENERAL DESCRIPTION OF THE RAW PROGRAM	9-3
9.2	BASIC ELIGIBILITY REQUIREMENTS	9-4
9.3	PROPOSED PROCEDURES	9-5
9.4	REGISTRATION PHASE	9-7
	9.4(a) Determination of Groups Allowed to Register	9-7
	9.4(b) Prior "Agricultural Employment" Requirement	9-8
	9.4(c) "Seasonal Agricultural Services"	9-10
	9.4(d) Denied and Unadjudicated SAW Applications	9-11
	9.4(e) Agricultural Workers Who Were Not Among the Eligible Rejected SAW Applicants	9-13
	9.4(f) Priority Consideration of Certain Registrants	9-13
	9.4(g) Registration Procedures	9-14
9.5	PETITION PHASE	9-15
9.6	INTERVIEW	9-16
	9.6(a) General Considerations About the Submission of Documents	9-18
	9.6(b) Proof of Identity and Age	9-19
	9.6(c) Evidence of Family Relationship	9-20
	9.6(d) Employment Documentation	9-21
	9.6(e) Admissibility	9-23
9.7	DECISION ON RAW APPLICATION	9-25

9.8	OBLIGATIONS OF TEMPORARY RESIDENTS UNDER THE RAW PROGRAM	9-27
9.9	RIGHTS OF TEMPORARY RESIDENTS UNDER THE RAW PROGRAM	9-29
9.10	PROCEDURE FOR ADJUSTMENT TO PERMANENT RESIDENCE STATUS	9-30
9.11	TERMINATION OF TEMPORARY RESIDENT STATUS AND DEPORTATION UNDER THE RAW PROGRAM	9-31

CHAPTER TEN
LEGALIZATION OF NATIONALS FROM COUNTRIES GRANTED EXTENDED VOLUNTARY DEPARTURE: POLES, ETHIOPIANS, UGANDANS, AND AFGHANS

10.1	BASIC ELIGIBILITY REQUIREMENTS FOR LEGALIZATION OF NATIONALS FROM COUNTRIES GRANTED EXTENDED VOLUNTARY DEPARTURE: POLES, ETHIOPIANS, UGANDANS AND AFGHANS WHO ENTERED THE UNITED STATES BEFORE JULY 21, 1984	10-3
10.2	CONFIDENTIALITY, FRAUD, AND RELATED CRIMINAL PENALTIES	10-5
	10.2(a) Confidentiality	10-5
	10.2(b) Fraud in the Making of an Application for Temporary Residence	10-5
10.3	COUNTRIES GRANTED EXTENDED VOLUNTARY DEPARTURE BETWEEN NOVEMBER 1, 1982 AND NOVEMBER 1, 1987	10-5
10.4	ENTRY INTO THE UNITED STATES BEFORE JULY 21, 1984	10-7
10.5	NONIMMIGRANTS MUST ESTABLISH EXPIRATION OF STAY BEFORE JANUARY 21, 1985 OR APPLICATION FOR ASYLUM BEFORE JULY 21, 1984	10-7
	10.5(a) Manner of Entry into the United States	10-7
	10.5(b) Nonimmigrants-Expiration of Authorized Stay before January 21, 1985; Duration of Status	10-8
	10.5(c) Nonimmigrants--Application for Political Asylum before July 21, 1984	10-9
	10.5(d) Nonimmigrants-Validity of the Nonimmigrant Visa	10-10
	10.5(e) Re-entry after July 21, 1984 on a Nonimmigrant Visa	10-10
	10.5(f) Nonimmigrants--Eligibility of Otherwise Qualifying Exchange Visitors	10-11

10.6	CONTINUOUS RESIDENCE IN THE UNITED STATES SINCE A DATE PRIOR TO JULY 21, 1984	10-11
10.7	CONTINUOUS PHYSICAL PRESENCE IN THE UNITED STATES SINCE DECEMBER 22, 1987	10-12
10.8	ADMISSIBILITY AS AN IMMIGRANT	10-12
	10.8(a) Introduction	10-12
	10.8(b) Excludability	10-13
	(1) Inapplicable Grounds of Excludability	10-13
	(2) Applicable Grounds of Excludability	10-14
	(3) Waivers of Excludability	10-16
10.9	OTHER DISQUALIFYING GROUNDS	10-17
10.10	BURDEN OF PROOF: THE ALIEN MUST ESTABLISH ELIGIBILITY BY A PREPONDERANCE OF CREDIBLE AND VERIFIABLE EVIDENCE	10-17
10.11	DOCUMENTATION	10-18
	10.11(a) Proof of Identity	10-19
	10.11(b) Proof of Nationality	10-19
	10.11(c) Proof of Residence	10-20
	10.11(d) Proof of Financial Responsibility	10-20
10.12	FILING AND PROCESSING THE APPLICATION	10-20
	10.12(a) Filing the Application	10-20
	10.12(b) INS Interview, Employment and Travel Authorization	10-21
10.13	DECISION AND APPEAL PROCESS	10-22
10.14	TERMINATION OF TEMPORARY RESIDENT STATUS	10-25
10.15	ADJUSTMENT FROM TEMPORARY TO PERMANENT RESIDENT STATUS	10-26

CHAPTER ELEVEN
REGISTRY

11.1	BASIC ELIGIBILITY REQUIREMENTS	11-3
11.2	CONTINUOUS RESIDENCE SINCE PRIOR TO JANUARY 1, 1972	11-4
	11.2(a) Date and Manner of Entry	11-5
	11.2(b) Continuous United States Residence Since Entry	11-5

11.3	ADMISSIBILITY	11-7
	11.3(a) Grounds of Excludability Applicable to Registry	11-7
	11.3(b) Waivers of Grounds of Excludability	11-7
11.4	GOOD MORAL CHARACTER	11-9
11.5	NOT INELIGIBLE FOR UNITED STATES CITIZENSHIP	11-11
11.6	DOCUMENTATION	11-11
11.7	PROCEDURE FOR APPLYING FOR REGISTRY	11-12
	11.7(a) Application	11-12
	11.7(b) Adjudication of the Application	11-13

CHAPTER TWELVE
ALTERNATIVE MEANS OF OBTAINING LAWFUL STATUS

12.1	BENEFITS AND RELIEF UNDER THE IMMIGRATION LAWS	12-3
12.2	THE "FAMILY FAIRNESS" PROGRAM	12-3
12.3	LEGAL ALTERNATIVES AVAILABLE UNDER THE INA	12-6
	12.3(a) Registry, INA §249	12-7
	12.3(b) Immediate Relative and Preference Categories, INA §§201-204	12-7
	12.3(c) Political Asylum, INA §208	12-9
	12.3(d) Suspension of Deportation, INA §244	12-10
	12.3(e) Extended Voluntary Departure (by Attorney General/Department of State Designation), INA §244	12-10
	12.3(f) Voluntary Departure, INA §244	12-12
	12.3(g) Derivative or Acquired United States Citizenship, INA §§320, 321, 341	12-12
	12.3(h) Non-Immigrant Visas, INA §214	12-13
	12.3(i) Other Remedies	12-13

EXHIBITS

List of SAW crops	1-104
Sample Denial of Legalization Application	5-85
Sample Appeal Notices	5-87
Freedom of Information Act Appeal	5-91
Regional Processing Facility Addresses	5-94
Issue Bank Ordering Information	5-96
Form I-213	7-17
List of INS forms	Appendix
Legalization Wires and Memoranda	Appendix
List of Civics Questions and Answers	Appendix
Grounds of Exclusion Chart	Appendix

COMMON ABBREVIATIONS

AFDC	Aid to Families with Dependant Children
AILA	Americal Immigration Lawyers Association
AAU	Administrative Appeals Unit
BIA	Board of Immigration Appeals
CSP	Certificate of Satisfactory Pursuit
CPF	Central Processing Facility
ETS	Educational Testing Service
ESL	English as a Second Language
EOIR	Executive Office for Immigration Review
EVD	Extended Voluntary Departure
FOIA	Freedom of Information Act
FAM	Foreign Affairs Manual
GR	General Relief
GA	General Assistance
HIV	Human Immunodeficiency Virus
HRC	Haitian Refugee Center
IJ	Immigration Judge
INA	Immigration and Nationality Act
INS	Immigration and Naturalization Service
IRCA	Immigration Reform and Control Act
JRAD	Judicial Recommendation Against Deportation
LAU	Legalization Appeals Unit
LULAC	League of United Latin American Citizens
LO	Legalization Office
NALEO	National Association of Latino Elected Officials
NCA	National Coordinating Agencies
OI	Operations Instructions
OSC	Order to Show Cause
QDE	Qualified Designated Entity
RAW	Replenishment Agricultural Worker
ROP	Record of Proceedings
RPF	Regional Processing Facility
SAW	Seasonal Agricultural Worker
SLIAG	State Legalization Impact Assistance Grant
SSA	Social Security Administration
SSI	Supplemental Security Income
TESL	Teachers of English as a Second Language
WIC	Women, Infants, and Children

CHAPTER ONE

CURRENT STATUS OF THE LEGALIZATION PROGRAMS

1.1	INTRODUCTION	1-5
1.2	THE LEGALIZATION PROGRAM, INA §245A	1-5
1.2(a)	Nonimmigrants: Unlawful Status in the United States Prior to January 1, 1982	1-6
(1)	Expiration of Authorized Stay; Duration of Status	1-7
(2)	Unlawful Status Known to the Government	1-8
(3)	Knowledge of Violation of Status by Government Agencies Other than the Immigration and Naturalization Service	1-16
(4)	Exchange Visitors	1-17
(5)	Unlawful Status Due to Fraud or Error in Visa Issuance	1-18
(6)	Other Qualifying Status Designations and Manners of Entry	1-20
1.2(b)	Continuous Unlawful Residence in the United States	1-22
(1)	Order of Deportation	1-24
(2)	Deportation Before January 1, 1982	1-27
(3)	Deportation After November 6, 1986	1-27
1.2(c)	Unlawful Status During Residence	1-28
1.2(d)	Continuous Physical Presence in the United States After May 1, 1987	1-29
1.2(e)	Statutory Bars Applicable to Legalization Applicants	1-31
(1)	In General	1-31
(2)	Misdemeanors and Felonies	1-31
(3)	Assisted in Persecution of Others	1-34
(4)	Selective Service Registration	1-34
1.2(f)	Burden of Proof: The Alien Must Establish Eligibility by a Preponderance of Credible and Verifiable Evidence	1-35
(1)	Preponderance of the Evidence	1-35
(2)	Proof of Identity	1-36
(3)	Proof of Residence and Physical Presence	1-36
(4)	Proof of Financial Responsibility	1-37
(5)	Other	1-38
1.2(g)	The Alien Must File the Application for Temporary Residence on Time	1-39
1.3	THE SPECIAL AGRICULTURAL WORKER (SAW) PROGRAM	1-42
1.3(a)	Ninety Days Employment in Seasonal Agricultural Services	1-43
1.3(b)	Fruits, Vegetables and Other Perishable Commodities	1-43

(1)	In General	1-43
(2)	Horticultural Specialties	1-47
(i)	Seasonal	1-48
(ii)	Critical and Unpredictable Labor Demands	1-48
(3)	Grains	1-49
(4)	Seed Crops	1-50
1.3(c)	Field Work	1-51
(1)	Duties Performed	1-51
(2)	Location of Work Performed	1-52
(3)	Nature of Employer's Business	1-53
1.3(d)	Man-days	1-54
1.3(e)	Physical Presence In and Entry To the United States	1-54
1.3(f)	Residence in the United States	1-56
1.3(g)	Additional Bars to Eligibility	1-57
1.3(h)	Burden of Proof: Qualifying Employment Proven by a Preponderance of the Evidence	1-58
(1)	In General	1-58
(2)	INS' Burden to Disprove Eligibility	1-60
(3)	Documentary Requirements	1-62
(i)	Proof of Identity	1-62
(ii)	Proof of Employment	1-63
(iii)	Proof of Fiscal Responsibility	1-68
1.3(i)	Timely Filing of the Application	1-68
1.3(j)	Overseas Processing	1-69
1.3(k)	Temporary Admission at Designated Ports of Entry on the Southern Land Border	1-70
1.4 ADMISSIBILITY		1-71
(a)	Excludability for Criminal Conduct Under INA §§212(a)(9) or (a)(10), and (a)(23)	1-71
(1)	Definition of Conviction	1-74
(2)	Offense Committed by an Alien Under Age 18	1-75
(3)	Former Federal First Offender Act	1-76
(4)	Foreign Convictions	1-77
(5)	Crime of Moral Turpitude	1-77
(6)	Petty Offenses	1-78
(7)	Controlled Substance Offenses	1-79
(8)	Post-Conviction Relief	1-80
(b)	Persons Likely to Become Public Charges, INA §212(a)(15)	1-82
(1)	Determining Likelihood of Becoming a Public Charge	1-82
(2)	Determining the Alternate Public Charge Inadmissibility Standard	1-86
(3)	Public Cash Assistance	1-89
(4)	Recipient of Public Cash Assistance	1-90
1.5 IMMIGRATION REFORM AND CONTROL ACT WAIVERS		1-92
1.5(a)	Standard for IRCA Waivers	1-92

(1)	Humanitarian Purposes	1-94
(2)	Family Unity	1-95
(3)	Public Interest	1-96
1.5(b)	Procedures for Applying for a Waiver	1-98
1.5(c)	Waivers Under §212 of the INA	1-99
1.6	CONFIDENTIALITY, FRAUD AND RELATED CRIMINAL PENALTIES	1-105
1.6(a)	Confidentiality	1-105
1.6(b)	Fraud in the Making of a Application for Temporary Residence	1-107

CHAPTER ONE

CURRENT STATUS OF THE LEGALIZATION PROGRAMS

1.1 INTRODUCTION

The first stage of the legalization and seasonal agricultural worker (SAW) programs created by the Immigration Reform and Control Act of 1986, has come to a conclusion. The litigation challenging INS' interpretations and regulations implementing these programs, however, continues. Throughout the course of both programs, frequent regulatory, policy, and court-ordered changes affected the fates of many applicants and would-be applicants for legal status. Because substantive requirements were changed midway or late in the programs, various courts have ordered extensions of the application period, a fact which has lead to additional controversy.[1] This chapter will attempt to summarize the developments in the law regarding both programs, focusing on the most recent changes and issues, as well as address stage one issues which have yet to be resolved. Chapter Five discusses many of these same issues in the context of administrative appeals of denials under the legalization and SAW programs.

One noteworthy characteristic of both programs has been the INS' long-term reliance on "interim regulations and on numerous internal memoranda interpreting substantive provisions. While it is true that IRCA authorized promulgation of "interim final" regulations in order to implement the legalization program in a timely manner[2] (there is no comparable "interim rule" authority under the SAW or RAW provisions), such determination of basic substantive rights would appear to be vulnerable to attack for violation of the notice and comment rulemaking procedures of the Administrative Procedure Act.[3]

1.2 THE LEGALIZATION PROGRAM, INA §245A

The basic eligibility requirements for the legalization program contained in the statute and regulations can be summarized as follows:

---

[1] See §1.2(g), infra.

[2] INA §245A(g)(3).

[3] 5 U.S.C. §551.

1. Unlawful or other qualifying status as of a date prior to January 1, 1982.[4]

2. Continuous residence in the United States in an unlawful status (or other qualifying status) from the pre-1982 date when unlawful status arose to the date the legalization application is submitted; certain brief and casual departures not disqualifying.[5] Unlawful status may be due to the manner of entry (e.g., without a valid visa) or due to events which occurred after entry (e.g., expiration of authorized stay or a violation of the terms of the visa which is "known to the government").[6]

3. Continuous physical presence in the United States between May 1, 1987 and the date application for temporary residence is submitted; brief, casual and innocent departures or absences authorized by the INS not disqualifying.[7]

4. Not inadmissible under certain of the grounds of excludability set forth at INA §212(a).[8]

5. Not ineligible under any one of three special statutory bars: 3 misdemeanors or 1 felony; persecution of others; failure to register for the Selective Service, if required.[9]

6. Application within time period provided, May 4, 1987 through May 4, 1988; and within 30 days of issuance of an Order to Show Cause; or pursuant to court-ordered extensions of these deadlines.[10]

1.2(a) Nonimmigrants: Unlawful Status in the United States Prior to January 1, 1982

Much of the litigation involving the legalization program has arisen due to restrictive requirements pertaining to nonimmigrants.

---

[4] INA §245A(a)(2)(A).

[5] INA §§245A(a)(2)(A), (B); 245A(g).

[6] INA §245A(a)(2)(B).

[7] INA §245A(a)(3).

[8] INA §§245A(a)(4), (d).

[9] INA §245A(a)(4).

[10] INA §245A(a)(1)(A), (B); court-ordered extensions are discussed in §1.2(g), infra.

Nonimmigrants, like all other applicants, must demonstrate that they entered or were in the United States in an unlawful status, or other qualifying status, as of any date prior to January 1, 1982. However, nonimmigrants, unlike all other entrants, must also prove that their unlawful status was known to the Government before January 1, 1982.

The implementing regulations often applied a very narrow interpretation of the statutory terms. In this context, issues involving the validity of the nonimmigrant visa, continuous residence, "known to the government," and re-entry to the United States on a nonimmigrant visa, have been resolved in favor of nonimmigrant applicants for temporary resident status.

1.2(a)(1) Expiration of Authorized Stay; Duration of Status

Nonimmigrants whose fixed departure date expired before January 1, 1982 clearly qualify under the regulations.[11] However, questions arise as to those nonimmigrants admitted to the United States for "Duration of Status" (A, G, F or J visas,).[12] They were admitted, not until a fixed date, but for as long as they maintained their status. There are two situations in which nonimmigrants admitted for duration of status can automatically satisfy the "unlawful status" requirement for legalization:

1. In the case of a alien admitted on an F, F-1, or F-2 student visa who prior to January 1, 1982 completes a full course of study, including practical training and time allowed to depart (if any), lawful status is deemed to have expired through the passage of time.[13] In 1981 there was no provision in the regulation adding 30 days after the completion of the course of study.

2. Those nonimmigrants who were admitted on "A, A-1, A-2, G, G-1, G-2, G-3 or G-4" visas for duration of status ("D/S"), attained unlawful status when their qualifying employment terminated or when

---

[11] 8 CFR §245a.2(b)(2).

[12] Their I-94 forms will have been endorsed "Duration of Status" or "D/S."

[13] Interim rule 8 CFR §245a.2(b)(12), 52 Fed. Reg. 43845 (1987); additional information can be found in Legalization Wire #26 dated July 14, 1987, which preceded publication of the interim rule.

they ceased to be recognized by the Department of State as being entitled to such classification.[14]

Effective February 23, 1981, all "duration of status" student admissions were automatically converted to a date certain, i.e., the date certified on the I-20 form as the date of expected graduation.[15] If the I-20 indicated an expected graduation date before January 1, 1982, than (barring the grant of an extension), the student's authorized stay expired through the passage of time.

In addition, nonimmigrants admitted for duration of status have been found to have ended their unlawful status "through the passage of time" by engaging in unlawful employment or otherwise violating the terms of their stay.[16]

1.2(a)(2) Unlawful Status Known to the Government

A nonimmigrant who violated the conditions of his or her nonimmigrant status, whose violation of status was "known to the Government" prior to January 1, 1982, is eligible for legalization under INA §245A(a)(2)(B). A nonimmigrant may violate that status by failing to comply with the conditions or requirements applicable to maintaining that status or by otherwise engaging in conduct in violation of that status. Common violations of status applicable to various nonimmigrant visa categories include:

(a) employment without having obtained the prior permission of the Immigration and Naturalization Service and any employment in those nonimmigrant categories in which aliens are not allowed to work under any circumstances;[17]

(b) employment other than that authorized by approval of particular nonimmigrant visa petition and/or grant of nonimmigrant status;[18]

---

[14] Interim rule 8 CFR §245a.2(b)(11), 52 Fed. Reg. 43845 (1987); see also Legalization Wire #36, dated August 25, 1987.

[15] See 8 CFR §214.2(f)(5)(iii).

[16] See Immigrant Assistance Project v. INS, ___F. Supp.___ (W.D. Wash. 1989).

[17] 8 CFR §§214.1 and 214.2.

[18] Id; note that some employment is permitted incident to student status and will not be deemed to violate that status. See 8 CFR §§214.2(f)(9) and (10); see also Legalization Wire #26, dated July 14, 1987.

(c) (students) school transfer without following the procedures prescribed by the Immigration and Naturalization Service;[19]

(d) (students) failure to pursue a full course of study;[20]

(e) willful failure to provide full and truthful information requested by the INS (whether or not requested information is material);[21]

(f) conviction in any United States jurisdiction of a crime of violence for which a sentence of more than one year may be imposed.[22]

(g) failure to file quarterly or annual alien address reports.[23]

(h) failure to maintain validity of passport 6 months beyond period of stay.[24]

Citations to the above provisions refer to current regulations. However to assess whether a violation of status existed prior to January 1, 1982, it is important to know the exact language of the pertinent regulations in effect throughout the nonimmigrant's stay prior to January 1, 1982.

---

[19] 8 CFR §§214.2(f)(8). Matter of Yazdani, 17 I&N Dec. 626 (BIA 1981); Shoja v. INS, 679 F.2d 447 (5th Cir. 1982). According to a letter from Assistant Commissioner for Legalization William S. Slattery, students who transfer schools without permission are not considered to have completed their studies under 8 CFR §245a.2(b)(12), see 65 Interpreter Releases, 6 (January 4, 1988); but see, Immigrant Assistance Project v. INS, supra, which held that such transfers create a rebuttable presumption of knowledge on INS' part.

[20] 8 CFR §214.2(f)(6). Those who completed a full course of study before January 1, 1982 may be eligible under interim rule 8 CFR §245a.2(b)(12). See the discussion in §1.2(a)(1) above.

[21] 8 CFR §214.1(f).

[22] 8 CFR §214.1(g).

[23] INA §§265, 266; 8 CFR §265.1 (1981). See Immigrant Assistance Project v. INS, supra. See also Klissas v. INS, 361 F.2d 529 (D.C. Circ. 1966); Caiozzo v. District Director, 158 F. Supp. 872 (S.D.N.Y. 1958); Matter of B-, 5 I&N Dec. 692 (BIA 1954).

[24] INA §212(a)(26), 8 CFR §214.2(f)(2)(1979). See Matter of Kazemi, Int. Dec. #2961 (BIA 1984).

Nonimmigrants must show that their unlawful status was "known to the Government" prior to January 1, 1982. Exceptions to this requirement include F-1 students who completed their course of study before January 1, 1982; certain "A" and "G" visa holders who were admitted for duration of status (as noted in §1.2(a)(1), supra); and those who applied for political asylum prior to January 1, 1982.[25]

Regulations promulgated by the INS defined the terms "known" and "Government" narrowly. Pursuant to 8 CFR §245a.1(d), the term "government" was equated with the "Immigration and Naturalization Service" alone; thus requiring that the alien prove that the INS knew of his or her violation of status before 1982 in order for the alien to meet the "known to the Government" requirement. The INS' restrictive definition of "known to the government," limiting those terms to "the INS" was struck down in Farzad v. Chandler.[26] In Farzad, the District Court for the Northern District of Texas held that the regulation limiting the term "government" to the INS was inconsistent with IRCA.

> Except in this section, Congress refers specifically to the Attorney General and INS throughout the Reform Act; here, by contrast, it consciously chose to use the term "the Government." In this court's view, Congress must have intended "the Government" to be a broader term than "the Attorney General" or "the INS." Accordingly, the INS' interpretation is impermissibly narrow...The court is of the opinion that Congress intended the phrase "the Government" to be broader than merely the INS, and at least broad enough to include the Internal Revenue Service and the Social Security Administration.[27]

In the Farzad decision, Social Security and Internal Revenue Service records were found to be sufficient to show that federal agencies (other than the INS) knew of the aliens employment in violation of status, thus satisfying IRCA's "known to the Government" requirement. Subsequently, in Ayuda, Inc. v. Thornburgh, the court articulated the standard as requiring that the alien show that before January 1, 1982, documentation existed in the files of any government agency which taken as a whole would warrant the finding that the nonimmigrant alien's status in the

---

[25] Interim rule 8 CFR 245a.2(b)(14), 52 Fed. Reg. 43845 (1987); see also Legalization Wire #35, dated August 24, 1987.

[26] Farzad v. Chandler, 670 F. Supp. 690 (N.D. Texas 1987) [hereinafter Farzad], discussed in section 2.3(c)(3)(F) below. See also Kalaw v. Ferro, 651 F. Supp. 1163 (W.D.N.Y.1987); Ayuda, Inc. v. Thornburgh, 687 F. Supp. 650 (D.D.C. 1988).

[27] Farzad at 694. See also Kalaw v. Ferro, supra.

United States was unlawful.[28] The INS did not appeal this portion of the court's ruling.[29]

Despite these rulings, the LAU has affirmed denials of temporary residence in 5 cases involving aliens on "A" and "G" visas who claimed eligibility based on their unauthorized employment before 1982.[30] In Immigrant Assistance Project v. INS, __F. Supp.___, (W.D. Wash., 1989), the court held that there is no rational bases for the LAU's distinguishing among the proof required of different nonimmigrants.

Although the courts in Farzad and Ayuda expanded the scope of the terms "known to the government" to encompass federal agencies than the INS, proof of unlawful status is most likely to exist only as to a handful of agencies [discussed in §1.2(a)(3) below]. The applicant who attempts to prove that INS itself directly knew of the unlawful status faces a number of evidentiary problems, as the regulations also restricted the scope of circumstances, procedures, records, or notices which it will consider as constituting its knowledge of an alien's unlawful status, i.e.,

(a) the alien must have made a clear statement or declaration of unlawful status to another federal agency, this declaration was reported to INS, and such information was recorded by INS in the alien's "A" file; or

(b) INS made an affirmative determination that the alien was subject to deportation proceedings; this must be proven by presentation of INS documents (e.g., I-94, I-210, I-221, I-541, I-213, I-205, I-265, etc.); or

(c) INS advised any other agency that a particular alien had no legal status or INS record; this must be proven by presentation of a copy of INS' notice to the other agency; or

(d) the applicant produces documentation that the school attended forwarded to the INS a report clearly indicating that the student violated student status, and the applicant was not subsequently reinstated to student status.[31]

---

[28] 687 F. Supp. 650 (D.D.C. 1988).

[29] Reported in 65 Interpreter Releases 590 (June 6, 1988).

[30] Reported in 66 Interpreter Releases 65-66 (January 13, 1989).

[31] 8 CFR §§245a.1(d)(1), (2), and (3); and interim rule 8 CFR §245a.1(d)(4), 52 Fed. Reg. 43845 (1987).

To these must be added the following consideration: evidence of notification of unlawful status may be acceptable even if INS was informed by the school after January 1, 1982;[32] two courts have held that once an alien has fallen out of status, subsequent action by the INS in granting permission to change schools or status does not return the alien to a lawful status;[33] in addition to presenting the above proof of actual knowledge by the INS, the alien may be able to prove presumptive knowledge by the INS.[34]

Each of the above four means of satisfying the "known to the government" presents enormous proof problems, among them the fact that

> [t]he vast majority of nonimmigrants do not have an official file with the INS unless and until they are somehow determined to have been in violation of their status...INS does not record how or when it initially learned of...a violation of status. Without such record keeping, INS would make it impossible, through its own practices, for an applicant to meet the burden required by its interpretation of the Act.[35]

Of the above four means of establishing that the INS itself "knew" of a violation, notification sent by school officials of the alien's violation of status is the only one which nonimmigrants might conceivably be able to satisfy. Obvious proof problems caused by schools' and the INS' destruction of records after several years have been mitigated by recent LAU decisions in which the declaration of the foreign student advisor, that he routinely reported foreign students in violation of status to the INS, was accepted as adequate proof that INS was notified.[36]

---

[32] See Leap Lines, Newsletter of the LEAP Immigration Project, Issue #14, December 15, 1987, reporting on informal comments by Associate INS Commissioner Richard Norton following announcement of the interim rule.

[33] CIPRA v. Meese, Civ. No. 88-1088 (D.D.C. 1988); Immigrant Assistance Project v. INS, ___F. Supp.____(W.D. Wash. 1988).

[34] See the discussion of Immigrant Assistance Project v. INS, infra.

[35] Farzad at 694.

[36] See LAU decision dated April 12, 1988 (available from the American Immigration Lawyer's Association's Legalization Appeals Project, LAU Decisions Digest order #L0788-249. Ordering information appears at the end of Chapter Five); LAU decision dated November 12, 1988 (LAU Decisions Digest order #L0288-080). But see LAU decision dated February 8, 1988 (LAU Decisions Digest order

Other examples of documentation which might be presented under this regulation are:

(i) <u>Student Advisor Reports (Form I-20B)</u>. Foreign student advisors are mandated by regulation to file regular reports with the Immigration and Naturalization Service listing those foreign students who failed to attend classes on a full-time basis.[37] Failure to file such reports can result in loss of INS' approval of the school for attendance by foreign students.[38] The names of students who stopped attending classes, who enrolled in classes for less than 12 credit hours, and who transferred schools without permission, should appear on these reports. Copies should be sought directly from the INS (through a FOIA request), as well as from the Foreign Student Advisor's office of the school in question.

(ii) <u>Statement of the Foreign Student Advisor</u>. If copies of the reports submitted to the INS are unavailable, the applicant should submit a statement from the foreign advisor that the school complies with federal regulations and reports non-fulltime foreign students to the INS as required, and/or that the school has never lost its INS approval for attendance by foreign students by reason of failure to file such reports. This should be accompanied by the applicant's transcript indicating failure to attend classes fulltime before 1982.[39]

(iii) <u>Regulations Governing Foreign Students, Foreign Student Advisors, and the Immigration and Naturalization Service</u>. Under regulations in effect prior to 1982 and up to now, there are many mechanisms in place which assure that the INS knew of a foreign student's failure to attend classes fulltime. Requiring foreign students to independently prove INS' knowledge of their failure to attend classes fulltime can only be grounded on the premise that foreign student advisors and INS employees were not, at least prior to 1982, abiding by <u>mandatory</u> regulations to report violations of status to the INS.[40] In <u>Immigrants Assistance Project v. INS</u>, the

---

#L0488-169); LAU decision dated March 11, 1988 (LAU Decisions Digest order #L0688-184), reported in 65 Interpreter Releases 636 (June 27, 1988).

[37] 8 CFR §214.3(g); Operations Instructions 212.2f.

[38] 8 CFR §214.4.

[39] <u>See Matter of ---</u>, (LAU June 6, 1988) (AILA reprint no. 81-118).

[40] <u>See</u>, e.g., 8 CFR §214.3(g) (1981); 8 CFR §214.3(h) (1980 and 1981); 8 CFR §214.4(a) (1980 and 1981).

court held that there is a presumption that school officials discharged their duties as mandated by the regulations. Accordingly, presentation of proof that the student failed to attend school fulltime as of a date prior to January 1, 1982, together with a copy of the regulations in effect on the date the student failed to attend school fulltime, gives rise to the presumption that this violation of student status was reported by the school to the Immigration and Naturalization Service; the applicant has satisfied his or her burden and has established a _prima facie_ case of eligibility for legalization under INA §245A. As with all _prima facie_ cases, the INS may produce evidence from its files which rebuts this presumption, such as proof that the particular school in question lost its approved status for failure to make regular reports to the INS, or proof that the applicant was enrolled as a graduate student and therefore, though enrolled in less than 12 semester hours of classes, was nonetheless considered to be a "fulltime" student, or by producing the actual report in question lacking the applicant's name. This issue is further explored in Chapter Five of this book, at §5.4(a)(3)(B)(i).

In _Immigrant Assistant Project v. INS_[41] the court also held that failure to file quarterly and yearly address reports constitutes an unlawful status that is known to the government for purposes of legalization eligibility.

There are many other instances in which the INS may have had actual knowledge of an alien's violation of his or her status, although it may have taken no official action in response nor created a file or record thereof. Such cases do not squarely fit within any of the above regulatory definitions of "known to the government," but nonetheless some investigatory work might yield documents which constitute undeniable proof that the INS knew or should have known of an alien's unlawful status.

The statute itself makes no mention of "determinations of deportability" or notations in alien files as required by the regulations. In some cases, it will be quite obvious that the INS had actual knowledge of an alien's violation of status. INS' inactivity could arguably be interpreted to mean that a "determination of deportability" was made _or could have been made_, even though the INS declined to act in the exercise of its prosecutorial discretion, thus bringing the applicant within the definition set by regulation. Moreover, it can be argued that evidence of _actual_ knowledge should satisfy the statutory standard without need to impute to INS a "determination of deportability."

Examples of situations in which the INS may have had actual knowledge of a violation of nonimmigrant status are:

---

[41] _Supra_.

(i) <u>Visa Petitions Filed Before January 1, 1982</u>. An application for extension of nonimmigrant stay or its supporting documents may on its face indicate violation of nonimmigrant status. An I-130 or I-140 visa petition may have been filed on behalf of an alien with the INS; these forms request information regarding the visa, if any, used by the alien for entry, the alien's status, and when and where the alien has been employed in the U.S., thus alerting the INS to a nonimmigrant's violation of status.[42]

(ii) <u>Iranian Reporting Requirement</u>. All Iranian students then admitted to the United States as F-1 students were required by regulation, <u>as a condition of maintenance of status</u>, to report to INS before December 19, 1979. Failure of an Iranian student to report as required arguably put the INS on notice of those students' unlawful status.[43]

(iii) <u>Employer's Records</u>. The Immigration and Naturalization Service has had a long-standing program pursuant to which the personnel records of cooperating employers are reviewed by the Service in order to locate aliens who are in the United States unlawfully or who are working without authorization. By comparing the name and birthdate information from an employee's record with data on the INS's MIRAC computer system, the Service knows of nonimmigrants who have violated status by working without INS authorization. If an alien worked for an employer contacted by INS, the INS arguably knew or should have known of the alien's violation of status.

(iv) <u>Reports</u>. The Immigration and Naturalization Service receives reports of aliens suspected of having violated the immigration laws from many other quarters, including anonymous callers, local and state law enforcement agencies, the Social Security Administration, other federal and state agencies administering public assistance and unemployment compensation programs, Assistant United States Attorneys, the Internal Revenue Service, the United States Passport Office, private individuals,

---

[42] In some cases the alien's pre-1982 interactions with INS should have suggested to them a failure to comply with the conditions of admission as a nonimmigrant. One such circumstance might be the filing with the INS of an I-130 visa petition or I-485 adjustment of status application prior to January 1, 1982. This normally indicated that the alien no longer maintained the intention of remaining in the U.S. only temporarily and departing to a permanent residence abroad.

[43] 8 CFR §214.5(a) (1979); <u>see</u> Matter of --- (LAU, August 6, 1988) (AILA reprint no. 102-1288).

and others.[44] Such reports, if available, often list the names of specific individuals suspected of being or working in the United States in violation of law. Investigations may or may not have been commenced by INS in response to such reports.

(v) _Foreign Student Advisors_. Some practitioners have raised the question of whether a foreign student advisor's knowledge of a violation of status can be attributed to the INS under general principles of agency law. The powers of foreign student advisors have steadily increased over the years and they may arguably be deemed to be agents of the INS in the exercise of their mandatory duties.

1.2(a)(3) Knowledge of Violation of Status by Government Agencies Other than the Immigration and Naturalization Service

While proof of any of the above will be sufficient to show that unlawful status was "known to the government" within the regulations, the proof required to show that unlawful status was known to agencies other than the INS may be more quickly or easily obtained. Agencies other than the INS which may possess evidence of an alien's violation of status include:

(i) _Social Security Administration_ The applicant's possession of W-2 forms, or the appearance of earnings on the SSA's Statement of Earnings, are proof that the SSA was aware of unauthorized employment.[45]

(ii) _Internal Revenue Service_ The alien who files a tax return under his or her own name and number thereby advises the IRS of his or her unlawful employment.[46]

The fact that an alien filed income tax returns using a Social Security number which belongs to another person, is unassigned, or

---

[44] For example, 8 CFR §214.2(f)(9)(v) automatically suspends employment authorization of a nonimmigrant student upon certification by the Secretary of Labor or his designee to the INS Commissioner of a strike or labor dispute at the place of authorized employment. See also Social Security Administration reporting requirements, discussed in §1.2(a)(3), infra, and the discussion of foreign student advisor reporting requirements, supra.

[45] In Farzad, the applicant presented an SSA statement of earnings and an IRS certification of tax returns filed for years preceding 1982.

[46] See Farzad at 694.

is different from that used in a previous year, will come to the IRS' attention when they cross check the numbers on tax returns with information from the Social Security Administration.

(iii) **The Filing of an Alien Labor Certification** Alien Labor Certification forms are filed with state labor departments and forwarded to the U.S. Department of Labor. More often than not, these forms will indicate the alien's visa status in the United States and that the alien is working in violation of that status. This will be of importance only in the cases of those nonimmigrants who were denied labor certification or who did not pursue their cases after filing, as all cases filed before 1982 will have been issued immigrant visas by now through the normal procedures.

Under the standard articulated in Ayuda v. Meese, the "known to the government" requirement is satisfied if any government agency possesses documentation which taken as a whole would warrant a finding that the alien's status in the U.S. was unlawful. Other agencies may possess documents or information indicating unlawful status, e.g., public assistance and housing agencies, state workers compensation boards, etc. Whether knowledge of unlawful status by state and local government agencies will satisfy the "known to the government" requirement has not yet been resolved.

1.2(a)(4) Exchange Visitors

INA §245A imposes an additional requirement upon any alien who has at any time been present in the United States as a nonimmigrant exchange visitor or exchange student (J-1, J-2 visa). Such an alien must establish that he or she has either satisfied the 2-year foreign residence requirement of INA §212(e) or obtained a waiver of the 2-year foreign residence requirement.[47] A "no objection" letter and proof that the USIA has recommended approval of the waiver is insufficient to overcome this bar. The applicant must seek and be granted a waiver.[48]

The practitioner should first ascertain whether the J visa holder is in fact subject to the two-year residence requirement, as not all exchange visitors are subject to this requirement.

---

[47] 8 CFR §245a.2(b)(4).

[48] See LAU decision dated March 31, 1988 (LAU Decisions Digest order #L0688-197); LAU decision dated April 11, 1988 (LAU Decisions Digest order #L0788-246).

1.2(a)(5) Unlawful Status Due to Fraud or Error in Visa Issuance

The LAU has held that an alien who entered on an immigrant visa obtained through fraud was never lawfully admitted to the United States and is therefore eligible to apply for legalization.[49] The LAU has reached a similar conclusion where the nonimmigrant visa was issued in error.[50]

If the nonimmigrant cannot meet the "known to the government" requirements, it may be worthwhile to consider the validity of the nonimmigrant visa, extension of stay, or change of status by themselves. A nonimmigrant visa is defined as a visa *properly issued to an eligible nonimmigrant*.[51] In construing the statutory grounds of deportability and excludability relating to documentary requirements, the courts have held that a visa obtained through a deception which amounted to a material misrepresentation is equivalent to no document at all.[52] An alien admitted either as a nonimmigrant or as an immigrant based upon presentation of an unlawfully obtained or an improperly issued visa is subject to exclusion or deportation as an immigrant not in possession of a valid immigrant visa.[53]

In certain cases, aliens who entered on nonimmigrant visas which would have expired before January 1, 1987, but who requested and were granted an extension of stay or change of nonimmigrant status can argue that the extension or change of status was invalid in that it was obtained through fraud or misrepresentation (e.g., through failure to disclose unauthorized employment or intention to remain permanently, etc.). This situation is analogous to that of aliens who re-entered the United States after 1982 pursuant to a nonimmigrant visa obtained by fraud, which is specifically

---

[49] *Matter of Salazar*, Int. Dec. #3094 (Comm'r December 19, 1988), digested in 65 Interpreter Releases 968-969 (September 19, 1988). See also *Matter of Hilbert*, undesignated, File A90-283-028 (LAU, July 11, 1988, and *Matter of Urena*, undesignated, File A90-235-087 (LAU, March 14, 1988), reported in 65 Interpreter Releases 907-910 (September 2, 1988).

[50] See *In Re---*, A90-204-392 (LAU December 24, 1987), reported in 65 Interpreter Releases 236 (March 14, 1988); *Matter of ---*, (LAU, June 6, 1988) (AILA reprint no. 81-1188).

[51] INA §101(a)(26).

[52] *Feodoranko v. United States*, 449 U.S. 490 (1981); *Fink v. Reimer*, 96 F. 2d 217 (2d Cir.1938); *Ablett v. Brownell*, 240 F. 2d 625 (D.C. Cir. 1957).

[53] INA §212(a)(20).

allowed,[54] and to those whose original entry was made pursuant to a fraudulently obtained nonimmigrant visa. In Matter of N,[55] the LAU sustained the appeal of a student who was reinstated to student status based on fraudulent representations concerning unauthorized employment.

While no case as yet has raised this issue as to the obtaining of the original nonimmigrant visa by fraud, the same reasoning would apply, i.e., an entry accomplished through presentation of an invalid nonimmigrant visa is not a nonimmigrant entry. This construction is similar to that employed in the context of eligibility for relief under INA §212(c), which interprets "lawfully admitted for permanent residence" as a status which includes only an alien whose immigrant visa was obtained lawfully. It also parallels cases which have held that persons who enter under a fraudulent claim to U.S. citizenship are deemed uninspected and thus ineligible for adjustment of status.[56]

IRCA regulations implicitly adopt this position. Interim rule 8 CFR §§245a.2(b)(9) and (10) provides that unlawful status is maintained despite a subsequent entry pursuant to a visa obtained by fraud. That is, when entry is achieved through fraud, it does not cloak the ensuing residence in a "lawful" status so as to interrupt the previously established unlawful residence, and therefore does not render the alien ineligible for legalization. Note that these regulations make no distinction between entries occurring before and after January 1, 1982. It is difficult to see what distinction could be drawn between initial entries on fraudulent nonimmigrant visas and subsequent entries on such visas.

If the doctrine is applied in this context as it has been in others, an alien who entered before January 1, 1982 using a nonimmigrant visa obtained by fraud or deception, would not have to establish either the timely expiration of an "authorized stay," or Government knowledge of an unlawful status. The mere fact of entry through presentation of an invalid document creates an unlawful rather than a lawful nonimmigrant entry. Instead, the alien would then be in the same position as an alien who had entered without inspection (EWI) and would have to satisfy only the requirements of INA §245A(a)(2)(A), i.e., he or she need not prove that the unlawful status was "known to the government."

---

[54] Interim rule 8 CFR §§245a.2(b)(9) and (10).

[55] I.D. #3080 (Comm'r 1988).

[56] Ex parte Saadi, 26 F. 2d 458 (9th Cir. 1928); Volpe v. Smith, 6 F. 2d 808 (7th Cir. 1933) aff'd on other grounds, 289 U.S. 422 (1933).

Obtaining entry by fraud or misrepresentation is a grounds of excludability under INA §212(a)(19), and the alien would have to apply for a waiver of that ground of excludability under INA §245A(d)(2)(B).

1.2(a)(6) Other Qualifying Status Designations and Manners of Entry

The legalization provisions of INA §245A establish eligibility for two groups: (a) those who entered as nonimmigrants, who must prove both entry and unlawful status known to the Government before 1982, as discussed in preceding sections of this Chapter; and (b) all other aliens, who must merely prove entry and unlawful residence since 1982.[57] Thus, those who entered the United States in a status which is not clearly a nonimmigrant status, fall under the more lenient provisions applying to all aliens "other than nonimmigrants."[58]

There are a number of different kinds of "entry," admissions or statuses which an alien may have had prior to January 1, 1982, which are neither true nonimmigrant classifications, nor undocumented entries. Certain other administrative immigration statuses acquired after entry also arguably fall short of lawful status. Some of these administrative statuses or benefits are specifically addressed in the regulations. These include:

1. Voluntary departure, extended voluntary departure, and deferred action status.[59] However, the regulations also require that the alien granted that status have resided continuously in such status until the date of application for legalization.

2. An alien paroled into the United States whose parole was terminated prior to January 1, 1982 and who has thereafter resided continuously in the United States "in such status" is eligible for legalization.[60] Those who departed and returned to an unrelinquished unlawful residence in the United States pursuant to parole before May 1, 1987 are also expressly

---

[57] See INA §245A(2)(A) and (B).

[58] INA §245A(2)(A).

[59] 8 CFR §245a.2(b)(5). These statuses are discussed in Chapter Twelve, infra. Temporary residence for nationalities granted extended voluntary departure is discussed in Chapter Ten.

[60] 8 CFR §245a.2(b)(6). See INA §212(d)(5); 8 CFR §§212.5(b) and (d).

1-20

eligible,[61] and those who were paroled into the United STates pursuant to the stateside criteria program after an unsuccessful visa interview.[62] However, those aliens paroled into the United States before January 1, 1982 whose parole status terminated or expired <u>after</u> January 1, 1982 are specifically excluded from legalization eligibility.[63]

It would appear that a failure to extend or maintain the above two administrative statuses would place the alien in a status no less unlawful than before. Also, it is hard to divine the rational basis for the distinctions in treatment of those paroled into the United States.

3. "Cuban-Haitian Entrants."[64]

4. Persons who were issued "<u>Silva</u> letters."[65]

5. Aliens who filed asylum applications prior to January 1, 1982.[66]

Other statuses or designations which fall short of "nonimmigrant" status and which are not mentioned in the regulations include:

1. Nonresident Border Crossing Card holders.

2. TrWOV--aliens in transit without a visa; authorized limited access to the United States for brief time periods sufficient to make connections during course of travel to a third country.

3. Deferred inspection--applicants for admission deferred for further inquiry as to admissibility.

4. Applicant/Excludee--aliens in exclusion proceedings or subject to unexecuted order of exclusion.

---

[61] Interim rule 8 CFR §245a.2(b)(15), 52 Fed. Reg. 43845 (1987).

[62] 8 CFR §245a.1(C) (52 Fed. Reg. 43846).

[63] 8 CFR §245a.2(c)(8).

[64] INA §245A(a)(4); 8 CFR §245a.2(b)(7); <u>see</u> wire dated July 30, 1980 from INS Commissioner Carmichael.

[65] Interim rule 8 CFR §245a.2(b)(13).

[66] Interim rule 8 CFR §245a.2(b)(14), 52 Fed. Reg. 43845 (1987); <u>see also</u> Legalization Wire #35, dated August 24, 1987.

5. Stowaway.

6. False claim to U.S. citizenship or presentation of false immigration documents.

1.2(b) Continuous Unlawful Residence in the United States

The applicant must establish that he or she has resided continuously in the United States in an unlawful status from the date before January 1, 1982 when such unlawful status arose through the date the application for temporary residence was filed.[67] During this time period, any time spent outside of the country pursuant to advance parole, however long or short, will not interrupt the alien's continuous U. S. residence.[68] Likewise, aliens who attended scheduled visa interviews in Canada or Mexico under the Stateside Criteria program and who were not issued a visa were paroled back into the United States. Such "parole" is regarded as "advance parole" under the regulations[69] and therefore does not break the alien's continuous residence, nor should it be counted in calculating the number of days the alien was outside of the country.[70]

IRCA requires the Attorney General to prescribe regulations establishing a definition of the term "resided continuously"; it also requires the Attorney General to specify individual periods and aggregate periods of absence which will break continuous residence, taking into account absences due merely to brief and casual trips abroad.[71]

Under the regulations the continuous residence requirement is met so long as the applicant's record is consistent with four articulated criteria:

---

[67] INA §§245A(a)(2); 245A(g)(1)(A).

[68] INA §245A(g)(2)(B)(ii). The regulations are worded differently; they provide that advance parole "shall not be considered as having interrupted...continuous residence..." 8 CFR §245a.1(c)(1).

[69] Interim rule 8 CFR §245a.1(c)(1), 52 Fed. Reg. 43846 (1987); see also Legalization Wire #25, dated July 14, 1987.

[70] See INA §§212(d)(5), 245A(g)(2)(B)(ii). Such parole status is normally indicated on a Form I-94 issued to the alien upon return to the United States.

[71] INA §245A(g).

(1) no single absence exceeded 45 days in length (unless emergent reasons prevented the alien's return during that time limit);

(2) the aggregate of all absences between January 1, 1982 and the date of application does not exceed a total of 180 days (unless emergent reasons prevented the alien's return during that time limit);

(3) the alien maintained a residence in the United States;

(4) departure from the United States was not pursuant to an order of deportation.[72]

Departures exceeding these time limits do not automatically disqualify the applicant. Under the statute the Attorney General may provide a waiver of the above time limits in the case of a brief absence caused by emergency or extenuating circumstances outside of the control of the alien.[73] The wording of the regulation differs somewhat, requiring the alien to show that due to emergent reasons return to the United States could not be accomplished in the time period allowed, i.e., within forty-five days.[74] A formal waiver procedure is not required, rather discretion can be exercised on a case-by-case basis.[75] This should not be interpreted to mean that waivers of the 45/180 day absence rule can be obtained only where prior plans to return to the United States within 45 days were frustrated by the occurrence of the unexpected. Rather, the statute's "emergency or extenuating circumstances" language, which appears to encompass both the original motive for the departure and subsequent events effecting the alien's return, should guide the preparation and adjudication of such waivers.

The terms "emergency," "extenuating circumstances," and "emergent reasons" are not defined in the statute or regulations. However, the LAU has defined the term "emergent" as "coming unexpectedly into being". In *Matter of C*, the LAU found that where the applicant, absent a total of 58 days, had intended to remain outside of the U.S. for a period of 30 days, but was unexpectedly delayed in returning because a letter from her husband containing the money for her return trip was delayed. These facts were found

---

[72] INA §245A(g)(2)(B)(i). 8 CFR §§245a.1(c)(1), 245a.2(h)(1).

[73] INA §245A(g)(2)(C).

[74] 8 CFR §§245a.1(c)(1)(i), 245a.2(h)(1)(i).

[75] *Hernandez v. Meese*, Civ. No. S-88-385 LKK-JFM (E.D. Cal. 1988).

to fit the enunciated standard for "emergent".[76] Other cases, although not designated for publication, also give an indication of the circumstances considered by the LAU to constitute "emergent reasons" for an extended departure. A 116 day absence was waived when problems encountered at the applicant's scheduled visa interview unexpectedly required him to remain in Mexico longer than the 2 weeks originally planned. In another case, an absence of over 7 months was waived when the applicant was twice prevented from returning to the U.S. by her inability to procure a B-2 visa from the American Consulate. In a similar case, two entry attempts which were thwarted by INS officials on the U.S.-Mexico border, were found to have unexpectedly delayed the applicant's timely return, resulting in an absence of 59 days. Lastly, a 59 day absence was waived when the 14-year old applicant was afraid to take the return flight back to the United States alone after a frightening flying experience, and had to wait until her father was able to bring her back to the U.S.[77]

"Emergent reasons" also logically encompass urgent family or business needs; travel emergencies; urgent or unanticipated social, cultural, personal or business matters; political emergencies or natural disasters; matters outside of the alien's control or any other change in circumstances which compelled the alien's departure or caused the absence to exceed the specified time period. Documentation in corroboration of "emergent reasons" might include medical reports, weather reports, news articles, correspondence, personal affidavits, death or birth certificates, long distance telephone or cable records, or other evidence probative of the emergency or extenuating circumstances.

Once an emergent reason is established, discretion should be exercised in favor of the applicant.[78]

1.2(b)(1) Order of Deportation

The statute provides that "an alien shall not be considered to have resided continuously in the United States if...the alien was outside the United States as a result of a departure under an order of deportation". Such a departure poses two problems:

---

[76] Matter of C, Int. Dec. #3087 (Comm'r Nov. 15, 1988); See also Hernandez v. Meese, Civ. No. S-88-385 LKK-JFM (E.D.Cal. 1988).

[77] Reported in 66 Interpreter Releases 66-67 (January 13, 1989).

[78] See Matter of T --, undesignated, (LAU, September 2, 1988) reported in 65 Interpreter Releases 1077 (October 17, 1988).

(1) it constitutes a "meaningful interruption" of the alien's continuous residence in the United States if it occurred after January 1, 1982;[79] and

(2) it also renders the alien excludable under INA §212(a)(17), discussed below.

Note that these provisions apply to deportation orders; aliens who departed the country under an order of exclusion are arguably not expressly barred from establishing continuous residence.[80]

A final order of deportation is an order issued after the exhaustion of all avenues of administrative direct appeal available under the statute and taken by the alien. It may include not only a finding of deportability, but the denial of all requests for relief in lieu of deportation.[81] A final order of deportation is subject to review by the Circuit Court of Appeals; timely filing of such an appeal provides an automatic stay of deportation.

Departure by an alien who has never been served with an Order to Show Cause is not a departure under an order of deportation. Departure pursuant to administrative voluntary departure, whether granted by an Immigration Judge or the District Director of INS; or voluntary departure under safeguards, whether or not at government expense, does not constitute departure based on an order of deportation and is not interruptive of an alien's continuous residence.

Often an alien who appears before an Immigration Judge is granted voluntary departure under INA §244(e) in lieu of deportation, with an alternate order of deportation should the alien fail to depart. If the alien fails to depart within the time granted by the Immigration Judge, or any extension of the Judge's order which has been granted by the Immigration Service, or if all requested relief is denied and an appeal either is not taken or is denied, the order of deportation will be executed by issuance of a warrant of deportation ordering the alien to surrender for deportation and ordering the alien's expulsion.[82] If the alien granted voluntary departure departs, but he or she departs <u>after</u> the time allowed by the Immigration Judge or after the expiration

---

[79] See INA §245A(g)(2)(B), 8 CFR §§245a.1(c)(1)(i), 245a.2(h)(1)(iii).

[80] Although aliens in such circumstances are excludable under INA §212(a)(16) and must seek a waiver of excludability under INA §245A(d)(2).

[81] See 8 CFR §243.1.

[82] See 8 CFR §243.2.

of any extension of the time period granted by the Immigration and Naturalization Service, or otherwise departs while an order of deportation is outstanding, the alien is considered to have "self-deported"; self-deportation carries the same legal consequences as departure under an order of deportation executed by the INS.[83]

If an alien granted voluntary departure *after* a deportation hearing departed within the required time period, yet verification of the departure was never received by the Immigration and Naturalization Service, INS records may show either a self-deportation or an outstanding Warrant of Deportation.

In some cases, an alien who appears before an Immigration Judge in deportation proceedings will be ineligible for, or will be denied, voluntary departure or other discretionary relief, and will be ordered deported. In recent years, many aliens have been ordered deported *in absentia*.[84] Such aliens may have unwittingly self-deported by leaving the country after their hearing *in absentia*, or they may have been arrested on the outstanding warrant of arrest for deportation and expelled.

The language of the statute and the regulations to the effect that a departure under an order of deportation breaks an alien's continuous residence raises many issues. One of the unsettled questions is whether the application and approval of Form I-212 Request for Permission to Reapply for Admission After Deportation, which forgives excludability under INA §212(a)(17) and criminality under INA §276, will also work to forgive the legal consequences of such departure for purposes of the continuous residence requirement for legalization. The retroactive grant of an I-212 "waiver" of a prior deportation has long been available on a *nunc pro tunc* basis in situations where the grant of a waiver would completely dispose of the matter at hand, e.g., an adjustment of status application under INA §245.[85] The procedures and standards applicable to Form I-212 waiver applications are discussed in *Immigration Law and Defense*, *supra*, at 5.3A.

Some practitioners, seeking to avoid the extremely harsh consequences of INA §245A(g)(2)(B), have questioned the use of the language "outside the United States as a result of a departure under an order of deportation," arguing that it is limited to those

---

[83] See 8 CFR §243.5.

[84] 8 CFR §3.24. EOIR procedures regarding deportation hearings in which the alien failed to appear for a deportation hearing, including procedures for *in absentia* hearings, were set forth in a memorandum from the Chief Immigration Judge dated March 7, 1984.

[85] 8 CFR §212.2.

orders of deportation signed by an Immigration Judge and executed by the INS through the physical expulsion of the alien, as opposed to voluntary departure/alternate orders of deportation and self-deportation.[86]

Some practitioners have successfully sought <u>nunc pro tunc</u> advance parole for departures after May 1, 1987 (<u>not</u> under an order of deportation). If <u>nunc pro tunc</u> advance parole were obtained as to departures under an order of deportation, the alien would be eligible for legalization under INA §245A(g)(2)(B)(ii). Pending further clarification of this issue, the deported alien's only alternative is to collaterally attack the deportation order.[87]

1.2(b)(2) Deportation Before January 1, 1982

As to a deportation which occurred <u>before</u> January 1, 1982, two forms of amelioration are available to overcome the alien's actual or potential inadmissibility under INA §212(a)(17). An alien may seek to waive this ground of excludability by seeking a waiver provided under INA §245A. An alien can also apply for "Permission to reapply for admission to the United States after deportation, removal or departure at government expense," pursuant to 8 CFR §212.2. These provisions are subject to adjudication under different standards (the latter being more stringent) and require different forms of supporting documentation.[88]

1.2(b)(3) Deportation After November 6, 1986

Deportations occurring after November 6, 1986, are subject to collateral attack if they violated the automatic stay of deportation provided by statute, and internal INS procedures set forth in Legalization Wires #1 and #8. Pursuant to those directives, aliens eligible for legalization who were under voluntary departure or deportation orders were to be advised that they need not leave the country. In some cases, orders of deportation were to be vacated. Aliens and their ineligible family members expelled on or after November 6, 1986 in violation of the

---

[86] <u>But see</u> 8 CFR §243.1, INA §101(g).

[87] <u>See</u>, e.g., <u>U.S. v. Mendoza-Lopez</u>, 107 S.Ct. 2148 (1987).

[88] A discussion of each ground of excludability and of the availability of waivers follows in §§1.4 and 1.5 below.

stay provision and INS directives were paroled into the country until May 5, 1988.[89]

Aliens who departed the United States after November 6, 1986, in compliance with voluntary departure or subject to an order of deportations (and those who did not file their applications within the first month of the application period), should argue that the Immigration and Naturalization Service had an affirmative duty to advise them that departure or late filing would effect their eligibility for temporary residence. This affirmative duty is reflected not only in the above instruction but in the statute, which requires that the INS publicize such provisions.[90]

1.2(c) Unlawful Status During Residence

The applicant's residence in the United States since before January 1, 1982 must not only be continuous, it must be continuously unlawful.[91] Of obvious concern is whether the alien's obtaining of a status or immigration benefit after January 1, 1982, albeit for a brief time, will be deemed a "lawful" status which interrupts the alien's continuous unlawful status; thus proving to be fatal to the alien's case. This arises in two situations: when the alien in unlawful status departs the United States and upon re-entry is inspected and admitted as a nonimmigrant, and when the alien is granted a benefit the Immigration and Naturalization Service while residing in the United States. Some of these eligibility questions have been resolved by the regulations.

Eligibility for legalization will not be affected by entries to the United States after January 1, 1982, that were not documented on Service Form I-94, Arrival-Departure Record.[92] Thus, post-1982 temporary entries such as those permitted Canadian citizens without the need for documentation, and post-1982 entries effected by presentation of nonresident alien Mexican or Canadian Border Crossing Cards (Form I-158, I-186), or of a Mexican border visitors permit (Form I-444), will not interfere with eligibility by interrupting an alien's continuous unlawful status for the

---

[89] Legalization Wire #1, dated November 14, 1986 and Legalization Wire #8, dated December 17, 1986, reproduced in the Appendix.

[90] See INA §245A(i).

[91] See 8 CFR §§245a.2(b)(1), (2) and (3).

[92] 8 CFR §245a.2(b)(8).

required period.[93] The regulations do not appear to require a waiver of such entries.

Likewise, an alien who re-enters the United States as a nonimmigrant in order to return to an unrelinquished unlawful residence is eligible for legalization. The regulations require the applicant to seek a waiver under INA §245A(d), based on the presumption that the applicant is excludable under INA §212(a)(19) as an alien who entered the United States by fraud.[94]

1.2(d) Continuous Physical Presence in the United States After May 1, 1987

Each applicant must establish that he or she has been continuously physically present in the United States since the date of enactment of the program, i.e., November 6, 1986 until the filing of the application. Applicants outside the United States on that date, or who departed after that date, are nonetheless eligible as long as they reentered the United States before May 1, 1987.[95] Absences during this time period which were "brief, casual, and innocent" will not break the alien's continuous physical presence.[96] The regulations define this requirement narrowly, holding that this provision requires an alien's actual continuous presence since May 1, 1987 until the filing of an application for legalization, with the exception of departures (1) pursuant to advance parole[97] for legitimate emergency or humanitarian purposes or (2) beyond the alien's control; or (3) where the otherwise eligible alien was outside of the United States on or after

---

[93] Compare interim rules 8 CFR §245.2(b)(10), which requires a waiver of those who reentered as nonimmigrants after January 1, 1982, referring to 8 CFR §245.2(b)(9) only; and 8 CFR §245.2(b)(8), regarding entries not recorded on an I-94, and referring to eligibility in mandatory terms.

[94] Interim rule 8 CFR §§245a.2(b)(9) and (10), 52 Fed. Reg. 43845 (1987). See also Legalization Wire #46, dated November 16, 1987; and October 8, 1987 statement of Commissioner Nelson, reproduced in the Appendix. See also LULAC v. INS, ____ F. Supp. __, Cv. No. 87-04757 WDK (JR,) (C.D. Cal. 1988).

[95] INA §245A(a)(3); the final regulations concerning the legalization program were promulgated on May 1, 1987. The May 1, 1987 last-date-of-reentry rule was successuflly challenged in Catholic Social Services v. Meese, Cv. No. S-86-1433 LKK (E.D. Cal. 1988).

[96] INA §245A(a)(3)(B).

[97] 8 CFR §212.5(e).

November 6, 1986, but returned prior to May 1, 1987,[98] (4) or departures due to wrongful expulsion after November 6, 1986.[99] The Court in <u>Gutierrez v. Ilchert</u> found the purpose of the departure determinative of whether the departure was "brief, casual and innocent" rather than the circumstances surrounding the manner of departure and re-entry (e.g., attempting to re-enter the U.S. with a counterfeit permanent resident card).[100]

The INS' requirement that all departures since enactment must be pursuant to advance parole or that reentry be accomplished without the issuance of Form I-94 was successfully challenged and enjoined in <u>Catholic Social Services V. Meese</u>; the INS has not appealed this portion of the decision.[101]

Physical presence should be established by evidence consistent with these and previous judicial and BIA interpretations of the term "brief, casual and innocent." Congress' recent express overruling of the Supreme Court's limitation on the applicability of the "meaningfully interruptive" standard to the requirement of continuous physical presence in INA §244(b), only underscores the propriety of considering the variety of factors which characterize a particular departure and reentry.[102]

Applicants should provide evidence of the purpose and length of any departures made since enactment of the new law. In addition, evidence in the form of affidavits concerning an applicant's lack of knowledge of the requirement now imposed by INS, and/or lack of knowledge of the availability of advance parole as a means of departure and reentry, and practical lack of access to advance parole (e.g., on weekends, in cases of emergency) should be provided. The statute and INS numerous references to it's public information campaign should be cited regarding INS' failure to inform aliens regarding advance parole provisions, as required.[103]

Legalization applicants who did depart the U.S. briefly without advance parole have been held for exclusion proceedings and

---

[98] 8 CFR §245a.1(f) and (g); <u>see also</u> Legalization Wire #14, dated June 30, 1987.

[99] <u>See</u> the discussion in §1.2(b)(3), <u>supra</u>.

[100] 682 F. Supp. 467 (N.D. Cal. 1988).

[101] <u>See also</u> <u>Bailey v. Brooks</u>, 688 F. Supp. 575 (W.D. Wash. 1986) and <u>Gutierrez v. Ilchert</u>, <u>supra</u>.

[102] <u>See</u> INA §244(b), as amended by IRCA §315.

[103] <u>See</u> Legalization Wire #8.

have had their legalization applications denied on the basis of their exclusion. These[104] practices are being challenged in an nationwide class action.

1.2(e) Statutory Bars Applicable to Legalization Applicants

1.2(e)(1) In General

Legalization applicants must establish that they are not within any of the three additional classes of aliens barred from temporary residence under INA §245A(a)(4), including:

(1) aliens convicted of one felony or of three misdemeanors committed in the United States;

(2) aliens who have assisted in the persecution of any person or persons on account of race, religion, nationality, membership in a particular social group, or political opinion;

(3) aliens who are required to register for the draft (males, ages 18 to 26) who have not done so or are not registering.

SAW workers are not subject to the above disqualifiers.

1.2(e)(2) Misdemeanors and Felonies

The statute makes ineligible for benefits under INA §245A any person convicted of "a single felony or three misdemeanors committed in the United States."

The regulations interpreting INA §245A define "misdemeanor" as:

a crime committed in the United States, either (1) punishable by imprisonment for a term of one year or less, regardless of the term such alien actually served, if any, or (2) a crime treated as a misdemeanor under 8 CFR §245a.1(p). For purposes of this definition, any crime punishable by imprisonment for a maximum term of five days or less shall not be considered a misdemeanor.[105]

---

[104] Bamondi v. INS, No. 88-1410-KG (S.D. Calif. 1988), reported in 65 Interpreter Releases 1018-1019 (October 3, 1988).

[105] 8 CFR §245a.1(o), 53 Fed. Reg. 963 (March 28, 1988).

The regulations define "felony" as:

> a crime committed in the United States, punishable by imprisonment for a term of more than one year regardless of the term such alien actually served, if any, except: When the offense is defined by the State as a misdemeanor and the sentence actually imposed is one year or less regardless of the term such alien actually served. Under this exception for purposes of 8 CFR §245a, the crime shall be treated as a misdemeanor.[106]

Thus, it is the potential punishment that determines how a crime is to be classified, not the time served or the state classification scheme. Many aliens will be prevented from legalizing their status due to the three misdemeanor bar. Many will have three misdemeanor convictions which arose from a single incident. It is critical in all cases to ascertain the potential penalties for even minor traffic offenses (such as parking violations) as many such violations carry potential, though rarely enforced, penalties of incarceration of more than five days. Above all, the practitioner should determine what the penalty was <u>at the time of the arrest and conviction</u>, not that which is assessed under current provisions of the law pertaining to the offense.

The definition produces unfortunate and unfair results due to the multiplicity of sentencing schemes which exists among the state and local governments. In states where traffic offenses are classified as misdemeanors by a state (as in Texas), but where no sentence to confinement is possible under the criminal code, the offense is not a misdemeanor for purposes of this requirement because the crime is always punishable by a term of less than five days. In other states, all traffic violations carry maximums of more than five days confinement. Thus, the legalization applicant's eligibility may turn on which state issued the traffic citations in question.

The impact of the 3 misdemeanor/1 felony rule extends far beyond the initial application for temporary resident status. Although an alien may be convicted of two misdemeanors before becoming ineligible for the benefits of adjustment of status under the legalization program, a third conviction will not only work to bar the alien from subsequent adjustment to permanent resident status under INA §245A, but will serve as a basis for the termination of temporary residence.[107] Thus, the applicant must not accumulate 3 misdemeanor convictions prior to the date that permanent residence is received, i.e., for up to 2 and 1/2 years after application for temporary residence. It is therefore

---

[106] 8 CFR §245a.1(p), 53 Fed. Reg. 963 (March 28, 1988).

[107] <u>See</u> 8 CFR §245a.2(u)(1)(iii).

important not only to vacate existing misdemeanor convictions if at all possible, but to avoid the entry of a misdemeanor conviction in the first instance during this time period.[108]

Foreign felony or misdemeanor convictions will not serve to bar the legalization applicant under the 3 misdemeanor/1 felony provisions, although they may still result in the exclusion of the applicant under INA §§212(a)(9), (a)(10), and (a)(23), discussed in §1.4(a) above.

As to those aliens who do have 3 misdemeanors or 1 felony in the United States, the discussion of "convictions" and post-conviction relief contained in §1.4(a), infra, should be consulted. However, there is an important distinction between the analysis of what constitutes a "conviction" for purposes of determining excludability under INA §212(a)(19), and the LAU's analysis of what consitutes a "conviction" under the 1 felony/3 misdemeanor bar for purposes of eligibility under the legalization program. In Matter of M---, the LAU determined that a conviction exists when:

1) a judge or jury has found the alien guilty or he has entered a plea of guilty or nolo contendere or has admitted sufficient facts to warrant a finding of guilty;

2) the judge has ordered some form of punishment or penalty, including but not limited to a fine or probation.

The opinion expressly left open the question of whether expungements or "other judicial acts" might be excepted from the general rule expressed above.[109] This holding is more severe than the already restrictive standard set forth in Matter of Ozkok.[110]

While no express authority is provided in INA §245A, it is reasonable to assume that Congress was aware of the existence of those mechanisms which ameliorate or eliminate the immigration consequences of criminal convictions in other contexts, and could have rejected their applicability with regard to the 3 misdemeanor/1 felony requirements specifically. Furthermore, the LAU departure from the BIA's holding in Ozkok appears to ignore 8 CFR §3.1(g) which renders BIA decisions binding on all INS

---

[108] See, §1.4(a), infra.

[109] Matter of M---, Int. Dec. #___ (Comm'r January 31, 1989).

[110] Int. Dec. #3044 (BIA 1988), see discussion in §1.4(a)(1) infra.

officers. The statutory mechanisms and the case law applicable in the context of defeating the immigration consequences of convictions in deportation and exclusion proceedings should continuee to be invoked in the context of the 1 felony/3 misdemeanor rule until this matter is resolved through litigation.

1.2(e)(3) Assisted in Persecution of Others

Assistance in the persecution of others originates in the INA definition section which defines "refugee," excluding from the definition one who assisted or participated in the persecution of others.[111] A developing body of administrative and judicial decision continues to refine that definition in the context primarily of review of applications for political asylum under INA §208, withholding of deportation under INA §243(h), and in Nazi denaturalization procedures and litigation (on grounds of violation of the Displaced Persons Act). Reference to extradition cases is also relevant to interpretation of this prohibition. A discussion of this prohibition is beyond the scope of this volume, but can be found in *Immigration Law and Procedure*, *supra*; additional analyses of these concepts are available in individual briefs and memoranda of law housed in the Brief Bank of the National Immigration Project of the National Lawyers Guild.

1.2(e)(4) Selective Service Registration

Pursuant to Presidential Proclamation of July 2, 1980, all males born on or after January 1, 1960 and between the ages of 18 and 26 must register for the Selective Service. INA §245A(a)(4)(D) and 8 CFR §245a.2(g) require proof of previous registration in the form of a letter of acknowledgment from the Selective Service System, or presentation of a completed registration form at the time of applying for legalization (to be forwarded to the Selective Service System by the INS). An alien no longer required to register as the result of age, but who did not register when so required will not be disqualified under this section, as his compliance would be impossible.

---

[111] *See* INA §101(a)(42)(A).

1.2(f) Burden of Proof: The Alien Must Establish Eligibility by a Preponderance of Credible and Verifiable Evidence

1.2(f)(1) Preponderance of the Evidence

An applicant for temporary resident status as a pre-1982 entrant must prove by a preponderance of the evidence that he or she,

(1) has resided in the United States for the requisite periods;

(2) is admissible to the United States under the provisions of INA §245A; and

(3) is otherwise eligible for adjustment of status.[112]

According to the regulations, the sufficiency of the evidence will be determined according to its probative value and credibility.[113] A complete application for adjustment of status filed under this part must be accompanied by documentation establishing proof of identity, proof of residence, and proof of financial responsibility.[114] The inference to be drawn from such evidence depends upon the extent of the documentation, its credibility and its amenability to verification.[115] INS' previous policy of rejecting all applications supported in whole or in part by affidavits without verifying the information or testing the affiant's credibility was successfully challenged in Loe v. Thornburgh.[116]

An alien must agree to assist the INS in verifying declarations the applicant has not received public assistance and does not have a criminal record.[117] An alien's failure to provide verifiable documentation or to authorize release to INS of

---

[112] 8 CFR 245a.2(d)(5).

[113] 8 CFR §245a.2(d)(6).

[114] 8 CFR §245a.2(d).

[115] 8 CFR §245a.2(d)(5).

[116] 88 Civ. 7363 PKL (S.D.N.Y. 1988).

[117] 8 CFR §245a.2(k)(5).

information protected by the Privacy Act or related laws, in order to adjudicate a claim may be cause for denial.[118]

A different standard is applied in those situations in which the potential legalization applicant seeks a related benefit such as employment authorization, advance parole, or a stay of deportation. The applicant must demonstrate *prima facie* eligibility in order to obtain these benefits.

1.2(f)(2) Proof of Identity

The regulations list what evidence will be accepted as proof of identity, in descending order of preference: passport, birth certificate, any national identity document from the alien's country of origin bearing photo and fingerprint (e.g., "cedula" or "cartilla"), drivers license or similar document with photo, baptismal or marriage record, or affidavits.[119] Other acceptable documents include: social security card, school records, family Bible, employment I.D. card, union I.D. card, state I.D. card.[120]

Those who have used an assumed name to satisfy any of the eligibility criteria must prove that documents under the assumed name actually pertain to them. Persuasive evidence of common identity would be: a document issued in the assumed name, with the photo, fingerprint or physical description of the applicant; affidavits by others regarding the use of the assumed name by the applicant and with the applicant's photo attached, preferably identifying the applicant by the assumed name, stating the relationship to the applicant, and the affiant's knowledge of the use of the assumed name; other affidavits; documents under the assumed name substantiated by documents corroborating the common identity.[121]

1.2(f)(3) Proof of Residence and Physical Presence

INA §245A(g)(2)(D) requires that both continuous residence and physical presence be proven through documents and independent corroboration of the information they contain. Emphasis is placed on the production of employment-related documents to meet this requirement:

---

[118] 8 CFR §245a.2(d).

[119] 8 CFR §245a.2(d)(1).

[120] INS, *Legalization Training Manual* M-283, at p. 58.

[121] *See* 8 CFR 245a.2(d)(2).

The Conferees prefer the use of employment-related documents whenever possible, because this type of documentation is viewed as the `best evidence' of continuous residence. H.R. Conf. Rep. No. 1000, 99th Cong., 2d Sess., pt. 2 (1986) at 92.

However, the House Judiciary Committee noted that:

>...some flexibility may be necessary in accepting documents in proof of continuous residence. While employment documents may constitute the most direct evidence of continuous residence, many undocumented aliens have been clandestinely employed and thus may not have the usual trail of records...Unnecessarily rigid demands for proof of eligibility for legalization could seriously impede the success of the legalization effort. Therefore, the Committee expects the INS to incorporate flexibility into the standards for legalization eligibility, permitting the use of affidavits of credible witnesses and taking into consideration the special circumstances relating to persons previously living clandestinely in this country. H.R. Rep. No. 682, 99th Cong., 2d Sess., pt.1 (1986), at 71-73.

8 CFR §245a.2(d)(3) lists those records which are acceptable proof of residence. These include in general, employment records, utility bills, school records, hospital and medical records, attestations by churches, unions, and other organizations, and various other forms of documentation tending to establish residence.[122]

1.2(f)(4) Proof of Financial Responsibility

The regulation's requirement of proof of financial responsibility is designed to allow the INS to determine the alien's admissibility under INA §212(a). The burden of proof is on the applicant to show, by affirmative proof, that he or she is not excludable under INA §212(a)(15), or to show a history of employment in the United States without receipt of public cash assistance. The traditional standard and the "special rule" applied in legalization cases is discussed in §1.4(b)(2) above. Generally, the proof submitted to establish residence will also demonstrate the alien's financial responsibility. If the applicant's period(s) of residence in the United States include significant gaps in employment, or if there is reason to believe the alien may have received public assistance while employed, he

---

[122] 8 CFR §245a.2(d)(3)(i)-(v).

or she may be required to submit proof he or she has not received public cash assistance.[123]

The construction of this regulation may result in the imposition of a greater rather than a lesser burden on the alien with regard to financial responsibility. The alien's burden is **not** to establish "no receipt of public cash assistance" **unless the alien is unable to show he or she is not likely to become a public charge**. While past receipt of benefits may be one factor relevant in determining whether or not the prospective ground of excludability "likely to become a public charge," it does not indicate *per se* that the applicant is inadmissible nor does it require denial of adjustment of status as a matter of law, as the regulation appears to suggest.[124] The INS acknowledges that the determination is a prospective one and states that length of time that an applicant received public cash assistance will be considered a significant if not dispositive factor.[125]

The following documents can be submitted by the applicant to satisfy the burden of proof as to financial responsibility:

(i) Evidence of a history of employment (i.e., employment letter, W-2 Forms, income tax returns etc.);

(ii) Evidence that he/she is self-supporting (i.e., bank statements, stocks, other assets, etc.); or

(iii) Form I-134, Affidavit of Support, completed by a spouse in behalf of the applicant and/or children of the applicant or a parent in behalf of children which guarantees complete or partial financial support. Acceptance of the affidavit of support shall be extended to other family members in unusual family circumstances, e.g., by aunts, uncles, foster parents, etc.[126]

1.2(f)(5) Other

To establish admissibility under INA §212(a)(1) through (5), the results of a medical examination by an approved physician must

---

[123] 8 CFR §245a.2(d)(4).

[124] Compare 8 CFR §245a.2(k)(4) which contains a special rule for determination of public charge excludability.

[125] See §1.4(b) *infra*.

[126] Interim rule 8 CFR §245a.2(d)(4) 52 Fed. Reg. 43845; INS Central Office cable dated August 14, 1987 and INS memorandum dated November 10, 1987.

be included with the application for Temporary Resident status.[127] The additional applicable grounds of excludability are listed on the application form with regard to which the alien must swear, under penalty of perjury, that he or she does not belong to any of the proscribed categories. Usually, the execution of this <u>jurat</u> will suffice as proof that the alien is not excludable under the enumerated grounds, however, the immigration examiner can request that additional documents be submitted to disprove excludability if the facts warrant it.

1.2(g) The Alien Must File the Application for Temporary Residence On Time

The alien who meets all of the above requirements for temporary resident must file the application forms and supporting documents <u>on time</u>, or temporary residence will be denied. The deadlines for filing the Application for Temporary Residence are as follows:

1. Aliens illegally in the United States since before January 1, 1982, have from May 5, 1987 through May 4, 1988, to file their applications. Aliens subject to an Order to Show Cause (OSC) prior to November 6, 1986, may file at any time during the twelve month filing period, regardless of whether they were ordered by an Immigration Judge or the BIA to file within 30 days.[128]

2. INS regulations provide that any alien apprehended,[129] in INS custody, or subject to an OSC after November 6, 1986 and before May 5, 1987, must apply before June 4, 1987.[130]

3. An alien subject to an OSC issued during the course of the legalization program, must apply within 30 days of the issuance of the OSC.[131]

---

[127] 8 CFR §245a.2(d).

[128] INA §245A(a)(1)(A); 8 CFR §245a.2(a); <u>In Re Teklay</u>, Int. Dec. #3027 (BIA 1987).

[129] The requirement that "apprehended" aliens file their applications within 30 days was modified by INS memorandum dated March 6, 1989. <u>See</u> <u>Doe v. Nelson</u>, 88 C. 6987 (N.D. Ill. 1988), reported in 65 Interpreter Releases 1066-1067 (October 17, 1988).

[130] 8 CFR §§245a.2(a)(2), 245a.2(c)(5).

[131] INA §245A(a)(1)(B); 8 CFR §245a.2(a)(2)(ii).

4. Any alien subject to an OSC after April 5, 1988 must apply before May 4, 1988.[132]

"Subject to an Order to Show Cause" means actual service of the Order to Show Cause upon the alien through the mail or by personal service.

The "filing" of the application means either (a) the presentation of the completed application form I-687 and supporting documents at the INS legalization office and the payment of the correct filing fee; or (b) the presentation of application form I-687 and the signing of a "Consent to Forward" form at the office of a Qualified Designated Entity (QDE) and the attachment of the appropriate filing fee to the completed application.[133] An unsuccessful Registry applicant cannot apply the Registry filing date an application for temporary resident status.[134] A denial based solely on a late filing cannot be reviewed on appeal.[135]

In a number of lawsuits the Courts have ordered extensions of the application filing deadline to allow persons newly eligible for IRCA, (due to a Court ruling or a change in INS policy), time within which to apply under INA §245A. The court-ordered extensions of the application deadlines are a continuing matter of controversy due to the U.S. Supreme Court's ruling in INS v. Pangilinan.[136] Pangilinan involved legislation passed in the wake of World War II according naturalization to certain Filipino war veterans allied with the U.S. military. Procedures required the submission of a naturalization petition to a certain authorized U.S. consular official within a set time period, however, this official was withdrawn from the Philippines, preventing would-be beneficiaries of the law from taking advantage of its provisions. A class action suit was filed on behalf of those who would have qualified for naturalization had the procedural means set-forth in the statute been available, however the Supreme Court held that the courts had no power to confer citizenship in violation of the statutory deadlines established by Congress.

Several courts have attempted to distinguish Pangilinan and continue to order INS to accept legalization applications for

---

[132] 8 CFR §245a.2(a)(2)(iii).

[133] 8 CFR §245a.2(f).

[134] Reported in 65 Interpreter Releases 959 (September 19, 1959).

[135] INA §245A(f)(2), 8 CFR 103.3(a)(2)(iv)(B).

[136] 486 U.S. ___, 108 S.Ct. 2210, 108 S.Ct. 2210, 100 L.Ed.2d. 882 (1988).

specific groups of aliens. Whether the INS will yield in its opposition to this equitable remedy fashioned by the courts to remedy unlawful denials, or whether the matter will be resolved only after further appeals, remains to be seen. These extensions of the application deadline apply only to those potential applicants who fall within the following specific classes:

1. Nonimmigrants whose unlawful status was known to any federal government agency before January 1, 1982, or who willfully failed to file quarterly address reports and who were advised they would be ineligible under the "known to the INS" standard, could submit a form "application" directly with the court prior to November 15, 1988.[137]

2. Aliens who briefly departed the United States on or after May 1, 1987 and who returned to the United States without advance parole were accorded an extension until November 30, 1988 to file their applications with the INS.[138]

3. Aliens who were discouraged by INS or others from applying due to regulations which replaced IRCA's two-tier analysis of "public charge" with an overly restrictive one-step analysis.[139]

4. Those who re-entered the United States at any time and whose entry was documented on form I-94 were granted until November 30, 1988 to file their applications with the INS.[140]

INS has allowed that in extreme situations a person who missed the legalization filing deadline may be granted some form of deferred action. Requests for such status must be made to the District Director.[141]

---

[137] Ayuda v. Meese, 687 F.Supp. 650 (D.D.C. 1988), Supplemental Order, October 31, 1988, reported in 65 Interpreter Releases 590 (June 6, 1988).

[138] Catholic Social Services v. Meese, No. CIV. S-86-1343-LKK (E.D.Cal, 1986). See 65 Interpreter Releases 1010-12 (October 3, 1988).

[139] Zambrano v. INS, ___ F.Supp. ___ Civ. No. S-88-455 EJG (E.D.Cal. 1988).

[140] LULAC v. INS, ___F.Supp.___ No. 87-4757-WDK (C.D.Cal. 1988).

[141] Reported in 65 Interpreter Releases 596 (June 6, 1988).

1.3 THE SPECIAL AGRICULTURAL WORKER (SAW) PROGRAM

The SAW program was characterized by reports of widespread fraud among SAW applicants, leading to stricter evidentiary standards and increased scrutiny of SAW applications. As a result, despite an unexpectedly high number of applicants (1.1 million), only approximately 25% of SAW applications have been approved. Numerous unresolved SAW issues await resolution at the administrative appeals level in the months ahead.

The basic eligibility requirements for temporary resident status contained in the statute and regulations can be summarized as follows:

1. Must have performed agricultural services for at least 90 man-days between May 2, 1985, and May 1, 1986.[142]

2. 3 months residence in the United States during the one-year period ending on May 1, 1986.[143]

3. Must be admissable to the United States; most grounds of excludability are waived or waivable.[144]

4. Burden of proof: must establish the length and type of qualifying employment by a preponderance of the evidence.[145]

5. Must apply within time period provided, June 1, 1987 through November 30, 1988.[146]

Unlike the legalization program, eligible aliens residing overseas could submit their applications to consular posts or at

---

[142] INA §210(a)(1)(B). SAW applicants who can establish that they worked 90 man days of seasonal agricultural services in each of the three years ending May 1, 1984; May 1, 1985; and May 1, 1986 can become permanent residents at stage two of the program one year before other SAWs. These applicants are designated "Group 1 SAWs." See Interim rules 8 CFR 210.1(f)(g).

[143] INA §210(a)(1)(B), Interim rule 8 CFR §210.3(b)(4). Those who qualify for "Group 1" SAW status must establish 6 months aggregate residence in the United States during each of the one-year periods ending May 1, 1984; May 1, 1985; and May 1, 1986.

[144] INA §210(a)(1)(C), 210(C).

[145] INA §210(b)(3).

[146] INA §210(a)(1)(A).

designated ports of entry in order to gain admission to the United States to work and gather documents in support of their applications.[147]

1.3(a) Ninety Days Employment in Seasonal Agricultural Services

According to the statute, "the alien must establish that he has--(i) resided in the United States, and (ii) _performed seasonal agricultural services_ in the United States for at least 90 man-days."[148] The term "Seasonal Agricultural Services" is defined by statute as the performance of (1) field work (2) related to planting, cultural practices, cultivating, growing and harvesting of (3) fruits and vegetables of every kind and other perishable commodities, as defined by the Secretary of Agriculture.[149]

The following key terms used in the definition of "seasonal agricultural services" have been defined by the Department of Agriculture and are discussed in detail below: field work, fruits, vegetables, and other perishable commodities.[150] Although the regulations separately define the term "seasonal," that term is already incorporated in both the statutory and regulatory definition of "seasonal agricultural work" and need not be independently proven.[151]

1.3(b) Fruits, Vegetables and Other Perishable Commodities

1.3(b)(1) In General

A controversial element of the definition of "seasonal agricultural services" are the fruits, vegetables and other perishable commodities which are the focus of the work being performed. The unambiguous language of the statute requires the inclusion of fruits and vegetables _of every kind_. Accordingly, the

---

[147] Interim rule 8 CFR §§210.1(k), (l), 53 Fed. Reg. 10065 (March 29, 1988).

[148] INA §210(a)(1)(B).

[149] INA §210(h); this definition is repeated in 7 CFR §1d.9.

[150] See, 7 CFR §§1d.4, 1d.5, 1d.7, 1d.10.

[151] The use of the word "seasonal" to define "other perishable commodities", is discussed in §1.3(b)(2)(i) below.

Department of Agricultural has adopted the scientific definitions of "fruit" and "vegetable". These terms are defined as follows:

> Fruit: the human edible parts of plants which consist of the mature ovaries and fused other parts or structures, which develop from flowers or inflorescence.[152]

> Vegetables: the human edible herbaceous[153] leaves, stems, roots, or tubers of plants, which are eaten, either cooked or raw, chiefly as the principal part of a meal rather than as a dessert."[154]

Any plant or plant product which meets the definition of fruit or vegetable, "without exception" constitutes a qualifying crop or plant product under the statute. Fruits and vegetables need not be perishable to qualify,[155] nor must they be destined for human consumption.[156]

> Other perishable commodities are defined as: those commodities which do not meet the definition of fruits or vegetables, that are produced as a result of field work, and have critical and unpredictable labor demands.[157] This is limited to Christmas trees, cut flowers, herbs, hops, horticultural specialties,[158] spanish reeds (arundo donax), spices, sugar beets, and

---

[152] 7 CFR §1d.5.

[153] 7 CFR §1d.10. Herbaceous plants are to be distinguished from woody plants; these distinctions are based on patterns of plant growth, i.e., herbaceous plants "die back" each year whereas woody plants grow by adding outward layers of plant cells.

[154] 7 CFR §1d.10, as amended, 53 Fed. Reg. 31630-31639 (August 19, 1988).

[155] See the Comments pertaining to fruits and vegetables published with the final regulations, 52 Fed. Reg. 20372-20376 (June 1, 1987).

[156] See LAU discussion dated February 8, 1988.

[157] The term "critical and unpredictable labor demands" is discussed in section 1.3(a)(2)(ii) below.

[158] Discussed in the following section.

tobacco. This is an exclusive list, and anything not listed is excluded.[159]

Examples of commodities that are not included as perishable commodities are animal aquacultural products, birds, [cotton,[160]] dairy products, earthworms, fish including oysters and shellfish, forest products, fur bearing animals and rabbits, hay[161] and other forage and silage,[162] honey, horses and other equines, livestock of all kinds including animal

---

[159] Whereas the proposed regulation listed Christmas trees, cut flowers, etc., as *examples* of "other perishable commodities", the final rule expressly excludes all commodities not on this short list. See proposed regulations published in 52 Fed. Reg. 13248 (April 22, 1987). The *inclusion* of Christmas trees, herbs, hops, nursery crops, Spanish reeds, spices, sugar beets, and tobacco on the list of perishable commodities has been upheld. See Northwest Forest Workers, 688 F. Supp. 1 (DDC, 9-30-87). Those items not on the list may nonetheless qualify under the definitions of fruit, vegetable, or horticultural specialty.

[160] The express exclusion of cotton was successfully challenged in National Cotton Council of America v. LYNG, ___ F. Supp.___, CA-5-87-0200-C (N.D. Tex. 1988) which held that cotton meets the statutory and regulatory definition of fruit. See also Valdez-Valencia v. Lyng, Civ. No. 87-630-TUC-RMB (D.Ariz., 9-21-80). Cotton was subsequently dropped from the "excluded" list in the final regulation published at 53 Fed. Reg 28628.

[161] Texas Farm Bureau v. Lyng, 697 F. Supp. 935 (E.D. Tex. 1988).

[162] Silage is produced from the stalks of corn plants, after the ears of corn have been harvested. Thus, although work performed in making and storing silage may not qualify, the employee also may have worked in the preceding phases of corn planting, cultivation and harvest, work which is qualifying work. See Legalization Wire #33, August 24, 1987. The LAU has determined that corn is a qualifying crop even though it is not meant for human consumption. See LAU decision, February 8, 1988, reported in 65 Interpreter Releases 410-411 (April 18, 1988).

specialties, poultry and poultry products, sod,[163] sugar cane,[164] wildlife, and wool.

Additional commodities have been found by the INS to qualify under the terms "fruits, vegetables, and other perishable commodities," e.g., wheat, rice, oats, barley, rye, and other grains produced primarily for human consumption; all corn, sweet and other; beans, including soybeans, berries, and melons grown for human consumption; grapes; potatoes; tree nuts and ground nuts grown for human consumption, including peanuts; and mushrooms...Together...fruits and vegetables <u>include all plant crops grown for human food</u>...[w]ith the exception of sugar cane...(emphasis supplied).[165]

The following products are <u>excluded</u> from classification as "fruits, vegetables" or "other perishable commodities, according to INS' directives:" sorghum,[166] milo,[167] millet,[168] alfalfa, clover,

---

[163] Although the proposed regulations failed to mention sod, it appeared in the final rule as an example of a commodity not included under the rubric "other perishable commodity". This was challenged in <u>Morales v. Lyng</u>, No. 87C 20522 (N.D. Ill., Dec. 1987). USDA then republished proposed and then final regulations, again excluding sod. <u>See</u> 53 Fed. Reg. 41339-41342 (October 28, 1988), 53 Fed. Reg. 50375-50381 (December 15, 1988).

[164] Sugarcane has been classified as a "perishable commodity" in other contexts, see <u>Maneja v. Waialva Agricultural Co.</u>, 349 U.S. 254, 257 (1955); <u>Wirtz v. Oscola Farms</u>, 372 F. 2d 584, 586 (5th Cir. 1967). Its exclusion from the list of eligible plants and plant products was challenged in <u>Northwest Forest Workers v. Yuetter</u>, 688 F. Supp.1 (D.D.C. 1987), which upheld the amended definition of "vegetable" which excluded sugarcane. Reported in 66 Interpreter Releases 254-255 (March 6, 1989).

[165] Legalization Wire #23, dated June 5, 1987. One of the problems with the INS directives is their failure to specify whether a plant or plant product is included on the basis of its being a fruit, a vegetable or a perishable commodity. Both INS adjudicators and practitioners are left to speculate as to the rationale for the inclusion of certain plants, and the extension of these exceptions to other plants.

[166] The exclusion of sorghum (which produces molasses) is also the subject of challenge; an administrative appeal brief on this issue is available through AILA, Legalization Issues Bank. <u>See also</u> the discussion of grains in section 1.3(b)(3) below.

[167] Discussed in § 1.3(b)(3) below.

timothy, and other grains and grasses grown primarily for forage and other uses aside from human consumption; gourds; seeds;[169] and flax.[170]

A chart of those items expressly determined to be included or excluded under the terms "fruit", "vegetable" or "other perishable commodity" is found at the end of this Chapter.

According to INS directives, SAW applicants who rely upon work in crops not included in the regulatory definitions of "fruits," "vegetables" or "perishable commodities" <u>are clearly ineligible for SAW status</u> ...District Directors have the discretion to deny such applications at the Legalization Office...District Directors are encouraged to deny such applications locally, notwithstanding whether inclusion of a particular crop in the USDA regulations is at issue in litigation (emphasis supplied)."[171]

1.3(b)(2) Horticultural Specialties

Although the definition of "other perishable commodities" purports to be an exclusive list, one of the more ambiguous items included on that list is that of "horticultural specialties." "Horticultural specialties" means field grown, containerized, and greenhouse produced nursery crops which include juvenile trees, shrubs, seedlings, budding, grafting and understock, fruit and nut trees, fruit plants, vines, ground covers, foliage and potted plants, cut flowers, herbaceous annuals, biennials and perennials, bulbs, corms, and tubers.[172] Because the list of horticultural specialties is not expressly exclusive, there exists some flexibility for the practitioner to argue in favor of the inclusion of other plants within the meaning of horticultural specialties. The terms "herbaceous annuals, biennials and perennials" may provide additional opportunity for creative lawyering. If a plant comes within the definition of horticultural specialty, i.e., field

---

[168] <u>Id</u>.

[169] <u>See</u> the discussion of seed crops in § 1.3(b)(4) below.

[170] Legalization Wire #23, June 5, 1987. Compare INS' less restrictive interim definition of perishable commodity, contained in Legalization Wire #9, December 30, 1986.

[171] <u>See</u> Legalization Wire #48, January 13, 1988, reproduced in the Appendix.

[172] 7 CFR §1d.6.

grown, containerized, and greenhouse produced nursery crops, it is presumably a perishable commodity.

1.3(b)(2)(i) Seasonal

The SAW applicant need not prove the seasonality of the crop or work performed in order to qualify for Temporary Residence. Work which meets the regulatory definition of "seasonal agricultural work," discussed in section 1.3(a), is by definition "seasonal." The regulations nonetheless provide a separate definition of the term "seasonal." "Seasonal" means:

> the employment pertains to or is of the kind performed exclusively at certain seasons or periods of the year. A worker who moves from one seasonal activity to another while employed in agriculture or performing agricultural labor, is employed on a seasonal basis even though she or he may continue to be employed during the year.[173]

According to the comments which accompanied the proposed regulations, this definition of "seasonal" was introduced in order to make clear the fact that year round employment did not preclude the alien from establishing seasonal agricultural employment.[174]

1.3(b)(2)(ii) Critical and Unpredictable Labor Demands

Under the proposed regulations, the term "horticultural specialties" identified a group of plants which, like "other perishable commodities" (a) is produced as a result of seasonal field work, and (b) have critical and unpredictable labor demands.[175] As neither the proposed definition of "horticultural specialties" nor that of "other perishable commodities" contained exclusive lists, the inclusion of a plant under either definition would have required proof that the plant met the above two criteria. The final regulations removed the need to meet this criteria by imposing an exclusive list of items, all of which by definition (a) are produced as a result of seasonal field work, and (b) have critical and unpredictable labor demands. This list includes horticultural specialties. The definition of "critical

---

[173] 7 CFR §1d.8.

[174] See 52 Fed. Reg. 13247 (April 22, 1987).

[175] See comments accompanying the proposed rules at 52 Fed. Reg. 13247 (April 22, 1987).

and unpredictable labor demands" was retained in the final regulations, although it is now superfluous.

It is possible that the INS may nonetheless require proof that a plant is seasonal or subject to unpredictable labor demands in order for it to qualify under the definition of "horticultural specialty." "Critical and unpredictable labor demands" means that the period during which field work is to be initiated cannot be predicted with any certainty 60 days in advance of need.[176] This is not a difficult test to meet in that, as explained by the Department of Agriculture, "[t]ypical of the circumstance which creates the critical, yet unpredictable demand for labor is weather or other climate conditions. As a result, a labor force would be needed on short notice."[177] In addition, the discussion of the reasons why various perishable commodities were found to have such labor demands is enlightening and may supply a basis for arguing in favor of other plants and plant products as "horticultural specialties". For example, the rationale for the inclusion of cut flowers was that "[i]n many instances, the timing of the planting and harvesting is dependent upon uncontrollable factors, and is, therefore, critical;" while activities involving nursery products "are highly subject to unpredictable weather influences".[178] This can be said of almost any plant product and would support the inclusion of numerous other items under "horticultural specialties". Other factors considered by the Department of Agriculture were the fact that certain critical activities could only be performed during a short period of time in the plant's growth cycle (Christmas trees, shape trees during a 10 day period; hops, 20-25 days harvest; Spanish reeds, 3 week harvest; tobacco, harvest at 10 day intervals). Also significant was the fact that certain crops are labor intensive (hops, Christmas trees).

1.3(b)(3) Grains

Grains arguably fall within the definitions of fruit and perishable commodities. The comments accompanying the final regulations allow that soybeans are a qualifying crop because they meet the definition of "fruit". Yet almost all grains meet the above definition of "fruit". While the INS directives recognize that such grains as wheat, oats, barley, rye, corn and beans are qualifying crops, the same directives disallow sorghum, milo and

---

[176] 7 CFR §1d.3.

[177] See comments to the proposed regulations, 52 Fed. Reg. 13247 (April 22, 1987).

[178] See comments accompanying the final regulations at 52 Fed. Reg. 20375 (June 1, 1987).

millet. It is difficult to understand the distinction between these grains, given the language of the definition of fruit. That sorghum, milo and millet are human edible is without question; they are, in fact, food staples in the Middle East and Africa. Nor can the INS exclude sorghum and millet by interpreting the definition of fruits to exclude those meant for human consumption outside of the United States, as these crops are also eaten or used in food products in the United States.[179]

1.3(b)(4) Seed Crops

As is noted in the comments accompanying the final regulations, the language of the statute is unambiguous, requiring the inclusion of fruits and vegetables of every kind. In light of this fact, the exclusion of certain seed crops (referred to in the comments accompanying the final regulations, but not incorporated into the regulations) is puzzling. Most of the excluded seed crops listed in the comments arguably come within all three of the qualifying kinds of plants or plant products, i.e., fruit, vegetables, and perishable commodities.

Seed crops are vegetables and other plants which are planted, cultivated, irrigated and grown to maturity, through the final stages of plant life including the blooming and the production of seeds. In the course of the plant's growth such plants as beets, cabbage, carrot, collards, kale, radish, rutabaga, spinach, and turnip are indistinguishable from the same vegetables planted for human consumption. Most of the labor required to bring these plants to maturity is the same as that required to cultivate harvestable vegetables; if anything, seed crops are more labor intensive than crops grown for human consumption.[180] Seed crops are

---

[179] Sorghum is used to make molasses; millet can be purchased in natural food stores and grocery stores throughout the United States. It may be true that these crops are grown for export and human consumption abroad or for other purposes in addition to human consumption, however, the same can be said of soybeans and corn, which was expressly allowed. The issue of whether employment performed in the production of sorghum is qualifying agricultural employment is currently the subject of an administrative appeal (briefs available through AILA's Legalization Issues Bank).

[180] The seed crop industry is subject to regulation by the federal and state Departments of Agriculture. Generally, fields and the seeds they produce must be certified to be 97% pure (as to the particular hybrid or line of plants being grown) and weed free before the seeds produced can be sold. To meet this rigorous standard, fields must be "rogued", i.e., all "contaminating" plants must be pulled by hand on a regular basis to prevent cross-

subject to the same vagaries of weather and the same critical and unpredictable labor demands as qualifying crops. In fact, the crop seed industry's labor needs are "critical" not only to the survival of a particular harvest or to the crop seed industry itself, but to the fruit and vegetable growers who would cease to exist without these seeds.

Seed production is a critical stage in the growth and production of plants for human consumption. It is difficult to understand the rationale for exclusion of agricultural labor performed on an otherwise qualifying crop, based solely on the fact that the plants, though consumable, were not produced for the purpose of human consumption but for the production of seeds, which are, according to USDA's own definition, fruit. By comparison, ornamental fruit trees are qualifying crops despite the fact that they are cultivated and grown for other than human consumption of their fruit. The same rationale for including ornamental fruit trees would appear to apply to seed crops as well.

1.3(c) Field Work

The SAW applicant must also satisfy another component of the definition of "seasonal agricultural services," i.e, "field work". Under 7 CFR §1d.4, "field work" is defined as any employment (1) performed on agricultural lands (2) for the purpose of planting, cultural practices, cultivating, growing, harvesting, drying, processing, or packing (3) any fruits, vegetables, or other perishable commodities.

1.3(c)(1) Duties Performed

As the definition recognizes, "field work" encompasses activities other than the harvest of crops. Operating tractors or machines which pick crops or shake trees, collecting, loading, and weighing fruit or vegetables, are an intrinsic part of field operations. Supervising those who perform seasonal agricultural work is expressly included.[181] Plowing, tilling, operating irrigation equipment and applying fertilizer and pesticides are also agricultural work, but these and other duties are not specifically mentioned in the statute or regulations. The comments accompanying the final regulations describe a variety of activities as within the scope of field work. INS directives have also expanded on allowable duties. These interpretations of the statute indicate that virtually anything done in order to produce fruits,

---

pollination.

[181] 7 CFR §1d.4.

vegetables or perishable commodities is included in "field work".

Some of the activities expressly mentioned as included in or excluded from the definition of "field work" are set forth in a chart at the end of this Chapter.

In order to test a SAW applicant's credibility, INS may ask the applicant to describe agricultural duties performed, including harvesting techniques, at the INS interview on the application.[182]

1.3(c)(2) <u>Location of Work Performed</u>

The regulation requires that these activities take place "on agricultural lands". "Agricultural lands" means <u>any land, cave, or structure, except packinghouses or canneries</u>, used for the purpose of performing field work.[183]

The activities which constitute "field work" have to be performed on agricultural land <u>in order to produce</u> fruits, vegetables, and other perishable commodities, as opposed to those activities that occur in a processing plant or packinghouse not on agricultural lands.[184] The regulation's exclusion of work performed in a processing plant or packinghouse is explained further by two INS memoranda. According to the INS,

> Such processing facilities as freezing plants, processing plants, packaging plants, etc. are included under the term "Packing Houses" and are not considered "agricultural lands" regardless of proximity to field production sites. Work performed in such facilities is not "field work" within the meaning of 7 CFR §1d.4. However, <u>stripping, grading, drying or packing performed in or adjacent to the field</u> where the produce is grown is "field work" if performed as an integral part of the picking and harvesting operation on that farm (emphasis supplied).[185]

Work performed in packing sheds at highways, railheads, or similar transportation points, or at central locations in cases of farms with separate, remote fields, qualifies as field work if: (a) it consists of activities such as stripping, grading, drying, or

---

[182] <u>See</u> § 1.3(h)(3)(ii) below.

[183] 7 CFR §1d.2.

[184] 7 CFR §1d.4.

[185] <u>See</u> Legalization Wire #23, June 5, 1987, reproduced in the Appendix.

packing, and (2) 85% or more of the produce packed has been produced by the grower/employer. Employment by an agricultural cooperative or commercial packinghouse does not constitute employment "by a farmer or on a farm" and is not field work.[186]

The drying, processing, or packing of fruits, vegetables, and other perishable commodities in the field, and the "on the field" loading of transportation vehicles are included.[187]

1.3(c)(3) Nature of Employer's Business

Given the language of the statute and the regulations, the size of the employer is irrelevant, as is the fact that the employer is not a farmer, the job site is not a farm, and the "crops" in question were not destined for a commercial market. Thus, persons who toil in a private vegetable garden or orchard may qualify if they were so employed for the requisite number of man-days.[188] It should be noted, however, that in INS' instructions to its field offices, distinctions are drawn, based on the type of employer, between workers who perform the same duties.[189] For example, workers whose duties involve beekeeping for pollination of fruits, vegetables and other perishable commodities are eligible if employed by the grower or producer; this is so even if the hives tended were rented from an apiarist. When the employee works for an apiarist tending hives rented to a grower _for pollination_ of a fruit, vegetable, or perishable commodity, the worker is disqualified _because the principle business of an apiarist is honey production_.[190] Likewise, the stripping and grading of fruits and vegetables constitutes qualifying employment if performed for a grower/producer, but not if done for an agricultural cooperative. According to INS, packing is considered agricultural employment if performed "by a farmer or on a farm."

Thus, although certain workers such as landscapers may appear to meet all of the requirements based on the regulations and the

---

[186] See Legalization Wire #33, dated August 14, 1987, reproduced in the Appendix.

[187] 7 CFR §1d.4.

[188] However, payment for these services is required by interim rule 8 CFR §210.1(i).

[189] See Legalization Wire #33.

[190] See Legalization Wire #33, August 28, 1987, reproduced in the Appendix.

statute, INS may introduce additional criteria relating to the nature of the employer's business to disqualify SAW applicants.

1.3(d) Man-days

SAW--Group 2 applicants must prove that they have worked for at least 90 "man days" in eligible agricultural employment from May 2, 1985 to May 1, 1986. SAW--Group 1 applicants must also prove that they have worked for 90 "man-days" in qualifying employment during each of the two preceding years. "Man-day" means the performance during any day of not less than one hour of such qualifying agricultural employment for wages paid. If employment records relating to an alien applicant show only piece rate units completed, then any day in which piece rate work was performed shall be counted as a man-day. Work for more than one employer in a single day shall be counted as no more than one man-day for the purposes of this part.[191] 8 CFR §210.3(b)(2) states that evaluation of the evidence submitted will include consideration of the fact that work performed by minors and spouses is sometimes credited to a principal member of a family.

A worker who moves from one seasonal activity to another, while employed in agricultural labor, is employed on a seasonal basis even though (s)he may continue to be employed during the year.[192]

Aliens who apply for SAW--Group 1 classification at the Legalization Office whose documents are deemed insufficient to establish eligibility for such classification may nonetheless have their applications considered for SAW--Group 2 classification. The denial of SAW--Group 1 classification is appealable.

1.3(e) Physical Presence In and Entry To the United States

SAW applicants must meet certain requirements regarding residence in the United States during the years when they were employed in qualifying agricultural work. However, unlike provisions of the legalization program, the statute establishing the SAW program does not require the applicant to establish <u>continuous</u> residence, physical presence, nor lawful or unlawful status in the United States during the required time period.

---

[191] Interim rule 8 CFR §210.1(i).

[192] 7 CFR §1d.8. SAW applicants are not required to prove the seasonality of the crop or work performed, as long as the work they performed involved the kinds of duties and plants described above.

1-54

The INS, in implementing the law, sought to impose various restrictions on potential SAW applicants based on the date and manner of last entry of the alien to the United States. The object of these restrictions was "to avert a potential flow of illegal immigrants and to eliminate any inducement to unlawful entry" by qualifying SAW workers living in Mexico.[193]

According to initial INS directives, SAW eligible aliens who had entered the United States after November 6, 1986, were not eligible to apply for temporary residence in the United States, but could apply at certain foreign consular posts outside of the United States.[194] The determinative entry date was pushed back to May 1, 1987,[195] then to June 1, 1987 (as of May 9, 1987).[196] The cut-off date was then moved to June 26, 1987, the date when border processing centers in Mexico were opened.[197] These cut-off dates were challenged in litigation and as a result the INS changed its policy directives to allow eligible SAW workers to apply for temporary residence regardless of the date on which they entered the United States.[198] On December 22, 1987 Amendments to INA §210 were enacted which expressly allow aliens to enter the United States in order to apply for temporary residence as SAWS.[199] Although this made the issue of the applicant's last date of entry irrelevant, those who enter the United States as nonimmigrants with the intention of applying for SAW status may be required to seek

---

[193] See Legalization Wire #37, November 3, 1987, reproduced in the Appendix.

[194] See Legalization Wire #1, November 14, 1986, and Legalization Wire #12, January 19, 1987, reproduced in the Appendix.

[195] See Legalization Wire #14, April 30, 1987.

[196] See Legalization Wire #19, May 8, 1987, reproduced in the Appendix.

[197] See Statement of Alan C. Nelson, INS Commissioner, on June 29, 1987, reproduced in the Appendix. See also INS memorandum dated September 26, 1987.

[198] See Legalization Wire #37, November 3, 1987.

[199] P.L. no. 100-202, 101 Stat. 1329 (1987); see also Legalization Wire #51, December 23, 1987.

a waiver due to excludability under INA §212(a)(19).[200] SAW applicants who had entered the United States on any date prior to June 26, 1987 or after December 22, 1987, could apply for temporary residence within the U.S. Those erroneously deported or excluded from the U.S. between November 6, 1986 and June 26, 1987 need not obtain of waiver to be eligible for temporary residence.[201]

1.3(f) Residence in the United States

The statute requires that the SAW applicant "ha[ve] resided in the United States." Under the regulations, SAW-Group 1 workers must prove that they have resided in the United States for (1) an aggregate of 6 months between May 2, 1983, and May 1, 1984, (2) an aggregate of 6 months between May 2, 1984, and May 1, 1985; and (3) an aggregate of 6 months between May 2, 1985, and May 1, 1986.[202] As to SAW--Group 2 workers, evidence of performance of the required 90 man-days of seasonal agricultural services shall constitute evidence of qualifying residence.[203] This allows "commuter" aliens who traveled to work from a residence abroad to qualify despite the lack of a U.S. residence.

Because residence need not be continuous, the number and length of departures during the applicant's United States residence is irrelevant. It is also important to remember that the residence requirement does _not_ require the applicant to establish 6 months aggregate _physical presence_. The term "residence," as interpreted in other contexts, means the place of general abode, i.e., his or her principal, actual dwelling place in fact, without regard to intent.[204] Thus, time periods during which the alien maintained a residence in the United States should be counted towards satisfaction of the SAW--Group 1 residence requirement, despite the

---

[200] See Legalization Wire #46, October 28, 1987; and Legalization Wire #37, November 3, 1987. Waivers are discussed in §1.5 below.

[201] See Catholic Social Services v. Meese, CIV-S-86-1343 LKK (E.D. Cal. 1988), reported in 65 Interpreter Releases 844-845 (August 22, 1988).

[202] See 8 CFR §210.1(f).

[203] Interim rule 8 CFR §210.3(c)(4).

[204] INA §101(a)(33); Matter of Young, 11 I.& N. 38, 40 (BIA 1965). See also the discussion in Chapter Eleven, §11.2(b); and Legalization Wire #10, January 14, 1987.

fact that the alien was outside of the country all or part of the time.

While SAW--Group 2 workers need not prove residence independent of the proof they present to substantiate the performance of 90 man-days qualifying work, SAW--Group 1 workers must prove 6 months aggregate United States residence. This distinction was explained as follows:

> The Conference Managers' Report expressly states that: "...the conferees intend `resided' to mean 6 months per year, in the aggregate, in the U.S. for `Group 1 workers....' A six-month residence requirement for Group 2 workers is mentioned in the Conference Managers' Report but this was reduced to a three-month residence requirement according to clarification provided in colloquies in the House and Senate.[205]

1.3(g) Additional Bars to Eligibility

Unlike legalization applicants, SAWs are not required to present proof of Selective Service Registration. Male SAWs between the ages of 18 and 26 who reside in the United States nonetheless have the obligation, under the Selective Service laws, to register for the Selective Service.[206]

Unlike legalization applicants, SAWs do not face an independent bar to eligibility due to conviction of a single felony or of three misdemeanors, nor due to having assisted in the persecution of any person or persons on account of race, religion, nationality, membership in a particular social group, or political opinion.

Under the regulations (but not the SAW provisions), an alien who at any time was a nonimmigrant exchange visitor under §101(a)(15)(J) of the INA who is subject to the two-year foreign residence requirement is ineligible to adjust status to that of temporary resident unless the alien has complied with that requirement or the requirement has been waived pursuant to the provisions of section 212(e) of the Act.[207]

---

[205] See 52 Fed. Reg. 16190 (1987) at 16195.

[206] Aliens who obtain Temporary Resident status under the SAW program may reside outside of the United States. In such cases, Selective Service registration may not be required.

[207] Interim rule 8 CFR §210.3(d)(1).

1-57

1.3(h) Burden of Proof: Qualifying Employment Proven by a Preponderance of the Evidence

1.3(h)(1) In General

The applicant for SAW status in the United States must prove by a preponderance of the evidence that (s)he has worked the requisite man-days, is admissible under INA §210(c), and, in SAW-Group 1 cases, has resided in the United States the requisite amount of time.[208] An alien can meet such burden of proof if the alien establishes that the alien has in fact performed seasonal agricultural services by producing sufficient evidence to show the extent of that employment as a matter of just and reasonable inference.[209] Although the regulations provide that the applicant cannot rely solely on uncorroborated personal testimony in order to meet his or her burden of proof,[210] one court has found that this imposes an impermissible burden on SAW applicants[211] although another, while finding this standard of proof to be permissible, interpreted "corroborating documentation" quite liberally, finding that the corroborating affidavit of a co-worker in support of the credible personal testimony of an applicant was sufficient to meet the applicant's burden.[212]

Aliens who are eligible for temporary residence by virtue of their agricultural work and who seek to enter the United States at Calexico, Otay Mesa or Laredo, under the regulatory admission procedures (and, between July 1 and November 1, 1987, under the temporary transitional admissions standard) must meet a far lower standard in order to be admitted to the United States for 90 days,[213] but must ultimately prove their eligibility by a

---

[208] See INA §§291, 210(b)(3)(B), and interim rule 8 CFR §210.3(b).

[209] INA §210(b)(3)(B)(iii).

[210] Interim rules 8 CFR §210.3(b)(2) and (3); see also Department of State cable dated May 27, 1987.

[211] See Haitian Refugee Center, Inc. V. Nelson, 694 F. Supp. 864 (S.D. Fla. 1988), applicable in the 11th Circuit. See also Ramirez-Fernandez v. Giugni, C.A. No. EP-88-CA-389 (W.D. Tex. 1988), which found voluntary compliance witht he order entered in Haitian Refugee Center.

[212] See UFW v. INS, Civil No. S-87-1064 LKK (E.D. Cal. 1988).

[213] Discussed in § 1.3(k) below.

preponderance of the evidence when pursuing their applications at INS Legalization Offices. This same standard of proof, under another name, is applied in those situations in which the potential SAW applicant seeks a related benefit. Applicants for transitional overseas processing, employment authorization, advance parole or a stay of deportation, must demonstrate that they have a nonfrivolous claim to SAW status in order to obtain these benefits.

Congress recognized that documentary evidence to establish SAW eligibility would be extremely difficult to obtain. For this reason, the statute at one part requires only a showing of a nonfrivolous claim to SAW status to qualify for a stay of deportation and employment authorization, whereas comparable provisions of the legalization program require the applicant to show <u>prima facie</u> eligibility. In addition, the Conference Report expressly incorporates Fair Labor Standard Act case law as a guide to remedying this objective obstacle in SAW cases to create an evidentiary inference in favor of an applicant's evidence.[214] The Congress contemplated that a lower burden of proof apply to SAW cases, and yet the burden of proof which emerges from the regulations is higher than that required of legalization applicants.

The regulations set-forth those documents which must be presented to prove the various elements of eligibility, but they also describe those cases in which the applicant will <u>not</u> be deemed to have met the burden of proof, i.e., where documentation of eligibility consists solely of personal testimony or affidavits of the applicant which is not corroborated, in whole or in part, by other credible evidence.[215] In practice, INS Legalization Offices are even more restrictive, routinely requiring employer records and pay stubs and recommending denial of all applications in which eligibility is established based on the applicant's personal testimony and on the affidavits of third parties; these affidavits are deemed non-corroborative without regard to their probative value or credibility. This contravenes the regulations which disallow applications based solely on the personal testimony or affidavit <u>of the applicant</u>. Thus, the regulations explicitly reject any proof of eligibility for temporary residence which is grounded on the SAW applicant's own sworn evidence, no matter how relevant, probative and credible the SAW applicant's testimony is. In essence, the regulation as written prejudges the credibility, probative value and relevance of the evidence and finds it wanting,

---

[214] <u>See</u> Joint Explanatory Statement of the Committee of Conference, H.R. Rep. No. 99-1000, 99th Cong., 2d Sess. (1986).

[215] Interim rules 8 CFR §§210.3(b)(2) and (3). <u>See also</u> 8 CFR §210.3(c)(3).

without having examined it.[216] Outright rejection of affidavit-supported cases has been found to impose an impermissible standard in SAW cases.[217]

As the case law interpreting the Fair Labor Standards Act reveals, many agricultural workers will find it impossible to obtain evidence which corroborates their employment of 90 days. In cases where corroborative evidence is not available, a detailed affidavit establishing eligibility and explaining the absence of corroborative evidence and the efforts made to locate evidence should be prepared and filed in support of the application.

Administrative regulations may not contravene an act of Congress.[218] A legal challenge to this restrictive interpretation is likely in light of the apparent inconsistency between the express legislative intent to create an "inference in favor of worker evidence" and the regulatory requirement not to accept worker evidence alone.

Yet it is not expected that INS will relax the rigid standard with which it assesses the sufficiency of the documents presented by the SAW applicant. According to the INS, fraud is rampant among SAW applicants; it has been estimated that in Florida fraud was detected in 50% of the SAW applications filed. Because the INS has not divulged the basis for their claims of widespread fraud, it is impossible to determine whether these claims are well-founded or exaggerated. INS has promised to prosecute such cases, but as this book goes to press, only a handful of indictments in Florida have been reported.

1.3(h)(2) INS' Burden to Disprove Eligibility

Once the applicant has established eligibility by a preponderance of the evidence, the burden shifts to the INS to disprove the alien's evidence with a showing which negates the reasonableness of the inference to be drawn from the evidence.[219] In VFW v. INS, the Court ruled that any credible documentation,

---

[216] Interim rule 8 CFR §210.3(b)(2).

[217] See Haitian Refugee Center, Inc. v. Meese, supra, applicable in the 11th Circuit, Ramirez-Fernandez v. Guigni, supra, but see VFW v. INS.

[218] See e.g., NCIR, Inc. v. Meese, 791 F. 2d 1351 (9th Cir. 1986).

[219] INA §210(b)(3)(B)(iii). See also Haitian Refugee Center, Inc. v. Meese, supra.

however sparse and incomplete is sufficient to shift the burden to the INS:

> [T]he applicant need only produce corroborating documentation that he or she performed some portion of the claimed qualifying work; once this is established his or her own testimony, if credible, as to the extent of the employment will suffice to shift the burden of proof to the INS. For example, the corroborating affidavit of a co-worker that the applicant worked for a particular farmer at some point during the claimed period will establish the _fact_ of employment; the applicant's own testimony that he or she worked for that farmer for the full 90 man-days establishes the _extent_ of the employment.[220]

The INS is not bereft of tools to meet this burden:

> "All evidence of identity, qualifying employment, admissibility, and eligibility submitted by an applicant for adjustment of status under this part will be subject to verification by the Service. Failure by an applicant to release information protected by the Privacy Act or related laws when such information is essential to the proper adjudication of an application may result in denial of the benefit sought. The Service may solicit from agricultural producers, farm labor contractors, collective bargaining organizations and other groups or organizations which maintain records of employment, lists of workers against which evidence of qualifying employment can be checked. If corroborating evidence is not available and the evidence provided is deemed insufficient, the application may be denied."[221]

Pursuant to INS Legalization wire #16, the INS recommends that Legalization Offices request records from local agricultural employers.

> "If it appears that the applicant may be inadmissable under §212(a)(15) of the Act, he or she may be required to submit documentation showing a history of employment without reliance on public assistance for all periods of evidence in the United States."[222]

> "At the discretion of the district director or consular officer, original documents, even if accompanied by certified

---

[220] Cv. No. S-87-1064-LKK/JFM (E.D. Cal. 1988).

[221] Interim rule 8 CFR §210.3(b)(3).

[222] Interim rule 8 CFR §210.3(c)(5).

1-61

copies, may be temporarily retained for forensic examination."[223]

1.3(h)(3) **Documentary Requirements**

According to regulations, a complete application for adjustment of status filed under this part must be accompanied by proof of identity, evidence of qualifying employment, evidence of residence and such evidence of admissibility or eligibility as is required and as may be requested by the examining immigration officer in accordance with such requirement.[224]

Any application for SAW status filed between June 15, 1987 and August 15, 1987 with a QDE comes within special procedures established to encourage the filing of additional applications. If an application filed within this time period is subsequently denied for lack of sufficient documentation, additional documentation can be submitted directly to the Regional Processing Facility within 60 days of the denial without the necessity of paying an additional fee for an appeal.[225]

1.3(h)(3)(i) **Proof of Identity**

The regulations list what evidence will be accepted as proof of identity, in descending order of preference: passport, birth certificate, national identity or military registration document bearing a photo or fingerprint or both, drivers license or similar document with photo, baptismal or marriage record, affidavits, or other documentation which establishes the identity of the applicant.[226]

Those who have an assumed name must prove that documents under the assumed name actually pertain to them. Persuasive evidence of common identity would be: a document issued in the assumed name, with the photo, fingerprint or physical description of the applicant; affidavits by others regarding the use of the assumed name by the applicant and with the applicant's photo attached;

---

[223] Interim rule 8 CFR §210.3(c).

[224] Interim rule 8 CFR §210.3(c).

[225] See letters from Richard Norton, dated June 16, 1987 and July 15, 1987.

[226] Interim rule 8 CFR §210.3(c)(1).

1-62

other affidavits; documents under the assumed name substantiated by documents corroborating the common identity.[227]

1.3(h)(3)(ii) Proof of Employment

Under the regulations, the alien can establish qualifying employment by presenting certain enumerated evidence. According to the regulations, the following documents constitute evidence of the performance of seasonal agricultural services:

> "...government employment records, or records maintained by agricultural producers, farm labor contractors, collective bargaining organizations and other groups or organizations which maintain records of employment, or such other evidence as worker identification issued by employers or collective bargaining organizations, union membership cards or other union records such as dues receipts or records of the applicant's involvement or that of his or her immediate family with organizations providing services to farmworkers, or work records such as pay stubs, piece work receipts, W-2 Forms or certification of the filing of Federal income tax returns on IRS Form 6166, or state verification of the filing of state income tax returns. Affidavits may be submitted under oath, by agricultural producers, foremen, farm labor contractors, union officials, fellow employees, or other persons with specific knowledge of the applicant's employment.[228]

Other documents which will establish qualifying employment include: employment records kept by foremen, unions including referral records from Union hiring halls, worker identification cards, referrals from the employment service, wage abstracts from the Department of Employment, normally given to unemployment insurance claimants, Social Security statement of wages, worker compensation claims and records, state disability insurance records in those states in which it exists, registry of farm labor contractors from the U.S. Department of Labor.[229]

In evaluating the evidence of residence and employment submitted by SAW applicants, adjudicators must apply the "just and reasonable inference" standard mandated by INA §210(b)(3)(iii).

---

[227] Interim rule 8 CFR §210.3(c)(2)(ii).

[228] Interim rule 8 CFR §210.3(c)(3).

[229] <u>Legalization Training Manual</u> (M-283), prepared by the INS Outreach Program.

Under this standard an applicant cannot be denied temporary residence for failure to establish a complete documentary record of the full periods of required employment and residence if it is reasonable to conclude, from the evidence presented and the interview, the likelihood that the applicant meets the eligibility requirements. In cases where eligibility is not fully documented, but may be reasonably inferred from the evidence provided and the personal testimony of the applicant at the interview, the adjudicator must either recommend approval or disprove the evidence.[230]

If an employer or farm labor contractor who employed the applicant has kept proper and adequate records, the alien's burden of proof may be met by securing timely production of those records under regulations promulgated by the Attorney General.[231] "Proper and adequate" employment records is not defined but presumably means a contemporaneous record kept in the normal course of business identifying the employee, the dates worked, and the wages paid. In response to litigation on this issue,[232] the INS promulgated regulations allowing for the subpoena of an employer's records. These provide:

> Securing SAW employment records. When a SAW applicant alleges that an employer or farm labor contractor refuses to provide him or her with records relating to his or her employment and the applicant has reason to believe such records exist, the Service shall attempt to secure such records. However, prior to any attempt by the Service to secure the employment records, the following conditions must be met: a SAW application (Form I-700) must have been filed; an interview must have been conducted; the applicant's testimony must support credibly his or her claim; and, the Service must determine that the application cannot be approved in the absence of the employer or farm labor contractor records. Provided each of these conditions has been met, and after unsuccessful attempts by the Service for voluntary compliance, the District Directors shall utilize section 235 of the Immigration and Nationality Act and issue a subpoena in accordance with 8 CFR §287.4, in such cases

---

[230] See Department of State cable, dated May 27, 1987; Haitian Refugee Center, Inc. v. Meese, supra.

[231] INA §210(b)(3)(B)(ii).

[232] United Farm Workers of America v. INS, Civil No. S-87-1064-LKK (E.D. Cal. 1988).

1-64

where the employer or farm labor contractor refuses to release the needed employment records.[233]

INS' internal directives recommend that the L.O.s contact employers directly for employment information and otherwise cooperate to assist applicants in obtaining needed documents.[234] Farmworkers have sued both employers[235] and crewleaders[236] directly for failure to provide them with the required corroborative evidence.

The problem of obtaining verification of employment from agricultural employers is substantial, not only because of haphazard recordkeeping but because many will be reluctant to provide records which implicate the employer in violations of laws. For example, the agricultural employer who has failed to report wages, FICA, state or federal withholding taxes will be unwilling to cooperate when an alien requests copies of employment records; in order to document that a child who helped his parents in the fields performed the requisite 90 man-days work, an employer may in the process admit to violating child labor laws. While some states have laws allowing employees access to their personnel files, these employee access laws may yield little or no evidence for those in agricultural occupations. They can nonetheless be used to compel uncooperative employers to produce needed records.

Lacking "proper and adequate" employment records, an alien can meet his or her burden of proof by establishing that (s)he in fact performed the qualifying work "by producing sufficient evidence to show the extent of that employment as a matter of just and reasonable inference."[237] If qualifying employment is shown by just and reasonable inference "the burden then shifts to the Attorney General to disprove the alien's evidence with a showing which negates the reasonableness of the inference to be drawn from the evidence."[238]

---

[233] Interim rule 8 CFR §210.3(b)(4), 54 Fed. Reg. 4758 (January 31, 1989).

[234] See Legalization Wire #16, June 19, 1987; Statement of Alan Nelson, INS Commissioner, dated June 29, 1987 regarding growers associations.

[235] Amarillas v. Sakakura (Superior Court, San Joaquin Co., No. 203883) (Nov. 16, 1987).

[236] Felix et al v. Jimmy Lee Hill (S.D. Fla.).

[237] INA §210(b)(3)(B)(iii).

[238] INA §210(b)(3)(B)(iii).

1-65

Examples of other documents which might meet this burden are an agricultural employer's cancelled paychecks issued to and endorsed by the applicant; crewleaders' transportation and other records which include the applicant's name; "Intake Sheets" or other records of Migrant Social Service agencies, Migrant Health Clinics, Migrant Education programs, and Migrant Legal Assistance programs. From such records it can reasonably be inferred that an alien and his family members were performing seasonal agricultural services.

Under the regulations, the inference to be drawn from the documentation provided shall depend on the extent of the documentation, its credibility and amenability to verification by the Immigration Service.[239] This language regarding a document's "amenability to verification" is problematic, however, in view of the legislative history which makes clear that due to problems of recordkeeping practices in agricultural industries, "fairness dictates they create <u>a presumption in favor of worker evidence, unless disproved by specific evidence adduced by the Attorney General.</u>[240] It is also ironic that INS insists on verification of those documents presented to it, in order to refute unverifiable claims, yet will not use verification of qualifying employment affirmatively, as ordered by statute, to obtain documents from recalcitrant growers.[241]

The INS and the Department of States have provided the following guidelines for SAW adjudicators:[242]

a. Evidence will frequently relate to piece-rate work and will show volume of product picked or harvested rather than hours or days worked over a period of time. Productivity may vary significantly from day to day based on number of hours worked, weather conditions, or assignment to other tasks. Site managers at LOs with a high volume of SAW applications should solicit information from employers, extension agents, collective bargaining organizations or other appropriate sources relative to average daily per-worker production. Such

---

[239] Interim rule 8 CFR §210.3(b)(1).

[240] Conference Comm. H. R. Rep. No. 99-1000, 99th Cong., 2nd Sess. (1986), page 97.

[241] <u>See</u> INA §210(b)(3)(B)(ii).

[242] <u>Legalization Training Manual</u> (M-283), prepared by the INS Outreach Program, pp. 23-25; Department of State cable dated May 27, 1987.

information will aid adjudicators in equating piece-rate records with man-days of employment.

b. Records of employment may be in the form of informal tallies of boxes, bushels, etc. Such records may not be dated and may identify the worker only by a first name or nickname or not at all. Such evidence is of extremely limited probative value if not supported by a Form I-705 affidavit or by other information permitting verification. District Directors or chief legalization officers at LOs with a high volume of SAW applicants should consider soliciting lists of former employees from local agricultural employers for their potential value as an aid to verifying employment claimed by applicants.

c. Piece-rate work performed by an entire family is sometimes credited to a single principal member of the family. Information relative to the average productivity of individual workers will be useful in weighing claims that piece-rate evidence relates to more than one individual.

d. Individuals who worked as crew members for a farm labor contractor may only have vague information concerning the name or producers or farmers for whom the crew worked or concerning the names and specific locations of the farms on which they worked. However, in all cases, experienced farm workers can readily provide information concerning the crops on which they worked, the methods of cultivation or harvesting employed for specific crops, and the general geographic areas where specific products are grown. Additionally, workers who claim to have harvested products which require field-sorting or selective harvesting should be able to describe selection criteria. The plausibility of documentary evidence is enhanced by an applicant's demonstration of familiarity with routine occupational information. Adjudicators should develop such information and test claims to eligibility against it in applicant interviews. However, an applicant's familiarity with particular agricultural operations, standing alone, does not serve to establish qualifying employment during the required period(s).

e. Employer associations may recruit, transport, house and supervise or provide only one of these services for a variety of employers, usually in a particular geographic area. They may do this directly or simply provide employee referral to the employer, usually an association member. Some associations may handle payroll only and thus be the only depository of records.

1.3(h)(3)(iii) Proof of Fiscal Responsibility

The burden of proof is on the applicant to show (s)he is not excludable.[243] Under the regulations, affirmative proof that the alien is not excludable under INA §212(a)(15) as likely to become a public charge is required. Generally, the proof submitted to establish employment will also

"serve to demonstrate the alien's financial responsibility. If it appears that the applicant may be inadmissible under section 212(a)(15) of the Act, he or she may be required to submit documentation showing a history of employment without reliance on public cash assistance for all periods of residence in the United States."[244]

1.3(i)   Timely Filing of Application

INS regulations and directives requiring the filing of a SAW application within 30 days of issuance of an OSC were challenged and have now been removed from the regulations.[245]

(a) All eligible agricultural workers have from June 1, 1987 through November 30, 1988, to file their applications and documents.[246]

(b) If the application is filed with a QDE, the application is deemed to have been filed as of the day the alien signs an authorization to forward the application to the INS.[247] Aliens who filed applications with a QDE had 60 days within which to present the application and pay the filing fee at the LO.

---

[243]   INA §291.

[244]   Interim rule 8 CFR §210.3(c)(5).

[245]   Interim rule 8 CFR §210.2(c). See Guzman et al v. Nelson, No. 87-12060-Civ. Ryskamp (S.D. Fla.). See also Florida Rural Legal Services v. U.S. Department of Justice, Civ. No. 87-999 (S. D. Fla. June 11, 1987).

[246]   Interim rule 8 CFR §210.2(c)(1).

[247]   8 CFR §210.2(b)(1).

(c) Aliens who presented an application at the port of entry had 90 days (until March 30, 1989) within which to file a completed application at an LO.[248]

The regulations allow the District Directors of the INS legalization offices, in their discretion, to permit the filing of applications by mail. The regulations do not indicate whether or not the filing date will be the date of postmark or the day the application is "fee receipted" in such cases. The decision whether an application is timely filed is to be made by the LAU, not the director of the RPF.[249]

On January 25, 1988, Sen. Alan Cranston (D-Cal.) introduced S. 2002 to extend the SAW application deadline by 6 months.

1.3(j) Overseas Processing

Unlike legalization applicants, SAWS residing outside of the United States can file an application for temporary residence with American consular posts. Presentation of a complete I-700 application and all required supporting documents[250] will enable consular officials to recommend approval or denial of the application. At the commencement of the SAW program, consular posts in Mexico City, Kingston, Bridgetown, Ottawa, Port-Au-Prince, Santo Domingo, Nassau, Guatemala, San Salvador, and Tegucigalpa were furnished with application I-700 forms. All other posts will be furnished with such forms upon request.

The standard for the adjudication of a SAW application overseas is the "just and reasonable inference" mandated by statute.[251] Generally, the requirements discussed in this Chapter apply in such cases, including requirements relating to waivers, timely filing, and payment of filing fees. As of February 17, 1988, all SAW applications filed overseas were subject to stateside verification before the SAW entry packet would be issued the alien.[252] Upon approval, applicants are given a SAW package, containing the form I-700 and other documents, and an entry

---

[248] Interim rule 8 CFR §§210.2(c)(4)(ii), (iii).

[249] Matter of M--S--, (LAU January 19, 1989), reported in 66 Interpreter Releases 170-171, (February 6, 1989).

[250] Interim rule 8 CFR §210.2(c)(3).

[251] See Department of State cable dated May 27, 1987.

[252] See Legalization Wire #55 dated February 17, 1988.

document and directed to present both at a port of entry within 30 days. Those whose applications are denied due to statutory ineligibility or admitted fraud are given 60 days within which to appeal.[253]

1.3(k) Temporary Admission at Designated Ports of Entry on the Southern Land Border

Between July 1, 1987 and November 1, 1987, the INS and the Department of State instituted a temporary Transitional Admission Standard to allow aliens who could not fully document their eligibility to enter the United States to work and to perfect their claims to SAW status. On March 29, 1988 the Admission Standard was promulgated in interim rules.[254] In such cases, aliens who presented completed I-700 applications which provided sufficient detail to indicate qualifying employment, which identify documentary evidence the applicant intends to submit, and whose credibility was tested at a personal interview, were to be granted entry and employment authorization for a period of 90 days. These Admission Standards applied to aliens seeking entry at certain ports of entry along the U.S.-Mexico border. Medical examination and evidentiary requirements were not waived but were deferred for completion in the United States at the Legalization Office. All aliens who proceeded to the United States under the Temporary Transitional Admission Standards were provisionally classified as SAW--Group 2 workers.[255]

The above program has now been extended by Congress to December 1, 1988, and the geographical limitations have been removed.[256] Effective December 23, 1987 through December 1, 1988, credible SAW applicants of any nationality submitting completed I-700 forms at the ports of entry of Calexico, Otay Mesa and Laredo, will be admitted and issued employment authorization valid for 90 days. Such applicants must submit a completed application, together with all supporting documents, at any legalization office

---

[253]   Id.

[254]   53 Fed. Reg. 10066.

[255]   8 CFR §210.6, 52 Fed. Reg. 28663 (1987). See also the statement of Alan C. Nelson, INS Commissioner, dated June 29, 1987; Legalization Wire #27, July 1, 1987; Department of State cable, dated July 1, 1987. SAWS whose cases were processed under the Transitional Admissions Standards cannot be assured of the protections of the confidentiality provisions of INA §210. See the discussion in § 1.6 below.

[256]   Pub. L. No. 100-202, 101 Stat. 1329.

within 90 days, or any extension of that time granted by the District Director.[257]

1.4 ADMISSIBILITY

Admissibility as an immigrant is required by INA §245A(a)(4).

Inapplicable Exclusion Grounds[258]   The following grounds of excludability do not apply during the first stage of the legalization and SAW programs:

(14) entered to work without labor certification;
(20) not in possession of a valid entry document;
(21) visa not issued per numerical limitations;
(25) illiterate over age 16;
(32) foreign medical graduate who has not taken the visa qualifying examination.

Exclusion Grounds Which Cannot Be Waived[259]   The following provisions of INA §212(a) <u>cannot be waived</u> during the first stage of the legalization and SAW programs:

(9) crime of moral turpitude;
(10) two crimes with aggregate sentence of 5 yrs. or more;
(15) likelihood of becoming a public charge [applies to SAW applicants only][260]
(23) drug-related convictions (except 30 grams of marijuana);
(27) likely to engage in activities prejudicial to the public interest;
(28) anarchists, communists, etc.;
(29) spy, saboteur, subversive;
(33) Nazi.

Waivable Grounds of Exclusion [261]   The following exclusion grounds under INA §212(a) are applicable but are waivable for humanitarian purposes, to assure family unity, or when it is otherwise in the public interest:

---

[257]   Interim rule 8 CFR §210.3(c)(4)(iii). Legalization Wire #51, December 23, 1987.

[258]   INA §§210(c)(2)(A), 245(d)(2)(A).

[259]   INA §§210(c)(2)(B)(ii), 245A(d)(2)(B)(ii).

[260]   INA §210(c)(2)(B)(ii).

[261]   INA §§210(c)(2)(B)(i), 245A(d)(2)(B).

(1) mentally retarded;[262]
(2) insane;[263]
(3) attack(s) of insanity;[264]
(4) psychopath, sex deviant, mental defect;[265]
(5) drug addict, alcoholic;[266]
(6) contagious disease;
(7) physical disability effecting ability to work;
(8) paupers;
(11) polygamy;
(12) prostitutes;
(13) entry to engage in immoral sex acts;
(15) public charge [applies to legalization applicants only];[267]
(16) excluded within 1 year;
(17) deported within 5 years;
(18) stowaway;
(19) fraud;
(22) ineligible for U.S. citizenship;
(24) arrived on non-signatory line;
(26) no valid visa, passport on entry;
(30) entry with excluded alien;
(31) smuggling.[268]

Inadmissibility under the above grounds can be overcome by a waiver which provides:

(i) In General.--Except as provided in clause (ii), the Attorney General may waive any other provision of Section 212(a) in the case of individual aliens for humanitarian purposes, to assure family unity, or when it is otherwise in the public interest.[269]

The IRCA waiver provisions <u>cannot</u> be used to overcome excludability based upon INA §212(a)(9), (10), (15) [as it applies

---

[262] INA §§212(a)(1) through (5) are also appealable under INA §§234 and 235.

[263] <u>Id</u>.

[264] <u>Id</u>.

[265] <u>Id</u>.

[266] <u>Id</u>.

[267] The "special rule" to determine excludability as a public charge is discussed in §1.4(b) below.

[268] INA §§245A(d)(2)(B), 210(c)(2)(B)(i).

[269] INA §§245A(d)(2)(B), 210(c)(2)(B)(i).

1-72

to applications for adjustment to permanent resident status], (23) [except as it applies to simple possession of less than thirty grams of marijuana], (27), (28), (29) and (33).[270] However, as to those grounds of excludability, there may be other waiver provisions in the Immigration and Nationality Act which may apply. A comparative chart of exclusion grounds and waivers is reproduced in the Appendix to this book and should be consulted to determine which INA §212 waivers are normally available to immigrants for the grounds of excludability at issue. The IRCA waiver provisions do not bar the use of these other waivers as a means of overcoming inadmissibility.

1.4(a) Excludability for Criminal Conduct Under INA §§212(a)(9) or (a)(10), and (a)(23)

Many legalization applicants who have criminal convictions will be automatically barred from legalization under the 3 misdemeanor/1 felony rule, discussed below, which is not waivable (SAW applicants are not subject to the 1 felony/3 misdemeanor bar).[271] The other bases for excluding certain types of admitted criminals are INA §§212(a)(9), (10), and (23). While there is overlap between these grounds and the 3 misdemeanor/1 felony rule, INA §212(a)(9) will work to bar a misdemeanor offender whose crime involved moral turpitude, those who are convicted of a crime of moral turpitude in a foreign country, as well as the person with no convictions whatsoever who admits to activity which constitutes a crime of moral turpitude.

INA §212(a)(9) excludes from entry non-citizens "who have been convicted of a crime involving moral turpitude or...who admit having committed such a crime, or...who admit committing acts which constitute the essential elements of such a crime".

Conviction of two crimes render an alien inadmissible under INA §212(a)(10) without regard to whether or not they arose in a single scheme or involved moral turpitude, if the aggregate sentence imposed was for more than five years. Concurrent sentences are treated as a single sentence for purposes of computing the time served within the meaning of this subsection. In order to determine the aggregate sentence imposed upon persons sentenced to consecutive terms, the individual sentences are added together and totaled.

The nature of the conviction, the finality of the order and the length and type of sentence imposed will be determinative as

---

[270] See INA §245A(d)(2)(B)(ii), 210(c)(2)(B)(ii).

[271] See §1.2(e)(2) supra.

to whether a conviction renders that alien excludable under INA §§212(a)(9) or (10).

INA §212(a)(23) will also work to exclude those convicted of misdemeanor or felony offenses involving controlled substances and those suspected of illicit trafficking in controlled substances. Other types of criminal activity may result in the exclusion of an alien under other sections of INA §212(a), e.g., polygamy, prostitution and procuring, and alien smuggling.

It should also be noted that INA §701 now admonishes the Attorney General to begin expeditious deportation proceedings against those aliens who are convicted of a criminal offense.

1.4(a)(1) Definition of Conviction

A final conviction by a federal, state or foreign tribunal may trigger immigration consequences. The pendency of criminal charges will not effect an alien's eligibility for immigration benefits unless and until there is a final conviction. A conviction will be considered final when direct appeals are either waived or exhausted.[272] Thus, a conviction being appealed or for which the appeal period has not tolled, may not be used as a disqualifying conviction for purposes of eligibility for temporary resident status under INA §§245A and 210. The mere possibility of obtaining post-conviction relief does not defeat the immigration consequences of the conviction.[273] A petition for a writ of habeas corpus or for a writ of coram nobis is considered a collateral appeal. Moreover, a conviction under collateral challenge will, in all likelihood, be deemed sufficiently final to be a disqualifying conviction under INA §§245A and 210.

The BIA has determined that a conviction exists when:

1) a judge or jury has found the alien guilty or he has entered a plea of guilty or nolo contendere or has admitted sufficient facts to warrant a finding of guilty;

2) the judge has ordered some form of punishment, penalty, or restraint on the person's liberty to be imposed, including but not limited to incarceration, probation, a fine or restitution, or community-based sanctions such as a rehabilitation program, a work-release or study-release program, revocation on suspension of a driver's

---

[272] Will v. INS, 447 F. 2d 529 (7th Cir.1971).

[273] Hernandez Valenzuela v. Rosenberg, 304 F. 2d 639 (9th Cir. 1962).

> license, deprivation of nonessential activities or privileges, or community service; and
>
> 3) a judgement or adjudication of guilt may be entered if the person violates the terms of his probation or fails to comply with the requirements of the court's order, without availability of further proceedings regarding the person's guilt or innocence of the original charge.[274] Under this standard, many alternative senting devices will be considered "convictions" for immigration purposes.

Note that while a criminal disposition might satisfy the above test and therefore not constitute a conviction for purposes of INA §212(a)(19) excludability, it may nonetheless constitute a conviction for purposes of the 1 felony/3 misdemeanor bar under the more stringent rule applied by the LAU in Matter of M---.[275]

1.4(a)(2) Offense Committed by an Alien Under Age 18[276]

Generally, a judicial finding of guilt in juvenile proceedings is not considered to be a conviction for immigration purposes.[277] A juvenile is defined as a person who has not attained his 18th birthday or, for an alleged act of juvenile delinquency, a person who has not attained his 21st birthday.[278] Nevertheless, a minor alien convicted of a crime of moral turpitude may be excludable if the court expressly forgoes the existing juvenile proceedings and treats the minor as an adult offender.[279]

A crime committed by a juvenile in a foreign country is assessed according to the standards of the Federal Juvenile

---

[274] In Re Ozkok, Int. Dec. #3044 (BIA 1988).

[275] Int. Dec. #____ (Comm'r, January 31, 1989); see also discussion in §1.2(e)(2).

[276] The effect of convictions for crimes committed when the alien was under the age of 18 is discussed in greater detail in Kesselbrenner and Rosenberg, Immigration Law and Crimes, Clark Boardman Co. Ltd., 1987, 1988, at §§2.4 and 4.7(b).

[277] Matter of C.M., 5 I & N Dec. 327 (BIA 1953); see also Tutrone v. Shaughnessy, 160 F. Supp. 433 (S.D.N.Y. 1958).

[278] 18 U.S.C. §5031.

[279] See Morasch v. INS, 363 F. 2d 30 (9th Cir. 1966); Matter of C.M., supra; Matter of Espinoza, 15 I&N Dec. 328 (BIA 1975).

Delinquency Act to determine whether the underlying conduct constitutes a conviction.[280]

1.4(a)(3) Former Federal First Offender Act

A disposition and discharge under the former Federal First Offender Act or its state counterparts prior to November 1, 1987 does not constitute a conviction.[281] Applicants who have been prosecuted under this statute have compelling arguments that such dispositions should not be considered convictions for purposes of INA §§245A and 210. Moreover, applicants with discharges under the first offender statutes of Wisconsin, Virginia, Michigan, and Georgia, should be afforded the same beneficial treatment as those applicants prosecuted under the federal statute. Significantly, while the BIA had held in Matter of Carillo,[282] that the Texas Code of Criminal Procedure 42.12 was not a state counterpart, it found that a sentence to probation under that provision did not constitute a conviction for immigration purposes.[283]

Those aliens convicted under the first offender acts of New Hampshire, Florida, Washington, and Texas have to overcome prior decisions that the laws in those states are not counterparts to the federal statute and as such trigger adverse immigration consequences.[284] Nevertheless, an argument may be made that dispositions under those state statutes are sufficiently similar to the former Federal First Offender Act not to be considered convictions for purposes of eligibility for benefits under INA §§245A and 210.

Dispositions under the Federal First Offender Act offer more relief for temporary resident applicants than expungement

---

[280] Matter of Ramirez-Rivero, 18 I & N Dec. 135 (BIA 1981), and Matter of De La Nues, 18 I & N Dec. 140 (BIA 1981).

[281] P.L. 91-513, 84 Stat. 1245 (1970); 21 U.S.C. 844(b)(1), repealed by Pub.L. 94-473, effective November 1, 1986. See INS Central Office memorandum dated April 22, 1988, reproduced in 65 Interpreter Releases 443-446 (April 25, 1988).

[282] Int. Dec. #2965 (BIA 1984).

[283] Matter of Garcia, Int. Dec. #2995 (BIA 1985).

[284] See, e.g., Matter of Zangwill, 18 I & N Dec. 22 (BIA 1981).

statutes[285] in that a discharge under the former Federal First Offender Act and its state counterparts is not a conviction.

1.4(a)(4) Foreign Convictions

Unlike IRCA's 3 misdemeanor/1 felony bar, INA §§212(a)(9), (a)(10), and (a)(23) apply to foreign convictions as well as to convictions obtained in the United States. In cases which involve a foreign conviction, a determination must first be made as to whether or not the conviction was for a felony or for a misdemeanor. It is often difficult to determine whether or not a conviction by a foreign tribunal constitutes conviction of a felony or of a misdemeanor. Since the United States system of classifying crimes into felonies and misdemeanors is not used worldwide, the Board of Immigration Appeals has developed a standard to determine how a foreign crime should be classified under United States law. This test, first elaborated to determine whether or not a foreign crime constitutes a petty offense in the context of INA §212(a)(9) excludability, is very difficult to apply. The adjudicator must first attempt to locate a comparable offense under the United States Code. If no such offense is found, the adjudicator must turn to Title 22 of the District of Columbia Code to identify the most similar offense under United States law.[286]

It is advisable to obtain a certified copy of the record of conviction and attempt to identify the most lenient equivalent statute. If possible, consultation with an experienced criminal attorney, as well as with an attorney or advocate with expertise in immigration consequences related to criminal convictions is advised.[287]

1.4(a)(5) Crime of Moral Turpitude

Whether or not a crime involves moral turpitude is based on the nature of the crime, not the specific conduct of the person convicted.[288] If the minimum conduct required to be convicted under the statute does not require vile and base (turpitudinous) conduct, the crime does not involve moral turpitude. Thus, an unusually

---

[285] Matter of Seda, supra; expungements are discussed in Chapter Eleven.

[286] See Matter of De La Nues, 19 I & N Dec. 140 (BIA 1981).

[287] See in particular Immigration Law and Crimes, supra, at Chapter Four.

[288] US ex rel. Robinson v. Day, 51 F. 2d 1022, 1022-23 (2d Cir. 1931).

flagrant violation of a crime for which non-flagrant conduct could also result in a conviction, is not a conviction for a "crime involving moral turpitude."

On the one hand, the phrase "moral turpitude" is not subject to a uniform definition. In <u>Jordan v. DeGeorge</u>, 341 U.S. 223 (1951), the United States Supreme Court held that the phrase "moral turpitude" was not void for vagueness. Generally, murder, rape, crimes in which fraud is an element, and larceny involve moral turpitude. On the other hand, prior case law only has value as precedent for the same statute and for statutes that provide an identical definition of the crime charged. For example, not all crimes related to illicit sexual conduct involve moral turpitude. Convictions for gross indecency,[289] and simple fornication,[290] have been held not to involve moral turpitude. Moreover, the same crime may involve moral turpitude in one state, but may not involve moral turpitude in another state. Crimes identified by the same name frequently are defined differently in different jurisdictions.

The elements of the crime as defined by the statute are often crucial factors in judicial determinations of whether or not a particular crime involves moral turpitude. A crime in one jurisdiction could have different elements required for conviction than a crime with the same name in another jurisdiction. For example, the Board of Immigration Appeals has held that the conviction under an Ohio criminal non-support statute did not involve moral turpitude,[291] but that a conviction under a Wisconsin statute for the same offense did involve moral turpitude.[292] Thus, with the exception of a few crimes that have been treated universally as involving moral turpitude, the crime for which the alien was convicted should be subjected to research and analysis to determine whether or not the crime involves moral turpitude.[293]

1.4(a)(6) Petty Offenses

INA §212(a)(9) was recently amended by the Comprehensive Crime Control Act of 1984 regarding that provision's exception for petty

---

[289] <u>Matter of Z</u>, I & N Dec. 316 (BIA 1945).

[290] <u>Matter of R</u>, 6 I & N Dec. 444 (BIA 1954).

[291] <u>Matter of E</u>, 2 I & N Dec. 134 (Aff'd A.G. 1944).

[292] <u>Matter of R</u>, 4 I & N 192 (BIA 1950).

[293] For an extensive analytical discussion of crimes of moral turpitude, see <u>Immigration Law and Crimes</u>, <u>supra</u>, at Chapter Six. This volume also contains a table of published decisions on this issue, organized by type of crime, at Appendix E-1.

offenses. Effective November 1, 1987, the petty offense exception will provide,

> An alien who would be excludable because of the conviction of an offense for which the sentence imposed did not exceed a term of imprisonment in excess of six months, or who would be excludable as one who admits the commission of an offense for which a sentence not to exceed one year's imprisonment might have been imposed upon him, may be granted a visa and admitted to the United States if otherwise admissable: provided, that the alien has committed only one such offense....

The law currently provides that a petty offense is a misdemeanor (defined as a crime for which the maximum sentence is less than one year) for which the sentence imposed did not exceed six months. 18 USC §1(1), (3). Given the language of the future as well as the present "petty offense" exception, it is critical to obtain a record of the sentencing order to determine whether the exception will apply to a particular offense. An applicant whose imposed sentence exceeds imprisonment for a period of six months cannot benefit from consideration under this provision of §212(a)(9) even though the applicant was released early on parole, or for good behavior. Probation or reduced sentences are not deemed to be imprisonment for a period of six months. Suspended sentences _do_ count as imprisonment.[294]

1.4(a)(7) Controlled Substance Offenses

An alien convicted for possessing or distributing designated controlled or narcotic substances is subject to harsh treatment under the immigration laws. Excludability under INA §212(a)(23) as a trafficker in controlled substances or narcotics does not require a conviction, but is based upon a "reason to believe" standard. The Immigration and Naturalization Service has issued instructions on the processing of those aliens _arrested_ for controlled substance offenses whom may be eligible for legalization.[295] Controlled substance and narcotics convictions are not ameliorated by a judicial recommendation against deportation, by a pardon, or under traditional expungement mechanisms.[296]

Nevertheless, some relief is available to aliens convicted under the former Federal Youth Corrections Act, former 18 USC 5021, and its state counterparts; those convicted under the former

---

[294] See Matter of Castro, Int. Dec. #1073 (BIA 1988).

[295] Legalization Wire #7, dated December 5, 1986. Reproduced in the Appendix.

[296] See discussion at §1.4(a)(8) below.

Federal First Offender Act and its state counterparts; and those convicted for possession of small quantities of marijuana. An alien convicted of possession of less than thirty grams of marijuana, and thus excludable under INA §212(a)(23), is eligible to apply for an IRCA waiver.[297]

1.4(a)(8) Post-Conviction Relief

If the alien's conviction falls squarely within the criminal conduct proscribed by INA §212(a)(9) or (10), it is possible that post-conviction remedies may have been obtained or may still be available to the convicted alien. There are a number of post-conviction remedies which may either obviate the conviction entirely or ameliorate the immigration consequences which would otherwise flow from the conviction and sentence. These remedies include,

(1) a motion to withdraw a plea of guilty and vacate judgment;

(2) a motion for coram nobis or habeas corpus relief;

(3) a motion to correct or reduce sentence;

(4) expungement of conviction;[298]

(5) former Federal Youth Correction Act amelioration;

(6) former Federal First Offender Act dispositions; and present federal first offender provisions, 18 USC 3607, yet to be construed by judicial decision;[299]

(7) Writ of audita querela;

(8) Judicial Recommendation Against Deportation.[300]

INA §241(b) provides that the sentencing judge may enter a judicial recommendation against deportation (JRAD) at the time of

---

[297] See 8 CFR §§245a.2(k)(3), 210.3(e)(3). Compare INA §212(h).

[298] See Matter of V., 560 33/701 (BIA 1943); Matter of O.T., 4 I & N 265 (BIA 1943); Matter of A-F, 8 I & N 429 (AG 1959).

[299] A discussion of these post-conviction remedies as well as sample pleadings, are contained in Chapter Four of Immigration Law and Crimes, supra.

[300] INA §241(b).

sentencing or shortly thereafter. If such a recommendation has been included in the criminal court records (except for convictions relating to controlled substances), the offense cannot be used as a basis for excluding the alien under §212(a)(9) or (10).[301] Similarly integral to amelioration of the effects of conviction of a crime of moral turpitude within the statutory scheme of INA §241, is a pardon. Neither a JRAD or a pardon will nullify the immigration consequences of a narcotics conviction.[302] INS has taken the position that a Judicial Recommendation Against Deportation does not bar the use of a conviction for purposes of determining IRCA eligibility.[303]

The writ of _audita querela_ has been successfully used to vacate both felony and misdemeanor convictions where the consequences of the conviction were unforseen due to the subsequent creation of a right to legal status under IRCA.[304]

A final order of expungement of a non-drug related offense will eliminate the conviction as a bar to IRCA eligibility. Also pardons and writs of coram nobis are treated as if no conviction had existed. Aliens "convicted" prior to October 12, 1984 under the Federal Youth Offenders Act or its state counterparts are not barred from eligibility under INA §245A by virtue of the offense.

The length of time required to obtain post-conviction remedies makes it imperative that steps be taken immediately following the initial consultation to set this process in motion. Nonetheless, inability to obtain post-conviction relief within the application period may force the alien to submit his or her application and face denial, in the hope that the post-conviction remedy is granted in time to submit it as evidence in the context of administrative appellate review. This strategy poses a judgment call, as proceeding to file an application on behalf of a previously undetected alien without first having obtained certain amelioration or waiver of grounds of excludability, notifies INS of his or her presence while eligibility for benefits are still less than certain. While the confidentiality provision should insulate the alien from INS action based on the application alone, the alien may be vulnerable to deportation proceedings initiated on a purportedly independent basis.

---

[301] See _Rasmussen v. Robinson_, 163 F. 2d 732 (3d Cir. 1947).

[302] _Matter of Lindner_, 15 I & N Dec. 170 (BIA 1970).

[303] See INS Central Office memorandum dated April 22, 1988, reproduced in 65 Interpreter Releases 443-446 (April 25, 1988).

[304] See _United States v. Salgado_, 692 F. Supp. 1265 (E.D. Wash. 1988); _U.S. v. Ghebreziabher_, 701 F. Supp. 115 (E.D. La. 1988).

1.4(b) Persons Likely to Become Public Charges, INA §212(a)(15)

INA §212(a)(15) bars the admission to the United States of any alien found likely to become a public charge. This ground of excludability applies to all legalization applicants; however, legalization applicants found to be excludable under the traditional test of INA §212(a)(15) benefit from a special rule whereby an alternate standard can be used to determine excludability. INA §245A(d)(2)(B)(iii) provides that an alien will not be ineligible for adjustment of status because of likelihood of becoming a public charge if the alien demonstrates a history of employment in the United States evidencing self-support without receipt of public cash assistance. Those legalization applicants who fail to satisfy both the traditional standard and the special rule may nonetheless qualify for a waiver of excludability. SAWs may also satisfy one or the other of a similar two-tiered test of public charge excludability, however no waiver is available to those SAWs ultimately found excludable under INA §212(a)(15).

Thus, under the statute, the inquiry into excludability under INA §212(a)(15) can be summarized as follows:

a) Is the applicant likely to become a public charge? The totality of the circumstances should be taken into account including affidavits of support, future employment prospects, etc.

b) If applicant appears to be likely to become a public charge under the above test, has the applicant nonetheless demonstrated a consistent employment history which shows the ability to support self and family? i.e., regularly attached to the workforce, income over a substantial period of the time, etc. (length of receipt of public cash assistance a significant factor).

c) (If a legalization applicant) If applicant is found to be likely to become a public charge under both of the above tests, would the granting of a waiver serve humanitarian purposes, assure family unity, or be in the public interest? Failure to advise an excludable alien of the availability of a waiver is a reversible error. Matter of A---, Int. Dec.___ (Comm'r December 29, 1988).

1.4(b)(1) Determining Likelihood of Becoming a Public Charge

The determination of whether or not an alien is likely to become a public charge arises traditionally in these contexts:

applications for adjustment of status to lawful permanent resident status; exclusion proceedings conducted within the United States by the Immigration and Naturalization Service or the Executive Office for Immigration Review; and the adjudication of immigrant and nonimmigrant applications made before the United States consulates abroad at the time an alien applies for a visa to come to the United States. Those cases which have construed INA §212(a)(15) reveal that the traditional test for determining whether or not an alien is likely to become a public charge is "a prediction based on the totality of the alien's circumstances" at the time he or she applies for admission.[305]

Unfortunately, INS regulations and policies did not clearly track the two-tier analysis of the statute. INS' regulations relating to public charge determinations were successfully challenged as unlawfully substituting a higher, single, standard of financial responsibility" (the special rule) for the two-tier analysis set-forth in the statute.[306] INS first determination, then, must be whether the alien meets the traditional "totality of the circumstances" test.[307]

The government must consider a variety of factors: age, health, mental and physical disabilities, the capacity to earn a living, prior receipt of public assistance, family situation, work history, the amount of funds available for self-support and the existence of others in the United States willing and able to offer their assistance.[308] Low income or prior receipt of public assistance, while relevant, are not determinative where other factors suggest the capacity to be self-sustaining.[309] Excludability under INA §212(a)(15) is not a penalty for past receipt of public assistance. Rather, all factors must be considered prospectively, to foretell whether or not there exists a likelihood that the alien will require public assistance in the future.

The INS makes a prospective evaluation of a variety of factors ("age, health, income and vocation") in determining likelihood of becoming a public charge. "The existence or absence of a

---

[305] Matter of Perez, 15 I & N Dec. 136, 137 (BIA 1974).

[306] Zambrano v. INS, No. CIV-88-455-EJG (E.D.Cal.1988).

[307] See also INS Central Office wire dated September 23, 1987.

[308] Matter of Perez, supra; Matter of Harutunian, 14 I & N Dec. 583, 588-90 (Reg. Comm. 1974); Matter of Martinez-Lopez, 10 I & N 409, 421 (Op. Atty. Gen. 1964).

[309] See Matter of Martinez-Lopez, supra.

particular factor should never be the sole criteria for determining if an alien is likely to become a public charge."[310] "Obviously an unemancipated child will be unable to provide a history of employment. Therefore the review of the public charge ground with respect to minor children should be much more flexible than that of an able bodied adult."[311]

The regulations implementing the legalization program which construe excludability under INA §212(a)(15) make specific reference to the Poverty Income Guidelines,[312] and the applicant should, if possible, present evidence of resources which to Poverty Income Guideline levels, however, the application of the guidelines should be challenged in those cases in which the totality of the circumstances indicate that the alien, despite a low income, will not become a public charge. INS has specifically instructed the legalization offices not to use the poverty Income Guidelines as a standard.[313] The "totality of the circumstances" test was applied by the LAU in Matter of A---[314] in which it found that a 33-year old mother of three, physically capable of working and presently employed, was not excludable despite the family's receipt of public assistance for 4 years. The LAU further observed that a mother's absence from the work force to care for her children is an insufficient basis to support public charge excludability.

Applicants for either adjustment of status or for consular visa processing can satisfy the standard for determining admissibility by presenting either tax records or an "Offer of Employment" form (DS-1743) or employer's letter demonstrating acceptable income potential. If the funds of the alien and of dependant family members do not indicate that the alien is admissible under INA §212(a)(15), affidavits of support can be submitted by relatives and friends in the United States. Affidavits of Support (Form I-134) are acceptable evidence in applications processed before consular officers, as well as in

---

[310] See INS Central Office wire dated September 23, 1987.

[311] See INS Central Office wire dated November 10, 1987, reproduced in the Appendix.

[312] The Poverty Income Guidelines are published at 45 CFR 1060.2, and are periodically updated in the Federal Register; the current Poverty Income Guidelines are found in 53 Fed. Reg. 4214 (February 12, 1988).

[313] See INS Central Office memorandum dated September 10, 1987.

[314] In Adjustment of Status Proceedings, designated by Commissioner, December 29, 1988.

establishing admissibility in applications filed within the United States.[315]

In legalization cases, the above-mentioned documents, as well as other forms of proof, can be presented as proof of admissibility under INA §212(a)(15). In addition, evidence of employment, if submitted to substantiate residence in the United States since 1982, will serve to overcome excludability under INA §212(a)(15).[316] Specifically, the applicant may provide:

1) Evidence of a history of employment (i.e., employment letter, W-2 forms, income tax returns, etc.);

2) Evidence that he/she is self-supporting (i.e., bank statements, stocks, other assets, etc.,); or

3) Form I-134, Affidavit of Support, completed by a spouse in behalf of the applicant and/or children of the applicant or a parent in behalf of children which guarantees complete or partial financial support. Acceptance of the Affidavit of Support shall be extended to other family members such as aunts or foster parents, in some circumstances.[317]

Other documents pertinent to the applicant's particular circumstances may be presented. It is important to remember that excludability under INA §212(a)(15) requires an analysis of what the applicant's financial status will be _in the future_, based on the totality of the circumstances. In this context, in can be argued that one of the circumstances which cannot be ignored in legalization cases is the fact that an alien who has worked in the United States since 1982 may have an income below the poverty income guidelines because his or her salary is artificially low because of exploitation of his or her past unlawful status. It is unrealistic to project this artificially low income into the future, ignoring the fact that the applicant's future lawful resident status should allow him or her to work for the prevailing wage in his or her present occupation. Therefore, in cases of low annual income, wage surveys indicating the actual prevailing wage for the applicant's occupation and area of employment might be presented as a more reliable predictor of future earning capacity than past income levels.

---

[315] See Foreign Affairs Manual, §40.7(a)(15), notes N6, N6.1, N6.2, N6.3, formerly §42.91(a)(15), Notes 4.1, 4.2, 4.3.

[316] 8 CFR §245a.2(d)(4)

[317] 8 CFR §245a.2(d)(4), as amended, 52 Fed. Reg. 43845 (November 11, 1987); Central Office Cable dated August 14, 1987, and INS memorandum dated November 10, 1987.

In most cases, an alien with no U.S. citizen or permanent resident dependents and no health or medical problems can simply argue that the five year ban on receipt of public assistance by temporary residents makes it virtually impossible to become a public charge in the future.

Lastly, the INA and the Foreign Affairs Manual provide for the posting of a public charge bond of at least $1000 in those cases in which the financial evidence submitted is not sufficient to establish beyond question that the alien will not become a public charge.[318] This provision can arguably be applied in legalization cases. According to the Foreign Affairs Manual, a public charge bond should be used in borderline cases. Where an alien appears prima facie likely to become a public charge (for example because of a physical condition and a lack of resources), the filing of a public charge bond would not serve a purpose. Public charge bonds may be cancelled when the District Director having jurisdiction over the alien's place of residence is satisfied that the alien is not likely to become a public charge. If no prior application for cancellation is made, the INS will inquire as to the continuing need for the bond when five years have elapsed following the alien's entry.[319] INA §213 provides that federal, state and local governmental units can recover the public charge bond money if the alien does become a public charge after entry.

1.4(b)(2) Determining the Alternate Public Charge Inadmissibility Standard

The same standard applied to determine whether a potential permanent resident is likely to become a public charge, i.e., the totality of the circumstances test, must be the standard applied to applicants for temporary resident status. Aliens who can satisfy this test are not excludable under 212(a)(15) and no further inquiry is required.[320]

Congress provided an alternate basis for an alien to establish admissibility with regard to the ground of excludability imposed upon those who are likely to become a public charge. The language of the alternate standard differs slightly as to the legalization and the SAW programs. Under the legalization program, the low-income alien who might otherwise be found excludable under the

---

[318] 8 CFR §213.1.

[319] See 22 CFR §42.91(a)(15)(iv); INA §§221(g), 213; Foreign Affairs Manual, §40.7(a)(15), Notes 6.5, N7, N7.1, formerly §40.7(a)(15)N7.1, formerly §42.91(a)(15), Note 5.

[320] Zambrano v. INS, No. CIV-88-455-EJG (1988).

traditional test because the totality of the circumstances indicate that the alien is likely to become a public charge, nevertheless may be eligible for temporary resident status if he or she can demonstrate "a history of employment in the United States evidencing self-support without <u>receipt of</u> public cash assistance."[321]

Given the two separate analysis of admissibility under INA §212(a)(15), the factors relevant under the alternative standard should have no bearing on the admissibility of the applicant able to satisfy the traditional public charge standard.

The alternative standard was introduced in recognition of the fact that applicants for the legalization program often will have earned the lowest of wages; Congress designed the provision to provide "<u>more flexibility than we have historically had in connection with the application of the Immigration Law</u>" (emphasis supplied).[322] The criteria focuses on "whether or not that person has a consistent employment history that shows the ability to support himself and his family even though his income may be below the poverty line."[323] The goal is that he be "self-sustaining", that he "be regularly attached to the work force, <u>has an income for a reasonable period of time, such as a year</u>, and demonstrates the capacity to exist on it and to maintain his family without recourse to public assistance (emphasis supplied)."[324]

Under the regulations implementing the special rule for those who would be excludable under the traditional public charge test,

> An alien who has a consistent history which shows the ability to support himself and his or her family, even though his income may be below the poverty level, may be admissible. The alien's employment history need not be continuous in that it is uninterrupted. It should be continuous in the sense that the alien shall be regularly attached to the workforce, has an income over a substantial period of the applicable time, and has demonstrated the capacity to exist on his or her income and maintain his or her family without recourse to public cash assistance. This regulation is prospective in that the Service shall determine, based on the alien's history, whether he or she is likely to become a public

---

[321] INA §245A(d)(2)(B)(iii).

[322] <u>See</u> 130 Cong. Rec. H 5908 (Daily Ed. June 15, 1984) (Statement of Rep. Brown).

[323] <u>Id</u>.

[324] <u>Id.</u> at H 5909.

charge. Past acceptance of public cash assistance within a history of consistent employment will enter into this decision. The weight given in considering applicability of the public charge provisions will depend on many factors, but the length of time an applicant has received public cash assistance will constitute a significant factor.[325]

Although the statutory provisions of both programs use slightly different terminology, the standard set forth in the regulations and policy memoranda is the same. However, it should be noted that "reliance" on public cash assistance (as would bar a SAW applicant) indicates a long-term dependance on cash assistance as a principal source of income. The legislative history provides support for this view. Although the provision would permit exclusion of an alien who "had been on welfare...for a substantial period of time,"[326]

The statute requires the INS to examine the <u>history of employment in the United States</u> evidencing self-support without receipt of (or reliance on) public cash assistance. Thus, if an examination of the applicant's employment since coming to the United States <u>as a whole</u> shows self-support without receipt of public cash assistance, the special rule allows the individual's admission. The regulations implement this provision by allowing for past acceptance of public assistance within the context of a history of consistent employment. Under factors articulated in the regulation, and in keeping with the traditional test, past receipt of benefits is only one relevant factor to determine the prospective ground of excludability "likely to become a public charge," but it does not indicate <u>per se</u> that the applicant is inadmissible nor does it require a denial of adjustment of status as a matter of law. The length of time an applicant has received public cash assistance will constitute a significant factor in determining whether the applicant is admissible under the special rule.[327]

One of the questions raised by the statute and regulations is <u>how far back</u> in an alien's past the INS can go in considering past receipt of public cash assistance. If any and all receipt of public cash assistance were to render an applicant ineligible for consideration under the special rule, such an interpretation would clearly violate the legislative intent behind the grounds of

---

[325] 8 CFR §245.2(k)(4), as amended by the 52 Fed. Reg. 43845 (November 17, 1987); 8 CFR 210.3(e)(4).

[326] 130 Cong. Rec. H5908 (Daily Ed. June 15, 1984) (Statement of Rep. Brown).

[327] <u>See</u> 8 CFR §§245a.1(i), 210.3(e)(4).

excludability and the special rule itself, both of which are intended to be predictive of future likelihood of becoming a public charge. This would be particularly problematic in the cases of those who had received cash public assistance for a short period of time or in the remote past.

1.4(b)(3) Public Cash Assistance

In the case of an alien who cannot establish admissibility under the traditional test, it is important to determine (a) whether or not it was public <u>cash</u> assistance and (b) whether or not the applicant was a direct <u>recipient</u> of public cash assistance. The regulations define both of these elements.

Because most undocumented aliens have long been ineligible for most cash public assistance programs, cases in which in alien has directly received public cash assistance will be limited to those cases in which the alien had a status such as "color of law" status (e.g., <u>Silva</u> letter holders), or cases in which local or state General Assistance programs did not exclude undocumented aliens, or cases in which the alien committed fraud in order to receive benefits.

The regulations define "public cash assistance" as follows:

> income or needs-based monetary assistance, to include but not limited to supplemental security income, received by the alien or his or her immediate family members[328] through federal, state, or local programs designed to meet subsistence levels. It does not include assistance in kind, such as food stamps, public housing, or other non-cash benefits, nor does it include work-related compensation[329] or certain types of medical assistance (Medicare, Medicaid, emergency treatment, services to pregnant women or children under 18 years of age, or treatment in the interest of public health).[330]

Programs such as Aid to Families with Dependant Children (AFDC), General Assistance (GA) or simple local relief programs, and cash payments made under energy assistance programs are cash assistance programs. Supplemental Security Income (SSI) is

---

[328] The attribution of benefits received by family members to the applicant has been challenged in <u>Zambrano v. INS</u> ___ F. Supp.___ Civ. No. 8-88-455 EJG (E.D. Cal. 1988).

[329] E.g., workman's compensation, unemployment compensation, social security retirement and disability insurance.

[330] 8 CFR §§245a.1(i); interim rule 210.1(m).

considered cash assistance only with regard to the person who receives it; it should not be attributed to immediate family members who reside with the recipient but who are not themselves recipients unless such benefits are the sole means of support of the family.[331] In-kind assistance, such as food stamps, public housing[332], work-related compensation, assistance earmarked for educational needs[333], and Medical Assistance (Medicaid), or payments made to third parties are not cash programs.[334] Foster care payments paid on behalf of the child were considered "cash assistance" received by the child,[335] but this policy was successfully challenged in City of New York v. Meese.[336] Conforming policy directives were subsequently issued.[337] Nor are foster care benefits counted as "public cash assistance" as to foster parents who apply for legalization. Determinations regarding the inclusion/exclusion of numerous other state and federal programs must be left to administrative and judicial interpretation.

1.4(b)(4) Recipient of Public Cash Assistance

The "receipt" of public cash assistance clearly applies to those cases in which an alien has received public cash assistance directly due to either personal eligibility for the assistance, or else through some degree of misrepresentation or presentation of false documents in order to qualify for the assistance. Aliens who have received public cash assistance by either means must divulge this information when applying for temporary resident

---

[331] See INS Central Office wire dated November 23, 1987; INS Central Office Wire dated April 21, 1988, reproduced in 65 Interpreter Releases 447-451 (April 25, 1988).

[332] See letter to Attorney Enrique Valdez dated June 17, 1988, reproduced in 65 Interpreter Releases 922 (September 2, 1988).

[333] See INS Central Office Wire dated June 10, 1988.

[334] See INS Central Office wire dated September 23, 1987, reproduced in the Appendix. See also letter from William Slattery reproduced in 66 Interpreter Releases 249-251 (March 14, 1988).

[335] See INS Central Office memoranda dated November 10, 1987 and December 1, 1987.

[336] 88-CIV-1570 (S.D.N.Y. 1988), reported in 65 Interpreter Releases 232-33 (March 14, 1988) and 65 Interpreter Releases 337-338, 357-358 (April 4, 1988).

[337] See INS Central Office Memorandum dated March 23, 1988, reproduced in 65 Interpreter Releases 357-358 (April 4, 1988).

status, or must sign a verifiable declaration to the contrary and risk prosecution for making a false statement. Those aliens who have received such assistance by fraudulent means may be denied temporary resident status as a matter of public charge ineligibility. Confidentiality provisions will still protect the alien from disclosure of this information to the public assistance agency concerned or to law enforcement authorities.[338] More problematic is the fact that the definition of "public cash assistance" includes cash assistance received by immediate family members.[339] INS' response to comments to the proposed regulations on this issue was "The position of INS is that the statute is clear regarding this subject and applicants may in fact be ineligible for legalization if such cash assistance was received by their U.S. citizen child."[340]

Public assistance programs and regulations draw a clear distinction between the "recipient" of assistance and the "representative payee" to whom the assistance is given for the recipient's benefit. In fact, because the regulations provide for penalties to be assessed against any representative payee who converts public assistance benefits to his or her own use, a representative payee can be prosecuted for personally "receiving" such funds intended for the eligible recipient. Under the regulations, the INS drew no such distinction and many applicants were found to be excludable due to their citizen children's receipt of cash benefits (AFDC). In February of 1988 the INS liberalized its position, stating that cash benefits received under AFDC would not be attributed to a payee parent.[341] This was followed by a class action alleging the wrongful denial of thousands of cases on public charge grounds prior to INS' change in policy.[342]

Those applicants for temporary resident status under the legalization provisions who are found likely to become public charges under the traditional test and under the special rule set forth in INA §245A(d)(2)(B)(iii), are eligible for a waiver of excludability for humanitarian purposes, to assure family unity or for reasons in the public interest. Unfortunately, no waiver of public charge excludability is available during Stage Two of the legalization program, nor is the IRCA waiver available to SAW

---

[338] INA §245A(c)(5), 210(b).

[339] See 8 CFR §§245a.1(i), interim rule 210.2(m).

[340] See Federal Register, Vol. 52, No. 84, May 1, 1987, at p. 16297.

[341] See letter from William Slattery, 66 Interpreter Releases 249-251 (March 17, 1988).

[342] Perales v. Meese, No. 88-CIV-2265 (S.D.N.Y. 1988).

applicants for either temporary or permanent resident stages.

1.5 IMMIGRATION REFORM AND CONTROL ACT WAIVERS[342]

1.5(a) Standard for IRCA Waivers

Legalization, SAW, and EVD Nationality applicants for temporary and permanent residence and for termination of temporary residence under INA §245A who are excludable may be granted a waiver under any of three independent grounds: a) humanitarian purposes; b) to assure family unity; or c) when it is otherwise in the public interest. In contrast to other INA waiver provisions, extreme or exceptional hardship need not be demonstrated.[343]

Although waiver applications are discretionary, the legislative history of IRCA shows that Congress contemplated that they be granted liberally. "In most cases, denials of legalization on the basis of the waivable exclusions should only occur when the applicant also falls within one of the specified nonwaivable grounds of exclusion."[344]

An internal INS memorandum directs legalization offices to apply a balancing test in adjudicating waivers on all of the above three grounds, i.e., if the equities presented are determined to outweigh the identified adverse factors, the application should be approved; if not, it should be denied.[345]

> ...the case law relating to applications for waivers under §212 of the Act remains instructive for the purpose of adjudication of waivers under the IRCA waiver criteria. Factors identified in the case law as heavily weighted adverse factors for the purposes of §212 remain so for the purposes of IRCA. Such factors, unless outweighed by the equities presented, will continue to be a correct basis for denial of a waiver.

---

[342] The specific grounds of excludability which apply to legalization, SAW, and EVD nationality applicants for temporary residence; Cuban-Haitian adjustment applicants; and Registry applicants; and the different waivers available to each of these groups, are set forth in a comparative chart at the end of this volume.

[343] See, for example, INA §§212(h), 212(e).

[344] H.R. Rep. No. 98-115, 98th Cong., 1st Sess. 69-70.

[345] See INS Central Office memorandum dated August 6, 1987.

The balancing of favorable and adverse factors discussed in the caselaw regarding §§212(c), (h), and (i) arises as to the issue of the exercise of discretion. Before this analysis of discretionary factors can be reached, however, the applicant must establish eligibility for the waiver under the statute, i.e., show extreme hardship to certain family members, etc. The same is true in the case of IRCA waivers; the applicant must premise his or her waiver request on one of three enumerated grounds: humanitarian concerns, family unity, and public interest. The exercise of discretion balancing test is not a substitute for the statutory waiver grounds, as one might believe from reading the above memorandum.

Having said this, it is noted that the favorable factors considered in the exercise of discretion overlap with the factors considered to be favorable in the context of INA §212 waivers and include the favorable factors of family unity, humanitarian purposes, and public interest. However, given the plain statutory language, Congress clearly intended that they be given far more weight than other factors. In the context of §212(c) waivers, the Board of Immigration Appeals (BIA) has stated that the minimum equities required to establish eligibility under the statute may be sufficient, in and of themselves, to warrant favorable discretionary action.[346]

Favorable factors which have been weighed in the exercise of discretion regarding §§212(h) and (i) waivers are:

(1) nature of the offense;
(2) circumstances which led to the offense;
(3) how recently the offense occurred;
(4) whether an isolated incident or part of a pattern of misconduct;
(5) evidence of reformation or rehabilitation;
(6) hardship factors such as the age, health, circumstances of the applicant and the relative(s) concerned;
(7) whether the applicant's relationship to the U.S. citizen or permanent resident relative is _bona fide_ and stable;
(8) Other considerations may apply in individual cases.[347]

Under INA §212(c), adverse factors must be balanced against social and humane considerations. Adverse factors include the nature and underlying circumstances of the exclusion ground at issue, the presence of additional significant violations of the

---

[346] <u>Matter of Marin</u>, 16 I.& N.581 (BIA 1978).

[347] <u>I.N.S. Examinations Handbook</u>, Part V, reproduced in Gordon and Rosenfield, <u>Immigration Law and Procedure</u> (Revised Ed., 1987), Vol. 4, p.23A-256. Obviously, most of the above factors are inapplicable in IRCA waiver cases.

immigration laws, the existence of a criminal record and, if so, its nature, recency and seriousness (particularly if a drug offense), and the presence of other evidence of bad character or undesirability. Favorable factors include family ties in the United States, long residence in the United States (particularly when the inception of residence occurred while the respondent was of young age), hardship to the respondent and family, military service, a history of employment, property or business ties, value and service to the community, proof of genuine rehabilitation if a criminal record exists, and good moral character (e.g., affidavits of family, friends, and responsible community representatives).[348]

However, it is important to remember, that

Given the difference between the terminology used for the IRCA waiver criteria and that employed in §212(h), it is clear that Congress intended to establish a distinct standard for implementation of the waiver provisions of IRCA.[349]

The breadth of the statutory language and the variety of factors considered leaves room for creative advocacy. An applicant's job, community activities, family ties, health history, personality traits and numerous other factors should be investigated to support eligibility for a waiver. Humanitarian concerns encompass medical problems, conditions in the home country such as war, persecution, economic conditions and other considerations. Public interest encompasses contributions to the community, the alien's special assistance to his/her employer, and other factors.

1.5(a)(1) Humanitarian Purposes

Though not defined in the regulations, a decision of the Northern RPF has elaborated on the term "humanitarian purposes." The RPF cited the dictionary's definition of "humanitarian" as "...the promotion of human welfare" and welfare as "health, happiness, and general well-being," referring to the LO's denial of temporary resident status due to a fourteen-year old deportation as "unfair to the point of being inhumane."[350] The term "humanitarian purposes" is also briefly discussed in internal INS memoranda. Generally, the term "humanitarian purposes" sets a less stringent or restrictive standard than the "extreme hardship"

---

[348] Matter of Marin, supra.

[349] See INS Central Office memorandum dated August 6, 1987.

[350] LAU decision summarized in AILA February 1989 mailing, p. 89, Reprint No. 101-1288.

requirement of §212(h).[351] "Humanitarian" purposes also encompass the following situation:

> Applicant does not admit the excludable condition, but when asked again as the result of INS records checks, admits the excludable act and submits a waiver. Although the applicant made a false statement...subjecting himself to possible criminal prosecution, the subsequent recantation falls within the humanitarian purposes of Congress. This would be a favorable action in all but the most egregious situations.[352]

1.5(a)(2) Family Unity

Family unity is defined as "maintaining the family group without deviation or change." The family group shall include the spouse, unmarried minor children under 18 years of age who are not members of some other household, and parents who reside regularly in the household of the family group."[353] Note that the terms of the definition of family unity do not require that the applicant _have_ a spouse, unmarried minor child under 18, or a parent in the household in order to qualify for a waiver; rather he or she must be a part of a family unit consisting of those relationships. Thus, the applicant can be the parent or the unmarried minor child described in the definition.

Thus, excludable applicants who are part of a family unit consisting of parents, spouse or minor unmarried children may have the grounds of excludability waived _solely to avoid severance of the family unit_. The immigration status of the other family members and whether the other family members rely on the applicant for support are irrelevant,[354] although copies of documents

---

[351] See INS Central Office memorandum dated August 6, 1987.

[352] See letter from Joseph L. Thomas, INS Western Regional Processing Facility Director, to Attorney Ron Tasoff, reproduced in 64 Interpreter Releases 1328 (November 23, 1987).

[353] 8 CFR §§245a.1(m); interim rule 210.1(e).

[354] Some INS officials have interpreted the family unity basis to apply to cases in which any immediate family member is dependant on the applicant financially, emotionally, or physically. See letter of Joseph Thomas, dated October 14, 1987, supra.
If other family members are U.S. citizens, permanent residents, or IRCA eligible; and if any rely on the applicant for full or partial support, these facts should also be included in the waiver application, as they are among the favorable factors considered in the exercise of discretion and come within the scope

substantiating family members' lawful status, if available, should be submitted.

Nonetheless, the definition may be overly restrictive, given the statute's focus on the family unit, not on specific blood relationships, as in other waiver provisions of the INA. Other provisions of the regulations have been relaxed to encompass non-nuclear family situations such as those in which a minor child resides with an aunt.[355] Common law relationships should also serve as a basis for approving a waiver on family unity grounds.[356] Waiver requests grounded on close relationships which fall outside of the strict regulatory definition should therefore be attempted.

1.5(a)(3) Public Interest

Although "public interest" in not defined in the regulations interpreting IRCA, the term has been interpreted by the LAU. In Matter of P--,[357] the LAU emphasized that waivers should be granted liberally. It also adopted the definition of "public interest" found in Black's Law Dictionary, finding that the applicant's commitment of time, money, and talent (in the job he performed) contributed to the betterment of the community and warranted the approval of a waiver for reasons in the public interest. Those found excludable due to a positive HIV test are required to make an additional showing in order to qualify for a waiver.[358] This may be subject to challenge. "Public interest" is also discussed in the regulations pertaining to parole of aliens into the United States. According to 8 CFR §212.5, the following aliens can be paroled into the United States for reasons deemed "strictly in the public interest:" pregnant women, juveniles, aliens with close family members in the United States who have filed visa petitions on their behalf, witnesses in judicial or governmental proceedings, aliens paroled to the custody of another prosecuting agency, aliens whose continued detention is not in the public interest.

---

of humanitarian considerations, another basis for an IRCA waiver.

[355] See cable from Richard Norton, INS Central Office, dated August 14, 1987, regarding affidavits of support.

[356] Restricting IRCA waivers to marital relationships sanctioned by law would allow estranged spouses to base their waiver applications on family unity.

[357] Int. Dec. #3090, In Legalization Proceedings, decided by INS Commissioner, November 23, 1988.

[358] See Central Office memorandum of July 29, 1988, reproduced in 65 Interpreter Releases 850-851 (August 22, 1988).

The INS has determined that the "public interest" criterion for IRCA waivers should be interpreted in a broader fashion than that utilized in the above regulation which is directed to the detention of alien applicants for admission. Instead, examples of reasons for the approval of an IRCA waiver "in the public interest" include, for example,

> because an alien is particularly eminent in his or her field of endeavor; because an alien has performed noteworthy charitable or public service; because an alien is employed in an occupation in which there is a shortage of workers; because an alien's admission would be beneficial to the national welfare or security or to the welfare of the locality in which he or she resides; or because an alien's admission would serve the interests of the government. These examples are not exhaustive.[359]

One example of a situation in which a waiver may be granted based on the public interest is the case of an applicant who admits the excludable condition on his application. The admission of the excludable act is a forthright indication of honesty and fits within the public interest intent of Congress to allow a long term illegal resident to obtain legal status.[360]

Those who test positive for HIV antibodies are eligible for a waiver under IRCA, however, the INS has substituted a different and stricter standard than that applied when the same waiver is sought for other grounds of excludability. Those seeking a waiver of INA §212(a)(6) due to a positive HIV antibody test must prove:

1. the danger to the public health of the U.S. is minimal;

2. the possibility of the spread of infection in minimal;

3. there will be no cost incurred by any level of government agency of the U.S. without prior consent of that agency.[361]

Application of this distinct standard in adjudicating IRCA waivers is nowhere supported in the statute or the regulations.

---

[359] See INS memorandum dated August 6, 1987.

[360] See letter from Joseph Thomas, supra.

[361] See Central Office Wire dated March 2, 1988, reprinted in 65 Interpreter Releases 239 (March 14, 1988); and CO Wire dated July 29, 1988, reprinted in 65 Interpreter Releases 850-851 (August 22, 1988).

1.5(b) Procedures for Applying for a Waiver

An application for a Waiver of Grounds of Excludability (Form I-690) can be filed jointly with the application for temporary residence or after the alien's preliminary interview at the legalization office. The regulations provide that if the waiver application is submitted after the interview, the waiver is forwarded to the appropriate regional processing facility. Therefore, because in many cases the issue of excludability will not arise until the interview itself, it is best not to file a hastily drafted waiver application on the spot but rather to prepare it after the interview and have it forwarded later to the regional processing facility.

The same procedures are followed by both legalization and SAW applicants found to be excludable. SAWs who apply for temporary residence at overseas processing posts file their waivers with the consular official in the same manner as those applying at legalization offices.[362] SAWs who seek admission at a port of entry must present a waiver of any applicable ground of excludability. All applications for waivers must be accompanied by a money order, cashier's check or bank check for $35.00. No personal checks or cash will be accepted.

The LAU has held that the failure of the INS to advise a temporary resident of the availability of a waiver is reversible error.[363]

The waiver application should be accompanied by as much documentation in support of the request as is possible. The circumstances of the particular case will often not fall into a neat category such as "humanitarian," "family unity" or " public interest" but rather, will contain elements of each of these grounds. Under the humanitarian aspects of a case, the applicant should present detailed doctors letters, medical records; materials commonly used in political asylum cases to document conditions of war and/or persecution, if applicable; documentation of economic conditions in the home country; psychological reports, etc. Family unity considerations can be highlighted by such supporting evidence as birth certificates of children; letters and/or affidavits from neighbors, teachers, ministers or priests, friends, relatives; family photographs, letters; tax returns, etc., and other evidence. Public Interest can be demonstrated by letters, affidavits or other documents evidencing the applicant's contributions to the

---

[362] See State Department cable dated May 27, 1987. But note that this cable indicates that the filing fee for such a waiver is fifty dollars, rather than thirty-five dollars.

[363] Matter of A---, Int. Dec. #_____ (Comm'r December 29, 1988).

community, school, church, or other organization; an employer's attestation of the applicant's special value to his business; records of school attendance, awards, and other evidence of self-improvement; etc. One of the sample appeal notices at the end of Chapter Five pertains to the denial of a waiver and can be adapted for use as an attachment to a waiver application.

In those cases involving clear statutory ineligibility or admitted fraud, the District Director may deny the waiver application rather than forward it to the regional processing facility (RPF).[364] However, not all fraud that is uncovered will result in an automatic denial of the application and/or waiver. Fraud is one of the grounds of excludability for which a waiver was expressly made available under the IRCA. If the alien makes a false statement in connection with the legalization application but, when questioned further, admits the excludable act, then a waiver may be granted for humanitarian reasons. However, if the alien does not admit the excludable act when confronted by INS, the waiver and application may be denied by the RPF.[365]

The waiver will be forwarded to the RPF. The applicant shall be notified of the decision and, if the application is denied, of the reason therefore. The applicant may appeal the decision within 30 days of the service of the notice of denial to the INS Administrative Appeals Unit.[366] SAWs who apply at overseas processing posts have 60 days within which to file an appeal at the post.[367]

1.5(c) Waivers Under §212 of the INA

§212 of the INA not only lists the various grounds of excludability, it also contains several provisions which waive those grounds of excludability in certain circumstances. There is nothing in IRCA which prevents the application of these waiver provisions to those grounds of excludability which cannot be waived by the more liberal waiver provisions of INA §245A(d)(2)(B)(i) and §210(c)(2)(B)(i); in fact, there are strong arguments supporting

---

[364] See 8 CFR §§245a.2(k)(2). Interim rule 210.3(e)(2).

[365] See letter of Joseph Thomas dated October 14, 1987. In lieu of issuing a recommendation and forwarding the application to the RPF for final decision, the legalization office can deny an application based on fraud admitted by the applicant, but not based on suspected fraud. 8 CFR §103.1(h).

[366] 8 CFR §§245a.2(k)(2) and 210.3(e)(2).

[367] See State Department cable dated May 27, 1987.

the applicability of INA §212 waivers to temporary residence applications.

As a practical matter, the applicability of several of the other waiver provisions of the INA will seldom, if ever, arise because they are by their terms limited to lawful permanent residents or returning resident aliens.[368] One of the INA waiver provisions which might be useful in some cases (e.g., a misdemeanor crime of moral turpitude) is the waiver provided in INA §212(h), available in those cases where the alien is determined to be excludable under INA §§212(a)(9), (10), or (12).[369]

The requirements for a waiver under INA §212(h) are:

1. The applicant must be a spouse, child (including minor unmarried, adopted child) of a United States citizen or permanent resident alien, or must have a son or daughter who is a United States citizen or a permanent resident alien; and
2. Extreme hardship would result to the United States citizen or permanent resident spouse, parent, son or daughter; and
3. Admission must not be contrary to the national welfare, safety or security of the United States; and
4. The Attorney General, pursuant to the terms, conditions and procedures as the regulations prescribe, must consent to the applicant's admission.

INA §101 defines spouse and child. The definition of spouse includes an estranged spouse and an INA §212(h) waiver has been granted in cases where the alien, though separated from his/her spouse, nonetheless supported his/her family.[370] If the alien applicant is an adult, (s)he cannot claim hardship to his lawful

---

[368] See, e.g., INA §212(c) waiver, limited to persons who have continuously resided as lawful permanent residents for more than seven years.

[369] It also is important to remember that in the case of a pre-1982 applicant, any waiver of crime related disqualifications must overcome both grounds of inadmissibility under INA §212(a)(9) or (10), and ineligibility based upon conviction of one felony or three misdemeanors. See discussion of post-conviction remedies, infra. at §1.4(a).

[370] Matter of Heller, 12 I&N 319 (1967); see also Silva v. Carter, 326 F.2d 315 (9th Cir.1963).

permanent resident or United States citizen parent, as such a relationship is not within the ambit of the statute.[371]

The alien applicant must also prove that "extreme hardship" would result to his or her citizen or lawful permanent resident spouse, parent, son or daughter. Extreme hardship to the applicant is irrelevant. A large body of caselaw has interpreted the term "extreme hardship" as applied under INA 244, and to a lesser extent, under 8 CFR §212.7(c) and 22 CFR §514.31.[372]

The INS has taken the contradictory position that section 212 waivers apply in some legalization cases, but do not apply in most cases. While on the one hand it concludes that the sole statutory authority for waivers in connection with legalization or SAW applications are the waiver provisions of §§210 and 245A, which are not available for §§212(a)(9) and (10); and that a previously obtained §212(h) waiver of these grounds is therefore without effect, it nonetheless allows the applicant to use a previously obtained INA §212(h) waivers of INA §212(a)(23) as it relates to simple possession of 30 grams or less of marijuana, and previously obtained INA §212(i) waivers of INA §212(a)(19) fraud grounds, in cases in which the family relationship or extreme hardship on which the waiver was based continues to exist.[373] This selective application of INA §212 waiver provisions is nowhere supported by the statutory language.

The INS restricts the latter §§212(i) and 212(h) waivers to legalization applicants who had "previously obtained" these waivers; it also instructs district offices which receive applications under §212(h) for waivers of §212(a)(9) or (10) from applicants who identify themselves solely as prospective SAW or legalization applicants to deny such applications based on the applicants' clear statutory ineligibility for legalization or for SAW status.

IRCA lists excludability grounds §§212(a)(9), (10), (23), (27), (28), (29), and in some cases (15), as grounds which cannot be waived..."under clause (i) [referring to the IRCA waiver for humanitarian purposes, etc.]" It does not say that these grounds

---

[371] See Chiaramonte v. INS, 626 F.2d 1093, 1100 (2d Cir. 1980).

[372] For a discussion of the factors considered in determining the establishment of "extreme hardship," see National Immigration Project, Immigration Law and Defense, Clark Boardman Co. Ltd., at p. 8-22.

[373] See the August 6, 1987 memorandum of INS Assistant Commissioner William Slattery, reproduced in the Appendix.

of excludability can never be waived.[374] The regulations state that "[n]otwithstanding any other provision of the Act (emphasis supplied), the following provisions [INA §§212(a)(9), (10), (27), (28), (29) and (33)] may not be waived under paragraph (k)(2) of this section [regarding IRCA humanitarian waivers]...",[375] implying that other waiver provisions under the Act may obtain.

Furthermore, the language of IRCA supports the general applicability of INA §212 waivers to the legalization and SAW programs. It is significant that IRCA requires that the alien be admissible, rather than requiring that the alien not be excludable under certain specified grounds of excludability. Admissibility and excludability are not two sides of the same coin. Admissibility is broader, encompassing qualitative, numerical, and documentary restrictions as set forth in both INA §§211 and 212 in their entirety; subsumed within INA §212 are the grounds of excludability.[376] INA §212 also contains, of course, waivers of those exclusion grounds which would otherwise render an alien inadmissible. The waiver provisions must be read together with INA §212(a) and INA §211 to construe the term "admissibility". By requiring "admissibility" Congress arguably intended all statutory provisions which define that concept to apply, not just the grounds of excludability.

That "admissibility" encompasses waivers of excludability under INA §212 is also supported by the fact that INA §212 waivers are available to both Cuban-Haitian adjustment applicants and Registry applicants. In both cases, the statute requires aliens to demonstrate "admissibility" to the United States; the statute was silent about the applicability of INA §212 waivers.[377] The INS, in interpreting these provisions, has nonetheless determined that §212 waivers are available to overcome excludability in these cases.[378]

---

[374] See INA §§245A(d)(2)(B)(i) and (ii); 210(c)(2)(A), (B).

[375] 8 CFR §245a.2(k)(3).

[376] See Gordon and Rosenfield, Immigration Law and Procedure, Vol. 1 §2.1b (revised ed. 1987) 2-12.

[377] See INA §249, and Note 10A, §202, Act of Nov. 6, 1986, P.L. 99-603, 100 Stat. 3359 providing for adjustment of Cuban/Haitian nationals.

[378] See letter from Richard Norton, Assistant Commissioner for Examinations to Warren Lieden, dated June 8, 1987; and see 8 CFR §249.1. Only INA §212(h) waivers are available to Registry applicants because the other INA §212 waivers apply to those grounds of excludability which are statutorily inapplicable to Registry cases.

In the case of crimes which may be waived under this waiver provision, it can be argued the INS' policy memorandum of August 6, 1987 exceeds the permissible scope of interpretation of INS' own regulation. Limiting qualified §212(h) waiver applicants' access to existing statutory means of removing the disability of a conviction for a crime of moral turpitude is beyond the scope of the relevant statutory section, and is _ultra vires_. According to this argument, under any of several principles of statutory interpretation, neither the statutory language nor the legislative history favor INS' regulatory and policy memo implementation limiting accessibility to these benefits.[379]

IRCA was an ameliorative statute and the new waiver provision was intended to provide a broader, more liberal provision, not to restrict existing avenues of relief. It is clear that Congressional intent in enacting the "humanitarian, family unity" waiver was not to prevent applicants for temporary and permanent residence under the SAW and pre-1982 legalization provisions from utilizing existing statutory mechanisms in order to qualify for benefits. The interpretation proposed by INS limiting access to the §212(h) waiver appears not only to be inconsistent with the statute and with legislative intent, but to be contrary to judicial practice and rational administrative policy. Case law previously interpreting the applicability of §212(h) has upheld its availability to those aliens who seek a waiver of deportability under §241(a), as well as its applicability to those who seek to overcome excludability under §212(a).[380] Thus, the BIA itself has recognized that it is logical, reasonable, and appropriate to extend the ameliorative provisions of §212(h) to disqualifications for immigration benefits or sanctions for immigration violations

---

[379] _See_ discussion of legal authority for challenging INS' restrictive interpretation of the statute at §1.5(c), _infra_.

[380] _See_ Matter of Millard, 11 I & N Dec. 175 (BIA 1965) (available in deportation proceedings to cure a charge of deportability under §241(a)(1) premised upon an alien's excludability at time of entry); Matter of P-, 7 I & N Dec. 713 (BIA 1958). _See also_ Matter of Sanchez, 17 I & N 218 (BIA 1980) (charge of deportability under §241(a)(4) rather than under §241(a)(1) [excludable at time of entry] does not preclude relief under §212(h)); Matter of Tanori, 15 I & N Dec. 566 (BIA 1976) (§212(h) available to waive excludability on same facts forming basis of charge of deportability under §241(a)(11), where §212(c) waiver would be granted permanent resident _nunc pro tunc_).

other than those associated literally with <u>admissibility</u> as an immigrant under INA §§203 and 204.[381]

The advocate should prepare and submit an application for a waiver under INA §212(h) whenever a waiver would otherwise be available to an applicant for an immigrant visa. The question then becomes where and how to file an application for a waiver under INA §212(h) (normally submitted on form I-601). Based on the premise that the waiver provisions are an integral part of INA §212 as it is applied to legalization applicants, and to bring such applications within IRCA's confidentiality protections, such waivers should be filed at the legalization office. Form I-601 should be used instead of form I-690. The fee for I-601 waivers is $35.

It is likely that the LO will reject the application on its face and deny the applicant temporary residence, or at best, will forward the application to the RPF where, according to current INS policy, it will be denied. This denial should be appealed. The INS policy is not only wrong as a matter of law, but is unsound as a matter of administrative policy. Denial of access to §210 or §245A benefits by failure to acknowledge the §212(h) waiver, is likely to result in one of two undesirable alternatives. On the one hand, it may require the applicant either to continue to live an underground, unlawful existence, contrary to IRCA's stated purpose, in order to remain in the United States. On the other hand, it may impose separation either from family or from a current employer who may have already obtained a labor certification from the Department of Labor indicating the need for the applicant's services.

It is critical that applicants who may have been turned away or advised they were ineligible be contacted so that initial applications can be submitted. As with any other decision to apply for temporary residence, this is, of course, the applicant's choice. Yet the alien incurs no risk by the filing of such an application, as even an applicant who is denied is protected by the confidentiality provisions of IRCA. If the INS ultimately is forced to recognize the applicability

---

[381] There have been other instances in which the Board or the courts have determined it appropriate to apply remedial and ameliorative provisions contained in the INA or regulations pursuant to it to closely related sections of the INA conferring benefits on otherwise eligible aliens. For example, in <u>Rasmussen v. Robinson</u>, 163 F.2d 732 (3rd Cir. 1947), the court held that the benefit of a judicial recommendation against deportation under §241(b) could be invoked by an alien seeking entry who must establish <u>admissibility</u>, as well as by an alien subject to charges of having violated the INA, who must establish that he or she is not deportable. <u>See</u> <u>also</u>, <u>Matter of K.</u>, 9 I&N 121 (BIA 196)).

of the waiver under INA §212(h), those who were denied and whose cases are pending before the LAU may benefit while others who never applied may be unable to obtain benefits. At the same time, if the argument for §212(h) waiver is successful, it may be possible to demand a post-application period adjudication for an applicant who never applied either due to misinformation from INS or a QDE following INS advice.

1.6 CONFIDENTIALITY, FRAUD AND RELATED CRIMINAL PENALTIES

1.6(a) Confidentiality

As with the first stage of the program, the contents of the application and supporting documentation provided by an applicant for permanent resident status under the legalization program are protected by a statutory guarantee of confidentiality. In this regard, two issues have arisen as the legalization program has evolved: first, the INS has taken the position that the confidentiality protections terminate once the alien is granted permanent resident status;[382] second, in some cities the U.S. Border Patrol and INS investigators routinely call the Legalization Office to "verify" whether a detained individual with a valid form I-688 or I-688A has in fact applied under INA §245A or 210, and to determine the status of the application. Both may violate the confidentiality provisions.

IRCA prohibits the use of the information furnished pursuant to an application for temporary residence by any official, employee, bureau or agency of the Department of Justice[383] for any purpose other than to: (a) make a determination on the application, or (b) enforce the criminal provisions prohibiting the submission of false statements or documents in the application for permanent residence. Also prohibited is the making of any publication whereby the information furnished by any particular individual can be identified; and permitting anyone other than the sworn officers and employees of the Department or bureau or agency or, with respect to applications filed with a designated entity, that designated entity, to examine individual applications.[384]

According to the terms of the confidentiality protection, the information provided on the application Form I-698 and in

---

[382] See interim rule 8 CFR §245a.3(m)(4).

[383] The Department of Justice includes, among others, the Immigration and Naturalization Service (INS), the Federal Bureau of Investigation, and the United States Attorney's office.

[384] INA §245A(c)(4); 8 CFR §245a.3(m); INA §210(b)(6); 8 CFR §210.2(e).

supporting documents can not be used to locate, apprehend, or deport undocumented family members listed on the application. It cannot be used as a basis for prosecuting an alien for apparent welfare fraud, tax evasion, or for other violations of law apparent in supporting documentation.

Because confidentiality provisions refer specifically to employees of the Department of Justice, SAW applications filed with the Department of State at overseas processing posts may fall outside of the confidentiality provisions; State Department employees were instructed to maintain copies of I-700 applications submitted to them.[385] Also, pursuant to Temporary Transitional Admissions Standards for SAWS, aliens who presented a completed and credible I-700 to Immigration officials at designated ports of entry were admitted to the United States for 90 days and instructed to apply for temporary residence at an INS Legalization Office within 90 days. INS officials at the ports of entry were also instructed to retain a copy of the I-700 before returning the original to the applicant for filing at the L.O.[386] Because the retention by INS of copies of the I-700 is not undertaken for the purpose of adjudication the application, nor, in most cases, to enforce the criminal provisions of IRCA, this practice appears to violate the confidentiality provisions. SAW applicants who are placed in deportation proceedings should ascertain whether and how INS obtained a copy of the SAW application.

Any person who believes that a criminal, civil, deportation or other proceeding was commenced based directly or indirectly on information filed in connection with any application for temporary resident status can: (a) request the suppression of such evidence as the "fruit of the poisonous tree,"[387] (b) request that the United States Attorney investigate and prosecute those who have violated confidentiality provisions under INA §245A(c)(15), which provides that anyone who uses, publishes, or permits information to be examined in violation of these provisions can be fined and

---

[385] Note the procedures described in the State Department cable of July 1, 1987, reproduced in the Appendix.

[386] See Legalization Wire #27, July 1, 1987.

[387] Whether this doctrine (derived from the Fourth Amendment) can be relied on in deportation proceedings is an open question; nevertheless egregious violations are subject to suppression under the Fifth Amendment. Matter of Garcia-Flores, 17 I & N Dec. 325 (BIA-1980); Matter of Toro, 17 I & N Dec. 340 (BIA-1980).

imprisoned for up to five years,[388] (c) seek money damages against those who violated the confidentiality provisions.[389]

Applicants who seek assistance from a Qualified Designated Entity (QDE) in the preparation of an application for permanent resident status are protected by INA §§245A(c)(4) and 210(b)(5).[390] According to these provisions, records maintained by the QDE are confidential and the Attorney General and the INS are forbidden access to the QDE's files without the consent of the alien. This confidentiality provision also insulates those aliens who sought advice or assistance from the QDE, but did not subsequently file their applications with the QDE, such as those who were informed by the QDE that they were ineligible for temporary residence.

Although the statute bars the Department of Justice from providing copies of the application to anyone other than those named above, the Freedom of Information Act (FOIA) still applies to legalization applications. Under its provisions, the applicant, or anyone with the signed and notarized authorization of the applicant, can have access to the file. Practitioners seeking access to an alien's "A90" legalization file should file a G-28 signed by the alien together with their FOIA request.[391]

1.6(b) Fraud in the Making of an Application for Temporary Residence

Although there are few reports of fraud among INA §245A legalization applicants, INS reports that fraud was widespread among SAW applicants. District Directors are authorized to deny[392] applications if the alien clearly fails to meet statutory requirements or the alien <u>admits</u> fraud or misrepresentation in the

---

[388] See also Legalization Wire #54, January 21, 1988, reproduced in the Appendix.

[389] The confidentiality provisions may create an implied cause of action for damages; <u>see also</u> National Immigration Project of the National Lawyers Guild <u>Remedies to Misconduct of the INS</u>, Skills Seminar Materials (1987).

[390] <u>See also</u> 8 CFR §§245a.2(t), 210.2(e)(2).

[391] A sample FOIA appeal can be found at the end of Chapter Five.

[392] As opposed to the normal procedure of issuing a <u>recommendation</u> that the Regional Processing Facility approve or deny an application.

application process.[393] INS' internal directives appear to exceed the regulations, allowing District Directors and overseas processing posts to deny applications containing "material inconsistencies or contradictory information or... serious discrepancies."[394] The INS must make available to the applicant any adverse information and must give the applicant an opportunity to rebut the adverse information <u>before</u> a decision is rendered.[395]

Under the regulations, if the INS determines that the alien has willfully misrepresented or concealed a material fact or provided a false writing or document, the matter shall be referred to the United States Attorney for prosecution of either the alien or the individual who created or supplied the false writing or document.[396]

If the fraud involves an application under the legalization program, INA §245A(c)(6) authorizes strict penalties for those who supply false information or documents in connection with an application:

> "Whoever files an application for adjustment of status under this section and knowingly and willfully falsifies, misrepresents, conceals or covers up a material fact, or makes any false, fictitious, or fraudulent statements or representations, or makes or uses any false writing or document knowing the same to contain any false, fictitious, or fraudulent statement or entry, shall be fined in accordance with title 18, United States Code, or imprisoned not more than five years, or both."[397]

The provisions pertaining to SAWs contain slightly different language, and have lead the INS to assert that fraud in regards to SAW applications is a strict liability crime which does not require proof of <u>scienter</u>.

---

[393] 8 CFR 103.1(n)(2).

[394] See Department of State wire, dated May 27, 1987; and Legalization Wire #45, November 3, 1987.

[395] 8 CFR §103.2(b)(2).

[396] 8 CFR §§210.2(e)(4), 245.2(t)(4). <u>See also</u> Legalization Wire #45, November 3, 1987, reproduced in the Appendix.

[397] <u>See</u>, e.g., 18 U.S.C. §§1005, 1015-1018, 1028, 1546, 3571, and 3581. Under these provisions, fines range up to $250,000. The language of INA §245A(c)(6) differs from that of its counterpart in the SAW program, INA §210(b)(7).

"Whoever (i) files an application for adjustment of status under this section and knowingly and willfully falsifies, conceals or covers up a material fact, or makes any false, fictitious, or fraudulent statements or representations, or makes or uses any false writing or document knowing the same to contain any false, fictitious, or fraudulent statement or entry, or (ii) creates or supplies a false writing or document for use in making such an application[398] shall be fined in accordance with title 18, United States Code, or imprisoned not more than five years, or both."[399]

Given the above language, INS has attempted to criminally prosecute an attorney who represented SAW applicants whose documentation was discovered to be fraudulent, arguing that the statute criminalized such activity on a strict liability basis, i.e., no guilty knowledge or intent need be proven.[400] Because one prosecution under this provision was dismissed on other grounds, the constitutionality of this provision has yet to be decided.

If prosecution of the applicant is declined, and if the U.S. Attorney returns the matter to the Service for initiation of deportation proceedings in lieu of prosecution, the INS may issue an Order to Show Cause and a warrant for arrest of the alien. However, in those cases in which prosecution for fraud is declined by the U.S. Attorney, INS cannot issue an Order to Show Cause based on information contained in the application or obtained in the subsequent fraud investigation, but must rely on information obtained independently.[401]

INS has directed its field offices to report U.S. Attorneys who consistently fail to prosecute legalization and SAW fraud cases.[402] The INS also plans to aggressively investigate reports

---

[398] Note that the language in subparagraph (ii) is not found in the fraud provisions governing the legalization program, INA 245A(c)(6).

[399] See, e.g., 18 U.S.C. §§1005, 1015-1018, 1028, 1546, 3571, and 3581. Under these provisions, fines range up to $250,000.

[400] See U.S. v. Chauvin, Cr. No. 88-00236-A (E.D. Va.), 66 Interpreter Releases 5-6 (January 2, 1989), 66 Interpreter Releases 35 (January 9, 1989).

[401] See Legalization Wire #54, January 21, 1988, reproduced in the Appendix; see also INS Central Office wire dated November 20, 1987.

[402] Legalization Wire #54, January 21, 1988.

of fraud and unscrupulous practices by notaries, consultants, attorneys and others.[403]

---

[403] See INS Central Office memo dated January 17, 1987, reproduced in the Appendix.

FRUITS AND VEGETABLES OF EVERY KIND
AND OTHER PERISHABLE COMMODITIES

INCLUDED:

all plant crops grown for human food[1]

barley[1]
beans[1]
berries[1]
biennials[2]
budding stock[2]
bulbs[2]
Christmas trees[3]
corms[2]
corn, sweet & other[1 & 6]
cotton[4]
cut flowers[2 & 3]
foliage plants[2]
fruit plants[2]
fruit trees[2]
fruits (scientific definition)[5]
grafting stock[2]
grains produced primarily for human consumption[1]
grapes[1]
ground covers[2]
ground nuts[1]
herbaceous annuals[2]
herbs[3]
hops[3]
horticultural specialties[2]
juvenile trees[2]
melons grown for human consumption[1]
mushrooms[1]
nut trees[2]
oats[1]
peanuts[1]
"other perishable commodities"[3 & 5]
perennials[2]
potatoes[1]
potted plants[2]
rice[1]
rye[1]
shrubs[2]
silage[6]
soybeans[1 & 8]
spanish reeds (arundo donax)[3]
spices[3]
sugar beets[3]
tobacco[3]

FRUITS AND VEGETABLES

tree nuts[1]
tubers[2]
understock[2]
vegetables (scientific definition)[5]
vines[2]
wheat[1]

EXCLUDED:

alfalfa[1 & 7]
animal aguacultural products[3]
animal specialities[3]
birds[3]
clover[1]
dairy products[3]
earthworms[3]
equines[3]
feedlots[8]
fish[3]
flax[1]
forage[3]
forest products[3]
fur bearing animals[3]
game birds[8]
gourds[1]
grains & grasses for forage & other uses aside from human consumption[1]
hay[7]
honey[3]
horses[3]
all livestock[3]
millet[1]
milo[1]
oysters[3]
poultry[3]
poultry products[3]
rabbits[3]
Seed Crops:[1 & 8]
   alfalfa
   beet
   cabbage
   carrot
   collard
   green panic
   kale
   kleingrass
   mustard
   radish
   rhodesgrass
   rutabaga
   spinach

turnips
sheep shearing[8]
shellfish[3]
sod[3&9]
sorghum[2]
sugar cane[3]
timothy[1]
turfgrass[8]
turkey hatching eggs[8]
wildlife[8]
wool[3]

[1] See, Legalization Wire #23, dated June 5, 1987, reproduced in 64 Interpreter Releases 777-778 (June 29, 1987).

[2] 7 CFR 1d.6.

[3] 7 CFR §1d.7

[4] National Council of American V. Lyng, ___F.Supp.___ (N.D. Tex. 1988); Valencia v. Lyng, No. CIV 87-630 TUC RMB (D. Ariz. Aug. 26, 1987).

[5] INA §210(h), 7 CFR §1d.5

[6] LAU Decision, February 8, 1988 (LAU Decision Digest Order No. L0488-174).

[7] Texas Farm Bureau v. Lyng, 697 F. Supp. 935 (E.D. Tex. 1988).

[8] As per the Comments accompanying the final regulations, 52 Fed. Reg. 20372-20376 (June 1, 1987).

[9] 7 CFR § 1d.7; 53 Fed. Reg. 50375-50381 (December 15, 1988); see Morales v. Lyng, 702 F. Supp. 161 (N.D.Il. 1988).

CHAPTER TWO

LEGALIZATION: STAGE TWO--SUBSTANTIVE REQUIREMENTS

2.1	BASIC ELIGIBILITY REQUIREMENTS FOR ADJUSTMENT FROM TEMPORARY RESIDENT TO PERMANENT RESIDENT STATUS UNDER INA §245A	2-3
2.2	TEMPORARY RESIDENT STATUS UNDER INA §245A	2-5
2.3	CONTINUOUS RESIDENCE REQUIREMENT	2-5
2.4	PHYSICAL PRESENCE REQUIREMENT	2-10
2.5	ADMISSIBILITY REQUIREMENT	2-10
	2.5(a) General Requirements	2-10
	2.5(b) Medical and Mental Exclusion Grounds	2-12
	2.5(c) Economic Grounds	2-13
	2.5(d) Immigration and Documentary Grounds	2-15
	2.5(e) Criminal Grounds	2-16
	2.5(f) Other Exclusion Grounds	2-17
	2.5(g) Waivers of Excludability	2-18
2.6	ONE FELONY/3 MISDEMEANOR DISQUALIFICATION	2-20
2.7	BASIC CITIZENSHIP SKILLS REQUIREMENT	2-21
	2.7(a) General Requirements	2-21
	2.7(b) Exceptions	2-21
	2.7(c) Basic Citizenship Skills--The Examination Option	2-22
	(1) INS Examination	2-23
	(2) ETS Examination	2-23
	2.7(d) Basic Citizenship Skills--The Class Attendance Option	2-24
	2.7(e) Rejection of the Certificate of Satisfactory Pursuit	2-26
	2.7(f) Class Sponsorship Requirements	2-27
2.8	THE APPLICATION PERIOD	2-31
	2.8(a) Advance Filing	2-33
	2.8(b) Failure to File the Application on Time	2-34
2.9	DELAYED GRANTS OF TEMPORARY RESIDENT STATUS	2-35

CHAPTER TWO

LEGALIZATION: STAGE TWO--SUBSTANTIVE REQUIREMENTS

2.1 BASIC ELIGIBILITY REQUIREMENTS FOR ADJUSTMENT FROM TEMPORARY RESIDENT TO PERMANENT RESIDENT STATUS UNDER INA §245A

Temporary resident aliens who obtained their status pursuant to the legalization program of the Immigration Reform and Control Act (i.e., based on their unlawful residence in the United States since January 1, 1982) must apply for adjustment to permanent resident status within a set time period or face reversion to their prior unlawful status. The basic eligibility requirements governing this "second stage" of the legalization program can be summarized as follows:[1]

a) the alien must be a temporary resident under INA §245A;[2]

b) the alien must have continuously resided in the United States since the date of adjustment to temporary resident status;[3] with certain exceptions, absences should not exceed 30 days (each absence), or 90 days total;[4]

c) the alien must be physically present in the United States at the time of application for adjustment to permanent residence;[5]

---

[1] Interim regulations governing the second stage of the legalization program were published in the Federal Register of October 31, 1986, Vol. 53, No. 210, pp.43993-43997. The Immigration and Naturalization Service has also issued a number of memoranda, letters and instructions regarding a variety of "second stage" issues.

[2] INA §245A(b)(1), 8 U.S.C. §1255a(b)(1); interim rules 8 C.F.R. §§245a.3(b), 245a.3(c)(4).

[3] INA §§245A(b)(1)(B), 245A(b)(3)(A); 8 U.S.C. §§1255a(b)(1)(B), 1255a(b)(3)(A); interim rule 8 CFR §245a.3(b)(2).

[4] Interim rule 8 CFR §§245a.1(c)(2), 245a.2(m)(2), (3); interim rules 245a.3(b)(2), 245a.3(g).

[5] Interim rule 8 CFR §245a.3(b).

d) the alien must not have been convicted of one felony or of three misdemeanors in the United States;[6]

e) the alien must be admissible as an immigrant (some grounds of excludability are automatically waived, some others are waivable under certain circumstances, others cannot be waived);[7]

f) the alien must demonstrate basic citizenship skills (unless applicant falls within certain exempt groups), i.e.:

   1) must meet the requirements of the naturalization examination relating to minimal understanding of ordinary English and a knowledge and understanding of the history and government of the United States);[8] or alternatively,

   2) must prove that he or she is "satisfactorily pursuing" a course of study recognized by the Attorney General to achieve a minimal understanding of ordinary English and a knowledge and understanding of the history and government of the United States.[9]

g) the alien must apply for adjustment during the one-year period beginning with the nineteenth month that begins after the date the alien was granted temporary resident status;[10]

Exceptions and interpretations of the above requirements are discussed below.

---

[6] INA §245A(b)(1)(C)(ii), 8 U.S.C. §1255a(b)(1)(C)(ii); interim rules 8 CFR §§245a.3(b)(3), 245a.3(c)(1).

[7] INA §245A(b)(1)(C)(i), 8 U.S.C. §1255a(b)(1)(C)(i); interim rules 8 CFR §§245a.3(b)(3), 245a.3(c)(2), 245a.3(f).

[8] INA §§312, 245A(b)(1)(D)(i), 8 U.S.C. §§1423, 1255a(b)(1)(D)(i); interim rule 8 CFR §245a.1(t). See interim rules 8 CFR §§245a.3(b)(4)(i)(A), 245a.3(b)(4)(iii)(A).

[9] INA §245A(b)(1)(D)(i), 8 U.S.C. §1255a(b)(1)(D)(i); interim rules 8 CFR §§245a.1(s). See interim rules §§ 245a.3(b)(4)(i)(B); 245a.3(b)(4)(iv), (v); 245a.3(b)(5).

[10] INA §245A(b)(1)(A), 8 U.S.C. §1255a(b)(1)(A); interim rules 8 CFR §§245a.3(a), 245a.3(b)(1), 245a.3(c)(3).

2.2 TEMPORARY RESIDENT STATUS UNDER INA §245A

Basic to the filing and processing of the application for permanent residence is the requirement that the alien have been admitted as a temporary resident under INA §245A. The statute pertaining to adjustment to permanent resident status expressly applies to "any alien provided lawful temporary resident status under [245A(a)]," and provides for calculating the application period from "the date the alien was granted such temporary resident status."[11] The interim regulations expressly require lawful admission for temporary resident status under §245A.[12] Various programs resulted in the issuance of an I-688 temporary resident card, therefore, if it is unclear under which program the alien became a temporary resident, check the face of the card which should carry the notation "245A." Because of strict application deadlines, all aliens must file their applications for permanent residence under INA §245A before a specific date, yet many will be prevented from doing so due to lengthy delays in the adjudication of their applications. This problem is discussed in §2.9 below.

2.3 CONTINUOUS RESIDENCE REQUIREMENT

Each applicant for temporary residence is required to establish that he or she has "continuously resided" in the United States since the date temporary residence was granted.[13] All absences occurring after the date of the fee receipt must therefore be examined to determine whether they interrupted the applicant's "continuous residence." Statutes and interim regulations pertaining to continuous residence can be very confusing and are expected to be clarified in the final regulations.[14]

The statute requires the Attorney General to promulgate regulations which (1) define "resided continuously," specifying individual and aggregate periods of absence which break continuous residence (taking into account absences due merely to "brief and casual" trips abroad),[15] and (2) provide for a waiver of these time periods in the cases of "brief temporary" trips required by

---

[11] INA §245A(b).

[12] Interim rules §§8 CFR 245a.3(b), 245a.4(c)(4).

[13] INA §245A(b)(1)(B)(i), 8 U.S.C. §1255a(b)(1)(B)(i); interim rule 8 CFR §245a.3(b)(2).

[14] Letter from Terrance O'Reilly to the author, February 17, 1989.

[15] INA §§245A(g)(1), (2); 8 U.S.C. §§1255a(g)(1), (2). See Interim rule 8 CFR §245a.1(h).

emergency or extenuating circumstances outside the control of the alien."[16] However, in limitation of the Attorney General's authority, the statute also provides that "continuous residence" shall not be considered lost as to the following absences permitted during the period the alien is in lawful temporary residence status: (1) "brief and casual"[17] trips abroad as are permitted by regulation and as reflect an intention to adjust to permanent resident status; (2) those which are "brief temporary" trips abroad permitted by regulation and occasioned by a family obligation involving an occurrence such as the illness or death of a close relative or other family need;[18] (3) those absences undertaken pursuant to advance parole.[19] Conversely, a departure under an order of deportation does break continuous residence.[20]

The regulations promulgated pursuant to the above statutory provisions clearly allow individual departures of 30 days and total departures of 90 days. This 30/90 day limit is set forth in a number of different regulatory provisions.[21] However, confusion results from the variety of exceptions set forth in the regulations for departures in excess of these limits. For example, one provision exempts longer absences wherein "due to emergent reasons the return to the United States could not be accomplished within the time period(s) allowed."[22] Another provision requires the alien to "establish that due to emergent reasons or circumstances beyond his or her control, the return to the United States could not be accomplished within the time period(s) allowed." Elsewhere, this same provision excepts longer departures if the alien "can establish to the satisfaction of the district director that he or she did not, in fact, abandon his or her residence in the United States during this such period."[23] A fourth provision exempts longer departures "in cases where the absence from the United States was due merely to a brief temporary trip abroad due to

---

[16] INA §245A(g)(2)(C), 8 U.S.C. §1255a(g)(2)(C).

[17] INA §§245A(b)(1)(B)(ii), 245A(b)(3)(A), 8 U.S.C. §§1255a(b)(3)(A). Defined at interim rule 8 CFR §245a.1(h).

[18] INA §§245A(b)(1)(B)(ii); 245A(b)(3)(A), 8 U.S.C. §§1255a(b)(1)(B)(ii), 1255a(b)(3)(A).

[19] INA §245A(g)(2)(B)(ii), 8 U.S.C. §1255a(g)(2)(B)(ii).

[20] INA §245A(g)(2)(B)(i), 8 U.S.C. §1255a(g)(2)(B)(i).

[21] 8 CFR §§211.1(d)(2), 245a.1(c)(2), 245a.3(b)(2), 245a.2(m)(3).

[22] 8 CFR §245a.1(c)(2).

[23] Interim rule 8 CFR §245a.3(b)(2).

emergent or extenuating circumstances beyond the alien's control (this language repeats the statutory language regarding waivers of longer departures).[24] One must add to this the general requirement that as to all departures, regardless of their length, the alien must establish a continuing "intention to adjust to lawful permanent resident status."[25]

The practitioner must be alert to the fact that most aliens who were issued I-688A work authorization cards upon the filing of their applications knew they could not depart the country. Those aliens who in fact left the U.S. during this time will be inclined to divulge only those departures undertaken after they received the I-688 permanent resident card. Given analogous caselaw and the retroactivity of the grant of temporary resident status, it is unlikely that such unauthorized departures will affect eligibility for permanent residence.[26] The practitioner should therefore press the applicant to inform him or her of all departures.

If the applicant departed prior to receipt of the I-688 and without advance parole, the practitioner should find-out whether the applicant committed fraud upon re-entry (i.e., using border crossing card, tourist visa, etc.). Such re-entries may render the alien excludable under fraud grounds (discussed below).[27] If the alien re-entered without inspection, this is among the grounds of excludability which are automatically waived and thus poses no excludability problems.[28]

---

[24] INA §245A(g)(2)(C), 8 U.S.C. §1255a(g)(2)(C); 8 CFR §245a.2(m)(3).

[25] INA §245A(b)(3)(A), 8 U.S.C. §1255a(b)(3)(A), interim rule 8 CFR §§245a.1(h), 245a.3(g). Note that these regulatory provisions differ from the term "resided continuously" defined for purposes of temporary residence eligibility. There, the regulations provided for a 45/180 day limit on absences from the United States after January 1, 1982, which would not be considered to break continuous residence. 8 CFR §§245a.1(c)(1)(i); 245a.2(h). It is unclear why a 45 day single absence would not break continuous residence for purposes of temporary residence but would break continuous residence for purposes of permanent residence.

[26] See Catholic Social Services v. Meese, No. S-86-1343 LKK (E.D. Cal. 1988).

[27] INA §212(a)(19), 8 U.S.C. §1182(a)(19).

[28] See INA §§212(a)(20), 245A(d)(2)(A), 8 U.S.C. §1182(a)(20), 1255a(d)(2)(A).

The practitioner should first determine whether a departure was undertaken pursuant to advance parole.[29] Advance parole departures do not interrupt the required continuous residence, regardless of their length, nor are they to be counted with other departures.[30] A great many aliens departed the United States pursuant to advance parole after they applied for temporary resident status but before they were issued their I-688 temporary resident cards.

As to all departures not made pursuant to advance parole, the practitioner should determine if any single departure exceeded 30 days and then determine whether the total of all departures exceeded 90 days. Absences after the filing or submittal of the second stage application and before the application is approved must also be considered. If the applicant's departures are within these time limits, the applicant meets the continuous residence requirements. If a departure approaches the 30/90 day limitations, the applicant should submit documentation showing continuous residence, i.e., proof of the departure and return dates.[31]

As to departures exceeding the 30/90 day limitations, the INS anticipates modifying the regulations to dispel the current confusing standards.[32] Pending this clarification, the practitioner, while arguing that eligibility under one of the exception clauses is sufficient, should try to present sufficient facts as to support eligibility under all of the following bases:

a) due to emergent reasons or circumstances beyond the alien's control return to the United States could not be accomplished within 30/90 days;[33]

b) the applicant did not abandon his or her residence in the United States during the departure(s);

---

[29] 8 CFR §212.5(e). See also 8 CFR §§245a.1(g), interim rule 245a.2(m), 245a.2(n)(2).

[30] INA §245A(g)(2)(B)(ii), 8 U.S.C. §1255a(g)(2)(B)(ii); 8 CFR §245a.1(c)(1).

[31] Minutes, NCA meeting with Raymond Penn, Assistant Commissioner, Legalization (October 27, 1989).

[32] Letter from Terrance O'Reilly, INS Central Office, to the author, February 17, 1989.

[33] See, e.g., Matter of C--, Int. Dec. 3087 (Comm'r Nov. 15, 1988) summarized in 65 Interpreter Releases 595-596 (June 6, 1988). See also Hernandez v. Meese, Civ. No. S-88-385 CKK-JFM (E.D. Cal. 1988) summarized in 65 Interpreter Releases 1065-1066 (October 17, 1988).

c)   the absence was a brief and casual trip reflecting an intention to adjust to permanent resident status;

d)   the absence was a brief temporary trip occasioned by illness or death of close relative or other family need;

e)   the absence was a brief temporary trip required by emergency or extenuating circumstances beyond the alien's control.

In a closely related context the LAU has had to construe the term "continuous residence" as to those departures after January 1, 1982 which exceeded the 45/180 day limitation imposed by regulation.[34] The reasoning applied to such extended departures will apply in the context of an application for permanent residence as well. Administrative appellate decisions have found the following factors to be relevant: the length of the trip, the location of family ties, property, and employment; reasons for traveling abroad, intent to maintain residence.[35] Examples of facts which might support eligibility under these bases are: illness or death of family member; impediments to a planned return, such as unexpected transportation (e.g. automobile repairs) or financial problems; the need to dispose of or deal with real estate, business or other legal problems; disruptions to travel plans or changes in circumstances due to weather, natural disasters or civil disturbances or fighting. The applicant must simultaneously stress the maintenance of U.S. ties, i.e., the presence of family ties, job, residence, bank accounts and other assets in the United States.

The LAU has found "emergent reasons" prevented the timely return of temporary resident applicants based on a variety of situations, including inability to secure a B-2 visa to re-enter the U.S. (223 day absence), inability to elude INS officers (59 days), fear of flying alone (59 days), unexpected postponement of Consular appointment (116 days), and inability to purchase return fare due to unexpected delay in receipt by mail of return airfare,[36]

---

[34]   See the discussions in Chapters One and Five.

[35]   Matter of Quijencio, 15 I&N 95 (BIA 1974).

[36]   See Matter of C--, Int. Dec. #3087 (Comm'r May 6, 1988), summarized in 65 Interpreter Releases 595-596 (June 6, 1988), and unreported LAU decisions discussed in 66 Interpreter Releases 66-67 (January 13, 1989).

2-9

and need to take sick mother to scheduled doctors appointments.[37]

If the temporary resident must leave the country and believes the departure may extend beyond the 30/90 day limits, he or she should request the issuance of advance parole to cover the anticipated length of the departure.

2.4 PHYSICAL PRESENCE REQUIREMENT

The regulations require physical presence in the United States at the time of filing.[38] As to those rare cases in which an application is filed while the applicant is outside the United States, it should be noted that physical presence is not required by the statute.

2.5 ADMISSIBILITY REQUIREMENT

2.5(a) General Requirements

The applicability of the grounds of excludability, normally applied to aliens seeking entry or adjustment of status either as immigrants or nonimmigrants, has been modified in the cases of temporary residents applying for adjustment to permanent resident status. With one exception, the grounds of excludability and the waivers of excludability apply to the same extent as they did during the first stage of the legalization program. Thus, many excludable aliens will have been either screened-out or had their grounds of excludability waived at the first stage. However, in some cases grounds for excludability may arise or become obvious only during the transitional temporary residence period (e.g., mental and physical problems, crimes, public assistance, visa or document fraud, smuggling). Those who are excludable, and whose excludability arose prior to the submittal of the first stage application, and who failed to admit excludability during the first stage, could face additional problems during the second stage. In such cases, the question of fraud in obtaining temporary resident status may arise and could lead to the termination of temporary residence, prosecution for fraud, deportation, and exclusion.[39] In no case should the applicant repeat incorrect information supplied during the first stage merely for the sake of conforming the

---

[37] Matter of T--, undesignated LAU opinion dated September 1, 1988, reported in 65 Interpreter Releases 1077 (October 17, 1988).

[38] 8 CFR §245a.3(b).

[39] INA §245A(c)(6), 8 CFR 245a.2(t)(4); INA §212(a)(19), 8 U.S.C. §1182(a)(19).

information on the applications. Rather, an explanation of the discrepancies should be attached.

Inapplicable Grounds Of Excludability

212(1)(14)	Aliens coming to perform skilled or unskilled work in the United States without a labor certification;
212(a)(20)	Aliens not in possession of a valid visa or passport;
212(a)(21)	Aliens entering with a visa issued in violation of INA §203 numerical limits;
212(a)(25)	Illiterates;
212(a)(32)	Graduates of foreign medical schools who have not passed the appropriate visa qualifying examination.

Grounds of Excludability Which Cannot be Waived

212(a)(9)	Aliens convicted of a crime of moral turpitude (other than a purely political offense and certain crimes committed while under the age of 18), or aliens who have admitted committed such a crime;
212(a)(10)	Aliens convicted of two or more offenses, regardless of whether they arose from a single trial or scheme, if the aggregate sentence of confinement was for five years or more;
212(a)(27)	Aliens who are threats to national security;
212(a)(28)	Anarchists, communists and subversives;
212(a)(29)	Threats to the national security and subversives;
212(a)(33)	Aliens who assisted in Nazi persecution.

Grounds of Exclusion Which Can be Waived

212(a)(1)	Aliens who are mentally retarded;
212(a)(2)	Aliens who are insane;
212(a)(3)	Aliens who have had one or more attacks of insanity;
212(a)(4)	Aliens afflicted with psychopathic personality, sexual deviation, or mental defect;
212(a)(5)	Narcotic drug addicts or chronic alcoholics;
212(a)(6)	Aliens afflicted with dangerous contagious diseases;
212(a)(7)	Aliens with a physical disability affecting ability to earn a living;
212(a)(8)	Paupers, professional beggars or vagrants;
212(a)(11)	Polygamists;
212(a)(12)	Procurers and prostitutes;
212(a)(13)	Aliens entering to engage in any immoral sexual act;
212(a)(15)	Aliens likely to become public charges;
212(a)(16)	Aliens excluded within one year prior to the date of application;
212(a)(17)	Aliens deported within five years prior to the date of application unless the Attorney General consents to their admission;
212(a)(18)	Stowaways;

212(a)(19)   Aliens who have procured or sought to procure a visa or other documentation by fraud or willful misrepresentation of a material fact;

212(a)(22)   Aliens who are ineligible to citizenship and draft evaders;

212(a)(23)   Any alien convicted of a drug related offense or in whose case there is reason to believe the alien engaged in trafficking;

212(a)(24)   Aliens who arrived on non-signatory transportation lines;

212(a)(26)   Aliens lacking valid passports;

212(a)(30)   Aliens accompanying an alien excluded due to physical or mental problems;

212(a)(31)   Aliens who assisted any other alien to enter the United States in violation of law.

2.5(b)   Medical and Mental Exclusion Grounds

All of the medical and mental grounds of exclusion, INA §§ 212(a)(1)-(a)(7), apply during the second stage of legalization, although all can be waived for humanitarian reasons, family unity, or the public interest (discussed below). These include:

212(a)(1)   Aliens who are mentally retarded;
212(a)(2)   Aliens who are insane;
212(a)(3)   Aliens who have had one or more attacks of insanity;
212(a)(4)   Aliens afflicted with psychopathic personality, sexual deviation, or mental defect;
212(a)(5)   Narcotic drug addicts or chronic alcoholics;
212(a)(6)   Aliens afflicted with dangerous contagious diseases;
212(a)(7)   Aliens with a physical disability affecting their ability to earn a living.

A complete medical examination is not required to determine excludability under the above provisions, nonetheless, in order to determine whether a person is excludable under INA §212(a)(6), the regulations require every permanent resident applicant age 15 or over to be given a serologic test for HIV (human immunodeficiency virus) either at the temporary resident stage, or now, at the permanent resident stage.[40] INS is apparently not requiring a test for syphilis and a chest x-ray for tuberculosis of those who turn 15 before submitting their applications for permanent residence (such tests were required of all those over 15 at the temporary residence level). Specifics regarding who must take the HIV are set forth in Chapter Three.

---

[40] See INA §245A(d)(2)(C), 8 U.S.C. §1255a(d)(2)(C); interim rules 8 CFR §245a.3(d)(4).

Those found excludable under INA §§212(a)(1) through 212(a)(5), in addition to seeking an IRCA waiver, can apply for review of the excludability determination under INA §234. Also, although the IRCA waiver (discussed below) does apply to those found excludable based on a positive HIV test, more stringent standards are being applied to such cases.[41] Lastly, some of those found excludable under the above physical and mental grounds, particularly those who test positive for HIV, may also encounter difficulties overcoming exclusion under the public charge grounds (discussed below), a grounds of exclusion which normally cannot be waived.

2.5(c) Economic Grounds

The poor may face possible exclusion under the following grounds:

212(a)(6)	Aliens afflicted with a dangerous contagious disease;
212(a)(7)	Aliens with a physical disability affecting ability to earn a living;
212(a)(8)	Paupers, professional beggars, vagrants;
212(a)(15)	Aliens likely to become public charges (determined by special rule, discussed below).

The first two grounds enumerated are briefly discussed in the preceding section, however, they are included here because they may also indicate that the person is likely to become a public charge.

The overall numbers of applications presenting public charge excludability problems during the second stage should be fewer than the number of such cases filed during the first stage, given the fact that all temporary residents are barred from receipt of governmental assistance for a period of 5 years.[42] However, the 5-year bar does not prohibit the receipt of government assistance by a temporary resident's U.S. citizen children. If an applicant's U.S. citizen children have received public assistance, this fact will in turn lead to increased INS scrutiny of the case during the second stage. Cases in which the applicant indicates on the I-698 application form (Question no. 17) that the applicant or his or her dependents have received public assistance and those in which the applicant admitted past receipt of public assistance during the first stage of the legalization program and was required then to seek a waiver, are likely to elicit requests for further documentation of the applicant's financial status. Such applicants

---

[41] See Central Office memorandum of July 29, 1988, reproduced in 65 Interpreter Releases 850-851 (August 22, 1988).

[42] INA §245A(h).

should therefore submit proof of financial responsibility at the time the application is filed.[43]

The two-step analysis of whom is likely to become a public charge, including the "special rule," applies to permanent resident applications in the same manner as it did to temporary resident applications.[44] The "special rule" will therefore still be available to those applicants who might otherwise be excluded from legalization benefits. This is of great practical importance because some who qualify under the general rule would not qualify under the special rule, and vice versa. The INS must first review the totality of the circumstances of the alien (age, health, income, vocation) to determine whether it is likely that the alien will receive public assistance in the future. The receipt of public assistance by an applicant's children is not attributable to the applicant, and will not, in and of itself, disqualify the applicant.[45] However, under the "totality of the circumstances" standard it is one of the factors which can be considered. If the totality of the circumstances indicate that the applicant is not likely to become a public charge, the alien is not excludable. Further inquiry into the applicants financial status is not necessary.

If the totality of the circumstances indicate likelihood of public charge problems, the special rule is applied, and if satisfied, will also result in a determination that the applicant is not excludable. The "special rule" requires that the alien demonstrate a history of employment in the United States evidencing self-support without receipt of public cash assistance, i.e., AFDC, SSI, GA or GR. Food stamps, foster care payments, unemployment compensation, public housing, Medicare, Medicaid, emergency medical treatment, WIC, among other programs, are not considered to be cash public assistance.[46] Thus a bifurcated analysis of the applicant's circumstances is undertaken.

Although a finding by the INS of public charge excludability cannot be waived during the second stage in most cases, an IRCA

---

[43] See, Minutes, NCA meeting with Raymond Penn, Assistant Commissioner, Legalization (October 27, 1988).

[44] INA §245A(d)(2)(B)(iii), 8 U.S.C. §1255a(d)(2)(B)(iii); interim rule 8 CFR §245a.3(f)(4). See also 8 CFR §245a.1(i).

[45] See, Matter of A--, Int. Dec. #___ (decided December 29, 1988), discussed in 66 Interpreter Releases 106-108 (January 23, 1988).

[46] INA §245A(d)(2)(B)(iii), 8 U.S.C. §1255a(d)(2)(B)(iii). For additional details, see the discussion of public charge excludability in Chapter One.

waiver is available in the cases of those who are aged (65 or over), blind or disabled "for the month in which such alien is granted lawful temporary residence status" in accordance with SSI eligibility requirements defining those terms. Such applicants need not be recipients of SSI to qualify for the IRCA waiver they must merely meet SSI's definition of "aged, blind, disabled." Given the language of the statute, it is unsettled whether those who become aged, blind, or disabled <u>after</u> the grant of temporary residence will be eligible for an IRCA waiver if found excludable under the public charge provision.[47]

2.5(d) Immigration and Documentary Grounds

212(a)(16)	Aliens excluded within one year prior to the date of application;
212(a)(17)	Aliens deported within five years prior to the date of application unless the Attorney General consents to their admission;
212(a)(18)	Stowaways;
212(a)(19)	Aliens who have procured or sought to procure a visa or other documentation by fraud or willful misrepresentation of a material fact;
212(a)(22)	Aliens who are ineligible to citizenship and draft evaders;
212(a)(26)	Aliens lacking valid passports;
212(a)(31)	Aliens who assisted any other alien to enter the United States in violation of law.

The fraud grounds covers a wide variety of conduct, including fraud or misrepresentation committed in order to secure a visa, passport, immigration document, or entry into the United States. Temporary Residents have been known to depart and re-enter the United States with old documents, i.e., border crossing cards, while their temporary resident applications were pending. This conduct comes within the fraud grounds of excludability. Fraud in securing temporary residence will also result in a finding of excludability.[48] INS has declined to adopt a "blanket" waiver policy for legalization fraud.[49]

If an applicant provided incorrect information when applying for temporary residence, the practitioner should determine if this omission was deliberate and if it materially affected the outcome

---

[47] <u>See</u> 1988 technical amendments. Title XVI of the Social Security Act, 42 U.S.C. §§1382C(a)(1)(A)(1982), (a)(2)(1982), (a)(3)(1982).

[48] INA §212(a)(19), 8 U.S.C. §1182(a)(19).

[49] <u>See</u> 65 Interpreter Releases 635 (June 27, 1988).

of the application. The INS may request an explanation of any discrepancies in the information provided at the first and second stage. The practitioner should not provide incorrect information on the permanent resident application in order that the information will conform with incorrect information previously provided at the first stage.

2.5(e) Criminal Grounds

Criminal activity can cause an alien to be excluded under a number of different grounds, including:

212(a)(5)	Narcotic drug addicts and chronic alcoholics;
212(a)(8)	Vagrants;
212(a)(9)	Aliens convicted of a crime of moral turpitude (other than a purely political offense, one "petty offense" and certain crimes committed while under the age of 18), or aliens who have admitted committing such a crime;
212(a)(10)	Aliens convicted of two or more offenses, regardless of whether they arose from a single trial or scheme, if the aggregate sentence of confinement was for five years or more;
212(a)(11)	polygamists;
212(a)(12)	Procurers and prostitutes;
212(a)(19)	Visa fraud;
212(a)(23)	Any alien convicted of a drug related offense or in whose case there is reason to believe the alien engaged in trafficking, except single offense marijuana possession 30 grams or less;
212(a)(31)	Alien smugglers.

If it appears that an applicant has engaged in any activity which might fall under the above grounds, the practitioner should determine: whether the crime involves moral turpitude, what the sentence was, whether it falls within the petty offense exception, whether the offense was a juvenile, youthful offender or first offender matter, whether the disposition constitutes a "conviction" for immigration purposes, whether it was drug-related. In order to determine what constitutes a crime of moral turpitude, reference must be made to the case law.[50]

To be excluded based on an "admission" of conduct constituting a crime of moral turpitude, the person must make a formal, knowledgeable admission to an official of each of the elements of a crime.

---

[50] Consult, e.g., Kesselbrenner and Rosenberg *Immigration Law and Crimes*, Clark Boardman Ltd. (revd. ed. 1989).

Portions of INA §§212(a)(9), (10), and (23) require a "conviction", which, given the variety of state court procedures and sentencing schemes, is not always a forgone conclusion. As to some provisions, a deferred adjudication of guilt may not constitute a "conviction" under state law. However, the LAU has held, in a recent decision, that a conviction exists pursuant to INA §245A(a)(4)(B) where

a)   a judge or jury has found the alien guilty or the alien has entered a plea of guilty or nolo contendere, and

b)   the judge has ordered some form of punishment or penalty, including but not limited to a fine or probation.

The fact that the judge has withheld an adjudication of guilt is irrelevant for purposed of IRCA eligibility.[51] Thus, the LAU is applying a more severe standard than that articulated by the BIA in Matter of Ozkok to legalization matters.[52]

Drug convictions and suspicion of drug trafficking render an alien excludable. "Drug" means any controlled substance. Only in cases where there is a single offense involving simple possession of up to 30 grams of marijuana or hashish is an IRCA waiver available.

Excludability for criminal offenses must be considered separately from the 1 felony/3 misdemeanor disqualification, considered below.

2.5(f)   Other Exclusion Grounds

Excludability grounds not listed in the above topical discussions include:

212(a)(13)	Aliens entering to engage in any immoral sexual act;
212(a)(27)	Aliens who are threats to national security;
212(a)(28)	Anarchists, communists and subversives
212(a)(29)	Threats to the national security and subversives;
212(a)(30)	Aliens accompanying an alien excluded due to physical or mental problems;
212(a)(33)	Aliens who assisted in Nazi persecution.

Except for excludability based on ideological grounds or those relating to former Nazis, the above grounds can be waived under IRCA.

---

[51]   Matter of M--, Int. Dec. #___, (Comm'r Jan. 31, 1989).

[52]   Int. Dec. #3044 (BIA 1988).

2.5(f) Waivers of Excludability

Inadmissibility under most of the exclusion grounds can be overcome by a discretionary waiver if the INS deems it warranted for humanitarian purposes, to assure family unity, or when it is otherwise in the public interest.[53] However, if a waiver was granted during the first stage of the legalization program for a particular grounds of excludability, no additional waiver of the same ground of excludability will be required when the alien applies for permanent resident status.[54] If the alien becomes excludable subsequent to the date temporary residence was granted, a waiver of the ground of excludability, if available, will be required before permanent resident status may be granted.[55] Because the waiver grounds are broad, you should argue that the applicant is eligible for a waiver under each of the three separate bases. Although a waiver was available to those found excludable under the public charge provisions during the first stage of the legalization program, no waiver of the public charge provisions is available during the second stage (with limited exceptions).[56]

To obtain a waiver "to assure family unity," requires proof that the waiver is required in order to maintain the family group without deviation or change. The regulations limit "family group" to the spouse, unmarried minor children under 18 who are not members of another household, and parents residing in the applicant's household.[57] Note that the Immigration status of such family members appears to be irrelevant, although copies of documents substantiating family members' lawful status, if available, should be submitted.

Neither "humanitarian purposes" nor "public interest" is defined in the regulations, although the LAU and the RPFs have elaborated on these terms during Stage One of the legalization program. In Matter of P--,[58] the LAU emphasized that waivers should be granted liberally. The Northern RPF cited the dictionary's definition of "humanitarian" as "...the promotion of human welfare"

---

[53] INA §245A(d)(2)(B)(ii).

[54] Interim rule 8 CFR §245a.3(f)(2).

[55] INA §245A(d)(2)(B), 8 U.S.C. §1255a(d)(2)(B); interim rule 8 CFR §245.3(f)(2).

[56] INA §245A(d)(2)(B)(ii), 8 U.S.C. §1255a(d)(2)(B)(ii).

[57] 8 CFR §245a.1(m).

[58] Int. Dec. #3090, In Legalization Proceedings, decided by INS Commissioner, November 23, 1988.

and welfare as "health, happiness, and general well-being," referring to the LO's denial of temporary resident status due to a fourteen-year old deportation as "unfair to the point of being inhumane."[59] The LAU has also adopted the definition of "public interest" found in Black's Law Dictionary, finding that the applicant's commitment of time, money, and talent (in the job he performed) contributed to the betterment of the community and warranted the approval of a waiver for reasons in the public interest. Additional details regarding waivers are discussed in Chapter One.

Those found excludable due to a positive HIV test are required to make an additional showing in order to qualify for a waiver.[60] Specifically, they must show:

1) The danger to the public health of the United States created by the alien's admission to the U.S. is minimal;

2) The possibility of spread of the disease created by the alien's admission to the U.S. is minimal;

3) There will no cost incurred by any level of government agency of the U.S. without prior consent of that agency.

Because the statute which provides for a waiver under IRCA draws no distinctions between the grounds of excludability which can be waived, the fact that a stricter standard must be met in order to obtain a waiver of one particular grounds of excludability, is subject to challenge.

In many cases it will be difficult to determine whether the facts support excludability. However, if the alien is clearly excludable (e.g., fraud in manner of entry to the U.S.), a waiver should be filed. The admission of excludability itself is a favorable factor which supports the approval of the waiver application.[61] If excludability is not clear, a waiver should not be filed, however, the facts and, if available, citations to legal authority, should be noted on the I-698 application, attachment or a cover letter. The RPF may then determine if a waiver is required and if so, will advise the applicant. It should be submitted on form I-690 (application for waiver of grounds of excludability),

---

[59] LAU decision summarized in AILA February 1989 mailing, p. 89, Reprint No. 101-1288.

[60] See INS Central Office memorandum of July 29, 1988, reproduced in 65 Interpreter Releases 850-851 (August 22, 1988); INS Central Office memorandum of March 2, 1988.

[61] See letter from Western RPF Director, reproduced in 64 Interpreter Releases, 328-29 (November 23, 1987).

the facts supporting approval should be amply developed, and all relevant supporting documents should be attached.

2.6 ONE FELONY/3 MISDEMEANOR DISQUALIFICATION

Temporary residents convicted of one felony or of three misdemeanors in the United States are barred from adjusting their status to permanent residence under INA §245A legalization provisions.[62] A felony is defined as any crime punishable by imprisonment of more than one year except where the offense is classified as a misdemeanor under state law and the sentence actually imposed was one year or less, regardless of the term actually served.[63] A misdemeanor is any crime punishable by a term of imprisonment between 6 days and 1 year, regardless of the term actually served.[64] An alien will be barred by this provision regardless of when the felony or 3 misdemeanor convictions occurred, i.e., convictions occurring before and after the temporary residence application was filed will be counted. This disqualification does not apply to foreign offenses. Those who have a total of 3 misdemeanors during temporary residence should immediately begin efforts to expunge or vacate 1 or more of their convictions. Those with two misdemeanors should apply for permanent residence at the earliest possible date.

Because of heightened awareness of the draconian effects of even the smallest misdemeanor offenses on an alien's immigration status, many criminal defense attorneys will have sought dispositions under alternative sentencing provisions, JRADs, expungements, pre-trial diversion, and other forms of relief. One creative solution has been advanced in recent cases, providing another remedy to the alien whose prior convictions render him or her ineligible for legalization. The ancient writ of <u>audita querela</u> has been revived and is now a viable means of vacating both misdemeanor and felony criminal convictions entered prior to the passage of IRCA.[65]

---

[62] INA §245A(b)(1)(C), 8 U.S.C. §1255a(b)(1)(C); interim rule 8 CFR §245a.3(c)(1).

[63] 8 CFR §245a.1(p).

[64] 8 CFR §245a.1(o).

[65] <u>U.S. v. Salgado</u>, 692 F. Supp. 1265; <u>U.S. v. Ghebreziabher</u> ____ F. Supp. ____Crim. Action No. 87-457 (E.D.La. 12-14-88);

2.7 BASIC CITIZENSHIP SKILLS REQUIREMENT

2.7(a) General Requirements

The statute also requires that each permanent resident applicant under INA §245A demonstrate "basic citizenship skills."[66] This requirement can be met in either of two ways:

1) by taking an examination similar to the naturalization examination (which tests minimal understanding of ordinary English and knowledge and understanding of the history and government of the United States), or

2) by demonstrating satisfactory pursuit of an INS-approved course of study to achieve an understanding of ordinary English and a knowledge and understanding of the history and government of the United States.[67]

All options should be reviewed by the temporary resident at the earliest opportunity to allow the applicant time for course attendance, if necessary. This is particularly important given the waiting lists for class attendance which are already developing in many parts of the country and predictions by course sponsors that there will be insufficient classroom space to accommodate all those who need to attend such classes. Even so, you should not assume that an applicant will be incapable of taking the examination. The examination administered by the Educational Testing Service (ETS) will be a viable option in many cases (discussed below).

2.7(b) Exceptions

Certain aliens are exempt from demonstrating "basic citizenship skills:"

a) those under the age of 16;[68]
b) those 65 years of age or older as of the date of application for permanent residence;[69]

---

[66] INA §245A(b)(1)(C).

[67] INA §245A(b)(1)(D)(i), 8 U.S.C. §1255a(b)(1)(D)(i).

[68] Interim rule 8 CFR §245a.3(b)(4)(ii).

[69] INA §245A(b)(1)(D)(ii), 8 U.S.C. §1255a(b)(1)(D)(ii); interim rule 8 CFR §245a.3(b)(4)(ii).

2-21

c) those over 50 years of age who submit evidence that they have resided in the United States for at least 20 years;[70]
d) those who are physically unable to comply;[71]
e) those who are developmentally disabled.[72]

2.7(c) Basic Citizenship Skills--The Examination Option

One alternative available to satisfy the statute's requirement regarding basic citizenship skills requires that the applicant meet the requirements of INA §312 relating to "minimal understanding of ordinary English" and a knowledge and understanding of the history and government of the United States.[73] INA §312 governs the examination of naturalization applicants. Thus, permanent resident applicants can opt to take a test similar to that administered for naturalization. The scope of the testing is limited primarily to subject matters covered in the Federal Textbooks on Citizenship.[74] The test is an oral examination given in the English language.

The applicant can choose the method of testing:

a) The test can be taken at the time of the interview for permanent residence, or

a) The test can be taken in advance in designated locations and the results mailed by the Educational Testing Service (ETS) to the INS.

Those temporary residents who opt to take the examination (in lieu of class attendance), whether it is administered by ETS or the INS, and who pass it, need not repeat the test at the time they naturalize (in most cases, 5 years after adjustment to permanent residence).[75]

---

[70] Interim rule 8 CFR §245a.3(b)(4)(ii).

[71] Id.

[72] INA §245A(b)(1)(D)(ii), 8 U.S.C. §1255a(b)(1)(D)(ii); Cong. Rec. H9839, October 7, 1988.

[73] INA §245A(b)(1)(D)(i), 8 U.S.C. §1255a(b)(1)(D)(i); interim rule 8 CFR §§245a.1(s), 245a.1(t), 245a.3(b)(4), (5).

[74] Interim rule 8 CFR §245a.3(b)(4)(iii).

[75] INA §245A(b)(1)(D)(iii), 8 U.S.C. §1255a(b)(1)(D)(iii).

2.7(c)(1) INS Examination

The INS has distributed a list of 100 questions from which examiners may select questions;[76] a copy of this list may be obtained at local INS offices. In choosing the subject matter and in phrasing questions, the INS must give due consideration to the extent of the petitioner's education, background, age, length of residence in the United States, opportunities available and efforts made to acquire the requisite knowledge, and any other elements or factors relevant to an appraisal of the adequacy of his or her knowledge and understanding.[77]

Regulations permit the applicant to demonstrate English comprehension "by speaking and understanding English during the course of the interview."[78] Because many of the grounds of excludability recited on the application form contain legal terms of art and archaic terminology which few people understand, a hurried review of the contents of the application with the applicant in English at the time of the interview may not meet the standard set forth in the law and regulations. At the examination the alien will also be asked to read and to write simple sentences in English.

Those who take the examination at their interview, and who do not pass the examination, are to be given a second opportunity to either pass the test or present alternative proof of satisfaction of the "Basic Citizenship Skills" requirement.[79] Standardized tests are currently being developed and are under consideration by the INS.[80]

2.7(c)(2) ETS Examination

In lieu of being tested by INS officials at the interview, the applicant has the option of advance testing by the Educational Testing Service (ETS). The ETS test is a 20 question multiple-choice test which can be taken at specified sites on specified dates. The test also requires the applicant to write a simple sentence in English. If the alien answers 12 of the 20 questions correctly, he or she passes the ETS test; his or her scores are

---

[76] Reproduced in 66 Interpreter Releases 109-113 (January 23, 1989).

[77] Interim rule 8 CFR §245a.3(b)(4)(iii).

[78] Interim rule 8 CFR §245a.3(b)(4)(iii)(A).

[79] Interim rule 8 CFR §245a.3(b)(4)(iii)(B).

[80] See 66 Interpreter Releases 181 (February 13, 1989).

forwarded to the INS in satisfaction of the testing requirement. The advantages of taking the ETS test are that it can be taken in advance, is administered in non-threatening surroundings, results are promptly released, and only passing grades are forwarded to the INS. Those who pass the ETS test will receive an official notification of their results by mail. The RPF will simultaneously receive notification. The applicant may present a certified copy of the notice at the interview, but should keep the original in a safe place for use when applying for naturalization at a later date.

The ETS test can be taken an unlimited number of times. ETS charges $10.00 per person to administer the test. ETS reports an 80%+ pass rate, higher than originally anticipated. ETS testing is not conducted in all cities. To find-out if ETS testing is offered in a specific city, contact NALEO at 1-800-446-2536; in California, call 1-800-346-2536. Local ETS test sites can then provide you with test dates and locations as well as test guide booklets with sample test questions.

The ETS test is slightly different from the combination home study/ proficiency test option, one of the class attendance options listed below. The state administered test does not require the applicant to write phrases in English. Also unlike the ETS examination, the state administered test can not be used in later satisfaction of the examination requirement when the alien applies for naturalization.

2.7(d) Basic Citizenship Skills--The Class Attendance Option

In lieu of taking a "civics" examination, the applicant may satisfy the "basic citizenship skills" requirement by proving "satisfactory pursuit" of a course of study recognized by the Attorney General to achieve a minimal understanding of English and a knowledge and understanding of the history and government of the United States. This can be done in any of several different ways:

(1) <u>Proof of enrollment in an INS-approved program and attendance for at least 40 hours of a minimum 60-hour course</u> as appropriate for his or her ability level, demonstrating progress according to the performance standards of the English/citizenship course prescribed by the recognized program in which he or she is enrolled (i.e.,
    (a) enrollment occurred on or after May 1, 1987 (and the program was approved by INS during the period of enrollment; some were approved retroactively);
    (b) course standards include attainment of particular functional skills related to communicative ability, subject matter knowledge, and English language competency; and

(c) attainment of these skills is measured either by successful completion of learning objectives appropriate to the applicant's ability level, or attainment of a determined score on a test or tests, or both of these);
(Local school diplomas or certificates will not be accepted as proof of school attendance. The alien must be issued a form I-699 Certificate of Satisfactory Pursuit by the program).

(2) <u>High school diploma</u> from a school in the United States;

(3) <u>G.E.D.</u> from a school in the United States; if G.E.D. was gained in a language other than English, applicant must prove that he or she passed the English proficiency test;

(4) <u>A letter from a state recognized, accredited learning institution</u> in U.S., certifying attendance for one academic year and that the curriculum included at least 40 hours instruction in English and U.S. government (there appears to be no limits on when school was attended - i.e., would include 1980-81 academic year);

(5) <u>Form I-699 (Certificate of Satisfactory Pursuit)</u>, Proof of attendance at courses certified by the INS Outreach Program or local District Director (retroactively to May 1, 1987 if necessary), conducted by employers, social, community, or private groups.

(6) <u>Applicant attests to 40 hours home study and passes a proficiency test</u> for legalization, administered by qualified administrators, indicating that the applicant is able to read and understand minimal functional English within the context of the history and government of U.S.[81] Nine of fifteen questions presented in a video/audio format must be answered correctly. For information on the availability of this last option, consult the local LO.

The District Director and Outreach Program shall compile and maintain lists of INS recognized courses at the district and the national level.[82] These lists of approved classes will be distributed at local INS offices. In many areas there may not be sufficient approved classes to teach all of the second stage applicants who wish to enroll. Several months into the second stage, some cities were reporting ever-lengthening waiting lists to get into approved classes. Applicants should enroll in such classes as soon as possible to insure receipt of a certificate before their application deadline.

---

[81] Interim rules 8 CFR §§245a.1(s), 245a.3(b)(4)(iv), (v).

[82] Interim rule 8 CFR §245a.3(b)(6).

The applicant need not be enrolled in any of the above classes at the time of application for permanent residence. If the course has not been completed by the day of the interview, the applicant should attempt to take the test or should be able to demonstrate that the course will be completed within 6 months or less if the interview is re-scheduled.

While those enrolled in approved classes or who have high school or G.E.D. diplomas may be tempted to rely on the class attendance option out of convenience, they should be encouraged to consider the examination option instead (producing proof of class attendance as a "back up" in case they fail the examination). Those passing the examination need not repeat it in order to become U.S. citizens and therefore are more apt to seek naturalization when eligible.

2.7(e) Rejection of Certificate of Satisfactory Pursuit

The Certificate of Satisfactory Pursuit (Form I-699), which is one of the six alternate methods for proving compliance with the "basic citizenship skills" requirement, as described above, does not guarantee, require, or certify that the applicant learned specific information or has reached a certain level of comprehension. It merely certifies attendance at a recognized program. A Certificate of Satisfactory Pursuit can only be rejected by the District Director:

(1) if fraudulent or fraudulently issued,[83] or
(2) if the District Director determined that the course provider is not complying with INS regulations.[84]

The Certificate of Satisfactory Pursuit may be accepted if the program is subsequently cited for deficiencies or decertified at a later date but no fraud was involved in the issuance of the certificate in question.[85] District Directors will accept Certificates once deficiencies have been satisfactorily corrected.[86] Because of these provisions, the burden is on the applicant to assure that the classes he or she attended meet INS requirements.

---

[83] Interim rule 8 CFR §245a.3(b)(10)(ii).

[84] Interim rule 8 CFR §245a.3(b)(10)(iii).

[85] Interim rule 8 CFR §245a.3(b)(10)(vi).

[86] Interim rule 8 CFR §245a.3(b)(10)(iv).

2.7(f) Class Sponsorship Requirements

Because a Certificate of Satisfactory Pursuit issued by an instructional program can be rejected by the INS due to the failure of the course sponsor to meet INS requirements, it is incumbent upon the applicant to check whether a program is complying with federal regulations. The following list sets-forth the requirements with which course sponsors must comply.

1. <u>The program must be recognized by the Attorney General.</u>[87] Such recognized programs include:

   a. established public or private institution of learning recognized by a qualified state certifying agency (inquiry must be made with the individual school or the state department of education to determine whether an institution is state-recognized);[88] or

   b. institutions of learning approved by the INS to issue Forms I-20 (schools authorized to issue I-20s will have been issued a school approval form I-516) by the INS);[89] or

   c. qualified designated entities ("QDEs") in good standing with the INS;[90] or

   d. courses certified by the District Director in whose jurisdiction the program is conducted, or certified on a national basis by the Director of the INS Outreach Program. Recognized courses are then placed on a list distributed by the local LO or INS District Director; some will have also been issued a Form I-804, Certificate of Attorney General Recognition.[91]

---

[87] INA §245A(b)(1)(D)(i)(II).

[88] Interim rule 8 CFR §245a.3(b)(5).

[89] <u>See</u> 8 CFR §214.3, interim rule 8 CFR §245a.3(b)(5).

[90] Interim rule 8 CFR §245a.3(b)(5). <u>See</u> INA §245A(c)(2), 8 U.S.C. §1255a(c)(2); 8 CFR §245a.1(l); interim rule 8 CFR §245a.1(r).

[91] In order to be recognized, the institution or program must have submitted a Notice of Participation before December 1, 1988 or within 30 days of the creation of the course of study either (1) to the District Director in whose jurisdiction a local program is conducted or (2) to the Director of the Outreach Program for national programs; or must file a form I-803 (Petition for Attorney General Recognition to Provide Courses of Study for Legalization, Stage II)," reproduced in 65 Interpreter Releases

2. *The program must have a curriculum* ("a defined course for an instructional program") on file at the school for each level of instruction provided in English and history and government. According to the final regulations, the curriculum must minimally prescribe what is to be taught, how the course is to be taught, with what materials, and when and where.[92] The curriculum must:

    a. teach words and phrases in ordinary, everyday usage;

    b. include the content of the Federal Citizenship Text series as the basis for curriculum development (other texts with similar content may be used in addition to, but not in lieu of, the Federal Citizenship Text series);[93]

    c. be designed to provide at least 60 hours of instruction per class level;

    d. be relevant and educationally appropriate for the program focus and the intended audience;

    e. be available for examination and review by INS as requested.[94]

3. *Courses of study must provide certain standards for the selection of teachers.* Since some programs may be in locations where selection of qualified staff is limited or where budget constraints restrict options, the following list of qualities for teacher selection is set forth in the regulations as guidance for teacher selection (teachers should possess as many of the following as possible): TESL training; classroom experience teaching adults; cultural sensitivity and openness; familiarity with competency-

---

872-874 (August 22, 1988). See interim rule 8 CFR §245a.3(b)(6).

[92] Interim rule 8 CFR §§245a.1(u)(5), 245a.3(b)(12)(i)(B). Pedogologically, the "what, how, when, and where," of a course of instructions the syllabus, not the curriculum. The proposed regulatory definition of curriculum was more in keeping with this dichotomy: "minimally, it prescribes what is to be taught. *It can also include suggestions* for how, when and with what materials." See 53 Fed. Reg. 29806 (August 8, 1988). See also "INS Draft Paper Discusses Legalization's Second Step Guidelines" 65 Interpreter Releases 179-180 (February 29, 1988).

[93] Interim rule 8 CFR §§245a.1(v), 245a.3(b)(5)(ii), 245a.3(b)(8). The Federal Citizenship Texts are reviewed in 65 Interpreter Releases 783-784 (August 8, 1988).

[94] 8 CFR §245a.1(u).

based education; knowledge of curriculum and materials adaptation; knowledge of a second language.[95]

4. <u>Certificates of Satisfactory Pursuit must be issued in accordance with regulations</u>;[96] i.e.,

    a. <u>Designated Official.</u> The head of the school system or school, the director of the QDE, the head of a program approved by the Attorney General, or the president or owner of other institutions recognized by the Attorney General must specify a "designated official" whose signature must appear on all Certificates of Satisfactory Pursuit (Form I-699). Each school or institution (or each campus in a multi-campus institution) may have up to 3 designated officials at any one time. The designated official may not delegate this designation to any other person.[97] The "designated official" must be a regularly employed member of the school administration whose office is located at the school and whose compensation does not come from commissions for recruitment of foreign students.[98] The designated official must read and be familiar with the "Requirements and guidelines for courses of study recognized by the Attorney General"[99] (available from the Director of INS' Outreach Program). The name, title, and sample signature of each designated official shall be on file with District Director in whose jurisdiction the program is conducted.[100]

    b. <u>Issuance of I699 Certificates of Satisfactory Pursuit</u> The Certificate of Satisfactory Pursuit shall be issued to an applicant who has attended a recognized course of study for at least 40 hours of a 60-hour course as is appropriate for his or her ability level and is demonstrating progress according to the performance standards of the English and U.S. history and government

---

[95] Interim rule 8 CFR §245a.3(b)(13).

[96] <u>See</u> interim rule 8 CFR §245a.3(b)(10).

[97] Interim rule 8 CFR §245a.3(b)(11)(iii)(A).

[98] Interim rule 8 CFR §245a.3(b)(11)(ii).

[99] Interim rule 8 CFR §245a.3(b)(11)(iii)(B).

[100] Interim rule 8 CFR §245a.3(b)(11)(iii)(C).

course prescribed in 8 CFR §245a.1(s).[101] Performance standards must conform with the following requirements:

(1) enrollment occurred on or after May 1, 1987;

(2) course standards include attainment of particular functional skills related to communicative ability, subject matter knowledge, and English language competency; and

(3) attainment of these skills is measured either by successful completion of learning objectives appropriate to the applicant's ability level, or attainment of a determined score on a test or tests, or both of these).[102]

INS recognized programs receive SLIAG reimbursement moneys for every hour a student attends the ESL/Civics classes. Incidents of refusal to issue CSPs and requiring students to enroll in additional courses have been reported.[103] According to the INS Outreach Program, certified programs may not routinely refuse to issue certificates after the required number of hours (40) have been completed. INS plans to monitor programs for such problems.[104]

5. <u>Records</u> must be maintained for three years on each temporary resident enrollee. The records must include the students name as it appears on his or her I-688 temporary resident card, "A" number, and a copy of the I-699 Certificate of Satisfactory Pursuit.

6. <u>Fees</u> (if any) assessed by course provider must not be excessive.[105]

Course providers which engage in fraudulent activities or fail to conform with INS regulations will be removed from the list of INS approved programs and their Certificates will not be

---

[101] Interim rule 8 CFR §245a.3(b)(10).

[102] Interim rule 8 CFR §245a.1(s)(1).

[103] Programs are reimbursed with SLIAG funds based on the total hours student attends classes.

[104] Minutes, NCA meeting with Raymond Penn, Assistant Commissioner, Legalization (October 27, 1989).

[105] Interim rule 8 CFR §§245a.3(b)(6)(vi), 245a.3(b)(7).

accepted.[106] A Certificate of Satisfactory Pursuit shall be rejected by the District Director if fraudulent or fraudulently issued[107] or if the District Director determined that the course provider is not complying with INS regulations.[108] The Certificate of Satisfactory Pursuit may be accepted if the program is subsequently cited for deficiencies or decertified at a later date but there was no fraud involved in the issuance of the certificate.[109] District Directors will accept Certificates once deficiencies have been satisfactorily corrected.[110]

2.8 THE APPLICATION PERIOD

The deadline for filing an application for permanent resident status will be different for each applicant. The beginning and ending dates of the application period are measured from the exact date (between May 5, 1987 and May 4, 1988) when each individual filed his or her application for temporary residence during the first stage. The exact language of the statute requires temporary residents to apply for such adjustment to permanent resident status "during the one year period beginning with the nineteenth month after the date on which temporary resident status was granted."[111] The statute and the regulations merely require the submittal of the application during this one-year period; the interview need not be scheduled nor the application adjudicated during this time in order to comply with the statute.[112]

To calculate the applicant's beginning and ending application dates, refer to the applicant's fee receipt, not the date of issue of the I-688, nor the date of the approval of the temporary residence application by the RPF.[113] The statute provides for the application period to begin "during the one year period beginning with the 19th month after the date temporary residence was

---

[106] Interim rule 8 CFR §245a.(b)(10)(v).

[107] Interim rule 8 CFR §245a.3(b)(10)(ii).

[108] Interim rule 8 CFR §245a.3(b)(10)(iii).

[109] Interim rule 8 CFR §245a.3(b)(10)(vi).

[110] Interim rule 8 CFR §245a.3(b)(10)(iv).

[111] INA §245A(b)(1)(A), 8 U.S.C. §1255a(b)(1)(A).

[112] INA §245A(b)(2)(C), 8 U.S.C. §1255a(b)(2)(C). See also 8 CFR §245a.3(b)(4)(iii)(B).

[113] 8 CFR §§245a.2(s); interim rule 245a.3(a).

granted."[114] This language is repeated in one part of the regulations yet in another provision, the interim regulations describe the application period in a slightly different way stating that "18 months after the granting of temporary resident status, [the alien] may make application for permanent resident status."[115] This variance in language can be confusing, yet it appears that the latter provision is the operational rule.

Adding to the confusion is the fact that the I-688 temporary resident card lists an "issue date" and an "expiration date." Unfortunately, many temporary residents will doubtless assume that temporary residence commenced as of the "issue date" and that they have until the "expiration date" to apply for permanent residence. However, it is the date on which the temporary residence application was "filed" which is the date of the "grant" of Temporary Residence. To ascertain the exact date of filing, you must refer to the date on the application fee receipt issued by the legalization office.[116] Although the "issue date" on the I-688 Temporary Resident card usually coincides with the fee receipt date, in some cases it does not, particularly in those cases in which the application was submitted by mail, or a "skeletal" application was filed towards the end of the application period, followed later by an interview. The I-688 "issue date" therefore cannot be relied on. Nor does the last day in which an application for permanent residence can be submitted correspond to the "expiration date" on the I-688. The "expiration date" was generally set one month after the end of the application period to provide additional time for those who reverted to unlawful status to prepare to depart the country (although it should be noted that on many cards the expiration date is not always a date 30 days after the application deadline.) Again, use the date of the individual's fee receipt (form I-689), when calculating the last day of the filing period.

Given the announced first date of filing, an applicant counts 18 months from the filing date to arrive at the beginning of the application period. Filing dates will not be later than May 4, 1988 unless the application was filed with a QDE towards the end of the application period, in which case the applicant had until July 3, 1988 to present the application at the LO and pay the fee, or unless the application was submitted pursuant to a court ordered extension. In determining when 18 months have transpired, if the calendar date falls on a weekend or a legal holiday it is moved to

---

[114] INA §245A(b)(1)(A), 8 U.S.C. §1255a(b)(1)(A).

[115] Interim rule 8 CFR §§245a.3(a), (b)(1), (c)(3).

[116] 8 CFR §§245a.2(s); interim rule 245a.3(a).

the next workday.[117] Thus, November 7, 1988 was the day on which early (May 5, 1987) filers for temporary residence became eligible to apply for permanent residence (because November 5 and 6, 1988 occurred on a weekend, their filing date is the next Monday).[118]

Certain cases will present anomalies because the length of months varies. For example, in cases in which temporary resident status dates from September 30, 1987, one couldn't simply move that date 18 months hence to February 30, 1989, as there is no such date (the same is true for those who filed on September 29, 1987 and January 31, 1988). It is best to approach these anomalies conservatively, i.e., in the above example, consider March 2, 1989 as the beginning date of the application period, and February 27, 1990 as the final date for application.

Determining the last date of the application period is far more important than determining the initial application date especially in those cases where the application will be filed in the last two months of the individual's application period. As the end of the application period approaches the application form and filing fee should be filed by themselves rather than delayed while tardy supporting documents are gathered, thus risking filing the application late. This "skeletal" application can be supplemented by the needed supporting documents later.

If the applicant has lost the fee receipt or filed the application by mail and was not issued a fee receipt, determine whether the applicant was represented by a QDE or attorney who will know the exact filing date. Otherwise, request that the LO check their computer bank for the date of filing.

Although the INS will allow QDEs in good standing to assist aliens in preparing second stage applications, and although the statute allows for the filing of second stage applications via the QDEs, unlike the first stage there is no second stage regulation allowing the execution of a "consent to forward" to constitute a "filing" provided the application was submitted to the INS in the following 60 days.

2.8(a) Advance Filing

Once the beginning date of the permanent residence filing period has been determined, the regulations allow applicants to submit their applications 60 days prior to the first day of eligibility. Such applications will be reviewed, held by the RPF and considered "filed" on the first day of the applicable

---

[117] 8 CFR §1.1(h).

[118] See Interim rule 8 §CFR 245a.3(a), 8 CFR §1.1(h).

application period.[119] Because the date of permanent residence, once granted, will be retroactive to the date of filing, applications filed 60 days in advance will be accorded permanent residence as of the first date of the application period. If the application is filed in advance, those substantive requirements which depend on the individual's age (HIV, basic citizenship skills, etc.) will apply based on the applicant's age as of the filing date (the first date of eligibility), not on age as of the advance submittal of the application.[120]

2.8(b) Failure to File the Application on Time

Failure to file an application within the one year application period will result in the automatic termination of temporary resident status at the end of the thirty-first month after the date the alien was granted temporary resident status (i.e., the 31-month validity of the temporary resident card covers 12 months as a temporary resident, plus 18 months permanent resident application period, plus 1 month grace period, presumably within which to depart the country).[121] Temporary resident status therefore automatically ends one month after the application period for permanent residence has ended. If the application is submitted after the expiration of the application period, and is denied, there is no review of late filings.[122] Because of confusion caused by the fact that the "issue date" noted on the I-688 Temporary Resident card is different from the actual filing date noted on the fee receipt, INS is considering acceptance of applications during the 12 months after the I-688 "issue date" in those cases found to be late filed because of mistaken reliance on the I-688 issue date.[123]

If an applicant is rejected due to late filing, ascertain the reasons which lead to the alien's misjudgment of the deadline, e.g., erroneous information provided by teachers; LOs; confusion regarding the "expiration date" on the I-688; waiting lists for class enrollment; etc. It should be noted that the language of the statute arguably lends itself to a slightly different formula for

---

[119] Interim rule 8 CFR §245a.3(a).

[120] Letter from Terrance O'Reilly to the author, February 17, 1987.

[121] INA §245A(b)(2)(C), 8 U.S.C. §1255a(b)(2)(C), 8 CFR §245a.2(u.(1)(iv). See also 8 CFR §245a.2(u)(4).

[122] INA §245A(f)(2), 8 U.S.C. §1255a(f)(2).

[123] Minutes, NCA meeting with Raymond Penn, INS Assistant Commissioner, Legalization (October 27, 1988).

calculating the application period than that used by the INS. It provides for the submittal of the application "during the one year period beginning with the nineteenth month after the date on which temporary resident status was granted." The term "month" can be construed to mean each separate, whole calendar month, i.e., if an applicant filed on September 6, 1987, October 1987 would be the first month after filing; March 1989 would be the nineteenth month after filing. Those whom the INS considers to be late filers may have to argue that this alternative method of calculating the time period follows the statutory language whereas the regulation does not.

2.9 DELAYED GRANTS OF TEMPORARY RESIDENT STATUS

Because temporary residence dates from the date of filing the temporary residence application,[124] and not the date of the decision to approve the application, the time limits placed on the filing of the second stage application run whether or not the temporary residence application has been adjudicated. Thus, those whose cases are unadjudicated after 18 months face a dilemma in that they are ineligible because they are not yet temporary residents; yet if they wait to be granted temporary resident status in order to file their applications, the adjudication may come after their statutory application period has ended, thus rendering them ineligible for temporary residence due to their tardy filing.

It is not known how many temporary residence applications remain pending after 18 months, nor how many appeals pending before the Legalization Appeals Unit (LAU) involved cases filed with the Legalization Office 18 months previously. The uncertainty caused by delayed adjudication of an application will have caused some applicants to defer enrollment in "civics" classes while they await a decision on their applications. Given the fact that the application period for permanent residence is rigidly fixed as of the day the alien applied for temporary residence, those whose temporary residence applications remain unadjudicated after 18 months and those granted temporary residence only after time-consuming administrative appeals, court actions, or long delays at the RPF, may find the actual time period within which they can act to fulfill the "basic citizenship skills" requirement and file an application for permanent residence to have diminished from the statutory one year period.

Excessive delays may be caused by a variety of reasons. In some cases the RPF is merely waiting for the location and transfer of a previous "A" file; in some cases the "A" file the Lo is waiting for is lost. The LO's review of the "A" file is not a prerequisite to adjudication but merely assists the INS in

---

[124] 8 CFR §245a.2(s).

rebutting the alien's prima facie application. There must be practical limits on the amount of time the INS may have to marshall its rebuttal evidence, particularly when delays encroach on the alien's permanent resident application period and his or her right to timely adjust to permanent residence. Dealing with such matters can be difficult given the practitioner's inability to communicate with the RPF directly regarding "problem" cases. An inquiry letter, sent by certified mail, should be mailed to the RPF when delays encroach on the alien's permanent residence application period to inquire about the cause of the delay; this may call attention to the problem.

Administrative appeals of denials of temporary residence leave the appellant in a delicate dilemma. An appellant may request a copy of the administrative record and in most cases must do so in order to adequately prepare the appeal. Yet most such requests delay adjudication of the appeal an enormous amount of time. To avoid this additional delay, the appellant forgoes his right to review the record, thereby prejudicing the chances of success on the merits, merely to receive a prompt review by the LAU which, if favorable, will preserve his or her right to file for permanent resident status.

The application deadline problems of delayed temporary residents is currently under review by the INS and may be corrected in the final regulations.[125] However, INS' position in related situations has been that INS v. Pangilinan 108 S.Ct. 2210 486 U.S. ___, (1988) prevents the extension of statutory application deadlines by the courts (and arguably by administrative agencies as well). Thus, if final regulations were to extend the filing deadline they might ultimately be found to be invalid. Nor may estoppel arguments be available in the absence of proof of willful or deliberate delay on INS' part.

Apart from filing a mandamus action, the unadjudicated temporary resident applicant should consider submitting a timely application for permanent resident status accompanied by a request for nunc pro tunc approval of temporary resident status.

It remains to be seen what approach to this problem will be adopted by the INS. If the delay is caused by administrative appeals to the LAU, one remedy for the shrinking permanent residence application period would be the tolling of the permanent resident application period during the pendency of administrative

---

[125] Letter from Terrance O'Reilly, INS Deputy Assistant Commissioner for Legalization, to the author, February 17, 1989.

appeals.[126] Alternatively, applicants may be compelled to challenge the regulation defining the commencement of Temporary Resident status as the day of the fee receipt (instead of the day of actual approval of Temporary Resident status), a challenge which would have a "ripple effect" impact on other provisions, i.e., the length and standard of permitted absences, the date of commencement of the 5-year public assistance bar, the date of eligibility to naturalize, etc.

---

[126] See, e.g., Zambrano v. INS, ___F. Supp.____ CV-88-455 EJG (E.D. Cal 1988). See also LULAC v. INS, ___F. Supp.____ No. 87-4757-WDK (C.D. Cal 1988); Catholic Social Services v. Meese, ___F. Supp.____ No. Civ. S-86-1343 LKK (E.D. Cal 1988).

CHAPTER THREE

PROCEDURES FOR APPLYING FOR ADJUSTMENT
TO PERMANENT RESIDENT STATUS

3.1	SUMMARY OF SECOND STAGE PROCEDURES	3-3
3.2	THE APPLICATION FORM I-698	3-5
	3.2(a) Who Can Assist the Alien Applicant	3-5
	3.2(b) Completing the Application Form	3-6
3.3	DOCUMENTS SUBMITTED WITH THE APPLICATION	3-9
	3.3(a) Considerations Regarding the Submission of Documents	3-12
	3.3(b) HIV Serologic Test	3-13
3.4	FILING THE APPLICATION	3-14
	3.4(a) Calculating the Application Period	3-14
	3.4(b) Last-Minute Filings	3-15
	3.4(c) Where to File the Application	3-15
3.5	INS PROCESSING OF THE APPLICATION	3-17
3.6	THE INTERVIEW AND DECISION	3-18
3.7	REQUESTS FOR ADDITIONAL INFORMATION	3-21
3.8	POST-ADJUDICATION MATTERS	3-21

CHAPTER THREE

PROCEDURES FOR APPLYING FOR ADJUSTMENT TO PERMANENT RESIDENT STATUS

3.1 SUMMARY OF SECOND STAGE PROCEDURES

During the 18 months preceding the time when temporary residents can make application for adjustment to permanent resident status, the INS plans to send a series of separate notices to all temporary residents providing them with information about the requirements and procedures for adjustment to permanent resident status. These notices will be sent to each temporary resident at his or her last known mailing address. The first notice was mailed to all applicants in the summer of 1988 and outlined the general requirements for permanent resident status. Approximately one month before each temporary resident's period for applying for permanent residence begins (i.e., approximately 17 months after the grant of temporary resident status), the Regional Processing Facility (RPF) will send a M-306 packet of application forms and information, or a notice to pick up the packet. The M-306 consists of two I-698 application forms, two I-690 waiver forms, and instructions for filing. The alien may immediately complete and file the application according to the instructions in the packet. The mailing of the M-306 will be followed by a notice sent when 6 months remain to file the application. The fourth and last notice will be sent when two months remain in the application period.[1]

Those temporary residents who have moved since receipt of their I-688 temporary resident cards should file a change of address card (I-697) with the LO or the RPF to insure receipt of the M-306 packet and notices. Those who have not received the M-306 by the beginning of their application period can obtain one at the LO.[2]

The completed permanent resident application forms, photographs and filing fee, must be submitted by mail to one of the four Regional Processing Facilities. In addition, medical exams will be required of aliens 15 and over who were not tested for HIV at the time of application for temporary residence.[3] Documents showing continuous residence and proof of financial responsibility

---

[1] See 65 Interpreter Releases 988-989 (September 26, 1988).

[2] See INS-CO wire dated December 13, 1988, reproduced in 66 Interpreter Releases 65 (January 13, 1989).

[3] See instructions accompanying M-306 packet.

will not be routinely required and therefore should not be submitted unless specifically requested by the RPF.[4] Applications which show that the applicant meets all eligibility requirements, i.e., those submitted with proof of compliance with the "basic citizenship skills" requirement, can be approved by the RPF. In such cases, no "interview" will be conducted at the LO, although the applicant will be given an appointment at the LO for "ADIT" processing (fingerprinting for issuance of I-551 card).

Once the application is filed and processed, notification of the receipt of the application by the RPF will be sent to the appropriate local INS district or sub-office or to one of the 41 legalization offices which will remain open to process permanent resident applications. If the application has not been automatically approved by the RPF, these offices will then interview the alien on his or her application.[5] Those who opt to take an examination in lieu of class attendance can be tested by the Educational Testing Service (ETS) prior to their interview or they can be tested by INS at their LO interview.[6] If the applicant has elected to be given the basic citizenship examination at the time of the interview, and fails to pass it, he or she must be given a second opportunity to pass the examination or otherwise comply with the basic citizenship skills requirement.[7]

If additional information or documentation is required in order to complete the processing of the application, the applicant will be notified and given 60 days to respond. If no response is received by the RPF, a second notice will be sent to the applicant and an additional 60 days will be allowed for a response before the application is adjudicated.[8]

Applications for permanent residence are considered to be within IRCA's confidentiality provisions and the contents of the application and supporting documents cannot be divulged to other agencies or individuals or to INS personnel other than legalization adjudicators.[9] However, INS has taken the position that once

---

[4] Letter from Terrance O'Reilly, INS Deputy Commissioner, Legalization, to the author dated February 7, 1989.

[5] Interim rule 8 CFR §245a.3(e).

[6] Interim rule 8 CFR §245a.3(b)(4)(iii)(A).

[7] Interim rule 8 CFR §245a.3(b)(4)(iii)(B).

[8] Interim rule 8 CFR §245a.3(d)(6).

[9] Interim rule 8 CFR §245a.3(m).

permanent resident status has been approved, IRCA's confidentiality provisions no longer apply.[10]

While second stage procedures appear to be simplified in comparison with those of the first stage, this can be deceptive, as the underlying legal requirements are not simple. The legal consequences of mistakes or misinformation can be severe.

3.2 THE APPLICATION FORM I-698

3.2(a) Who Can Assist the Alien Applicant

The first stage of the legalization program provided for the preparation and filing of temporary residence applications with voluntary and other non-profit agencies termed "Qualified Designated Entities" (QDEs).[11] During the first stage, approximately 17% of all temporary residence applications were processed by QDEs. Others sought assistance from private attorneys or certified representatives and many filed their applications pro se.

The second stage of the legalization program promises to be vastly different. First of all, the INS has elected not to renew its cooperative agreement with the QDEs for the processing of second stage applications (after January 1, 1989). QDEs will also not receive federal reimbursement moneys for work undertaken during the second stage. Nor do the regulations allow for QDEs to forward applications to the INS within 60 days of the applications "filing" with the QDE, removing one advantage to tardy filers. As a result, many QDEs will no longer be providing assistance to those who need assistance in completing the second stage processing. QDEs in good standing who wish to do so will be allowed to provide application assistance during the second stages and may charge a reasonable fee, e.g., $50.00.[12]

Additionally, teachers have replaced the QDEs as a necessary preliminary contact point before submittal of the second stage application. In view of these changes, many applicants will turn to ESL/Civics teachers for advice on legal requirements or assistance in the completion of the application form. Although some former QDEs are now offering second stage "civics" classes, most ESL/Civics teachers have had little, if any, training in the most elementary aspects of second stage requirements. These

---

[10] Interim rule 8 CFR §245a.3(m)(4).

[11] 8 CFR §245a.1(l); interim rule 8 CFR §210.1(n).

[12] Minutes, NCA meeting with Raymond Penn, Assistance Commissioner, Legalization (October 27, 1989).

teachers may apply logic and common sense in responding to an applicant's requests for assistance, thus unwittingly exposing the alien to future problems with the INS.

Furthermore, the federal regulations limit the completion of immigration applications to the following persons:

a) the applicant, *pro se*;

b) attorneys;

c) law students and law graduates supervised by an attorney in a clinical or legal aid program and whose appearance is permitted by the INS officer before whom he or she wishes to appear;

d) reputable individuals with a pre-existing relationship to the applicant who file a declaration that they receive no payment for their services and whose appearance is permitted by the INS officer before whom he or she wishes to appear;

e) BIA accredited representative;

f) officials of the alien's home country;

g) foreign-licensed attorneys;[13]

h) Qualified Designated Entities (QDEs).[14]

Temporary residents with questions about the law and the procedures for the Second Stage are best served by referral to those who specialize in Immigration law matters.

3.2(b) Completing the Application Form

Applicants can use the Form I-698 form included in the M-306 packet received by mail, or obtain copies of these forms from the local district INS office or to those LOs which will be adjudicating applications during the second stage of the Legalization program. I-698 applications are also available through the Government Printing Office at $18.00 per 100, serial no. 027-002-00375-6. If the applicant has not received the application form I-698 or the M-306 packet by mail, application

---

[13]   8 CFR §292.1.

[14]   8 CFR §245a.1(l); interim rule 8 CFR 210.1(n).

forms can be obtained from the LO; photocopies of the form can also be used.

Many have found the instructions in the M-306 to be confusing, incomplete, and in some cases incorrect. For example, two I-698 application forms, two I-690 waiver forms, and an I-693 medical examination form are included in all M-306 packets sent to Temporary Residents. The M-306 includes two I-698 application forms, apparently intending that one form be used as the applicant's "draft" copy. Most applicants will not need to file I-690 waiver forms. Yet the instructions nowhere advise applicants that they needn't complete and submit all copies of these forms. The medical form does not indicate that it is only for use by those over 15 not previously tested for HIV;[15] alternative methods of satisfying the "Basic Citizenship Skills" requirement are not mentioned, and other problems.[16]

Most of the information sought on the application form is self-evident. However, certain concerns will arise regarding the completion of the application form:

1. <u>INS mailing label</u>. INS prefers that applicants use the pre-printed label with the bar code on the M-306 mailed to them as it helps INS sort and process applications automatically.

2. <u>Name changes</u>. Name changes (including names misspelled on the I-688 temporary resident card) should be indicated on the form and supporting documentation showing the name change should be attached, if available, e.g., marriage certificate, divorce or name change order. Married women may file under either their maiden or married name. If the person's name was listed incorrectly on the temporary residence card, an explanation should be attached.

3. <u>Absences</u>. List all absences from the date of application for temporary residence (the date on the fee receipt). If an absence was undertaken pursuant to advance parole, this fact should be noted on the form or on an attached explanation. Absences in excess of the 30/90 day limits should be accompanied by an explanation on a separate sheet (see the discussion of continuous residence in Chapter Two <u>supra</u>).

4. <u>Criminal arrests</u>. If the applicant has been arrested since the date of application for temporary residence, court documents pertaining to the arrest (indicating the nature of the offense), and the disposition should be obtained and filed. If convicted, a copy of the statute or ordinance indicating the maximum sentence

---

[15] <u>See</u> 66 Interpreter Releases 1, 13 (January 2, 19890.

[16] <u>See</u> 66 Interpreter Releases 57 (January 13, 1989). <u>See also</u> 65 Interpreter Releases 988-989 (September 26, 1988).

which can be imposed for the offense may need to be obtained. If an expungement or other post-conviction remedy has been obtained, this should be indicated on the form at Question 15 and pertinent documents should be attached.

5. <u>Public assistance</u>. If the applicant has received public assistance since the date of application for temporary residence, proof of the type of assistance and the dates of receipt may need to be obtained and submitted.

6. <u>Excludability</u>. The excludability grounds are not fully set-forth on the form. While applicants filing the form <u>pro se</u> cannot be held to a knowledge of excludable conduct not obvious from the plain meaning of the words on the form, attorneys, certified representatives and QDEs will be. If the applicant is excludable, this should be indicated on the form. Determine if the applicant filed a waiver of this grounds of excludability at the time of application for temporary residence. If so, note this in writing on the application or in an attachment; no new waiver need be filed. If excludability arose after the date of application for temporary residence, and the grounds of excludability is waivable, file an I-690 waiver application and the $35.00 filing fee. If a waiver is submitted, a detailed discussion of family unity, humanitarian, and public interest considerations present in the case should be attached, together with supporting documentation. If you are in doubt as to whether the facts indicate excludability, do not file a waiver application; explain the facts at the interview or in a separate attachment.

7. <u>Inconsistencies with Temporary Residence application</u>. The applicant should not misstate information in order to conform it to information supplied on the previously submitted I-687 application for temporary residence. Explanations of known discrepancies should be provided.

8. <u>Confidentiality</u>. As in the first stage of the legalization program, all information provided in the application and interview are covered by IRCA's confidentiality protections (with the exception of cases involving fraud). However, it appears that in some cities INS Investigators and Border Patrol agents routinely call LO offices to "verify" through their computer system whether an application was filed by a specific individual under INA §245A or §210, and its status.

9. <u>Required signatures</u>. The person who completes the form at the alien's request must sign the form at No. 24. In so doing he or she certifies that the form provides accurate and complete information concerning the facts of which he or she has knowledge. The alien's signature certifies that all facts provided are all

true and complete. The sanctions for providing false information on the application are severe.[17]

3.3 DOCUMENTS SUBMITTED WITH THE APPLICATION

The application and supporting documents should be submitted by mail to the RPF with jurisdiction over the applicants' place of residence. The following items should be included:

1. Completed application form I-698 (one for each applicant).[18]

2. One color, glossy photograph, taken within 30 days of the application (2 additional photographs will be required at the time of the interview). The applicant's I-688 name and "A90" number should be written on the back of each photograph in pencil.[19]

3. Medical Examination Form I-693 indicating HIV test results, original signed copy, if the applicant is age 15 or over and was not tested for HIV at the temporary resident stage.[20]

4. Money Order, cashiers check or certified bank check in the amount of $80.00 per individual applicant, or $240.00 per family (mother, father, and unmarried children under the age of 18).[21]

If family members file separately, a cover letter should be included with each application setting forth the names of all family members, their "A90" numbers, relationship, date of application for permanent residence (as to those previously filed)

---

[17] INA §245(c)(6), 8 U.S.C. §1255a(c)(6).

[18] Interim rule 8 CFR §§245a.3(d)(1), 245a.3(d)(3).

[19] All of these photographs must be 3/4 profile with the right side of the face, right ear and both eyes visible. The face must be against a white background and must measure one inch from the chin to the top of the hair. Photograph instruction sheets setting forth the required dimensions of photographs are available from the LO or the INS District Office.

[20] Interim rule 8 CFR §245a.3(d)(4), [see the discussion in §3.3(b)]. Medical examinations can only be performed by INS-certified civil surgeons in the area. The LO or the INS District Office distributes lists of certified civil surgeons.

[21] Interim rule 8 CFR §245a.3(d)(3). No personal checks or currency will be accepted.

and the amount of fee paid. A copy of any fee receipt received from the RPF by any family member should also be attached.[22]

5. Proof of compliance with "basic citizenship skills" requirement if applicant is between the ages of 16 and 64, i.e.,

a) "Proof of satisfactory pursuit of classes" (Form I-699), issued by a program recognized by INS and showing enrollment in classes after May 1, 1987 and 40 hours attendance. Diplomas issued by such approved programs are not acceptable proof of compliance with these provisions.

b) High School diploma; or

c) G.E.D. in English; or

d) G.E.D. in another language, and proof that applicant passed the English proficiency part of the G.E.D. examination; or

e) A letter from a state accredited school certifying that the applicant attended school during one academic (nine month) year and that such study included 40 hours in English and Civics instruction (those currently or previously enrolled in high school and who did not graduate from high school may obtain such letters to comply with the requirements); or

f) Attestation of 40 hours of home study and proof that the applicant has passed a proficiency test administered by the state (currently being offered pursuant to a pilot program established in California).[23]

Barring submission of any of the above documents, the applicant must indicate one of the following on the application form at Item No. 18:

a) the applicant will be able to produce one of the above at the time of the examination; or

b) the applicant wants to take the examination at the time of the interview (this option should be marked if the applicant plans to submit ETS test results); or

c) the applicant falls within one of the groups exempted from the "Basic Citizenship skills" requirement.

---

[22] See footnote 4, supra.

[23] Interim rule 8 CFR §§245a.1(s), 245a.3(b)(4)(iv).

3-10

6. Optional Documents:

a. Completed and signed form G-28, if represented by an attorney, or accredited representative, or other person authorized under the regulations.[24]

b. Waiver form I-690, supporting documents, and $35.00 (money order) waiver filing fee, if required by INS. No waiver need be submitted if the same basis for excludability was waived during the first stage.

c. Explanation and documentation of the cause of extended absence(s) exceeding 30 days (individual) or 90 days (aggregate), e.g., medical records, doctor's letter, death certificate, pharmacy receipt, affidavits, letters, etc., as well as proof that the applicant intended to maintain his or her U.S. residence, e.g., credit card, utility, and other bill payment records, rent receipt, evidence of the continuous maintenance of bank accounts, proof of location of family members and personal and real property.

d. Copies of criminal arrest records, dispositions, and sentencing statutes, expungement records, pardons, and other post-conviction records, if applicable.

e. Documents pertaining to name changes, e.g., marriage certificate, divorce or other court decree.

f. Documents pertaining to receipt of public assistance, indicating type of assistance and for whom. If applicant indicates receipt of public assistance on the I-698 or filed a waiver of the public charge grounds at the first stage, the applicant should now submit proof of financial responsibility.

g. Translations of any document in a foreign language.

h. Form I-772, Declaration of Intending Citizen, may be filed with the application or at the interview (optional). To be covered by IRCA's employment discrimination provisions, this form must first be filed with the INS or the General Counsel's office.

i. Request for Waiver of Interview Requirement. If the applicant is under 14 or an interview is impractical due to the applicant's health or advanced age, the interview may be waived (although the

---

[24] 8 CFR §292.1. QDEs may not file a G-28 unless they have an attorney or accredited representative on their staff. Due to IRCA's confidentiality provisions, LOs are requiring the applicant's signature on all G-28s. Indicate attorney or certified representative number at the bottom of the form.

applicant must still go to the LO for ADIT processing). Documentation of health or other problems should be attached.

3.3(a) Considerations Regarding the Submission of Documents

In preparing the application and supporting documentation, keep in mind the following:

(1) If in doubt as to whether any of the above documentation is required in a particular case, set forth the underlying facts on separate paper or cover letter. If the RPF determines the facts warrant additional information or documents, they will advise the applicant.

(2) Submit the original, signed application form I-698 and the original medical examination results. As to all other documents, the applicant should submit certified[25] copies of any required original documents and retain the originals for presentation at the interview. QDEs in good standing, attorneys, and accredited representatives can certify documents as true and complete copies. Any original documents submitted directly to the INS will be kept by them.[26]

(3) As with all other applications filed with the INS, you should make a copy of the application form and all supporting documents being submitted, so that the packet of documents can be easily reconstructed in the event that the original application form and documents are lost in the mail.

(4) Certain documents submitted must be certified as true and complete by the party that maintained them and must bear their seal or signature or the signature and title of persons authorized to act in their behalf: official government records, employment or employment-related records maintained by employers, unions, or collective bargaining organizations, medical records, school records maintained by a school or school board or other records maintained by a third party.[27]

(5) Submit the application by certified mail, return receipt requested, in order to have proof of filing and receipt by INS.

---

[25] 8 CFR §245a.3(d)(2), 8 CFR §204.2(j)(1) or (2).

[26] Interim rule 8 CFR §245a.3(d)(2).

[27] Interim rule 8 CFR §245a.3(d)(2).

3.3(b) HIV Serologic Test

The test for HIV can only be performed by civil surgeons recognized by the INS.[28] The results of the test must be indicated on INS form I-693 (medical examination of aliens seeking adjustment of status). Both the list of civil surgeons and the INS form I-693 can be obtained at the local INS office. Any person who filed an application for temporary residence _after_ December 1, 1987, and who was age 15 or older at the time need not take another medical examination, as all such applicants were automatically tested for HIV.[29]

Most applicants who filed their applications _before_ December 1, 1987, were not tested for HIV, however, in some cases the applicant's medical doctor administered a test for HIV even though it was not required. This is particularly likely as to medical examinations given in October and November of 1987. If available, check the medical examination results indicated on the applicant's copy of form I-693. If the applicant filed his or her application for temporary residence before December 1, 1987 but nonetheless was tested for HIV, no new medical examination need be taken, rather, the applicant should note this fact on the application form or submit the previous medical examination results.

If the alien does not have a copy of the I-693 medical examination results form, he or she should contact the facility which conducted the medical examination. If the applicant is unable to determine if he was tested for HIV, he or she should note this on the application form I-698. If the INS examiner determines that the HIV test is required but the alien's file indicates it was not previously administered, the applicant will be notified on form I-72 (INS request for additional information or documents) or on the notice scheduling the applicant for his or her interview.

All applicants for temporary resident status under the age of 15 at the time they filed their applications for temporary residence were normally not tested for HIV, regardless of the date they filed their applications. Some of those who were 12, 13 or 14 at the time of application for temporary residence will have turned 15 on the date they file their application for permanent residence. If so, they must be tested for HIV. Therefore, all potential permanent resident applicants aged 15, 16, and 17 (specifically, those born between 5-6-72 and 10-31-75) should be checked to determine whether they were under 15 at the time of application for Temporary Residence and therefore must now be tested for HIV.

---

[28] Interim rule 8 CFR §245a.3(d)(4).

[29] Interim rule 8 CFR §245a.3(d)(4).

Those who submit their applications 60 days in advance are considered to have filed their applications on the first day of eligibility. A person who is 14 when the application is submitted under advance filing procedures, but who is 15 on the first date of eligibility (the true filing date) must be tested for HIV.

Those who test positive for HIV should be referred to another clinic for re-testing to assure that the applicant is not held excludable based on a "false positive."

3.4 FILING THE APPLICATION

3.4(a) Calculating the Application Period

The earlier an applicant files for permanent residence, the more likely he or she is to avoid the crush which will occur during the last half of the program. Those who file late in the program will undoubtedly, due to their sheer numbers, encounter a slower processing and adjudication of their applications.

Also, given the fact that permanent resident status, once approved, dates retroactively from the date of filing at the Regional Processing Facility (RPF), those interested in ultimately becoming U.S. Citizens effectively shorten the time they must wait for U.S. citizenship by filing their form I-698 (application to adjust status from temporary to permanent resident) as early as possible.

The method of calculating the application period is set-forth in Chapter Two. Once you have determined the beginning date of the permanent residence filing period, it should be noted that the regulations allow applicants to file their applications 60 days prior to the first day of eligibility. Such applications will be reviewed, held by the RPF and considered "filed" on the first day of the applicable application period.[30] Because the date of permanent residence, once granted, will be retroactive to the date of filing, applications filed 60 days in advance will be accorded permanent residence as of the first date of the application period. If filing in advance, those substantive requirements which depend on the individual's age (HIV, basic citizenship skills, etc.) will apply based on age as of the filing date (the first date of eligibility), not on age as of the advance submittal of the application.[31]

---

[30] Interim rule 8 CFR §245a.3(a).

[31] See footnote 4, supra.

The application should be mailed to the RPF at least two weeks before the final deadline to allow for mail delivery or by express mail service.

3.4(b) Last-Minute Filings

Given the severe consequences of late filings as the end of the application period approaches you should file the application form and filing fee by themselves rather than wait for tardy supporting documents and risk filing the application late. The application can be supplemented by the needed supporting documents later. Be sure to calculate the last day of the application period with care. If the application is being submitted close to the end of the application period, express mail service is advisable.

3.4(c) Where to File the Application

The application and documents must be mailed to the Regional Processing Facility having jurisdiction over the applicant's current residence.[32] Unlike Stage One applications, submittal to a QDE does not constitute "filing" the application.

(1) Northern Region. The Northern Region includes these states: Alaska, Colorado, Idaho, Illinois, Indiana, Iowa, Kansas, Michigan, Minnesota, Missouri, Montana, Nebraska, North Dakota, Ohio, Oregon, South Dakota, Utah, Washington, Wisconsin, Wyoming. The address of the Northern RPF is:

Northern Regional Processing Facility
Federal Building and U.S. Courthouse
1000 Centennial Mall North, Room #B-25
Lincoln, NE 68508

(2) Southern Region. The Southern Region includes these states: Alabama Arkansas, Florida, Georgia, Kentucky, Louisiana, Mississippi, New Mexico, North Carolina, Oklahoma, South Carolina, Tennessee, Texas. The address of the Southern RPF is:

Southern Regional Processing Facility
P.O. Box 569570
Dallas, TX 75356-9570

(Note that this address is _different_ from the RPF address used for the filing of appeals).

(Address for overnight/express mail services:)

---

[32] Interim rule 8 CFR §245a.3(d)(1).

Southern Regional Processing Facility
1825 Market Center Blvd.
Dallas, Texas 75207

(3) Eastern Region. The Eastern Region includes these states: Connecticut, Delaware, District of Columbia, Maine, Maryland, Massachusetts, New Hampshire, New Jersey, New York, Pennsylvania, Puerto Rico, Rhode Island, Vermont, Virginia, Virgin Islands, West Virginia. The address of the Eastern RPF is:

Eastern Regional Processing Facility
Post Office Box 968
Williston, VT 05495

(Note that this address is _different_ from the RPF address used during Stage One).

(Address for overnight/express mail services:)

Windersport Lane and Industrial Avenue
Williston, VT 05495

(4) Western Region. The Western Region includes these states: Arizona, California, Hawaii, Nevada. The address of the Western RPF is:

Western Regional Processing Facility
Post Office Box 30030
Laguna Niguel, CA 92677-0030

(Note that this address is _different_ from the RPF address used during Stage One).

(Address for overnight/express mail services:)

Chet Holifield Federal Building
24000 Avila Rd.
Laguna Niguel, CA 92677

To assure receipt by the RPF of the application, it should be mailed by certified mail, return receipt requested. Some of the LOs have an alternate filing procedure available: some LOs will accept I-698s or have set-up a "drop off box" for I-698 applications which are then forwarded to the RPF. The applicant should check with the LO to determine if there is a "drop off box" available at the LO, and whether the filing date will be that of submission to the LO or that of receipt by the RPF.

Some RPFs have more than one Post Office Box. One is used for appeals and other matters related to first stage temporary resident applicantions, the other is used for second stage permanent resident applications. If the applicant submits an application at the wrong post office box, RPF personnel will forward it to the appropriate handling unit. The filing date is the date the application is stamped as being received by the RPF.

If the application is being submitted close to the end of the application period, express mail service is advisable. Some express mail services will only deliver to a street address, not to a P.O. Box.

3.5 INS PROCESSING OF THE APPLICATION

The date of adjustment to Permanent Resident status is the date of the fee receipt, i.e., the date on which the filing fee is received and logged-in by the RPF. An exception is made in cases of "early filings," i.e, cases submitted 60 days before commencement of the application period. In such cases the application is processed and held; the application will be considered "filed" on the first day of the application period.[33]

Once the application is received at the RPF, its contents will be entered into a computer file pertaining to the applicant. If the applicant and supporting documents indicate satisfaction of all of the eligibility requirements, including the Basic English skills requirement, the application will be approved by the RPF. In lieu of a full interview at the LO, the applicant will merely be processed for his or her I-551 permanent resident card.

If the RPF determines that additional information or documents are needed, they may mail a "Request for Additional Information," form I-72 to the applicant (in which case the requested items should be mailed to the RPF) or advise the applicant to bring certain data or documents with them to the interview. If requested items are not received within 60 days, a second I-72 request must be mailed. If no response is received within 60 days of the second notice, the application will be adjudicated based on the existing record.[34]

If it appears that the applicant may have difficulties responding to an I-72 request, a request for an extension of the 60-day reply period should be filed as soon as possible. This request should explain the circumstances, respond to the request to the extent possible and provide alternate documents if available.

If in processing the application the RPF encounters inconsistencies with the information provided during the first

---

[33] Interim rule 8 CFR §245a.3(a).

[34] Interim rule 8 CFR §245a.3(d)(6). But see 8 CFR §§103.2(b)(2).

stage, the applicant will be asked to provide additional information or documentation to clarify the discrepancies. If the matter cannot be resolved at the RPF, the applicant will be scheduled for an interview at the LO or local INS field office.[35]

Once the data has been entered into the computer, the computer record will be transmitted to the LO. The RPF will simultaneously send a notice to the alien scheduling him or her for an interview at the LO. Although processing times will vary at each RPF, it is anticipated that it will take approximately 30 to 90 days from receipt of the application by the RPF to schedule the interview.[36] The application and documents themselves will be retained at the RPF unless the RPF determines that a denial is likely. In such cases the file will be forwarded to the LO. The entire file must be reviewed before the LO can issue a final decision in such cases.[37]

The applicant's Temporary Resident card (Form I-688) will be extended in one year increments, if necessary, during the processing of the Permanent Resident application.[38]

3.6 THE INTERVIEW AND DECISION

The applicant will be notified by mail of the interview date, time and place. The interview can be waived in the following cases:

a) children under 14,

b) where impractical because of the alien's health or advanced age;[39]

c) where the RPF determines that the applicant has met all of the eligibility requirements and has approved the application.

In all of the above cases, the alien will nonetheless be notified to appear at the LO for "ADIT" processing, i.e.,

---

[35] Interim rule 8 CFR §245a.3(h); see also footnote 4, supra.

[36] See footnote 4, supra.

[37] Interim rule 8 CFR §245a.3(h).

[38] Interim rule 8 CFR §245a.3(d)(5).

[39] Interim rule 8 CFR §245a.3(e).

fingerprinting and signature on the card used to manufacture the I-551 permanent resident card.

The following documents should be submitted at the Legalization Office interview:

1. Appointment letter;
2. Two photographs (Note name and A-number on back in pencil);
3. Temporary Resident card (Form I-688);
4. The original documents of those submitted to the RPF with the application;[40]
5. Other documents requested by the INS;
6. Proof of compliance with Basic Citizenship skills requirement (if required, and if not submitted at the time the application was filed).
7. If the applicant has lost his or her I-688, he or she should bring one form of identification, a completed I-695 application for replacement I-688A and the $15.00 filing fee.

If an applicant is unable to attend a scheduled interview, he or she should advise both the LO and the RPF in writing of the reasons therefore and request that the interview be re-scheduled. A second interview may be granted if the alien was unable to attend the first "for good cause."[41]

The INS estimates that the average interview will take approximately 10 minutes. At the interview, the information from the application will be reviewed. If the INS file or the interview uncovers any adverse information or inconsistencies, the applicant must be given an opportunity to provide additional information and/or documentation to clarify any discrepancies. If the applicant appears to be excludable under an exclusion grounds which can be waived, INS must inform the applicant of the availability of a waiver. If the applicant is between 16 and 65 and does not submit proof of class attendance, he or she will be given an oral examination similar to the naturalization examination at the time of the interview. If the applicant passes the test, he or she will be given no proof thereof by the LO. It will be noted on the Memorandum of Creation of Record of Lawful Permanent Residence (Form I-181). INS has stated that when such aliens later seek to naturalize they will not need to prove that they have passed the exam, as INS will have access to their legalization files.[42] If the applicant elects to take the test but fails it, he or she must be given a second appointment at least 6 months in the future, or

---

[40] Interim rule 8 CFR §245a.3(d)(2).

[41] Interim rule 8 CFR §245a.3(e).

[42] See footnote 4, supra. See also 8 CFR §245a.3(m)(4).

sooner if requested by the applicant.[43] In lieu of attempting the examination a second time, the applicant may present other proof of compliance with the Basic Citizenship Skills requirement (e.g., a Certificate of Satisfactory Pursuit, G.E.D., etc.) immediately or at the time of the second interview. An applicant whose 12 month application period expires prior to the 6 month re-test shall be accorded the entire 6 months within which to be re-tested.[44]

The INS adjudicator at the local office will, with limited exceptions, make the final decision on the application. The INS must render its decision in writing.[45] If the local INS adjudicator is unable to decide a case based on the facts presented, he or she may give an applicant form I-72 requesting additional information or documentation. These items must be submitted directly to the LO. The case may also be continued if the adjudicator deems that a waiver of a grounds of excludability must be submitted. If a case involves an unusually complex or novel question of law, the local INS office or the RPF may certify the application to the Legalization Appeals Unite (LAU), who will then make the final decision.[46] If the question is certified, the applicant has 30 days within which to submit a brief.[47]

If approved, the applicant will be informed at the interview, and a sticker will be placed on the reverse side of the I-688 temporary residence card as temporary (6 months) evidence of adjustment to permanent resident status. Once approved the alien can travel outside the United States and can file second preference visa petitions. Those who have lost their I-688s may be immediately photographed for a replacement so that the sticker can be placed on their replacement card. However, a completed I-695 application for replacement of the I-688, and the $15.00 filing fee will be required. The ADIT card (form I-89) will be completed (the applicant's fingerprint and signature will be taken) and forwarded by the local INS office to the card manufacturing facility in Arlington, Texas for manufacture of the Alien Registration Receipt Card, form I-551 (permanent resident card)., which will be sent by mail directly to the applicant within 3 to 6 months.

If the application is denied (form I-692), the applicant must be provided with specific reasons for the denial in writing. If the denial is based on adverse information or inconsistencies, the

---

[43] Interim rule 8 CFR §245a.3(b)(4)(iii)(B).

[44] Interim rule 8 CFR §245a.3(b)(4)(iii)(B).

[45] Interim rule 8 CFR §245a.3(h).

[46] Interim rule 8 CFR §245a.3(k).

[47] Interim rule 8 CFR §245a.3(i).

applicant must have first been given an opportunity to explain or rebut the information.[48] A denial cannot be issued unless the LO has reviewed the entire file, not just the computer record forwarded by the RPF. Appeals of denials of Permanent Residence must be filed on Form I-694 (in triplicate) within 30 days of the date of the denial. If the denial is mailed (instead of personally served on the applicant at the interview), add 3 days to the appeal period.[49] If the time period for submitting an appeal has passed and if the grounds for denial can be overcome, the applicant should consider filing a new I-698 (if still within the application period).[50] The filing fee for an appeal is $50.00;[51] the RPF will mail the appellant a receipt. If the application is denied due to INS' rejection of the Certificate of Satisfactory Pursuit (Form I-699), refer to the Chapter Two, supra.

The RPF can also re-open and reconsider adverse decisions, however this possibility should not be pursued in lieu of filing an appeal. Requests for re-opening or reconsideration should be filed simultaneously or after the filing of an appeal. Because the LO has rendered the "final" decision without prior review by the RPF, the RPF may be persuaded to take a different view. All appeals should therefore request reopening or reconsideration by the RPF.

3.7 REQUESTS FOR ADDITIONAL INFORMATION

If the RPF, LO or INS requests additional information, the applicant has 60 days within which to respond. If no response is received, a second request will be made, again according the applicant 60 days within which to respond. If there is still no response, the application will be adjudicated based on what has been submitted up to that point.[52]

3.8 POST-ADJUDICATION MATTERS

If Permanent Residence is approved, the manner in which the applicant satisfied the "Basic Citizenship Skills" requirement will be noted on the Memorandum of Creation of Record of Permanent

---

[48] Interim rule 8 CFR §§245a.3(h), 103.2(b)(2).

[49] Interim rule 8 CFR §§245a.3(i), 103.3(a)(2), 103.5a(b).

[50] See 8 CFR interim rule §245a.3(h).

[51] 8 CFR §103.7(b).

[52] Interim rule 8 CFR §245a.3(d)(6).

Residence (Form I-181) so that the applicant who passed an examination and who subsequently seeks to naturalize need not re-take the examination. However, INS has taken the position that once permanent residence is achieved the confidentiality provisions no longer apply and the entire contents of the legalization file may be reviewed to render a decision on naturalization.[53]

If approved for permanent residence, the alien may wish to have his or her passport stamped in order to freely travel abroad. Those contemplating possibly lengthy trips abroad should apply (on form I-131) for a Re-entry Permit (Form I-327) before departing. He or she may also immediately file I-130 visa petitions under the second preference for spouses and unmarried children.

Applications which are denied do not result in the automatic termination or expiration of temporary residence. Temporary resident continues until the end of the appeal period or the expiration date of the I-688, whichever is later. If an appeal of the denial is filed, extensions of the I-688 will be granted during the pendency of the appeal. I-688 card-holders have work authorization by operation of regulation.[54]

Because the information in the application and interview is confidential it cannot be used to arrest or deport an individual unless the case involved fraud.

If the application is denied and the applicant files an appeal, the RPF will forward the entire file to the Legalization Appeals Unit (LAU). If the alien has requested the RPF to reconsider or reopen the LO's denial, it will review the case. If it decides to re-open it will enter an order, request additional information or documents or remand it to the LO with instructions.

---

[53] Interim rule 8 CFR §245a.3(m)(4).

[54] Interim rule 8 CFR §245a.3(h).

CHAPTER FOUR

PERMANENT RESIDENCE FOR S.A.W.S UNDER INA §210

4.1	INTRODUCTION	4-3
4.2	REQUIREMENTS FOR ADJUSTMENT OF STATUS TO PERMANENT RESIDENT STATUS UNDER INA §210	4-3
4.2(a)	Maintenance of Status as a Temporary Resident	4-3
4.2(b)	Deportable as Excludable at Entry	4-6
4.3	DATE OF ADJUSTMENT TO PERMANENT RESIDENCE STATUS	4-8
4.4	PROCEDURES FOR ADJUSTMENT TO PERMANENT RESIDENT STATUS	4-9
4.5	OTHER PROVISIONS RELATING TO SECOND STAGE SAWS	4-10
4.5(a)	Numerical Limitations	4-10
4.5(b)	Stay of Deportation and Employment Authorization	4-10
4.5(c)	Administrative and Judicial Review of Denials	4-10
4.5(d)	Permanent Resident Status	4-11

CHAPTER FOUR

PERMANENT RESIDENCE FOR S.A.W.S UNDER INA §210

4.1 INTRODUCTION

As with the first stage of IRCA's amnesty programs, the second stage substantive and procedural requirements for SAWs differ greatly from those of the general legalization program, INA §245A. The following discussion is based on interim regulations which were promulgated on March 29, 1988.[1] As the date approaches for the submittal of permanent residence applications (i.e., December 1, 1989), additional regulations will probably be required in order to clarify some of the problems suggested by the current regulations.

4.2 REQUIREMENTS FOR ADJUSTMENT OF STATUS TO PERMANENT RESIDENT STATUS UNDER INA §210

Under the statute, there are very few requirements exacted of second stage SAWs. They must be temporary residents, and they must submit an application for adjustment.[2] Once these requirements are met, their adjustment to permanent resident status is mandatory as of a date determined by the provisions of the SAW statute under which they applied and the date they were adjusted to temporary resident status. Current regulations introduce controversial provisions requiring the SAW temporary resident to appear at the LO or INS district office for an interview where the alien is required to execute an affidavit stating he or she has maintained status as a temporary resident in that he or she does not fall within any of the grounds of deportability.

4.2(a) Maintenance of Status as a Temporary Resident

At the interview to determine whether the alien has maintained status, the INS officer must determine whether the applicant falls under any of the grounds of deportability under INA §241.[3] The information provided by the alien concerning his or her maintenance of status will serve as the basis for the determination and is

---

[1] 53 Fed. Reg. 10064-10070.

[2] INA §§210(a)(2); 210(b)(1).

[3] Interim rules 8 CFR §210.5(b)(2).

subject to verification by the INS.[4] The interim regulations provide that the SAW temporary resident must not come within any of the following grounds of deportability at the time of the interview [INA §241(a)]:

(1) Aliens who are excludable at entry, i.e., within any of the 33 grounds of excludability as of any entry to the United States or adjustment of status (discussed below);
(2) Entered without inspection or in violation of the INA;
(3) Has become institutionalized at public expense within 5 years of entry to the U.S.;
(4) Convicted of a crime of moral turpitude within 5 years of entry and sentenced to 1 year confinement; or convicted of two crimes of moral turpitude not stemming from the same scheme of criminal conduct;
(5) Failed to notify INS of change of address;
(6) Anarchists and communists;
(7) Subversives;
(8) Has become a public charge within 5 years of entry to the U.S.;
(9) Failed to maintain nonimmigrant status;
(11) Became narcotic drug addict after entry to the U.S.; narcotics conviction;
(12) Prostitution;
(13) Alien smuggler (for gain);
(14) Automatic/semiautomatic weapons violations;
(15)-(16) Violations of Alien Registration Act;
(17) Violations of the neutrality laws;
(18) Convicted of importing alien for immoral purposes;
(19) Nazis;
(20) RAWs who fail to comply with work requirements.

If the INS believes that a SAW temporary resident is deportable under INA §241, the interim regulations provide that an Order to Show Cause (OSC) will be issued.[5] No IRCA waiver is available for any of the above grounds of deportability.[6] However, other forms of relief from deportation may be available to the alien under other provisions of the INA depending on the facts of each case. If after institution of the proceedings the alien is found to be deportable by an immigration judge, temporary residence status is deemed automatically terminated and the alien must surrender his or her I-688 on demand.[7]

---

[4] Interim rules 8 CFR §§210.5(b)(1), (2).

[5] Interim rule 8 CFR §210.5(b)(2).

[6] With certain exceptions as to INA §241(a)(1).

[7] Interim rules 8 CFR §§210.5(b)(2), 210.4(d).

These contemplated procedures raise a number of issues. The details of how the INS proposes to implement such procedures are not known, but several obvious problems deserve to be considered. First is the obvious fact that the statute contains no requirement that a determination regarding the deportability of an applicant be made prior to the granting of permanent resident status during the second stage. Indeed, the admissibility requirements for achieving status under IRCA's programs are explicitly set forth as to the first and second stage of the legalization program, and as to the first stage of the SAW program. The statute contains no comparable provision for the second stage of the SAW program. Yet the interim regulation introduces the requirement that the applicant show nondeportability under the 20 listed grounds of deportation, one of which encompasses all 33 grounds of excludability as of the date of adjustment to temporary residence and all subsequent entries to the U.S. Because SAW applicants were free to travel since the day they filed their nonfrivolous application for temporary residence, many--perhaps most--did so. The grounds of excludability will therefore apply in addition to the grounds of deportability in the majority of cases. Thus, although the statute is completely silent as regards admissibility and deportability requirements, the regulatory requirements are far more onerous than the admissibility requirements imposed on legalization and Stage One SAW applicants.

Second, IRCA's confidentiality provisions apply to both Stages One and Two of the SAW program, thus preventing the use in deportation proceedings of any information obtained during any second stage procedures established as prerequisites to permanent resident status. The procedures contemplated make the execution of a statement that the applicant has maintained status an integral part of second stage processing; as such it is covered by the confidentiality provisions and cannot be used for the issuance of an Order to Show Cause in the manner provided by the regulations.

Next, one must consider the exception to the confidentiality protections, i.e., to investigate or enforce the law regarding "false statements in applications." Can INS thwart the intent of Congress by introducing a requirement which will serve to give them easy access to IRCA files? If in the course of a routine matter, an INS agent determines that a SAW permanent resident alien falls within a ground of deportation or excludability (e.g., infection with a dangerous contagious disease, convicted of a crime of moral turpitude, or failure to notify INS of a change of address)[8] at any time between the date of application for temporary resident status and the date of application for permanent residence (a time span which can approach 4 and 1/2 years), will the INS claim the right to access the otherwise confidential IRCA file on the grounds that the alien made a false statement as part of his Second Stage

---

[8] INA §§212(a)(6), 212(a)(9), 241(a)5).

application when he executed the affidavit stating that he had maintained status? Can the INS rescind permanent residence, terminate temporary residence or exclude an alien, not on the basis of the examples listed, but on the grounds of fraud? The materiality and relevancy of the false statement to the determination of eligibility will be relevant as to excludability for fraud and also as to whether the confidentiality provisions apply. According to the statute, deportability and excludability under the grounds mentioned are irrelevant to a determination on a second stage application and would not permit access by the INS to the alien's IRCA file.[9]

In essence, what the INS has done is to convert the provision relating to the <u>termination</u> of temporary residence, wherein INS has the burden of proving that the temporary resident is deportable under INA §241, into an affirmative requirement, hereby shifting the burden to the alien to prove non-deportability under INA §241. The statute provides that "During the period of temporary resident status" the INS may terminate the status only upon a determination that the alien is deportable.[10]

Obviously, for purposes of administrative convenience, the INS seeks to screen all applicants during the second stage for deportability in order to facilitate their investigation and termination of temporary resident status. The statute allows for termination of termination of temporary resident status "during the period of temporary resident status." This "period of temporary resident status" arguably ends as of the date fixed by statute for the alien's adjustment to permanent resident status. If they have not found a basis for terminations of status prior to that date, they arguably lose their authority to terminate.

Can the applicant refuse to answer an INS officer's questions pertaining to deportability and still proceed with his or her confidential second stage application? Perhaps changes in the present regulations will render these unanswered questions moot.

4.2(b) Deportable as Excludable at Entry

If the alien is deportable on the grounds that he or she was excludable at the time of adjustment to temporary resident status [INA §241(a)(1)], he or she must be advised of the waiver application procedures, if a waiver is available under INA §210(c).

---

[9] It should be noted that INS may use another basis for its claim to the right to access confidential IRCA files. INS has taken the position that IRCA files are confidential only until the applicant is granted permanent resident status.

[10] INA §210(a)(3).

The subsequent approval of the waiver does not effect the date of adjustment to permanent resident status.[11]

However, this ground of deportability has far broader applicability; a determination of "excludability at the time of entry" can be made as to any entry made subsequent to the filing of the temporary residence application. SAWs issued I-688A work authorization cards were free to travel and a great many SAWs did so. INS therefore can review the alien's excludability as of each return trip to the United States after the filing of the application for temporary residence.

Although nothing in the statute or in deportation grounds INA §241(a)(1) limits the applicability of any of the exclusion grounds to be applied to returning I-688A holders, (or Temporary Residents or SAW Permanent Residents) and IRCA waivers do not expressly apply in such a context, INS is arguably limited in the exclusion grounds it may apply and must arguably allow for IRCA waivers. This is illustrated by cases of temporary residence applicants who fall within grounds of excludability which were automatically waived at the first stage (e.g., illiteracy).[12] If such grounds were inapplicable at the temporary resident stage yet applied as to every return trip to the United States the alien would be effectively trapped within the United States, i.e., unable to leave for fear of exclusion upon re-entry. If such grounds are permanently inapplicable, then those grounds which were waivable at the first stage are also arguably waivable in subsequent years. Thus IRCA's limitations on the applicability of certain exclusion grounds and provision of waivers arguably extends to subsequent entries.

If excludability arose after application for adjustment to temporary resident status, and the alien has not departed the United States since the grounds of excludability arose, the alien is not subject to termination of temporary resident status.[13] However, such excludable aliens face future problems if they leave the United States due to the "re-entry doctrine," i.e., the alien may be excluded at the port of entry upon his or her return or may be admitted but subsequently placed in deportation proceedings as deportable for having been excludable at the time of entry.[14]

---

[11] Interim rule 8 CFR §210.5(b)(2).

[12] INA §212(a)(25).

[13] Interim rule 8 CFR §210(b)(2).

[14] INA §241(a)(1).

4.3 DATE OF ADJUSTMENT TO PERMANENT RESIDENCE STATUS

According to the language of the statute, the dates of adjustment to permanent resident status will vary depending on whether the alien was a "Group 1 SAW" or a "Group 2 SAW" and depending on the date the application was filed. SAW Group 1 temporary residents are those who were able to prove they performed seasonal agricultural services for 3 years ending on May 1, 1986.[15] SAW Group 2 temporary residents are those who were able to prove they performed seasonal agricultural services for one year ending May 1, 1986.[16]

Those who were classified SAW Group 1 shall be adjusted to permanent resident status after one year from either the date the alien was granted temporary residence, or the last day of the application period for Stage One (November 30, 1988), whichever is later. This provision applies to the first 350,000 SAW Group 1 applications for permanent resident status that are filed (it is doubtful this numerical limit will be reached).[17]

All other temporary residents (SAW Group 2) shall be adjusted to permanent resident status after two years from either the date the alien was granted temporary residence, or the last day of the application period for Stage One (November 30, 1988), whichever is later.[18] Most SAW applicants fall within the Group 2 classification.

Thus, to determine the date on which an alien is eligible to adjust to permanent resident status, you must know whether the alien was accorded SAW Group 1 or SAW Group 2 classification at the time of application for temporary residence, as well as the date on which the alien was adjusted. The date of adjustment to temporary resident status is generally the date of the fee receipt.[19] The date of adjustment to permanent resident status will usually be fairly easy to determine, as most temporary resident status applicants, will have filed their temporary resident applications and adjusted to temporary resident status prior to November 30, 1988 (the last day of the SAW Stage One application period). Thus, the vast majority will have a December 1 date--in 1990 for SAW Group 1 workers, and in 1991 for SAW Group 2 workers.

---

[15]   INA §210(a)(2)(A).

[16]   INA §210(a)(2)(B).

[17]   INA §§210(a)(2)(A), (C); interim rule 8 CFR §210.5(a)(1).

[18]   INA §210(a)(2)(B), §210(a)(2)(C); interim rule 8 CFR §210(a)(2).

[19]   Interim rule 8 CFR §210.4(a).

However, others will be considered to have filed after November 30, 1988 and they will come within the other provisions of the regulations regarding the calculation of the filing date for permanent resident status. They must count one year from their filing date. Such late filers fall into two groups: those who filed towards the end of the application period (in October and November, 1988) by signing a Consent to Forward with a QDE, may have physically submitted the application and paid the application fee at the LO up to 60 days after the November 30, 1988 application deadline.[20] In such cases the date of adjustment is the date on the fee receipt. Secondly, those who applied for temporary resident status at an overseas processing office, though required to submit their application and pay the filing fee before the November 30, 1988 deadline, were adjusted as of the date of their admission into the United States.[21] Because SAWs approved overseas had 120 days within which to present themselves at a port of entry,[22] some SAWs who were processed overseas may have had their status adjusted after November 30, 1988.

Thus, as to all who filed their applications within the United States, you must determine from the fee receipt the date of "adjustment;" as to those who filed at overseas processing posts the date of adjustment will be the date of entry to the United States (normally indicated on the I-688 as the "Issue Date.")

In issuing the temporary resident cards to SAWs, the INS has indicated an expiration date on the I-688; this date is one year and one month after the above dates (depending on which group the alien falls within) thus indicating that the INS plans to establish a one year "application period" within which SAWs will be adjusted to permanent resident status.

4.4 PROCEDURES FOR ADJUSTMENT TO PERMANENT RESIDENT STATUS

As yet, the application for Adjustment to Permanent Resident status has not been distributed and the fees and other details of the application procedure have not been determined.

An application must be submitted to either the INS or to a Qualified Designated Entity (QDE) (by signing a consent to forward

---

[20] Interim rule 8 CFR §210.2(b).

[21] Interim rule 8 CFR §210.4(a).

[22] Department of State wire dated May 27, 1987, reproduced in 64

form).[23] The information furnished in the application is confidential and cannot be used for law enforcement purposes, except in cases of fraud; violators are subject to criminal penalties.[24] The files of QDEs are also confidential.[25]

The SAW temporary resident must appear at the LO or INS district office for an interview. At the interview an I-89 ADIT card will be completed (i.e., applicant's fingerprint and signature required for manufacture of the I-551) and the applicant will be required to execute an affidavit stating he or she has maintained status as a temporary resident. Given the regulations' focus on deportability, rather than excludability, second stage SAWS should not have to submit HIV test results.

4.5 OTHER PROVISIONS RELATING TO SECOND STAGE SAWS

4.5(a) Numerical Limitations

INA §§201 and 202 numerical limitations do not apply to applications by SAWs for adjustment to permanent resident status.[26]

4.5(b) Stay of Deportation and Employment Authorization

Applicants for adjustment who have filed a nonfrivolous application during the application period may not be excluded or deported and may be issued employment authorization "until a final determination on the application has been made."[27]

4.5(c) Administrative and Judicial Review of Denials

There will be a single level of administrative appeal to review adjustment determinations. Appellate review will be based solely upon the administrative record established at the time of the determination on the application and upon such additional or newly discovered evidence as may not have been available at the

---

[23] INA §210(b)(1)(A).

[24] INA §§210(b)(6), (7).

[25] INA §210(b)(5).

[26] INA §210(c)(1).

[27] INA §210(d)(2), amended by P.L. No. 100-202, 101 Stat. 1329. See also Chapter Five.

time of the determination.[28] Judicial review may be had only in the review of an order of exclusion or deportation under INA §106. Judicial review shall be based solely upon the record at the time of the administrative appeal and the findings of fact and determinations contained in such record shall be conclusive unless the applicant can establish abuse of discretion or that the findings are directly contrary to clear and convincing facts contained in the record considered as a whole.[29]

4.5(d) Permanent Resident Status

Aliens adjusted to permanent residence as SAWs are considered lawfully admitted to permanent residence under INA §101(a)(20).[30]

Aliens granted temporary resident status as SAWs are ineligible for certain forms of public assistance for five years after the date on which they were granted temporary residence.[31] This public assistance bar will therefore extend into the period of permanent residence up to a date five years from the date of adjustment of temporary resident status.

---

[28] INA §210(e)(2).

[29] INA §210(e)(3).

[30] INA 210(g).

[31] INA §210(f).

CHAPTER FIVE

LEGALIZATION AND SAW APPEALS

5.1	DENIAL OF TEMPORARY RESIDENCE	5-3
	5.1(a) Denial of the Application	5-3
	5.1(b) Notice of Denial and Right of Appeal	5-4
5.2	POST-DECISION MOTIONS AND CERTIFICATIONS	5-6
5.3	ADMINISTRATIVE APPEALS TO THE LEGALIZATION APPEALS UNIT	5-8
	5.3(a) Procedure and Preparation of the Appeal	5-9
	(1) Reviewing the Record of Proceedings	5-10
	(2) The Notice of Appeal and Appeal Brief	5-11
	5.3(b) Decision by the L.A.U.	5-14
5.4	SUBSTANTIVE AND PROCEDURAL GROUNDS OF APPEAL	5-15
	5.4(a) Grounds of Appeal in INA §245A Denials	5-17
	(1) Denials Based upon Failure to Establish Continuous Residence	5-17
	(A) Insufficient Documentation	5-17
	(B) Continuous Residence Broken by Absences in Excess of 45/180 Days	5-21
	(C) Denials Based upon Departure Caused by Deportation Order	5-25
	(2) Denials Based upon Failure to Establish Continuous Physical Presence	5-30
	(3) Denials Based upon Failure to Establish Unlawful Status	5-31
	(A) Expiration of Authorized Stay; Duration of Status	5-32
	(B) Unlawful Status "Known to the Government"	5-34
	(i) School Report of Violation of Nonimmigrant Status to the INS	5-37
	(C) Unlawful Status Due to Fraud	5-40
	(4) Denials Based upon Public Charge Grounds	5-40
	(5) Denials Based upon Criminal Grounds	5-48
	(A) The Finality of a Conviction	5-49
	(B) The Effect of Post-Conviction Relief	5-51
	(C) Denials Based upon the Unavailability of INA §212(h) Waivers	5-52
	(6) Denials Based Upon Untimely Filing of the Application	5-56

5.4(b) Appeal of Denials of SAW Applications under
INA §210   5-61
 (1) INS Suspicion of Fraud in SAW Program   5-61
 (2) Denials Based upon Insufficient Evidence
  or the Lack of Corroborative
  Documentation of Qualifying Employment   5-63
 (3) Denials Based upon Determination that
  Applicant did not Perform Ninety Days of
  Employment in Seasonal Agricultural
  Services   5-68
  (A) Denials Based upon Determination
   that Crop was not A Fruit, Vegetable
   or Other Perishable Commodity   5-68
   (i) Horticultural Specialties   5-72
   (ii) Grains and Seed Crops   5-73
  (B) Denials Based on a Finding that the
   Applicant did not Engage in
   Qualifying Field Work   5-75
 (4) Denials Based upon Grounds of Exclusion   5-77
  (A) Denials Based upon Public Charge
   Grounds   5-78
 (5) Denials Based upon Untimely Filing   5-79

5.5 APPEAL OF DENIAL OF WAIVER OF INELIGIBILITY   5-80

CHAPTER FIVE

LEGALIZATION AND SAW APPEALS

5.1 DENIALS OF TEMPORARY RESIDENCE

5.1(a) Denial of the Application

With limited exceptions, the Regional Processing Facility (RPF) has the sole authority to issue a final approval or denial of temporary resident applications under INA §§245A and 210. The District Director of the Legalization Office may deny an application filed under INA §245A or an application for a waiver of a ground of excludability, without forwarding it to the RPF, only if an alien fails to meet the statutory requirements or admits fraud or misrepresentation in the application process.[1] The Legalization Office (LO) District Director has discretion to approve those cases in which an alien establishes eligibility for a waiver of excludability after referral for re-interview from the Regional Processing Facility.[2] In adjudicating SAW applications filed at overseas processing posts, the consular official may deny the application if the applicant fails to meet his or her burden of proof, or if fraud is suspected.[3] A sample denial notice is included at the end of this Chapter.

The RPF makes the final determination on an application for temporary resident status under INA §245A or §210 based upon the record of proceedings received from the District Director of the Legalization Office (LO), as well as information contained in any investigatory reports or pre-existing immigration file ("A file") pertaining to the applicant.[4] The record of proceedings from the LO includes the application form, all supporting documentation, any and all records or notations made by the INS examiner concerning the legalization interview, as well as the LO's recommendation to approve or deny the application.

---

[1] 8 CFR §§103.1(n)(2). See also 245a.2(k)(2), 210.3(e)(2). Improper exercise of the District Director's limited authority to make final adjudications is subject to appeal.

[2] 8 CFR §§245a.2(k)(2), 210.3(e)(2).

[3] 8 CFR §210.3(e)(2). See also Department of State Cable dated May 27, 1987, reproduced in 64 Interpreter Releases 697-703 (June 1, 1987).

[4] See 8 CFR §103.1(t).

The regulations require the disclosure of any derogatory evidence considered by the INS and of which the applicant is unaware. The applicant must be offered an opportunity to rebut such adverse evidence and to present an explanation and/or evidence which shall be included in the record and considered _prior_ to the rendering of a decision.[5] Although the regulations do not limit the time allowed for a rebuttal, the INS has indicated that it will normally issue a Form I-72 "Request for Additional Information" notifying the applicant of the adverse information, and granting the applicant 30 days to respond.[6] An appeal of a denial in which the decision was predicated upon adverse evidence not made available to the applicant should provide additional evidence rebutting the adverse information and challenging the INS' reliance upon it without having given the applicant an opportunity to rebut it in the first instance. The appeal should include a request that the RPF reopen the case and reconsider its denial.[7]

5.1(b) Notice of Denial and Right of Appeal

If the application for adjustment of status is denied either by the LO District Director or by the Director of the RPF, the applicant must be notified of the denial and of his or her appeal rights. According to the regulations, the applicant must be provided with the following:

(a) written notice of the denial of temporary residence on Form I-692, Notice of Denial;[8]

(b) a statement of the _specific_ reasons for the denial;[9]

(c) written notice that the decision may be appealed; that such appeal must be taken within (30) days after service

---

[5] See 8 CFR §103.2(b)(3)(i).

[6] See INS memorandum dated April 11, 1988 from Associate Commissioner Richard Norton entitled "Denial and Appeal Procedures in Legalization Process," reproduced in 65 Interpreter Releases 403 (April 18, 1988).

[7] The RPF will reopen all cases in which a denial based on adverse information was issued without first providing the information to the applicant or an opportunity to present information or evidence in rebuttal. See INS memorandum dated April 11, 1988 by Associate Commissioner Richard Norton, reproduced in 65 Interpreter Releases 403 (April 18, 1988).

[8] 8 CFR §§245a.2(o), 210.2(f).

[9] 8 CFR §§245a.2(o), 210.2(f), 103.3(a)(2).

of notice of the decision; that such appeal may be accompanied by any additional new evidence, and a supporting brief, if desired;[10]

(d) written notice that if a timely appeal is not submitted, employment authorization shall be automatically revoked on the final day of the appeal period;[11]

(e) notice that in the case of failure to file an appeal of the decision, the denial on Form I-692 will serve as a final notice of ineligibility.[12]

The denial notice containing the above information accompanied by a copy of Form I-694 Notice of Appeal, will be sent to the applicant at his or her last known address and to his or her attorney or accredited representative.[13] Applicants who move prior to receiving notification of the decision from the RPF should file an I-697 Change of Address form with the LO or the RPF.

INS has conceded that 3 days will be added to the appeal time when the denial is served by mail. Thus, the applicant will have 33 days from the date the denial is mailed within which to file an appeal. The Notice of Appeal must be received by the RPF within this period. Note that where the filing deadline falls upon a weekend, a holiday, or other non-business day, the deadline is carried over to the next regular business day. Note also that three days are not added to the appeal deadline if the denial notice is not served by mail, i.e., is personally served on the applicant at the LO.[14] Applicants at overseas processing posts are allowed sixty (60) days from the date of denial in which to file an appeal of the decision.[15] A timely filed notice of appeal should include a request for a copy of the record of proceedings and a request for an extension to file a written brief and additional supporting documentation. In response to such a request, the RPF will grant an automatic extension of 30 days from the time the record of proceedings is mailed for the submission of a brief and any additional evidence. Extensions can also be granted for good

---

[10] 8 CFR §§245a.2(o), 210.2(f), 103.3(a)(2).

[11] 8 CFR §245a.2(n)(4).

[12] 8 CFR §103.3(a)(2)(i).

[13] 8 CFR §§245a.2(o), 103.3(a)(2).

[14] 8 CFR §§1.1(h), 103.5a.(b), 245a.2(p), 103.3(a)(2).

[15] See Department of State cable dated May 27, 1987, footnote 3, supra.

cause shown.[16] Details regarding prosecuting an administrative appeal are discussed below.

5.2 POST-DECISION MOTIONS AND CERTIFICATIONS

The regulations do not provide an opportunity for an applicant to directly initiate reopening, reconsideration or certification of a denied application. In its regulations, the INS has restricted the applicant's ability to seek reopening, limiting authorization for such actions to the RPF acting sua sponte. This will occur when a notice of appeal is filed with the RPF and the Director of the RPF, on his own motion, reopens or reconsiders an adverse decision; or when the INS is obliged to reopen or reconsider specific kinds of cases or denials pursuant to Court order or a change in the law or INS policy since the adjudication of the application. The RPF Director's new decision must be served on the appealing party within 45 days of receipt of any briefs and/or new evidence, and upon expiration of the time allowed for the submission of any briefs.[17]

Reopening and reconsideration allows the RPF to correct clear errors of law and factual mistakes. It is particularly appropriate to request that the Director of the RPF reopen and reconsider cases where the applicant is submitting new evidence that would alter the initial decision or if evidence previously submitted was not considered in the decision. Moreover, a discretionary request to the RPF to reopen and reconsider may be the only vehicle to obtain review of a denial where an applicant has missed the 30/33 day deadline for filing an appeal. An appeal should always raise the option of reopening and reconsideration of the initial denial by requesting that the RPF act sua sponte. However, requests to reopen and reconsider are not alternatives to filing an appeal. The applicant will lose his or her right to appeal if he or she does not file a Notice of Appeal within the required time. Thus, a request to reopen and reconsider should be made either simultaneously with the filing of a Notice of Appeal or with the filing of the appeal brief. The request should be brought to the attention of the Director of the RPF and should be clearly marked as such on the envelope. Currently, the RPF must reopen and reconsider denied applications in the following situations:

---

[16] See INS memorandum dated April 11, 1988 by Associate Commissioner Richard Norton, reproduced in 65 Interpreter Releases 403 (April 18, 1988). See the discussion at §5.3(a)(1), infra.

[17] 8 CFR §§103.5(b), 210.2(g), 245a.2(q).

(a) denials based on adverse information which was not provided to the applicant for the opportunity to rebut;[18]

(b) denials based on lack of sufficient evidence when the application was filed with a Qualified Designated Entity (QDE) between June 15, 1987 and August 15, 1987;[19]

(c) denials of SAW applications at the LO for failure to submit corroborative documentation (in the Eastern Region);[20]

(d) denials based upon the ground that the applicant was ineligible due to re-entry to the United States on a nonimmigrant visa after January 1, 1982;[21]

(e) denials based on the INS' erroneous interpretation of "known to the government";[22]

---

[18] See 8 CFR §§103.2(b)(3)(i) and INS memorandum dated April 11, 1988 by Associate Commissioner Richard Norton, reproduced in 65 Interpreter Releases 403 (April 18, 1988). See also Haitian Refugee Center v. Nelson, 694 F. Supp. 864 (S.D. Fla. 1988).

[19] According to letters issued by INS Associate Commissioner Richard Norton, dated June 16, 1987 and July 15, 1987, such applications may be resubmitted with additional documentation directly to the RPF within 60 days of denial. There is no official policy, however, indicating that the 30/33 day appeal period will be stayed in cases of those applicants who take advantage of this procedure and submit additional documentation.

[20] Loe v. Thornburgh, No. 88 CIV. 7363 (PKL) (S.D.N.Y. 1989).

[21] See 8 CFR §§245a.2(b)(9) and (10). As a result of LULAC v. INS, F. Supp. (C.D. Cal.) No. 874757 WDK July, 18, 1988, the INS amended its regulations to allow an alien who departed the U.S. and subsequently reentered with a nonimmigrant visa in order to return to an unrelinquished unlawful residence to qualify for legalization. The applicant, however, must also submit a waiver of excludability under INA §212(a)(19) as an alien who entered the United States by fraud. Pursuant to the court's order in LULAC, INS must continue to accept legalization applications from such aliens. See 65 Interpreter Releases 767 (August 1, 1988).

[22] See Ayuda v. Meese, 687 F. Supp. 650 (D.D.C. 1988). Civ. Ac. No. 88-0625. in which the district court ordered the INS to suspend its regulations defining "known to the Government." See 65 Interpreter Releases, 1131 (October 31, 1988). See also discussion at §5.4(a)(3)(B) of this Chapter, infra.

(f) denials based upon the ground that the applicant did not establish continuous physical presence in the United States due to a brief, casual and innocent departure that was not previously authorized by the INS;[23]

(g) denials based on actions taken with regard to F-1 students (permission to change schools, renewal, change of status) constituting a reinstatement to lawful status.[24]

Further examples of the many instances in which the law regarding eligibility requirements for temporary resident status has changed are provided in the discussion of substantive and procedural grounds of appeal at § 5.4 of this Chapter. Although the RPF has been directed to reopen such cases, the advocate should always make a request to reopen denials of applications in instances where a change in the law would affect the decision.

When a case involves a novel question of law or fact, the RPF may seek certification and review by the INS Associate Commissioner, Examinations.[25] This avenue has been taken in cases presenting a variety of issues such as factors constituting emergent reasons for an extended absence, and circumstances constituting unlawful entry prior to 1982, not addressed by agency policy.[26] An applicant whose case presents a novel or controversial issue may wish to suggest by motion or other correspondence that such action be taken by the Director of the RPF in a case recommended for denial.

5.3 ADMINISTRATIVE APPEALS TO THE LEGALIZATION APPEALS UNIT

The Legalization Appeals Unit (LAU) is the part of the Administrative Appeal Unit (AAU) of the Immigration and Naturalization Service which reviews denials of applications for temporary resident status under INA §§245A and 210. The scope of administrative appellate review is limited to the administrative

---

[23] See Catholic Social Services v. Meese, No. S-86-1343-LKK (E.D. Calif. 9th Cir., 1987, 1988), in which the district court struck down INS' restrictive definition of a brief, casual and innocent absence as ultra vires. See 65 Interpreter Releases, 1010 (October 3, 1988). See discussion at §5.4(a)(2) of this Chapter, infra.

[24] CIPRA v. Meese, No. 99-1088 (D.D.C. January 3, 1989).

[25] 8 CFR §§103.4, 210.2(h), 245a.2(r).

[26] See discussion of substantive and procedural grounds of appeal, at §5.4, infra.

record established at the time of the determination on the application and such newly discovered evidence "as may not have been available at the time of the determination."[27]

5.3(a) Procedure and Preparation of the Appeal

The regulations set forth the following procedures to be followed in an appeal of the denial of an application for temporary residence:

(a) The Form I-694 Notice of Appeal must be filed in triplicate at the Regional Processing Facility[28] within 30 days of the notice of denial(the appeal period includes an additional three days for mailing, extending the period to thirty-three (33) days for decisions mailed by the RPF and an additional 30 days for overseas SAW processing cases);[29]

(b) The Form I-694 Notice of Appeal must be accompanied by the filing fee of $50.00, remitted in the form of a cashier's check or a money order;[30]

(c) The Notice of Appeal should be accompanied by any additional new evidence and a supporting brief if desired; if a copy of the record of proceedings is requested, the supporting brief may be filed within 30 days of its receipt.[31]

The addresses of the four Regional Processing Facilities and the Legalization Appeals Unit are reproduced in the Appendix.

---

[27] INA §§210(e)(2)(B), 245A(f)(3)(B).

[28] 8 CFR §§103.3(a)(2)(i), (ii); 210.2(f); 245a.2(p).

[29] See notes 3, 14 and 15, supra. As the mailing date is often different from the date of the decision, it is advisable to verify the precise date of mailing from the postmark on the envelope. It is also recommended to send the appeal by certified mail in order to have a record of the date the appeal was received by the RPF. Some regions have adopted an emergency filing method which allows appeals to be filed on the last day of the 30/33 day filing period at the LO. Check with the RPF and local LO before attempting to utilize this method in cases where a timely appeal cannot be accomplished by mail to the RPF.

[30] 8 CFR §103.7(b).

[31] 8 CFR §103.3(a)(2)(i). See note 16 and accompanying text, supra.

5.3(a)(1) Reviewing the Record of Proceedings

The first step in preparing an administrative appeal is obtaining and reviewing the record. This is particularly important in cases where the advocate handling the appeal did not represent the alien at the application stage. According to procedures outlined by the INS in an April 11, 1988 directive issued by Associate Commissioner Richard Norton, a request for a copy of the record of proceedings can be made on the I-694 Notice of Appeal. The record of proceedings includes the application, supporting documentation, the examiner's worksheet, investigative reports as well as the contents of any previously existing immigration file ("A file") pertaining to the applicant. If review of the record of proceedings is requested with the Notice of Appeal, an automatic thirty day extension for filing the appeal brief will be granted from the date the record is mailed by the RPF.[32]

Notwithstanding the INS' policy to allow access to the record of proceedings and to provide adverse information allowing an opportunity for the applicant to rebut such adverse information, it may still be advisable to file a separate request for documents under the Freedom of Information Act (FOIA) on INS form G-641, if this was not previously done. A FOIA request should seek copies of documents stored in any of the applicant's INS files which may affect the applicant's eligibility, not simply those stored in the A90 file created at the time of the temporary residence application. A FOIA request may be appealed if the agency has not responded within ten working days.[33]

The record of proceedings does not include a written record of the initial temporary residence interview beyond that provided by the examiner's notes. The advocate should therefore meet with the applicant and any former representative to determine what statements were made by either the applicant or the examiner during the interview. If the applicant's statements were misunderstood or misconstrued, or if the examiner made statements or assumptions later relied upon by the RPF in denying the application, the advocate will want to prepare an affidavit from the applicant

---

[32] See INS memorandum dated April 11, 1988 by Associate Commissioner Richard Norton, reproduced in 65 Interpreter Releases 403 (April 18, 1988). See note 16, supra. A sample Notice of Appeal appears at the end of this Chapter.

[33] 8 CFR §103.10(c). See sample FOIA request, prepared by advocates at the Georgetown University Law Center, reproduced at the end of this Chapter. INS' consistent failure to respond to FOIA requests within the required time has been challenged in Mayock v. INS, N.D. Cal. NOC-85-5169-CAL, July 6, 1988), reported in 65 Interpreter Releases 734 (July 25, 1988).

and/or the former representative. The affidavit should rebut the examiner's conclusions, or may allege the mishandling of the interview, and recount the actual statements and responses made at the interview. This will be particularly important in preparing appeals of denials of SAW applications, where the interview process is utilized to test the applicant's knowledge and understanding of the agricultural work which forms the basis of his or her application.

5.3(a)(2) The Notice of Appeal and Appeal Brief

In preparing an appeal, examine the notice of denial carefully and identify and analyze each of the specific grounds upon which the denial was based. If the factual and legal grounds for the decision appear to be insufficient and are not properly specified, this should be highlighted in the Notice of Appeal.[34] The Notice of Appeal should outline the grounds for appeal in a clear and succinct manner and indicate what new evidence is being submitted.[35] As mentioned above, the Notice of Appeal should also include a request to review the record of proceedings and should include any requests for an extension of time to file the appeal brief. A sample Notice of Appeal is included at the end of this Chapter.

The administrative appeal should always be supported by a written brief, arguing the facts and the evidence provided in the

---

[34] The regulations require that the notice of denial explain the specific reasons for the denial. 8 CFR §§103.3(a)(2); 245a.2(o); 210.2(f). Many of the denial notices issued by the RPF have been deficient in this regard. The failure to adequately specify the reasons for denials issued in SAW cases has been challenged in three separate federal court actions: Haitian Refugee Center v. Nelson, 694 F. Supp. 864 (S.D. Fla. 1988); United Farm Workers of America v. INS, Civ. No. S-87-1064-LKK/JFM (E.D. Cal.); and Ramirez-Fernandez v. Giugni, No. EP-88-CA-389 (W.D. Tex. November 23, 1988).

[35] A Notice of Appeal that fails to state the reasons for the appeal will be summarily dismissed. 8 CFR §103.3(b). See also, Matter of Valencia, Int. Dec. 3006 (BIA 1986) and Reyes-Mendoza v. INS, 774 F.2d 1364 (9th Cir. 1985). If the advocate preparing the appeal did not represent the alien at the application stage, he or she should request a copy of the record of proceedings, give a general statement of the reason for the appeal and reserve the right to amend the Notice of Appeal after receiving and reviewing the administrative record. See note 16, supra.

initial application which support approval of temporary residence.[36] The brief should argue that the RPF's decision was wrong and state the reasons why it was not supported by the evidence provided in the initial application. The appellate brief should also discuss reasons why the denial is erroneous as a matter of law and cite the statutory sections, agency regulations and policy memoranda which support a finding in the applicant's favor. Administrative and judicial decisions supporting the basis of the appeal should be discussed. Pertinent sections should be quoted in the brief and attached if appropriate.

Certain appeals may focus upon the INS' failure to follow its own regulations. Others will be premised upon the theory that the INS' regulations are too restrictive, or at odds with the legislative purposes and statutory terms enacted by Congress.[37] Arguments supporting such appeals should cite and address the statutory section, legal principles, or legislative history with which the regulation is at odds.[38] The LAU will be unable to overturn sections of the statute challenged on constitutional grounds. Nevertheless, the appeal may raise these objections in order to preserve the challenge for further judicial review.

In addition to arguing the applicant's substantive eligibility and entitlement to adjustment of status under the appropriate section of IRCA, the facts may give rise to challenges to the significant limitations on the applicant's due process rights to a hearing which characterize the application process. The applicant's ability to satisfy his or her burden of proof is severely restricted by an initial application procedure, which is limited to a cursory non-adversarial interview in which the applicant is not allowed an opportunity to present witnesses on his or her behalf. These deficiencies are particularly glaring where credibility is at issue, such as in cases denied on grounds of

---

[36] Sample briefs on a variety of appeal issues are available from the Legalization Issues Bank, a joint effort of a number of groups nationwide. An index and particular briefs may be obtained from the American Immigration Lawyers Association, 1000 16th Street NW Suite 1604, Washington, D.C. 20036, Attn: Legalization Issues Bank. Tel. 202-331-0046.

[37] See, for example, the discussion of an appeal of a denial based upon INS' position that INA §12(h) waivers are not available to legalization applicants, at §5.4(a)(5)(C) of this Chapter, infra.

[38] The underlying intent of Congress that the legalization program be administered in a generous and liberal fashion should provide the context for both substantive and procedural appeal arguments. See, H.R. No. 99-682-(I), 99th Cong. 2d Sess. (1986) at 72. See discussion at §5.4 of this Chapter, infra.

insufficient documentary evidence, or in those cases denied on the basis of alleged fraud. Further, as the regulations preclude reopening or reconsideration of the application except on the RPF's own motion, the applicant's only opportunity to present additional, new evidence is in the context of an administrative appeal.

New evidence may be submitted with an appeal and will be considered during the course of administrative review.[39] The applicant should take advantage of this provision to submit additional or collateral evidence which may establish entitlement to adjustment of status. For example, a denial based upon a conviction for a disqualifying crime might be overcome by submitting an order of expungement of the conviction obtained after the initial application was submitted.[40] Appeal of a denial which arguably can be cured through submission of a waiver under any provision of the INA should be accompanied by the requisite waiver form and supporting documents. Additional documentation which was not previously available or which the applicant did not submit with the original application should be submitted to overcome a denial based upon a failure to establish continuous residence through sufficient documentation. In every case, it is appropriate to submit additional documentation in order to meet the applicant's burden of proof, which, it may be argued, was already satisfied in the first instance

The appeal is filed with the RPF, and, as mentioned previously, should always include a request to the RPF to reopen the case sua sponte pursuant to 8 CFR §103.5(b). In situations where the LO denied the case and the decision was erroneous as a matter of law, or in cases in which the INS policy has changed since the time of the original adjudication, it may be possible to obtain approval from the RPF. Similarly, cases which are now well-documented may also be candidates for approval by the RPF without the necessity of referral to the LAU. Cases which raise issues of INS policy under dispute, or in which the RPF believes it will prevail, are certain to be forwarded to the LAU.

---

[39] 8 CFR §103.3(a)(2).

[40] The INS changed its policy on the effect of expungements on convictions for legalization purposes toward the end of the filing period. In an April 22, 1988 memorandum by Associate Commissioner, Richard Norton, the INS announced that complete expungements of convictions of other than controlled substance offenses will eliminate the conviction as a bar to legalization eligibility. Reproduced in 65 Interpreter Releases 443-446 (April 25, 1988). See discussion in §5.4(a)(5)(B) of this Chapter, infra.

5.3(b) Decision by the LAU

Upon receipt of an appeal, the RPF will forward the administrative record to the LAU for review and decision. The decision on the appeal shall be in writing and if dismissed shall include a final notice of ineligibility. A copy of the decision shall be served upon the applicant and his or her attorney or representative of record.[41]

According to the regulations the following appeals will be summarily dismissed:

(a) an appeal that fails to state the reason for the appeal; or

(b) an appeal filed _solely_ to challenge a denial for failure to apply in a timely manner; or

(c) an appeal that is patently frivolous.[42]

No further administrative appeal shall lie from the decision,[43] nor may the application be filed or reopened before an Immigration Judge or before the Board of Immigration Appeals during exclusion or deportation proceedings.[44] Any alien served with an Order to Show Cause after November 6, 1986 who fails to file an application for temporary residence under INA §245A within the 30 day period provided by regulation, and who is thereafter found to be deportable by decision of the Immigration Judge, shall not be permitted to appeal the finding of deportability based solely on refusal of the Immigration Judge to entertain such application in deportation proceedings.[45]

Thus, judicial review of a denial of temporary residence by the LAU may be extremely difficult to obtain. An alien who fails to file an appeal to the LAU or an alien whose application is denied by the LAU may continue in an unlawful status without employment authorization and will be subject to deportation if apprehended by the INS.[46] Methods of obtaining judicial review through collateral federal court actions or by appealing an order

---

[41] 8 CFR §103.3(a)(2)(iii).

[42] 8 CFR §103.3(a)(2)(iv). But see notes 16 and 32, _supra_.

[43] 8 CFR §103.3(a)(2)(iii).

[44] _Id_.

[45] 8 CFR §242.21(b).

[46] But see the discussion at Chapter Seven, §7.1(a), _infra_.

of an Immigration Judge and the BIA in deportation proceedings are discussed in the chapter seven.

The Associate Commissioner for Examinations and the LAU are given the authority to reopen and reconsider any decision rendered by the LAU.[47] Given the difficulty of obtaining judicial review, an alien whose appeal is dismissed by the LAU should consider requesting that the proceedings be reopened and the denial reconsidered, particularly in cases where there is a clear error of law or fact.

5.4 SUBSTANTIVE AND PROCEDURAL GROUNDS OF APPEAL

Denials of applications for temporary residence under INA §§245A and 210 will be based on a determination that the applicant has failed to satisfy one or more of the eligibility requirements identified in the statute and implementing regulations. Since the inception of the legalization program, INS' interpretation of the statutory provisions of the IRCA has been the subject of continuing controversy and litigation, which has resulted in numerous changes in the law affecting eligibility determinations. Many of these actions are pending final decision in the federal courts and many contain orders extending the filing deadline for aliens who did not submit a timely application due to their belief that they were not eligible under INS' erroneous interpretation of the statutory eligibility requirements.[48]

---

[47]   8 CFR §103.5.

[48]   Federal court actions which have extended the filing deadlines for applications under INA §245A, or are considering requests to extend the application period include:
   Ayuda, Inc. v. Meese, 687 F. Supp. 650 (DDC 1988). The Court found that those who did not apply for legalization by the filing deadline due to the INS' restrictive definition of "known to the Government" could file for relief from the court. See discussion at §5.4(a)(3), infra.
   Catholic Social Services v. Meese, No. S-86-1343-LKK (E.D. Calif. 9th Cir. 1987, 1988). The Court extended the filing deadline for aliens who did not apply for legalization due to INS' restrictive definition of "brief, casual and innocent absence." See discussion at §5.4(a)(2), infra.
   Doe & Roe v. Nelson, No. 88-C-6987 (N.D. Ill. 1988). The plaintiffs have requested the extension of the filing deadline for aliens apprehended after November 6, 1986 who were not issued Orders to Show Cause and did not apply for legalization because they believed they were ineligible under the INS regulations. See discussion at §5.4(a)(6), infra.
   Hernandez v. Meese, No. S-88-385 LKK (E.D.Calif. 1988). The plaintiffs have requested an extension of the filing deadline for

In preparing an appeal, it is therefore critical for the advocate to be aware of the developments in the various federal court actions challenging the regulations, as well as INS' patterns and practices in interpreting the statutory and regulatory provisions governing applications for temporary residence. The Legalization Appeals Project of the American Immigration Lawyers Association issues reports on developments in these cases on a regular basis. In addition, the Project has compiled a pleadings bank on the substantive and procedural appellate issues in legalization cases, as well as a digest of LAU decisions. In a joint effort with a variety of immigrant advocate groups, pleadings are collected, catalogued by issue and reproduced for ordering. The advocate should consult these resources in identifying the grounds of appeal and in preparing the appeal argument. Information on how to order from the Project, including an index to the Project's Legalization Issues Bank, is included at the end of this Chapter.

There are a variety of grounds which may be raised in an administrative appeal of a denial of an application for temporary resident status. It is beyond the scope of this volume to identify and discuss all of these grounds. Rather, some of the more common substantive and procedural grounds of appeal in denials of applications for temporary residence are discussed below.

---

aliens who did not apply by the deadline because they believed that their absence(s) of over 45 days made them ineligible. See discussion at §5.4(a)(1)(B), infra.

LULAC v. INS, No. 87-4757-WDK (C.D. Calif. 1988). The Court granted an extension of the filing period for aliens who reentered the United States after January 1, 1982 on nonimmigrant visas and did not apply because they believed they were ineligible under the INS' initial regulations.

Perales v. Meese, CV No. 2265-88 (S.D.N.Y. 1988). The plaintiffs have requested an extension of the filing period for those who believed themselves ineligible because of the confusion generated by INS policy regarding the public charge rule.

Zambrano v. Meese, No. S-88-455 EJG-M (E.D.Calif. 1988). The Court extended the deadline for those who failed to apply because they believed themselves ineligible under the public charge rule. See discussion at §5.4(a)(4).

The INS has contested all orders extending the filing deadline on the basis of the Supreme Court's decision in INS v. Pangilinan, 486 U.S.___, 108 S.Ct. 2210 (Nos. 86-1992, 86-2019, June 17, 1988) which held that courts are powerless to ignore such time limitations fixed by Congress. The Courts in Zambrano, LULAC and Catholic Social Services, Inc. have all distinguished Pangilinan. See 65 Interpreter Releases 818-819 (August 15, 1988).

5.4(a) Grounds of Appeal in INA §245A Denials

An applicant for temporary residence under INA §245A must establish that he or she has resided continuously in an unlawful immigration status since before January 1, 1982, that he or she has been physically present in the United States since November 6, 1987 and that he or she is not inadmissible on the basis of certain criminal, medical, moral and economic grounds of excludability set forth at INA §212(a). The application must have been timely filed within the application period (May 5, 1987 until May 4, 1988), and within 30 days of the issuance of an Order to Show Cause.[49] Applications for temporary residence under INA §245A must be supported by documentary proof of the applicant's identity, continuous residence and financial responsibility. Denials will be based upon a determination that the applicant has failed to meet his or her burden of establishing eligibility according to these requirements.

5.4(a)(1) Denials Based upon Failure to Establish Continuous Residence

Many applicants for legalization will be denied benefits due to a determination that they did not submit sufficient evidence documenting their continuous residence in the United States since before January 1, 1982 or that their continuity of residence was broken by an extended absence or absences or by departure under an order of deportation.

5.4(a)(1)(A) Insufficient Documentation

An applicant must establish his or her eligibility for temporary resident status by a preponderance of the evidence.[50] The sufficiency of the evidence will be determined according to its probative value, credibility and amenability to verification.[51]

The INS has not provided any meaningful or consistent directions on the sufficiency of documentation to establish continuous residence from before January 1, 1982. Consequently, the nature and extent of documentation required for approval has varied significantly between regions. Appeals challenging this ground of denial should be framed in the context of Congress' intent to administer the legalization program in a liberal and

---

[49] INA §245A(a)(1)(B).

[50] 8 CFR §245a.2(d)(5).

[51] 8 CFR §245a.2(d)(5), (6).

generous fashion,[52] and should argue that the evidence in the case is reliable and sufficient to establish eligibility.

Additional documentary evidence establishing continuous residence should always be submitted when available, along with a detailed explanation of why the evidence was not originally presented with the application.[53] If the applicant is unable to provide much documentary evidence and relies in large part on personal affidavits to establish continuous residence, the practitioner should elicit the special circumstances of the alien's "clandestine" life[54] in the United States which explain why he or she is not able to present corroborating documentation such as employment records, rent receipts, telephone and utility bills, financial records and medical records for each year dating from January 1, 1982 to the time the application was filed.[55] Form affidavits are of minimal probative value and should not be submitted to overcome a denial based upon insufficient evidence. Rather, affidavits by relatives, friends, neighbors, landlords and organizational associates should specify in detail the identity of the affiant, his or her relationship to the applicant and the nature and extent of the contact between the affiant and the applicant during the course of their relationship. Such affidavits should be supplemented by all available evidence corroborating the relationship between the applicant and the affiant.

An evaluation of recent LAU decisions reveals a pattern of affirming denials of applications supported entirely or in large part by personal affidavits. The LAU has held that affidavits "in and of themselves" do not establish the requisite entry, residence or presence unless they are used in conjunction with "documents from established institutions or organizations,"[56] reasoning that a person living in the United States for a number of years should

---

[52] H.R. Rep. No. 99-682(I) 99th Cong. 2nd Sess. (1986) at 72. See also, Matter of C, I.D. 3087 (Comm'r 1988) Matter of N, I.D. #3080 (Comm'r 1988), digested in 65 Interpreter Releases 1063 (October 17, 1988).

[53] INA §245A(f)(3)(B) requires an appeal to be based upon "the administrative record at the time of the determination of the application, and on newly discovered evidence as may not have been available at the time of the determination."

[54] H.R. Rep. No. 682, 99th Cong., 2nd Sess., pt. 1 (1986) at 71-73.

[55] See 8 CFR §245a.2(d)(3).

[56] LAU, July, 27, 1988. Order No. L1088-388 from the Legalization Issues Bank, LAU Decision Digest. Ordering information appears at the end of this Chapter.

have some documents to corroborate affidavits.[57] While the LAU has rejected seemingly reasonable explanations for the lack of documentary evidence, such as the fact that the applicant lived on the farms where he worked for the requisite period of residence,[58] it has accepted other explanations, including the loss of documents in a fire,[59] and the inability of a fifteen year old girl who quit school and did not speak English, to obtain other than affidavit evidence of her residence for the critical period of 1981-1982.[60]

The rejection of an affidavit, particularly in the context of an administrative structure which does not provide for any procedure by which to verify the credibility of the affiant or the veracity of his or her sworn statements, arguably contravenes Congressional intent to administer the program in a liberal and generous fashion and violates due process.[61] Although INA

---

[57] LAU, October 7, 1988. Order No. L1288-424 from the Legalization Issues Bank, LAU Decision Digest. Ordering information appears at the end of this Chapter. See also, Matter of --- A90 255 040 (LAU, October 20, 1987), a LAU decision which rejected an application that relied on the affidavit of the applicant's cousin to establish residence for 1982, noting that the applicant was 20 years old at the time and could have engaged in activities reasonably calculated to bring his presence here to the attention and knowledge of persons other than his cousin. Reported in 65 Interpreter Releases 76 (January 25, 1988).

[58] LAU, September 9, 1988. Order No. L1288-428 from the Legalization Issues Bank, LAU Decision Digest. Ordering information appears at the end of this Chapter.

[59] LAU, November 1, 1988. Order No. L1288-425 from the Legalization Issues Bank, LAU Decision Digest. Ordering information appears at the end of this Chapter.

[60] LAU, June 14, 1988. Order No. L0988-324 from the Legalization Issues Bank, LAU Decision Digest. Ordering information appears at the end of this Chapter.

[61] This argument is advanced in Leo v. Thornburgh, No. 88 Civ. 7363 (PKL) (S.D.N.Y. 1988), a pending class action in the INS' Eastern Region, which alleges that the INS has adopted a policy of rejecting applications for legalization that are supported wholly or in part by affidavit proof, without attempts to verify the affidavits or to test the credibility of the affiants at the interview. Plaintiffs assert that the failure of the INS to provide a hearing in which to test the credibility of the affiants is violative of due process. The INS agreed to temporarily stop issuing denials in cases where the evidence consists solely of affidavits and to reopen such cases previously denied. Copies of the pleadings and supporting briefs may be obtained from AILA's

§245A(g)(2)(D) requires that both continuous residence and physical presence be proven through documents and independent corroboration of the information they contain, the House Judiciary Committee noted that:

> ...Unnecessarily rigid demands for proof of eligibility for legalization could seriously impede the success of the legalization effort. Therefore, the committee expects the INS to incorporate flexibility into the standards for legalization eligibility, permitting the use of affidavits or credible witnesses and taking into consideration the special circumstances relating to persons previously living clandestinely in this country.[62]

The initial application procedure is limited to a cursory, non-adversarial interview in which the legalization applicant is not allowed an opportunity to present witnesses in support of his eligibility. This truncated interview procedure is unusual in the immigration context, where a more exacting interview is usually afforded applicants seeking to establish eligibility for other forms of relief such as political asylum. A denied applicant who relies primarily on affidavit evidence should argue that this procedure severely limits his due process rights to a hearing, to examine adverse evidence, and to present and cross-examine witnesses. In support of such an argument, the applicant should submit an affidavit describing the inadequacies of his or her individual interview at the LO with regard to making credibility determinations. If the LO examiner did not allow an applicant to present a witness in order to verify the statements made in his or her affidavit, an attestation to this effect should be included with the appeal.

In denials of applications based on insufficiency of evidence, it is particularly appropriate to request that the RPF reopen and reconsider its decision _sua sponte_[63] where additional evidence is being presented on appeal tending to establish eligibility for temporary resident status.

Legalization Issues Bank. Ordering information appears at the end of this Chapter.

[62] H.R. Rep. No. 682, 99th Cong., 2nd Sess., pt. 1 (1986) at 71-73.

[63] 8 CFR §§103.5(b), 245a.2(q). _See_ discussion at §5.2 of this Chapter.

5.4(a)(1)(B) Continuous Residence Broken by Absences in Excess of 45/180 Days

INS regulations state that continuous residence is broken when an applicant has been absent from the United States for a single 45-day period or 180 days in the aggregate, unless the applicant can establish that due to "emergent reasons" his or her return to the United States could not be accomplished within the time period allowed.[64]

The LAU has defined the term "emergent" as "coming unexpectedly into being," noting that "in seeking to interpret and apply the term, we are mindful of the Congressional intent that the legalization program should be administered in a liberal and generous fashion..."[65] The LAU has further held that, as a general rule, once there is a finding of an emergent reason, discretion should be exercised in favor of the alien.[66]

A review of recent LAU decisions in this area indicate that it has sustained appeals of cases involving lengthy absences[67] where the emergent reasons for failing to return within the requisite time period are reasonable, credible and corroborated by independent evidence. Examples of circumstances held to be emergent include those involving the need to care for sick relatives abroad,[68] as well those in which the applicant's attempt

---

[64] 8 CFR §245a.1(c)(1)(i).

[65] Matter of C, Int. Dec. 3087 (Comm'r Nov. 15, 1988.) digested in 65 Interpreter Releases 596-597 (June 6, 1988). In this case, the LAU sustained the appeal of an applicant who was absent for 58 days, finding that she had intended to remain outside of the U.S. for a period of 30 days, but that she was unable to return within the required time period because a letter from her husband containing the money for her return trip was delayed.

[66] Matter of T, LAU, Sept. 2, 1988, reported in 65 Interpreter Releases 1077 (October 17, 1988). See note 68, infra.

[67] The LAU has excused an absence of 233 days (LAU, May 19, 1988), see note 69, infra., as well as absence of 307 days in the case of a 13 year old girl (LAU, July 29, 1988). Order No. L1088-382 from the Legalization Issues Bank, LAU Decision Digest. Ordering information appears at the end of this Chapter.

[68] LAU, June 15, 1988, see note 70 infra.; LAU, May 19, 1988, see note 69 infra.; and Matter of T, (LAU, Sept. 2, 1988), in which the LAU excused a 61 day absence in the case of an applicant who returned to Mexico to visit his sick mother and couldn't return within 45 days because he was the oldest child and had to take his mother to her doctor's appointments. Reported in

to return to the United States within the requisite time period was thwarted by events beyond the applicant's control, such as unsuccessful attempts to obtain a visa;[69] unsuccessful attempts to cross the border without inspection;[70] car problems;[71] and even the inability to find a smuggler with enough room in his car to take the applicant across the border.[72] The decisions stress that the applicant need not have departed the United States for an emergent reason, rather he or she must have been prevented from returning within 45 days due to an emergent reason.[73]

---

65 Interpreter Releases 1077 (October 17, 1988).

[69] LAU, May 19, 1988. The LAU excused a 233 day absence where the applicant had gone to Japan to visit her elderly mother who had recently suffered a stroke. The applicant made 2 unsuccessful attempts to obtain a tourist visa from the American Consulate to return to the U.S. The LAU found that she had every intention to return to the U.S. as quickly as possible to rejoin her husband and children. Order No. LO988-333 from the Legalization Issues Bank, LAU Decision Digest. See also, LAU, June 27, 1988, in which the LAU excused a 116 day absence in the case of an applicant who returned to Mexico for an immigrant visa appointment and was unable to return within the anticipated two weeks due to delays caused by the Consulate. Order No. LO988-334, from the Legalization Issues Bank, LAU Decision Digest. Reported in 65 Interpreter Releases 66-67 (January 13, 1988). Ordering information appears at the end of this Chapter.

[70] LAU, June 15, 1988. The LAU excused a 59 day absence in the case of an applicant who left the U.S. to visit his seriously ill father. The applicant argued that his plans to return were frustrated by 2 unsuccessful attempts to illegally cross the border. The illness was documented by medical evidence and personal affidavits. Reported in 66 Interpreter Releases 67 (January 13, 1989). Order No. LO988-355 from the Legalization Issues Bank, LAU Decision Digest. Ordering information appears at the end of this Chapter.

[71] LAU, October 7, 1988. Order No. L1288-438, from the Legalization Issues Bank, LAU Decision Digest. Ordering information appears at the end of this Chapter.

[72] LAU, Sept. 2, 1988. Order No. L1288-435, from the Legalization Issues Bank, LAU Decision Digest. Ordering information appears at the end of this Chapter.

[73] LAU, July 11, 1988. Reported in 65 Interpreter Releases 66 (January 13, 1988). Order No. LO988-332 from the Legalization Issues Bank, LAU Decision Digest. Ordering information appears at the end of this Chapter.

In addition to focusing on the emergent reasons preventing an applicant from returning to the United States within the requisite 45 day period, the argument on appeal should emphasize that the applicant maintained a residence in the United States from January 1, 1982 until the time of filing, including any period of absence.[74] The concept of residence is well established in other provisions of the immigration laws, most commonly being applied in the context of registry[75] and naturalization. It is defined in the Immigration and Nationality Act as "the place of general abode or principal, actual dwelling place in fact, without regard to intent."[76]

Factors considered for determining continuous residence in suspension of deportation[77] and registry cases[78] as well as in cases involving the abandonment of permanent resident status,[79] may be used as guidelines by the legalization applicant to establish continuous residence. For example, in determining whether or not a particular absence breaks the continuity of residence required in registry cases under INA §249, the Board of Immigration Appeals has treated the nature of the ties maintained by the applicant in the United States and abroad as a more significant indicia of intent to abandon U.S. residence than the length of the alien's absence. However, mere maintenance of ties in the U.S., and the intent to reside in the U.S., will be insufficient if the alien's actual abode is elsewhere.[80] Other factors considered significant in the context of determining eligibility for registry have included the fact that no residence or business was established outside the United States during the absence; that the alien maintained a mailing address in the United States; that the alien did not intend to abandon United States residence; that the alien's

---

[74] 8 CFR §245a.1(c)(1)(ii).

[75] INA §249.

[76] INA §101(a)(33). See also, Legalization Wire #10, dated January 14, 1987.

[77] See Rosenberg v. Fleuti, 374 U.S. 449 (1963); Wadman v. INS, 329 F.2d 812 (9th Cir. 1964); Matter of Wong, 12 I & N Dec. 271 (BIA 1967).

[78] INA §249. See note 81, infra.

[79] See Matter of Kane, 15 I & N Dec. 258 (BIA 1975); Matter of Muller, 16 I & N Dec. 637 (BIA 1978); Matter of Morcos, 11 I & N Dec. 740 (BIA 1966); INS v. Gamero, 367 F. 2d 123 (9th Cir. 1963).

[80] Matter of Harrison, 13 I & N Dec. 540 (D.D. 1970); Matter of Oution, 14 I & N Dec. 6 (BIA 1972); Matter of Ting, 11 I & N Dec. 849 (BIA 1966); Matter of Jalil, I.D.#3070 (Comm'r 1988).

personal property or financial interests remained in the United States; that the alien's immediate family did not reside outside the United States; that the alien pursued other forms of relief under the immigration laws; and that the alien did not represent his or her intent to remain in the United States temporarily upon reentry.[81]

Thus, the appeal brief should characterize the applicant's absence as a brief interlude in the many years of his or her residence in the United States and highlight the indicia of the applicant's ties to the United States during his or her absence. The motivation behind the applicant's departure from the United States,[82] as well as the subsequent events which prevented his or her early return should be presented in this context. Finally, since the LAU has indicated that it will exercise its discretion in excusing absences exceeding 45 days, an appeal should also include a discussion of the equities presented by the applicant's case, including close family ties as well as other humanitarian or public interest considerations.

Many applicants were not informed by the LO's that their absences for a period of over 45 days could be waived or excused for an emergent reason and therefore they did not include a written explanation of their failure to return within 45 days with their initial applications.[83] On appeal, the applicant should explain in as much detail as possible the emergent or unexpected circumstances which prevented his or her earlier return and request that the RPF reopen and reconsider the case sua sponte.[84] The appeal should be supported by documentation corroborating the circumstances alleged by the applicant, including medical records,

---

[81] See Matter of Harrison, 13 I & N Dec. 540 (D.D. 1970); Matter of Lee, 11 I & N Dec. 6 (BIA 1972); Matter of Outin, 14 I & N Dec. 6 (BIA 1972); Matter of Lettman, 22 I & N Dec. 878 (Reg. Comm'r 1966). For a more detailed discussion of continuous residence requirements, see Zacovic, "Registry Applicants: Eligibility and Procedure," 16 Immigration Newsletter, No. 2 (Mar.-Apr. 1987).

[82] INA §245A(g)(2)(c) provides for a waiver of absences due to a brief trip abroad required by emergency or extenuating circumstances outside the alien's control. This language appears to encompass both the original motive for the departure, as well as subsequent events affecting the alien's return.

[83] See Hernandez v. Meese, No. S-88-385 LKK (E.D. Calif. 1988). Reported in 65 Interpreter Releases 1065-1066 (Oct. 17, 1988). See note 86, infra.

[84] 8 CFR §§103.5(b), 245a.2(q). See discussion at §5.2 of this Chapter, supra.

weather reports, newspaper articles, birth, death and marriage certificates, employment records and personal affidavits.

Other applicants for temporary resident status who were absent from the United States for brief periods exceeding 45 days may not be able to demonstrate that their return was delayed by emergent reasons. For example, students may have returned to their home countries during summer vacation, intending to return to the United States after a two month period to resume their studies and continue their residence here.[85] Such applicants can premise an appeal on the theory that INS regulations limiting individual absences to 45 days and aggregate absences to 180 days are too restrictive and at odds with the legislative purposes and statutory terms enacted by Congress.[86] The appeal should argue that while Congress may have intended the agency to determine a particular period of time consistent with its mandate that noninterruptive absences must be brief and casual, the imposition of an absolute and inflexible figure is inconsistent with judicial interpretation of such departures and frustrates the ameliorative purpose of the legalization program.[87] Congress is presumed to be aware of existing case law when it enacts new legislation.[88] Moreover, other IRCA provisions requiring proof of continuous residence have been interpreted to allow temporary (even extended) absence from the primary dwelling place[89] without regard to emergent reasons preventing return.

---

[85] An alien who entered the United States as a nonimmigrant student will also have to prove that he or she was in an unlawful status that was "known to the Government" as of January 1, 1982. INA §245A(a)(2)(B). See discussion at §5.4(a)(3) of this Chapter, infra.

[86] But see Hernandez v. Meese, No. S-385 LKK (E.D. Calif. 1988), where the district court ruled that the 45/180 absence provision of the regulations is sufficient under IRCA and consistent with Congress' intent to create a generous amnesty program. Reported in 65 Interpreter Releases 1065-1066 (October 17, 1988).

[87] Fleuti v. Rosenberg, 374 U.S. 449 (1963).

[88] Russelo v. United States, 464 U.S. 16 (1983).

[89] See Department of State Cable dated January 9, 1987.

5.4(a)(1)(C) Denials Based upon Departure Caused by Deportation Order

INA §245A(g)(2)(A)(ii) provides that "an alien shall not be considered to have resided continuously in the United States if... the alien was outside the United States as a result of a departure under an order of deportation."[90] This provision has been applied to aliens who have "self-deported", as well as to those that were physically removed by the Immigration Service pursuant to a final order of deportation issued by an Immigration Judge.[91]

An alien is considered to have "self-deported" if he or she departs the United States at any time after the issuance of a deportation order by an Immigration Judge. For example, often an alien who appears before an Immigration Judge is granted voluntary departure under INA §244(e) in lieu of deportation, with an alternate order of deportation which becomes effective should the alien fail to depart. If the alien fails to depart within the time period accorded in the Judge's order, or any extension of time granted by the Immigration Service, or if all requested relief is denied and an appeal either is not taken or is denied, the order of deportation will be executed by issuance of a warrant of deportation ordering the alien to surrender for deportation and ordering the alien's expulsion.[92] If an alien granted voluntary departure leaves the United States after the time allowed by the Immigration Judge or after the expiration of any extension of the time period granted by the Immigration and Naturalization Service, or otherwise departs on his or her own while an order of

---

[90] Deportations which occurred prior to January 1, 1982 will not, of course, break the requisite period of continuous residence. However, INA §212(a)(17) renders excludable those aliens who have been deported within the five previous years, if such aliens have not obtained the permission of the Attorney General to reenter the United States. Aliens who reentered the United States within five years of their deportation or "self-deportation," can apply for such permission *nunc pro tunc* pursuant to 8 CFR §212.2. Such an application, however, is not necessary in the legalization context as the §212(a)(17) ground of exclusion may be overcome by IRCA's more generous humanitarian waiver at INA §245A(d)(2)(B)(i). Legalization waivers are discussed in Chapter One. While a waiver of these exclusion grounds is available regardless of the date of deportation, aliens who were deported after January 1, 1982 must establish their eligibility under the more onerous continuous residence requirement.

[91] Self-deportation carries the same legal consequences as a departure under an order of deportation executed by the INS. 8 CFR §243.5.

[92] *See* 8 CFR §§243.1, 243.2.

deportation is outstanding, the alien is considered to have "self-deported." In the past few years, Immigration Judges have oftentimes conducted hearings in absentia and entered deportation orders in those cases in which an alien has not appeared for his or her hearings. Those who depart unaware of an in absentia deportation order will have self-deported.

Many unrepresented applicants for temporary residence who were unaware of outstanding deportation orders issued against them will be denied on the ground that any departure constituting a deportation which occurs after January 1, 1982 breaks the continuity of residence required and therefore renders the alien ineligible under INA §245A. In representing such an applicant on appeal, the advocate should first verify that a deportation order was actually issued by requesting a copy of the order and a record of the deportation proceedings, as well any notices sent to the alien by the INS after the issuance of the order.[93] The advocate should question the applicant regarding his or her understanding of the deportation proceedings and knowledge of the existence of the deportation order. Finally, the circumstances of the applicant's departure should be fully explored, including the dates of the departure and return and the reasons motivating the departure. If the alien departed the United States unaware of an outstanding deportation order or for reasons wholly unrelated to the deportation order, he or she can challenge a denial on this ground by arguing the statute provides that only departures resulting from orders of deportation break the period of continuous residency and that the INS regulations and policy interpreting the statute are overly broad. For example, if an alien was ordered deported in a hearing held in absentia[94] and later departed the United States unaware of the deportation order to attend the funeral of a parent, the applicant could argue that she was not outside the United States as a result of the deportation order, as she had no knowledge of the order and her trip was precipitated by a totally unrelated occurrence. This argument was advanced in, Jane Doe v. INS, 42 Civil No. C88-257 (W.D. Wash. June 1, 1988), an individual action which sought a declaratory judgment invalidating the INS policy of denying legalization to persons who left the United States briefly after January 1, 1982 while a

---

[93] A request for a copy of the record of proceedings may be made with the filing of a Notice of Appeal. In cases which involve a prior deportation order, it is advisable to file a separate FOIA request with the INS. See discussion at §5.3(a)(1) of this Chapter.

[94] INA §242(b); 8 CFR §3.24. EOIR procedures regarding deportation proceedings in which the alien fails to appear for a deportation hearing, including procedures for in absentia hearings, are set forth in a memorandum by the Chief Immigration Judge, dated March 7, 1984.

deportation order was pending, but whose departures were not caused by the deportation order. The action asserted that the regulations promulgated by the INS at 8 CFR §245a.1(c)(iii), are inconsistent with the statutory language and contradict the intent of Congress that the legalization program be administered in a liberal fashion. The action further alleged that the INS interpretation violates the equal protection clause of the Fifth Amendment by distinguishing between legalization applicants who remained continuously in the United States after a deportation order was entered and those who also remained in the United States after an order of deportation was entered but briefly went abroad for reasons unrelated to the order. The case was dismissed on the basis of lack of jurisdiction under the IRCA, thus not reaching the merits of this issue.[95]

The only other way to overcome this ground of denial would be to actually remove the deportation order or the legal effect of the order. This may be accomplished by requesting the Immigration Service, Immigration Judge or Board of Immigration Appeals to reinstate voluntary departure <u>nunc pro tunc</u> or by requesting the Immigration Service to grant advance parole <u>nunc pro tunc</u>. It is important to note, however, that IRCA's confidentiality provisions do not apply in this context to protect an alien who makes such requests to the Immigration and Naturalization Service, an Immigration Judge or the Board of Immigration Appeals. An alien should therefore fully consider the risks involved in exposing him or herself to the Immigration Service before pursuing such requests.

In addition, those aliens who meet all of the requirements for legalization but for the fact that they departed under an order of deportation after January 1, 1982 may wish to test the applicability of I-212 "permission to re-apply after deportation" to the legalization provisions.[96] The I-212 is commonly referred to and functions as a waiver of excludability under INA §212(a)(17). The Attorney General exercises broad power in approving an I-212 waiver. An alien can escape prosecution for a felony under

---

[95] Reported in 65 Interpreter Releases 1237 (Nov. 21, 1988). Copies of the pleadings and briefs may be obtained from the Legalization Issues Bank. Ordering information appears at the end of this Chapter.

[96] 8 CFR §212.2. Although the I-212 is commonly referred to as a waiver, its technical name is "Permission to Reapply for Entry after Deportation, Removal or Departure at Government Expense." If granted, it forgives excludability under INA §212(a)(17) and criminality under INA §276, and allows the deportee to apply for admission to the United States. Standards applicable to Form I-212 waivers are discussed in <u>Immigration Law and Defense</u>, National Lawyers Guild, (Clark Boardman, Co., Ltd.) §5.3A.

INA §276 (criminal prosecution for re-entry after deportation) by obtaining an I-212 waiver which is applied retroactively to the admitted felonious conduct. This broad authority and the retroactive applicability of I-212 waivers should arguably be extended to the much less onerous civil offense of deportation, especially given the enormous penalty to the alien if the prior deportation is not waived, i.e., ineligibility for legalization.

The INS and the LAU, however, have taken the position that an approval of an application for permission to reapply for admission after deportation has no effect on the applicant's eligibility if the deportation occurred after January 1, 1982.[97] On appeal, the applicant should argue that the provisions establishing eligibility for temporary residence under the IRCA must be read in the context of the INA as a whole, and that an approved I-212 "waiver" should work to forgive the legal consequences of a departure based upon an order of deportation for purposes of the continuous residence requirement for legalization. As IRCA's confidentiality protections do not apply to such collateral applications to the Immigration Service, the applicant should submit the waiver application pursuant to 8 CFR §212.2 directly to the RPF or LAU on the legalization waiver application form I-601.

A final alternative is to collaterally attack the validity of the deportation order.[98] For example, deportations occurring after November 6, 1986 (the effective date of IRCA) are subject to collateral attack if they violated the automatic stay of deportation provided by statute and internal INS procedures set forth in Legalization Wires #1, dated November 14, 1986 and #8, dated December 17, 1986. Pursuant to those directives, aliens eligible for legalization who were under voluntary departure or deportation orders were to be advised that they need not leave the country. In some cases, orders of deportation were to be vacated. Aliens and their ineligible family members expelled on or after November 6, 1986 in violation of the stay provision and INS directives were to be paroled into the country until May 5, 1988. Aliens who departed the United States after November 6, 1986, subject to an order of deportation, may claim on appeal that the Immigration and Naturalization Service had an affirmative duty to advise them that departure would effect their eligibility for temporary residence. This affirmative duty is reflected not only in the above instruction, but in the statute, which requires that the INS publicize such provisions. As to deportations occurring prior to November 6, 1986, collateral attacks of the deportation

---

[97] See LAU decision August 19, 1988. Order No. L1288-440 from the Legalization Issues Bank, LAU Decision Digest. Ordering information appears at the end of this Chapter.

[98] See U.S. v. Mendoza-Lopez, 107 S. Ct. 2148 (1987).

order, similar to that successfully attempted in U.S. v. Mendoza-Lopez, may be necessary.

5.4(a)(2) Denial Based upon Failure to Establish Continuous Physical Presence

Superimposed upon the requirement of continuous unlawful residence since before January 1, 1982 is the requirement that the applicant be "continuously physically present" in the United States since the date of enactment, November 6, 1986.[99] The statute specifically allows for "brief, casual and innocent" absences during this period.[100] INS regulations defined this phrase narrowly as meaning a departure after May 1, 1987 authorized by the Immigration Service by way of advance parole or a departure beyond the alien's control.[101] This restrictive definition of "brief, casual and innocent" is contrary to a rich body of judicial decisions interpreting this phrase in the context of suspension of deportation cases under INA §244(a)(1) and was struck down as ultra vires by the district court in Catholic Social Services v. Meese, No. S-86-1343-LKK (E.D. Calif, 9th Cir. 1987, 1988). The Court enjoined the Service from enforcing its regulations and held that such absences must be reviewed on a case-by-case basis to determine whether they were "brief casual and innocent."[102]

The INS must reopen and reconsider all denials based upon the previous definition of "brief, casual and innocent," including cases that have been appealed to the LAU. Thus, an applicant denied on this basis should request that the RPF reopen and

---

[99] INA §245A(a)(3)(A).

[100] INA §245A(a)(3)(B).

[101] 8 CFR §245a.1(g).

[102] The government has withdrawn its appeal from the district court's decision overturning the INS' construction of the "brief, casual and innocent" provision of INA §245A(a)(3)(B). However, it is continuing its appeal concerning the remedies ordered by the Court, which instructed the INS to accept legalization applications from persons who failed to apply on time because they believed themselves ineligible due to INS' wrongful interpretation of the statute. See discussion in 65 Interpreter Releases 1010-1011 (October 3, 1988). A Form for Determination of Class Membership in Catholic Social Services v. Meese is reproduced at 65 Interpreter Releases 1216 (October 24, 1988).

reconsider his or her case sua sponte.[103] The applicant should specify the exact dates of his or her absence and explain the precise purpose of the departure. Wherever possible, corroborating documentation of the length and purpose of the trip should be included with the appeal.

In Gutierrez v. Ilchert, ___F. Supp.___, (N.D. Cal., No. C-88-0585 EFL, March 28, 1988), the district court found that the definition of "brief, casual and innocent" is made in a case-by-case inquiry using the standards developed in the suspension of deportation context. In Gutierrez, the INS had concluded that an alien who attempted to reenter the United States after a three week visit to his seriously ill mother in May 1987 was plainly ineligible for legalization because his departure was not "brief, casual and innocent." The Court found that the applicant's absence was within the definition and overturned the denial.[104]

Thus, in arguing that an alien's departure from the United States after May 1, 1987 was a brief, casual and innocent one, the applicant should rely on the interpretation of the phrase developed in the context of suspension of deportation cases under INA §244(a)(1).[105] The applicant should argue that his departure was not intended to be "meaningfully interruptive" of his residence[106] and emphasize his or her commitment to this society through the establishment of roots and the development of future plans.[107]

5.4(a)(3) Denials Based upon Failure to Establish Unlawful Status

IRCA's legalization provisions were designed to help those who had been continuously residing in the United States in an unlawful status since January 1, 1982. Entry on a nonimmigrant visa is

---

[103] 8 CFR §103.5b. See discussion at §5.2, supra.

[104] A copy of this decision may be obtained from the Legalization Issues Bank. Ordering information appears at the end of this Chapter.

[105] See Rosenberg v. Fleuti, 374 U.S. 449, 83 S.Ct. 1084, (1963); Wadman v. INS, 329 F.2d 812 (9th Cir. 1964); Matter of Wong, 12 I & N Dec. 271 (BIA 1967); Di Pasquale v. Karmuth, 158 F. 2d 878 (2nd Cir. 1947); Delgadillo v. Carmichael, 332 U.S. 388 (1947); Kamheangpatiyooth v. INS, 597 F. 2d 1253, 1256 (9th Cir. 1979).

[106] Rosenberg v. Fleuti, 374 U.S. 449, 83 S.Ct. 1084 (1963).

[107] Kamheangpatiyooth v. INS, 597 F.2d 1253 (9th Cir. 1979).

presumably lawful, therefore, in order to satisfy the requirement of "unlawful status" in the United States, an alien who entered on a nonimmigrant visa must prove (1) that his or her period of authorized stay as a nonimmigrant expired before January 1, 1982 or (2) that s/he violated one of the conditions necessary to maintain lawful nonimmigrant status, and that the resulting unlawful status was "known to the Government" prior to January 1, 1982,[108] or (3) the nonimmigrant visa was obtained through error or fraud, rendering the subsequent stay unlawful.

There are a myriad of unresolved eligibility issues posed by aliens who entered the United States on nonimmigrant visas prior to January 1, 1982. Some of the more common basis of denials and possible grounds of appeal are reviewed below.

5.4(a)(3)(A) Expiration of Authorized Stay; Duration of Status

An applicant who entered on a nonimmigrant visa before January 1, 1982 and whose authorized stay expired before such date through the passage of time, qualifies for legalization, without having to establish that his or her unlawful status was known to the government.[109] For those nonimmigrants who are admitted until a fixed date, it is relatively simple to determine whether their authorized stay expired prior to January 1, 1982 by examining their I-94 entry document. Certain nonimmigrants, however, are admitted for "duration of status"[110] and are authorized to stay in the United States for as long as they maintain their status.

The INS recognizes that the lawful status of an alien admitted on a "F-1" or "F-2" student visa will have expired through the passage of time in cases where the alien has completed a full course of study, including practical training and time allowed to depart, prior to January 1, 1982.[111] However, the INS has adopted a policy and practice of denying legalization to aliens on student visas who failed to maintain their status by dropping out of school, by failing to enroll in 12 or more units of study or by transferring schools without permission, or by engaging in

---

[108] INA §245A(a)(2)(B).

[109] INA §245A(a)(2)(B).

[110] See, e.g., 8 CFR §214.2(f)(5)(i) (students); 8 CFR §214.2(g) (international organizational aliens); 8 CFR §214.2(a) (foreign government officials); and 8 CFR §214.2(i) (representatives of foreign information media).

[111] 8 CFR §214.2(f)(5)(iii).

unauthorized employment unless the failure to maintain status was "known to the Government" before January 1, 1982.[112]

Denied applicants who were admitted for "duration of status" and failed to maintain student status by dropping out of school, failing to enroll in a full course of study or transferring schools without permission, prior to January 1, 1982, can present two theories on appeal in support of the argument that their authorized stay expired before that time.

First, the INS' own regulations indicate that a student who has committed these violations of status has overstayed his or her authorized stay by operation of law. Under INS regulations, "duration of status" is defined as "the period during which the student is pursuing a full course of study in one educational program; plus thirty days following completion of the course of study...within which to depart from the United States."[113] The regulations further provide that a student who has not been pursuing a full course of study at the school he or she was last authorized to attend may not obtain an extension of stay unless the student first applies for reinstatement to student status.[114] It is therefore clear that although a student visa or I-94 entry document does not specify a fixed expiration date, a student's authorized stay terminates when he or she is no longer pursuing a full course of study at the school he or she was authorized to attend. This is true for students who terminate their studies after successful completion of their program, as well as for other students who violate the conditions of their stay. Thus, the applicant who was admitted to the United States on a student visa for the duration of his or her status and who violated student status prior to January 1, 1982 can argue that the decision requiring the applicant to demonstrate that his or her unlawful status was "known to the Government" conflicts with INS' own regulations.[115]

---

[112] See Letter of William S. Slattery, Assistant Commissioner, Legalization, dated November 25, 1987. Reported in 65 Interpreter Releases 6 (January 4, 1988).

[113] 8 CFR §214.2(f)(5)(iii).

[114] 8 CFR §214.2(f)(7)(i).

[115] See "Legalization Appeals," by Peter Schey & Carlos Holguin, in Vol. 2 of the 42nd Annual Symposium of the American Immigration Lawyers Association, June 15-19, 1988, San Diego, Calif., editors Edwin R. Rubin, Robert E Juceum, at pp. 403-05, for a detailed presentation of this argument.

Second, an applicant can challenge this type of denial on equal protection grounds by contrasting the distinction drawn by the IRCA regulations between "A" and "G" visa holders admitted for duration of status and other nonimmigrants, including "F" visa holders, who were admitted for duration of status. The regulations provide that nonimmigrants who were admitted on "A," "A-1," "A-2," "G," "G-1," "G-2," "G-3" or "G-4" visas for duration of status attain unlawful status when their qualifying employment terminated or they ceased to be recognized by the Department of State as being entitled to such classification.[116] If these events occurred prior to January 1, 1982, the alien meets the unlawful status requirement for legalization under INA §245A without having to demonstrate that the unlawful status was known to the government.[117] On the other hand, as discussed above, an alien student admitted for duration of status who violated his or her status by dropping out of school, failing to take a full course of study or transferring schools without permission must establish that such violation was "known to the Government" in order to qualify for legalization. The argument on appeal should assert that there is no rational basis or legitimate governmental interest upon which to justify this distinction between these similarly situated nonimmigrant visa holders.[118]

Thus, an applicant who was admitted to the United States for "duration of status" and violated the conditions of his or her stay by dropping out of school, failing to take a full course of study or transferring schools without permission before January 1, 1982, should argue on appeal that he or she should not be required to prove that the unlawful status was "known to the Government." In the alternative, the applicant should also argue that the violation of status should be presumed to be "known to the Government" because the school was required to report these infractions to the INS. This argument is presented in greater detail in §5.4(a)(3)(B)(i) of this Chapter.

---

[116] 8 CFR §245a.2(b)(11).

[117] But see the series of LAU decisions between March and September, 1988 dismissing appeals of applicants who entered on "A" and "G" visas and violated their status by working without permission prior to January 1, 1982. Reported in 66 Interpreter Releases 65-66 (January 13, 1989).

[118] "Legalization Appeals," by Peter Schey and Carlos Holguin, supra. at pp. 405-506.

5.4(a)(3)(B) Unlawful Status "Known to the Government"

If an alien who entered the United States on a nonimmigrant visa cannot establish that the period of his or her authorized stay expired before January 1, 1982, the alien must prove, through documentation, that his or her unlawful status was "known to the Government" prior to January 1, 1982.

The INS promulgated excessively restrictive and convoluted regulatory interpretations of "known to the Government," which went far beyond the statutory language or the legislative intent in requiring an applicant to prove that the INS itself knew of the unlawful status. These regulations, however, have been successfully challenged. In <u>Farzad v. Chandler</u>, 670 F. Supp. 690 (N.D. Texas 1987), the Court held that "Congress intended the phrase "the Government" to be broader than merely the INS, and at least broad enough to include the Internal Revenue Service and the Social Security Administration."[119] Thus, the Court ruled that the Internal Revenue Service and the Social Security Administration's receipt of information that an alien who entered with a student visa had worked without authorization satisfied the requirement that his illegal status be "known to the Government."

Similarly, in <u>Ayuda v. Meese</u>, 687 F. Supp. 650 (D.D.C. 1988), a nationwide class action, the Court ordered the INS to suspend implementation of its regulations defining "known to the Government," and to propose new regulations for the Court's approval. The Court held that the "known to the Government" requirement is satisfied if any government agencies currently possesses a document that shows the applicant violated his or her legal status prior to January 1, 1982. Moreover, to meet this test, the nonimmigrant alien must establish only that documentation existed in the files of one or more government agency, which, taken as a whole, would warrant the finding that the alien's status in the United States was unlawful. The agency does not have to have made the determination from those documents that the alien was in the United States unlawfully. Finally, the Court enjoined the INS from denying legalization to nonimmigrant aliens who meet all other applicable conditions for legalization and credibly contend that they violated their status prior to January 1, 1982 by willfully failing to comply with the mandatory quarterly or annual registration requirements of INA §265.[120]

---

[119] <u>Id.</u> at 694.

[120] Although the Government has appealed the portion of the Judge's order with regard to the eligibility of students who failed to comply with the quarterly or annual registration requirements, it has indicated that it will not appeal the other portions of the Judge's order regarding the interpretation of "known to the

The Ayuda court did not render its decision until shortly before the application deadline of May 4, 1988. The Court therefore established a procedure by which aliens who claim that their unlawful status was known to the government before January 1, 1982 and who did not file for legalization by May 4, 1988 because the INS or a QDE misled or dissuaded them from applying, may file for relief through the Court. Additionally, the court ordered that the INS notify those denied on the basis of "known to the Government" about the new standard and reconsider those applications using the new test at no additional cost to the applicant.[121]

Applicants who filed notices of appeal prior to the decision in Ayuda and who believe they can now establish eligibility under the new standard should therefore request that the RPF reopen and reconsider their cases sua sponte.[122] The request should be supported by documentation showing that a government agency knew of the applicants violation of status prior to January 1, 1982.

Those eligible for legalization under the new standard of "known to the Government" include:

(1) Aliens who entered the United States on nonimmigrant visas who worked without permission prior to January 1, 1982 and can demonstrate that a government agency had knowledge of their unauthorized employment prior to January 1, 1982;

(2) Aliens who entered the United States on student visas and failed to maintain status prior to January 1, 1982 by dropping out, transferring schools without permission or failing to maintain a full course of study and can demonstrate that their violation of status was known to a government agency prior to January 1, 1982;

(3) Aliens who willfully failed to file mandatory quarterly or annual registration forms in 1981.

Although the applicant does not have to demonstrate that a government agency actually made a determination that he or she was in an unlawful status, the applicant must submit specific

---

Government." Reported in 65 Interpreter Releases 590 (June 6, 1988). See also Immigrant Assistance Project v. INS, No. C88-379 (W.D. Wash. 1988).

[121] The Court's supplemental orders regarding relief are reproduced in 65 Interpreter Releases 1012-1014 (October 3, 1988).

[122] 8 CFR §103.5(b). See discussion at §5.2 of this Chapter, supra.

documentation establishing that as of January 1, 1982 sufficient information existed in the files of the United States Government to warrant a conclusion that the applicant was in the United States in an unlawful status. In the case of a nonimmigrant alien who worked without authorization, documentation demonstrating that the applicant's work was reported to the Internal Revenue Service, the Social Security Administration or the Department of Labor should be submitted.[123] In *Farzad v. Chandler*, 670 F. Supp. 650 (D.D.C. 1988), the court accepted an SSA statement of earnings and an IRS certification of tax returns filed for years preceding 1982 as sufficient to establish that the applicant's unlawful employment was "known to the Government." Similarly, in *Matter of P*, I.D. ____ (Comm'r Nov. 23, 1988), the LAU found that tax returns from 1979 through 1986 "left no doubt that as of January 1, 1982, there existed sufficient information in the files of the United States Government to warrant a conclusion that the applicant was in the United States in an unlawful status."[124]

5.4(a)(3)(B)(i) School Report of Violation of Nonimmigrant Status to the INS

The nature and extent of the documentation required by students who violated their status by dropping out of school, transferring schools without permission or failing to maintain a full course of study has not been resolved. Recognizing that the INS and most schools destroy student records after five years, the INS has agreed to accept an affirmation from the school that it forwarded to the INS a report that clearly indicated the applicant had violated his or her nonimmigrant student status before January 1, 1982.[125]1 If the school doesn't have sufficient records to make such an affirmation, an applicant on appeal should argue that his or her violation of status can be presumed "known to the

---

[123] The issue of whether knowledge by a city or state governmental agency satisfies the "known to the Government" requirement has not been resolved. For example, an alien who applied for a vendor's license from a municipality might submit a copy of the application or license in order to satisfy the "known to the Government" requirement.

[124] The decision also discusses the standards in adjudicating legalization waivers of excludability on public interest grounds. A copy of this decision may be ordered from the Legalization Issues Bank, Order No. L1288-422. Ordering information appears at the end of this Chapter.

[125] 8 CFR §245a.1(d)(4). The school need not have available a copy of the report actually sent to the INS. *See* 65 Interpreter Releases 635 (June 27, 1988).

Government" because the school was required to report these infractions.[126]

In support of such an appeal, the applicant should submit a statement from the foreign student advisor that the school complies with federal regulations and reports non-fulltime foreign students to the INS as required, and/or that the school has never lost its INS approval for attendance by foreign students by reason of failure to file such reports.[127] This should be accompanied by the applicant's transcript indicating failure to attend classes fulltime before 1982.

The legal argument should offer the following analysis of the regulatory framework concerning maintenance of student status. Under the regulations in effect prior to 1982 and up to now, there are many mechanisms in place which assure that the INS knew of a foreign student's failure to attend classes fulltime. Requiring foreign students to independently prove INS' knowledge of their failure to attend classes fulltime can only be grounded on the absurd premise that foreign student advisors and INS employees were not abiding by mandatory regulations (see footnote 24 below).

The 1981 regulations at 8 CFR 214.3(g) provided:

> Reporting requirements. Each approved school, upon receiving Service notification of arrival in the United

---

[126] This issue is raised in Immigrant Assistance Project v. INS, No. C88-379 (W.D. Wash. 1988), a pending class action covering the Northern and Western Regions which seeks mandamus and a declaratory judgment with respect to several other INS rules and policies regarding the "known to the Government" requirement. Copies of the pleadings may be obtained from the Legalization Issues Bank. Ordering information appears at the end of this Chapter.

[127] See Matter of --- (LAU, June 6, 1988), an undesignated decision, sustaining the appeal of an applicant who submitted a letter from the school's Director of International Student Services, stating it was the practice of the University to notify INS when a foreign student is no longer authorized to attend. The decision accepted this statement as evidence that the applicant's unlawful status was known to the Government, finding that "it is not possible to hold the applicant accountable for something over which he had no control and no longer exists." This decision may indicate that the LAU is easing its standards for determining whether a student's unlawful status was "known to the Government." Order No. L1088-403 from the Legalization Issues Bank. Ordering information appears at the end of this Chapter. But see Matter of --- (LAU, March 11, 1988), which reached the opposite conclusion. Reported in 65 Interpreter Releases 636 (June 27, 1988).

States of a nonimmigrant student destined to that school...shall submit immediately to the office of the Service...a report, in writing, if the student fails to register personally at the school within 60 days of the time he was expected to do so. <u>An immediate report shall also be made in the case of each nonimmigrant student who fails to carry a full course of study</u> as defined in Sec. 214.2(f)(1a), fails to attend to the extent normally required, or terminates his attendance at the institution. The report shall be made on Form I-20B. (emphasis supplied).

Furthermore, District Directors were mandated to regularly review each INS-approved school within their districts, "to determine whether the school...has complied with the reporting requirements of paragraph (g) of this section."[137] The regulations provided that INS approval of a school for the attendance of the nonimmigrant students "shall be withdrawn if the school...fails to submit reports required by sec. 214.3(g)..."[138]

In addition, the regulations in effect in 1981 provided for the establishment of a special group at the Central Office of the INS to enforce the regulations governing students:

<u>Enforcement of student regulations by Immigration and Naturalization Service</u>. There shall be established in the Central Office a coordinating group of employees to coordinate enforcement of the student regulations throughout the country. This group shall coordinate liaison between Service officers in the field and the schools. Officers in the field <u>shall</u> be responsible for conducting periodic reviews on the campuses under their jurisdiction for the purpose of determining whether students are complying with Service regulations...Any apparent violations of the provisions of these regulations found by the Service officers shall be referred to the district director for appropriate action (emphasis supplied).

The regulations cited above are those in effect on January 1, 1981, however, regulations for the preceding years, also relevant in legalization cases, contain identical or similar language. INS Operations Instructions provide additional details regarding the responsibilities of student advisors and INS personnel.[139]

---

[137] 8 CFR §214.3(h) (1980 and 1981).

[138] 8 CFR §214.4(a) (1980 and 1981).

[139] <u>See</u> Operations Instructions 212.2f.

It must be assumed that school officials charged with the above reporting duties, and employees of the Immigration and Naturalization Service, discharged their duties as mandated by the regulations. It is a well-established evidentiary presumption that official actions by public officers are presumed to have been regularly and legally performed.[140]

Accordingly, presentation of proof that the student failed to attend school fulltime as of a date prior to January 1, 1982, together with a copy of the regulations in effect on the date the student failed to attend school fulltime, gives rise to the presumption that the violation of student status was reported by the school to the Immigration and Naturalization Service. The applicant has thus established a *prima facie* case of eligibility for legalization under INA §245A. As with all *prima facie* cases, the INS may produce evidence from its files which rebuts this presumption, such as proof that the particular school in question lost its approved status for failure to make regular reports to the INS, or proof that the applicant was enrolled as a graduate student and therefore, though enrolled in less than 12 semester hours of classes, was nonetheless considered to be a "fulltime" student.

To require the applicant to prove that the report was actually forwarded to the INS requires the assumption that foreign student advisors routinely fail to comply with mandatory federal reporting requirements, and that the INS, when it did not receive the required reports from a school, routinely did not comply with its mandatory regulations by rescinding approval of the school for attendance by foreign students.

5.4(a)(3)(C)   Unlawful Status Due to Fraud

Another unresolved appeal issue in this area is whether a fraudulently obtained nonimmigrant or immigrant visa, or a fraudulently obtained status subsequent to the applicant's initial entry, renders the applicant's status "unlawful" for legalization

---

[140] See McCormick on Evidence, at 969, (3rd Ed. 1984), §343, note 11, citing Thompson v. Consol. Gas Utilities Corp., 300 U.S. 55 (1937); S.S. Kresge Co. v. Davis, 277 N.C. 654, 178 S.E. 2d 382 (1971) (good faith administration of the law by law enforcement officers and city officials is presumed); State ex. rel. Lawrence v. Burke, 253 Wis. 240, 33 N.W. 2d 242 (1948) (habeas corpus after judgment of conviction; judge presumed to have informed accused of right to counsel; West's Ann. Cal. Evid. Code, §644; 9 Wigmore, Evidence §2534 (Chadbourne rev. 1981); Dec. Dig. Evidence §82, 83; Hammond v. Brown; 323 F. Supp. 326, 355 (N.D. Ohio 1971), aff'd 450 F.2d 480 (6th Cir.). See also U.S. v. Chemical Foundation, 272 U.S. 1, 14-15, 47 S. Ct. 1, 6 (1926); Citizens to Preserve Overton Park v. Volpe, 401 U.S. 415, 393 S.Ct. 814 (1971).

purposes. This issue can arise in three contexts: 1) an applicant who entered on a fraudulently obtained nonimmigrant visa; 2) an applicant who was in unlawful status prior to January 1, 1982 and was subsequently reinstated to lawful status through fraudulent representations and 3) an applicant who entered the United States on an immigrant visa obtained through fraud.

An applicant who entered on a fraudulently obtained nonimmigrant visa prior to January 1, 1982 whose authorized stay did not expire until after January 1, 1982 may wish to argue that the nonimmigrant visa itself was invalid. A nonimmigrant visa is defined as a visa <u>properly issued to an eligible nonimmigrant</u>.[141] Entry accomplished through the presentation of an invalid nonimmigrant visa is arguably not a nonimmigrant entry for purposes of INA §245A.

For example, if an alien entered the United States on a tourist visa with the knowledge that he or she intended to remain and work in the United States on an indefinite basis, he or she could assert that the tourist visa was obtained by a misrepresentation of a material fact. In construing the statutory grounds of deportability and excludability relating to documentary requirements, the courts have held that a visa obtained through a deception which amounted to a material misrepresentation is the equivalent of no document at all.[142] An alien admitted either as a nonimmigrant based upon presentation of an unlawfully obtained or an improperly issued visa is subject to exclusion or deportation as an immigrant not in possession of a valid immigrant visa.[143] The mere fact of entry through presentation of an invalid document creates an unlawful rather than a lawful nonimmigrant entry. The alien would therefore arguably be in the same position as an alien who had entered without inspection and would not have to establish either the timely expiration of an "authorized stay," or Government knowledge of an unlawful status.

IRCA regulations implicitly adopt the position that a visa obtained through fraud is unlawful for purposes of establishing eligibility for legalization. 8 CFR §245a.2(b)(9) provides that unlawful status is maintained despite a subsequent entry pursuant

---

[141] INA §101(a)(26).

[142] <u>Feodoranko v. United States</u>, 449 U.S. 490 (1981); <u>Fink v. Reimer</u>, 96 F. 2d 217 (2nd Cir. 1938; <u>Ablett v. Brownwell</u>, 240 F. 2d 625 (D.C. Cir. 1957).

[143] INA §212(a)(20).

to a nonimmigrant visa obtained by fraud.[144] That is, when entry is achieved through fraud, it does not cloak the ensuing residence in a "lawful" status so as to interrupt the previously established unlawful residence, and therefore does not render the alien ineligible for legalization. The regulation makes no distinction between entries occurring before and after January 1, 1982. An applicant who entered the United States with a fraudulently obtained nonimmigrant visa should therefore argue that no legal distinctions can be drawn between initial entries on fraudulent nonimmigrant visas and subsequent entries on such visas.

Indeed, the LAU has recognized this principle in an analogous context. In Matter of N, ___ Int. Dec. ___ (In Adjustment of Status Proceedings, Decided by Commissioner, September 26, 1988),[145] the LAU sustained the appeal of a student who was reinstated to student status in December, 1983 based upon fraudulent representations concerning unauthorized employment. Citing 8 CFR §245a.2(b)(9), which permits a legalization applicant who reentered as a nonimmigrant after January 1, 1982 to establish that the return was to an unrelinquished unlawful residence, the LAU reasoned:

> ...because the Service is now permitting aliens who reentered as nonimmigrants to establish eligibility notwithstanding a "lawful" reentry, we can find no statutory basis that permits us to draw a distinction between nonimmigrant aliens who commit fraud at entry and those who commit fraud at the time of reinstatement to nonimmigrant status.

Thus, the alien who was in an unlawful status prior to January 1, 1982 and was subsequently reinstated to lawful status based upon fraudulent representations of material fact, should argue that the reinstatement was not lawful and therefore does not break his or her continuity of residence in an unlawful status for purposes of determining eligibility for temporary residence.

The LAU reached a similar conclusion with regard to a legalization applicant who entered before January 1, 1982 on a

---

[144] INS amended its regulations to allow an alien who reentered as a nonimmigrant after January 1, 1982 to qualify for legalization, if he or she obtains a waiver of the excludability ground INA §212(a)(19). See LULAC v. INS, No. 87-4757-WDK (C.D. Calif. 1988).

[145] Reported in 65 Interpreter Releases 1075-76 (October 17, 1988).

fraudulently obtained immigrant visa. In Matter of Salazar,[146] the LAU receded from its position in previous decisions that a lawful permanent resident remains in "lawful status" for legalization purposes until a final adjudication of deportability by an immigration judge or the BIA. Citing Matter of T, 6 I & N Dec. 136 (A.G. 1984) and Feodoranko v. United States, 449 U.S. 490 (1981), the LAU reasoned that an immigrant alien who is not admitted in accordance with the immigration laws, and is excludable at entry, has not been admitted lawfully to the United States. Thus, the LAU ruled that a legalization applicant who entered the United States in 1980 with a fraudulently obtained immigrant visa successfully established continuous residence in the United States in an unlawful status since before January 1, 1982 and remanded the case to the RPF to allow the applicant to apply for a waiver of INA §212(a)(19) excludability.[147]

An applicant's statement alone that the visa or benefit was obtained through fraud or misrepresentation will rarely be sufficient to establish eligibility, particularly in cases where the applicant alleges that he or she fraudulently obtained a tourist visa by misrepresenting his or her intentions to immigrate. On appeal, an applicant should submit documentation which establishes or infers his or her fraudulent conduct in obtaining the visa or interim immigration benefit. For example, the student in Matter of N, supra., submitted credible evidence establishing that he had worked without authorization. An applicant who obtained an immigrant visa through fraud, such as the alien in Matter of Salazar, supra., will most probably have to make a concession of deportability in deportation proceedings in order to establish eligibility.

5.4(a)(4) Denials Based upon Public Charge Grounds

INA §212(a)(15) bars the admission to the United States of any alien likely to become a public charge. This ground of excludability applies to all legalization applicants, who must

---

[146] LAU decision, September 8, 1988, File A90 283 120, in Legalization Proceedings under INA §245A. Digested in 65 Interpreter Releases 968-69 (September 19, 1988). Note that the "known to the Government" requirement does not apply to an alien who entered on an immigrant visa.

[147] While an alien may establish threshold eligibility for temporary resident status using this strategy, obtaining entry or immigration benefit by fraud or misrepresentation is a ground of excludability under INA §212(a)(19), and the alien would have to apply for a waiver under INA §245A(d)(2)(B).

establish their admissibility as immigrants.[148] The traditional test utilized by the INS for determining whether an alien is likely to become a public charge is a prospective one, taking into consideration the totality of the alien's circumstances, including his or her age, health, income, vocation, capacity to earn a living, mental and physical disabilities, prior receipt of public cash assistance, the amount of funds available for self-support and the existence of others in the United States willing and able to offer their assistance in supporting the applicant, as evidenced by the submission of an affidavit of support.[149] The applicant must establish that he or she will have an income above the federal poverty income guidelines,[150] which are published at 45 CFR 1060.2 and are periodically updated in the Federal Register.

In addition to the traditional test, Congress formulated a special rule for determining public charge which provides that an alien is not ineligible to adjust status if he or she can show a history of employment without receipt of public cash assistance.[151] The special rule applies to applicants at the initial temporary resident stage as well as the final lawful permanent resident stage.

The legislative history indicates that the purpose of this "special rule" was to preclude the use of the federal poverty guidelines as the sole criteria for determining excludability under §212(a)(15).[152] In passing IRCA, Congress recognized that many applicants for legalization would be low wage workers whose incomes did not meet the poverty level guidelines, but who were unlikely to rely on welfare. The special rule was therefore meant to liberalize the public charge test for the working-poor; it was not meant to exclude prior recipients of public cash assistance from

---

[148] INA §245A(a)(4). See also INA §245A(d)(2).

[149] See June 17, 1988 letter from INS General Counsel, Raymond M. Momboisse, to Enrique Valdez, citing Matter of Vindman, 16 I & N Dec. 131, 132 (Regional Commissioner 1977) and Matter of Perez, 15 I & N Dec. 136, 137 (BIA 1974), reproduced in 65 Interpreter Releases 922 (September 2, 1988). See also April 21, 1988 memorandum by Associate Commissioner Richard Norton, citing FAM, Part III, Vol. 9, note 3.5 to 22 CFR §42.91(a)(15)(iii) reproduced in 65 Interpreter Releases 447-451 (April 25, 1988).

[150] 22 CFR §42.91(a)(15)(iii).

[151] INA §245A(d)(2)(B)(iii).

[152] 130 Cong. Rec. H5909 (daily ed. June 15, 1984).

meeting the eligibility requirements of IRCA under the traditional public charge test.[153]

Although the statutory framework clearly indicates that the special rule is only to be applied if the applicant cannot satisfy the traditional test in determining whether he or she will become a public charge, the LOs frequently required applicants to prove consistent employment without receipt of public cash assistance in order to be eligible for legalization. Thus, many applicants who received public cash assistance in the past were erroneously denied without taking into consideration the totality of their financial circumstances; many others were discouraged from applying.

In <u>Zambrano v. Meese</u>, No. S-88-455 EJG-M (E.D. Calif. 1988), the Court issued a preliminary injunction rejecting INS' proof of financial responsibility requirements and ordered the reopening of cases denied on public charge grounds. The court found that the INS should first apply the traditional prospective test for determining whether someone is likely to be a public charge. If the applicant cannot meet that test, the INS should then apply the "special rule." Although <u>Zambrano</u> is a class action within the 9th Circuit only, applicants in other regions who were erroneously denied temporary resident status on public charge grounds should request the RPF reopen and reconsider their cases <u>sua sponte</u>.[154]

In appealing a denial based upon a finding that the applicant is excludable under INA §212(a)(15), the advocate should carefully scrutinize the denial notice to determine whether it is based on the traditional public charge test or the special rule. If the applicant received public cash assistance in the past and is currently working, he or she should submit evidence of his or her present employment and argue, pursuant to the traditional rule for determining public charge, that a consideration of the totality of the applicant's circumstances, including age, health and present ability to work, establishes that he or she is unlikely to be a public charge in the future. The applicant's economic situation can be compared to that of the alien in <u>Matter of Perez</u>, 15 I&N Dec. 136 (BIA 1974). In <u>Matter of Perez</u>, the Board found that an alien who was young, healthy and capable of securing employment was not likely to become a public charge, despite the fact that she had no employment history and that both she and her children had received welfare for a significant period of time. Finally, the applicant should provide an explanation as to the circumstances which led the applicant to receive public cash assistance in the past and point to circumstances in the applicant's current life

---

[153] <u>See</u> Charles Wheeler and Beth Zacovic, "The Public Charge of Exclusion for Legalization Applicants," 65 Interpreter Releases 1047 (September 14, 1988).

[154] 8 CFR §103.5(b). <u>See</u> discussion at §5.2, <u>supra</u>.

which indicate that receipt of such assistance is unlikely to occur in the future.

If an applicant whose income has been significantly below the federal poverty income guidelines can demonstrate self-support and has not personally received public cash assistance, the special rule should be applied to render the applicant eligible for legalization. Such an applicant should submit verification from the Department of Welfare that the applicant has not received AFDC benefits, as well as an affidavit or documentary proof of how the applicant has been supporting him or herself since January 1, 1982. The applicant may also argue that obtaining legalization and employment authorization will facilitate his or her ability to obtain steady employment at a prevailing wage, which may have been previously impeded by his or her past unlawful status. Finally, affidavits of support from close family members should be submitted, accompanied by the affiant's income tax returns, letters verifying employment and bank letters. Affidavits may be submitted by other relatives however such affidavits will not be given as much weight.[155]

As a final strategy, an applicant who cannot satisfy the INS that he or she is not likely to become a public charge might offer to post a public charge bond pursuant to 8 CFR §213.1. According to this regulation, the INS may accept the posting of a bond of at least $1000 in those cases in which the financial evidence submitted by an applicant for an immigrant visa is not sufficient to establish beyond question that the alien will not become a public charge. This provision can arguably be applied in the legalization context, particularly in light of the legislative intent to administer the legalization program in a liberal and generous manner.

If an applicant was denied temporary residence on public charge grounds because his or her dependent children received AFDC or SSI, he or she should request that the RPF reopen and reconsider the case sua sponte.[156] One of the major controversies in this area concerns the effect that receipt of such benefits by a dependent child has on an alien parent's eligibility for legalization. While the regulations at 8 CFR §245a.1(i) imply that receipt of such benefits by any family member may render the applicant ineligible for legalization, INS has publicly stated a policy that, as a general rule, receipt of SSI and AFDC benefits by a member of a

---

[155] See INS cable from Associate Commissioner Richard Norton, dated August 14, 1987. 8 CFR §245a.2(d)(4) provides that the acceptance of an affidavit of support as evidence of financial responsibility shall be extended to other family members in unusual family circumstances.

[156] 8 CFR §103.5(b).

legalization applicant's family is not attributed to the applicant for the purpose of determining whether the applicant will become a public charge.[157] The confusion generated by this conflict is the subject of litigation in Perales v. Meese, Civil Action No. 2265-88, a class action on behalf of New York state residents whose family members have received welfare.[158]

Similarly, an applicant denied legalization on public charge grounds because he or she received foster care payments on behalf of a child should request the RPF to reopen and reconsider the case sua sponte. INS has changed its policy regarding such payments and has indicated that foster care payments are not attributable to the parent for purposes of legalization.[159] Moreover, such payments will not render a child in foster care ineligible on public charge grounds. In such cases, a copy of the judicial order placing the child in foster care should be submitted.[160]

If a denial based upon public charge grounds cannot be overcome on appeal, the applicant for temporary residence should apply for a waiver based on family unity, humanitarian or public interests grounds.[161] Single mothers, who comprise the majority of the applicants denied temporary resident status on public charge grounds,[162] should be able to present a compelling case for approval of such a waiver application. Care must be taken during the second

---

[157] See INS memorandum dated November 23, 1987 for policy with regard to SSI benefits, reproduced in 65 Interpreter Releases 1-4 (January 25, 1988). See also memorandum by Richard Norton, dated April 21, 1988, for INS policy with regard to AFDC benefits, reported in 65 Interpreter Releases 447-451 (April 25, 1988). This memorandum was issued in response to Perales v. Meese, CA No. 2265-88 (S.D. N.Y 1988), filed on April 1, 1988, challenging INS implementation of the public charge grounds of exclusion.

[158] See April 21, 1988 memorandum by Richard Norton, reproduced in 65 Interpreter Releases 439 (April 25, 1988).

[159] See 65 Interpreter Releases 1-4 (January 25, 1988).

[160] See INS memorandum dated March 23, 1988.

[161] INA §245A(d)(2). The procedures and standards for adjudicating waiver applications are discussed in Chapter One.

[162] In Zambrano v. INS, CV-88-455 EJG (E.D. Cal. 1988), the plaintiffs contend that the vast majority of persons denied legalization under INA §245a.2(d)(4) are women who have received AFDC or other similar benefits and that the INS regulations violate the equal protection clause because they are discriminatory on the basis of sex. Reported in 65 Interpreter Releases 486 (May 9, 1988).

stage of the legalization program however, as the financial circumstances of an applicant who was granted a waiver of the public charge ground of exclusion at the first stage of the legalization process will most likely be carefully scrutinized at the second stage. This is particularly significant since a waiver of this ground of excludability is not available to applicants at the second stage of applying for lawful permanent residence.[163] An exception, however, has been made for the aged, blind and disabled eligible for benefits under Title XVI of the SSA or §212 of Public Law 93-66, who may apply for a waiver of the public charge ground of exclusion during the second stage permanent application process. It is therefore preferable to contest a finding that the applicant is likely to become a public charge during the first stage rather than submit a waiver. If a waiver application must be filed and is granted, the temporary resident should be advised that receipt of public cash assistance during the period of temporary residence could render him or her ineligible for permanent resident status at the second stage.

5.4(a)(5) Denials Based upon Criminal Grounds

Denials of applications for temporary resident status under INA §245A based upon criminal grounds arise in two contexts. First, the statute renders any person convicted of "a single felony or three misdemeanors committed in the United States" ineligible for legalization.[164] This provision constitutes an absolute bar to legalization as no waivers are available.

In addition to the 1 felony/3 misdemeanor rule, an applicant with a criminal conviction or an applicant who admits to having committed certain criminal offenses may be excludable under INA §§212(a)(9), (10) or (23). INA §245A provides that no waiver is available under the humanitarian waiver provisions of INA §245A(d)(2)(B)(i) for excludability under INA §§212(a)(9), (10) and (23), with the exception of applicants convicted of possession of less than thirty grams of marijuana.[165]

The INS has taken the position that other waivers provided by the INA at §212, including §212(h) and 212(i) waivers, are not

---

[163] INA §245A(d)(2)(B)(ii)(II).

[164] INA §245A(a)(4)(B). See Chapter One for a discussion of the 1 felony/3 misdemeanor bar.

[165] INA §§245A(d)(2)(i) and (ii); 8 CFR §§245a.2(k)(3)(i) and (ii). An alien convicted of possession of 30 grams or less of marijuana is excludable under INA §212(a)(23), but may apply for a legalization waiver.

available to legalization applicants.[166] Given this position, it is critical that post-conviction relief be pursued on behalf of the applicant to ameliorate the effect of a criminal conviction under these provisions. As discussed below, post-conviction relief for aliens with disqualifying convictions under one of the grounds of exclusion or the 1 felony/3 misdemeanor rule should be sought through the final stages of an appeal.

Some of the major issues raised on appeal in denials of temporary residence based upon criminal grounds include:

(a) the definition of a "final conviction" and whether the applicant was actually "convicted" of the crime or crimes rendering the applicant ineligible for benefits under the 1 felony/3 misdemeanor rule or excludable under INA §§212(a)(9), 212(a)(10) or 212(a)(23);

(b) the definition of "misdemeanor" and "felony" and whether the applicant was actually convicted of a felony rendering the applicant ineligible for benefits under the 1 felony/3 misdemeanor rule;

(c) the definition of a crime of moral turpitude and whether the applicant was convicted of or has admitted committing a crime of moral turpitude rendering the applicant excludable under INA §212(a)(9);

(d) whether an alien convicted of two crimes was sentenced to an aggregate sentence of 5 years or more rendering the applicant excludable under INA §212(a)(10);

(e) whether a post-conviction remedy obviates the conviction entirely or ameliorates the immigration consequences of a conviction which would render an applicant ineligible for benefits under the 1 felony/3 misdemeanor rule or excludable under INA §§ 212(a)(9), (10) or (23);

(f) whether a waiver under INA §212(h) is available to an applicant excludable under INA §212(a)(9);

(g) whether a crime of moral turpitude falls within the petty offense exception of INA §212(a)(9).

Appeal issues concerning the finality of a conviction, the ameliorative consequences of post-conviction relief and the availability of INA §212(h) waivers are discussed below. There are numerous other issues involving criminal offenses and their impact on INA provisions are beyond the scope of this volume. The practitioner is advised to consult <u>Immigration Law and</u>

---

[166] <u>See</u> memorandum of INS Assistant Commissioner William Slattery, dated August 6, 1987.

Crimes[167] for an in-depth treatment of issues concerning the finality of a conviction, the classification of a crime as one of moral turpitude, the definition of a felony, and the different forms of post-conviction remedies available which ameliorate the immigration consequences of a conviction in non-legalization contexts.

5.4(a)(5)(A) The Finality of a Conviction

The INS has declared that the existing case law that applies to determinations of what constitutes a conviction for purposes of deportation or exclusion, will be applied when determining whether an applicant has been convicted of a felony or misdemeanor for purposes of legalization eligibility.[168] Thus, the standards set forth in Matter of Ozkok, Interim Decision 3044 (BIA January 26, 1988) with regard to what constitutes a conviction with sufficient finality for immigration purposes will be applied to legalization adjudications.

The BIA's wide-ranging decision in Matter of Ozkok overruled portions of former precedent decisions in holding that a "final conviction" includes situations in which an adjudication of guilt has been withheld, and

(1) there has been a finding of guilt by judge or jury, or entry of a plea of guilty or nolo contendere, or an admission of facts sufficient to warrant a finding of guilty;

(2) the judge has ordered some form of punishment, penalty or restraint on the person's liberty; and

(3) a judgment or adjudication of guilt may be imposed without further proceedings, regarding the person's guilt or innocence of the original charge, if the person violates the terms of probation or fails to comply with the requirements of the court's order.[169]

Based upon Ozkok, the LAU has affirmed the denial of applications where the alien was sentenced to a conditional

---

[167] D. Kesselbrenner and L. Rosenberg, Immigration Law and Crimes (Clark Boardman, Co., Ltd.), (1989 rev. ed).

[168] Memorandum by INS Associate Commissioner Richard Norton, dated April 22, 1988, reproduced in 65 Interpreter Releases 433 (April 25, 1988).

[169] Ozkok, at pp. 5 & 6. See discussion of post-conviction forms of relief at Chapter One.

discharge program[170] and where the alien received a six-year deferred adjudication probation.[171] Appeals which raise the issue of what constitutes a final conviction should attempt to distinguish the criminal disposition in the applicant's case from Ozkok. The applicant should also argue on appeal that Ozkok was wrongly decided and is contrary to the Supreme Court's ruling in Pino v. Landon, 349 U.S. 901 (1955), which held that a conviction which had been placed "on file" was not a final conviction within the meaning of the INA. Under the broad Ozkok standards for determining the finality of a conviction, the criminal disposition specifically held not to be a final conviction in Pino would be considered sufficiently final under Ozkok.

5.4(a)(5)(B) The Effect of Post-Conviction Relief

In all appeals of denials of applications for temporary resident status based upon criminal convictions, the applicant should simultaneously pursue a strategy of seeking post-conviction relief whenever possible. Contrary to its previously stated positions that expungements must have been obtained by the time of the legalization interview, the INS has declared that a final order of expungement may be accepted by the RPF at any time prior to rendering a decision in the case.[172] It will also be accepted in response to a Notice of Denial or in support of an appeal or a request to reopen and reconsider. The LAU will defer adjudication of an appeal if given notice that the applicant is in the process of getting an expungement. This policy should apply to other forms of post-conviction relief as well.

Thus, if an application for temporary resident status is denied because of an existing disqualifying conviction, the applicant should continue with the appeal and, at the same time, attempt to vacate the judgment of conviction. The applicant should include documentary verification of his or her application for post-conviction relief with the appeal or request to reopen. If the applicant failed to file a timely appeal due to a final order of conviction and later obtained a form of post-conviction relief that would eliminate the conviction for legalization purposes, the applicant should submit a certified record of the expungement, vacation of judgment or other form of relief to the RPF and request

---

[170] LAU, October 15, 1988. Order No. L1288-443 from the Legalization Issues Bank, LAU Decision Digest. Ordering information appears at the end of this Chapter.

[171] LAU, October 5, 1988. Order No. 1288-442 from the Legalization Issues Bank, LAU Decision Digest. Ordering information appears at the end of this Chapter.

[172] See 65 Interpreter Releases 1321 (December 19, 1988).

that the RPF reopen and reconsider the case sua sponte pursuant to 8 CFR §103.5(b).

An alien denied temporary residence on the basis of a criminal conviction should always seek post conviction relief. In its April 22, 1988 memorandum concerning the determination of what constitutes a conviction for purposes of legalization,[173] the INS finally clarified its position that expungements for non-drug offenses eliminate the conviction as a bar to legalization eligibility. Similarly, a full and unconditional pardon by the President of the United States or by the Governor of any state will eliminate the conviction, as will a writ of coram nobis, which vacates or corrects a judgment in the absence of any other remedy.

The INS, however, draws a distinction between these post-conviction remedies and the judicial recommendation against deportation (JRAD) pursuant to INA §242(b)(2), commenting that while expungements and pardons affect non-immigration benefits and privileges of the recipient, JRADs simply prevent the conviction from forming the basis of deportability pursuant to INA §241(a)(4). Since there is no specific application of the JRAD to a benefit such as legalization, the INS reasons that a JRAD will not nullify a conviction for purposes of legalization eligibility.[174]

The applicant should argue on appeal that a JRAD should eliminate the consequences of a conviction for legalization purposes in the same way a pardon or expungement does. In Rasmussen v. Robinson, 163 F.2d 732 (3rd Cir. 1947), the Court held that a judicial recommendation against deportation under INA §241(b) could be invoked by an alien seeking entry who must establish admissibility, as well as by an alien subject to charges of having violated the INA, who must establish that he or she is not deportable. The requirement of INA §245A(a)(4) that a legalization applicant establish "admissibility" to the United States as an immigrant, should not be read in isolation from other provisions of the INA and established judicial precedent. A JRAD should similarly ameliorate the consequences of a conviction under the 1 felony/3 misdemeanor bar in light of Congressional intent to administer the legalization program in a liberal and generous manner.

---

[173] Reproduced in 65 Interpreter Releases 433 (April 25, 1988).

[174] The LAU has followed this position regarding JRAD's. LAU, July 29, 1988. Order No. 1088-397 from the Legalization Issues Bank, LAU Decision Digest. Ordering information appears at the end of this Chapter.

5.4(a)(5)(C) Denials Based upon the Unavailability of INA §212(h) Waivers

An applicant who is convicted of a felony crime of moral turpitude is both excludable under INA §212(a)(9) and is ineligible for legalization under the 1 felony/3 misdemeanor bar. Such an applicant would therefore not benefit from a waiver application under INA §212(h), which, if approved, would eliminate the §212(a)(9) exclusion ground, but would not eliminate the bar to a felony conviction under INA §245A(a)(4)(B). A legalization applicant convicted of a misdemeanor crime of moral turpitude, however, is not ineligible under INA §245A(4)(B) and would benefit from a §212(h) waiver of INA §212(a)(9) ground of exclusion. If such an applicant has the requisite family relationships to meet the threshold eligibility requirements for a waiver under INA §212(h), the applicant should submit a waiver application on appeal to the LAU on form I-601.[175] Given INS policy concerning the unavailability of such waivers to legalization applicants, the RPF will reject the waiver application and issue a Notice of Denial. The denial should be appealed to the LAU.

The applicant's brief accompanying the appeal may rely on the theory that the INS exceeded it's authority under the statute in determining that such waivers are not available to legalization applicants. The brief should first examine the statutory sections pertaining to inadmissibility and waivers.[176]

INA §245A(d) addresses the "Waiver of Numerical Limitations and Certain Grounds for Exclusion." Subsection (2)(B), "Waiver of Grounds of Exclusion.---" states in pertinent part:

> In the determination of an alien's admissibility under subsection (a)(4)(a),(b)(1)(C)(i) and (B)(2)(B)--(B) Waiver of Other Grounds...(i) In general. Except as provided in clause (ii), the Attorney General may waive any other provision of §212(a) in the case of individual aliens for humanitarian purposes, to assure family unity, or when it is otherwise in the public interest." [Emphasis supplied].

Clause (ii), entitled "Grounds that may not be waived.---" states "the following provisions of §212(a) may not be waived by the Attorney General under clause (i)" [emphasis supplied] and then

---

[175] The requirements and standards for adjudicating waivers under §212(h) of the INA are discussed in Chapter One.

[176] See discussion of grounds of exclusion at Chapter One.

specifies in pertinent part, (I) paragraphs (9) and (10) (relating to criminals).[177]

After setting forth the applicable statutory provisions, the applicant should argue that the scope of the regulations promulgated by the INS with regard to inadmissibility and the availability of any waiver of such ineligibility for benefits under IRCA is limited by the specific terms of the statute.[178] If the language of the statutory waiver section is read literally, it bars only the availability of the "humanitarian" waiver at INA §245A(d)(2)(B), clause (i) to waive the grounds enumerated in clause (ii), including INA §212(a)(9) concerning the conviction of a crime of moral turpitude. It is silent as to the effect of other existing waivers which an applicant may seek to invoke. Thus, in enacting the SAW and legalization provisions of the IRCA, Congress did not explicitly bar the applicability of the INA §212(h) waiver. Any restriction of the Attorney General's authority to waive grounds of excludability in general must be confined to the language of this "humanitarian" waiver.

The brief's statutory analysis should be placed in the context of the strict rules of statutory interpretation, which hold that the plain language of the statute controls its application.[179] With regard to the statutory scheme of the INA, the Supreme Court has already held and reaffirmed that it is bound to assume "that the legislative purpose is expressed by the ordinary meaning of the

---

[177] The identical argument can be made for SAW applicants. The applicable statutory and regulatory provisions are found at INA §§210(c)(2)(B)(i) and (ii); 8 CFR §§210.3(d)(3); 210.3(e)(2) and (3).

[178] Compare 8 CFR §245a.2(c)(3), "Ineligible aliens...(3) An alien excludable under the provisions of section 212(a) of the Act whose grounds of excludability may not be waived, pursuant to §245A(d)(2)(B)(ii) of the Act," and 8 CFR §245a.2(k)(2), "Waiver of grounds of exclusion...(2) Except as provided in paragraph (3) of this section, the Service may waive any other provision of section 212(a) of the Act only in the case of individual aliens for humanitarian purposes, to assure family unity, or when the granting of such waiver is in the public interest..."

[179] See Sutherland, *Statutory Construction*, §45.01 (4th ed.). See also, Cardoza-Fonseca v. INS, 107 S. Ct. 1207, 1212 (1987); citing Russello v. United States, 464 U.S. 16, 21 (1983); Ernst & Ernst v. Hochfelder, 425 U.S. 185 (1976) (The ordinary and obvious meaning of a phrase is not to be lightly discounted).

words used."[180] If the language of the statute is not clear on its face, it is appropriate to look at the legislative intent.[181] If the language of the waiver section is clear on its face, but its application deviates from the intent of the legislation, or there is a "clearly expressed legislative intention," it is appropriate to look at the legislative history.[182] This is particularly appropriate when the statute being construed is a statute in a case of first impression.[183]

Moreover, Congress is presumed to be aware of existing statutes and existing case law when it enacts new legislation, and to act intentionally when it includes language in one section of a statute but omits it in another section of the same Act.[184] Provision for a waiver of excludability under §212(h) of the INA preceded enactment of the IRCA. Congress must be presumed to have been aware of the language of this section when it enacted IRCA and enumerated exclusions from eligibility for the "humanitarian, family unity, public interest" waiver contained "in clause (i)."[185]

---

[180] INS v. Phinpathya, 464 U.S. 183, 189 (1984) quoting American Tobacco Co. v. Patterson, 456 U.S. 63, 68 (1982), in turn quoting Richards v. United States, 369 U.S. 1, 9 (1962).

[181] Blum v. Stanton, 465 U.S. 896 (1984).

[182] Cardoza-Fonseca v. INS, 107 S.Ct. 1207, 1213, n. 12 (1987), citing U.S. v. James, 478 U.S. ___ (1986).

[183] Escobar-Ruiz v. INS, ___F.2d___ (9th Cir. 1988) (No. 83-7501, January 11, 1988), citing United States v. Dadanian, 818 F.2d 1443, 1448 (9th Cir. 1987).

[184] Russello v. United States, supra., at 23 (quoting United States v. Wong Kim Bo, 472 F. 2d 720, 722 (5th Cir. 1980).

[185] This argument is strengthened by the fact that INS itself has recognized the applicability of expungements as overcoming inadmissibility and ineligibility based upon criminal convictions. Thus, the agency has acknowledged the effect of ameliorative mechanisms other than the "humanitarian" waiver to overcome ineligibility, and in fact, has given effect to certain pre-existing post-conviction remedies traditionally recognized as curing grounds of inadmissibility. See April 25, 1988 memorandum by Richard Norton, supra. See discussion at §5.4(a)(5)(B), supra. It should also be noted that IRCA provisions regarding the similarly structured adjustment program for Cubans and Haitians were also silent as to the availability of waivers. The INS nonetheless has determined the INA §212 waivers are available in Cuban-Haitian adjustment cases. See letter from INS Associate Commissioner Richard Norton dated May 11, 1987, reprinted in 64 Interpreter Releases 733-734 (June 8, 1987).

Furthermore, the language of IRCA supports the general applicability of INA §212 waivers to the legalization and SAW programs. The IRCA requires that the alien be <u>admissible</u>, rather than requiring that the alien <u>not be excludable</u> under certain specified grounds of excludability. Admissibility and excludability are not two sides of the same coin. Admissibility is broader, encompassing qualitative, numerical, and documentary restrictions, as set forth in both INA §§211 and 212 in their entirety. INA §212 (pertaining to admissibility) contains both the grounds of excludability, as well as waivers of those exclusion grounds which would otherwise render an alien inadmissible.[186] The waiver provisions must be read together with INA §212(a) and INA §211 to construe the term "admissibility." By requiring "admissibility," Congress intended all statutory provisions which define that concept to apply, not just the grounds of excludability.

Thus, the appeal brief should conclude that INS' policy of limiting qualified INA §212(h) waiver applicants' access to existing statutory means of removing the disability of a conviction for a crime of moral turpitude in the context of a SAW or legalization application, exceeds the permissible scope of interpretation of INS's own regulations, is beyond the scope of the relevant statutory section, and is <u>ultra vires</u>. Neither the statutory language nor the legislative history favor INS' regulatory and policy memo implementation limiting accessibility to these benefits. IRCA is an ameliorative statute and the new waiver provision was intended to provide a broader, more liberal provision, not to restrict existing avenues of relief. It is clear that Congressional intent in enacting the "humanitarian, family unity, public interest" waiver was not to prevent applicants for temporary and permanent residence under SAW and pre-1982 legalization provisions from utilizing existing statutory mechanisms in order to qualify for benefits.

It is critical that the advocate explore the possibilities of submitting a waiver application pursuant to INA §212(a)(9) in cases of applicants denied on the basis of a misdemeanor conviction for a crime of moral turpitude. If the applicant meets the threshold requirements for a §212(h) waiver and a waiver application was not submitted with the original legalization application, the advocate should prepare and submit the §212(h) waiver (application form I-601) on appeal. Indeed, if an applicant is unable to obtain post-conviction relief ameliorating the consequences of a conviction for a crime of moral turpitude, a waiver pursuant to INA §212(h) may be the only means by which to establish eligibility for legalization. Although it is likely that the LAU will deny the

---

[186] <u>See</u> Gordon and Rosenfield, <u>Immigration Law and Procedure</u>, Vol. 1, §2.1b (revised ed. 1987) 2-12.

application, it is imperative that the issue of the availability of such waivers be raised for further judicial review.[187]

5.4(a)(6) Denials Based Upon Untimely Filing of the Application

An alien who meets all of the eligibility requirements for temporary residence must file the application forms and supporting documentation on time, or temporary residence will be denied. The deadlines for filing the Application for Temporary Residence pursuant to INA §245A were as follows:

(1) Aliens illegally in the United States since before January 1, 1982, including aliens subject to an Order to Show Cause prior November 6, 1986,[188] must have filed their applications by May 4, 1988.[189]

(2) Aliens who became subject to OSCs after November 6, 1986 and prior to May 5, 1987, must have filed their applications between May 5 and June 3, 1987. INS regulations interpret this to mean that any alien apprehended, in INS custody, or subject to an OSC after November 6, 1986 and before May 5, 1987, must have applied by June 3, 1987.[190]

(3) Aliens who became subject to an OSC during the course of the legalization program between May 5, 1987 and April

---

[187] See discussion of judicial review in Chapter Seven.

[188] Aliens who were subject to an OSC prior to November 6, 1986 were permitted to file at any time during the twelve month filing period, regardless of whether they were ordered by an Immigration Judge or the BIA to file within 30 days. In re Teklay, Int. Dec. 3027 (BIA 1987).

[189] 8 CFR §245a.2(a)(1).

[190] 8 CFR §§245a.2(a)(2), 245a.2(a)(2)(i), 245a.2(c)(5). The practitioner should be aware that a nationwide class action, Doe & Roe v. Nelson, 88-C-6987 (N.D.Ill. 1988), challenges the 30-day limitation imposed by this regulation on the filing of legalization applications under INA §245A by aliens "apprehended" by the INS on or after November 6, 1986 and before May 5, 1987, and who were not served with Orders to Show Cause. The complaint charges that the regulation violates the terms of the statute and further asserts that the INS did not provide the plaintiffs and class members with notice of the 30 day application period at the time of their apprehension or thereafter. Reported in 65 Interpreter Releases 1066-67 (October 17, 1988).

4, 1988, must have applied prior to the thirty-first day after the issuance of the OSC.[191]

(4) Aliens who became subject to an OSC after April 5, 1988, must have applied by the May 4, 1988 deadline.[192]

According to the statute, when an application under INA §245A is denied because it was not filed in a timely manner, denial on such grounds by itself may not be reviewed in any administrative or judicial proceeding.[193] Nevertheless, this provision does not preclude the District Director, in individual cases, or the Immigration and Naturalization Service, as a matter of policy, from accepting applications which are not filed on time. In such cases, the practitioner should request that the District Director exercise his discretion to permit the filing of an application after the required filing period. The language of the regulations provides for dismissal of any appeal based solely upon a denial for an untimely filing.[194] Thus, cases which raise other procedural or substantive issues, such as refusal to accept a late filing, or others discussed above, should arguably be entitled to appellate review.

Whether or not an application pursuant to INA §245A is untimely filed may be a disputed issue. In many cases, the alien may argue that he or she should not be subject to a 30-day filing period, while the Service may take the position that the filing deadline applies. Many aliens subject to Orders to Show Cause were unaware of the need to file an application within thirty days.[195] Moreover, certain aliens who were subject to an Order to Show Cause did not file within the thirty-day time period because they were not prima facie eligible under the regulations in force at that time and only became eligible later as a result of orders issued in federal court actions.[196] Other aliens eligible for benefits

---

[191] 8 CFR §§245a.2(a)(2)(ii), 245a.2(c)(6).

[192] 8 CFR §§245a.2(a)(2)(iii), 245a.2(c)(7).

[193] INS §245A(f)(2).

[194] 8 CFR §103.3(a)(2)(iv)(B).

[195] Such aliens can assert a due process argument that they were entitled to specific notice of the restrictive 30-day filing deadline at the time they were served with the Order to Show Cause. See also INA §245A(i).

[196] Immigrant Assistance Project v. INS, No. C88-379 (W.D. Wash. 1988), a class action covering the INS Northern and Western Regions, raises this issue with regard to such applicants who qualify for legalization as "known to the Government," as defined

under both the legalization and SAW programs applied for SAW status during the 18 month application period and were later denied, only to have missed the one-year deadline for filing an application under the legalization program. Each of these examples presents the issue of whether or not the filing was late and therefore not subject to review under the provisions for administrative and judicial review.

Given the bar to administrative and judicial review of a determination that the application is late, the applicant may wish to request that the Regional Processing Facility or the District Director certify the issue of the application's timeliness to the Administrative Appeals Unit pursuant to 8 CFR §§245a.2(r), 210.2(i) and 103.4(b). A request of this nature should not challenge the validity of the regulations or statute, but rather raise issues involving a factual dispute or other collateral considerations. The request for certification should be documented in writing and supported with evidence where possible.

An appeal of a denial on grounds of untimely filing may be justified on the grounds that INS or QDEs, acting upon INS' instructions or interpretation of the law, wrongfully prevented a timely filing. For example, INS has revised its requirements regarding the quality and quantity of documentation necessary to establish continuous residence in pre-1982 cases, but both the INS and the QDEs did not contact each and every applicant erroneously dissuaded from applying under the earlier, more strict, policy. Similarly, countless applicants otherwise eligible for benefits actually were dissuaded from filing by the LOs or the QDE's or turned away at the LOs under an erroneous interpretation of the statutory eligibility requirements. This group includes persons who had single absences in excess of 45 days who were not apprised of the possibility of establishing the existence of emergent reasons,[197] as well as those who returned from brief trips on non-immigrant visas,[198] non-immigrants whose violation of status was

---

in Ayuda v. INS, 687 F. Supp. 650 (D.D.C. 1988). See LEAP Immigration Project Memorandum of July 5, 1988.

[197] See Hernandez v. Meese, No. S-88-385LKK (E.D. Calif. 1988).

[198] See LULAC v. INS, No. 87-4757-WDK (C.D. Calif. 1988).

known to the government but not to the INS,[199] and those having criminal convictions ameliorated by expungement.[200]

The basis of such an argument in support of a late filing, certification to the RPF or an appeal to the LAU would resemble an estoppel theory that the applicant's reliance upon incorrect direction from the LO or an agency acting under its authority prevented the applicant from submitting a timely application. In such a case, the harm to the applicant is clear. The applicant can argue that the Immigration and Naturalization Service had an affirmative duty to disseminate information regarding the legalization eligibility requirements and filing deadlines, including information regarding changes in these requirements[201] and that its failure to do so deprived the applicant of all notice of the need to submit an application within a specific period of time.

This argument finds support in two district court decisions extending the filing deadline for legalization applicants who did not submit timely applications due to their belief that they were not eligible under INS' erroneous regulatory interpretations of certain statutory eligibility requirements. In Zambrano v. INS, ___ F. Supp.___ , Civ. No. S-88-455 EJG (E.D. Cal. August 9, 1988), the Court found that applicants discouraged from applying for legalization by reliance on an illegal INS regulation had been denied the 12-month application period contemplated by Congress.[202] Similarly, the Court in LULAC v. INS, found that legalization applicants are entitled under the statute to a 12-month filing period.[203] The Court held that the applications of those who did not apply by the May 4, 1988 deadline, in reliance on erroneous information by the INS that they were ineligible, were not "late"

---

[199] See Ayuda, Inc. v. Meese, 687 F. Supp. 650 (D.D.C. 1988).

[200] See April 22, 1988 memorandum from Associate Commissioner Richard Norton entitled "What Constitutes a Conviction for Purposes of Legalization." Reproduced in 65 Interpreter Releases 433 (April 15, 1988).

[201] INA §245A(i). See also Legalization Wires #1, 8; Press Conference statements of Alan C. Nelson, dated November 26, 1986; Department of State cable dated May 27, 1987 and INS memoranda dated June 29. 1987.

[202] Zambrano v. INS dealt with INS regulations concerning the public charge ground of exclusion. See discussion in 65 Interpreter Releases 817 (August 15, 1988).

[203] ___ F. Supp.___, No. 87-4757-WDK (C.D. Cal., August 12, 1988).

because the applicants had not been given the filing period prescribed by the statute.[204]

The grounds of an appeal of this nature do not challenge the lawfulness of the statutory provision, but rest upon collateral, factual considerations. The argument should address the INS' offending patterns and practices in implementing the IRCA, including administrative delay in supplying needed information and forms; delays in opening offices; the provision of erroneous and inadequate information in response to applicants' questions regarding the legalization programs or related procedures; mid-application period changes in procedures and requirements; or long lines, limited office hours and limited filing procedures at certain Legalization Offices due to inadequate staffing. Late-filed applications and appeals of denials based upon untimely filing should always be well-documented and corroborated with the statements of the applicant, the QDE, or other advocates advised erroneously by INS personnel. Written documentation of changes in INS policy and of unresolved issues presently in litigation should be included.

In addition to making the above arguments in the context of an administrative appeal, the applicant should explore the alternative avenue of seeking declaratory and injunctive relief, individually or on a class basis.[205] Such actions might address the INS' offending patterns and practices in implementing the IRCA, as discussed above, as well as challenging the validity and constitutionality of aspects of the regulations or the statute, particularly upon due process grounds.

5.4(b) Appeal of Denials of SAW Applications Under INA §210

The Special Agricultural Worker (SAW) provisions of IRCA allow those aliens who have been employed as seasonal agricultural

---

[204] LULAC v. INS challenged the now changed INS policy of denying legalization to those who used a fraudulently obtained visa or other document to reenter the United States after January 1, 1982 to resume an unlawful residence. See discussion in 65 Interpreter Releases 819 (August 15, 1988).

[205] See for example, Doe & Roe v. Nelson, No. 88-C-6987 (N.D. Ill. 1988) which seeks a declaratory judgment invalidating INS rules denying legalization to persons who were apprehended after November 6, 1986, but were never issued an OSC, and who did not apply for legalization by June 3, 1987. The action challenges the scope of the regulations and raises due process considerations of inadequate notice. Copies of the pleading in this action may be obtained from the Legalization Issues Bank. Ordering information appears at the end of this Chapter.

workers (SAWS) in the United States for at least ninety days between May 1, 1985 and May 1, 1986 to become temporary residents.[206] Of these, those who can document their employment in seasonal agriculture for ninety days during each of three years, i.e., the years ending May 1, 1984; May 1, 1985 and May 1, 1986 are classified with SAW-Group 1 status and are eligible for permanent resident status one year earlier than other SAWs, who are classified with SAW-Group 2 status.[207] Applicants for SAW-Group 1 status under INA §210(a)(2)(A) may appeal the portion of the decision denying them SAW-Group 1 status.[208]

5.4(b)(1) INS Suspicion of Fraud in SAW Program

The SAW program has been the subject of considerable controversy. The Immigration and Naturalization Service has reported that by the end of the filing deadline on November 30, 1988 there were over one million SAW applications filed, which is more than twice the anticipated number of applicants. Some INS officials have indicated that they suspect that up to 50% of SAW applications may be fraudulent.[209] This percentage, however, is not reflected in the approval rate thus far. As of March 9, 1989, approximately 93% of SAW applications which had been adjudicated, had been approved, compared to an approval rate of approximately 97% for INA §245A legalization applications. Unfortunately, a mere 25% of SAW applications had been adjudicated as of that date. The INS speculates that the incidence of fraud rose dramatically in the last days of the program and expects the rate of denial to increase significantly in the remaining period of adjudication.

INS suspicion of fraud in SAW applications has resulted in a wide range of abuses towards SAW applicants who have attempted to return to the United States after travelling abroad with their work authorization cards, as well as those who seek to enter the United States after filing a preliminary SAW application at a designated port of entry. A nationwide class action, Lopez v. Ezell, seeks injunctive, mandamus and declaratory relief on behalf of SAW

---

[206] INA §210(a)(1)(B).

[207] INA §§210(a)(2)(A) and (B).

[208] 8 CFR §210.2(f). The one-year difference in the period in which SAW-Group 1 temporary residents and SAW-Group 2 temporary residents can apply for permanent resident status could be very significant in cases where an alien wishes to petition for ineligible family members. See Chapter Twelve on Ineligible Family Members.

[209] See "1.1 Million Apply for SAW Amnesty", 65 Interpreter Releases 1257 (December 5, 1988).

applicants who were either interrogated and denied reentry upon return or coerced into withdrawing their preliminary applications.[210]

The high degree of suspicion which pervades the INS' adjudication of SAW applications under INA §210, will undoubtedly taint the appeal process as well. The practitioner is advised to make a determination as to the merits of the case before filing the notice of appeal. If this is impossible to accomplish given the brief 30 day filing period,[211] the notice of appeal must be filed in order to preserve the applicant's appeal rights. If, after inspection of the record of proceedings or further investigation, the practitioner determines that the appeal appears to be without merit, he or she can withdraw from the case without filing a brief or submitting additional documentation.[212]

5.4(b)(2) Denials Based upon Insufficient Evidence or the Lack of Corroborative Documentation of Qualifying Employment

Perhaps the most common ground of denial will be that the applicant failed to submit sufficient documentation to establish eligibility under INA §210. To qualify for SAW legalization, the applicant must prove by a preponderance of the evidence that he or she has worked the requisite man-days, is admissible under INA §210(c), and, in SAW-Group 1 cases, has resided in the United

---

[210] No. 88-1825-JLI (S.D. Calif. 1988) reported in 65 Interpreter Releases 1255 (December 5, 1988). INS has issued a cable dated January 1, 1989 establishing a policy regarding confiscation of work authorization documents which addresses many of the concerns raised in this action. See 66 Interpreter Releases 61-63 (January 13, 1989).

[211] The limited 30-day filing period for appealing SAW denials has been challenged in United Farmworkers v. INS, No. 87-1064-LKK (E.D. Calif).

[212] Practitioners should be aware that the government indicted an attorney on 10 counts of conspiracy under INA §210(b)(7)(A)(ii) for creating a false writing or document in making a SAW application. The government contended that the statute criminalizes the conduct described without requiring a showing of scienter, mens rea, or guilty knowledge or intent. The Court dismissed the charges after granting the defendant's motion to suppress illegally seized evidence, leaving unresolved the constitutional issue posed by the Government's "strict liability" construction of the statute. Reported in 65 Interpreter Releases 1313 (December 19, 1988) and 66 Interpreter Releases 35 (January 9, 1989).

States for the requisite amount of time.[213] An alien can meet this burden of proof if the alien establishes that he or she has in fact performed seasonal agricultural services by producing sufficient evidence to show the extent of that employment as a matter of just and reasonable inference. In such cases, the burden then shifts to the Attorney General to disprove the alien's evidence with a showing that negates the reasonableness of the inference to be drawn from the evidence.[214]

Congress recognized that documentary evidence to establish SAW eligibility would be extremely difficult to obtain as a result of the failure of agricultural employers to maintain records of employment or to cooperate with employees in documenting their past employment. For this reason, the statute at one part requires only a showing of a nonfrivolous claim to SAW status to qualify for a stay of deportation and employment authorization, whereas comparable provisions of the legalization program require the applicant to show *prima facie* eligibility. Moreover, the Conference Report expressly incorporates Fair Labor Standard Act case law as a guide to remedying this objective obstacle in SAW cases to create an evidentiary inference in favor of an applicant's evidence.[215] Finally, anticipating the difficulties to be encountered by SAW applicants in obtaining documentary evidence, Congress directed the INS to assist farmworkers in meeting their burden of proof.[216]

---

[213] See INA §§291, 210(b)(3)(B), 8 CFR §210.3(b).

[214] INA §210(b)(3)(B)(iii). The INS is not bereft of tools to meet this burden. 8 CFR §210.3(b)(3) provides that all evidence of identity, qualifying employment, admissibility, and eligibility submitted by an applicant will be subject to verification by the Service...The Service may solicit lists of workers, against which evidence of qualifying employment can be checked, from agricultural producers, farm labor contractors, collective bargaining organizations and other groups or organizations which maintain records of employment. See also 8 CFR §210.3(b)(4).

[215] See Joint Explanatory Statement of the Committee of Conference, H.R. Rep. No. 99-1000, 99th Cong., 2d Sess. (1986). This case law establishes that, in the absence of employer records, an employee can meet the burden of proof with inexact or approximate evidence, including his or her own sworn declaration. Belize v. W.H. McLeon & Sons Packing Co., 765 F. 2d 1317 (5th Cir. 1985); Donovan v. New Floridian Hotel, Inc., 676 F. 2d 468 (11th Cir. 1982).

[216] See 8 CFR §210.3(b)(4). The INS did not promulgate such regulations until July 1988, as a result of the Court's order in United Farmworkers v. INS, No. 87-1064-LKK (E.D. Calif).

Thus, Congress deliberately lowered the burden of proof for SAW applicants to establish eligibility for temporary resident status. The statutory provisions, read as a whole, indicate that SAW applicants are to be given the benefit of a just and reasonable inference that they performed the qualifying agricultural employment based upon all available evidence, including their own testimony.[217]

Although Congress clearly contemplated that a lower burden of proof apply to SAW cases, the burden of proof which emerges from the regulations is higher than that required of legalization applicants. In addition to setting forth those documents which must be presented to prove the various elements of eligibility, the regulations provide that an applicant will not meet the burden of proof where documentation of eligibility consists solely of personal testimony or affidavits of the applicant which are not corroborated, in whole or in part, by other credible evidence.[218] Thus, the regulations explicitly reject any proof of eligibility for temporary residence which is grounded on the SAW applicant's own sworn evidence, no matter how relevant, probative and credible the testimony is. In essence, the regulation prejudges the credibility, probative value and relevance of the evidence and finds it wanting, without having examined it.

Three major class action lawsuits have challenged a number of INS practices and policies regarding the SAW program, including the imposition of an improper burden of proof on applicants. The first action, Haitian Refugee Center v. Nelson, No. 88-1066 (S.D. Fla. 1988), limited to the 11th Circuit, was successful in preliminarily enjoining the INS from (1) continuing to impose an improper burden of proof on applicants; (2) failing to re-issue denial notices that gave incorrect information regarding appeal procedures or inadequate information as to the basis of the denial; (3) conducting interviews without competent translators; and (4) denying cases on the basis of adverse information without first providing the information to the applicant and affording an opportunity to rebut.[219]

As a result of this litigation, the INS issued instructions to correct the practice of denying applications based solely upon an employer affidavit (Form I-705) verifying the alien's performance of the qualifying employment. Unless there is evidence to negate the just and reasonable inference created by an employer

---

[217] See "Legalization Appeals," by Peter Schey and Carlos Holguin, supra. at 394.

[218] 8 CFR §§210.3(b)(2) and (3). See also 8 CFR §210.3(c)(3).

[219] Reported in 65 Interpreter Releases 692 (July 11, 1988).

affidavit, the affidavit is sufficient evidence of employment to support approval of a SAW application if the statements in the application are credible.[220] Applicants who received denials which reject employer affidavits as sufficient evidence to establish eligibility should request the RPF to reopen and reconsider the decision sua sponte pursuant to 8 CFR §103.5(b). The request should cite the INS cable and the decision in Haitian Refugee Center v. Nelson.

In a second action, United Farm Workers of America v. INS, CV. No. S-87-1064-LKK/JFM (E.D. Cal.), the plaintiffs claimed that the INS had misapplied the statutory test for adjudicating SAW applications by requiring applicants to produce particular documentary evidence in addition to the alien's own testimony before the burden of proof shifted to the government. The court disagreed, finding that "Congress explicitly intended to require SAW applicants to submit some corroborating documentation...as a predicate to a final adjudication under section 210(b)(3)(B)(iii)." However, the court ruled that any credible documentation, "however sparse and incomplete," is sufficient to shift the burden of proof to the INS:

> The applicant need only produce corroborating documentation that he or she performed some portion of the claimed qualifying work: once this is established, his or her own testimony, if credible, as to the extent of that employment will suffice to shift the burden of proof to the INS. For example, the corroborating affidavit of a co-worker that the applicant worked for a particular farmer at some point during the claimed period will establish the fact of the employment; the applicant's own testimony that he or she worked for that farm for the full 90 man-days establishes the extent of the employment. (Emphasis in the original).[221]

In a third action, Ramirez-Fernandez v. Giugni, No EP-88-CA-389 (W.D. Tex. November 23, 1988) covering the regions of Texas and New Mexico, the Court denied the plaintiff's motion for a preliminary injunction.[222] The plaintiff's argued that the INS was applying an illegal burden of proof to SAW applicants and requested an order enjoining the Service from using a procedurally deficient SAW interview process which does not provide for transcripts, the

---

[220] INS CO Cable dated September 14, 1988, reproduced in 65 Interpreter Releases 985 (September 26, 1988).

[221] Reported in 65 Interpreter Releases 1256 (December 5, 1988).

[222] Reported in 65 Interpreter Releases 1256-1257 (December 5, 1988).

opportunity to present live witnesses and the opportunity to be confronted with and rebut adverse evidence. In denying the request for a preliminary injunction, the court noted that the INS Southern RPF had agreed to apply the practices and procedures ordered by the Court in <u>Haitian Refugee Center v. Nelson</u> to all legalization offices in the region and to reopen and readjudicate all cases denied prior to August 22, 1988 in the region. The Court further held that neither IRCA nor the Constitution requires transcripts of legalization interviews.

Thus, appeals of denials based upon insufficient documentation should begin with a discussion of the legislative intent to ease the burden of proof required of SAW applicants and to administer the program in a liberal and generous fashion. The brief should challenge the heightened burden of proof required by INS regulations and adjudication procedures as contrary to the plain meaning, intent, and purpose of the statute. <u>American Tobacco Co. v. Patterson</u>, 456 U.S. 53, 68 (1982); <u>see</u> also <u>Ford Motor Credit Company v. Cenance</u>, 452 U.S. 155 (1981). The argument should then proceed to analyze the nature and scope of the evidence presented by the applicant according to the standards developed in the case law under the Fair Labor Standard Act referred to above.

The appeal should evaluate each piece of evidence submitted by the SAW applicant in terms of its probative value and argue that the evidence, taken as a whole, supports a just and reasonable inference that the alien performed the qualifying employment. According to the standards set forth in <u>United Farmworkers of America v. INS</u>, <u>supra</u>., an applicant's own testimony in the form of a sufficiently detailed and credible affidavit, coupled by an affidavit from an employer or co-worker, or other documentary proof corroborating the performance of a portion of the claimed qualifying work, is sufficient to shift the burden of proof to the INS. If the Service does not introduce any evidence refuting the veracity or credibility of the evidence, the applicant has established eligibility for temporary residence benefits under the statute.

The LAU will carefully scrutinize all documentary evidence for inconsistencies, alterations and erasures which diminish the document's credibility and probative value. It is therefore extremely important to offer a reasonable explanation for any inconsistencies or apparent irregularities in the documentary evidence initially presented by the applicant.

In all appeals of denials for insufficient evidence, the applicant should attempt to supplement the record with further corroborating evidence whenever possible. For example, the applicant should attempt to supplement his or her own statement with a sworn statement from an agricultural producer, foreman, farm labor contractor, union official, fellow employee or any other individual who has specific knowledge of the applicant's employment. The affidavit should be sufficiently detailed and state the affiant's willingness to personally verify the information provided.[223] Standard "fill-in-the-blank" affidavits will not be given much weight.[224] If an unrepresented alien submitted a "fill-in-the-blank" affidavit with the original application, the advocate should contact the affiant and prepare a more thorough and detailed affidavit according to the requirements of 8 CFR 210.3(c)(3). Other documentation, such as personal letters, receipts and bills establishing the applicant's residence in the area of work, will also contribute to an inference that the alien performed the qualifying employment. An explanation as to why the evidence was not available at the time of filing should accompany any additional evidence submitted. If additional evidence is not available and the applicant is relying solely on his or her own affidavit, he or she should include a detailed explanation regarding the efforts made to obtain corroborating documentation.

In cases where the applicant's efforts to obtain verification of employment has been frustrated by an uncooperative employer, the applicant should request that the INS issue a subpoena to obtain such documentation from the employer or contractor. The applicant may also seek to stay the processing of an appeal while the request for the issuance of a subpoena is pending.[225]

5.4(b)(3) Denials Based upon Determination that Applicant did not Perform Ninety Days of Employment in Seasonal Agricultural Services

According to the statute, "the alien must establish that he has -- (i) resided in the United States, and (ii) performed seasonal agricultural services in the United States for at least 90 man-days."[226] The term "seasonal agricultural services" is defined by statute as the performance of (1) field work, (2)

---

[223] 8 CFR §210.3(c)(3). The LAU has indicated that if such affidavits do not conform to the strictures of 8 CFR §210.3(c)(3), it is quite possible that the applicant will fail to reach the just and reasonable inference standard. LAU, June 9, 1988. Order No. L0888-280 from the Legalization Issues Bank, LAU Decisions Digest. Ordering information appears at the end of this Chapter.

[224] LAU, June 16, 1988. Order No. L0888-283, from the Legalization Issues Bank, LAU Decision Digest. Ordering information appears at the end of this Chapter.

[225] See "Legalization Appeals," by Peter Schey and Carlos Holguin, supra. at 397.

[226] INA §210(a)(1)(B).

relating to planting, cultural practices, cultivating, growing and harvesting of (3) fruits, and vegetables of every kind and other perishable commodities, as defined by the Secretary of Agriculture.[227]

5.4(b)(3)(A) Denials Based upon Determination that Crop was not A Fruit, Vegetable or Other Perishable Commodity.

One of the most controversial issues in the adjudication of SAW applications has been the determination of what constitutes a fruit, vegetable or other perishable commodity. The unambiguous language of the statute requires the inclusion of fruits and vegetables <u>of every kind</u>. Accordingly, the Department of Agriculture has adopted the scientific definitions of "fruit" and "vegetable." These terms are defined as follows:

<u>Fruit</u>: the human edible parts of plants which consist of the mature ovaries and fused other parts or structures, which develop from flowers or inflorescence.[228]

<u>Vegetables</u>:[229] the human edible herbaceous leaves, stems, roots or tubers of plants. Any plant or plant product which meets the definition of a fruit or vegetable, "without exception" constitutes a qualifying crop under the statute. Fruits and vegetables need not be perishable to qualify.[230]

"Other perishable commodities" are defined as those commodities which do not meet the definition of fruits or vegetables, that are produced as a result of seasonal field work, and have critical and unpredictable labor demands.[231] The regulations at 7 CFR §1d.9 provide an inclusive list of crops which

---

[227] INA §210(h). This definition is repeated in 7 CFR §1d.9.

[228] 7 CFR §1d.5.

[229] 7 CFR §1d.10. Herbaceous plants are to be distinguished from woody plants; these distinctions are based on patterns of plant growth; i.e., herbaceous plants "die back" each year whereas woody plants grow by adding outward layers of plant cells.

[230] <u>See</u> the Comments pertaining to fruits and vegetables published with the final regulations, 52 Fed. Reg. 20372-20376 (June 1, 1987).

[231] "Critical and unpredictable labor" demands mean that the period during which field work is to be initiated cannot be predicted with any certainty 60 days in advance of the need. 7 CFR §1d.3.

qualify as perishable commodities, as well as an exclusive list of those crops which do not meet this definition.

<u>Includes</u>: Christmas trees, cut flowers, herbs, hops, horticultural specialties, spanish reeds, (arundo donax), spices, sugar beets, and tobacco.[232]

<u>Excludes</u>: Animal aquacultural products, birds, cotton,[233] dairy products, earthworms, fish including oysters and shellfish, forest products, fur-bearing animals and rabbits, hay[234] and other forage and silage,[235] honey, horses and other equines, livestock of all kinds including animal specialties, poultry and poultry products, sod,[236] sugar cane[237], wildlife, and wool.

---

[232] The inclusion of Christmas trees, herbs, hops, nursery crops, spanish reeds, spices, sugar beets, and tobacco on the list of perishable commodities was unsuccessfully challenged in <u>Northwest Forest Workers v. Lyng</u>, CA 87-1487 (DDC, Sept. 3, 1987).

[233] The express exclusion of cotton was successfully challenged in <u>National Cotton Council of America v. Lyng</u>, CA-S-87-0200-C (N.D. Tex. 1988), which held that cotton meets the statutory and regulatory definition of fruit. This order is final, as the government did not appeal. <u>See</u> also <u>Valdez-Valencia v. Lyng</u>, Civ. No. 87-630-TUC-RMB (D.Ariz. 1988).

[234] The exclusion of hay from the list of perishable commodities was unsuccessfully challenged in <u>Texas Farm Bureau v. Lyng</u>, No. M-88-0095-CA (E.D.Tex. 1988). Reported in 65 Interpreter Releases 1102 (October 24, 1988).

[235] Silage is produced from the stalks of corn plants, after the ears of corn have been harvested. Thus, although work performed in making and storing silage may not qualify, the employee also may have worked in the preceding phases of corn planting, cultivating and harvesting which is qualifying work. <u>See</u> Legalization Wire #33, August 24, 1987. <u>See also</u>, Matter of - --- (LAU, Feb. 8, 1988), holding that harvesting all corn will be considered qualifying employment, reported in 65 Interpreter Releases 403 (April 18, 1988).

[236] The exclusion of sod from the definition of other perishable commodities is the subject of litigation in <u>Morales v. Lyng</u>, No. 87C 20522 (N.D. IL, Dec. 1987). The district court invalidated the USDA regulations excluding sod, however the USDA repromulgated its regulation and continues to exclude sod.

[237] Sugarcane has been classified as a "perishable commodity" in other contexts. <u>See</u> <u>Maneja v. Waialva Agricultural Co.</u>, 349 U.S. 254, 257 (1955); <u>Wirtz v. Oscola Farms</u>, 372 F.2d 584, 586 (5th Cir. 1967). Its exclusion from the list of eligible plants and

According to INS' internal directives, the following products are included under the terms fruit, vegetables and other perishable commodities:

> "wheat, rice, oats, barley, rye and other grains produced primarily for human consumption; all corn, sweet and other beans, including soybeans, berries, and melons grown for human consumption; grapes; potatoes, tree nuts and ground nuts grown for human consumption, including peanuts; and mushrooms...Together, fruits and vegetables <u>include all plant crops grown for human food</u>, with the exception of sugar cane..."(emphasis supplied).[238]

The following crops are excluded from classifications as fruits, vegetables, or other perishable commodities according to INS directives: sorghum;[239] milo; millet; alfalfa; clover; timothy, and other grains and grasses grown primarily for forage and other uses aside from human consumption; gourds; seeds; and flax.

According to INS directives, SAW applicants who rely upon work in crops not included in the regulatory definitions of fruits, vegetables or other perishable commodities are clearly ineligible for SAW status.[240] Thus, if a SAW applicant is denied on this ground, the advocate should determine whether the crop the applicant worked on is included in the Department of Agriculture regulations at 7 CFR §1d.9 or whether INS has acknowledged its inclusion in policy memoranda or directives. At the end of this Chapter there is a chart of those items expressly determined to be included or excluded under the terms fruit, vegetable or other perishable commodity which the advocate can consult in making this determination.

---

plant products is the subject of litigation in <u>Northwest Forest Workers</u>, <u>supra</u>. The USDA has repromulgated its regulations and continues to exclude sugarcane.

[238] Legalization Wire #23, dated June 5, 1987. One of the problems with the INS directives is their failure to specify whether a plant or plant product is included on the basis of its being a fruit, a vegetable or a perishable commodity. Practitioners are left to speculate as to the rationale for the inclusion of certain plants, and the extension of these exceptions to other plants.

[239] An administrative appeal brief challenging the exclusion of sorghum (which produces molasses) is available through the Legalization Issues Bank. Ordering information appears at the end of this Chapter.

[240] <u>See</u> Legalization Wire #48, January 13, 1988.

If the crop is specifically excluded by the regulations and INS directives, the advocate should determine whether the crop is the subject of a federal court challenge. For example, the exclusion of sugar cane has been challenged in <u>Northwest Forest Workers Assoc. v. Lyng</u>, C.A. No. 87-1487 consolidated with <u>Augustine Valdez Valencia v. Lyng</u>, C.A. No. 87-3303 (D.D.C. April 25, 1987).[241] The exclusion of sod has also been challenged in <u>Morales v. Lyng</u>, 702 F. Supp. 161 (N.D. Ill. 1988).[242] Although the Department of Agriculture continues to exclude these crops, the advocate should file an appeal pending a final adjudication of the federal court actions. Citations to the pending court actions should be included in the appeal.

If an applicant who performed qualifying agricultural services in cotton was denied prior to the redefinition of cotton as a fruit, the advocate should file an appeal and request that the RPF reopen and reconsider its decision <u>sua sponte</u> pursuant to 8 CFR §103.5(b).

On appeal, the advocate should look for creative ways in which to argue for the inclusion of a specific crop within the definition of fruit, vegetable or perishable commodity. Some arguments based upon apparent ambiguities or inconsistencies in the regulatory definitions are discussed below.

5.4(b)(3)(A)(i) <u>Horticultural Specialties</u>

The regulations include "horticultural specialties" in the list of perishable commodities, however the list of crops which fall within this classification is not expressly exclusive. The advocate should therefore determine whether the applicant worked on a crop than can be classified as a horticultural specialty. "Horticultural specialties" mean field grown, containerized, and greenhouse produced nursery crops which include juvenile trees, shrubs, seedlings, budding, grafting, and understock, fruit and nut trees, fruit plants, vines, ground covers, foliage and potted plants, cut flowers, herbaceous annuals, biennials and perennials, bulbs, corms, and tubers.[243]

---

[241] The Court ordered the USDA to determine if sugarcane could be defined as either a vegetable or perishable commodity. New regulations issued by INS continue to exclude sugarcane. <u>See</u> 65 Interpreter Releases 693 (July 11, 1988).

[242] In response to the Court's order, the USDA repromulgated its regulation and continues to exclude sod from eligibility.

[243] <u>See</u> 7 CFR §1d.6.

If the applicant worked with a plant product or other field grown, containerized, and greenhouse produced nursery crop which is not specifically named, he or she should present proof that the plant is seasonal or subject to unpredictable labor demands. The regulations at 7 CFR §1d.3 provide that critical and unpredictable labor demands exist when the period during which field work is to be initiated cannot be predicted with any certainty 60 days in advance of need. Typical of the circumstances which create a critical, yet unpredictable demand for labor is weather or other climate conditions which require the employment of a labor force on short notice.[244]

The discussion of reasons why various perishable commodities were found to have such labor demands may supply a basis for arguing in favor of other plants and plant products as "horticultural specialties." For example, cut flowers were included because "[i]n many instances, the timing of the planting and harvesting is dependent upon uncontrollable factors, and is, therefore, critical." Similarly, activities involving nursery products "are highly subject to unpredictable weather influences."[245] This can be said of almost any plant product and would support the inclusion of numerous other items under "horticultural specialties."

5.4(b)(3)(A)(ii)   Grains and Seed Crops

An applicant denied on the basis of the exclusion of sorghum, milo and millet can argue on appeal that these grains fall within the definition of fruit and perishable commodities. INS directives recognize that such grains as wheat, oats, barley, rye, corn and beans are qualifying crops and further recognize soybeans as a fruit. The applicant should argue that there is no distinction among these grains, which are all used for human consumption. Sorghum, milo and millet are human edible. They are food staples in the Middle East and Africa and are also eaten or used in food products in the United States.[246] Thus, the characterization of

---

[244] See comments to the proposed regulations, 52 Fed. Reg. 13247 (April 22, 1987).

[245] See the comments accompanying the final regulations at 52 Fed. Reg. 20375 (June 1, 1987).

[246] Sorghum is used to make molasses. Millet can be purchased in natural food stores and grocery stores throughout the United States. While it may be true that these crops are grown for export and human consumption abroad or for other purposes in addition to human consumption, the same can be said of soybeans and corn, which are expressly allowed. See Matter of---, (LAU, Feb. 2, 1988), holding that harvesting all corn will be considered

such grains as grown primarily for forage and other uses aside from human consumption should be challenged.

Similarly, the rationale for excluding certain grains and seed crops from the list of fruits, vegetables and perishable commodities is puzzling and should be susceptible to challenge. An applicant denied on the basis of the exclusion of certain seed crops should argue on appeal that these crops come within the definition of fruit, vegetables and perishable commodities. Seed crops are vegetables and other plants which are planted, cultivated, irrigated and grown to maturity, through the final stages of plant life including the blooming and the production of seeds. In the course of the plant's growth, such plants as beets, cabbage, carrot, collards, kale, radish, rutabaga, spinach, and turnip are indistinguishable from the same vegetables planted for human consumption. Most of the labor required to bring these plants to maturity is the same as that required to cultivate harvestable vegetables. In fact, seed crops are more labor intensive than crops grown for human consumption.[247] Seed crops are subject to the same vagaries of weather and the same critical and unpredictable labor demands as qualifying crops. The crop seed industry's labor needs are "critical" not only to the survival of a particular harvest or to the crop seed industry itself, but to the fruit and vegetable growers who would cease to exist without these seeds.

Seed production is a critical stage in the growth and production of plants for human consumption. It is difficult to understand the rationale for exclusion of an agricultural labor performed on an otherwise qualifying crop, based solely on the fact that the plants, though consumable, were not produced for the purpose of human consumption but for the production of seeds, which are fruit, according to the USDA's own definition. By comparison, ornamental fruit trees are qualifying crops despite the fact that they are cultivated and grown for other than human consumption of their fruit. The applicant should argue on appeal that the same

---

qualifying employment. The end use of a crop is Irrelevant under the statute, as long as a crop is a fruit, vegetable or perishable commodity. Reported in 65 Interpreter Releases 403 (April 18, 1988).

[247] The seed crop industry is subject to regulation by the federal and state Departments of Agriculture. Generally, fields and the seeds they produce must be certified to be 97% pure (as to the particular hybrid or line of plants being grown) and weed free before the seeds produced can be sold. To meet this rigorous standard, fields must be "rogued," i.e., all "contaminating" plants must be pulled by hand on a regular basis to avoid cross-pollination.

rationale for including ornamental fruit trees should apply to seed crops.

Finally, in representing an applicant denied on this ground, the advocate should carefully review with the applicant all of the crops on which the applicant worked during his or her employment on a particular farm, ranch or other agricultural site. The applicant may have worked on other crops not listed on the original application because the crop was not the primary crop the applicant worked on. A "man-day" of qualifying work, however, constitutes only one hour of work in a given day. Thus, it may be possible that the applicant did perform a sufficient amount of field work in a qualifying crop which, as a result of the applicant's ignorance of the complicated regulatory requirements, was not included on his or her original application for temporary resident status.

5.5(b)(3)(B) Denials Based on a Finding that the Applicant did not Engage in Qualifying Field Work

The work performed by the SAW applicant on a particular crop must fall within the definition of "field work" in order for the applicant to establish eligibility for temporary resident status. The regulations at 7 CFR §1d.4 define "field work" as any employment (1) performed on agricultural lands (2) for the purpose of planting, cultural practices, cultivating, growing, harvesting, drying, processing or packing (3) any fruits, vegetables, or other perishable commodities. "Field work" encompasses activities other than the harvest of crops. Operating tractors or machines which pick crops or shake trees, collecting, loading, and weighing fruit or vegetables, are an intrinsic part of field operations. Plowing, tilling, operating irrigation equipment and applying fertilizers and pesticides are also agricultural work, but these and other duties are not specifically mentioned in the statute or regulations. INS interpretations of the statute, however, indicate that virtually anything done in order to produce fruits, vegetables or perishable commodities is included in "field work."

If an applicant was denied on the basis that he or she did not perform "field work", the advocate should explore all of the agricultural activities the applicant engaged in the applicant and determine whether the activities were properly described in the application. The advocate should then determine whether the applicant's work could be construed as "field work" under the statute and regulations. Some of the activities expressly mentioned as included in or excluded from the definition of "field work" are set forth in a chart at the end of this Chapter.

In determining whether the applicant engaged in qualifying "field work," the advocate should first establish the location where the work was performed. The regulations require that "field work" take place "on agricultural lands." "Agricultural lands" means any land, cave or structure, except packinghouses or canneries, used for the purpose of performing "field work."[248]

Activities that occur in a processing plant or packinghouse not on agricultural lands do not qualify as "field work."[249] According to the INS, such processing facilities as freezing plants, processing plants, packaging plants, etc. are included under the term "Packing Houses" and are not considered "agricultural lands" regardless of proximity to field production sites. Work performed in such facilities is not "field work" within the meaning of 7 CFR §1d.4. However, stripping, grading, drying or packing performed in or adjacent to the field where the produce is grown is "field work" if performed as an integral part of the picking and harvesting operation on that farm (emphasis supplied).[250]

Work performed in packing sheds at highways, railheads or similar transportation points, or at central locations in cases of farms with separate, remote fields, qualifies as "field work" if: (1) it consists of activities such as stripping, grading, drying, or packing and (2) 85% or more of the produce packed has been produced by the grower/employer. Employment by an agricultural cooperative or commercial packing house does not constitute employment "by a farmer or a farm" and is not "field work."[251]

The drying, processing, or packing of fruit, vegetables, and other perishable commodities in the field is considered "field work," as is on-the-field loading of transportation vehicles.[252]

If an applicant is denied because of a finding that he or she did not work on "agricultural lands," the advocate should carefully explore with both the applicant and the employer whether the work performed was an integral part of the picking and harvesting operation of the farm. Additional affidavits describing the entire operation of the farm should be provided in support of the appeal.

---

[248] 7 CFR §1d.2.

[249] 7 CFR §1d.4.

[250] See Legalization Wire #23, June 5, 1987, reproduced in 64 Interpreter Releases 777-778 (June 29, 1987).

[251] See Legalization Wire #33, August 14, 1987, reproduced in 64 Interpreter Releases 971-972 (August 24, 1987).

[252] 7 CFR §1d.4.

In addition to considering the location of the work performed by the applicant, the advocate should evaluate the nature of the employer's business to determine whether the applicant engaged in qualifying field work. For example, beekeeping, canning and packing may qualify as field work, depending upon the context of the activity and the type of employer. Workers whose duties involve beekeeping for pollination of fruits, vegetables and other perishable commodities are eligible if employed by the grower or producer, even in cases where the hives tended were rented from an apiarist. However, when the employee worked for an apiarist tending hives rented to a grower for <u>pollination</u> of a fruit, vegetable, or perishable commodity, the worker is disqualified <u>because the principle business of an apiarist is the production of honey</u>,[253] which is excluded from the definition of fruit, vegetable or perishable commodity. Similarly, the stripping and grading of fruits and vegetables constitutes qualifying employment if performed for a grower/producer, but not if done for an agricultural cooperative. Packing is considered agricultural employment if performed "by a farmer or on a farm," but not if performed in a packing house.

Many SAW applicants denied temporary resident status were not represented during the application period. Given the complexities of the regulatory definitions of qualifying seasonal agricultural employment, the lack of due process safeguards that characterize the cursory legalization interview, and the limited language skills of many applicants,[254] it is not surprising that many qualified applicants did not present the full nature and extent of their employment history on the application form. In preparing an appeal of a denial based upon the failure of the applicant to demonstrate the performance of seasonal agricultural services for the requisite time period, the advocate should obtain a full explanation of the nature and location of the employer's business, as well as a complete list of all of the tasks performed by the applicant on each and every crop grown by the employer. The advocate should present additional evidence on appeal to overcome the basis of the denial and offer an explanation as to why the information was not provided in the first instance. Appeals which include significant additional evidence should include a request that the RPF reopen and reconsider the decision denying benefits pursuant to 8 CFR §103.5(b).

---

[253] <u>See</u> Legalization Wire #33, footnote 251.

[254] 90% of IRCA applicants speak Spanish; the majority have between three and six years of schooling. 70% have only rudimentary literacy skills. <u>See</u> NCA letter to Raymond Penn, citing study by the Refugee Policy Group for the American Public Welfare Association, reprinted in 66 Interpreter Releases 78 (January 13, 1989).

5.4(b)(4) Denials Based upon Grounds of Exclusion

As with pre-1982 legalization applicants, all aliens who apply for temporary residence as SAWs must establish they are admissible as immigrants under INA §212, which sets forth thirty-three categories of undesirable characteristics constituting grounds of excludability which preclude an alien's admission to the United States.[255] Most, but not all, of these grounds of excludability apply to applicants for temporary resident status as SAWs. Many of the grounds that do apply can be waived.[256]

Many SAW applicants will be denied under the criminal grounds of exclusion at INA §§212(a)(9), 212(a)(10) and 212(a)(23). The discussion of appeals of denials based on the criminal grounds of exclusion at §5.4(a)(5) of this Chapter applies to the SAW program as well. The discussion of excludability, however, should not be confused with the 1 felony/3 misdemeanor bar which presents an additional hurdle for legalization applicants under INA §245A, but does not apply to the SAW program.

5.4(b)(4)(A) Denials Based upon Public Charge Grounds

Many other SAW applicants will be denied benefits under the public charge ground of exclusion at INA §212(a)(15). It is important to note that the standards for assessing whether a SAW applicant is likely to become a public charge differs from similar provisions under INA §245A regarding legalization of those who entered before 1982. Under the legalization provisions, those who apply for temporary resident status and who are found to be excludable as likely to become public charges can satisfy an alternate test of "past employment without receipt of public cash assistance." Failing that test, pre-1982 legalization applicants for temporary residence can seek a waiver under INA §245A for humanitarian purposes, family unity or for reasons in the public interest. In contrast, SAW applicants found excludable under the traditional test for determining public charge, may satisfy an alternate test requiring work history without "reliance upon public cash assistance."[257] No humanitarian waiver provisions are available for SAW applicants who fail both the traditional and alternate test.

---

[255] See INA §210(a)(1)(C).

[256] See INA §210(c). See Chapter One for discussion of the applicability of the exclusion grounds to SAW applications and the availability of waivers.

[257] INA §210(c)(2)(C); 8 CFR §210.3(e)(4).

In arguing that a SAW applicant is not excludable under the traditional test for determining public charge, the totality of the applicant's financial circumstances should be presented in the context of the standards set forth in the applicable case law. The INS must consider a variety of factors, including age, health, mental and physical disabilities, the capacity to earn a living, prior receipt of public cash assistance, family situation, work history, the amount of funds available for self-support and the presence of others in the United States willing and able to offer their financial assistance to the applicant. Matter of Perez, supra.; Matter of Harutunian, 14 I & N Dec. 583, 588-90 (Reg. Comm'r 1974); Matter of Martinez-Lopez, 10 I & N 409, 421. Low income or prior receipt of public cash assistance, while relevant, are not determinative where other factors suggest the capacity to be self-sustaining. Matter of Martinez-Lopez, supra. All factors must be considered prospectively, to foretell whether there is a likelihood that the alien will require public assistance in the future. Section 5.4(a)(4) of this Chapter should be consulted for a more detailed discussion of appeal strategies in denials based upon a finding that the applicant is likely to become a public charge under the traditional test.

If an applicant cannot pass the traditional public charge test, the alternative test will apply. An applicant who may have received public cash assistance for a brief period or periods of time during his or her years of residence in the United States should compare Congress' use of the phrase "reliance on public cash assistance" with the legalization program's special rule and its reference to "past receipt of public cash assistance."[258] "Reliance" indicates a long-term dependence on cash assistance as a principal source of income. The SAW applicant who is denied temporary resident status based on a finding that he or she is likely to become a public charge should argue that, although the provision would permit exclusion of an alien who "had been on welfare...for a substantial period of time,"[259] acceptance of some assistance is not preclusive. The argument should be supported by a discussion of the circumstances in the applicant's life which indicate a continuing prospect of future employment or the ability to be self-sustaining.

Given the unavailability of a waiver of INA §212(a)(15) for SAW applicants, it is particularly important that an applicant denied on this ground submit evidence of current employment with the filing of an appeal.

---

[258] Compare INA §§210(c)(2)(C) and 245A(d)(2)(B)(iii).

[259] See 103 Congressional Record H5908 (Daily Ed. June 15, 1984).

5.4(b)(5) Denials Based upon Untimely Filing

SAW applicants who were unable to submit their applications before the November 30, 1988 filing deadline[260] should consider appealing denials on this basis. Unlike INA §245A applicants, there is no provision in the statute barring SAWs from seeking administrative or judicial review of applications under INA §210 denied due to untimely filing.[261] SAW applicants who were prevented from filing timely applications because of various defects in the application procedure at the LOs or QDEs or due to INS' offending patterns and practices in implementing the IRCA should raise these issues on appeal.

For example, the INS has changed its regulations with regard to restricting the filing period for certain SAW applicants on at least two occasions. The regulations at 8 CFR §§210.2(b)(2) and 210.3(d)(2) initially required aliens who were apprehended by the INS or issued Orders to Show Cause after November 6, 1986 and before June 1, 1987 to file SAW applications within 30 days. The INS later rescinded these regulations, but it is not clear whether previous denials on this basis have been reopened. This is currently the subject of litigation in Guzman et al v. Nelson, No. 87-12060-Civ. Ryskamp (S.D. Fla.). Similarly, 8 CFR §210.2(c)(1), which required SAW applicants who reentered the United States after June 26, 1987 to apply from abroad, was also subsequently rescinded. Applicants who were erroneously denied on the basis of these regulations should seek to have their cases reopened and reconsidered pursuant to 8 CFR §103.5(b).

Aliens who met the eligibility requirements for temporary resident status under INA §210 and did not file timely applications due to misinformation by the INS regarding statutory eligibility and documentary requirements should consider making estoppel and due process arguments on appeal. These arguments are reviewed in the discussion of appeals of denials based upon untimely filings of pre-1982 legalization applications at §5.4(a)(6) of this Chapter, supra. Examples of aliens who might utilize such a strategy include cotton workers who were initially turned away by the LO's before the regulations at 7 CFR §1d were amended to make

---

[260] 8 CFR §210.1(b).

[261] But see 8 CFR §103.3(a)(2)(iv)(B) which provides that an appeal will be summarily dismissed if filed solely on the basis of a denial for failure to file an application under both INA §§210 or 245A in a timely manner.

cotton a qualifying agricultural commodity,[262] those who were not permitted to file their applications because they did not present employer records.[263]

5.5 APPEAL OF DENIAL OF WAIVER OF INELIGIBILITY

As discussed in Chapter One, a legalization applicant who seeks to overcome grounds of excludability under INA §245A(d)(2)(B)(i) and an applicant for SAW benefits under INA §210(c)(2)(B)(i) may be granted a waiver of certain specified grounds of ineligibility. A waiver may be issued under a combination or any one of the following three grounds: humanitarian purposes; to assure family unity; or when it is otherwise in the public interest.[264] As noted previously, in contrast to other waiver provisions under the INA, the applicant need not demonstrate extreme or exceptional hardship to obtain a waiver.[265]

The denial of an application for a waiver on grounds of family unity, humanitarian considerations or reasons in the public interest renders the alien ineligible for temporary residence as an excludable alien and will therefore be followed or combined with a decision denying the application. This may be appealed within 30 days in accordance with procedures set forth in §§5.1(a) and 5.1(b) of this chapter.

Denials of waiver applications should be subject to the same standard of review as that applied to the applications in chief. It therefore should be possible to supplement the waiver application on appeal with additional evidence not previously available.[266] Any additional documentation submitted should be accompanied by an explanation as to why the documentation was not presented with the original application. The applicant's personal affidavit, setting forth the grounds for the waiver, should be

---

[262] See National Cotton Council of America v. Lyng, CA-S-87-0200-C (N.D. Tex. 1988).

[263] See, Haitian Refugee Center v. Meese, ___F. Supp.___ (S.D. Fla) No. 88-1066 (Civ. Atkins, August 22, 1988).

[264] INA §§245A(d)(2)(B)(i); 210(c)(2)(B)(i).

[265] Compare, for example, INA §§212(h) and 212(e). Although the INS has clearly indicated that the legalization humanitarian and public interest waivers are to be adjudicated under a less strict standard, the applicant for a legalization waiver should draw from the concept of extreme hardship as developed in §212(h) waiver cases, as well as in suspension of deportation cases.

[266] 8 CFR §§103.3(a)(2), 210.2(f), 245a.2(p)

supported by objective documentary evidence or affidavits from other individuals, such as employers, community leaders, religious advisors, and relatives.

Although waiver applications are discretionary, IRCA's legislative history reveals that Congress contemplated that waivers under INA §§245A and 210 be granted liberally. "In most cases, denials of legalization on the basis of waivable exclusions should only occur when the applicant also falls within one of the specified nonwaivable grounds of exclusion."[267] Thus, it may be argued on appeal that there should be a presumption that waivers be granted consistent with the legislative intention that otherwise eligible applicants be accorded a lawful status in the United States.[268]

The regulations do not provide a definition of "humanitarian" or "public interest." The LAU, however, has indicated that these terms will be defined very broadly, consistent with the congressional intent to liberalize the standards for excludability waivers. In Matter of P,[269] the LAU granted a waiver of §212(a)(19) as in the public interest, citing the definition of public interest provided by Black's Law Dictionary as "something in which the public, the community at large, has some pecuniary interest, or some interest by which their legal rights or liabilities are affected.[270] Similarly, the LAU has defined humanitarian as "the promotion of human welfare..." and welfare as "health, happiness, and general well-being."[271] These are very broad standards that

---

[267] H.R. Rep. No. 9-115; 98th Cong., 1st Sess. 69-70. See also, INS Central Office Memorandum dated August 6, 1987.

268 Even the presence of adverse factors should not necessarily preclude the granting of a waiver. Compare, Matter of Mogharrabi, Int. Dec. #3208 (BIA-1987); Matter of Pula, Int. Dec. 3033 (BIA-1987) (in the absence of adverse factors, political asylum should be granted as a matter of discretion).

[269] Int. Dec _____ (Comm'r November 23, 1988). A copy of this decision can be obtained from the Legalization Issues Bank, Order No. L1288-422. Ordering information appears at the end of this Chapter.

[270] In Matter of P, the applicant was a businessman with significant monetary investments in the United States and was associated for seven years with a civic improvement organization for which he raised over 2 million dollars.

[271] LAU (August 23, 1988). A copy of this decision may be obtained from the Legalization Issues Bank, Order No. L1088-400. Ordering information appears at the end of this Chapter.

5-82

offer an opportunity for creative arguments, drawing on all aspects of an applicant's life.

"Family unity," on the other hand, is defined by the regulations as "maintaining the family group without deviation or change." The family group includes the spouse, unmarried minor children under 18 years of age who are not members of some other household, and parents who reside regularly in the household of the family group.[272] An applicant who has other family members in the United States who do not fit this restrictive definition should argue that other provisions of the regulations have been relaxed to encompass non-nuclear family situations, consistent with Congressional intent to administer the legalization program in a liberal and generous fashion.[273] If an applicant has family members, particularly U.S. citizens or lawful permanent residents, who do not reside in the household or who otherwise do not fit the above definition, he or she should also argue eligibility for a waiver under the broad humanitarian and public interests provisions, which encompass the concept of family unity.

The appeals brief should clearly specify upon which ground or grounds the applicant is basing his or her waiver application and the evidence which establishes eligibility under each ground. The brief should then identify each of the positive factors which would support a discretionary approval of the application. In cases where the applicant admitted the excludable act in the initial application, it should be argued that the admission of the excludable act is a forthright indication of honesty and fits within the public interest intent of Congress to allow a long term illegal resident to obtain legal status.[274] The positive factors should be weighed against any adverse factors that have been identified in the denial notice. Adverse factors will be present in all cases involving waiver applications, including the nature and underlying circumstances of the exclusion ground at issue; e.g., reliance on public welfare, the commission of fraud at entry or prior deportation from the United States. Other adverse factors, including violations of the immigration laws, may also surface in the presentation of the legalization application. Relying on guidelines utilized in the exercise of discretion in

---

[272] 8 CFR §§245a.1(m); 210.1(e).

[273] See cable from Richard Norton, INS Central Office, dated August 14, 1987, regarding affidavits of support, reproduced in 64 Interpreter Releases 970 (August 24, 1987).

[274] See letter from Joseph Thomas, INS Western Regional Processing Facility Director, to Attorney Ron Tasoff, reproduced in 64 Interpreter Releases 1328 (November 23, 1987).

other administrative applications,[275] the applicant should argue on appeal that the equities clearly outweigh the adverse factors and compel the approval of the waiver application as a matter of discretion.

The denial notice should indicate that the RPF has weighed and balanced all of the relevant factors in its exercise of discretion.[276] The federal courts, as well as the Board of Immigration Appeals, have required the INS to articulate the reasons behind its decisions in light of a full and fair evaluation of the record, in order for due process to be satisfied.[277] A denial based upon the failure of the RPF to properly consider all of the evidence of the record as a whole is arbitrary and an abuse of discretion.

An applicant who is excludable under INA §212(a)(9) for a conviction of a crime of moral turpitude may also wish to seek a waiver pursuant to INA §212(h), if he or she has the qualifying family relationships necessary to establish eligibility.[278] The INS has taken the position that waivers under INA §212(h) are not available to aliens applying for temporary resident status under §§245A and 210 and will therefore deny a waiver application pursuant to this provision. A discussion of how to present the argument on appeal of the denial of an INA §212(h) waiver appears at §5.4(a)(5)(C) of this Chapter, supra.

---

[275] See Matter of Marin, 16 I. & N. 581 (BIA 1978) [enumeration of factors to be considered in assessing eligibility for a waiver under INS §212(c)].

[276] See Universal Camera Corporation v. N.L.R.B., 340 U.S. 474, 488 (1951) (proper exercise of administrative authority requires that "(t)he substantiality of the evidence must take into account whatever in the record fairly detracts from its weight").

[277] See Santana-Figueroa v. INS, 644 F. 2d 1354 (9th Cir. 1981); Sida v. INS, 665 F. 2d 851 (9th Cir. 1981). See also, Matter of Correa, Int. Dec #2974 (BIA 1984).

[278] INA §212(a)(9) is not a waivable ground of exclusion under the legalization waiver provisions of INA §§245A(d)(2) and 210(c)(2). See discussion at §5.4(a)(5)(C) of this Chapter.

DATE:

88 JUL 27

UNITED STATES DEPARTMENT OF JUSTICE
IMMIGRATION AND NATURALIZATION SERVICE
SOUTHERN REGIONAL PROCESSING FACILITY
P.O. BOX 569710
DALLAS, TEXAS 75356-9710

▇▇▇▇▇▇▇▇▇▇▇▇
▇▇ La Vega Court SW
Albuquerque, NM 87105

REFER TO FILE NO:
A90▇▇▇▇▇▇

DECISION

Upon consideration, it is ordered that your Application for Temporary Resident Status (Form I-687) under Section 245A of the Immigration Reform and Control Act of 1986 be denied for the following reason(s):

SEE ATTACHMENT

You may appeal this decision to the Administrative Appeals Unit by completing the enclosed Form I-694, (NOTICE OF APPEAL) <u>in triplicate</u> and mailing them to this office together with one $50.00 fee in the form of a money order, cashier's check, or bank draft. Your NOTICE OF APPEAL must be received <u>within 30 days of the date of this notice</u>. Additional evidence, a brief, or other written statement in support of your appeal may be submitted with the NOTICE OF APPEAL. If no appeal is filed within the time allowed, this decision is final.

If a timely appeal is not submitted, all employment authorization previously granted by this Service will be automatically revoked.

Any questions which you may have will be answered by the local Legalization Office or by writing to the Regional Processing Center shown in the heading of this letter.

Sincerely,

[signature]

William J. Chambers
Director,
Regional Processing Facility

Enclosures: I-694

(Form I-692)

cc: ▇▇▇▇▇▇▇▇▇▇
    Attorney at Law

<u>DENIAL NOTICE</u>
5-85

gm

Attachment to Form I-692
A90[redacted]

On June 26, 1987 you filed an application to classify yourself as a temporary resident under section 245A of the Immigration Reform and Control Act of 1986.

Section 212(a) of the Immigration and Nationality Act states in part:

> "...the following classes of aliens shall be ineligible to receive visas and shall be excluded from admission into the United States:"

212(a)(17) excludes aliens who have been deported, arrested, have fallen into distress, or have been removed at government expense, unless consent to apply for admission has been granted by INS.

Further, 8 CFR 245a.2 (k) (2) states in part:

> :...the Attorney General may waive any other provision of section 212(a) of the Act only in the case of individual aliens for humanitarian purposes, to assure family unity, or when the granting of such a waiver is in the public interest. If an alien is excludable on grounds which may be waived as set forth in this paragraph, he or she shall be advised of the procedures for a waiver of grounds of excludability on Form I-690..."

You claim eligibility as an alien who illegally entered the United States at a place other than a designated port of entry in November 1978 and that you resided in the United States continuously in unlawfully status since that date.

Service records reveals that you were deported from Calexico, California to Mexico, on August 17, 1977 you failed to wait the five year period as required under Section 212(a).(17) of the Immigration and Nationality Act.

The documents submitted with your Application for Status as a Temporary Resident and Application for Waiver of Grounds of Excludability failed to establish you meet the criteria for approval of the waiver, in that you have no immediate family ties in the United States and there is no indication that your admission into the United States would serve in the public interest or humanitarian purposes.

You have been found to be excludable under Section 212(a)(17) of the Immigration and Nationality Act, in that you reentered into the United States within five (5) years from the date of deportation.

You have been found to be excludable under Section 212(a)(17) of the Immigration and Nationality Act. Insofar as the waiver you submitted has been denied, your application must be and is denied.
gm

DENIAL NOTICE
5-86

U.S. Department of Justice
Immigration and Naturalization Service

Notice of Appeal of Decision under Section 210 or 245A of the Immigration and Nationality Act.

OMB #1115-0135

In the Matter of: MOLINA- ███████	FEE STAMP
Application for: ☐ Permanent Residence ☒ Temporary Residence ☐ Waiver of Grounds of Excludability	File No.: A90 ███████ DOB ███████ A -

I hereby appeal to the Commissioner from the decision, dated **01-13-89** in the above entitled case.

☐ My written brief or statement is attached.   **Please see below.**

☐ I waive the right to submit a written brief or statement.

Briefly, state reasons for this appeal.

A. The undersigned requests a copy of all materials contained in the administrative record related to the applicant, including copies of the application, supporting documents, examiners worksheet, the entire contents of the INS "A" file and other material or information which was relied on as a basis for the denial.

B. The undersigned hereby requests 30 days from receipt of the record within which to file a brief in support of appeal.

APPELLANT (OR ATTORNEY OR REPRESENTATIVE) Please complete the following.

Name *(Type or Print)*

Address *(Street Name and Number)*

(City or Town)   *(State)*   *(ZIP Code)*

Title or Relationship to Appellant, if other than appellant.

Signature   Date
X

Form I-694 (04/01/87)   IMPORTANT - See instructions on Reverse Side of this Notice.

APPEAL NOTICE #1

Form I-694 Notice of Appeal Attachment
T---, R---; A90-_____

A. The undersigned requests a copy of all materials contained in the administrative record related to the applicant, including copies of the application, supporting documents, examiners worksheet, "A" file and other material or information which was relied on as a basis for the denial.

B. The undersigned hereby requests 30 days from receipt of the record within which to file a brief in support of appeal.

C. In addition to such other issues as may become apparent upon review of the record, appellant bases his appeal of the denial of his application for temporary resident status on the following:

1) The denial is based primarily on the applicant's alleged "fail[ure] to provide sufficient evidence of family unity, humanitarian or public interest reasons to qualify for [a waiver under 8 CFR §245a.2(k)(2)]." The denial is arbitrary, capricious and an abuse of discretion, and is against the weight of the evidence.

a) <u>Family Unity considerations</u> As regards family unity considerations, the RPF had ample evidence of the existence of such considerations in the applicant's case. On the applicant's I-687, submitted simultaneously with the waiver application form I-690, and made a part of the record to be considered by the Regional Processing Facility (RPF) at the time of the decision on the I-690, the applicant indicated that his brother Reynaldo B--- is a United States citizen; that his brother Jesus B--- is a United States citizen; that his brother Hugo M--- is an applicant for legalization; and that his brother Jose T---, also an applicant for legalization. The application further indicates that all of the applicant's above-named siblings reside in Albuquerque, New Mexico, as does the applicant. Furthermore, applicant's mother is an applicant for legalization and his step-father is a United States citizen. The applicant's brother Hugo and his mother have since been approved for Temporary Residence and have been issued I-688s. Documentation establishing Mr T---'s family member's status is attached. Inasmuch as the denial requires the applicant to prove eligibility for a waiver without reference to the I-687 application form, such a denial is arbitrary, capricious and an abuse of discretion. The fact that the denial of applicant's I-690 would result in his separation from his family was never considered in adjudicating his application and as such was arbitrary, capricious and an abuse of discretion.

If the denial could be upheld by the applicant's failure

APPEAL NOTICE #2 (ATTACHMENT)

to attach supporting documents regarding the status of his family members, and inasmuch as the status of certain family members has changed from that of legalization applicants to that of Temporary Residents, supporting documents are attached to the instant appeal. 8 CFR §103.3(a)(2)(i) allows for the consideration of new additional evidence on appeal. In view of the attached documentation and in view of such other reasons as are set forth in the instant appeal, applicant has met his burden and merits favorable discretion; the denial of the I-690 therefore should be overturned.

b) <u>Humanitarian considerations</u> Applicant also qualifies for a waiver under 8 CFR §245a.2(k)(2) based on humanitarian considerations. Applicant, previously employed as a freight handler, is currently unable to work due to a serious back injury suffered on the job which causes him pain on standing, sitting, and walking. He has been under the care of a doctor and receives worker's compensation payments. His need for regular medical attention, including back surgery, continues to this date. Documentation of his condition is attached. According to 8 CFR §103.3(a)(2)(i) additional new evidence can be presented and considered on appeal. In view of these reasons, applicant meets his burden of proof as to his waiver application based on humanitarian considerations; the denial of the application therefore should be overturned.

c) <u>Public Interest considerations</u> Applicant also qualifies for a waiver under 8 CFR §245a.2(k)(2) based on public interest considerations. In a letter written by Joseph L. Thomas, director of INS' Western Regional Processing Facility regarding the standard for the adjudication of waivers (attached), the forthrightness of the applicant in admitting entry pursuant to a Border Crossing Card obtained while maintaining a United States residence, in and of itself, qualifies the applicant for a waiver based on the public interest. This factor was not listed in the denial and was not considered by the RPF; the denial is therefore arbitrary, capricious, and an abuse of discretion.

d) The purpose of IRCA is ameliorative in nature. In passing IRCA, Congress intended that the legalization program be implemented in a liberal and generous fashion. <u>See</u> H.R. Rep. No. 99-682 Part One, 99th Cong., 2nd Sess. 72 (1986); <u>Ayuda v. Meese</u>, ___F.Supp.___ (D.D.C., Civil Action No. 88-0625, March 30, 1988). The legislative history of IRCA indicates that a waiver of excludability is to be granted unless some additional ground of excludability also applies. <u>"In most cases, denials of legalization on the basis of the waivable exclusions should only occur when the applicant also falls within one of the specified non-waivable grounds of exclusion."</u> H.R. Rep. No. 98-115, 98th cong., 1st Sess. 69-

APPEAL NOTICE #2 (ATTACHMENT)

70. In Mr. T---'s case, no other non-waivable ground of excludability exists. Mr. T--- also merits the favorable exercise of discretion. In this case, the RPF's interpretation of the waiver provisions contravenes the specific intent and purpose of the law.

2) The denial lacks specificity in that it is based, in part, on an alleged "fail[ure] to submit the required supporting documentation, specifically: proof of residence." The RPF's failure to specify what proof of residence was lacking provides inadequate notice of the defects in the application, and thereby prevents the applicant from preparing a response or curing said defects, in violation of due process. Furthermore, a denial on this basis is arbitrary, capricious and against the weight of the evidence. Supporting documentation presented at the Legalization Office establishes the required U.S. residence by a preponderance of the evidence.

D. As noted above, additional new evidence is submitted with this appeal pursuant to 8 CFR §103.3(a)(2)(i). This evidence, when viewed in combination with that previously presented, meets applicant's burden of proof as to eligibility for temporary residence under INA sec. 245A and as to a waiver under INA sec. 245A(d).

F. In view of the above, undersigned requests that the RPF reopen and grant the application sua sponte.

G. I reserve the right to amend this appeal upon receipt of the record in this matter and to submit additional documents for the Legalization Appeal Unit's consideration in accordance with 8 CFR §103.3(a)(2)(i).

APPEAL NOTICE #2 (ATTACHMENT)

GEORGETOWN UNIVERSITY LAW CENTER

Institute for Public Representation
Douglas L. Parker
Director
Laura Macklin
Associate Director
Elizabeth Fine
Yolanda R. Gallegos
S.E. Pietrafesa
Robert E. Richardson
Fellows
Sabrina Phoenix
Administrator

MEMORANDUM

To: Legalization Advisors

From: Virginia Garcia, Elizabeth Fine and Laura Macklin

Re: Freedom of Information Act Appeals

Date: December 17, 1987

Attached is a sample Freedom of Information Act appeal letter. The letter is essentially complete, although it contains blanks in which you can fill in information pertinent to each of your clients who need a Freedom of Information Act appeal. In addition, each appeal letter should have the words "Freedom of Information Appeal" clearly marked on both the letter and the envelope. Also, if you can describe the documents requested in more detail, this additional information may also be helpful to expedite agency action.

We would encourage you to routinely file appeal letters ten working days after filing the initial FOIA request. The advantages to this are, first, this may in fact expedite an agency response, and second, your client will be deemed to have exhausted his or her administrative remedies under 28 C.F.R. 16.7(e) in the event that no determination is made on his appeal within the twenty day time period and your client decides to pursue relief in federal district court. This additional step is also helpful in order to better show a need to review the administrative record in the event that the application for temporary residency is denied.

We hope that the above information and the attached sample appeal letter prove helpful. If you have any questions please do not hesitate to call Laura Macklin or Elizabeth Fine at (202) 662-9535.

Street Address: 25 E Street NW 3rd Floor Washington DC
Mailing Address: 600 New Jersey Avenue NW Washington DC 20001
202-662-9535

FOIA APPEAL
5-91

[SAMPLE] FREEDOM OF INFORMATION ACT
APPEAL LETTER

Date

Attorney General
Attention: Freedom of Information Appeals Unit
Department of Justice
Washington, D.C. 20530

Re: Freedom of Information Appeal
_____ (Name of Applicant)
_____ (A#)

Dear Madam or Sir:

We are writing on behalf of _____, (name of applicant) an applicant for temporary residency under §§245A and 210 of the Immigration and Nationality Act as amended by §§201 and 302 of the Immigration Reform and Control Act of 1986 ("IRCA"). This letter is to appeal the Immigration and Naturalization Service's failure to respond to his/her Freedom of Information Act request made pursuant to 5 U.S.C. §552(a)(b).

_____ (name of applicant) filed a Freedom of Information Act request on the Immigration and Naturalization Freedom of Information Act Form G-639 on _____ (date). He/she requested his/her A-file and included his/her date of birth _____, place of birth _____, his/her alien registration number _____, and (any other relevant information) _____ in order to help the Immigration and Naturalization Service locate his/her A-file. He/she submitted this Freedom of Information Act request to the Immigration and Naturalization Service District Office at _____ (address). [OPTIONAL: A photocopy of hes/her/ FOIA request is attached to this appeal letter.] Because _____ (name of applicant) did not receive a reply within the ten working day statutory time limit, he/she may treat this delay as a denial of his/her request and may file an appeal under 8 U.S.C. 103.10 and 29 C.F.R. 16.7.

We request a reply to _____'s (name of applicant) Freedom of Information Act appeal in an expeditious manner as legalization under the IRCA is a program of limited duration.

FOIA APPEAL

We expect a determination within the 20 working day time period under 28 U.S.C. 16.7(c). We understand that we have the right to seek judicial review under 28 U.S.C. 16.7(e) if the 20 working day time limit is not met. If you wish to discuss this appeal, please call or write to us at:

      Name of Qualified Designated Entity or Attorney
      Address:
      Phone number:

Thank you for your consideration.

                              Sincerely,

                            _____

[OPTIONAL: Attachment: FOIA Request]

<u>FOIA APPEAL</u>

REGIONAL PROCESSING FACILITY ADDRESSES

Northern Region
Alaska, Colorado, Idaho, Illinois, Indiana, Iowa, Kansas, Michigan, Minnesota, Missouri, Montana, Nebraska, North Dakota, Ohio, Oregon, South Dakota, Utah, Washington, Wisconsin, Wyoming.

The address of the Northern RPF is:

>   Federal Building and U.S. Courthouse
>   1000 Centennial Mall North, Room #B-25
>   Lincoln, NE 68508

Southern Region
Alabama, Arkansas, Florida, Georgia, Kentucky, Louisiana, Mississippi, New Mexico, North Carolina, Oklahoma, South Carolina, Tennessee, Texas.

>   Southern Regional Processing Facility
>   P.O. Box 569570
>   Dallas, TX 75356-9570

(Note that this address is _different_ from the RPF address used for the filing of appeals).

(Address for overnight/express mail services:)

>   1825 Market Center Blvd.
>   Dallas, Texas 75207

Eastern Region
Connecticut, Delaware, District of Columbia, Maine, Maryland, Massachusetts, New Hampshire, New Jersey, New York, Pennsylvania, Puerto Rico, Rhode Island, Vermont, Virginia, Virgin Islands, West Virginia. The address of the Eastern RPF is:

>   Post Office Box 968
>   Williston, VT 05495

(Note that this address is _different_ from the RPF address used during Stage One).

(Address for overnight/express mail services:)

>   Windersport Lane and Industrial Avenue
>   Williston, VT 05495

<u>Western Region</u>
Arizona, California, Hawaii, Nevada. The address of the Western RPF is:

>   Post Office Box 30030
>   Laguna Niguel, CA 92677-0030

(Note that this address is <u>different</u> from the RPF address used during Stage One).

(Address for overnight/express mail services:)

>   Chet Holifield Federal Building
>   24000 Avila Rd.
>   Laguna Niguel, CA 92677

Legalization Issues Bank

DESCRIPTION

The Legalization Issues Bank (LIB) is a joint effort of a number of different groups and organizations nationwide. Its purpose is to make sample briefs, pleadings, waiver applications, and other products of legal research available to assist representatives in filing appeals and litigation.

THE INDEXES

Access to the LIB can be obtained through four listings. The <u>Order Number Index</u> is a simple listing of the documents in the LIB. It is arranged numerically by the identifying number assigned to each included document.

The <u>Subject Index</u> lists the documents under the subjects to which they apply. The subjects are arranged alphabetically, and many are broken down into subtopics. This index does not include LAU decisions, which are covered in the fourth index, described below.

The <u>Sections Index</u> is arranged by section of the statute and the regulations. Under each section the documents are listed that directly address issues arising under that section.

The <u>LAU Decision Digests</u> lists summaries of recent decisions of the LAU under the subjects to which they apply.

THE ORDER NUMBER

To preserve the confidentiality of applicants, appeal briefs and decisions are "sanitized" : all identifying information is removed. Each document, therefore, is assigned an order number to act as a unique identifier. This number should be used when ordering a document.

The letter "L" is always a prefix to an LIB order number. Its sole purpose is to tell AILA, which maintains other brief and pleading banks, that this order pertains to the Legalization Bank. The L is followed by a four-digit number which indicates what month and year the document was added to the Bank. This is followed by a hyphen, then the actual number of the document.

Therefore, the number L0188-017, for example, indicates the 17th document that was added to the LIB in January 1988.

TO CONTRIBUTE DOCUMENTS

Sample briefs, waiver applications, and pleadings are still needed for all issues relating to legalization (including SAWs and Cuban-Haitian adjustment). To contribute a document, please block out all identifying information, and send to:

Crystal Williams
American Immigration Lawyers Association
1000 16th Street, NW
Washington, D.C. 20036
(202) 331-0046

HOW TO ORDER A DOCUMENT

Five organizations are acting as distributors for the LIB. Documents can be ordered from any one of them.

To obtain a document, send the order number(s) of the document(s) you want to any one of the distributors, along with a check made out to that distributor in the total amount of your order (prices are next to the order number). **If you are ordering from AILA, and you are located in Washington, D.C., please add 6% sales tax.**

Prices are to cover the actual costs incurred by the distributors in copying and mailing documents.

Order from any <u>one</u> of these organizations:

American Immigration Lawyers Association
1000 16th Street, NW
Suite 604
Washington, D.C. 20036
attn: Legalization Issues Bank
(202) 331-0046

Midwest Immigrant Rights Center
327 S. LaSalle, Rm. 1500
Chicago, IL 60604
attn: Craig Mousin
(312) 435-4500

Public Counsel
3535 West 6th Street
Suite 100
Los Angeles, CA 90020
attn: Susan Alva
(213) 385-2977

Texas Legal Services Center
815 Brazos, Suite 1100
Austin, TX 78701
attn: Jeff Larsen
(512) 477-6000

Volunteers of Legal Services
99 Hudson Street
New York, NY 10013
attn: Randye Retkin
(212) 966-4400

CHAPTER SIX

DENIALS OF PERMANENT RESIDENCE

6.1 APPEALS OF DENIALS OF PERMANENT RESIDENT STATUS   6-3

6.2 APPELLATE PROCEDURES   6-4

CHAPTER SIX

DENIALS OF PERMANENT RESIDENCE

6.1 APPEALS OF DENIALS OF PERMANENT RESIDENT STATUS

Administrative and judicial review of a denial of permanent resident status under both the legalization and SAW programs is limited by statute in the same manner as are applications for temporary resident status.[1] Administrative appellate review is based solely upon the administrative application and upon such additional or newly discovered evidence as may not have been available at the time of the determination.[2] Judicial review of a denial can only be had in the judicial review of an order of deportation under INA §106.[3] Such judicial review shall be based solely upon the administrative record established at the time of the review by the appellate authority and the findings of fact and determinations contained in such record shall be conclusive unless the applicant can establish abuse of discretion or that the findings are directly contrary to clear and convincing facts contained in the record considered as a whole.[4]

Applications which are denied do not result in the automatic termination or expiration of temporary residence. If the denied permanent resident applicant is still within the application period the I-688 remains valid. If the applicant is able to overcome the grounds of denial within the application period, than he or she may submit another application for permanent resident status with the correct fee.[5] If an appeal of the denial is filed, extensions of the I-688 will be granted during the pendency of the appeal. An alien whose application is denied will not be required to surrender his or her temporary resident card (I-688) until such time as the appeal period has tolled, or until the expiration date of the I-688, whichever is later.[6] Denied permanent resident applicants with valid I-688s have work authorization by operation of

---

[1] INA §245A(f)(1); INA §210(e)(2).

[2] INA §245A(f)(3)(B).

[3] INA §245A(3).

[4] INA §245A(f)(3); INA §210(e)(3).

[5] Interim rule 8 CFR §245a.3(h).

[6] Interim rule 8 CFR §245a.3(h).

regulation.[7] Employment authorization continues until a final decision has been rendered on an appeal or until the I-688 expiration date, if no appeal is filed.[8]

If the application is denied and the applicant does not file an appeal, the information in the application and obtained at the interview is protected by the confidentiality provisions and cannot be used to arrest or deport an individual, except in these cases involving fraud.

If the application is denied and the applicant files an appeal, the RPF will forward the entire file to the Legalization Appeals Unit (LAU). If the alien has requested the RPF to reconsider or reopen the LO's denial, it will review the case. If it decides to re-open it will enter an order, request additional information or documents or remand it to the LO with instructions.

If the application is denied the applicant will normally still maintain a valid I-688 with which he or she may seek to travel to and from the United States. What will happen when such denied aliens seek to reenter the United States is an open question. If the reasons for the denial of permanent residence do not constitute a grounds of excludability (e.g., 3 misdemeanors), the alien who retains a valid I-688 cannot be excluded and therefore should be able to deport and return to the United States without problems prior to the I-688 expiration date. If the denial stems from grounds which also render the alien excludable, the INS may not be able to exclude the alien as long as the I-688 remains valid. If the denial is on appeal to the Legalization Appeals Unit and is based on grounds which render the alien excludable, the practitioner must consider the questions of (1) whether the departure constitutes an abandonment of the appeal to the LAU, and (2) whether the departure was brief, casual and innocent and therefore noninterruptive of continuous residence so as to allow the alien's status to be determined in deportation rather than exclusion proceedings. It remains to be seen how the INS will approach these questions. Pending resolution of these issues, however, the departing alien must be realistic about the possibility of ultimately losing his or her case on the merits and must take certain precautions in order to place him or herself in the best possible legal position when departing. In all legal cases, deporting aliens should take care that departures will be viewed in the future as having been "brief, casual, and innocent," i.e., the temporary resident should document the date of departure, date of return, reason for departure, and proof of maintenance of U.S. residence.

---

[7] 8 CFR §245a.2(n).

[8] Interim rule 8 CFR §245a.3(h).

6.2 APPELLATE PROCEDURES

Under the legalization program,[9] certain rights and procedures attend the denial of a permanent residence application:

1. The applicant must be notified in writing of the decision.

2. If denied, the applicant must be notified of the specific reasons for the denial.[10]

3. No denials can be issued at local INS offices (district offices, suboffices, and legalization offices) until the entire record of proceeding has been reviewed.

4. No denials can be based on adverse information not previously furnished by the alien to the INS without providing the alien an opportunity to rebut the adverse information and to present evidence in his or her behalf.

    If inconsistencies are found between information submitted with the adjustment application and information previously furnished to the Service, the applicant shall be afforded the opportunity to explain discrepancies or rebut any adverse information.

Adverse decisions may be appealed to the Administrative Appeals Unit.[11] The procedures established for appealing the denial of an application for permanent residence are the same as those established for appealing the denial of an application for temporary resident status. The appeal form I-694 must be submitted to the Regional Processing Facility within 30 days of the Notice of Denial (3 days are added if the Notice of Denial is sent by mail). A notice of appeal received after the 30 days is tolled will not be accepted. The appellant has the right to submit additional or merely discovered evidence for consideration upon appeal.[12]

A brief in support of the appeal may be submitted with the Notice of Appeal or within 30 days of receipt of the appeal form

---

[9] Regulations regarding the appeal of a denial of permanent resident status under the SAW program have not been published as this book goes to press, but procedures should be substantially similar to those of the legalization program.

[10] Interim rule 8 CFR §245a.3(g).

[11] 8 CFR 103.1(f)(2).

[12] INA §245A(f)(3)(B).

at the Regional Processing Facility.[13] The interim regulations governing appeals of denials of permanent resident status under INA §245A are at variance with similar procedures governing appeals of temporary resident status. In both programs, the appellant or his or her representative may request a copy of the Record of Proceedings. However, according to Second Stage appellate procedures, once a review of the Record of Proceedings is requested,

> ...an additional thirty (30) days will be allowed for this review from the time the Record of Proceeding is photocopied and mailed. A brief may be submitted with the appeal form or submitted up to thirty (30) calendar days from the date of receipt of the appeal form at the Regional Processing Facility...For good cause shown, the time within which a brief supporting an appeal may be submitted may be extended by the Director of the Regional Processing Facility.

A clarification of this regulation is needed, as it appears to require the filing of an appellate brief prior to the review of the Record of Proceedings. The whole point of reviewing the Record of Proceedings is to adequately prepare the brief and respond to the basis of the denial.

In summary, the procedures for appealing an adverse decision are as follows:

1. File appeal notice I-694 in triplicate with he RPF within 30 days of the denial (within 33 days if the denial was mailed).

2. Include $50.00 filing fee in form of money order or cashier's check.

3. Request copy of record of proceedings and extension of time within which to file a brief, if necessary.

4. Submit new additional evidence, if available.

5. File brief within 30 days of submittal of notice of appeal or within time of extension granted by RPF.

---

[13] Interim rule 8 CFR 245a.3(i).

CHAPTER SEVEN

FEDERAL COURT LITIGATION AND REVIEW

7.1	DIRECT REVIEW OF ADMINISTRATIVE DENIALS	7-3
7.1(a)	Getting Into Deportation Proceedings	7-3
7.1(b)	Post-Deportation Procedures	7-7
	7.1(b)(1) Applicants with No Outstanding Orders of Deportation	7-7
	7.1(b)(2) Applicants Subject to Final Orders of Deportation	7-8
7.2	STRATEGIES FOR JUDICIAL REVIEW	7-9
7.2(a)	The Bitter With the Sweet?	7-9
7.2(b)	"Collateral" Judicial Review	7-12

CHAPTER SEVEN

FEDERAL COURT LITIGATION AND REVIEW

7.1 DIRECT REVIEW OF ADMINISTRATIVE DENIALS

There are a number of circumstances in which it may become necessary to seek federal judicial review or intervention in legalization cases. The most straightforward, though to date least common, situation is that of an applicant whose appeal is denied by the Legalization Appeals Unit (LAU). These applicants face an immediate and often painful dilemma.

As to the denial of both temporary resident status and permanent resident status, IRCA provides:[1]

"(A) Limitation To Review of Deportation--There shall be judicial review of such a denial only in the judicial review of an order of deportation under section 106."[2]

In order to understand the full import of this provision, its companion, INA §245A(f)(4)(B), 8 U.S.C. §1255a(f)(4)(B), must also be considered:

"Such judicial review shall be based solely upon the administrative record established at the time of the review by the appellate authority and the findings of fact and determinations contained in such record shall be conclusive unless the applicant can establish abuse of discretion or that the findings are directly contrary to clear and convincing facts contained in the record considered as a whole."

(Provisions for direct judicial review of denials of SAW worker's applications for temporary residence and for permanent residence contain identical wording).[3]

In addition, the practitioner should also note that INA §245A(f)(2), [8 U.S.C. §1255a(f)(2)(e)], purports to preclude all

---

[1] INA §245A(f)(4)(A), 8 U.S.C. §1255a(f)(4)(A).

[2] INA §106, 8 U.S.C. §1105a, provides, inter alia, that jurisdiction to review final orders of deportation is vested exclusively in the United States Courts of Appeal. Judicial review of final orders of exclusion must be accomplished by habeas corpus proceedings.

[3] See INA §§210(e)(3)(A) and (B), 8 U.S.C. §§1160(e)(1)(3).

7-3

review, administrative or judicial, of a denial of adjustment of status "based on a late filing of an application of such adjustment."[4]

It is thus apparent that direct judicial review of an administrative denial of benefits under IRCA was intended by Congress to occur exclusively in the courts of appeals and under a very deferential standard. This apparently simple scheme raises a number of complicated issues.

7.1(a) Getting Into Deportation Proceedings

An applicant whose case is denied by the LAU and who desires direct judicial review must somehow commence deportation proceedings. In most cases the only way to do this will be to physically present oneself to INS and to request the issuance of an Order To Show Cause.[5] Difficult as this may be emotionally, the applicant may face practical problems, as well. Some INS offices are reluctant to process those who simply "walk-in" requesting deportation. Therefore, the local Deportation section should be contacted to determine the most efficacious procedure.

Initially, it should be noted that this procedure may involve, for all practical purposes, the waiver by the applicant of the confidentiality protections of IRCA. This is not to say that an admission made to INS officials of foreign nationality or of the denial of the temporary residence application, constitutes a waiver of confidentiality which then allows INS to examine and use the contents of the application. It is clear that in the absence of fraud INS cannot divulge the application's contents to its own enforcement officers under penalty of criminal sanctions. Rather, the intent and purpose behind the statutory confidentiality protections is nullified if these protections do not extend to the review of agency actions. In enacting the confidentiality provisions the Congress, drawing from other country's experiences with "amnesty" programs, recognized the existence of a high level of distrust of the INS which would make many aliens reluctant to come "out of the shadows" and would seriously diminish the program's success. This fear of the INS and its power to deport which the Congress recognized is not diminished when a temporary residence application is denied, in fact it is likely to be heightened. Thus, for those whose applications for temporary

---

[4] But see, Doe and Roe v. Nelson, 1988 U.S. Dist. LEXIS15062 (challenge to regulation itself, independent of facts of individual case, held permissible). Note also that SAW applications are not barred from administrative or judicial review of denials based upon late filing.

[5] See 8 CFR §242.1.

residence are denied, IRCA's confidentiality provisions protect, at best, the names of family members, leaving the principal alien vulnerable to deportation.

Because of these potential consequences and the general fearfulness of those who have hidden from INS for so many years, it seems extremely unlikely that many applicants will submit to the statutory procedures. In making the decision whether to enter deportation proceedings, one significant factor to consider is the availability of other remedies within the authority of the Immigration Judge. Most applicants, for example, will likely be at least <u>prima facie</u> eligible for suspension of deportation under INA §244, 8 USC §1254.[6] Some might also be eligible for Political Asylum or Withholding of Deportation.[7] In such cases they could also be granted employment authorization <u>pendente lite</u>.[8] Even in these cases, however, a significant tactical dilemma is apparent. The IRCA denial cannot be raised before the Immigration Judge.[9] If the IRCA appeal seems more likely to succeed than other forms of relief, the applicant may be tempted not to fully prepare or present the suspension or political asylum case. As discussed more fully below, this could be a major procedural mistake in light of the difficulty in having a deportation hearing re-opened, should the IRCA denial be sustained. However, from the applicant's

---

[6] Such applicants must, in general:
1. Be deportable;
2. Have been physically present in the U.S. for a continuous period of not less than seven years immediately preceding the date of application (excluding "brief, casual and innocent absences" which do not "meaningfully interrupt the continuous physical presence");
3. Prove "good moral character" during the seven year period;
4. Prove that their deportation would result in "extreme hardship to the alien or to his [sic] spouse, parent, or child who is a citizen of the United States or an alien lawfully admitted for permanent residence."

<u>See</u> INA §244, for special restrictions on suspension of deportation for aliens deportable under INA §241(a)(4), (5), (6), (7), (11), (12), (14), (15), (16), (17), (18), (19), and aliens admitted pursuant to INA §101(a)(15)(J), <u>See also</u>, 8 CFR §244.

[7] <u>See</u> INA §101(a)42, 8 USC §1101(a)(42); INA §208, 8 USC §1158; INA §243(h), 8 USC §1253(h).

[8] 8 CFR §§208.4; 274a.12(c)(8), (10).

[9] INA §245A(f)(1) and (3), 8 USC §1255a(f)(1) and (3). For a contrary approach see INA §245, 8 USC §1255 (Adjustment of Status) and 8 CFR §245.2 (<u>de novo</u> hearing before Immigration Judge in deportation or exclusion proceeding after administrative denial).

perspective, the primary purpose of the deportation hearing under IRCA is as a jurisdictional prerequisite to judicial review of the IRCA denial. Few would surrender to pursue a suspension of deportation application. And those with strong political asylum cases would generally be better off first presenting the case "affirmatively" to the District Director.[10]

Employment authorization is also likely to be a major concern for applicants who are administratively denied under IRCA. While IRCA's regulations provide for work authorization during the pendency of a temporary resident application and subsequent appeal,[11] they are silent about work authorization after a denial by the LAU. The statute, on the other hand, provides for work authorization and a stay of deportation

> in the case of an alien who presents a prima facie application for adjustment of status under subsection (a) [relating to applications for temporary residence] during the application period, <u>and until a final determination on the application has been made</u> in accordance with this section (emphasis added)."[12]

Thus, the alien whose temporary residence application is denied at the LAU has a right to be issued work authorization until there is a "final determination," i.e., until and during deportation proceedings and direct judicial review result in a final determination, as set-forth in IRCA. SAW provisions also mandate work authorization for those who file and seek review of either a nonfrivolous temporary resident or permanent resident application "until a final determination on the application has been made in accordance with this section..."[13]

In such cases denied applicants would appear to qualify for work authorization whether or not an OSC were issued. Of course the question of whether the application presented a <u>prima facie</u> or nonfrivolous case might be raised to deny work authorization. Nonetheless, those who request employment authorization at INS will undoubtedly be interviewed for issuance of an OSC.[14]

---

[10] <u>See</u> 8 CFR §208.1.

[11] 8 CFR §§245a.2(n), 210.4(b).

[12] INA §245A(e)(1), 8 U.S.C. §1255a(e)(1).

[13] INA §210(d), 8 U.S.C. §1160(d).

[14] Query whether the statute can be read to require that employment authorization be issued by the LO (as opposed to the INS district office).

In most cases the INS will complete a form I-213 (reproduced at the end of this chapter) and the alien's admissions in response to the interviewing officer's questions will serve as the basis for the issuance of the Order to Show Cause, thus avoiding breach of IRCA's confidentiality provisions by INS.[15] In addition, the possibility that the applicant could be immediately arrested and placed in an INS Detention Facility cannot be overlooked.[16] Although most INS offices take the position that "those who walk-in, walk out", the authority to arrest is clear. The procedure at the hearing will likely be, to paraphrase Hobbes, "nasty, brutish and short": a simple concession of deportability. In order to achieve expeditious judicial review, the applicant is essentially compelled to waive all substantive and procedural protections available in deportation proceedings.[17] It is also not inconceivable that the applicant could be asked to disclose the identities of family members and friends at the hearing, depending on the form of relief, if any, sought.

7.1(b) Post-Deportation Procedures

7.1(b)(1) Applicants with No Outstanding Orders of Deportation

Assuming that the applicant has undergone deportation proceedings and been found deportable by the Immigration Judge, the next decision will be whether to appeal to the Board of Immigration Appeals (BIA).[18] If there were no collateral remedies sought in the deportation hearing, then there seems no reason to appeal. In this situation, the decision of the Immigration Judge would be "final" within the meaning of INA §242(b), 8 USC 1252(b) and INA §106 upon expiration of the appeal period.[19] If the applicant has been denied other relief, however, the tactical dilemma re-emerges. An appeal to the BIA will be time-consuming and may be expensive.

---

[15] See 8 CFR §242.1 (b).

[16] See INA §242(a), 8 USC §1252(a); 8 CFR §242.2.

[17] See, e.g., Wong Yang Sung v. McGrath, 339 U.S. 33, 70 S. Ct. 445, 94 L.Ed. 616 (1950) (general requirements of due process); Woodby v. INS, 385 U.S. 276 (1966), (INS must prove deportability by clear and convincing evidence); INS v. Lopez-Mendoza, 468 U.S. 1032, 104 S. Ct. 3479, 82 L.Ed.2d 778 (1984) (evidence obtained in fundamentally unfair manner or through egregious conduct by INS is suppressible).

[18] See 8 CFR §3.0, 8 CFR §292, OI 3.1-3.3. See also, INA §236(c), 8 USC §1226(c) regarding appeals of exclusion orders.

[19] 8 CFR §242.20 and 8 CFR §3.37.

The applicant may not have been granted employment authorization. Moreover, the IRCA administrative record, to which judicial review is confined per INA §245A(f)(3)(B), will become "stale" during the course of an administrative appeal, leaving the reviewing court with fewer options and making further proof, in the event of a remand, very hard to obtain. Thus, the applicant will again have to weigh all of these factors and assess both the relative likelihood of success on the merits of the legalization case versus other remedies and the relative benefits available from such remedies.[20]

7.1(b)(2) Applicants Subject to Final Orders of Deportation

Applicants who are subject to final orders of deportation from previous proceedings face special problems in seeking judicial review of denials under IRCA.[21] First, such applicants must consider the prospect of being arrested and deported within as little as 72 hours if the INS moves to execute an outstanding deportation order.[22] Also, if the applicant attempts to petition the Court of Appeals for review of the deportation order, it is likely that the court will dismiss the petition because INA §106(a)(1) mandates that, " a petition for review may be filed not later than six months from the date of the final deportation order."

The best procedural avenue in this scenario would appear to be a motion to re-open or re-consider pursuant to 8 CFR §§3.2 and 3.8., if the case was appealed to the BIA, and pursuant to 8 CFR §242.22 if there was no appeal.[23] This strategy, however, is far from simple. The immediate problem is that no automatic stay of deportation accompanies a motion to re-open or re-consider.[24]

---

[20] A successful asylum claim will eventually result in adjustment to permanent resident status. INA §209(b), 8 USC §1159(b); 8 CFR §209.2; see also, INA §244.

[21] See INA §245A(e)(i), 8 USC §1255a(e)(i); INA §245A (g)(2)(B)(i), 8 USC §1255a(g)(2)(B)(i); 8 CFR §245a (2)(a)(2).

[22] See INA §§242(c),(d) and (e), 8 USC §1252(c),(d) and (e); and 8 CFR §243.

[23] See 8 CFR §§103.5 and 103.7 for fees and requirements.

[24] Stays are automatic pending direct appeal of orders of deportation and exclusion. 8 CFR §3.6(a). A stay "may" be granted by the IJ or the BIA pending a decision on a motion to re-open or re-consider. 8 CFR §3.6(b), 8 CFR §242.22. See also, 8 CFR §243.4 regarding the authority of the District Director to grant a stay.

Therefore, the motion must be accompanied by a request for a stay. If the stay is denied, the denial itself must be appealed.[25]

The other problem with filing a motion to re-open or reconsider in the situation described above is that the applicant is really asking for nothing more than the entry of a new deportation order for the sole purpose of obtaining judicial review of the legalization denial. Generally, such a motion would be denied by the Immigration Judge or the BIA.[26] It is possible, of course, that the BIA, realizing the Scylla and Charybdis of the statute, will allow such motions as a matter of policy. If not, the applicant will have to seek review of the denial in the Court of Appeals pursuant to INA §106(a).[27] The applicant might also, in that proceeding, logically request review of the legalization denial as well, though the express language of INA §245A(f)(4)(A) seems to the contrary (judicial review of denial is permissible "only in the judicial review of an order of deportation...") (emphasis added).

7.2 STRATEGIES FOR JUDICIAL REVIEW

7.2(a) The Bitter With the Sweet?

It is apparent that the statutory scheme for judicial review presents substantial hurdles to the applicant for legalization whose case is denied. There are, however, a number of viable legal strategies available to the applicant who wishes to either avoid the deportation scenario or to achieve some review of a denial based upon late filing.

First, it is critical to understand that the restrictions imposed by IRCA on judicial review apply only to "denials". Both the plain language of the relevant sections and their interplay

---

[25] Such review must be sought in the District Court, generally pursuant to a Habeas Corpus petition.

[26] See Matter of D--, 5 I&N Dec.520 (BIA 1953), (IJ cannot re-open case solely to permit late appeal); Matter of Lennon, 15 I&N Dec. 9 (BIA 1974) (refusal to delay administrative proceedings to allow time for collateral remedies in federal courts), reversed on other grounds, Lennon v. INS, 527 F.2d 187 (2d Cir. 1975), See, generally, Martin, Judicial Review of Legalization Denials, 65 Interpreter Releases, 757 (August 1, 1988).

[27] For examples of how the Circuit Courts have dealt with applicants who may be eligible for legalization and who have cases pending on other issues see, De Preciado v. INS, 842 F.2d 240 (9th Cir. 1988); Arguelles-Vasquez v. INS, 844 F.2d 700 (9th Cir. 1988; Lopez-Rayas v. INS, 828 F.2d 1134 (5th Cir. 1987).

make this clear.[28] Thus, a variety of what might be termed "collateral" federal court actions, discussed in §7.2(b) below, are permissible. Initially, however, one might question whether Congress can constitutionally compel applicants for amnesty to surrender to deportation proceedings in order to obtain judicial review of denials under IRCA. Although a full analysis of this "bitter with the sweet" approach is beyond the scope of this work, a sketch of the dilemma may be useful.

There is no question that Congress has the power to limit appellate review of immigration matters, including denials under IRCA.[29] It is, however, extremely doubtful that Congress could preclude all judicial review of administrative action denying benefits.[30] Whenever the government seek to deprive any person of a constitutionally protected interest, due process is required by the Fifth Amendment. As the Supreme Court recently made clear, in a case involving termination from public employment:

> "...the Due Process Clause provides that certain substantive rights--life, liberty and property--cannot be deprived except according to constitutionally adequate procedures. The categories of substance and procedure are distinct..."Property" cannot be defined by the procedures provided for its deprivation anymore than can life or liberty..."[31]

---

[28] For example, the fact that INA §245A(f)(3)(B) mandates that judicial review be based, "solely upon the administrative record...", indicates that INA §245A(f)(1), which states, "There shall be no administrative or judicial review of a determination respecting an application for adjustment of status under this section except in accordance with this subsection" can only apply where there is a complete administrative record, i.e., in the case of a denial.

[29] See, e.g., Foti v. Immigration and Naturalization Service, 375 U.S. 217, 11 L.Ed 2d 281, 84 S. Ct. 306 (1963).

[30] See Hart, The Power of Congress to Limit the Jurisdiction of Federal Courts: An Exercise in Dialectic, 66 Harv. L.Rev. 1362 (1953); Traynor v. Turnage, 108 S. Ct. 1372 (1988); Interestingly, early Senate versions of IRCA did preclude all judicial review. S. Rep. No. 62, 98th Cong. 1st Sess. 53 (1983). S. 529, sec.301(a), 98th Cong., 1st Sess., 129 Cong. Rec. 6982-83 (1983).

[31] Cleveland Board of Education v. Loudermill, 470 U.S. 532, 541 (1984). See also, Board of Pardons v. Allen, 107 S. Ct. 2415, 2422 (1987) (parole denial); Mathews v. Eldridge, 424 U.S. 319 (1976) (social security benefits).

The constitutional requirement of due process certainly applies to aliens.[32] On proper facts, it is certainly possible to argue that a sufficient liberty interest is engendered by years of residence in the United States, close family ties,[33] or, perhaps, by the statutory benefit itself.[34] Due process is "flexible"[35], but in every case there must be an opportunity to be heard "at a meaningful time and in a meaningful manner".[36] The compulsion to surrender to deportation proceedings in order to vindicate rights under IRCA amounts to a deprivation of liberty which is not "preceded by notice and opportunity for hearing appropriate to the nature of the case".[37] This is true even though deportation has formalistically been held not to be punishment.[38] The alien, as discussed above, would be subject to arrest per INA §242 and would have to forfeit IRCA's guarantees of confidentiality.

For a variety of pragmatic reasons it seems generally more advantageous for the practitioner to proceed in one of the ways described in §7.2(b) below. For example, it is not clear what

---

[32] See Wong Wing v. U.S., 163 U.S. 228 (1896) (right not to be imprisoned at hard labor without judicial process); Russian Volunteer Fleet v. U.S., 282 U.S. 481 (1931) (property rights of non-resident aliens); Mathews v. Diaz, 426 U.S. 67, 77 (Fifth Amendment protects even one whose presence in this country is "unlawful, involuntary or transitory"); Plyler v. Doe, 102 S. Ct. 2382 (1982) (right to education for children of undocumented aliens).

[33] See, e.g., Ali v. INS, 661 F. Supp. 1234, 1246 (D. Mass. 1986), Chan v. Bell, 464 F. Supp. 125, 130 (D.D.C. 1978). See also, Polovchak v. Meese, 774 F.2d 731 (7th Cir. 1985) ("Liberty interest of family association" relevant to INS proceedings). But see, Kelly v. Smith, 684 F. Supp. 1113 (D. Mass. 1988), (close family ties held not to overcome congressional plenary power over immigration matters).

[34] See Loudermill, supra.

[35] Morrissey v. Brewer, 408 U.S. 471, 481 (1972)

[36] Mathews, 424 U.S. at 333.

[37] Mullane v. Central Hanover Bank and Trust Co., 339 U.S. 306, 313 (1950), Boddie v. Connecticut, 401 U.S. 371, 379 (1971). See also, Ostereich v. Selective Service System Local Board No.11, 393 U.S. 233, 243 (1968); Breen v. Selective Service System Local Board No. 16, 396 U.S. 460 (1970); Cf. Clark v. Gabriel, 393 U.S. 256 (1968); Fein v. Selective Service System Local Board No. 7, 405 U.S. 365 (1972).

[38] See INS v. Lopez-Mendoza, 468 U.S. 1032 (1984).

relief a District Court could grant even if the restrictions of IRCA were found unconstitutional. The affirmative grant of jurisdiction to the Courts of Appeals seems constitutional once the deportation component is removed. Therefore, a challenge of this sort appears likely to be brought only by an applicant, neither in detention nor facing imminent deportation, who is denied legalization by the LAU and who challenges no practices or regulations of INS. Nevertheless, it seems useful in all circumstances to endeavor not to lose sight of the forest for the trees.

7.2(b) "Collateral" Judicial Review

In order to challenge the constitutionality of particular aspects of IRCA, or its interpretation or administration by INS, the practitioner should consider alternatives to the draconian statutory requirements of administrative review followed by deportation proceedings. In order to do this, however, the action must be distinguished from a "denial".

Such cases may be brought in the District Courts, based upon the following:

a) INA §279, 8 U.S.C. §1329, which provides, inter alia:

> "The district courts of the United States shall have jurisdiction of all causes, civil and criminal, arising under any of the provisions of this title..."

b) 28 U.S.C. §2201 (The Declaratory Judgment Act):

> "In a case of actual controversy within its jurisdiction...any court of the United States...may declare the rights or other legal relations of any interested party seeking such declaration, whether or not further relief is or could be sought..."[39]

---

[39] See Navarro v. District Director of United States Immigration and Naturalization Service, 574 F.2d 379 (7th Cir. 1978), cert. denied, 439 U.S. 861.

c) 28 U.S.C. §2241:

"Writs of Habeas Corpus may be granted by...the district courts..." (See also, U.S. Constitution, Art.1, Sec.9, cl.2)[40]

d) 28 U.S.C. §1331:

"The district courts shall have original jurisdiction of all civil actions arising under the Constitution, laws or treaties of the United States."

e) 5 U.S.C. §701-706 (The Administrative Procedure Act), which provides for comprehensive judicial review of agency action except where such review is expressly precluded by statute.[41]

Collateral actions have arisen from a wide variety of situations. Some of the first cases involved applicants who claimed *prima facie* eligibility for legalization but who were denied stays of deportation. Cases of this type will almost invariably involve a request for the issuance of a Writ of Habeas Corpus.[42]

---

[40] Actual custody is not necessarily a jurisdictional prerequisite to habeas corpus relief. See, Flores v. United States Immigration and Naturalization Service, 524 F.2d 627 (9th Cir. 1975); U.S. ex.rel. Pon v. Esperdy, 296 F. Supp. 726 (D.C.N.Y. 1969); But see, Garcia v. Smith, 674 F.2d 838 (11th Cir. 1982).

[41] See Jean v. Nelson, 711 F.2d 1455 (11th Cir. 1983); But see, Abdelhamid v. Ilchert, 774 F.2d 1447 (9th Cir. 1985) (USIA refusal to grant waiver not reviewable); Hotel and Restaurant Employees Union Local 25 v. Att'y General of U.S., 804 F.2d 1256 (D.C. Cir. 1986) (decision not to grant extended voluntary departure not reviewable under 5 U.S.C. §701).

[42] See, e.g., Farzad v. Chandler, 670 F. Supp. 690 (N.D. Texas 1986), No.3-87-0256-6 (N.D. Texas 1988) (challenge to deportation order base on INS alleged misinterpretation of "known to the government"); Doe v. District Director, INS, 697 F. Supp. 694 (S.D.N.Y. 1988); (unsuccessful challenge to deportation order and detention; failure to exhaust administrative remedies held dispositive); Bailey v. Brooks, 688 F. Supp. 575 (1987) (detention upon re-entry from brief trip to Canada); Gutierrez v. Ilchert, 682 F. Supp. 467 (N.D. Cal. 1988) (detention upon re-entry from 3 week visit to Mexico in May 1987); Hernandez v. Gregg, 813 F.2d 633 (3d Cir. 1987) (incarceration of "Mariel" Cuban parolee upheld pending resolution of legalization case; Kalaw v. Ferro, 651 F. Supp. 1163 (W.D.N.Y. 1987) (preliminary injunction granted staying deportation pending LAU review of "known to the government" case.

In cases that do not involve immediate threats of imprisonment or deportation, practitioners have generally sought relief pursuant to the Administrative Procedure Act and the Declaratory Judgment Act. Although such cases have involved a wide variety of specific challenges to INS actions, they must initially be distinguished from reviews of "denials" [which could not be reviewed by a District Court under INA §245A(f)].

Simply attempting to characterize such a case, in general terms, as a challenge to INS regulations or practices may not be sufficient.[43] The District Courts have, however, appeared generally willing to decide cases that are clearly distinguished from mere challenges to specific, individual denials.[44] Though applicants are, of course, required to exhaust administrative remedies.[45]

For obvious reasons, cases which can be certified as "class actions" pursuant to F.R.C.P. Rule 23 are less likely to be viewed as attempts to circumvent INA §245A (f).[46] But see, Doe and Roe v. Nelson, supra, "...the INS cannot seriously argue that a pattern of constitutional violations becomes intolerable only once a threshold number of people are victimized..."

After LAU denial, District Court permitted further judicial review in context of Habeas Corpus petition.)

[43] See Kashani v. Nelson, 793 F2d 818,823 (7th Cir. 1986), cert. denied, 479 U.S. 1006 (1986).

[44] See, e.g., Doe and Roe v. Nelson, No. 88-C-6987 (N.D. Ill. 1988), in which plaintiffs challenged the "30 day rule" of 8 CFR §245a (2)(a)(2)(i). The government argued, inter alia, that the suit was barred by INA §245A(f)(2). The Court, noting that plaintiffs challenged "the methods" of INS and not the specific denial, allowed the cause of action to go forward. See also, Haitian Refugee Center, Inc., v. Nelson, 694 F. Supp. 864 (S.D. Fla. 1988); Vargas v. Meese, 682 F. Supp. 591 (D.D.C. 1987); Hernandez v. Meese, No.8-88-385 (E.D. Cal. Aug. 11, 1988); Zambrano v. INS, No. 8-88-455 (E.D. Cal. Aug. 9, 1988).

[45] See, e.g., MacDonnell v. INS, 693 F.Supp. 1439 (SDNY 1988).

[46] See LULAC v. INS, No.87-4757-WDK (C.D. Cal. 1988); Ayuda, Inc. v. Meese, 687 F. Supp. 650 (1988); Bamondi v. INS, No. 88-1410-KG (S.D.Cal. 1988); Catholic Social Services v. Meese, No. 5-86-1343-LKK (E.D. Cal. 1987); 813 F.2d 1500 (1987); CIPRA v. Meese, No.99-1088 (D.D.C. 1988); HRC v. Nelson, supra; Hernandez v. Meese, supra.

A full analysis of the specific challenges which have been brought involving IRCA is beyond the scope of this work. Generally, however, the cases are based upon the following:

1. An INS practice or regulation that conflicts with the language of the statute.

Challenges to agency regulations must first look to the plain language of the relevant statute. If this is clear, it obviously must control.[47] If a court determines that Congress has not directly addressed the precise question at issue, the court must determine whether the agency's construction generally comports with the congressional intent.[48] Courts will grant considerable deference to an executive agency's construction of the statute it is entrusted to administer.[49] Historically, this has been especially true of immigration laws.[50] In determining the intent of Congress, courts will look to the legislative history of prior enactments, the specific history of the statute, committee reports and, to some extent, prior agency interpretations.[51] Also, all parts of a statute are to be construed, if possible, to be harmonious.[52] Regarding IRCA, it appears clear that the fundamental intent of Congress, at least as to legalization, was that it be implemented "in a liberal and generous fashion."[53]

2. An INS practice or regulation that conflicts with other INS regulations.

This argument has been made primarily in opposing INS denial of legalization to students who withdrew from school prior to January 1, 1982. Other regulations make clear that such students

---

[47] Chevron U.S.A., Inc, v. Natural Resources Defense Council, Inc., et al., 467 U.S. 837, 842, 81 L.Ed.2d 694, 104 S. Ct. 2778 (1984).

[48] See FEC v. Democratic Senatorial Campaign Committee, 454 U.S. 27, 32 (1981).

[49] See Chevron, supra.

[50] See Landon v. Plascencia, 459 U.S. 21 (1982); Kleindienst v. Mandel, 408 U.S. 753 (1972).

[51] See Ford Motor Company v. Cenance, 452 U.S. 155 (1981).

[52] Richards v. United States, 369 U.S. 1 (1962).

[53] See H.R. Rep. No. 99-682(I), 99th Cong., 2d Sess. (1986) at 72.

were considered by INS to be out of status.[54] INS must follow its own regulations and certainly cannot disregard prior-enacted regulations in adjudicating legalization cases.

3. An INS practice or regulation violates due process or equal protection.

Where, for example, INS has prevented the timely filing of applications by failing to provide proper information or forms, a court could find a potential deprivation of liberty without due process. As noted above, although the due process rights of undocumented aliens are limited, they are cognizable.

Similarly, if INS has drawn a distinction, such as that between individuals on "A" and "G" visa who terminated their employment before January 1, 1982 and students who quit school before January 1, 1982, which appears arbitrary and irrational, it may violate an applicant's equal protection rights.[55] Although constitutional claims are obviously complex and difficult to win, practitioners should remember that courts recognize a strong presumption that Congress intended review of constitutional questions.[56]

A more comprehensive discussion of all federal court remedies and jurisdictional issues is beyond the scope this work. However, a detailed discussion can be found in *Immigration Law and Defense*, Clark Boardman (1988), Chapter Ten, Federal Judicial Review, by National Immigration Project member Ira Kurzban. Extensive seminar materials on federal court remedies are also available from the National Immigration Project.

---

[54] See 8 CFR §214.2(f).

[55] See *Plyler v. Doe*, supra.

[56] See *Doe and Roe*, supra, quoting *Traynor v. Turnage*, 108 S. Ct. 1372 (1988).

RECORD OF DEPORTABLE ALIEN

FORM I-213

CHAPTER EIGHT

TERMINATION OF TEMPORARY RESIDENCE

8.1 GROUNDS FOR TERMINATION OF TEMPORARY RESIDENT STATUS
    OBTAINED THROUGH THE LEGALIZATION PROGRAM, INA §245A   8-3

    8.1(a)   Waiver of Excludability Grounds   8-4
    8.1(b)   Procedure for Termination of Temporary
                 Resident Status   8-5
    8.1(c)   Effect of Termination of Lawful Temporary   8-6
                 Resident Status   8-8

8.2 REVOCATION OF TEMPORARY RESIDENCE - SAWS   8-9

    8.2(a)   Grounds for Termination of Temporary Resident
                 Status Obtained through the SAW program,
                 INA §210   8-9
    8.2(b)   Grounds of Deportation   8-10

CHAPTER EIGHT

TERMINATION OF TEMPORARY RESIDENCE

INA §§245A and 210 provide for the "termination" of temporary resident status, causing the alien to return to the unlawful status held prior to becoming a temporary resident. The grounds and procedures for termination of temporary resident status vary depending upon the program through which the alien was granted status.

8.1 GROUNDS FOR TERMINATION OF TEMPORARY RESIDENT STATUS OBTAINED THROUGH THE LEGALIZATION PROGRAM, INA §245A[1]

An alien lawfully admitted for temporary resident status under INA §245(a)(1) may have his or her status terminated at any time in accordance with INA §245A(b)(2). According to this provision, temporary resident status may be terminated upon the occurrence of any of the following:

(1) if it appears that the alien was in fact not eligible for temporary resident status under INA §245A (eligibility requirements are summarized in Chapter One); or

(2) if the alien commits an act which renders him or her inadmissible as an immigrant, except as to those exclusion grounds which are inapplicable or as to those grounds which can be waived as provided under INA §245A(d)(2) (set forth below), and a waiver is secured;

(3) the alien is convicted of a felony, or of three or more misdemeanors committed in the United States; or

(4) at the end of the thirty-first month beginning after the date the alien was granted status, unless the alien has filed an application for adjustment of status to lawful permanent resident and the application period has not been denied[2] (however the exact method of calculating the application should be carefully reviewed).[3]

---

[1] IRCA provisions relating to termination of temporary residence were incorporated into the legalization program for EVD nationals. See Pub. L. No. 100-204, 902; 101 Stat. 1332.

[2] INA §245A(b)(2), 8 CFR §245a.2(u)(1).

[3] See the discussion in Chapters Two and Three, supra.

Under the first two provisions, a variety of conduct, particularly conduct prescribed by the 33 grounds of exclusion, could result in the termination of temporary resident status. However, termination is governed by the same limitations on the application of the exclusion grounds as applied to the original application for temporary residence. Thus the following grounds of excludability, normally applicable to aliens seeking entry either as immigrants or nonimmigrants, have been circumscribed by IRCA in their applicability to the termination of temporary resident status:

Inapplicable Grounds Of Excludability

212(1)(14)	Aliens coming to perform skilled or unskilled work in the United States without a labor certification;
212(a)(20)	Aliens not in possession of a valid visa or passport;
212(a)(21)	Aliens entering with a visa issued in violation of INA §203 numerical limits;
212(a)(25)	Illiterates;
212(a)(32)	Graduates of foreign medical schools who have not passed the appropriate visa qualifying examination.

Grounds of Excludability Which Cannot be Waived

212(a)(9)	Aliens convicted of a crime of moral turpitude (other than a purely political offense and certain crimes committed while under the age of 18), or aliens who have admitted committing such a crime;
212(a)(10)	Aliens convicted of two or more offenses, regardless of whether they arose from a single trial or scheme, if the aggregate sentence of confinement was for five years or more;
212(a)(27)	Aliens who are threats to national security;
212(a)(28)	Anarchists, communists and subversives;
212(a)(29)	Threats to the national security and subversives;
212(a)(33)	Aliens who assisted in Nazi persecution.

Grounds of Exclusion Which Can be Waived

212(a)(1)	Aliens who are mentally retarded;
212(a)(2)	Aliens who are insane;
212(a)(3)	Aliens who have had 1 or more attacks of insanity;
212(a)(4)	Aliens afflicted with psychopathic personality, sexual deviation, or mental defect;
212(a)(5)	Narcotic drug addicts or chronic alcoholics;
212(a)(6)	Aliens with dangerous contagious diseases;
212(a)(7)	Aliens with a physical disability affecting ability to earn a living;
212(a)(8)	Paupers, professional beggars or vagrants;
212(a)(11)	Polygamists;
212(a)(12)	Procurers and prostitutes;

212(a)(13)	Aliens entering to engage in any immoral sexual act;
212(a)(15)	Aliens likely to become public charges;
212(a)(16)	Aliens excluded within one year prior to the date of application;
212(a)(17)	Aliens deported within five years prior to the date of application unless the Attorney General consents to their admission;
212(a)(18)	Stowaways;
212(a)(19)	Aliens who have procured or sought to procure a visa or other documentation by fraud or willful misrepresentation of a material fact;
212(a)(22)	Aliens who are ineligible to citizenship and draft evaders;
212(a)(23)	Any alien convicted of a drug related offense or in whose case there is reason to believe the alien engaged in trafficking;
212(a)(24)	Aliens who arrived on non-signatory transportation lines;
212(a)(26)	Aliens lacking valid passports;
212(a)(30)	Aliens accompanying an alien excluded due to physical or mental problems;
212(a)(31)	Aliens who assisted any other alien to enter the United States in violation of law.

8.1(a) Waiver of Excludability Grounds

INA §245A(d)(2) states that in determining admissibility for purposes of INA §245A(b)(2)(B) [termination of temporary resident status], all of the exclusion grounds and waiver provisions applicable to Phase I applications apply.[4] This would include termination based on ineligibility for temporary resident status at the time of application and termination based on conduct which arose after obtaining temporary residence and which falls within the grounds of excludability.[5] The procedures for waiving such grounds are unclear. However, the regulations provide for termination if

"The alien commits an act which renders him or her inadmissible as an immigrant, unless a waiver is secured pursuant to §245a.2(k)(2) [regulation relating to waiver of exclusions grounds]."

---

[4] INA §245A(d)(2).

[5] The statute allows for termination "if the alien commits an act that (i) makes the alien inadmissible except as otherwise provided under subsection (d)(2) [specifying inapplicable grounds, providing for a waiver of certain other grounds] [emphasis added]."

This would indicate that if the INS contemplates terminating temporary residence based on the commission of an act which comes within one of the grounds which is waivable, INS must first give the alien the opportunity to seek a waiver.

As to the grounds of excludability set forth above, IRCA provides that these grounds of excludability may be waived for reasons of family unity, humanitarian considerations or the public interest.[6] The implementing instructions and caselaw which discuss the factors considered in adjudicating such waivers are discussed in Chapter One.

8.1(b) Procedure for Termination of Temporary Resident Status

Statutory and regulatory provisions relating to the termination of temporary resident status set forth the following procedures:

1. <u>Notice of Intent to Terminate</u>. The regulations do not specify who has the authority to issue a Notice of Intent to Terminate, although given IRCA's confidentiality protections, the RPF is the most logical and probable candidate. Due process would require that the Notice of Termination set forth with specificity the reasons for the termination. The alien must be given an opportunity to offer evidence in opposition to the grounds alleged 1for termination. Such evidence must be submitted within thirty (30) days of service of the Notice of Intent to Terminate.[7]

2. <u>I-690 Waiver of Grounds of Excludability</u>. If the INS seeks to terminate temporary resident status due to ineligibility for that status because the alien was excludable at the time of application, and if the grounds of excludability is one that is waivable under IRCA, the alien must be given the opportunity to seek a waiver. Likewise, if termination is based on conduct occurring after obtaining temporary resident status and that conduct falls within a grounds of excludability which is waivable under IRCA, the alien must be given an opportunity to seek a waiver. Note that a waiver of excludability under the public charge provisions, INA §212(a)(15) is only restricted as to applicants for

---

[6] INA §245A(d)(2).

[7] 8 CFR §245a.2(u)(2).

permanent resident status; a waiver of those grounds is available in the termination context.[8]

The request for a waiver should be submitted to the RPF on Form I-690 within 30 days of the Notice of Intent to Terminate.

3. **Notice of Termination.** If after receipt and review of the administrative record, the INS decides to terminate status, the Director of the Regional Processing Facility will notify the alien of the decision on Form I-692 (Notice of Denial), of the reasons for termination, and that any Form I-94, Form I-688, employment authorization, advance parole, or travel document will be declared void by the director of the Regional Processing Facility if no appeal of the termination decision is filed within 30 days.[9] The notice must include copies of the Form I-694 Notice of Appeal and must advise the alien that any appeal may be accompanied by new evidence and a supporting brief, if desired. The notice must also advise the alien that if he or she fails to appeal, the Form I-692 will serve as a final notice of ineligibility.[10] The Notice of Termination of the alien's status must be made only by certified mail directed to the alien's last known address, and to his or her representative.[11]

4. **Appeal of Termination.** The alien may appeal the decision to terminate lawful temporary resident status to the Associate Commissioner, Examinations (Administrative Appeals Unit)[12]. The notice of appeal must be filed in triplicate with the required fee shall be filed within thirty (30) days after the service of the notice of termination to the alien on Form I-690.[13] The appeal may be accompanied by new evidence and a supporting brief, if desired. The decision on the appeal must be in writing, and if dismissed, must include a final notice of ineligibility. A copy of the decision must be served upon the applicant and his or her attorney or

---

[8] INA §§245A(d)(2), 245A(b)(2)(B).

[9] 8 CFR §245a.2(u)(2).

[10] 8 CFR §§103.3(a)(2)(i), (ii).

[11] 8 CFR §245a.2(u)(2).

[12] 8 CFR §103.1(f)(2).

[13] 8 CFR §§245a.2(u), 103.3(a)(2)(i), (ii).

representative of record. No further administrative appeal shall lie from this decision. The application may not be filed or reopened before an immigration judge or the Board of Immigration Appeals during exclusion or deportation proceedings.[14]

5. <u>Failure to Appeal Termination</u>. If no appeal is filed temporary resident status is terminated and the I-94, I-688 or other official document shall be deemed void, and must be surrendered without delay to an immigration officer or to the issuing INS office.[15] If the alien fails to appeal, the form I-692 will serve as a final notice of ineligibility.[16]

6. <u>Judicial Review</u>. Although the regulations provide that "[t]he entry of a final order of deportation is not necessary in order to terminate temporary resident status,"[17] the statutory scheme pertaining to judicial review of determinations under IRCA applies to termination proceedings, i.e., judicial review of a decision to terminate temporary resident status can only be had through appeal of a deportation order under INA §106. The application may not be filed or reopened before an immigration judge or the Board of Immigration Appeals during exclusion or deportation proceedings.[18]

8.1(c) Effect of Termination of Lawful Temporary Resident Status

Termination of the status of an alien granted lawful temporary residence under INA §245A(2) shall act to return the alien to the unlawful status held prior to the adjustment. This renders the alien amendable to exclusion or deportation proceedings under §§ 236 or 242 of the INA, as appropriate.[19] However, the confidentiality provisions will prevent the use of the information contained in the application for temporary residence in deportation proceedings, unless the grounds for termination pertain to fraud in the making of the application.

---

[14] 8 CFR §§103.3(a)(2)(i), (iii).

[15] 8 CFR §245a.2(u)(2).

[16] 8 CFR §103.3(a)(2)(i), (ii).

[17] 8 CFR §245a.2(t).

[18] 8 CFR §103.3(a)(2)(i), (iii).

[19] 8 CFR §245a.2(u)(4).

8.2 REVOCATION OF TEMPORARY RESIDENCE - SAWS

8.2(a) Grounds for Termination of Temporary Resident Status Obtained through the SAW program, INA §210

In contrast to the grounds for termination of temporary residence obtained through the legalization program, a SAW's temporary residence may be terminated "during the period of temporary resident status...only upon a determination under this Act that the alien is deportable."[20] The regulations amplify this by providing that

> The temporary resident status of a special agricultural worker is terminated automatically and without notice under section 210(a)(3) of the Act <u>upon entry of a final order of deportation</u> by an immigration judge based on a determination that the alien is deportable under section 241 of the Act.[21]

This poses many practical problems, given the fact that the contents of the application are confidential, with the exception of investigations of fraud in the obtaining of temporary residence. Thus, in most cases the INS must seek termination of temporary resident status based on the alien's subsequent acts which render him or her deportable, without reference to the contents of the SAW application.

Because one of the grounds of deportability is excludability at the time of admission or application for temporary residence, the INS can to some extent review whether the alien was excludable when applying for temporary residence. If the alien is determined or suspected of having been excludable at the time of application for temporary residence, INS investigators cannot proceed on the assumption that this excludability was deliberately concealed in order to obtain temporary residence, hence fraud was committed, and hence they may review the file regarding the temporary residence application. Rather, INS investigators must forward information regarding the basis for the grounds of excludability to the Director of the RPF who can determine whether a waiver of excludability was granted so that a determination can be made on the question of excludability or fraud in the securing of temporary resident status.

---

[20] INA §210(a)(3), 8 U.S.C. §1160(a)(3); interim rule 8 CFR §210.4(d)(1).

[21] Interim rule 8 CFR §210.4(d)(1).

8.2(b) Grounds of Deportation

The following are grounds for deportation under INA §241(a):

(1) Excludable at entry, i.e., within any of the 33 grounds of excludability as of any entry to the United States or adjustment of status (discussed below);*

(2) Entered without inspection or in violation of the INA;

(3) Has become institutionalized at public expense within 5 years of entry to the U.S.;

(4) Convicted of a crime of moral turpitude within 5 years of entry and sentenced to 1 year confinement; or convicted of two crimes of moral turpitude not stemming from the same scheme of criminal conduct;*

(5) Failed to notify INS of change of address;

(6) Anarchists and communists [same as INA §212(a)(28)];

(7) Security risks, subversives [same as INA §§212(a)(27), (29)];

(8) Became a public charge within 5 years of entry to the U.S.;

(9) Failed to maintain nonimmigrant status;

(11) Became narcotic drug addict after entry to the U.S.; narcotics conviction;*

(12) Prostitution [same as INA §212(a)(12)];*

(13) Alien smuggler (for gain);

(14) Automatic/semiautomatic weapons violations; after 1-1-89, possession of a firearm or bomb;

(15)-(16) Violations of Alien Registration Act;

(17) Violations of the neutrality laws;

(18) Convicted of importing alien for immoral purposes;

(19) Nazis;

(20) RAWs who fail to comply with work requirements.

An asterisk (*) indicates that the excludability grounds may be waivable under INA §241(f)(1) or §212(h). In the event the alien is granted a waiver, any proceedings to terminate the alien's status will be concluded, and the alien will be so informed.[22] It must be noted that "excludable at the time of entry" refers to <u>any</u> entry to the United States undertaken after temporary resident status was granted.

An alien who is excludable under INA §210(c), but who is not deportable under INA §241, is not subject to termination of temporary resident status provided that the ground of excludability arose subsequent to the adjustment of the alien's status to temporary resident.[23]

In circumstances in which the alien is deportable under INA §241(a)(1) because he or she was excludable at the time of his or her adjustment of status to temporary resident, the alien shall be advised of the procedures for applying for a waiver of grounds of excludability on Form I-690, if such a waiver is available under INA §210(c).

An alien whose temporary resident status has been terminated shall, upon demand, promptly surrender to the District Director having jurisdiction over the alien's place of residence or (in the case of a commuter) place of employment, the Form I-688, Temporary Resident Card, issued at the time of the grant of Temporary Resident status.[24]

---

[22] 8 CFR §210.4(d)(2).

[23] 8 §CFR 210.4(d)(1).

[24] 8 CFR §210.4(d)(3).

CHAPTER NINE

REPLENISHMENT AGRICULTURAL WORKERS PROGRAM

9.1	GENERAL DESCRIPTION OF THE RAW PROGRAM	9-3
9.2	BASIC ELIGIBILITY REQUIREMENTS	9-4
9.3	PROPOSED PROCEDURES	9-5
9.4	REGISTRATION PHASE	9-7
9.4(a)	Determination of Groups Allowed to Register	9-7
9.4(b)	Prior "Agricultural Employment" Requirement	9-8
9.4(c)	"Seasonal Agricultural Services"	9-10
9.4(d)	Denied and Unadjudicated SAW Applications	9-11
9.4(e)	Agricultural Workers Who Were Not Among the Eligible Rejected SAW Applicants	9-13
9.4(f)	Priority Consideration of Certain Registrants	9-13
9.4(g)	Registration Procedures	9-14
9.5	PETITION PHASE	9-15
9.6	INTERVIEW	9-16
9.6(a)	General Considerations About the Submission of Documents	9-18
9.6(b)	Proof of Identity and Age	9-19
9.6(c)	Evidence of Family Relationship	9-20
9.6(d)	Employment Documentation	9-21
9.6(e)	Admissibility	9-23
9.7	DECISION ON RAW APPLICATION	9-25
9.8	OBLIGATIONS OF TEMPORARY RESIDENTS UNDER THE RAW PROGRAM	9-27
9.9	RIGHTS OF TEMPORARY RESIDENTS UNDER THE RAW PROGRAM	9-29
9.10	PROCEDURE FOR ADJUSTMENT TO PERMANENT RESIDENCE STATUS	9-30
9.11	TERMINATION OF TEMPORARY RESIDENT STATUS AND DEPORTATION UNDER THE RAW PROGRAM	9-31

CHAPTER NINE

RAW PROGRAM

9.1 GENERAL DESCRIPTION OF THE RAW PROGRAM

The Replenishment Agricultural Workers (RAW) program was established under the Immigration Reform and Control Act of 1986 (IRCA) to address the concerns of growers that labor shortages might result as alien farmworkers granted status under the Legalization and SAW Programs retired or left to go into non-agricultural work.[1] The RAW Program is a two-stage program providing for the admission and adjustment of selected aliens to temporary resident status during fiscal years 1990, 1991, 1992, and 1993 in exchange for their promise to work in seasonal agricultural work for 90 days during 3 successive years. Completion of these agricultural work obligations will be followed by the alien's adjustment from temporary to permanent resident status. Each year's admission of RAWs will be subject to numerical limitations, determined by use of a "shortage number" or a formula specified in the statute, whichever number is less.[2] The number for fiscal year 1990 will be determined prior to October 1, 1989 by the Secretaries of Agriculture and Labor.[3]

Proposed regulations implementing the RAW program were published on March 6, 1989.[4] These proposed regulations differ radically from the preliminary draft regulations which were circulated by the INS earlier.[5] According to the proposed regulations, the RAW program will be open to applicants from all countries, however it does require previous employment in agricultural occupations in the United States. Due to the limited number of openings for RAW workers, preference will be given to certain applicants based on their relationship to aliens who have achieved lawful status in the United States.

---

[1] H.R. Rep. No. 99-62, 99th Cong., 2d Sess. (1986)(Part 1) at 83-84.

[2] INA §210A(c)(1). This number shall include a reasonable margin for a possible emergency increase during the fiscal year. See, proposed 8 CFR §210a.2(a).

[3] Proposed 8 CFR §210.2(a).

[4] 53 Fed. Reg. 9054-9061, reproduced in 66 Interpreter Releases 270-277 (March 6, 1989).

[5] "INS RAW Regs Summarized," 65 Interpreter Releases 854-867 (August 22, 1988).

9.2 BASIC ELIGIBILITY REQUIREMENTS

Based on the proposed regulations, the following minimum requirements must be met to qualify for temporary resident status under the RAW program:

1. **Age:**
   Applicants must be 18 years of age or older by October 1, 1989.[6]

2. **Work experience requirements:**
   Each applicant must have performed at least 20 man-days of "agricultural employment" in the United States during any 12 consecutive months between May 1, 1985 and November 30, 1988;[7]

   "Man day" means the performance during any day of not less than one (1) hour of agricultural employment or seasonal agricultural services for wages paid, or any day in which piece rate work was performed.[8]

3. **Prospective work requirements:**
   Each applicant must certify he or she is willing and able to perform 90 work-days of "seasonal agricultural services" during each of three successive years following the grant of temporary resident status.[9]

4. **Admissibility:**
   Each applicant must be admissible as an immigrant (certain grounds of excludability inapplicable, others waivable).[10]

---

[6] Proposed 8 CFR §210a.3(a)(1)(i).

[7] Proposed 8 CFR §245a.3(a)(1)(iii).

[8] Work for more than one employer in a single day shall be counted as no more than one man-day for purposes of this part. INA §210A(g)(4). Proposed 8 CFR §210a.1(c).

[9] INA §210A(d)(5)(A); proposed 8 CFR §§210a.3(a)(1)(iv), 210a.1(h).

[10] INA §210A(c)(1); INA §210A(e); proposed 8 CFR 210a.3(a)(1)(ii).

"Work day" is defined as any day in which at least four (4) hours work in seasonal agricultural services was performed.[11]

5. <u>Entry into the United States</u>:
Must not have entered the United States illegally after November 6, 1986.[12]

6. <u>Meets registration standard</u>:
Membership in a group to whom registration for the RAW program has been opened (minimally, aliens denied SAW status whom the INS determines may meet the age and work experience requirements; other groups to be added depending on the predicted shortage number).[13]

<u>Most of the above requirements are based on proposed regulations only and are subject to change.</u>

9.3 PROPOSED PROCEDURES

The system contemplated for choosing workers for the RAW program under the proposed regulations is fairly complicated. It follows several basic steps, discussed in greater detail below:

1. <u>Determination of Shortage Number and of Groups Allowed to Register under the RAW Program</u> Once a shortage number (i.e., an estimate of the shortage of agricultural workers for the upcoming fiscal year) is determined by the Secretaries of Agriculture and Labor, registration is opened to a defined group or groups of aliens. The larger the shortage number, the more groups may participate.

2. <u>Rejected SAW applicants</u> The first group consists of SAW applicants denied Temporary Residence under the SAW program and whose files contain documents indicating fulfillment of the age and agricultural work requirements. They will be placed on a list and mailed RAW registration forms.

3. <u>Registration for the RAW Program</u> Aliens in the specified group(s) who meet the minimum requirements may register by filing a registration form with the Central Processing Facility (CPF) of the INS.

---

[11] <u>See</u> proposed 8 CFR §210a.1(h). <u>See</u> also 29 CFR §502.

[12] Proposed 8 CFR §§210a.3(a)(2); 210a.2(b)(2), (3), and (4); 210a.4(g).

[13] Proposed 8 CFR §210a.3(b).

4. **Processing of the Registration Forms** Registration forms are then separated into two distinct groups: those who are the spouses or the unmarried sons or daughters of aliens with "approved applications under IRCA," and those who have no such relationship. Each group of registrants is then put in random order on separate lists.

5. **Invitation to Petition** Beginning with the group having relatives in the United States with approved applications under IRCA, aliens are "invited to petition" for the RAW program in the order they appear on the list, i.e., are scheduled for an interview at which the petition for temporary resident status under the RAW program is filed. The group with no such relatives in the United States is next invited to petition in the order they appear on the list. Only the number of aliens needed to meet the predicted shortage number will be invited to file a petition.

6. **Interview; Filing of the Petition** As to those registrants who are selected, interviews will be conducted at the INS and consular posts at which time the alien will submit the petition and all supporting documents which prove he or she meets all eligibility requirements. If recommended for approval, the alien will be issued Form I-688A employment authorization card, valid for six months, while record checks are conducted.[14] If subsequently approved, the alien will be either adjusted or admitted as a temporary resident under INA §210A and will be issued a Form I-688 Temporary Resident Card valid for approximately twelve months.

7. **Re-issuance of I-688 After Compliance with Initial Work Requirements** Once the RAW temporary resident fulfills his first required 90 work-days in seasonal agricultural employment (at any time during the first twelve months after the grant of temporary resident status), a second card will be issued to him or her, valid the remainder of the 3 year temporary residence period.

8. **Adjustment to Permanent Resident Status** Three years after the date temporary resident status was granted, the temporary resident must apply for adjustment to permanent resident status and must prove that he or she has worked 90 work-days in seasonal agricultural services during each of the twelve month periods following the grant of temporary resident status.

9. **Naturalization** Aliens who achieved permanent resident status under the RAW program may not become naturalized U.S. citizens

---

[14] Proposed 8 CFR §210a.5(i)(1).

unless they work 90 man-days in seasonal agricultural services for each of any two years after achieving permanent resident status.[15]

Details of each of the above steps are set forth below.

9.4 REGISTRATION PHASE

9.4(a) Determination of Groups Allowed to Register

The Secretaries of Agriculture and Labor must estimate the shortage of workers in seasonal agricultural services for the upcoming fiscal year. The shortage number is arrived at by following formulas set forth in the statute,[16] and shall include a reasonable margin for a possible emergency increase during the fiscal year.[17] A determination of the shortage number for fiscal year 1990 will be made prior to October 1, 1989.

The shortage of agricultural workers anticipated for fiscal year 1990 constitutes the number of RAW workers who will be adjusted or admitted for that fiscal year.[18] The registration for RAW-temporary resident status, and the beginning and ending dates of the registration period, will be publicized and announced in the Federal Register.[19] Depending on how large the shortage number is, different groups of people will be eligible to register. Therefore, the INS proposes to establish four "registration standards":

1. *Qualifying Rejected SAWS* First, those denied status under the SAW program who meet the age and prior "agricultural employment" requirements (except SAWs denied based on fraud or a non-waivable ground of exclusion), will be placed on a list of those eligible for the RAW program.[20] There must be credible documentation of qualifying employment and age in the file in order to be placed on the list of denied SAWs who are

---

[15] INA §210A(d)(5)(B).

[16] See INA §§210A(a), 210A(b)(1), 210A(c)(1).

[17] Proposed 8 CFR §210a.2(a).

[18] Proposed 8 CFR §210a.1(l).

[19] Proposed 8 CFR §210a.2(c).

[20] Proposed 8 CFR §210a.2(b).

eligible for the RAW program.[21] All those on the list will be furnished form I-807 to be completed and returned by those wishing to be considered under the RAW program. Depending on how many denied SAWs appear to qualify, there may be no need to solicit further registrants. (As of March 6, 1989, the date of the proposed RAW regulations, c.22,000 SAW applications had been denied and c.938,000 were unadjudicated. Of these, it is not known how many will meet the above requirements for selection for the RAW program.)

2. "Seasonal Agricultural Services in the U.S. After the above registration is completed, if the shortage number exceeds the number of eligible denied SAW applicants by up to 50,000, eligible aliens in the United States who have performed 20 man-days of qualifying work in "seasonal agricultural services" in the United States between May 1, 1985 and November 30, 1988 may register.

3. Agricultural Employment in the U.S. After the first registration is completed, if the shortage number exceeds the number of eligible denied SAW applicants by more than 50,000 but less than 200,000, eligible aliens in the United States who have performed 20 man-days in any kind of "agricultural employment" in the United States between May 1, 1985 and November 30, 1988 may register.

4. Agricultural Employment in the U.S. by workers abroad If, after the first registration is completed, the shortage number exceeds the number of eligible denied SAW applicants by more than 200,000, eligible aliens in and outside the United States who have performed 20 man-days in any kind of "agricultural employment" in the United States between May 1, 1985 and November 30, 1988 may register.[22]

9.4(b) Prior "Agricultural Employment" Requirement

In the above requirements and in various other provisions of the proposed regulations, a clear distinction is drawn between the terms "agricultural employment" and "seasonal agricultural services." In order to apply for the RAW program, most aliens will have to prove prior employment (1) for 20 "man-days" (2) during 12 consecutive months (3) between May 1, 1985 and November 30, 1988

---

[21] This group will not be required to prove qualifying employment at their subsequent interview (if selected). Proposed 8 CFR §210a.3(e)(3).

[22] Proposed 8 CFR §210a.2(b).

(4) in "agricultural employment."[23] Once approved for temporary resident status under the RAW program, the alien will be obliged to work for 90 "work-days" for each of the succeeding 3 years in "seasonal agricultural services."

"Agricultural employment" is liberally defined to include any employment:

1. On a farm[24] in connection with cultivating the soil, or in connection with raising or harvesting any agricultural or horticultural commodity, including raising, shearing, feeding, caring for, training, and management of livestock, bees, poultry, and fur-bearing animals and wildlife;

2. By a farm operator in connection with the operation or maintenance of the farm,[25] its tools and equipment, or with salvaging timber or clearing land of brush and other debris left by a hurricane, if the major part of such service is performed on a farm;

3. In connection with the production or harvest of any agricultural commodity or in connection with the operation or maintenance of ditches, canals, reservoirs, or waterways, not owned or operated for profit, used exclusively for supplying and storing water for farming purposes;

4. By the operator(s) of a farm[26] in handling, planting, drying, packing, packaging, processing, freezing, grading, storing, or delivering to storage or to market or to a carrier for transportation to market, in its unmanufactured state, any agricultural or horticultural commodity, does not include service performed in connection with commercial canning or commercial freezing or in connection with any agricultural or horticultural commodity after its delivery to a terminal

---

[23] All registrants must prior work in "agricultural employment" except for the second group of aliens eligible to register (i.e., those eligible to register if the difference between the shortage number and eligible aliens denied SAW status is less than 50,000); this group must prove prior work in "seasonal agricultural services."

[24] "Farm" includes stock, dairy, poultry, fruit, fur-bearing animals, and truck farms, plantations, ranches, nurseries, ranges, greenhouses, or other similar structures used primarily for the raising of agricultural or horticultural commodities, and orchards. Proposed 8 CFR §210a.1(d).

[25] See footnote 24.

[26] See footnote 24.

market for distribution for consumption or service not in the course of the employer's trade or business or domestic service in a private home of the employer.[27]

The regulations require 20 "man-days" of such agricultural employment. The term "man-day" means any day in which not less than one (1) hour of paid agricultural employment or seasonal agricultural services was performed, or any day in which piece rate work was performed. Work for more than one employer in a single day counts as one man-day.[28]

Documentation establishing that the alien meets the 20 man-days of agricultural employment need not be submitted by those persons who are registered based on their having been placed on the registration list of eligible aliens who were denied SAW status (see §9.6(d) infra).[29]

9.4(c) "Seasonal Agricultural Services"

If there are not sufficient eligible workers who were previously denied SAW status to meet the shortage numbers, the second group of aliens allowed to register under the proposed registration standards are those with prior experience in "seasonal agricultural services.[30] Also, once an alien is admitted as a temporary resident under the RAW program, the law requires that each temporary resident perform (1) 90 man-days of (2) seasonal agricultural services (3) during each of three one-year periods after the date temporary resident status was obtained.[31]

Because "man-day" was previously defined in other regulatory provisions to constitute days in which at least one hour of work was performed, the RAW regulations have changed to require 90 "work-days" defining "work day" as any day in which at least four (4) hours work in seasonal agricultural services was performed, in keeping with the statute's requirement.[32]

---

[27] Proposed 8 CFR §210a.1(c).

[28] Proposed 8 CFR §210a.1(g). See also 8 CFR §210.1(i).

[29] Proposed 8 CFR §210a.3(e)(3).

[30] See §proposed 8 CFR §210a.2(a)(2).

[31] INA §210A(d)(5)(A).

[32] See proposed 8 CFR §210a.1(h). See also 29 CFR §502.

"Seasonal Agricultural Services" is defined as it was for purposes of establishing eligibility for the SAW program:[33]

> ...the performance of field work related to planting, cultural practices, cultivating, growing, and harvesting of fruits and vegetables of every kind and other perishable commodities.[34]

Department of Agriculture regulations further define the terms "field work," "fruits," "vegetables" and "other perishable commodities" contained in the definition of Seasonal Agricultural Services.[35] A chart setting-forth which crops and plants come within these definitions can be found at the end of Chapter One.

There are important differences in the above terms which those granted temporary resident status must fully understand in order to preserve their new status. First of all, while much agricultural work will fall within both terms, "agricultural employment" is not a term which automatically encompasses work considered to be "seasonal agricultural services." "Agricultural employment" in most cases requires that the employment be on a farm or for a farm operator, a consideration largely irrelevant in determining whether work constitutes "seasonal agricultural services." RAW temporary residents cannot continue or resume the very work which qualified them for RAW status if this work related to livestock, the operation of irrigation systems, or farming operations devoted to most kinds of grains, forestry, dairies, etc.

9.4(d)   Denied and Unadjudicated SAW Applications

The first group eligible to apply for RAW temporary resident status under the proposed regulations will be those denied under the SAW program. INS will establish a list of those denied SAW status (except SAWs denied based on fraud or a non-waivable ground of exclusion), who meet the age and prior "agricultural employment" requirements. Qualifying employment must be supported by credible documentation in the file in order to be placed on the list. Such aliens will be furnished registration form I-807 which they must

---

[33]   INA §210A(g)(2).

[34]   Proposed 8 CFR §210a.1(j). <u>See also</u> INA §210(h); 7 CFR §1d.9.

[35]   <u>See</u> 7 CFR §§1d.4, 1d.5, and 1d.10.

complete and return if they desire to be considered for RAW status.[36]

These proposals enable the following SAWs to have a second chance to legalize their status under the RAW program:

1. SAW applicants who were unable to prove that they had worked 90 man-days of seasonal agricultural services in order to qualify for SAW status, but did have proof of at least 20 man-days of agricultural employment _after May 1, 1985_.

2. Those denied SAW status because their agricultural employment did not fit the definition of "seasonal agricultural services" required for SAW eligibility. The employment they sought to prove may fit under the broader RAW requirement of "agricultural employment" which encompasses work in the cattle, dairy, forestry, and other agricultural industries.

Rejected SAWs whose sole proof stems from work undertaken prior to May 1, 1985, will not be eligible for consideration.

The proposed regulations raise some practical problems regarding their implementation. The first problem concerns how the INS will review and select denied SAW applicants for placement on their list of potential registrants. As of March 6, 1989, the date when the proposed regulations were published, 1.3 million SAW applications had been filed; 25% had been approved and 1% had been denied.[37] Thus, the INS need only review a relatively small number of already denied SAW cases (i.e., c.22,000) for RAW eligibility, and can concentrate its review process on the majority of the SAW applications which are pending unadjudicated at the RPF (c. 938,000). Thus, in rendering a decision on these pending SAW applications, the RPF may simultaneously review rejected applications for RAW eligibility. Indeed, the low adjudication rate for SAW applications may be a result of the proposed RAW regulations, i.e., the RPFs are deferring adjudication of most SAW applications to facilitate review of such cases should the current proposals be implemented.

Of the 22,000 already denied SAW status, almost all would have to be reviewed again (except those denied due to fraud or a nonwaivable grounds of excludability), as the general denials issued by the LO in SAW cases (e.g., "insufficient documentation," "no qualifying employment") will give no indication of whether the applicant meets the criteria for inclusion on the RAW program list.

---

[36] Proposed 8 CFR §210a.2(b)(1).

[37] Per the IRCA Clearinghouse, National Immigration, Refugee and Citizenship Forum, as of March 9, 1989.

The fact that qualifying employment in "agricultural employment" <u>must be supported by credible documentation in the file</u> in order to be placed on the list of denied SAW applicants eligible to register for the RAW program poses problems. SAW applicants who presented documentation demonstrating that they had worked in the cattle or dairy industries (for example), or evidence that they worked in agricultural occupations <u>after</u> May 1, 1986, were most likely to have these documents returned to them by the LO as documentation irrelevant to the SAW program. Thus, credible documentation demonstrating such applicants eligibility for the RAW program, though available, will not be "in the file" and they will not be included on the list of eligible SAW applicants. Because exclusion from the list of SAWs selected for registration under the RAW program is not appealable,[38] eligible aliens will be unfairly denied an opportunity to legalize their status under the RAW program. Such aliens will apparently not know that they have not been included on the list. If registration is opened up to those other than denied SAW applicants, such aliens may presumably register at that time.

Given the preference given rejected SAWs with proof of agricultural employment in file, all pending SAWs should immediately submit to the RPF any proof they may have of qualifying "agricultural employment" for inclusion in their files.

Of the remaining unadjudicated SAW applications, the question becomes one of which cases will be reviewed for the RAW program. Will each case file and documents be reviewed or will the RPF base review on the LO interviewer's recommendation, i.e., his or her indication of the basis for a recommended denial? If the basis for denial recommended by the LO interviewer is used, it will be too general to accurately determine who qualifies under the RAW program.

9.4(e) **Agricultural Workers Who Were Not Among the Eligible Rejected SAW Applicants**

If the number of rejected SAW applicants who are eligible for the RAW program is insufficient to meet the shortage number, other agricultural workers will be eligible to register for the SAW program, according to the established registration standard as set forth in §9.4(a), <u>supra</u>.

9.4(f) **Priority Consideration of Certain Registrants**

Of all those who meet the above eligibility requirements, priority consideration will be given to registrants who are the

---

[38] Proposed 8 CFR §210a.2(h).

9-13

spouses or the unmarried sons or daughters (18 years of age or older) of aliens who have "filed an application under IRCA" which has been approved.[39] The term "application under IRCA" has been defined to mean approved applications filed by any alien under INA §245A (general amnesty or legalization), §210 (SAWs), and §202 of IRCA (Cuban/Haitian Adjustment), although H-2A workers should arguably be included.[40] All registration forms timely received at the CPF, will be sorted by separating all applicants who are eligible for this priority consideration. The cases of registrants who are eligible for priority consideration will then be randomly sorted; these registrants will then be eligible to apply for RAW status according to their place on the list.[41] Those without such family relationships will also be randomly sorted and will be invited to petition for RAW temporary resident status in the order of their appearance on the list if those given priority consideration were insufficient to meet the shortage number. There is no appeal from a failure to be placed on a list of registrants or to be placed on a list of registrants or to be granted priority consideration.[42]

9.4(g) Registration Procedures

According to the draft regulations, registration form I-807 will be distributed at all INS district, legalization, and sub-offices. These forms are then completed by the alien and sent by regular domestic or international surface or airmail mail to an INS Central Processing Facility (CPF) location (to be determined).[43] The form cannot be submitted in person or by any means other than by mail. Registration forms requiring any form of written

---

[39] Proposed 8 CFR §210a.2(e).

[40] Proposed 8 CFR §210a.2(f). Because the program granting temporary resident status to EVD nationals (Ugandans, Ethiopians, Afghans, and Poles) was not a part of IRCA, a relationship to an alien approved under those programs would not qualify one for priority consideration under the RAW program.

[41] Proposed 8 CFR §210a.2(f).

[42] Proposed 8 CFR §210a.2(h).

[43] If registration is expanded to include those outside of the United States, registration forms will also be available at American Embassies and consular posts. Proposed 8 CFR §§210a.2(d)(1), (2); see proposed 8 CFR §210a.2(b)(4).

acknowledgment or confirmation of the receipt will also be rejected.[44]

A separate registration form must be filed be each registrant. No fee will be required.[45] Only one registration form will be allowed per registrant; if multiple registration forms are submitted by an alien, all of the forms will be rejected.[46] Registrants must designate the priority classification they qualify for on the registration form. Registration forms containing information which is incomplete or which cannot be read will be discarded.[47]

No registration form will be returned. The INS will not respond to status inquiries concerning the registration process.

If fraud or willful misrepresentation of a material fact is found in the registration process, the registration form I-807 will be rejected or the subsequent petition will be denied. Such fraud or willful misrepresentation will subject the person to deportation and referral to a U.S. Attorney for possible prosecution.[48]

Neither employment authorization nor any other benefit shall derive from filing a registration form I-807, being placed on the register, or being invited to petition for RAW status.[49]

If the alien moves after having submitted his or her I-807 registration form, he or she should file a form I-697A change of address card for RAWs with the CPF, as well as provide the U.S. Postal Service with his or her forwarding address.

9.5 PETITION PHASE

Registrants will be selected in the order of their appearance on the register, beginning with the highest ranked registrant among those accorded priority consideration, and continuing through the remainder of the register until the shortage number is reached or

---

[44] Proposed 8 CFR §210a.2(d)(2).

[45] Proposed 8 CFR §210a.2(d)(5).

[46] Proposed 8 CFR §210a.2(d)(3).

[47] Proposed 8 CFR §210a.2(d)(4).

[48] Proposed 8 CFR §210a.2(g).

[49] Proposed 8 CFR §210a.2(i).

the supply of registrants is exhausted,[50] will be invited to petition and will be sent the following materials:

1. Instructions for completing all required forms.

2. Form I-805, Petition for Temporary Resident Status as a Replenishment Agricultural Worker (RAW).

3. Form I-697A, change of address card for RAWs.

4. Form FD-258, fingerprint card.

5. Form I-693, medical examination of alien seeking adjustment of status card.

6. ADIT Photograph instruction sheet.[51]

Petitions are mailed to the address of the alien which was supplied on the registration form. If the registrant changes address prior to the "invitation to petition," he or she must file a form I-697A Change of Address card as well as notify the U.S. Postal Service so that the petition package may be forwarded to the current address. If the petition package mailed by the CPF is returned as undeliverable because of an insufficient address or because the registrant has moved and left no forwarding address, he or she will be placed at the end of the list and the next registrant on the register will be selected in his or her place.[52] This provision may be problematic in that the CPF may have misaddressed the package to the registrant and may then automatically put the registrant to the end of the list if the package is returned undelivered.

9.6 INTERVIEW

If the rank and order number of a registrant is within the shortage number, he or she will be invited to an interview at the Consulate or INS Office with jurisdiction over the alien's residence.[53] Registrants will be scheduled for an interview for purposes of filing the petition for admission or adjustment as a

---

[50] Proposed 8 CFR §210a.2(j).

[51] Proposed 8 CFR §210a.5(a).

[52] Proposed 8 CFR §210a.5(b).

[53] Proposed §210a.5(c).

RAW worker.[54] The alien who seeks admission or adjustment of status as a RAW worker has the burden of proof in establishing each of the eligibility requirements.[55] The following items will be required at the interview:

1. Form I-805. (Visa petitions will by submitted by those outside of the United States, Adjustment of Status applications by those in the United States).[56]

2. A $185 filing fee, in the form of a money order, bank or cashier check if petitioner is in the United States, or in foreign currency if at a consular post.[57]

3. Proof of identity.

4. Proof of age.

5. Evidence of eligibility, including:

   a. Proof of family relationship (if seeking priority consideration);
   b. Proof of qualifying agricultural employment, if required (not required of denied SAW applicants notified by INS)

6. Evidence of admissibility.

7. Complete certified translations of foreign language documents submitted.

8. Form I-693, medical examination results.[58]

9. Photographs.[59]

10. FD-258 Fingerprint card.

---

[54] Proposed 8 CFR §210a.5(c).

[55] Proposed 8 CFR §210a.3(b)(2).

[56] INA §§210A(c)(1), (2).

[57] Proposed 8 CFR §210a.5(f). The application fee cannot be refunded or waived.

[58] Medical examination results, including the HIV test, are not required if previously submitted in connection with a SAW application. Proposed 8 CFR §210a.5(g).

[59] Proposed 8 CFR §§210a.5(c)(2), 210a.3(b)(1), (2).

The immigration or consular officer will judge the sufficiency of the documents submitted and may require additional documentation needed to establish eligibility.[60]

9.6(a) General Considerations About the Submission of Documents

Original documents are to be presented at the interview wherever possible.[61] If at the time of the interview the petitioner wishes the return of original documents, they must be accompanied by notarized copies or copies certified as true and complete by the petitioner's representative.[62] Copies of records maintained by parties other than the petitioner which are presented in evidence must be certified as true and complete by such parties and must bear their seal or signature or the signature and title of persons authorized to act in their behalf. At the discretion of the District Director or the Consular Officer, original documents even if accompanied by certified copies, may be temporarily retained for further examination.[63] Documents in a foreign language must be accompanied by a complete English translation certified by the translator. Summary translations, acceptable for legalization and SAW applications, are not permitted by the proposed RAW regulations.[64]

All information and evidence of identity, age, admissibility and family relationship and prior agricultural employment will be subject to verification by the INS or the consular post abroad a the time of the interview.[65] If any material fact cannot be verified, the petition will be denied;[66] if fraud or willful misrepresentation is found in the petition process, the petition will be denied. If the petitioner is in the United States, he or

---

[60] Proposed 8 CFR §210a.3(b)(3).

[61] Proposed 8 CFR §210a.3(f).

[62] See 8 CFR §204.2(j)(1) and (2).

[63] Proposed 8 CFR §210a.3(f)(1).

[64] Proposed 8 CFR §210a.3(f)(1), (2).

[65] Proposed 8 CFR §210a.5(c)(4).

[66] Proposed 8 CFR §210a.5(c)(2).

she will be subject to deportation and/or referral to the United States for possible prosecution.[67]

No information furnished as part of the RAW registration or petitioning process, including documents furnished by their parties, shall be used to identify or locate aliens for the purpose of removing them form the United States unless the Service has information that the alien entered the United States illegally after November 6, 1988. The INS will not furnish any such information to any government agency for the purpose of identifying or penalizing persons for violation of law.[68]

9.6(b) Proof of Identity and Age

The following documents may be submitted to prove identity and age:

A. Passport;
B. Birth Certificate;
C. National identity document from the alien's country of origin bearing a photograph and/or fingerprint (e.g. "cedula", "cartilla", "carte d'identite", etc.);
D. Driver's license or similar state I.D. with a photograph;
E. Baptismal record or marriage certificate;
F. Affidavits;
G. Other documentation which may establish the identity and age of the petitioner.[69]

Assumed names: If the petitioner claims to have met the eligibility criteria under an assumed name, he or she has the burden of proving that he or she is the person who used that name. After the petitioner's true identity has been established and documents submitted under the assumed name, the petitioner must submit evidence that the petitioner was known under both names. The most persuasive proof of common identity is a document issued in the assumed name which identifies the petitioner by photograph, fingerprint, or detailed physical description. Other evidence which will be considered are affidavits by persons made under oath which identify by name, address, and relationship to the petitioner and set forth the basis for affiant's knowledge of petitioner's assumed name. Affidavits accompanied by a photograph identifying the individual under the assumed name will carry greater weight.[70]

---

[67] Proposed 8 CFR §210a.5(l).

[68] Proposed 8 CFR §210a.3(g).

[69] Proposed 8 CFR §210a.3(c)(1).

[70] Proposed 8 CFR §210a.3(c)(2).

9.6(c) Evidence of Family Relationship

The following documents must be submitted to establish entitlement to priority consideration:

(1) If the petitioner claims eligibility for priority consideration based on marriage to an alien who was approved under IRCA, the petitioner must submit a certificate of marriage between the petitioner and the legalized alien as well as documents showing termination of all prior marriages by either party (divorce decree, death certificate, etc.).

(2) If the alien claims eligibility for priority consideration because his or her mother is a legalized alien, he or she should submit the birth certificate of the petitioner showing the name of the mother.

(3) If the alien claims eligibility for priority consideration because his or her father was legalized under IRCA, the petitioner must submit their birth certificate showing the name of the father and the marriage certificate of the parents.

(4) If the legalized alien is a step-parent, the petitioner must present his or her birth certificate showing the names of both natural parents, the marriage of the parent to the step-parent, and proof of a legal termination of the prior parties of the parent and step-parent.

(5) If the child was born out of wedlock, and the father is a legalized alien, evidence must be provided that a parent/child relationship exists or existed, e.g., the child's birth certificate showing the father's name and evidence that the father supported the child.

(6) If the child is adopted, a certified copy of an adoption decree and a statement showing the dates and places the child and adoptive parents lived together must be submitted.[71]

Secondary Evidence:

If any of the above documents are not available,[72] secondary evidence may be submitted, such as:

1. Church records (containing the church's seal), such as Baptismal records or comparable rites showing the date and

---

[71] Proposed 8 CFR §210a.3(d).

[72] Proposed 8 CFR §210a.3(d).

place of the child's birth and the names of the child's parents.

2. School records, a letter from school officials at the first school attended showing the date of admission, the date and place and birth of the child, and the names and places of birth of the parents, if shown in the school records.

3. State or federal census records, census records showing the name, place of birth, and date of birth for the age of the person listed.

4. Sworn affidavits of two persons who were living at the time and who have personal knowledge of the event the petitioner is trying to prove. The affidavit must give full information concerning the event and complete details concerning how the person acquired knowledge of the event. The affidavit must include the affiant's full name, address, date and place of birth, and his or her relationship to the petitioner, if any.

If documents are unavailable, the INS may require a statement from the appropriate authority certifying that the needed document is not available.[73]

Registrants who claim priority based on a family relationship that cannot be verified by the INS or the Consulate will be randomly ranked within that portion of the register established for qualifying aliens not entitled to priority consideration based on family relationship.

9.6(d) Employment Documentation

Except for registrants from the list of rejected SAW applicants,[74] all petitioners must submit employment documentation.

The following documents can be submitted to prove agricultural employment:

1. Government employment records;

2. Records maintained by agricultural producers, farm labor contractors, collective bargaining organizations, and other groups or organizations which maintain records of employment;

3. Worker identification issued by employers or unions;

---

[73] Proposed 8 CFR §210a.3(d)(s).

[74] Proposed 8 CFR §210a.3(e)(3).

4. Union cards or other union records, such as dues receipts;

5. Other records of the applicant's involvement with organizations providing services to farm workers (e.g., migrant education programs, migrant legal assistance, migrant health clinics);

6. Work records such as pay stubs, piece work receipts, W-2 forms, etc.;

7. Certification of filing income tax returns on IRS form 6166;

8. State verification of the filing of state income tax returns.[75]

Affidavits shall **not** be acceptable to document work performed to qualify for temporary resident status as a RAW.[76] If any material fact required by the announced registration standard claimed seasonal agricultural services is necessary to establish eligibility and cannot be verified, the petition will be denied.

When a RAW petitioner alleges that an employer refuses to provide him or her with work records relating to his or her employment and the petitioner has reason to believe such records exist, the service shall attempt to secure such records in the following cases:

1. The RAW petition must have been filed;

2. An interview must have been conducted;

3. The alien must have made a good faith effort to secure the documentation from the employer;

4. The alien's testimony must credibly support his or her claim;

5. The INS must determine that the petition cannot be approved in the absence of the employer records.[77]

---

[75] Proposed 8 CFR §210a.3(e)(1).

[76] Proposed 8 CFR §210a.3(e)(2).

[77] Proposed 8 CFR §210a.5(d).

If the above conditions are met, the district director may issue a subpoena in accordance with federal regulation for purposes of obtaining needed employment records.[78]

9.6(e) Admissibility

The law requires that all petitioners for temporary resident status be admissible.[79] In determining whether a registrant under the RAW program is admissible, the following provisions of INA §212(a) <u>do</u> <u>not</u> <u>apply</u>:

<u>Inapplicable Exclusion Grounds</u>
(14) entered to work without labor certification;
(20) not in possession of a valid entry document;
(21) visa not issued per numerical limitations;
(25) illiterate over age 16;
(32) foreign medical graduate who has not taken the visa qualifying examination.[80]

The following provisions of INA §212(a) <u>cannot be waived</u> under the RAW provisions [INA §210A(e)(2)(A)]:

<u>Exclusion Grounds Which Cannot Be Waived</u>
(9) crime of moral turpitude;
(10) two crimes with aggregate sentence of 5 yrs. or more;
(23) drug-related convictions (except 30 grams of marijuana);
(27) likely to engage in activities prejudicial to the public interest;
(28) anarchists, communists, etc.;
(29) spy, saboteur, subversive;
(33) Nazi.[81]

The following exclusion grounds under INA §212(a) are applicable but are waivable for humanitarian purposes, to assure family unity, or when it is otherwise in the public interest.[82]

<u>Waivable Grounds of Exclusion</u>

---

[78] Proposed 8 CFR §210a.5(d)(3).

[79] INA §§210A(c)(1), 210A(e). <u>See</u> also proposed 8 CFR §210a.4(a).

[80] INA §210A(e)(1), 8 CFR §210 a.5(c)(2).

[81] INA §210A(e)(2)(B), draft 8 CFR §210a.5(c)(5).

[82] INA §210A(e)(2)(A), draft 8 CFR §210a.5(c)(4).

(1) mentally retarded;[83]
(2) insane;[84]
(3) attack(s) of insanity;[85]
(4) psychopath, sex deviant, mental defect;[86]
(5) drug addict, alcoholic;[87]
(6) contagious disease;
(7) physical disability effecting ability to work;
(8) paupers;
(11) polygamy;
(12) prostitutes;
(13) entry to engage in immoral sex acts;
(15) public charge;
(16) excluded within 1 year;
(17) deported within 5 years;
(18) stowaway;
(19) fraud;
(22) ineligible for U.S. citizenship;
(24) arrived on non-signatory line;
(26) no valid visa, passport on entry;
(30) entry with excluded alien;
(31) smuggling.

To determine excludability under INA §§212(a)(1) through (5), a medical examination is required.[88] At the time of notification of the interview, form I-693 medical examination form will be sent to the applicant. The results of the medical exam must be submitted at the time of the interview. Unless medical examination results, including HIV testing, have been previously submitted in connection with a SAW application, all aliens must submit the results of a medical examination conducted by a designated civil surgeon or (if outside the United States) a panel physician designated to perform medical examinations for immigrant visa applicants. The results of the medical examination must be submitted on form I-693 at the time of the interview. Those certified under INA §212(a)(1) - (5) may appeal to the Board of

---

[83] INA §§ 212 (a)(1) through (5) are also appealable under INA §§234 and 235; proposed 8 CFR §210a.5(g).

[84] Id.

[85] Id.

[86] Id.

[87] Id.

[88] INA §210A(e)(3).

Medical Officers of the U.S. Public Health Service as provided in INA §§234 and 235.[89]

In determining excludability under INA §212(a)(15), the statute provides for a "special rule" similar to that set-forth in the legalization and SAW provisions. Under the special rule for public charge, the applicant must demonstrate a history of employment in the U.S. evidencing self-support without reliance on public cash assistance.[90] This provision is identical to that set-forth under legalization program, INA §245A(d)(2)(B)(iii), and the construction given it by the courts and through agency memoranda will likewise apply to the RAW program. "Public cash assistance" is defined as income or needs-based monetary assistance, including supplemental security income (SSI) received by the alien or immediate family members the federal, state or local programs designed to meet subsistence levels. It does not include in-kind assistance such as food stamps, public housing, or other non-cash benefits, work-related compensation, Medicare, Medicaid, emergency services, WIC or treatment in the interest of public health.[91]

Those previously admitted as exchange visitors must show compliance with the 2 year foreign residence requirements or the receipt of a waiver thereof.[92]

The INS may waive any grounds of excludability for humanitarian purposes, to assure family unity, or when the granting of such a waiver is in the public interest. If an alien is excludable on a grounds which may be waived, he shall be advised of the procedures for applying for a waiver on form I-690.[93]

9.7 DECISION ON RAW APPLICATION

The district director or the consular officer has authority to deny or to recommend approval of the petition based on information supplied at the interview regarding eligibility, agricultural employment experience and family relationship to an

---

[89] Proposed 8 CFR §210a.5(g).

[90] INA §210A(e)(2)(C), 8 CFR §210a.5(c)(3).

[91] Proposed 8 CFR §210a.1(h). Public charge excludability is discussed in Chapter One.

[92] Proposed 8 CFR §210a.4(f).

[93] Proposed 8 CFR §210a.4(d). Waivers are discussed in Chapter One.

IRCA legalized alien.[94] If the petitioner is unable to substantiate family relationship, and fraud has not been established, the petitioner will be randomly re-ranked within that portion of the register established for those without family preference. In such event the petition will be held in abeyance until such time as the petitioner is again invited to petition.

If approval is recommended, the INS will conduct record checks to verify the admissibility of the petitioner. During the pendency of the petition, the alien will receive work authorization and permission to travel abroad on Form I-688A, employment authorization card, for a period not to exceed six months from the date of filing.[95]

If the record check does not reveal adverse information concerning the petitioner, the petitioner will be issued Form I-688, temporary resident card, valid for 18 months from the date of filing the petition. This card may be renewed, extended, or reissued for the remainder of the three-year period upon a finding by the INS that the alien has completed the first required 90 workdays of employment in seasonal agricultural services as required.[96]

Those petitioners who are approved at an embassy or consular post will be provided with an entry document to enable admission to the United States. The petitioner must present this entry document at a port of entry, and must then appear at a service office within 30 calendar days of admission in order to be processed for a Form I-688 a temporary resident card (valid for 18 months).[97]

The date of adjustment for petitions approved by the INS shall be the date on which the petition was filed. Aliens admitted from consular or embassy posts abroad shall be issued a visa and admitted for temporary residence as of the date of their entry into the United States.[98]

If the petitioner fails to meet his or her burden of proof, or if record checks are returned with adverse information that render the petitioner ineligible for status as a RAW, the petition

---

[94] Proposed 8 CFR §210a.5(h).

[95] Proposed 8 CFR §210a.5(i)(1).

[96] Proposed 8 CFR §210a.5(i)(1)(ii).

[97] Proposed 8 CFR §210a.5(i)(2).

[98] Proposed 8 CFR §210a.5(k).

will be denied.[99] If any material fact necessary to establish eligibility cannot be verified, the petition will be denied.[100] If fraud or willful misrepresentation is found in the petition process, the petition will be denied,[101] and if the petitioner is in the United States, he or she will be subject to deportation and referral to the U.S. Attorney for possible prosecution.

The regulations state that no appeal shall lie from the decision to deny a petitioner temporary resident status,[102] and indeed, the statute is also silent regarding the review mechanisms available in cases of denial. However, due process would require some form of review of such denials.

9.8 OBLIGATIONS OF TEMPORARY RESIDENTS UNDER THE RAW PROGRAM

Registrants whose names are selected and who are issued temporary resident status must work for 90 man-days[103] (according to the regulations, "work-days"),[104] for each of 3 years commencing on the date the alien obtained temporary resident status.[105] A work-day is any day in which the person worked a minimum of 4 hours in seasonal agricultural services.[106] The number of work-days required is subject to decrease by the Secretaries of Agriculture and Labor.[107]

It is important for the newly legalized temporary resident to realize the distinction between "agricultural employment" and the "seasonal agricultural services" as it is the latter, not the former, which is required in order to maintain temporary resident status and to achieve permanent resident status afterwards. While many RAWs will achieve that status because of work in "agricultural employment", which encompassed the care of animals, the harvest of

---

[99] Proposed 8 CFR §210a.5(j).

[100] Proposed 8 CFR §210a.5(d)(3).

[101] Proposed 8 CFR §210a.5(l); see also proposed 8 CFR §210a.2(g).

[102] Proposed 8 CFR §210a.5(j).

[103] INA §210A(d)(5)(D).

[104] Proposed 8 CFR §210a.6(b)(1).

[105] INA §210A(d)(5)(A). Proposed 8 CFR §210a.6(b).

[106] INA §210A(g)(4). See INA §210(h); INA §210A(g)(2).

[107] INA §210A(d)(5)(D), see proposed 8 CFR §210a.6(c).

grains, forestry work, the operation of irrigation systems, and other qualifying "agricultural employment," they cannot continue or resume that kind of work for purposes of satisfying their "seasonal agricultural services" work requirement as a temporary resident. The only kind of work which will satisfy the work required for three years after achieving temporary resident status is that work which involves the cultivation and harvest, etc., of fruits, vegetables, and other perishable commodities as defined under the SAW regulations at 7 CFR §1(d). Failure to perform the required "seasonal agricultural services" renders the alien deportable.[108]

The burden is on the RAW temporary resident or permanent resident to collect, maintain, and have available for inspection evidence that he or she has performed the requisite number of work days of seasonal agricultural services for each year required.[109] Such evidence may consist of certificates provided to employees by employers or the same type of documentation as may be submitted to establish eligibility for SAW status.[110]

When a RAW worker alleges that an employer refuses to provide him or her with work records relating to his or her employment and the petitioner has reason to believe such records exist, the service shall attempt to secure such records in the following cases:

1. The alien must be approved as a RAW

2. The alien must have made reasonable attempts to secure the documentation from the employer

3. The alien's testimony must credibly support his or her claim

4. The service must determine that temporary resident's status is in jeopardy in the absence of the employer records.[111]

---

[108] INA §241(a)(20).

[109] Proposed 8 CFR §210a.6(d)(1).

[110] Proposed 8 CFR §210a.6(d)(2). See the discussion of SAW documentation in Chapter One.

[111] Proposed 8 CFR §210a.6(e).

If the above conditions are met, the district director may issue a subpoena in accordance with federal regulation for purposes of obtaining needed employment records.[112]

The alien must work an additional 2 years in agricultural employment in order to subsequently naturalize.[113]

Temporary residents may not receive public assistance for 5 years with these exceptions: food stamps, Legal Services Corporation assistance, and Title V of the Housing Act.[114]

9.9 RIGHTS OF TEMPORARY RESIDENTS UNDER THE RAW PROGRAM

An alien who is granted temporary resident status under the RAW program is considered to be an alien lawfully admitted for permanent residence (with certain exceptions under the INA).[115] RAW workers cannot file visa petitions for family members and cannot receive any benefit or consideration under the INA accorded lawful permanent residents.[116] RAW temporary residents stand on an equal footing with permanent resident aliens in other contexts, however. Tuition rates, scholarships, loans, employment opportunities, military service, and other concerns which may require permanent resident status must by law be accorded to RAW temporary residents to the same extent as permanent residents.

RAW temporary residents may reside in the United States or they may commute from a residence abroad.[117] They are eligible to be issued a work authorization document I-688A or I-688,[118] and are free to travel to and from the United States in the same manner as lawful permanent residents.[119]

Upon a finding that the alien has completed the 90 work-days required during the first 12-month period, a second Temporary

---

[112] Proposed 8 CFR §210a.6(d)(3).

[113] INA §210A(d)(5)(B); proposed 8 CFR §210a.6(b)(3).

[114] INA §210A(d)(6).

[115] INA §210A(d)(4); see INA §101(a)(20).

[116] Proposed 8 CFR §210a.6(g).

[117] INA §210A(d)(3); proposed 8 CFR §210a.6(a).

[118] INA §210A(d)(3), proposed 8 CFR §210a.6(a).

[119] INA §210A(d)(3), proposed 8 CFR §210a.6(a).

Resident Card (Form I-688) will be issued, valid through the remainder of the 36 month period.[120]

Employers of RAW workers who provide transportation to RAW workers must provide the same or comparable transportation to other workers;[121] civil penalties apply to violators.[122] The statute also prohibits farm labor contractors, and agricultural employers or associations from providing false or misleading information to a RAW worker about the terms, conditions, or existence of agricultural employment;[123] civil penalties apply to violators.[124] Lastly, the rights and protections of the Migrant and Seasonal Agricultural Worker Protection Act (MASAWPA) apply to RAW workers.[125] Violators will be assessed civil penalties in accordance with MASAWPA.[126]

Temporary residents may not receive public assistance for 5 years with these exceptions: food stamps, Legal Services Corporation assistance, and Title V of the Housing Act.[127]

9.10 PROCEDURE FOR ADJUSTMENT TO PERMANENT RESIDENCE STATUS

An alien who has been accorded temporary resident status under the RAW program is eligible to adjust status to that of permanent resident 3 years after the date that temporary residence was granted,[128] if he or she has maintained status under the INA.[129] In order to adjust to permanent resident status, the alien must prove he or she has performed the required work in seasonal agricultural

---

[120] Proposed 8 CFR §210a.6(f).

[121] INA §210A(f)(1).

[122] INA §210A(f)(4).

[123] INA §210A(f)(2).

[124] INA §210A(f)(4).

[125] INA §§210A(f)(3), (4).

[126] INA §210A(f)(4).

[127] INA §210A(d)(6).

[128] INA §210A(d)(1).

[129] Proposed 8 CFR §210a.7(a)

services for 3 years by presenting the kinds of documents as were required under the Seasonal Agricultural Worker (SAW) program.[130]

Once the RAW temporary resident has adjusted his or her status to that of a permanent resident alien, he or she cannot naturalize unless prior to petitioning for naturalization he or she performs 90 man-days of seasonal agricultural services during each of two years in addition to the three years of such work performed as required while a temporary resident.[131]

9.11 TERMINATION OF TEMPORARY RESIDENT STATUS AND DEPORTATION UNDER THE RAW PROGRAM

According to the statute, during the period of temporary resident status granted the alien under the RAW program, temporary resident status may be terminated by the Attorney General only upon a determination under the Immigration and Nationality Act that the alien is deportable.[132] The regulations regarding the implementation of this provision can be confusing. They provide for termination by the INS upon a finding that the alien is deportable under INA §235 (inspection of aliens seeking admission), §236 (exclusion proceedings), §237 (deportation of excluded aliens), and §241 (grounds of deportation).[133]

Under these provisions the INS appears to contemplate termination of RAW temporary resident status upon a finding of deportability by the Immigration Judge in deportation proceedings or upon entry of an order of exclusion and deportation in exclusion proceedings. The grounds of deportation were amended by IRCA to include the failure of an alien admitted under the RAW program to fulfill the yearly seasonal agricultural work obligations of the RAW program "by the end of the applicable period."[134] Indeed, INA §210A(d)(5)(A), regarding employment requirements for new RAW workers is captioned "For 3 Years to Avoid Deportation."

Neither the statute nor the proposed regulations make provision for administrative or judicial review of a termination decision. Nor does the statute contain the restrictions on judicial and administrative review as are contained in the

---

[130] INA §210A(d)(5)(C).

[131] INA §210A(d)(5)(c).

[132] INA §210(d)(2).

[133] See proposed 8 CFR §210a.6(h).

[134] INA §241(a)(20); proposed 8 CFR §§210a.6(h)(1), 210a.6(b)(3). See INA §210A(d)(5).

legalization and SAW provisions. However, given the fact that deportation proceedings are the avenue for termination proceedings, an order entered in such proceedings after a finding of deportability would be reviewable through the normal channels of administrative and judicial review open to all aliens in deportation proceedings.

The I-688 Temporary Resident Card shall not be issued, reissued or extended and shall lose its validity if temporary resident status has been terminated.[135] An alien whose status is terminated must promptly surrender his or her I-688A or I-688 upon demand to the INS district director.[136]

---

[135] Proposed 8 CFR §210a.6(f)(2).

[136] Proposed 8 CFR §210a.6(h)(1).

CHAPTER TEN

**LEGALIZATION OF NATIONALS FROM COUNTRIES
GRANTED EXTENDED VOLUNTARY DEPARTURE:
POLES, ETHIOPIANS, UGANDANS, AND AFGHANS**

10.1	BASIC ELIGIBILITY REQUIREMENTS FOR LEGALIZATION OF NATIONALS FROM COUNTRIES GRANTED EXTENDED VOLUNTARY DEPARTURE: POLES, ETHIOPIANS, UGANDANS AND AFGHANS WHO ENTERED THE UNITED STATES BEFORE JULY 21, 1984	10-3
10.2	CONFIDENTIALITY, FRAUD, AND RELATED CRIMINAL PENALTIES	10-5
	10.2(a) Confidentiality	10-5
	10.2(b) Fraud in the Making of an Application for Temporary Residence	10-5
10.3	COUNTRIES GRANTED EXTENDED VOLUNTARY DEPARTURE BETWEEN NOVEMBER 1, 1982 AND NOVEMBER 1, 1987	10-5
10.4	ENTRY INTO THE UNITED STATES BEFORE JULY 21, 1984	10-7
10.5	NONIMMIGRANTS MUST ESTABLISH EXPIRATION OF STAY BEFORE JANUARY 21, 1985 OR APPLICATION FOR ASYLUM BEFORE JULY 21, 1984	10-7
	10.5(a) Manner of Entry into the United States	10-7
	10.5(b) Nonimmigrants-Expiration of Authorized Stay before January 21, 1985; Duration of Status	10-8
	10.5(c) Nonimmigrants--Application for Political Asylum before July 21, 1984	10-9
	10.5(d) Nonimmigrants-Validity of the Nonimmigrant Visa	10-10
	10.5(e) Re-entry after July 21, 1984 on a Nonimmigrant Visa	10-10
	10.5(f) Nonimmigrants--Eligibility of Otherwise Qualifying Exchange Visitors	10-11
10.6	CONTINUOUS RESIDENCE IN THE UNITED STATES SINCE A DATE PRIOR TO JULY 21, 1984	10-11
10.7	CONTINUOUS PHYSICAL PRESENCE IN THE UNITED STATES SINCE DECEMBER 22, 1987	10-12
10.8	ADMISSIBILITY AS AN IMMIGRANT	10-12
	10.8(a) Introduction	10-12
	10.8(b) Excludability	10-13

	(1)	Inapplicable Grounds of Excludability	10-13
	(2)	Applicable Grounds of Excludability	10-14
	(3)	Waivers of Excludability	10-16

10.9 OTHER DISQUALIFYING GROUNDS   10-17

10.10   BURDEN OF PROOF: THE ALIEN MUST ESTABLISH ELIGIBILITY BY A PREPONDERANCE OF CREDIBLE AND VERIFIABLE EVIDENCE   10-17

10.11   DOCUMENTATION   10-18

10.11(a)	Proof of Identity	10-19
10.11(b)	Proof of Nationality	10-19
10.11(c)	Proof of Residence	10-20
10.11(d)	Proof of Financial Responsibility	10-20

10.12   FILING AND PROCESSING THE APPLICATION   10-20

10.12(a)	Filing the Application	10-20
10.12(b)	INS Interview, Employment and Travel Authorization	10-21

10.13   DECISION AND APPEAL PROCESS   10-22

10.14   TERMINATION OF TEMPORARY RESIDENT STATUS   10-25

10.15   ADJUSTMENT FROM TEMPORARY TO PERMANENT RESIDENT STATUS   10-26

CHAPTER TEN

LEGALIZATION OF NATIONALS FROM COUNTRIES GRANTED EXTENDED VOLUNTARY DEPARTURE: POLES, ETHIOPIANS, UGANDANS, AND AFGHANS

10.1 BASIC ELIGIBILITY REQUIREMENTS FOR LEGALIZATION OF NATIONALS FROM COUNTRIES GRANTED EXTENDED VOLUNTARY DEPARTURE: POLES, ETHIOPIANS, UGANDANS AND AFGHANS WHO ENTERED THE UNITED STATES BEFORE JULY 21, 1984

Pursuant to legislation enacted on December 22, 1987, nationals of countries granted extended voluntary departure ("EVD") at any time between November 1, 1982 and November 1, 1987 (i.e., Poland, Ethiopia, Uganda, and Afghanistan) who have continuously resided in the United States since a date prior to July 21, 1984 are eligible to apply for temporary resident status. Both the requirements and the procedures for obtaining temporary residence under these provisions are similar to those of the legalization program, INA §245A. Over 10,000 people are expected to apply under this program.[1] The basic eligibility requirements contained in the statute can be summarized as follows:

1. National of Poland, Ethiopia, Uganda, or Afghanistan;[2]

2. Entered the United States prior to July 21, 1984;

3. Those who entered the United States as nonimmigrants must also establish:

   a) the period of unauthorized stay as a nonimmigrant expired not later than January 21, 1985;

   or

   b) the alien applied for asylum before July 21, 1984.

4. Continuous residence in the United States since a date before July 21, 1984 (certain brief and casual departures not disqualifying);

---

[1] See 65 Interpreter Releases 411-412 (April 18, 1988).

[2] Nicaragua is also arguably a country whose nationals were granted Extended Voluntary Departure. See the discussion at §10.3 infra.

10-3

5. Continuous physical presence in the United States since December 22, 1987 (brief, casual and innocent departures or absences authorized by INS not disqualifying);

6. Not inadmissible under certain grounds of excludability set forth at INA §212(a);

7. Must not have been convicted of one felony or three misdemeanors committed in the United States;

8. Must not have assisted in the persecution of any person or persons on account of race, religion, nationality, membership in a particular social group, or political opinion;

9. Must register under the Military Selective Service Act if required;

10. Application within time period provided, March 21, 1988 through December 22, 1989.

The text of these provisions can be found in Pub.L. No. 100-204, section 902; 101 Stat. 1332; 133 Cong. Rec. H11297-11351 (daily ed. December 14, 1987); H.R. Conf. Rep. No. 100-475, 100th Cong., 1st Sess. (1987). Interim regulations were published in the Federal Register of March 21, 1988, Vol. 53, No. 54, at pp. 9274-9280. Final regulations were published in the Federal Register at 54 Fed. Reg. 6504-6512 (February 13, 1989). Each of the above requirements is discussed in detail below.

Although similar in most respects to IRCA's general legalization program under INA §245A, the following provisions of the legalization program were <u>not</u> incorporated <u>by</u> <u>the</u> <u>statute</u> into the temporary residence program for EVD nationals:

1. No requirement to file application within 30 days of issuance of Order to Show Cause;
2. Residence since July 21, 1984 need not be continuously "unlawful";
3. No obligation to provide information regarding relatives on application form;
4. Exchange visitors are not compelled to obtain INA §212(e) waivers;
5. No provision barring the admission of aliens into the U.S. in order to apply for benefits under this program;

10-4

6. No filing with QDEs;[3]
7. No confidentiality protections;[4]
8. No temporary stay of deportation;
9. No employment authorization upon presentation of *prima facie* application.[5]

10.2 CONFIDENTIALITY, FRAUD AND RELATED CRIMINAL PENALTIES

10.2(a) Confidentiality

Legalization provisions regarding confidentiality, the filing of applications through a Qualified Designated Entity (QDE), and extending confidentiality protections to applications filed with QDEs were also not incorporated in the amendments to the statute pertaining to nationals from countries granted EVD. The INS has nonetheless decided to keep its records confidential.[6] Also, because the regulations allow EVD nationals to file applications with the QDEs, the confidentiality of QDE files under INA §245A(c)(4) presumably applies.

10.2(b) Fraud in the Making of an Application for Temporary Residence

INA §245A(c)(6), which was incorporated in the INA amendments which accord temporary resident status to nationals of countries granted EVD, authorizes strict penalties for those who supply false information or documents in connection with a legalization application.[7] These provisions are discussed in greater detail in Chapter One, and should be consulted.

---

[3] The regulations allow for QDE filing of applications. Interim rule 8 CFR §245a.4(b)(5)(i).

[4] But *see* discussion in §10.2(a) *infra*.

[5] The regulations provide for employment authorization. Interim rule 8 CFR §245a.4(b)(14)(ii).

[6] *See* INS Memo of March 17, 1989, reprinted in 65 Interpreter Releases 269-270 (March 21, 1989).

[7] *See also* interim rule 8 CFR §245a.4(a)(5).

10.3 COUNTRIES GRANTED EXTENDED VOLUNTARY DEPARTURE BETWEEN NOVEMBER 1, 1982, AND NOVEMBER 1, 1987

The recent amendments to the Immigration and Nationality Act extend temporary resident status to nationals of certain countries previously granted EVD. The individual alien need not have sought and obtained Extended Voluntary Departure from the INS in order to qualify. Specifically, the law provides:

> ...any alien who is a national of a foreign country the nationals of which were provided (or allowed to continue in) "extended voluntary departure" by the Attorney General on the basis of a nationality group determination at any time during the 5-year period ending November 1, 1987...[8]

Since 1960, EVD has been granted, for varying periods of time, to nationals of Cuba, Dominican Republic, Czechoslovakia, Chile, Cambodia, Vietnam, Laos, Lebanon, Ethiopia, Hungary, Rumania, Uganda, Iran, Nicaragua, Afghanistan, and Poland.[9] During the 5-year period ending November 1, 1987, EVD was provided or continued for nationals of Poland, Ethiopia, Uganda, and Afghanistan. The regulations limit the grant of temporary residence to nationals of these countries.[10] Note that the individual applicant need not demonstrate that he or she was granted extended voluntary departure, merely that he or she is a member of a nationality granted EVD.

Also within the above 5-year time period, Attorney General Edwin Meese signed a memorandum directing INS offices to grant employment authorization of up to one year and stays of deportation to Nicaraguans who filed asylum applications. This action ratified earlier, more expansive action taken by the District Director of the INS office in Miami, Florida, who had announced in April of 1986 that he would not deport nationals of Nicaragua, whether or not they had filed for asylum.[11] Although the Attorney General's announcement stopped short of calling the action "Extended Voluntary Departure," referring to it as "deferred departure," nationals of Nicaragua may have an argument that they, too, come within the temporary residence

---

[8] See 133 Cong. Rec. H11297-11351, supra, at H11318.

[9] See 64 Interpreter Releases 1093 (September 21, 1987).

[10] Interim rule 8 CFR §245a.4(a)(9).

[11] Pursuant to INA §103, 8 CFR §103.1, the District Director is the agent of the Attorney General.

provisions for those accorded EVD status, as the status they were granted is essentially the same as EVD.[12]

10.4 ENTRY INTO THE UNITED STATES BEFORE JULY 21, 1984

Every applicant for temporary resident status under the temporary residence provisions for EVD nationals is required to demonstrate that he or she entered the United States as of any date prior to July 21, 1984.[13] According to the INS, American Samoa, Western Samoa, Micronesia, the Marshall Islands, or the Northern Marianas Islands are not included in the definition of the United States in INA §101(a)(38), thus entry to and residence in these islands does not meet this requirement.[14]

Although "entry" is a term of art used to distinguish those aliens whom the INS recognizes as having arrived in the United States, lawfully or otherwise, and those regarded as outside of the United States awaiting a determination of their admissibility, IRCA's implementing regulations construe that word more broadly, specifically allowing certain parolees to apply for legalization. The same rule should apply in this context.

This requirement does not mandate physical presence in the United States as of July 21, 1984. Aliens who reentered the United States after that date, having previously resided in the U.S., may nonetheless qualify if their continuous U.S. residence began prior to July 21, 1984 and other legalization requirements are met. In this context, the discussion of multiple entries into the United States, in Chapter One and in Chapter Five at §5.4(a)(1) should be consulted.

10.5 NONIMMIGRANTS MUST ESTABLISH EXPIRATION OF STAY BEFORE JANUARY 21, 1985 OR APPLICATION FOR ASYLUM BEFORE JULY 21, 1984

10.5(a) Manner of Entry into the United States

The legalization provisions of the recent amendments establish eligibility for two groups: (a) those who entered as nonimmigrants, who must prove either expiration of authorized

---

[12] See 64 Interpreter Releases 821-822 (July 13, 1987), and 63 Interpreter Releases 342 (April 18, 1986).

[13] See INA §245A(a)(2); 8 CFR §§245a.2(b)(6) and (7).

[14] See 65 Interpreter Releases, 77 (January 25, 1988).

stay prior to January 21, 1985 or application for political asylum before July 21, 1984; and (b) <u>all other aliens</u>, who must merely prove entry and continuous residence since July 21, 1984.[15] Thus, those who entered the United States in a status which is not clearly a nonimmigrant status, e.g., parole, without inspection, etc., fall under the more lenient provisions applying to all aliens other than nonimmigrants. Those who entered pursuant to a nonimmigrant visa must comply with certain additional requirements, discussed below.

10.5(b) <u>Nonimmigrants-Expiration of Authorized Stay before January 21, 1985; Duration of Status</u>

A nonimmigrant whose authorized admission, including any extension and/or change of status, expired before January 21, 1985 through the passage of time is eligible to apply for temporary residence under these provisions.[16] The term "authorized stay" denotes the date on which the authorized period of an alien's admission in a nonimmigrant status expires. The expiration date is marked either on Form I-94 or on the INS admission stamp placed in the alien's passport, or both. It does not correspond to the expiration date of the visa stamp in the alien's passport. If the authorized stay, or any subsequent extensions thereof granted by INS, expired prior to January 21, 1985, the alien meets this requirement.

Although an alien whose nonimmigrant stay was extended by the INS beyond January 21, 1985 normally would be found to be ineligible, if such extension was obtained by fraud or misrepresentation the alien is arguably in the same position, legally, as the applicant who re-entered the United States with a nonimmigrant visa after July 21, 1984. The regulations provide that an otherwise eligible applicant who reenters the United States as a nonimmigrant in order to return to an unrelinquished residence is eligible for temporary residence under this program provided he or she seeks and is granted a waiver of INA §212(a)(19) excludability grounds for fraud.[17] Likewise, EVD nationals who obtained extensions of their stays based on fraud or misrepresentation may argue that such

---

[15] Interim rule 8 CFR §245a.4(a).

[16] Interim rules 8 CFR §§245a.4(a)(12), 245a.4(b)(2)(i)(B).

[17] Interim rule 8 CFR §245a.4(b)(2)(D).

extensions are also invalid and should be ignored.[18] Decisions interpreting INA §245A's "unlawful residence" requirement lend support to this position.[19]

Certain nonimmigrants are admitted to the United States for "Duration of Status" (A, G, F or J visas); their I-94 forms are endorsed "Duration of Status" or "D/S." They are admitted, not until a fixed date, but for as long as they maintain their status.[20] Those admitted on "A" or "G" visas for Duration of Status must show that their qualifying employment terminated or that they ceased to be recognized by the Department of State as qualified for that visa classification prior to January 21, 1985.[21] Those admitted on an "F" visa for duration of status must show the completion of a full course of studies, including practical training or time to depart (if any) prior to January 21, 1985.[22] Those students who were retroactively restored to student status (which would otherwise preclude their eligibility) must present evidence that they had otherwise terminated their status during the requisite time period in order to qualify.

A dependent F-2 alien otherwise eligible who was admitted into the United States with a specific time period, as opposed to duration of status, documented on Service Form I-94, Arrival-Departure Record that extended beyond July 21, 1984 is considered eligible if the principal F-1 alien is found eligible.

10.5(c) Nonimmigrants--Application for Political Asylum before July 21, 1984

Nonimmigrants who cannot prove that their authorized stay expired through the passage of time must prove that they applied

---

[18] A waiver of excludability under INA §212(a)(19) would also be required in such cases.

[19] See Chapter Five, §5.4(a)(3)(c).

[20] For details regarding nonimmigrant admissions for duration of status, and when such status is deemed to have terminated, consult Chapter Five, §5.4(a)(3)(a).

[21] Interim rule 8 CFR §245a.4(b)(2)(E).

[22] Interim rule 8 CFR §245a.4(b)(2)(F).

for political asylum before July 21, 1984.[23] If the exact date of filing is not known, the applicant should file a form G-639 Freedom of Information Act (FOIA) request to obtain access to INS's files.

10.5(d) Nonimmigrants--Validity of the Nonimmigrant Visa

The visa itself, and the subsequent admission, is arguably invalid if obtained by fraud or misrepresentation. A nonimmigrant visa is defined as a visa <u>properly issued to an eligible nonimmigrant</u>.[24] In construing the statutory grounds of deportability and excludability relating to documentary requirements, the courts have held that a visa obtained through a deception which amounted to a material misrepresentation is equivalent to no documents at all.[25] An alien admitted either as a nonimmigrant or as an immigrant based upon presentation of an unlawfully obtained or an improperly issued visa is subject to exclusion or deportation as an immigrant not in possession of a valid immigrant visa.[26] The alien is thus in the same position as one who entered without inspection, except that he or she must obtain a waiver of the grounds of excludability pertaining to fraud.[27]

10.5(e) Re-entry after July 21, 1984 on a Nonimmigrant Visa

Otherwise eligible applicants who, after July 21, 1984, departed the United States and returned to an unrelinquished U.S. residence on a nonimmigrant visa are eligible provided they seek and are granted a waiver of INA §212(a)(19) excludability grounds for fraud.[28]

---

[23] Interim rule 8 CFR §245a.4(b)(2)(C).

[24] INA §101(a)(26).

[25] <u>Feodoranko v. United States</u>, 449 U.S. 490 (1981); <u>Fink v. Reimer</u>, 96 F. 2d 217 (2d Cir.1938); <u>Ablett v. Brownell</u>, 240 F. 2d 625 (D.C. Cir. 1957).

[26] INA §212(a)(20).

[27] <u>See</u> the discussion in Chapter One.

[28] Interim rule CFR §245a.4(b)(2)(D).

10.5(f) Nonimmigrants--Eligibility of Otherwise Qualifying Exchange Visitors

Unlike the legalization program, provisions governing those nationalities accorded EVD status do not require nonimmigrant exchange visitors or exchange students (J-1, J-2 visa) to demonstrate either compliance with the 2-year foreign residence requirement of INA §212(e) or obtain a waiver of the 2-year foreign residence requirement.

10.6 CONTINUOUS RESIDENCE IN THE UNITED STATES SINCE A DATE PRIOR TO JULY 21, 1984

The applicant must establish that he or she has resided continuously in the United States from before July 21, 1984, to the date of enactment of the amendments, i.e., December 22, 1987. The interim regulations define "resided continuously" as follows:

(a) no single departure from the country exceeded 45 days, and the aggregate of all absences between July 21, 1984 and the date of application does not exceed 180 days, unless due to emergent reasons return to the United States could not be accomplished within these time periods;

(b) the alien maintained a residence in the United States;

(c) the alien's departure was not based on an order of deportation.[29]

(d) any absence pursuant to advance parole or stateside criteria program parole does not interrupt the applicant's continuous residence.[30]

Note that unlike the legalization program, applicants under the provisions governing EVD nationals are *not* required to prove their "unlawful status" throughout the period of their continuous residence. However, according to the regulations, those in the United States before July 21, 1984 and who left and

---

[29] Interim rules 8 CFR §§2451.4(a)(3), 245a.4(b)(8).

[30] Id.

re-entered on nonimmigrant visas after July 21, 1984 must show that they were in an unlawful status before that date.[31]

The effect of departures on "continuous residence" is also discussed in Chapter Five, §5.4(a)(1).

10.7 CONTINUOUS PHYSICAL PRESENCE IN THE UNITED STATES SINCE DECEMBER 22, 1987

Superimposed upon the requirement of continuous residence since before July 21, 1984, is the requirement that the applicant be "continuously physically present" in the United States since the date of enactment, December 22, 1987. This requirement can be met by those outside of the United States after December 22, 1987 if they reentered the United States before March 21, 1988.[32] Absences after March 21, 1988 which are "brief, casual, and innocent" will not break the alien's continuous physical presence. The interim regulations define "brief, casual and innocent departures" as those that are: a) authorized by the Service (advance parole)[33] for not more than 30 days for legitimate emergency or humanitarian purposes unless a further period of authorized departure has been granted in the discretion of the district director; or b) beyond the alien's control.[34]

Other departures might also be considered brief, casual, and innocent. The discussion in Chapter Five, §5.4(a)(2) should be consulted in this regard.

10.8 ADMISSIBILITY AS AN IMMIGRANT

10.8(a)   Introduction

The provisions relating to EVD nationals require that an applicant be admissible as an immigrant as required by INA §245A(a)(4). Under this provision both the grounds of excludability and the waiver provisions which apply to the legalization program are incorporated into the provisions

---

[31] Interim rule 8 CFR §245a.4(b)(2)(D). Reentry on a nonimmigrant visa may require the filing of a waiver.

[32] Interim rule 8 CFR §§245a.4(a)(6), 245a.4(b)(12)(i).

[33] 8 CFR §212.5(e).

[34] Interim rules 8 CFR §§245a.4(a)(7), 245a.4(b)(12)(ii).

governing the legalization of Poles, Ethiopians, Ugandans, and Afghans.

10.8(b) Excludability

Section 212 of the INA sets forth thirty-three grounds of excludability which define various classes of aliens who are inadmissible to the United States. Most, but not all, of these grounds of excludability apply to applicants for temporary residence as EVD nationals. Many of the grounds of excludability that do apply can be waived "for humanitarian purposes, to assure family unity, or when it is otherwise in the public interest."[35] The standard governing this waiver differs favorably in comparison to the standard generally applied in adjudicating requests for excludability waivers applicable to applicants for immigrant or nonimmigrant status.[36]

10.8(b)(1) Inapplicable Grounds of Excludability

The following grounds of excludability, normally applicable to aliens seeking entry either as immigrants or nonimmigrants, are automatically waived in cases of EVD nationals:

212(a)(14)	Aliens coming to perform skilled or unskilled work in the United States without a labor certification;
212(a)(20)	Aliens not in possession of a valid visa or passport;
212(a)(21)	Aliens entering with a visa issued in violation of INA §203 numerical limits;
212(a)(25)	Illiterates;
212(a)(32)	Graduates of foreign medical schools who have not passed the appropriate visa qualifying examination.[37]

---

[35] See INA §245A(d)(2)(B)(i), incorporated by reference in Pub. L. No. 101-204, 101 Stat. 1332 relating to EVD nationals.

[36] A comparative chart of exclusion grounds and waivers available to applicants for different forms of relief under the INA is reproduced in the Appendix.

[37] Interim rule 8 CFR §245a.4(b)(11).

10.8(b)(2)   Applicable Grounds of Excludability

Applicants must, however, show that they are not inadmissible based upon any of the remaining grounds of excludability contained in INA §212, which include,

212(a)(1)*	Aliens who are mentally retarded;
212(a)(2)*	Aliens who are insane;
212(a)(3)*	Aliens who have had one or more attacks of insanity;
212(a)(4)*	Aliens afflicted with psychopathic personality, sexual deviation, or mental defect;
212(a)(5)*	Narcotic drug addicts or chronic alcoholics;
212(a)(6)*	Aliens afflicted with dangerous contagious diseases;
212(a)(7)*	Aliens with a physical disability effecting ability to earn a living;
212(a)(8)*	Paupers, professional beggars or vagrants;
212(a)(9)	Aliens convicted of a crime of moral turpitude (other than a purely political offense and certain crimes committed while under the age of 18), or aliens who have admitted committing such a crime;
212(a)(10)	Aliens convicted of two or more offenses, regardless of whether they arose from a single trial or scheme, if the aggregate sentence of confinement was for five years or more;
212(a)(11)*	Polygamists;
212(a)(12)*	Procurers and prostitutes;
212(a)(13)*	Aliens entering to engage in any immoral sexual act;
212(a)(15)**	Aliens likely to become public charges (determined by a special rule, discussed below);
212(a)(16)*	Aliens excluded within one year prior to the date of application;
212(a)(17)*	Aliens deported within five years prior to the date of application unless the Attorney General consents to their admission;
212(a)(18)*	Stowaways;
212(a)(19)*	Aliens who have procured or sought to procure a visa or other documentation by fraud or willful misrepresentation of a material fact;
212(a)(22)*	Aliens who are ineligible to citizenship and draft evaders;
212(a)(23)**	Any alien convicted of a drug related offense or in whose case there is reason to believe the alien engaged in trafficking;

212(a)(24)*	Aliens who arrived on non-signatory transportation lines;
212(a)(26)*	Aliens lacking valid passports;
212(a)(27)	Aliens who are threats to national security;
212(a)(28)	Anarchists, communists and subversives
212(a)(29)	Threats to the national security and subversives;
212(a)(30)*	Aliens accompanying an alien excluded due to physical or mental problems;
212(a)(31)*	Aliens who assisted any other alien to enter the United States in violation of law;
212(a)(33)	Aliens who assisted in Nazi persecution.[38]

To establish admissibility under INA §§212(a)(1) through (6), the results of a medical examination by an approved physician must be included with the application for temporary resident status.[39] The additional applicable grounds of excludability are listed on the application form with regard to which the alien must swear, under penalty of perjury, that he or she does not belong to any of the proscribed categories. Usually, the execution of this <u>jurat</u> will suffice as proof that the alien is not excludable under the enumerated grounds, however, the immigration examiner can request that additional documents be submitted to disprove excludability if the facts warrant it.

Any applicant certified under exclusion grounds INA §212(a)(1) through (5) above may appeal pursuant to INA §§234 and 235 as well as seek a waiver of excludability.[40]

Excludability based on likelihood to become a public charge is determined by application of a "Special rule" similar to that provided by the general legalization provisions, INA §245A. Excludability under this provision can be avoided if the applicant can show that (a) based on the totality of the circumstances he or she is unlikely to become a public charge or (b) he or she shows a "consistent employment history show[ing] the ability to support himself of herself and his or her family...without recourse to public cash assistance."[41]

Public cash assistance is defined in the regulations as income or needs-based monetary assistance, including SSI,

---

[38] Interim rule 8 CFR §245a.4(b)(11).

[39] Interim rule 8 CFR §245a.4(b)(9).

[40] Interim 8 CFR §245a.4(b)(9).

[41] Interim rule 8 CFR §245a.4(b)(11)(iv).

received by the applicant or his or her immediate family members. It does not include in-kind assistance such as food stamps, public housing, workers compensation, Medicare, Medicaid, emergency treatment, or WIC.[42]

Additional details concerning grounds of excludability are also discussed in Chapters One and Five.

10.8(b)(3)   Waivers of Excludability

Inadmissibility under any of the grounds above that are marked by an asterisk (*) can be overcome by a waiver under IRCA which provides:

(i) In General.--Except as provided in clause (ii), the Attorney General may waive any other provision of Section 212(a) in the case of individual aliens for humanitarian purposes, to assure family unity, or when it is otherwise in the public interest.[43]

A waiver application is submitted by filing a completed form I-690 and the $35.00 filing fee. The standard for waivers is discussed in Chapter Five, §5.5.

Two asterisks (**) are used to indicate those grounds of excludability which can be waived under limited circumstances. Specifically, INA §212(a)(15), barring the adjustment of those determined to be likely to become public charges, can be waived under INA §245A(d)(2)(B) as to applications for <u>temporary resident status,</u> but not as to applications for permanent resident status.[44] In the case of excludability under INA §212(a)(23), the IRCA waiver under INA §245A(d)(2)(B) is available in those cases in which excludability is based on a conviction for simple possession of under 30 grams of marijuana or hashish.

The IRCA waiver provision <u>cannot</u> be used to overcome excludability based upon INA §§212(a)(9), (10), (15) [as it applies to applications for adjustment to permanent resident

---

[42]   Interim rule 8 CFR §245a.4(a)(10).

[43]   INA §245A(d)(2)(B), incorporated by reference in the provisions relating to EVD nationals; interim rule 8 CFR §245a.4(b)(11)(ii).

[44]   For a discussion of this ground of excludability, the applicable standard and the applicability of INA §245A(d)(2)(B) waiver provisions, Chapter One.

status], (23) [except as it applies to simple possession of less than thirty grams of marijuana], (27), (28), (29) and (33).[45]

10.9 OTHER DISQUALIFYING GROUNDS

The statute bars any applicant who falls within the following disqualifying grounds:

1) convicted of one felony or three misdemeanors committed in the United States;

2) those who assisted in the persecution of any person or persons on account of race, religion, nationality, membership in a particular social group, or political opinion[46];

3) males age 17 to 25 who have not registered under the Military Selective Service Act, if the alien is required to be so registered under that Act (applicants may register at the time they file the I-687 application).[47]

These requirements are identical to those imposed on legalization applicants under INA §245A.

10.10 BURDEN OF PROOF: THE ALIEN MUST ESTABLISH ELIGIBILITY BY A PREPONDERANCE OF CREDIBLE AND VERIFIABLE EVIDENCE

An applicant for temporary resident status as an EVD national must prove eligibility by a preponderance of the evidence. An applicant will be required to prove that he or she:

(1) has resided in the United States for the requisite periods;

(2) is admissible to the United States under the provisions of INA §245A; and

(3) is otherwise eligible for adjustment of status.[48]

---

[45] See INA §245A(d)(2)(B)(ii).

[46] Interim rule 8 CFR §245a.4(b)(3).

[47] Interim rule 8 CFR §245a.4(b)(7).

[48] Interim rule 8 CFR §245a.4(b)(4)(vi).

The inference to be drawn from such evidence depends upon the extent of the documentation, its credibility and its amenability to verification. The sufficiency of all the evidence produced by the applicant will be judged according to its probative value and credibility. To meet his or her burden of proof, an applicant must provide evidence of eligibility apart from his or her own testimony. In judging the probative value and credibility of the evidence submitted, greater weight will be given to the submission of original documentation.[49] An alien must agree to assist the INS in verifying declarations that the applicant has not received public assistance and does not have a criminal record.[50] All documentation submitted will be subject to Service verification. Applications submitted with unverifiable documentation may be denied. Failure by an applicant to authorize release to INS of information protected by the Privacy Act and/or related laws in order for INS to adjudicate a claim may result in denial of the benifit sought.

10.11 DOCUMENTATION

To establish eligibility under this program, the applicant must submit:

1) application Form I-687;

2) if age 14 or older, fingerprint card (Form FD-256);

3) completed medical report (Form I-693);

4) proof of identity (discussed below);

5) proof of nationality (discussed below);

6) proof of residence (discussed below);

7) proof of financial responsibility (discussed below);[51]

8) photographs;

---

[49] Interim rule 8 CFR §245a.4(b)(4)(vi).

[50] Interim rule 8 CFR §245a.4(b)(11)(v).

[51] Interim rule 8 CFR §245a.4(b)(4)(v).

9) if male, age 17 to 25, proof of Selective Service registration or completed form SSS-1;[52]

10) $50.00 filing fee in the form of money order or cashiers check;

11) if any of the eligibility criteria is established under an assumed name, documentation establishing a common identity;[53]

12) Waiver form I-690 and $35.00 filing fee.[54]

10.11(a) Proof of Identity

Documents which can be presented to establish identity are, in descending order of preference:

1) Passport;

2) Birth certificate;

3) Any national identity document from the alien's

4) Driver's license or similar document issued by a state if it contains a photo;

5) Baptismal Record/Marriage Certificate; or

6) Affidavits.[55]

10.11(b) Proof of Nationality

Documents which can be presented to prove nationality include:

1) Passport;

2) Birth certificate;

---

[52] Interim rule 8 CFR §245a.4(b)(7).

[53] Interim rule 8 CFR §245a.4(b)(4)(iii).

[54] Interim rule 8 CFR §245a.4(b)(11)(ii).

[55] Interim rule 8 CFR §245a.4(b)(4)(i).

3) Any national identity document from the alien's country of origin bearing photo and fingerprint;

4) Other credible documents, including those created by, or in the possession of the INS, or any other documents (excluding affidavits) that, when taken singly, or together as a whole, establish the alien's nationality.[56]

10.11(c) Proof of Residence

Any document which establishes continuous residence since July 21, 1984 may be presented in support of the application, including employment-related documents, tax documents, utility bills, school records, medical records, attestations of churches, union, or other organizations or other documents.[57]

10.11(d) Proof of Financial Responsibility

Generally, employment documents submitted as proof of residence will be accepted as proof of financial responsibility as well. Bank statements or proof of assets may also be submitted. If the alien's period(s) of residence in the United States include significant gaps in employment or if there is reason to believe that the alien may have received public assistance while employed, the alien may be required to provide proof that he or she has not received public cash assistance.[58]

10.12 FILING AND PROCESSING THE APPLICATION

10.12(a) Filing the Application

The alien who meets all of the above requirements for temporary resident must file the application forms and supporting documents <u>on time</u>, or temporary residence will be denied. Eligible aliens from the qualifying nationalities have from March 21, 1988 through December 22, 1989, to file their applications.[59] The statute does <u>not</u> require those

---

[56] Interim rule 8 CFR §245a.4(b)(4)(ii).

[57] Interim rule 8 CFR §245a.4(b)(4)(iv).

[58] Interim rule 8 CFR §245a.4(b)(4)(v).

[59] Interim rules 8 CFR §§245a.4(b)(1)(i),(ii).

apprehended or served with an Order to Show Cause to file their applications within 30 days.

The date the alien submits a completed application to a Service office or designated entity shall be considered the filing date of the application. Designated entities are required to forward completed applications to the appropriate Service office within 60 days of receipt.[60] The status of an alien whose application for temporary resident status is approved shall be adjusted to that of a lawful temporary resident as of the date indicated on the application fee receipt issued at the Service Office.[61] Because of the retroactivity of the grant of temporary residence, those who contemplate leaving the United States after filing the application but before it is approved should review the departure restrictions discussed below.

To file an application under the EVD national program, the alien must submit for I-687 with all supporting documents and a $185 fee to the legalization office nearest his or her residence or at an office of a qualified designated entity (QDE). If the application is filed with a designated entity, the alien must have consented to having the designated entity forward the application to the Service office. The applicant should alter the form at block No. 1 in that neither Item A nor B apply. The applicant should add a "C", stating: "temporary residence as an alien eligible to apply under section 902".

10.12(b) <u>INS Interview; Employment and Travel Authorization</u>

Each applicant, regardless of age, must appear at the appropriate Service office and must be fingerprinted for the purpose of issuance of Forms I-688A and I-688. Each applicant shall be interviewed by an immigration officer, except that the interview may be waived for a child under 14 years of age, or when it is impractical because of the health or advanced age of the applicant.[62]

If an appointment cannot be scheduled within 30 days of the filing of the application, authorization to accept employment will be granted, valid until the scheduled appointment date. The appointment letter will be endorsed with the temporary

---

[60] Interim rule 8 CFR §§245a.4(b)(5), 245a.4(b)(6).

[61] Interim rule 8 CFR §245a.4(b)(19).

[62] Interim rule 8 CFR §245a.4(b)(10).

employment authorization. Form I-688A, Employment Authorization, will be given to the applicant after an interview has been completed by an immigration officer unless a formal denial is issued by a Service office. This temporary employment authorization will be restricted to six-months duration, pending final determination on the application for temporary resident status.[63]

During the time period from the date that an alien's application establishing *prima facie* eligibility for temporary resident status is reviewed at a Service office and the date status as a temporary resident is granted, the alien applicant can be readmitted to the United States provided his or her departure was authorized under the Service's advance parole provisions contained in 8 CFR §212.5(e).[64]

If fraud, willful misrepresentation or concealment of a material fact, knowingly providing a false writing or document, knowingly making a false statement, or representation, or other prohibited activity is established during the process of making the determination on the application, the INS will refer the matter to the United States Attorney for prosecution of the alien or of any person who created or supplied the false writing or document.[65]

10.13 DECISION AND APPEAL PROCESS

The applicant shall be notified in writing of the decision on his or her application. Temporary Residence applications and waiver applications will be approved or denied by the Director of the Regional Processing Facility except in cases involving clear statutory ineligibility or fraud, in which case the Director of the LO may deny the application. The Director of the LO may also approve the application if it was sent to the LO by the RPF for re-interview.[66]

Upon grant of an application for adjustment to temporary resident status by a Regional Processing Facility, the processing facility will forward a notice of approval to the alien at his or her last known address, or to his or her legal representative. The alien will be required to return to the

---

[63] Interim rule 8 CFR §245a.4(b)(14).

[64] Interim rule 8 CFR §245a.4(b)(14).

[65] Interim rule 8 CFR §245a.4(b)(5).

[66] Interim rule 8 CFR §245a.4(b)(11)(ii).

Service office where the application was initially received, surrender the I-688A previously issued, and obtain Form I-688, Temporary Resident Card, authorizing employment and travel abroad.[67]

Once an alien's application for temporary resident status has been approved, certain restrictions on travel apply. To preserve the temporary residents eligibility to subsequently apply for permanent resident status, the following restrictions governing departures should be kept in mind:

1. Must not depart while under deportation proceedings, such proceedings have been instituted subsequent to the approval of temporary resident status. A temporary resident alien will not be considered deported if that alien departs the United States while under an outstanding order of deportation issued prior to the approval of temporary resident status;

2. Must not be absent from the United States for more than 30 days on the date application for admission is made; and

   Must not be absent from the United States for an aggregate period of more than 90 days since the date the alien was granted lawful temporary resident status (unless emergent reasons prevented return within these time periods);[68]

3. Must present Form I-688 upon re-entry to the U.S;

4. Must present himself of herself for inspection;

5. Must be otherwise admissible;[69] and

6. Must show a continuing intention to adjust status to permanent residence.[70]

The periods of time that an alien can be absent from the United States may be waived at the discretion of the Attorney General in cases where the absence from the United States was

---

[67] Interim rule 8 CFR §245a.4(b)(14).

[68] Interim rule 8 CFR §245a.4(a)(4).

[69] Interim rule 8 CFR §245a.4(b)(13).

[70] Interim rule 8 CFR §245a.4(a)(6).

due merely to a brief and casual trip abroad due to emergent or extenuating circumstances beyond the alien's control.

IRCA's bar on the receipt of most forms of public assistance for a period of five years applies to aliens achieving temporary resident status under the EVD program.

If the application is denied, the reason(s) for the decision shall be provided to the applicant. Upon denial of an application for adjustment to temporary resident status, the alien will be notified that if a timely appeal is not submitted, employment authorization shall be automatically revoked on the final day of the appeal period.[71] An adverse decision under this part may be appealed to the Associate Commissioner, Examinations (Administrative Appeals Unit). Any appeal shall be submitted to the Regional Processing Facility (RPF) on Form I-694 with the required $50.00 fee within 30 days after service of the Notice of Denial. An appeal received after the 30-day period for submission of an appeal will not be accepted. If the denial is mailed to the applicant, the 30-day period for submission of the appeal begins three days after the Notice of Denial is mailed.[72]

The alien or his or her representative may request a copy of the Record of Proceedings (ROP) at the time the Notice of Appeal is filed. A brief may be submitted with the appeal form or submitted up to 30 calendar days from the date of receipt of the appeal form at the RPF or 30 days after receipt of the Record of Proceeding by the applicant, if requested. Briefs filed after submission of the appeal should be mailed directly to the RPF. For a good cause shown, the time within which a brief supporting an appeal may be submitted may be extended by the Director of the RPF.

The Regional Processing Facility director may *sua sponte* reopen and reconsider any adverse decision. When an appeal to the Associate Commissioner, Examination (Administrative Appeals Unit) has been filed, the INS director of the Regional Processing Facility may issue a new decision granting the benefit which has been requested. The director's new decision must be served on the appealing party within 45 days of receipt of any briefs and/or new evidence, or upon expiration of the time allowed for the submission of any briefs. Motions to

---

[71] Interim rule 8 CFR §245a.4(b)(14)(iv).

[72] Interim rule 8 CFR §245a.4(b)(16); *see* 8 CFR §103.5a(b).

reopen a proceeding or reconsider a decision shall not be considered.[73]

The Regional Processing Facility director may also, in accordance with 8 CFR §103.4, certify a decision to the Associate Commissioner, Examinations (Administrative Appeals Unit) when the case involves an unusually complex or novel question of law or fact.[74]

10.14 TERMINATION OF TEMPORARY RESIDENT STATUS

Temporary resident status obtained under the provisions for EVD nationals can be terminated by the director of the Regional Processing Facility for the following reasons:

(1) It is determined that the alien was ineligible for temporary residence;

(2) The alien commits an act which renders him or her inadmissible as an immigrant, unless a waiver is obtainable under IRCA for the exclusion grounds in question;

(3) The alien is convicted of any felony or three or more misdemeanors;

(4) The alien fails to adjust status to permanent residence within 31 months of the date granted temporary residence.

Prior to termination, the alien must be given an opportunity to offer evidence in opposition to the grounds alleged for termination of his or her status. This evidence must be submitted within 30 days after service of the "Notice of Intent to Terminate". The Regional Processing Facility must notify the alien of the decision by certified mail to his or her last known address (and to his or her representative). The notice to terminate must also advise the alien that any INS employment authorization, travel authorization, or Form I-688 temporary resident card previously issued to the alien shall be declared void within 30 days if no appeal of the termination is filed within that period. Appeals of the termination decision must be filed with the RPF on Form I-694 within 30 days. If the termination decision is not appealed within 30 days, any INS document issued to the alien must be surrendered to the INS upon

---

[73] Interim rule 8 CFR §245a.4(b)(17).

[74] Interim rule 8 CFR §245a.4(b)(18).

demand. Failure to appeal shall act to return the alien to the status held prior to adjustment.[75]

10.15   **ADJUSTMENT FROM TEMPORARY TO PERMANENT RESIDENT STATUS**

After the alien has been in temporary residence status for 18 months, he or she may apply for permanent residence status during a twelve month period which begins after a full 18 months of temporary residence status has been completed. Because temporary residence status, once approved, is retroactive to the date of filing, all calculations of deadlines should be made based on temporary residence having commenced as of the date of the filing of the application and payment of the application fee. The INS will begin accepting applications by EVD national temporary residents on September 21, 1989.

The provisions of IRCA's general legalization program relating to the adjustment of temporary resident to permanent resident status apply to the program for EVD nationals. Thus, upon applying for permanent resident status, the alien must demonstrate that he or she does not fall within any of IRCA's excludability grounds. Additionally, he or she must establish that no departure during the time of temporary residence exceeded 30 days (for any single departure), or 90 days (aggregate), unless emergent reasons prevented his or her return within these time periods.[76] The substantive and procedural requirements for adjustment to permanent resident status under the general legalization program, contained in Chapters Two and Three of this book, should be consulted.

---

[75]   Interim rule 8 CFR §245a.4(b)(20).

[76]   Interim rule 8 CFR §245a.4(a)(4).

CHAPTER ELEVEN

REGISTRY

11.1	BASIC ELIGIBILITY REQUIREMENTS	11-3
11.2	CONTINUOUS RESIDENCE SINCE PRIOR TO JANUARY 1, 1972	11-4
	11.2(a) Date and Manner of Entry	11-5
	11.2(b) Continuous United States Residence Since Entry	11-5
11.3	ADMISSIBILITY	11-7
	11.3(a) Grounds of Excludability Applicable to Registry	11-7
	11.3(b) Waivers of Grounds of Excludability	11-7
11.4	GOOD MORAL CHARACTER	11-9
11.5	NOT INELIGIBLE FOR UNITED STATES CITIZENSHIP	11-11
11.6	DOCUMENTATION	11-11
11.7	PROCEDURE FOR APPLYING FOR REGISTRY	11-12
	11.7(a) Application	11-12
	11.7(b) Adjudication of the Application	11-13

CHAPTER ELEVEN

REGISTRY

11.1 BASIC ELIGIBILITY REQUIREMENTS

An alien who has resided continuously in the United States since before January 1, 1972, is eligible to apply for lawful permanent resident status under the "registry" provision of the statute, INA §249. The Registry provision previously applied to those who could prove entry prior to June 30, 1948 and was therefore seldom used; with the enactment of IRCA on November 6, 1986, it became available to those who entered before January 1, 1972. The granting of a registry application results in lawful permanent residence.

Interim rules pertaining to registry applications were published in the Federal Register of March 3, 1987, Vol. 52, No. 41, at pages 6322-6323.

The applicant must satisfy these basic requirements, discussed in greater detail below:

1. Entry to the United States prior to January 1, 1972;

2. There must be no record that the applicant was at any time a lawfully admitted permanent resident;

3. Continuous residence in the United States since the qualifying date of entry;

4. Must not be inadmissible under grounds of excludability relating to criminals, procurers, other immoral persons, subversives, controlled substance violators or smugglers of aliens (waivers are available in some cases);

5. Good moral character;

6. Must not be ineligible for United States citizenship due to court martial for desertion or exemption from military service based on alienage;

7. The applicant must warrant the favorable exercise of discretion.

The burden of proof is on the applicant to establish compliance with the above requirements.

The major advantages of registry over temporary residence pursuant to INA §245A are: (1) permanent residence upon approval; (2) inapplicability of most exclusion grounds, including medical, mental, and public charge grounds; (3) waivability of certain other exclusion grounds; (4) inapplicability of 1 felony/3 misdemeanor bar; (5) manner of entry and lawfulness/unlawfulness of residence is irrelevant; (6) no obligatory filing period; (7) lower filing fee; (8) more flexible "continuous residence" standard as regards departures.

The major disadvantages are: (1) because applications are not protected by confidentiality provisions, denied registry cases can, and generally will, be followed by the issuance of an Order to Show Cause commencing deportation proceedings against the unsuccessful applicant; (2) applicants must present documents and other proof demonstrating residence for 15 years or more; (3) registry is discretionary with the district director or the Immigration Judge.

11.2 CONTINUOUS RESIDENCE SINCE PRIOR TO JANUARY 1, 1972

11.2(a) Date and Manner of Entry

The applicant must establish entry before January 1, 1972. Because all departures subsequent to January 1, 1972 do not necessarily preclude eligibility for registry, the pre-1972 entry need not be the alien's *last* entry to the United States.

The manner of entry is irrelevant. Those aliens who entered unlawfully, without inspection, or who were inspected and admitted on lawful nonimmigrant visas (whether or not they have maintained their nonimmigrant status), or who were admitted as lawful permanent residents (if no record of such admission can be found) are eligible for the benefits of registry if such entry occurred before 1972.[1]

Once an alien has been admitted as a lawful permanent resident, and a record of such lawful entry created, he or she is not eligible for registry. Permanent residents whose status was subsequently rescinded and who were deported for violation of the immigration laws, or who reentered the United States illegally are therefore ineligible for registry.

---

[1] See INS Central Office memoranda dated November 19, 1986 and May 19, 1987, reprinted in 63 Interpreter Releases 1080-1081 (November 24, 1986) and 64 Interpreter Releases 622 (May 26, 1987).

11.2 (b) Continuous United States Residence Since Entry

Eligibility for benefits under the registry provision does not require that an alien establish actual physical presence in the United States during the requisite period. Rather, it requires only that the applicant "has had his residence in the United States since such entry (before 1972)...." This language varies only slightly from that used to define eligibility for legalization benefits under INA §245A, which also requires an applicant to have "resided continuously" in the United States during the defined period of time.[2] While legalization provisions authorize INS to specify the periods of departure which interrupt "continuous residence" under INA §245A, no comparable provisions disqualify registry applicants. Rather, existing administrative and judicial interpretation of the concept of continuous residence govern in this context.[3]

The Board of Immigration Appeals has held that "[a]lthough the residence since the critical date must be continuous, the statute does not require actual physical presence in the United States during the entire period. Temporary absence, without abandonment of residence in the United States, will not preclude establishment of the required residence...."[4] Residence is defined as the "place of general abode; the place of general abode of a person means his principal, actual dwelling place in fact, without regard to intent."[5]

In determining whether or not a particular absence breaks the continuity of residence required by INA §249, the Board of Immigration Appeals has treated the nature of the ties maintained by the applicant in the United States and abroad as a more significant indicia of abandonment of U.S. residence than the length of the alien's absence. For example, an absence of as long as three years and five months resulting from an alien's performing foreign military service was found not to interrupt continuous residence.[6] A merchant seaman was found not to have broken his continuous residence, despite having been

---

[2] INA §245A(a)(2)(A).

[3] See INS Central Office memorandum of May 19, 1987, supra, footnote 1.

[4] Matter of Young, 11 I.& N. 38, 40 (BIA 1965).

[5] Id., citing INA §101(a)(33).

[6] Matter of Harrison, 13 I & N Dec. 540 (D.D. 1970).

absent from the United States fifty-three times in five years.[7] Conversely, an absence of only five months was found to break continuous residence where the alien reentered the United States using a renewed nonimmigrant visa (requiring alien's assertion of intent not to abandon a residence abroad).[8] In a recent decision of the Commissioner the issue was framed as one involving the nature of the circumstances of the applicant's trips outside the U.S., rather than the length or number of departures.[9]

Examples of factors considered in the context of determining eligibility for registry have included whether

(1) a residence or business was established outside the United States during the absence;

(2) the alien maintained a mailing address in the United States;

(3) the alien did not intend to abandon United States residence;

(4) the alien's personal property or financial interests remained in the United States;

(5) the alien's immediate family did not reside outside the United States;

(6) the alien pursued other forms of relief under the immigration laws; and

(7) the alien did not represent his or her intent to remain in the United States temporarily upon reentry.[10]

Yet the mere maintenance of assets in the U.S., including a home, business connections, financial interests and personal property, can not be equated with a "dwelling place in fact,"

---

[7] *Matter of Outin*, 14 I & N Dec. 6 (BIA 1972).

[8] *Matter of Lettman*, 11 I & N Dec. 878 (1966).

[9] *Matter of Jalil*, Int. Dec. 3070 (Decided by the Comm., June 13, 1988).

[10] See *Matter of Harrison*, supra; *Matter of Lee*, 11 I & N Dec. 34 (BIA 1965); *Matter of Outin*, supra; *Matter of Lettman*, supra. For a more detailed discussion of the residence requirements, see Zacovic, "Registry Applicants: Eligibility and Procedure," 16 *Immigration Newsletter*, (Mar.-Apr. 1987).

and where an applicant established an abode in a third country, where she was employed for three years before returning to the United States, she was found not to meet the statute's continuous residence requirement.[11]

An alien's departure under an order of deportation has been found to break continuous residence.[12] Departure under an order of voluntary departure does not break continuous residence.[13]

11.3 ADMISSIBILITY

11.3(a) Grounds of Excludability Applicable to Registry

Most of the grounds of excludability set forth in INA § 212(a) do not apply to registry cases. The following grounds of excludability are applicable:

212(a)(9)*	Aliens convicted of or who admit to commission of a crime of moral turpitude;
212(a)(10)*	Aliens convicted of any two crimes and sentenced to five or more years confinement;
212(a)(12)*	Aliens who are prostitutes and procurers;
212(a)(13)	Aliens seeking entry to the United States to engage in immoral sexual acts;
212(a)(23)*	Aliens convicted of a drug related offense or in whose case there is reason to believe the alien engaged in drug trafficking;
212(a)(27)**	Aliens who are threats to the national security;
212(a)(28)**	Aliens who are anarchists, communists or subversives;
212(a)(29)**	Threats to national security or subversives;

---

[11] Id.

[12] Mrvica v. Esperdy, 376 U.S. 560 (1964); Matter of P, 8 I.& N. 167 (1958); Matter of S-J-S, 8 I.& N. 463 (1959); Chong v. Esperdy, 191 F. Supp. 935 (S.D.N.Y. 1961); but see Matter of Ting, 11 I.& N. 849 (BIA 1966).

[13] See Matter of Young, supra; Matter of Benitez-Saenz, 12 I & N 593 (BIA 1967); Matter of Contreras-Sotelo, 12 I & N 596 (BIA 1967).

212(a)(31)   Aliens who have smuggled aliens for gain.

According to the statute, all other grounds of excludability are inapplicable. However, the Immigration and Naturalization Service has taken the position that exchange visitors who have not obtained a waiver of the two year foreign residency requirement are ineligible for registry; that the excludability of a foreign medical graduate under INA §212(a)(32) is to be viewed as a serious negative factor to be given great weight in a discretionary decision under INA §249; and that aliens excludable under INA §212(a)(33) are precluded from establishing good moral character.[14] This position is highly questionable, given the language of the statute.

11.3(b)   Waivers of Grounds of Excludability

As to those grounds of excludability listed above which are marked by an asterisk (*), those aliens who are otherwise admissible but for a disqualification under either INA §§ 212(a)(9), (10), (12), or INA §212(a)(23) so far as it relates to the possession of 30 grams or less of marijuana or hashish, may seek a waiver under INA §212(h) if eligible to do so.[15]

As to those grounds of excludability marked by two asterisks (**), aliens excludable as subversives under INA §212 (a)(28) "may apply for the benefits of 212(a)(28)(I)(ii)" if they can establish five years of active opposition to the doctrine rendering them excludable.[16] Furthermore, under Pub.L. 100-204, enacted on December 23, 1987, no alien whose application for registry is pending between January 1, 1988 and March 1, 1989 can be denied registry due to excludability under INA §§(27), (28), or (29) because of any past, current or expected beliefs, statements, or associations which, if engaged in by a United States citizen, would be protected under the Constitution of the United States.[17]

---

[14]   See INS Central Office memorandum of May 19, 1987, supra, footnote 1.

[15]   See 8 CFR §249.1; Matter of S., 8 I& N Dec. 288 (BIA 1969); Silva v. Carter, 326 F. 2d 315, cert. den. 377 U.S. 917 (9th Cir. 1963).

[16]   8 CFR §249.1.

[17]   Additional details regarding these grounds of excludability are provided in Chapter One on legalization under INA §245A. Applications pending when the pertinent parts of the INA are

The requirements for a waiver under INA §212(h) are:

1. The applicant must be a spouse, child (including minor unmarried, adopted child) of a United States citizen or permanent resident alien, or must have a son or daughter who is a citizen or a permanent resident alien; and

2. Extreme hardship would result to the United States citizen or permanent resident spouse, parent, son or daughter; and

3. Admission must not be contrary to the national welfare, safety or security of the United States;[18] and

4. The Attorney General, pursuant to the terms, conditions and procedures as the regulations prescribe, must consent to the applicant's admission.

A request for any necessary waiver is to be submitted at the time the application for registry is filed at the registry interview. INA §212(h) waivers are submitted on form I-601. See Chapter One for a more detailed discussion of waivers under INA §212(h).

11.4 GOOD MORAL CHARACTER

Applicants for registry must establish good moral character.[19] There is no fixed time period within which good moral character must be demonstrated, although presumably the applicant must be able to establish good moral character at the time the application is filed. The District Director or the Immigration Judge can look at the applicant's conduct for a

---

amended are to be considered under the new law, Matter of P--, supra.

[18] The effect of changes in the law regarding denials of immigration benefits based on political beliefs is discussed in Chapter One.

[19] For a more detailed discussion of the issue of good moral character, see National Immigration Project of the National Lawyers Guild, Immigration Law and Defense, (1987) Clark Boardman, at §§8.4 and 11.6, and Rosenberg and Kesselbrenner, Immigration Law and Crimes, (1987), Clark Boardman, at §9.2.

reasonable time prior to the adjudication of the application to assess his or her present good character.[20]

The standard against which the alien's background is tested for purposes of determining good moral character is not one of "moral excellence" but rather the "moral standard of the average person."[21] INA §101(f) precludes a person from establishing good moral character who is or has been,

(1) a habitual drunkard[22]
(2) a member of these classes inadmissible under INA §212(a)(9):
  (a) polygamists;
  (b) involved in prostitution;
  (c) aided in alien smuggling for gain;
  (d) convicted of a crime of moral turpitude;
  (e) two convictions and sentenced to five years;
  (f) drug-related convictions (except under 30 grams of marijuana or hashish);
(3) a gambler;
(4) convicted of two gambling offenses;
(5) anyone who has given false testimony to obtain an immigration benefit;
(6) confined a total of 180 days;
(7) convicted of murder.[23]

Good moral character is not limited to these prohibitions, however. A finding of good moral character is subject to the adjudicator's discretion and can be denied for reasons other than those specified in INA §101(f). Failure to pay child support, for example, can indicate a lack of good moral character.[24] Arrests not resulting in conviction do not preclude

---

[20] See INS Examinations Handbook, reproduced in Gordon and Rosenfield, Immigration Law and Procedure, supra, at §23A-132.

[21] Petition of Denessy, 239 F. Supp. 126 (E.D. Pa. 1965); see also Matter of DeLucia, 11 I.& N. 565 (BIA 1966).

[22] The INS may be precluded from considering alcoholism as a bar to good moral character in Registry cases, given the fact that the ground of excludability for alcoholics, INA §212(a)(5) is inapplicable in Registry cases.

[23] But see Matter of Martin-Arencibia, 13 I.& N. Dec. 166, cited in I.N.S. Examinations Handbook, supra.

[24] In Re Malaszenko, 204 F. Supp. 744 (N.J. 1962).

the establishment of good moral character[25] nor do numerous immigration law violations.[26] Those excludable under INA §212(a)(33) for being Nazi collaborators are deemed to lack good moral character.[27]

11.5 NOT INELIGIBLE FOR UNITED STATES CITIZENSHIP

Aliens who are ineligible for United States citizenship are ineligible for the benefits of registry. Ineligibility for United States citizenship is defined in INA §101(a)(19). Basically, it refers to those aliens who have been court martialled for desertion, or who claimed exemption from the draft based on their alienage.

11.6 DOCUMENTATION

According to the I.N.S. Examinations Handbook:

All section 249 applications must be accompanied by sufficient evidence to establish eligibility for the status sought. Exact, complete proof of continuous residence is not required; however, evidence should be submitted to show a pattern which will logically lead to the conclusion that the applicant has continuously resided in the U.S. for the period of time alleged. Though complete proof is not necessary, the alien should be required to submit evidence of residence in the U.S. during the periods of our history when aliens were leaving rather than entering this country; i.e., the depression and war years.

To prove continuous residence in the United States since prior to January 1, 1972, an alien must provide credible documentation similar to that required to prove residence eligibility for adjustment of status under the legalization program in INA §245A. Pursuant to 8 CFR §§249.2 and 103.2(b), all documents must be submitted in the original, accompanied by a copy and a translation, if necessary. Documents may include:

(a) records of official or personal transactions;

---

[25] Petition of Orphandis, 178 F. Supp. 872 (N.D. W. Va. 1959); see also Matter of Seda, 17 I.& N. 550 (BIA 1980).

[26] Matter of Carbajal, 17 I.& N. Dec. 272 (Comm. 1978), cited in I.N.S. Examinations Handbook, supra.

[27] See INS Central Office wire of May 19, 1987, supra, footnote 1.

(b) recordings of events occurring during period of United States residence;
(c) affidavits of credible witnesses;
(d) persons unemployed or lacking evidence in their own names may present evidence in the names of parents or others with whom living, if affidavits of parents or others are submitted attesting to residence.[28]

According to the I.N.S. Examinations Handbook,

[t]hough affidavits are acceptable evidence which should be considered, an applicant should be able to produce additional evidence to support the claim.

11.7 PROCEDURE FOR APPLYING FOR REGISTRY

11.7(a) Application

Unlike IRCA's temporary residence programs, there is no limitation on the application period for persons eligible for registry benefits; an application can be filed at any time. Registry applications may be filed with the District Director of the Immigration and Naturalization Service, or if the alien is subject to an Order to Show Cause such applications may be filed in proceedings before the Immigration Judge.

Jurisdiction to adjudicate applications for registry lies with either the District Director having jurisdiction over the alien's place of residence or the Immigration Judge, if an alien has been served with an Order to Show Cause.[29] In some cases, deportation proceedings may be terminated and jurisdiction granted to the district director.[30]

A complete application for registry will include the following items:

1. Completed Form I-485;
2. Completed Form G-325A;
3. $50.00 filing fee;
4. Fingerprint chart;
5. Two photographs conforming to the instructions on application Form I-485;

---

[28] See 8 CFR §249.2 (1986), and interim rule 8 CFR §249.2 found in 52 Fed. Reg. 6323 (1987).

[29] See 8 CFR §249.2(a).

[30] See INS Examinations Handbook, supra, at 23A-129.

6. Documents proving continuous residence since prior to January 1, 1972 (Originals or certified copies, if available; original documents to be returned to the applicant at the time of the interview); and/or
8. Affidavits of credible witnesses; and/or
9. Affidavits and evidence in the names of parents or other persons with whom the applicant was living, if the applicant is unemployed or unable to furnish evidence in his or her own name;[31]
10. Copies of all original documents;
11. Translations of all foreign language documents;
12. Waiver Form I-601, if required.

Note that because none of the grounds of excludability relating to health problems apply to registry cases, the results of a medical examination are not required.[32]

If, during the course of the interview, it should develop that the applicant is excludable under INA §§212(a)(9), (10), (12), or (23) as it relates to possession of under 30 grams of marijuana, and the applicant appears to be prima facie eligible for an INA §212(h) waiver by virtue of a relationship to a United States citizen or lawful permanent resident, a waiver form I-601 will be given the applicant for completion. The filing fee for waivers under INA §212(h) is $35.00.

11.7(b) Adjudication of the Application

While most registry applicants are interviewed by an immigration official regarding their application, this is not uniformly required. Due to lengthy backlogs in some offices of the INS, registry interviews are waived in "well documented" cases.[33]

If the applicant files a waiver under INA §212(h), a decision on the waiver will be rendered before a final decision on the registry application is made.[34]

---

[31] Interim rule 8 CFR §249.2(a), 52 Fed. Reg. 6323 (1987).

[32] See also INS Central Office memorandum dated May 19, 1987, supra, footnote 1.

[33] National Center for Immigrants Rights, Legalization Update, Vol. 1, Issue 9, December 29, 1987.

[34] See I.N.S. Examinations Handbook, supra.

Applications for registry that are filed with the District Director and which are subsequently denied are renewable by the alien in deportation proceedings.[35] Denials of registry in deportation proceedings are appealable under INA §106. Those denied Registry may not subsequently have their case considered under the legalization provisions, INA §245A[36] (separate application under INA §245A prior to May 4, 1988 deadline permitted).

If Registry is granted, an ADIT card (Form I-89) will be completed and the alien will be issued a Form I-181 approval notice, or an I-94 card as temporary proof of lawful admission as a permanent resident, and shortly thereafter will receive a Permanent Resident Card (Form I-551) by mail. The date of permanent resident status is the date the registry application is granted.

---

[35] 8 CFR §249.2(b).

[36] See 65 Interpreter Releases 959 (September 19, 1988).

CHAPTER TWELVE

ALTERNATIVE MEANS OF OBTAINING LAWFUL STATUS

12.1	BENEFITS AND RELIEF UNDER THE IMMIGRATION LAWS	12-3
12.2	THE "FAMILY FAIRNESS" PROGRAM	12-3
12.3	LEGAL ALTERNATIVES AVAILABLE UNDER THE INA	12-6
12.3(a)	Registry, INA §249	12-7
12.3(b)	Immediate Relative and Preference Categories, INA §§201-204	12-7
12.3(c)	Political Asylum, INA §208	12-9
12.3(d)	Suspension of Deportation, INA §244	12-10
12.3(e)	Extended Voluntary Departure (by Attorney General/Department of State Designation), INA §244	12-10
12.3(f)	Voluntary Departure, INA §244	12-12
12.3(g)	Derivative or Acquired United States Citizenship, INA §§320, 321, 341	12-12
12.3(h)	Non-Immigrant Visas, INA §214	12-13
12.3(i)	Other Remedies	12-13

CHAPTER TWELVE

ALTERNATE MEANS OF OBTAINING LAWFUL STATUS

12.1 BENEFITS AND RELIEF UNDER THE IMMIGRATION LAWS

The implementation of the legalization program has seen a gradual relaxation of many of the initial restrictive requirements which characterized its beginnings, resulting in an average approval rate of approximately 76% of all temporary residence applications received. The SAW program, on the other hand, had only a 25% approval rate, while 74% of all SAW applications were unadjudicated as of March of 1989.[1] Early surveys among legalization applicants indicated that approximately 44-48% of all IRCA eligible aliens had ineligible family members.[2] Thus, while IRCA was able to adjust the unlawful immigration status of many, it contained no provisions for the legalization of the spouses and children of newly-legalized aliens, resulting in the "divided family" phenomena. In some of these cases other provisions of the immigration laws may provide benefits.

12.2 THE "FAMILY FAIRNESS" PROGRAM

In an October 8, 1987 Press Conference, INS Commissioner Alan Nelson announced the "Family Fairness" program, INS' proposed partial resolution to the problem of "divided families" wherein some families members qualified to legalize their status while others did not.[3] This "program" is open to family members of those who have obtained lawful temporary status under either the legislative program, (INA §245A) or the SAW program, (INA §210).[4] According to the program, the following ineligible family members can be granted "indefinite voluntary departure":

---

[1] As of March, 1989, per IRCA Clearinghouse, National Immigration, Refugee and Citizenship Forum.

[2] 65 Interpreter Releases 75 (January 25, 1988), citing a report in the Los Angeles Times, December 17, 1987, Part I, p. 30, Col. 4.

[3] Reported in 64 Interpreter Releases 1145 (October 9, 1987).

[4] See INS-CO wire dated October 17, 1988, reproduced in 65 Interpreter Releases 1259 (December 5, 1988).

1. In those cases where both parents have been granted temporary resident status but their minor children have not, the INS will not deport the children. This encompasses only unmarried children under the age of 18 who can establish that they were in unlawful status in the U.S. before November 6, 1986 and who reside with the parents.

2. In single parent households, if the parent is legalized, minor children will be eligible.

3. Spouses who were unable to legalize will generally be ineligible for indefinite voluntary departure by virtue of the marriage itself unless they can show "compelling or humanitarian factors."[5]

4. In cases where one parent is eligible but the other is not and/or one or more children are not, INS officials will decide the matter on a case by case basis.

5. The program will generally not be available to ineligible parents of legalized or U.S. Citizen children. However, such parents can apply for discretionary relief under 8 CFR §242.5.[6]

Because the confidentiality provisions of IRCA prevent the INS from using information in legalization applications to seek out and deport ineligible family members, those who wish consideration under this program must come forward and voluntarily present themselves to the INS. On the other hand, IRCA's confidentiality provisions do not extend to "Family Fairness" requests; thus, those rejected under the program can and will be placed in deportation proceedings. If such individuals otherwise come to the INS' attention, Commissioner Nelson urged local INS District Directors to use their discretion to "be fair."[7]

The procedures established require the alien to submit a written request for voluntary departure under the "Family Fairness" program to the district director in whose jurisdiction the ineligible spouse or child resides. The request must include the name, address, and A90 number of the principal

---

[5] See INS policy statement reproduced in 64 Interpreter Releases 1191-1192, 1200-1204.

[6] See INS policy statement reproduced in 64 Interpreter Releases 1191-1192, 1200-1204.

[7] See footnote 3 supra.

alien; proof of the relationship to the legalized alien; the names, addresses, and immigration status of the ineligible spouses's minor children, if any; and the grounds for requesting voluntary departure. Each alien will be fingerprinted and a form I-213 will be completed (the I-213 is the form used to determine the charges to be lodged when issuing an Order to Show Cause and placing an individual in deportation proceedings) by an INS Investigator.

Under the procedures established by the INS, no decision will be made by the District Office. Rather, the applicant will be given an I-94 form marked "Application Pending - Valid to (date not to exceed 120 days from date of action)." During the first 45 days of the "Family Fairness" Program, District Directors were instructed to forward the requests to the Regional office with a recommendation. There a panel was charged with reviewing all requests to insure uniformity.

After a determination is made, the alien is put under docket control and the Detention and Deportation branch assumes responsibility for the case. Employment authorization requests must conform with the regulations at 8 CFR §274.12.[8]

The advantages of participating in such a program are next to none and the disadvantages are potentially enormous. Some INS offices have interpreted the articulated guidelines to mean that no adults qualify; any adult seeking consideration under the program is automatically processed for an Order to Show Cause. In many offices, employment authorization is refused eligible participants in all cases. Often INS investigators who are "processing" minor children view the occasion as an opportunity to interrogate the newly legalized parents about their eligibility for temporary resident status. Minor children are given a form I-210 for 4 months which supposedly protects them from expulsion while their case is under consideration, yet most minor children need not fear expulsion if apprehended anyway, with the possible exception of those aged 16 to 18.[9] Even if arrested by INS, aliens who fit the above categories

---

[8] See Central Office memorandum dated November 13, 1987, reproduced in 64 Interpreter Releases 1368, 1380-81. See also correspondence from Terrance M. O'Reilly, Deputy Assistant Commissioner for Legalization, INS to Attorney Michael Maggio, reproduced in 65 Interpreter Releases 165-166 (February 22, 1988).

[9] Conversely, parents who have requested consideration under the Family Fairness program for children who happened to have entered the United States after November 6, 1986, have had Orders to Show Cause issued and deportation proceedings commenced against children as young as five years old.

have sufficient equities to be released on their own recognizance pending a hearing. Thus, children have little to gain by participating in the program.

Most practitioners are warning aliens who inquire about the program not to "participate". Unfortunately, many newly legalized aliens are given false hope by the very name of the program, and on their own turn their spouses and children in to the Immigration and Naturalization Service only to watch them be deported. If a particular case fits within the "family fairness" criteria and, due to its unique facts, the program offers some advantage which is desireable, it is important to learn from local practitioners how the INS is handling such cases before considering submitting a "family fairness" request.

Thus, there appears to be little, if any, advantage to any alien to participate in the "family fairness" program. In essence, the INS undertakes all necessary preliminary steps to deport the "family fairness" applicant, while offering nothing more than a promise to take the problem of "divided families" under advisement, and then only as to a handful of children.

12.3 LEGAL ALTERNATIVES AVAILABLE UNDER THE INA

The Immigration and Nationality Act provides various forms of relief from deportation and various means of admission to the United States, each having complex and distinct eligibility requirements. In order to determine whether or not the particular circumstances in a given case are sufficient to meet the threshold eligibility requirements for a specific kind of relief or benefit, it will be necessary to elicit from a client numerous facts. This approach requires a lengthy and thorough initial interview. Samples of interview forms are found in other publications of the Immigration Project of the National Lawyers Guild, such as Immigration Law and Defense, (3rd ed. 1987), at App. A-61; and in Gordon and Rosenfield, Immigration Law and Procedure, (revised ed. 1987), at App. 34D-2.

Although a thorough discussion of the substantive and procedural details of these remedies is outside the scope of the present volume, a brief overview of the more common remedies will serve to direct the interviewer to possible alternatives which may warrant further research in the appropriate case.

12.3(a) Registry, INA §249

Basic Requirements:

(1) Entry before January 1, 1972;
(2) Continuous residence in the United States since the time of such entry;
(3) Good moral character;
(4) Not inadmissible under certain of the thirty-three grounds of excludability relating to criminals, immoral persons, subversives, or smugglers of aliens (some waivers available).

Registry is subject to the discretion of either the District Director of the INS or of the Immigration Judge, if the relief is sought in the context of deportation proceedings. Applicants are granted permanent resident status rather than temporary resident status. Details of the relevant law and filing procedures are discussed in Chapter Eleven of this book.

12.3(b) Immediate Relative and Preference Categories, INA §§201-204[10]

Basic Requirements:

(1) Aliens must fall within one of the following groups of intending immigrants:

   Immediate Relatives: spouses, single children under age 21 of United States citizens, and parents of United States citizens who are over age 21;

   First Preference: unmarried sons and daughters of United States citizens;

   Second Preference: spouses and unmarried sons and daughters of lawful permanent residents;

   Third Preference: members of the professions and persons of exceptional ability in the sciences or the arts whose services are sought by a United States employer;

---

[10] For a detailed explanation of the eligibility requirements and procedures for immigrating as an immediate relative or under the preference system, see Chapter 4 of *Immigration Law and Defense,* by the National Immigration Project of the National Lawyers Guild (Clark Boardman), 1986.

> Fourth Preference: married sons and daughters of United States citizens;
>
> Fifth Preference: brothers and sisters of United States citizens who are over 21 years old;
>
> Sixth Preference: aliens coming to perform skilled or unskilled labor in positions for which there is a shortage of employable and willing persons in the United States.

(2) Most third and sixth preference category immigrants must obtain a Labor Certification from the Department of Labor before the employer's visa petition will be considered by INS or the State Department.

(3) Alien must not be excludable under INA §212.[11]

The immigrant visa petition is the most widely available and commonly pursued route to permanent resident status. The alien classifiable as an "immediate relative" beneficiary of a petitioning United States citizen can apply for and obtain permanent resident status, subject only to the delays entailed in gathering the required documents and the administrative processing of the application. Other applicants may be subject to delays of varying lengths depending on the preference category in which classification is sought, the country of origin, and the country in which the application is being processed.

As to the preference categories, visa availability is subject to numerical limits imposed by the category-wide allocation of a finite worldwide ceiling on annual immigrant admissions. An applicant classified in any category in which the demand for visas exceeds the supply is assigned a place on a waiting list, designated by the filing date of the petition (or labor certification application), known as the "priority date." To determine whether or not delay due to such oversubscription will follow the filing of a visa petition on behalf of an alien in one of the above categories, call the State Department at (202) 646-0508 for a tape recorded message, updated approximately ten days into the month, providing the filing or "priority" dates which have been reached for issuance of a visa, by category and by country.

Aliens who achieve permanent residence under the legalization, SAW, Cuban-Haitian, or other program of the INA, can file a second preference petition for spouses and unmarried

---

[11] See the chart of excludability grounds reproduced in the Appendix of the volume.

children by the submittal of an I-130 visa petition to the INS. The petition, if approved, is sent to the American Consulate in the beneficiary's country of origin, or to the nearest INS office if the beneficiary is eligible to adjust status.[12] If denied, the denial can be appealed to the Board of Immigration Appeals.[13]

For most countries, there is currently a backlog of about 1 and 1/2 years before a second preference visa is issued.[14] Unfortunately, 73% of all legalization applicants are from "over-subscribed" countries. For example, permanent residents from Mexico who file second preference petitions can expect a wait of 11 years or more before being reunited with their spouses and children. In most cases, the only means of shortening this delay is if the petitioner becomes a United States Citizen (which itself requires a 5 year wait). If the petitioner and the beneficiary are from different countries, or if the beneficiary is entitled to a derivative priority date, the wait may also be greatly decreased.[15]

Also, any alien granted temporary resident status under INA §§245A or 210 may simultaneously pursue and be granted permanent resident status under the preference system.[16] Such a course is advantageous in that eligibility under a preference category would allow a beneficiary's spouse and children to be issued visas simultaneously.

12.3(c) Political Asylum, INA §208

Basic Requirements:

(1) Alien is "unable or unwilling to return to his or her native country because of persecution or well founded fear of persecution on account of race, religion, nationality, membership in a particular social group or political opinion" and is classifiable as a refugee;

---

[12] INA §245.

[13] 8 CFR §103.3.

[14] See Visa Bulletin, Department of State, Bureau of Consular Affairs.

[15] See 22 CFR §42.62(d); INA §202(b); Immigration Law and Procedure, Gordon and Rosenfield, §2.27j.

[16] See 65 Interpreter Releases 615 (June 13, 1988).

(2) Not firmly resettled or subject to other preclusions related to criminal conduct, public safety, national security;
(3) Entitled to a favorable exercise of discretion.

A realistic and practical discussion of this remedy, and the related remedy of withholding of deportation under INA §243(h), can be found in <u>Immigration Law and Defense</u>, <u>supra</u>, at §8.6. The National Immigration Project and the Central American Refugee Defense Fund (CARDF) also publish in-depth analysis and practice pointers on political asylum law and procedure as it develops, as well as information on conditions existing in various countries and referrals to experts and advocates, for use in the preparation of political asylum cases. The U.S. Committee for Refugees has published a report on the INS' approval/denial rate for 27 countries, entitled <u>Despite a Generous Spirit: Denying Asylum in the United States</u>.[17]

12.3(d) Suspension of Deportation, INA §244

<u>Basic Requirements:</u>

(1) Seven years continuous residence in the United States (ten in certain cases);
(2) Good moral character; and
(3) Proof of extreme hardship to the applicant or his/her United States citizen or lawful permanent resident spouse, parent or child (this is often the most difficult requirement to meet).

Many of those denied legalization under IRCA may be eligible for suspension of deportation, which requires a minimum of 7 years residence in the United States. Suspension of deportation is a form of discretionary relief from deportation, and can only be granted by an Immigration Judge in the context of a deportation hearing. A detailed discussion of eligibility requirements and procedures involved in Suspension of Deportation cases is found in <u>Immigration Law and Defense</u>, section 8.4. Additional practical materials on Suspension are available directly from the National Immigration Project.

---

[17] Copies of this report can be obtained from:

U.S. Committee for Refugees
815 Fifteenth Street, N.W., Suite 610
Washington, D.C. 20005
(202) 667-0782

12.2(e) Extended Voluntary Departure, (by Attorney General/Department of State designation), INA §244

In recent years, a non-statutory remedy referred to as "Extended Voluntary Departure" (EVD) has been granted to nationals of certain specified countries who are unwilling or unable to return to those countries because of conditions of "widespread fighting, destruction, and breakdown of public services and order" existing there.[18] EVD is authorized by the Attorney General upon receipt of a favorable recommendation by the Department of State. While not a recognized "status," "extended voluntary departure" means that the alien will not be subject to deportation for a specified period of time and may be granted employment authorization in the interim.

Currently, aliens from the following countries are eligible for "extended voluntary departure" (EVD):

(1) Nationals of Poland who entered the United States before July 21, 1984 are granted EVD (in one year increments);

(2) Natives of Afghanistan who entered the United States before December 2, 1980 are to be granted EVD in 1 year increments;

(3) Natives of Ethiopia who entered the United States before June 30, 1980, are granted EVD indefinitely.

Natives of Uganda were granted EVD on June 8, 1978; this was periodically extended.

Other nationalities have been granted this status for varying lengths of time.[19]

Under recent Amendments to the INA, aliens who are nationals of Poland, Ethiopia, Uganda, and Afghanistan are now eligible for temporary resident status if they entered the United States before July 21, 1984, and meet the other requirements for temporary residence. These requirements are set forth in Chapter Ten.

---

[18] 127 Cong. Rec. 9508 (1981). See O.I. 242.10e(3).

[19] See 64 Interpreter Releases 1093 (September 21, 1987).

12.2(f) Voluntary Departure, INA §244

Voluntary departure pursuant to INA §244(e) may be granted and extended by a District Director in individual cases which warrant relief from deportation on humanitarian grounds, depending on the circumstances of each case. The INS has exercised its authority to consider granting such relief in the cases of individual aliens unable and unwilling to return to Lebanon. A "sense of Congress" calling for the exercise of similar agency discretion in the cases of nationals of El Salvador endangered by the ongoing civil strife and recent earthquake destruction was passed in late 1986, but apparently has not been acknowledged by the Attorney General.

In individual cases, voluntary departure can be granted by a District Director prior to the initiation of deportation proceedings. 8 CFR §242.5 and INS Operations Instructions (O.I.) 242.10 set forth procedures and requirements for voluntary departure in such cases.

In deportation proceedings, the Immigration Judge may grant a period of voluntary departure under INA §244(e) if the following conditions are met:

(1) the applicant must not be deportable under certain specified grounds of deportation;

(2) the applicant must have maintained good moral character as defined in INA §101(f) for the previous five years;

(3) the applicant must be willing and have the financial means to depart the United States;

(4) the applicant must be worthy of a favorable exercise of discretion.

The voluntary departure date granted by the Immigration Judge can be extended by the District Director.[20]

12.2(g) Derivative or Acquired United States Citizenship, INA §§320, 321, 341

Basic Requirements:

(1) (Acquired Citizenship): Birth in a foreign country; one or both parents were or are United States

---

[20] See 8 CFR §§244.1, 244.2, and O.I. 244.4.

citizens; certain residence or retention requirements may apply, depending on the date of birth.[21]

(2) <u>(Derivative Citizenship)</u>: Naturalization of one or both parents; permanent resident status; under the age of sixteen at the time of parent(s) naturalization.[22]

Details regarding the eligibility requirements and procedures regarding both forms of citizenship are provided in Chapter Eleven of <u>Immigration Law and Defense</u>.

12.2(h)   Nonimmigrant Visas, INA §214

Nonimmigrant visas may be available to those aliens who wish to come to the United States temporarily. These include tourists, students, businessmen, temporary workers, and others. The eligibility requirements for each such type of nonimmigrant visa are set forth in Chapter Three of <u>Immigration Law and Defense</u>.

12.2(i)   Other Remedies

Private bills initiated before Congress and leading to lawful permanent resident status, and deferred action status granted by the INS in lieu of deportation are forms of extraordinary relief granted in meritorious cases. The procedures required for obtaining either form of relief are set forth in <u>Immigration Law and Procedure</u>, Gordon and Rosenfield, §§7.12 and 5.3e(7). While there are no fixed eligibility guidelines, it is fair to expect that both forms of relief will be very difficult to obtain in the wake of passage of the IRCA.

---

[21]   <u>See</u> INA §320 (1978) and prior provisions.

[22]   <u>See</u> INA §§321 and 341.

APPENDIX

List of INS Forms

Legalization Wires and Memoranda

Civics Questions and Answers

Excludability Chart

INS Forms

G-28	Notice of Entry of Appearance as Attorney or Representative. This blue form notifies the INS that the alien is represented by an attorney or accredited representative. Copies of all INS notices must be served on the attorney or representative of record.
G-639	Freedom of Information Act Request. Used to obtain copies of documents contained in an alien's INS file.
I-20	Certificate of eligibility for nonimmigrant student status. Form issued by school to foreign nation certifying his or her eligibility for school attendance.
I-72	Request for additional information. INS request for supplementary information or documents sent to an applicant.
I-94	Arrival-Departure record. Card or small form attached to passport indicating date of entry, visa category and length of permitted stay; also issued or endorsed by INS when employment authorization is granted.
I-130	Visa Petition for Alien Relative. Petition filed with INS by U.S. Citizen or permanent resident alien requesting immigrant visa issuance to alien relative.
I-134	Affidavit of Support. Form affidavit detailing economic status and intent to support alien relative if necessary.
I-327	Re-entry Permit. Document issued to permanent resident prior to embarking on lengthy departure as evidence of his or her intention not to abandon U.S. residence.
I-512	Advance Parole Form issued to alien permitting departure and return to the U.S. while application for status is pending.
I-516	Notice of School Approval
I-551	Alien Registration Receipt Card. INS I.D. card evidencing admission as a permanent resident alien.
I-687	Application for Status as a Temporary Resident. "First stage" legalization application for those residing in the U.S. since January 1, 1982.
I-688A	Employment Authorization Card. INS I.D. and work authorization card issued upon filing application for temporary residence.
I-688	Temporary Resident Card. INS I.D. card evidencing adjustment to temporary resident status.
I-689	Fee Receipt. Computer-generated card indicating amount and date of payment of filing fee for legalization or SAW forms.
I-690	Application for Waiver of Grounds of Excludability. Form submitted to overcome certain waivable grounds of excludability for legalization and SAW applicants.
I-693	Medical Examination form. INS form used by certified civil surgeons for medical examination for immigration purposes.
I-694	Notice of Appeal. Form for appealing a decision denying temporary or permanent residence under INA secs. 245A and 210, or for termination of temporary resident status.

I-695	Application for replacement of form I-688A or I-688. Form for requesting re-issuance of lost or destroyed temporary resident I.D. or work authorization card.
I-697	Change of Address card. Notification to INS of change of address of temporary resident applicants.
I-698	Application to Adjust Status from Temporary to Permanent Resident. "Second Stage" application for permanent residence by temporary residents who resided in the U.S. since January 1, 1982.
I-699	Certificate of Satisfactory Pursuit. Issued by INS-recognized schools evidencing 40 hours attendance at a 60 hour program in English and Civics.
I-700	Application for Status as a Temporary Resident (INA §210)
I-700R	Petition for RAW classification.
I-705	Affidavit to Corroborate Agricultural Employment.
I-772	Declaration of Intending Citizen. Filing prerequisite to a charge of discrimination based on lack of citizenship.
I-803	Petition for Attorney General Recognition to provide Course of Study for legalization Phase II. Application form submitted by English/Civics course sponsors seeking INS authorization to offer courses to second stage legalization applicants.
I-804	Certificate of Attorney General Recognition. Form issued to course sponsors approved by the INS to offer English/Civics classes for second stage legalization applicants.
M-306	A Temporary Resident's Guide to Applying for Permanent Residence. Packet of forms and instructions for temporary residents applying for permanent residence under the legalization program ("Stage Two").

Index to INS Legalization Wires
Memoranda and Correspondence

7-3-80	**Cuban-Haitian Program**
3-7-84	Memo from Chief Judge Robie re Failure to Appear **Cases** (Not Reproduced)
11-7-86	Memo from Chief Judge Robie to all Immigration Judges **IRCA Eligible Aliens in Deportation or Exclusion Proceedings Optional procedures for Immigration Judges**
11-14-86	Legalization Wire #1 **Entry after 11-6-86:** Aliens apprehended attempting to enter the U.S. are to be processed for removal as they have been in the past; Aliens apprehended in the U.S.; others apprehended will be questioned to determine if they are eligible for legalization or status under the special agricultural workers section; Instructions to INS officers on how to process these cases **Non-frivolous claim to SAW eligibility Prima facie legalization eligibility RSC addresses Family Unity Departures/Advance Parole Aliens with pending deportations/absondees INS public education campaign**
11-19-86	Legalization Wire #2 **Registry**
11-25-86	Press Conference Statement, Alan C. Nelson Commissioner of INS **INS Public Information campaign**
11-25-86	Legalization Wire #5 **Special I-94s:** Use only for work authorization as to those apprehended yet IRCA eligible, not at POE for regular I-94/admission.
12-5-86	Legalization Wire #7 **IRCA: Narcotics Violators** Treatment of aliens, arrested for narcotics violations, who can establish prima facie eligibility for legalization or non-frivolous SAW claim.
12-8-86	Legalization Wire #6 **Apprehended Alien procedures RSC addresses; correction**
12-12-86	Letter from Ninth Circuit, Chief Judge Cases on Appeal where alien is IRCA eligible; Proposed Internal procedures for cases pending in front of the Ninth Circuit wherein appellant appears to be IRCA eligible.
12-17-86	Legalization Wire #8 **Advance Parole;** standard & procedures; to 5-5-88 for non-friv. SAW applicants, to 12-5-88 for PF Legalization applicants; **Order of Deportation, voluntary departure;** Vacate order; publicize fact that those PF/non-friv. eligible need not depart **Public Information campaign;** advise those under deport and V/D order that they needn't depart; advise those who intend to apply under IRCA not to depart unless get advance parole. **Parole;** those wrongfully expelled or who unknowingly departed after 11-6-86 should be paroled in. **Departures after 11-6-86;** advise those under deport and V/D order that they needn't depart; advise those who intend to apply under IRCA not to depart unless get advance parole.
12-30-86	Legalization Wire #9 **Non-friv. SAW, PF Legalization Claim:** Standards; perishable commodities, exclusion grounds **Aliens apprehended at entry vs. in the interior Selective Service Requirements prior to application period Criminal SAWs**
1-9-87	DOS Telegram **G Visa holders:** Procedures for granting Special Immigrant Status to G visa holders under amendments made by IRCA
1-14-87	Legalization Wire #10 **G Visa Holders** Explains Special Immigrant and Nonimmigrant classifications for G visa holders and procedures for legalizing them under special IRCA provisions
1-14-87	Legalization Wire #11 **Adjustment, Sec. 245** Elaborates on IRCA amendments to Adjustment of status provisions (INA 245) regarding requirement

App-5

that certain A/S applicants be in status at time of filing

1-16-87 INS Memo Aliens in deportation proceedings who are IRCA eligible: Sets-forth procedures it recommends that INS Trial Attorneys follow when a pending deportation or exclusion case involves an IRCA eligible alien.

1-17-87 INS Memo from Office of General Counsel to Regional & District Counsels to Unscrupulous Notaries, attorneys, etc.; All INS investigative units are to aggressively investigate reports of unscrupulous individuals taking advantage of amnesty applicants, i.e., notaries, attorneys, etc. Proceudres to be followed set-forth.

1-19-87 Legalization wire #12 Apprehended Aliens Guidelines for when an apprehended alien should be questioned as to legalization or SAW eligibility

3-24-87 Legalization wire #13 Advance Parole requests: INS procedures, addresses

3-25-87 Letter from INS, CO-Adjudications Citizenship test: INS is revising its citizenship book & consultant hired to do same set to finish in September 1987. Examining INS officers will be required to use only questions from this book. Development of standardized test is under discussion.

4-30-87 Legalization Wire #14 Aliens apprehended or in custody: If in U.S. before 5-1-87, INS must inquire as to IRCA/SAW eligibility. Procedures to be, followed to determine eligibility & process. If entered U.S. after 5-1-87, not eligible to file for Legalization or SAW. SAWs can apply outside of U.S.

4-30-87 Legalization Wire #15 Addenda to Instruction to Forms I-687 and I-700: original documents vs. copies; receipt of public aid by family members; brief, casual & innocent departures before 5-1-87 O.K.

5-5-87 Social Security Administration Instructions SS-5 Applications: SSA & INS procedures

5-8-87 Legalization Wire #19 SAWS/Employer records: Recommends that LO directors solicit employment records from agricultural employers

5-11-87 Letter from Norton, INS C.O.-Examinations, to Lieden Cuban-Haitian Adjustments--Eligibility for 212 Waivers: Excludable Cuban-Haitian aliens, if eligible, can apply to waivers under 212(g),(h), & (i)

5-11-87 Legalization Wire #17 Cost & availability of forms

5-19-87 Legalization Wire #20 Incomplete applications: when returning application to alien, put copy of I-72 and of application in file.

5-19-87 Memo from CO Registry: Requirements, waivers, procedures

5-27-87 Legalization Wire #21 IRCA antidiscrimation provisions.

5-27-87 DOS Cable SAWS: Overseas processing

5-29-87 RSC Addresses & phones

5-29-87 Memo from Leiden & Haynes Social Security Applications: Explains procedures that will be followed re misuse of SS cards & numbers. SSA will not prosecute aliens for misuse of SS-5s.

6-4-87 Cable SAWS--Qualifying Employment: Elaborates on final USDA rule re perishable commod., etc. & employment

6-5-87 Legalization wire #23 (See Legal. wire #33 for additional info.)

6-9-87 INS Cable SS-5 forms: Not mandatory

6-9-87 INS Wire to all regional Legalization offices Expungements: approve & certify for decision

6-15-87 CO cable to all INS Offices SAWS, not in U.S. before 5-1-87: Overseas processing and entry procedures SAWS--Travel on I-688A

App-6

6-16-87	Legalization--Departures during pendency of I-687; Advance Parole; those apprehended who left without Advance Parole after I-688 issued; Passport & visa waiver required of those from non-adjacent countries
6-16-87	INS Wire to all Southern regional & District INS Offices
6-17-87	Letter from Richard Norton to QDEs Inadequately documented applications filed 6/15/87 to 7/15/87: QDE applications submitted between June 16 and July 15, 1987 denied for lack of documentation can later be resubmitted w/in 60 days as M/R w/out new fee.
6-17-87	AIDS: Clinical Suspicion of AIDS; procedures
6-23-87	CO Cable to all INS field offices
6-23-87	Texas D.W.I.s are Felonies
6-29-87	Announcement to House & Senate by Alan Nelson (See the following "statement" of 6-29-87 for more details)
6-29-87	SAWS: Physical presence date in U.S. moved from 5-1-87 to 6-26-87.
6-29-87	SAWS Consular processing: Border processing center opened in Calexico, Hermosillo, Monterrey, Mexico City
6-29-87	INS Public Information Campaign to be expanded to Mexico to reach SAWS
6-29-87	Statistics: As of June 24, 10,281 SAWS applied
6-29-87	Statement on Immigration Reform and Agricultural Labor SAWs: Physical presence date in U.S. moved from 5-1-87 to 6-26-87, date Calexico opened. SAWS consular processing; Border processing center opened in Calexico, Hermosillo, Monterrey, Mexico City Overseas processing procedures delineated INS Public Information Campaign to be expanded to Mexico. As of June 24, 10,300 SAWS applied; 4,000 applications distributed in Mexico City
6-29-87	Telex to INS Regional LOs Departure with I-688A LOs told to tell aliens in writing that I-688A is not for travel
7-1-87	DOS Cable to all consular posts in Central & South America
7-1-87	Overseas Processing Procedures for SAWS ; from 7-1-87 to 11-1-87; procedures
7-1-87	Legalization Wire #27 Overseas Processing of SAWs: Transitional Admission Standard; 7-1-87 to 11-1-87; where; procedures when entering the U.S.; procedures after entering the U.S.; procedures Statistics: 24,171 SAW applications received as of July 1, 1987
7-6-87	INS Cable to all INS field offices AIDS: Use of old forms; new forms must indicate clinical observation; standard for granting waiver of AIDS exclusion This cable inaccurately said applicants cannot file old medical forms done before June 8 but filed after August 8. Should say old forms done before July 8. See IR, p. 945.
7-7-87	INS Telex Documentation: QDEs & Attorneys can certify all documents with a cover sheet. Large, voluminous submissions of docs. not necessary. Unnecessary docs. will be returned to alien.
7-9-87	INS-CO memo re: Employment Authorization for Nonfrivolous Asylum Applicants
7-14-87	Legalization Wire #25 Parole into the U.S. after unsuccessful visa appointment: does not interrupt continuous residence
7-14-87	Memo-Final regs re 212(c)
7-14-87	Legalization Wire #26 F-1 Students: Those who completed studies & 30 days before 1-1-82 are eligible. See Wire for additional details.
7-15-87	INS Telex Inadequately documented cases filed 6-15-87 to 8-15-87: Temporary Policy (from 6-15-87 to 7-15-87) to allow QDEs to file application & then supplement them later without a fee if they are denied, has been extended to 8-15-87.
7-17-87	Legalization wire #30 Self-certification for employment through 9/1/87 Forms G-641 and G-845 not to be used as employment

App-7

7-24-87   Letter from Slattery to Bernsen re
             Fraudulent Entry: INS refuses to commit itself
             on whether an alien who entered on a fraudulently
             obtained visa is considered to be residing in the
             U.S. unlawfully.

7-31-87   Legalization wire #29
             Advance Parole
             Instruction to maintain list of aliens granted
             advance parole.

7-31-87   Employment Authorization to Nicaragua Who File for
             Asylum
             (Not Reproduced)

7/8 1987   IRS Press Release
             No Date, but was published in July-August 1987
             AILA mailing

             IRCA eligible aliens need not be reported to IRS
             under the Tax Reform Act of 1986.

             IRCA applicants tax obligations have not been
             reduced or forgiven. No special enforcement
             programs will be implemented, will follow standard
             procedure.

8-6-87   Memo from the Central Office, INS to all regional
             & district Legalization Officers
             IRCA Waivers: Legalization Officers
             standard; 212 caselaw helps
             identify what is considered adverse and what is
             not; 212(h) Waivers: Not available, except marijuana
             and fraud

8-8-87   INS to prepare sample Legalization and SAW cases
             denials

8-10-87   Memo Western Region, L.O. Consistency; sample
             denials

8-14-87   Legalization Wire #32

8-14-87   Legalization Wire #33
             SAWS:
             Beekeeping for Pollination is SAW work if done
             in field, not so if in apiary
             Packinghouse Work; describes when this will
             qualify & when it will not

8-14-87   Telex from Norton, INS C.O. – Examinations to all
             INS regional offices
             Affidavits of Support: Can be filed by other than
             immediate family members

8-14-87   Cable from Norton
             Minors/Financial Responsibility: Each minor
             needn't show financial responsibility, if filed
             with parent.

8-19-87   Legalization Wire #35
             IRCA–Asylum Applicants: if filed before 1-1-82
             & not approved, are IRCA eligible

8-25-87   Legalization Wire #36
             A and G Nonimmigrants with Duration of Status:
             if qualifying employment terminated or DOS
             recognition ceased, are to be considered
             "authorized admission expired through the passage
             of time" & therefore IRCA eligible. Date of this
             event must be clearly documented.

9-10-87   INS Central Office wire
             Public Charge: LOs should not use Poverty Income
             Guidelines, should check for consistent employment
             history

9-11-87   Prior Deportations

9-23-87   Public Charge Issues

9-25-87   Legalization Wire #43
             Transfer of INS files relating to IRCA applicants

9-26-87   Memo from CO to all regional & district
             Legalization officers
             SAWS who enter after 6-26-87: check date on I-
             700 & reject these

9-87   Legalization Wire #42
             Minors cases held pending Adjud. of parent(s)
             case(s)

9-30-87   Expediting RPF processing

             SAWS–Corroborating evidence

10-5-87   Memo from CO
             New Medical Forms I-693: & HIV test required of
             all cases filed after 12-1-87. Details re test
             date vs. filing date provided.

10-6-87   SAW Temporary Residents–Commuter Status

10-8-87   Memo to Designated Physicians/AIDS

10-8-87   Press Conference, Alan Nelson
             I-94 or nonimmigrant visa entries after 1-1-82:

App-8

10-9-87	eligible under IRCA, but must apply for waiver. *Family Unity question*: case-by-case decision
10-9-87	Memo from Norton *Documentary requirements*: INS to use flexible approach, quality, not necessarily quantity; sample checklist
10-14-87	Letter from Joseph Thomas, Western RPF re: *IRCA Waivers*. [Reprinted in 65 Interpreter Releases 1328 (November 23, 1987)].
10-15-87	Memo from Norton *FOIA requests*: LOs should accept IRCA applications even though missing documentation, if the same is in the aliens regular "A" file.
10-21-87	Statement of Alan Nelson *Family Unity*: Legislative history & intent; procedures; standard for voluntary departure *Statistics*: 865,000 applications filed by 10-16-87; 85% directly with INS
10-24-87	*Family Unity*
10-27-87	SAWs: Can file at any L.O.
10-27-87	SAWs-POE processing
10-27-87	SAW commuters
10-27-87	INS Wire SAWS: Re-entry to U.S with expired I-688A SAWS who relocate can be issued new card at any LO
10-28-87	Legalization wire #46 *Entry after 1-1-82 on nonimmigrant visa*: Eligible, but must file waiver for fraud; procedure for "pipeline" cases.
11-2-87	CO-Advance Parole
11-3-87	Legalization Wire #37 SAWS who enter the US after 6-26-87: if enter lawfully, can obtain TR in US, needn't go to Mexico.
11-3-87	Legalization Wire #45 *Denials at LOs for Fraudulent Applications*: If application has serious inconsistencies or material discrepancies, deny & advise of appeal rights.
11-10-87	Extending I-688A

App-9

2-24-88 Legalization Wire #58
         SAWs: Summary Judgement that cotton is a fruit

2-25-88 INS Central Office Wire
         SAWs: cotton

3-2-88   CO Wire
         Excludability due to HIV infection

3-7-88   INS Central Office Wire
         Copies of denials to QDEs

3-9-88   INS Central Office Wire
         Legalization Applications accepted regardless of applicants place of residence. [Reprinted in 65 Interpreter Releases 411 (April 18, 1988)].

3-15-88 INS Central Office Wire
         Reduction of Denial Backlog at RPF; Denials at LO. [Reprinted in 65 Interpreter Releases 338 (April 4, 1988)].

3-17-88 INS Central Office Wire
         EVD Nationals: procedures. [Reprinted in 65 Interpreter Releases 270 (March 21, 1988)]

3-22-88 INS Central Office Wire
         Filing procedures during last month of legalization program. [Reprinted in 65 Interpreter Releases 422-423 (March 22, 198)].

3-23-88 INS Office of Examinations
         Eligibility of foster children for Legalization Benefits

3-24-88 IRS press release
         SSA numbers on federal income tax returns

4-1-88   INS Central Office Wire
         Ayuda "known to the government" instructions. [Reprinted in 65 Interpreter Releases 375 (April 11, 1988].

4-4-88   INS Central Office Wire
         Former J-1 legalization applicants. [Reprinted in 65 Interpreter Releases 465 (May 2, 1988)].

4-11-88 INS Office of Examinations
         Denial and Appeal Procedures in Legalization Process

4-11-88 INS Central Office Wire
         Ayuda "known to the government" procedures

4-15-88 INS Central Office Wire

4-19-88 INS Central Office Wire
         LO hours on May 4, 1988

4-21-88 Ayuda "known to the government" instructions. [Reprinted in 65 Interpreter Releases 439 (April 25, 1988)].

4-22-88 INS Office of Examinations
         Effect of the Receipt of AFDC Benefits on Eligibility for Legalization

4-30-88 INS Office of Examinations
         What constitutes a conviction for purposes of legalization

5-1-88   Department of State Cable
         Ayuda "known to the government" instructions. [Reprinted in 65 Interpreter Releases 461-462 (May 2, 1988)].

5-4-88   INS Central Office Wire
         Ayuda "known to the government" instructions. [Reprinted in 65 Interpreter Releases 484-486 (May 2, 1988)].

5-12-88 INS Central Office Wire
         SAWs with Class A or B medical illness

5-26-88 INS Central Office Wire
         Confiscation of the Form I-688 Temporary Resident Cards

6-1-88   INS Central Office Wire
         QDEs can file through July 5, 1988

6-2-88   INS Central Office Wire
         CSS v. Meese: brief, casual & innocent departures

6-10-88 INS Central Office Wire
         I-772 Declaration of Intending Citizen

6-17-88 Office of the General Counsel
         Receipt of Educational Assistance: Impact on legalization eligibility

6-30-88 INS Central Office Wire
         CSS v. Meese: brief, casual & innocent procedures

7-12-88 INS Central Office Wire
         SAWs: Sugarcane workers procedures

         INS Central Office Wire
         SAWs: Sugarcane workers procedures

App-10

7-27-88 INS Central Office Wire Migrating SAW applicants. [Reprinted in 65 Interpreter Releases 845-846 (August 22, 1988)].

7-29-88 INS Central Office Wire Waiver for HIV or AIDS

8-10-88 INS Central Office Wire SAWs: Sugarcane workers procedures

8-26-88 INS Central Office Wire Haitian Refugee Center litigation: specificity of denials, opportunity to examine and rebut adverse information, appeal procedures. [Reprinted in 65 Interpreter Releases 877-879 (August 29, 1988)].

9-9-88 INS Central Office Wire Ayuda "known to the government" standard. [Reprinted in 65 Interpreter Releases 958-959 (September 19, 1988)].

9-14-88 INS Central Office Wire SAW fraud; verification. [Reprinted in 65 Interpreter Releases 983-985 (September 26, 1988)].

9-20-88 INS Central Office Wire LULAC decision, reentry on tourist visa. [Reprinted in 65 Interpreter Releases 987 (September 26, 1988)].

9-26-88 INS Central Office Wire I-689 Fee Receipts with Employment Authorization stamp

10-17-88 INS Central Office Wire Family Fairness

10-24-88 INS Central Office Wire Fraud prosecutions: procedures

10-26-88 INS Central Office Wire Cuban-Haitian Adjustment applications: Last filing day

10-27-88 INS Central Office Wire SAWs: Last filing day procedures

10-31-88 INS Central Office Wire Cuban-Haitian Adjustment Act: skeletal applications

11-1-88 INS Central Office Wire SAWs: Procedures for last day of filing

11-4-88 INS Central Office Wire Employment Authorization to those denied at LO

11-7-88 INS Central Office Wire SAWs: refunds to inadmissible S-9s

11-15-88 INS Central Office Wire SAWs: transfer of case to POE for interview

12-13-88 INS Central Office Wire Distribution of M-306 handbook

12-16-88 INS Central Office Wire Use of I-689 fee receipt as a travel document

12-22-88 INS Central Office Wire SAWs: filing deadline for S-9 applicants

1-9-89 INS Central Office Wire Confiscation of I-688A and I-688 Employment Authorization and Temporary Resident cards; Commencement of Exclusion of Deportation Proceedings

1-16-89 INS Central Office Wire SAWs: Social Security number applications

1-18-89 INS Central Office Wire LO must afford the applicant an opportunity to examine and rebut adverse evidence.

1-19-89 INS Central Office Wire Update of Standard 100 U.S. History and Government Questions/Answers

1-26-89 INS Central Office Wire Catholic Social Services v. Meese

2-17-89 DOS cable Travel letters for temporary residents/applicants with lost I-688A, I-688, expired I-512

App-11

[Facsimile Copy - Retyped from original]

FROM: Andrew J. Carmichael, Commissioner USINS
ACTION: PRIORITY
FILE: CO 242.1-P
DATE: July 3, 1980
TO: ALL REGIONAL COMMISSIONERS
ALL DISTRICT DIRECTORS
ALL OFFICERS IN CHARGE (EXCEPT FOREIGN)
ALL FILES CONTROL OFFICES (EXCEPT FOREIGN)
ALL CAMP DIRECTORS (EBLIN, FT. CHAFFEE, INDIANTOWN GAP, FT. MCCOY)
RE: Cuban boatlift program, project 069.

This has further reference to my telegraphic message of June 17, 1980 with respect to the manner in which Cuban boatlift aliens were to be processed at the end of the first period of sixty-day deferred inspection. That instruction is now revised in substantial part. Cubans who have arrived in the U.S. during the period April 21-June 19, 1980 and who are in INS proceedings as of June 19, 1980 and all Haitians who are in INS proceedings as of June 19, 1980 will have their parole (voluntary departure) into the country reviewed until January 15, 1981 as "Cuban/Haitian entrant (status pending)".

Take special note of the classes covered and the fact that the covered classes are limited to those aliens only Cuban and Haitian who were in INS proceedings as of midnight, June 19. "In INS proceedings" is interpreted as meaning any Cuban or Haitian officer and has been documented in some fashion. In the case of many Haitians, voluntary departure, rather than parole, will be extended. These instructions do not relate to any Cuban or Haitian who arrived in the U.S. on June 20, 1980 or since that date.

Beginning July 8, all Cuban and Haitian aliens affected will be called into district and files control offices pursuant to local announcements for extension of their current status. Forms I-94 currently in the aliens' possession will be stamped "Cuban/Haitian entrant (status pending) reviewable January 15, 1981." Stamps to be used for this purpose have been obtained at the Central Office and will be distributed under separate cover throughout the service in the number believed necessary for each district. Stamps are to be affixed on the alien's I-94 from the lower left corner to the upper right corner using security ink repeat security ink. Immigration officers will initial just below the word "authorized". Stamps themselves are to be maintained under security conditions. It is estimated that some 75,00 Cubans and over 15,000 Haitians in the covered classes are located in the South Florida area. Over 30,000 aliens remain in the processing camps. Thus there are approximately 9,000 Cubans and a relatively few Haitians located throughout the rest of the U.S. Beginning July 8, all Cuban aliens out-processed from the camps will have their I-94's stamped in the above manner and will not be required to report to a district office for that purpose. The appearance of the above stamp on I-94 will signal to HHS (formerly HEW) officials the availability of certain services and benefits pursuant to the administration's announcement of June 20. Each district and files control office depending on its volume of cases will make local announcements to accomplish this reparole (voluntary departure) process as quickly as possible. Most district and files control offices should be able to complete the project in less than one week. In order to accelerate the processing, especially in areas where the volume is greatest, a 5 x 7 card is to be prepared showing the alien's name, alien registration number and date of birth. At the time the I-94 is stamped, the card will be similarly stamped and later placed in the relating "A" file. All files relating to Cuban and Haitian aliens covered as above will be maintained seperately from other files.

Should a Cuban or Haitian alien who had not come before the service as of June 19, 1980 be encountered, those will be placed under docket control and the Central Office notified. Under no circumstances will these persons receive a document bearing the Cuban/Haitian stamp. No action is to be taken with respect to applications for Asylum, Form I-589. Further instructions will follow later on that category. Each region will report by telephone to the Acting Associate Commissioner, Examinations before close of business on Friday, July 11, 1980 as to the number of aliens both Cuban and Haitian whose processing has been completed up to that time. Any questions concerning this phase of Cuban/Haitian processing are to be directed to the Acting Associate Commissioner, Examinations.

COMMR

[Facsimile Copy - Retyped from Original]

11-7-86
EOIR

DATE: November 7, 1986
FOR: All Immigration Judges
FROM: William R. Robie
Chief Immigration Judge
SUBJECT: Operating Policies and Procedures Memorandum No. 86-9: Immigration Reform and Control Act of 1986

On Thursday, November 6, 1986, President Reagan signed the Immigration Reform and Control Act of 1986 (hereafter IRCA). I have attached a copy of the Congressional Record for October 14, 1986, containing the complete Conference Report on IRCA as enacted into law for your reference. As you will discover upon reading IRCA, no structural decisions were made by Congress regarding implementation of the legalization provisions, or for the placement of the Administrative Law Judges (ALJs) under either the employer sanctions provisions or the discrimination provisions. I am certain you already know that ALJs are selected from a register maintained by the Office of Personnel Management. Applications for the ALJ register were closed some time ago.

With the enactment of this bill into law, we must focus on those provisions having an immediate impact upon Immigration Judge proceedings.

1. Legalization Provisions. One of the first effects of IRCA will occur during a deportation hearing when an alien represents that he/she is prima facie eligible for legalization. It is important to note that IRCA does not authorize a stay of the deportation proceedings; it stays only the actual deportation by the Immigration and Naturalization Service of an alien who demonstrates prima facie eligibility for legalization. See Section 201(e) of IRCA ("Temporary Stay of Deportation and Work Authorization for Certain Applicants").

The following alternatives are available for handling cases in which the question of legalization is raised:

(1) If the Service moves to terminate the Order to Show Cause, you may, of course, grant the motion. (Please keep in mind that there is no current authority for any conditional termination of an Order to Show Cause, i.e., until the legalization application is adjudicated).

11-7-86
EOIR

(2) If both parties request that the case be administratively closed, you may grant the motion. If the motion is granted, the following language must be included in the Immigration Judge's order:

As both parties have so requested, it is hereby ordered that the case be administratively closed and is to be considered no longer pending before the Immigration Judge. No further action will be taken in this matter until such time as the case is presented for recalendaring and further proceedings.

The administrative closing order must be signed and delivered to the parties during the hearing.

(3) If the attorneys/representatives/applicants move to withdraw other applications for relief (without prejudice to the filing of a motion to reopen to reapply for the withdrawn relief if legalization is denied) and seek voluntary departure instead, and the Service agrees, you may grant a reasonable period of voluntary departure that will allow the alien to apply for legalization during or after that period (when the stay provisions apply). This option will eliminate the need for any hearing or decision by the Immigration Judge on prima facie eligibility for legalization because the Service's agreement will presume that they have reviewed any necessary evidence.

(4) Proceed as usual and render a decision in the normal manner.

Because IRCA does not authorize a stay of deportation proceedings to apply for legalization, it is not necessary to continue the deportation proceeding until eligibility for legalization is determined. It would also be inappropriate to consider or grant motions to reopen to apply for legalization in cases that have already been decided.

App-13

Date: January 9, 1989
From: Richard E. Norton, INS Associate Commissioner for Examinations, and Clarence M. Coster, INS Associate Commissioner for Enforcement
To: All Service field offices
File: CO 1588-C
Subject: SERVICE CONFISCATION OF THE TEMPORARY RESIDENT CARD (FORM I-688A) AND THE EMPLOYMENT AUTHORIZATION CARD (FORM I-688); COMMENCEMENT OF EXCLUSION OR DEPORTATION PROCEEDINGS
Reference: RESCINDS CO-1588-C DATED JUNE 20, 1988, CONCERNING THE SAME SUBJECT. REPLACES COLEG WIRE OF DECEMBER 27, 1988 TO INCLUDE THE LAST PARAGRAPH INADVERTENTLY OMITTED FROM THE ORIGINAL.

The purpose of this wire is to correct previous instructions on confiscation of forms I-688A and I-688 and to provide instructions on commencement of exclusion or deportation proceedings for aliens holding such forms. Legalization and SAW confiscation procedures are separated due to the variances of those programs. This wire applies to applicants for legalization or SAW status who are in possession of their own genuine documents. Aliens presenting counterfeit or altered documents or an otherwise valid document belonging to another person are not legalization or SAW applicants and are not protected from deportation or exclusion by IRCA.

Special Agricultural Workers (SAWs)-Section 210.

1. Aliens with an I-688A (Section 210 Work Authorization) who present themselves at a port of entry and appear to have obtained the I-688A through fraud in their SAW application or who appear excludable may not be excluded or deported until a final determination on their SAW application has been made. The I-688A may not be confiscated until a final determination on the application is made. Any adverse information obtained at the port of entry should be forwarded to the Regional Processing Facility having jurisdiction over the Legalization Office where the alien filed the SAW application for possible prosecution for fraud. Pending a final determination on the SAW application, such aliens with an I-688A at the port of entry should be released on parole, except that such aliens may be detained if they appear excludable under grounds of exclusion that may not be waived under IRCA (8 CFR 210.3(E)(3)). Exclusion charges against such aliens may not be based on information obtained from the SAW application. Because of the difficulties of proving fraud on a SAW application without submitting the application into evidence (which is prohibited by the confidentiality provisions of IRCA), exclusion charges should be based on grounds other than 212(a)(19) with relation

to the SAW application. See Legalization Wire #54, dated January 4, 1988.

However, should an alien present a counterfeit or altered I-688A or should the alien be an imposter presenting an otherwise valid I-688A belonging to another person, the alien should be processed for an exclusion hearing pursuant to standard service operation procedure.

2. An alien in possession of an I-688A (Section 245A temporary resident status) who is within the United States, may have that status terminated on the grounds provided in 8 CFR 245A.2(U)(1)(I-III). The I-688 may be confiscated upon completion of the termination proceedings. An alien whose status has been terminated shall not be referred to examination or enforcement for exclusion or deportation proceedings. Such an alien encountered independently by an investigatory or border patrol agent may be placed in deportation proceedings. However, deportation charges may not be based on information from the 245A application or fraud detected on that application. Information relating to fraud should be forwarded to the RPF for determination of the Phase II application and presented to the United States Attorney for prosecution. The I-68 of a Section 245A alien in deportation proceedings may not be confiscated until there is a final administrative order of deportation.

S-9 Aliens with I-94s and I-700s (Preliminary SAW applicants)

1. An alien who presents an S-9 preliminary application may be deemed inadmissible by a legalization officer of by an immigration inspector upon a finding that the alien has not presented a credible application or upon a finding that the alien is excludable under the INA. If such an alien requests an exclusion hearing, the alien should be charged in the same manner as nay other alien seeking admission without a visa. However, the exclusion charge may not be based on any information from the preliminary application or on any detected fraud in that application.

2. S-9s with I-94s who are encountered within the interior of the United States are treated in the same manner as aliens encountered within the interior of the United States with I-688As. See #2 and #3 on SAWs, above.

App-14

11-14-86
LEGALIZATION WIRE #1*

[Facsimile Copy - Retyped from Original]

FROM: Immigration and Naturalization Service Central Office
Washington, D.C.
ACTION: PRIORITY
DATE: November 14, 1986
TO: All Regional Commissioners
All Regional Legalization Officers
All District Directors
All Chief Patrol Agents
All Officers in Charge
ODTF GLYNCO
FILE: CO 1558-P

The President signed into law the Immigration Reform and Control Act of 1986 on November 6. The new law alters substantially the service's operational procedures and resource levels. However, it is of critical importance that the changes required to run employer sanctions, Legalization and Special Agricultural Worker (SAW) provisions occur smoothly with minimal adverse impact on existing programs. Except as noted below, operations are to continue in normal fashion. These guidelines are to be implemented on an interim basis, and will be finalized after consultation with regional and field offices. Comments from regions, district directors and chief patrol agents should be submitted to CODEP by November 29, 1986.

Although it is expected that the number of aliens to which the service will need to give special consideration during the next six months will not be large, these guidelines will establish an orderly transition during this period and ensure that aliens eligible for special benefits are given proper documentation:

1. Border operations, both at and between ports of entry, are to continue in accordance with present priorities; in these locations it will be business as usual.

2. Aliens apprehended in the interior of the United States are to be questioned to determine whether or not they fit criteria which make them eligible for Legalization or "SAW" status. Those who appear to qualify are to be documented as outlined below; aliens who are clearly ineligible (criminal aliens and those who entered the United States after January 1, 1982, and those who are not eligible for "SAW" status) are to be processed for deportation.

*Portions amended by wires #6 and #32

LEGALIZATION WIRE #1

3. Aliens who walk in to service offices claiming eligibility for Legalization or "SAW" status and requesting work authorization are to be advised to wait until their applications can be handled at a Legalization office.

4. Existing employer cooperation programs are to remain in effect.

5. Search warrants are required for service officers to enter outdoor agricultural operations without consent of the owner (except as provided in Section 287(a)(3).

The new law provides that certain aliens may immediately qualify for a temporary stay of deportation or exclusion and for work authorization. It creates two categories of aliens who may be eligible for these benefits: (1) aliens who claim eligibility under Section 210 (Special Agricultural Workers), and (2) aliens who claim eligibility under Section 245(a) (Legalization). Also, effective immediately the law restricts warrantless entries of outdoor agricultural operations.

Therefore, effective immediately, and until further notice, an alien apprehended in the interior shall be given the opportunity to establish a non-frivolous claim to eligibility as a Special Agricultural Worker under Section 210 and a prima facie case of eligibility for Legalization under Section 245A. In completing Form I-213, Record of Deportable Alien, officers shall ask whether the alien (1) performed seasonal agricultural service in the United States for three months or more from May, 1985 to May, 1986 and (2) has resided in the United States since January 1, 1982. The questions and the alien's response should be recorded on the I-213. If the alien's response to the first question is affirmative, explain the eligibility criteria under section 210 and if the alien claims eligibility proceed as indicated under Section 1 of this telegram. If the alien's response to the second question is affirmative, explain the eligibility criteria under Section 245A, and if the alien claims eligibility, proceed as indicated under Section 2. If the alien's response to both questions is affirmative, explain the eligibility criteria under both sections and allow the alien to choose to claim eligibility under one or the other. Explain that the alien may apply during the application period for temporary residence status under either or both sections.

For aliens already in custody proceed as above except that questions (1) and (2) above and the alien's responses should be recorded on the affidavit.

App-15

LEGALIZATION WIRE #1*
11-14-86

(1) Special Agricultural Workers

In general Section 210(a) provides that an alien who can establish that he resided in the United States and performed agricultural field labor in perishable commodities in the United States for at least 90 man-days in the twelve month period ending May 1, 1986, and is admissible as an immigrant to the United States may be granted temporary resident status. Application for such status may be made in the United States, or, at a U.S. consulate abroad during the eighteen month application period beginning on June 1, 1987. (It should be noted that this section waives the exclusion provisions at Section 212(a) (14), (20), (21), (25), (32) and (15) if the alien is otherwise qualified and has not relied on public cash assistance.)

Section 210(d)(1) provides that an alien who is apprehended prior to the application period beginning June 1, 1987 who can establish a non-frivolous case of eligibility to be a Special Agricultural Worker under Section 210 may not be deported or excluded and must be granted work authorization through June 30, 1987.

Aliens who enter the United States subsequent to enactment are not eligible for a stay of deportation or exclusion under Section 210(d), but under the statute may pursue their application at an American Consulate.

An alien who is apprehended or who is currently in INS custody, whose last entry was prior to enactment shall be given the opportunity to establish a non-frivolous claim to eligibility. Such claim must be made in the form of an affidavit (Form I-215B) under penalty of perjury that the alien was in the United States and employed in seasonal agricultural services for at least 90 days from May 1, 1985, to May 1, 1986. Seasonal agricultural services are defined in the legislation as "the performance of field work related to planting, cultural practices, cultivating, growing and harvesting of fruits and vegetables of every kind and other perishable commodities." The affidavit shall include the following information pertaining to such employment to the best of the alien's recollection:

1) The name and location of the farm(s) where such work was performed, and for each farm:
2) The period of employment and number of days worked;
3) The name of the employer;
4) Type of work and crop (i.e., planting strawberries) and

*Portions amended by wires #6 and #32

LEGALIZATION WIRE #1

5) The type of documentation the alien can produce to verify such employment.

The following must appear above the alien's signature: "I intend to apply to the Immigration and Naturalization Service for temporary residence status as a Special Agricultural Worker and to produce the documentation listed above at that time. I have read (or have had read to me) the statements that I have given. The grounds for exclusion have been explained to me. I declare under penalty of perjury that I am not excludable from the United States under Section 210(a) and that the statements which I have made are true and correct to the best of my knowledge and belief. I acknowledge that, if any of these statements are found to be false, I may be subject to criminal penalties under Title 18 of the United States code and subject to deportation or exclusion proceedings and further that I may be barred from admission to the United States under Section 212(a) (19) of the Immigration and Nationality Act."

Aliens who establish a non-frivolous claim to eligibility under Section 210 will by issued Form I-94, endorsed to show employment authorized through June 30, 1987. The I-94 shall include the alien's right index fingerprint as a means of positive identification. Security counterfoils will be provided to all service locations. These are to be affixed to the departure portion of the I-94 in the admission stamp area (the blank space in the upper right hand corner of the form). The counterfoil serial number shall be listed under "Comments" on line 26. The right index fingerprint shall be placed in the top-center area of the "Departure Record" portion of the I-94 in such a manner to slightly overlap the counterfoil. The "Employment Authorized thru (blank)" stamp shall be placed above the red line on the "Departure Record" portion of the I-94 in such a manner as to slightly overlap the counterfoil. The I-94 will show a "Code of Admission" (COA) of "S-1" in the space provided on the I-94 arrival record portion, but this is for statistical purposes only and is not considered an admission. On line 21 of the I-94 insert the three letter code of the appropriate regional service center having jurisdiction over the alien's intended place of residence. The codes are as follows:

Northern Region - LIN;	Western Region - WAC;
Eastern Region - EAC;	Southern Region - SRC

On the line designated for "A" Number on "Departure Record" insert the "A" Number assigned to the alien followed by "S" indicating a non-frivolous claim to eligibility under Section 210. Do not enter an 80 million series "A" Number.

App-16

11-14-86
LEGALIZATION WIRE #1*

LEGALIZATION

Section 245A provides for legalizing the status of certain aliens. The eligibility requirements for this section are divided into three parts: Residence, Physical Presence and Admissibility.

Residence: The alien must establish that he has been in the United States continuously in an unlawful status since January 1, 1982. If he was initially admitted as a non-immigrant the alien must establish that either his lawful status expired prior to January 1, 1982, or that his unlawful status was known to INS as of January 1, 1982. If the alien at any time was in J-1 status he must establish either that the provisions of 212(e) do not apply or that he has obtained a waiver of the provisions of 212(e).

Physical Presence: The alien must establish that he has been continuously physically present in the United States since enactment. However, "brief, casual and innocent" absences will not break the continuous physical presence. An alien outside the United States on the date of enactment may not be admitted to the United States in order to apply for adjustment of status under the legalization provision.

Admissibility: The alien must establish his general admissibility to the United States. The exclusion provisions in Section 212(a) (14), (20), (21), (25) and (32) do not apply to aliens applying for the benefits of the new Section 245A. An alien is not inadmissible under Section 212(a) (15) if the alien demonstrates a history of employment in the United States without receipt of public cash assistance. Further, the alien must establish that he has not been convicted of any felony, or of any drug offense (except for a single offense of simple possession of 30 grams or less of marijuana) or of three or more misdemeanors in the United States. Finally, if so required by law, the alien must establish that he has registered or is registering with the Selective Service.

Section 245A (e) provides that an alien who is apprehended and can establish prima facie eligibility for Legalization under Section 245A may not be deported. In addition the alien will be granted employment authorization through June 3, 1987.

*Portions amended by Wires #6 and #32

11-14-86
LEGALIZATION WIRE #1

To be eligible for employment authorization under Section 245A (e) of the reform legislation, the alien must present sufficient documentation to the processing officer to establish a prima facie eligibility for the benefits of Section 245A.

An alien who is apprehended in the interior of the United States or who is currently in service custody shall be given the opportunity to establish a prima facie claim to eligibility. Such a claim must be made in the form of an affidavit (Form I-215B), in which, under penalty of perjury, the alien asserts that he has resided continuously in the United States in an unlawful status since January 1, 1982. The I-215B will contain the following information:

1) The date, place and manner of entry.
2) The date, place and manner in which lawful status was violated (if entry was by lawful means).
3) A certification that the alien has resided continuously in the United States in an unlawful manner since January 1, 1982 through the date of the affidavit.
4) A certification that the alien has not been convicted of any felony or of three or more misdemeanors.

The following must appear above the alien's signature:

"I intend to apply to the Immigration and Naturalization Service for temporary residence status and to produce the required documentation. I have read (or have had read to me) the statements that I have given. The grounds for exclusion have been explained to me. I declare under penalty or perjury that I am not excludable from the United States under Section 245A and that any documents I have provided and statements which I have made are true and correct to the best of my knowledge and belief. I acknowledge that, if any of these statements are found to be false, I may be subject to criminal penalties under Title 18 of the United States Code and subject to deportation or exclusion proceedings and further that I may be barred from admission to the United States under Section 212 (a) (19) of the Immigration and Nationality Act."

Once prima facie eligibility has been established, the alien will be issued special Form I-94, endorsed to show Employment Authorized Through June 3, 1987. The I-94 shall include the alien's right index fingerprint as a means of positive identification. Security counterfoils will be provided to all service locations. These are to be affixed to the departure portion of the I-94 in the admission stamp area (the blank space in the upper right hand corner of the form). The counterfoil serial number

App-17

LEGALIZATION WIRE #1*

shall be listed under "Comments" on line 26. The right index fingerprint shall be placed in the top-center area of the "Departure Record" portion of the I-94 in such a manner to slightly overlap the counterfoil. The "Employment Authorized thru (blank)" stamp shall be placed above the red line on the "Departure Record" portion of the I-94 in such a manner as to slightly overlap the counterfoil. The I-94 will show a "Code of Admission" (COA) of "W-1" in the space provided on the I-94 arrival record portion, but this is for statistical purposes only and is not considered an admission. On line 21 of the I-94 insert the three letter code of the appropriate regional services center having jurisdiction over the alien's intended place of residence. The codes are as follows:

Northern Region - LIN;   Western Region - WAC;
Eastern Region - EAC;   Southern Region - SRC

On the line designated for "A" Number on "Departure Record" insert the "A" Number assigned to alien followed by "W" indicating a prima facie eligibility under Section 245A. Do not enter an 80 million series "A" Number.

All service personnel processing aliens under either the Special Agricultural Workers program or under Legalization as set out above will insure that the following is done:

1) Check the central index data base for relating "A" file:
   (A) If an "A" file exists open a work folder using that number and place it on the file tab.
   (B) If no relating file is found, create one. In either case make certain that the I-94 serial number and the counterfoil serial number are written on the inside cover of the file or work folder.

2) It will not be necessary to prepare G-361. This will be done by an exchange of tapes from NIIS to CIS.

Special I-94's completed under this project shall be batched, covered with the G-808 (white copy) and secured by crisscrossing rubber bands. The package shall be forwarded to: ACS/NIIS, Box 150, London, KY 40741.

District and sub-offices familiar with the regular I-94 submission process should follow normal procedures.

Border Patrol sectors and service processing centers shall forward the yellow copy of Form G-808, each Saturday covering the previous week's transactions, under separate cover to: ACS/NIIS, Box 150, London, KY 40741.

The yellow copy of the G-808 is for audit purposes only.

Since the counterfoils are secured documents care must be taken to record their usage. To ensure uniformity in the record keeping, each office shall maintain a record of each counterfoil used or voided, indicating the serial number, to whom the counterfoil was assigned, the date it was issued and the person who issued the counterfoil. When the counterfoil is voided, a short explanation shall be given.

All documents relating to the eligibility claim shall be placed in an "A" file or work folder and forwarded to the regional service center having jurisdiction over the alien's intended place of residence.

The Regional Service Center addresses are:

Northern Region Service Center
U.S. Immigration & Naturalization Service
Federal Building and U.S. Courthouse
100 Centennial Mall, Room 393
Lincoln, Nebraska 65808

Eastern Region Service Center
U.S. Immigration & Naturalization Service
Federal Building, P.O. and Custom House
St. Albans, VT 05478

Western Region Service Center
U.S. Immigration & Naturalization Service
728 East San Ysidro Blvd.
San Ysidro, CA 92073

Southern Region Service Center
U.S. Immigration & Naturalization Service
311 North Stemmons Freeway
Dallas, TX 75207

Spouses and Children of aliens protected by Section 210(d)(1) or Section 245A(e) who are in the United States on or before the day of enactment and who do not qualify in their own right for Special Agricultural Worker or Legalization status shall be given voluntary departure or a Stay of Deportation to coincide with the principal alien's employment authorization expiration date.

Aliens whose entry date is subsequent to enactment or who apply for entry before the application period, or whose claim to eligibility is patently frivolous will not be

*Portions amended by Wires #6 and #32

11-14-86
LEGALIZATION WIRE #1

App-18

11-14-86
LEGALIZATION WIRE #1*

granted employment authorization. They will be placed in deportation or exclusion proceedings as appropriate. Prior to removal of any alien whose status under the new law is questionable, the officer should consult with his or her appropriate supervisor and the district counsel.

An alien who makes an unauthorized departure and illegal reentry after enactment shall be considered to have broken his period of continuous physical presence and thus will be ineligible for legalization under Section 245A. Therefore the following procedure shall be used to authorize departure and readmission for humanitarian reasons.

An alien who has not been apprehended but has an urgent need to depart the United States for a brief period of time, may be authorized advance parole in accordance with procedures for class (3) aliens as specified in operations instruction at 212.5(c). The alien must first establish a prima facie claim to eligibility for legalization under Section 245A. The claim shall be made on affidavit (Form I-215B) in accordance with the procedures set forth at Section (2) of this telegram. Such alien shall be issued a special I-94 but shall not be granted employment authorization.

An alien who has been apprehended and has been issued a special I-94 in accordance with the procedures at Section (1) or (2) of this telegram, who has an urgent need to depart the United States for a brief period of time may be authorized advance parole in accordance with procedures for class (3) aliens at operations instruction 212.5(c).

Officers are reminded that aliens who are outside the United States on the date of enactment may not be admitted to the United States in order to apply for temporary residence status under Section 245A.

Aliens who walk in to district and sector offices seeking work authorization under Section 210(d) or Section 245A(e) prior to the application period, will not be processed for employment authorization but will be advised to make application during the application period at a legalization office.

Pending further instructions from this office all inquiries concerning these procedures should be directed to the following regional coordinators as appropriate.

*Portions amended by wires #6 and #32

11-14-86
LEGALIZATION WIRE #1

WRO - William King - 8-795-6603
SRO - William Zimmer - 8-729-6005
ERO - Edward Wildblood - 8-832-6410
NRO - James Bailey - 8-725-4471

In addition to the Legalization and Special Agricultural Worker provisions the Reform act contains an employer sanction provision which prohibits persons and entities including local, state and federal agencies from hiring, recruiting or referring unauthorized aliens for employment in the United States.

The Reform Act provides for a six month public education period which commences on December 1, 1986. During this period, the service along with other agencies, shall disseminate forms and information to employers, employment agencies, and organizations representing employees and provide public education respecting the requirements of this section. The service is precluded from conducting any proceedings or issuing any order based on any violation of the employer sanctions provisions of the act alleged to have occurred during this period.

In the context of service enforcement duties and priorities, the following instructions are to be adopted immediately by enforcement personnel as interim policy guidelines.

(3) Fingerprints, photograph and Form I-213 will be prepared on apprehended aliens under Section 1 or 2 above and placed in the file with the affidavit of the alien. Form I-265 is not required. The file will be forwarded to the RAC without the issuance of form I-210 or an Order to Show Cause.

(4) Core training for employer education will be provided by COENF. Defer commencement of education programs to employers and others until after the core training session.

(5) The act requires the service to expeditiously begin deportation proceedings as soon as possible after conviction for any alien convicted of an offense which makes him subject to deportation.

Investigations will not receive line 516 absconder cases involving aliens who are prima facie eligible for legalization or Special Agricultural Worker status. Cases in progress regarding such aliens will be completed administratively and the file returned to the deportation branch. If the application for the benefit is eventually denied, deportation procedures may be resumed.

(6) continue to place in progress line 513 fraud cases

App-19

11-14-86
LEGALIZATION WIRE #1*

particularly cases relating to the sale of fraudulent documents for the purposes of employment or obtaining benefits under this act. Title 18 USC 1546 has been amended to prohibit counterfeiting, alteration, distribution or use of false documents, or false allegations to obtain employment or to establish lawful entry or status in the United States. If you receive information about document packages being sold by counterfeiters or arrangers in your area, to potential applicants, accept and place in progress under line 513.2. Obtain copies of documents and retain for intelligence purposes.

(7) Service officers may not enter the premises of a farm or outdoor agricultural operation for the purpose of interrogating persons believed to be aliens as to their right to be or remain in the United States without the consent of the owner, or agent thereof, or a properly executed warrant. Consultation should be held with the district counsel regarding these requirements.

This does not preclude the entry onto private lands, but not dwellings, within 25 miles from any external boundary for purposes of patrolling the border as specified in Section 287(a)(3).

Influxes in apprehensions or reports of buildups of potential illegal entrants along the border are to be immediately reported to COBOR by all sectors.

Detention and deportation will maintain a separate statistical count in each district and report in the monthly CDD-34 the total number of prima facie eligible legalization aliens and non-frivolous Special Agricultural Worker issued a form I-94 and the number released from custody on the basis of their eligibility.

Questions concerning instructions (3) through (7) should be directed to Dave Nachtsheim, COINV, 633-2997/98, Art Harkness, COBOR, 633-3079, or Margo Creelman, CODDP, 633-2871.

These instructions are the result of lengthy discussions with field and regional office representatives, enforcement, examinations and general counsel. We will fully discuss these instructions at the commissioner's conference to ensure that these guidelines provide

*Portions amended by Wires #6 and #32

11-14-86
LEGALIZATION WIRE #1

necessary controls and do not impede normal service operations.

App-20

11-19-86

TO: ALL ROCOMS, ALL DIDIRS/EX FOR, ALL OICS/EXCEPT FOREIGN
FROM: RICHARD E. NORTON, ASSOCIATE COMMISSIONER, EXAMINATIONS, INS
DATE: NOVEMBER 19, 1986
RE: REGISTRY, INA SEC. 249
FILE: CO 249-P (WIRE #2)

Effective November 6, 1986, with the signing of the Immigration Reform and Control Act of 1986 (P.L. 99-603), Section 249 of the INA was updated to January 1, 1972. Regulations reflecting this change are being promulgated, and Form I-485 will be revised at the next printing. In the interim, applications for registry under the new date are to be accepted now and processed under existing Section 249 instructions, with exception of the registry date, which is January 1, 1972 in place of June 30, 1948. Adjudicators must keep in mind the fact that applicants for registry may also be eligible for legalization under the Reform Act, or may have been in lawful status since arrival prior to January 1, 1972. In either case, both applicants, if otherwise qualified under Section 249, eligible for creation of a record of admission as lawful permanent residents. Forms I-485 given to potential Section 249 applicants must be modified at instruction 1.E. and 4.B.(5)D. to reflect the January 1, 1972 date.

INS PRESS CONFERENCE

ALAN C. NELSON, COMISSSIONER
U.S. IMMIGRATION & NATURALIZATION SERVICE
NOVEMBER 25, 1986
PRESS CONFERENCE STATEMENT
ON IMMIGRATION REFORM LEGISLATION

The President signed into law on November 6 immigration reform legislation that will protect the proud heritage of immigration to the United States.

This legislation reflects both a resolve to strengthen law enforcement to control immigration and the humanitarian concern of the nation for certain persons who have been illegally in the country. The theme of this legislation is that the key to maintaining the immigration tradition of the United States is the firm, fair enforcement of laws designed to encourage the continued flow of legal immigrants, while closing the back door to illegal entry.

IMPLEMENTATION APPROACHES

Now we turn to the important task of implementing this land-mark legislation. Our planning is underway to carry out its provisions. Besides granting legal status to those qualified aliens who have been here continuously since prior to 1982, the law also serves notice to employers for the first time that they cannot continue to hire illegal aliens.

Effective implementation of the immigration bill requires deliberate and thorough planning and phased-in implementation. The legislation wisely includes such orderly phase-in provisions, particularly in the major elements of employer sanctions and legalization. As a critical part of such planning we are seeking advice from many sources as we prepare the implementation procedures and regulations. In coming weeks INS officials will be meeting with concerned groups, both to brief them on our preliminary planning and to solicit their comments. These will include business organizations, labor unions, ethnic organizations, voluntary agencies, church groups and attorney associations.

INS has taken a number of actions to begin the implementation of the legislation since the President signed it into law on November 6.

We have sent initial instructions to our field offices to begin operations under the provisions of the Act. In addition, there was considerable discussion of the legislation among INS management at our annual Commissioner's Conference last week, which was attended by all the operating heads of INS field offices and senior managers from headquarters and regional offices.

The first of the meetings with voluntary agencies and other groups has already been held. A questionnaire has been prepared (copy in press kit) to solicit comments from the public.

An organizational structure has been put into place, which includes two new assistant commissioner positions for legalization and employer-labor relations.

We have also met with Senator Simpson and Congressman Mazzoli and their staffs to brief them on our early implementation actions and to solicit their comments.

Attached are several charts which outline various aspects of our preliminary planning. These charts describe the major provisions of the Act, identify the implementation phases and indicate initiatives and timetables. Also included are charts which address the concerns of employers and potential applicants for legalization.

Instructions sent to field offices after the President signed the bill provided for special consideration to aliens apprehended who may be eligible for one of the legalization programs.

The wire directed the following:

Aliens apprehended attempting to enter the U.S. are to be processed for removal as they have been in the past;

Others apprehended will be questioned to determined if they are eligible for legalization or status under the special agricultural workers section;

Those apprehended who appear to be eligible are to be allowed to remain in the U.S. to pursue a claim for temporary residence;

Aliens who have entered subsequent to November 6 are ineligible for legalization and are ineligible for a stay of deportation;

Those who claim eligibility for legalization must sign an affidavit under penalty of perjury stating that they meet the criteria.

11-25-86

EMPLOYER SANCTIONS

The major enforcement provision of the law is employer sanctions, which will be a vital tool for keeping illegal aliens off employment rolls and will lead to control over illegal immigration.

It serves the national interest for employers to hire U.S. citizens and aliens legally entitled to work in this country, and the public has indicated through several opinion polls that it strongly supports this kind of law.

We will seek to make this work through employer education and voluntary compliance. Most employers will obey this law, as they do others. To ensure that they are knowledgeable about the law we will meet with employer groups, business organizations, labor unions and others to inform and help them. We will also continue our cooperative programs, which have been in place for several years, and which provide assistance to employers in verifying status of aliens applying for jobs. As additional personnel become available under the reform legislation we expect to expand this cooperative activity.

We have set up a new position for an Assistant Commissioner, Employer/Labor Relations, John Schroeder, who will have lead responsibility for his major initiative.

Through the LAW program, which stands for Legally Authorized Workers, we, together with interested business, labor, community groups, and other agencies want to work with employers to help ensure an adequate workforce for those employers who have until now relied primarily on illegal aliens.

One aspect involves working with local private organizations, labor unions, community organizations and others for referral to job sites where illegal aliens have been removed.

The LAW program is in the beginning stage but can be widely developed as a very positive program, which has other important benefits for reducing unemployment rates and providing employment opportunities for many citizens and legal aliens, particularly minorities.

Listed below are several broad recommendations for employers to consider at this time pending further information to be issued during the next six months:

11-25-86

1. Be alert for compliance information from the government during the 6-month education period.

2. State intention to hire only legal workers.

3. Inform all newly hired employees that when guidelines are received they must provide proof of work eligibility.

4. Do not discharge present employees or refuse to hire new employees based on foreign appearance or language.

5. Assist applicants for legal status under the legalization or agricultural worker programs who request summaries of employment history to help prove their residence.

LEGALIZATION

We are soliciting advice from many sources before we begin accepting applications in May 1987.

An Assistant Commissioner for Legalization, William Slattery, has been appointed to oversee the legalization effort. This is a new position in INS.

We anticipate opening a number of special legalization offices around the country, where we will conduct interviews and accept applications. These special offices will offer easier access to greater number of people, and will minimize the impact of the legalization processing on ongoing INS operations. We do not have an exact number or location of projected sites determined at this time but anticipate about 100. We will provide additional information as it develops.

We will utilize centralized automated processing to provide the most efficient means of adjudicating the large number of applications we expect to receive.

The assistance of voluntary agencies in preparing applications and counseling applicants will be sought.

INS will soon initiate a nationwide public information campaign to encourage qualified applicants to seek legal status and inform them how and where to apply.

There are several broad principles that will apply to the program:

INS employees will adjudicate the applications promptly.

App-23

The legalization program will not be used as an enforcement tool or to locate illegal aliens. Its sole purpose will be to approve those who legally qualify to remain in the U.S.

While we will grant status promptly to those who qualify, we will not grant approvals without adequate documentation.

INS will prosecute those who attempt to obtain legal status through fraud.

Listed below are general recommendations for potential legalization applicants to consider at this time, pending further information to be issued during the next six months:

1. Watch and listen to English and non-English newspapers, radio and TV for information on applying for legalization.

2. Do not contact INS now. No applications will be accepted by INS until May 5, 1987.

3. Watch and listen for information regarding making contact with local voluntary agencies, such as a church or local community or ethnic group or an attorney for information or assistance in applying for legalization. INS will certify organizations authorized to provide assistance.

4. Begin compiling documents and other information that will help prove your continuous residence in the U.S. since prior to January 1, 1982. These could include: employment-related documents, utility payments, tax, school or medical records and rent receipts.

5. Do not attempt to prove residence by using false documents. Documentation will be checked closely. Fraud could result in penalties, including ineligibility to legalize, deportation, fines and imprisonment.

6. Legalization can only be granted by INS. Beware of persons charging fees and promising they can obtain legalization.

OTHER ELEMENTS

11-25-86

While the employer sanctions and legalization are viewed as the major provisions of the legislation, there are others that are highly significant as well.

AGRICULTURAL WORKERS

Temporary resident status will be provided for certain aliens who can prove they have lived in the United States and have worked at least 90 days for 3 years in agriculture for each of those years. Temporary status is also provided for aliens who worked 90 days in agriculture between May 1985 and May 1986. There are also provisions for permanent status for both groups after a waiting period. As in the other areas INS is soliciting input and is preparing implementing regulations and plans for carrying out this part of the new law.

ENTITLEMENT

States are required to verify the status of non-citizens applying for public aid, such as food stamps, welfare programs, public housing and unemployment compensation. This will utilize the INS data base and is in line with the INS SAVE program, which has been in place for about two years and has resulted in savings of hundreds of millions of dollars. SAVE stands for Systematic Alien Verification for Entitlements.

ENHANCED RESOURCES

INS will require significant additional resources to successfully implement this law. The legislation authorizes an additional $422 million in fiscal 1987 and $419 million in fiscal 1988 for INS to administer the new statutes. This includes a 50 percent increase in Border Patrol staffing.

An enhanced capability for drug interdiction, particularly on our southern border is another positive aspect of immigration reform. A few months ago Attorney General Meese and I stressed at a press conference that illegal drugs and illegal aliens traffic were closely linked. The addition of INS enforcement resources will improve our capability, both to control illegal immigration and to interdict drugs. As the latest example, last Friday INS seized over one-half ton of cocaine, valued at $35 million dollars, near Kingsville, Texas.

MEXICO

In the implementation of this legislation we are aware and will continue to be sensitive to the concerns of

App-24

11-25-86

Mexico. In the past we have had good mutual cooperation and we anticipate this will continue. The Attorney General and I have met on several occasions with our counterparts in Mexico to ensure this mutual cooperation, and further bi-lateral meetings will occur.

SUMMARY AND CONCLUSION

The historic passage of immigration reform legislation will have many positive impacts upon our nation.

The nation now has immigration legislation that is balanced, fair and enforceable. INS will receive additional resources to enable us to administer and enforce this law. I have every confidence that we will be successful.

11-25-86
LEGALIZATION WIRE #5

[Facsimile Copy - Retyped from Original]

TO: All Regional Commissioners, All District Directors (Except Foreign) All Officers In Charge (Except Foreign), All Chief Patrol Agents, All Regional Legalization Officers
FROM: Richard E. Norton, Associate Commissioner, Examinations
DATE: November 25, 1986
FILE: CO-1588-P
RE: Legalization Wire #5

It has come to our attention that some special I-94's designed as employment authorization documents for apprehended aliens who claim eligibility under the Legalization or Special Agricultural Worker provision of reform legislation, are being used at POE's as regular I-94's.

The special I-94's are to be used only as outlined in the commissioner's telegram of November 14, 1986. Please ensure those instructions are followed.

11-25-86
LEGALIZATION WIRE #5

12-5-86
LEGALIZATION WIRE #7

[Facsimile Copy - Retyped from Original]

FROM: Immigration and Naturalization Service
ACTION: Immediate
DATE: December 5, 1986
TO: Immediate. ROCOMS, DIDIRS, BPSH's, OIC's

On October 27, 1986, the President signed into law the Anti-Drug Abuse Act of 1986. That Act amends certain provisions of the Immigration and Nationality Act (INA). The amendments impose significant responsibilities on the service. Regulations and Operations Instructions are being prepared and will be disseminated to the field shortly. In the interim, the policy guidance of this wire should be implemented immediately.

SUMMARY

Subtitle M of the Anti-Drug Abuse Act, entitled the "Narcotics Traffickers Deportation Act", amends the following provisions of the INA:

--Section 212(a)(23) is amended to render excludable any alien convicted of a violation involving controlled substances which are included in schedules I - V of Title 21 of the United States Code.

--Section 241(a)(11) is also amended to render deportable any alien convicted of a violation involving controlled substances included in those schedules, which may be found at 21 CFR Part 1308.

--Section 287 is amended by new subsection (d)(3) to require that when the service is expeditiously informed that an unlawful alien has been arrested for a violation of any law relating to controlled substances, the service must promptly determine whether or not to issue a detainer.

POLICY GUIDANCE

Effective immediately, the following guidelines should be adopted:

When an alien who has been arrested for a narcotics violation is encountered at a jail or institution, prior to conviction, DO NOT issue a detainer (1) if the alien is a permanent resident or a nonimmigrant in lawful status against whom deportation charges do not exist, absent a

12-5-86
LEGALIZATION WIRE #7

conviction; or (2) if the alien is illegally or unlawfully in the U.S. but can establish a prima facie claim to eligibility under the Legalization or Special Agricultural Worker (SAW) provisions of the Immigration Reform and Control Act. Under the provisions of that Act, an alien is ineligible if previously convicted of a felony or three misdemeanors committed in the U.S.

In the case of (2) above, the procedures listed below will apply: prepare I-213 and sworn affidavit; fingerprints (FD-249) and photographs should be obtained; create an "A" file; and give alien the information brochure relating to Legalization or SAW. If the brochure is not available, verbally advise the alien of eligibility and application requirements and so note on the I-213. Send the "A" file to the files control office. The following language should be included in the affidavit:

"I intend to apply to the Immigration and Naturalization Service for Legalization or as a Special Agricultural Worker and to produce the documentation listed above at that time. I have read (or have had read to me) the statements that I have given. The grounds for exclusion have been explained to me.

"I declare under penalty of perjury that the statements which I have made are true and correct to the best of my knowledge and belief. I acknowledge that, if any of these statements are found to be false, I may be subject to criminal penalties under Title 18 of the United States Code and subject to deportation or exclusion proceedings and further that I may be barred from admission to the United States under Section 212(a)(19) of the Immigration and Nationality Act."

COENF

BENED ROCOMS, DIDIRS, BPSH's, OIC's.

App-27

12-8-86

LEGALIZATION WIRE #6

[Facsimile Copy - Retyped from Original]

FROM: COINF
United States Immigration and Naturalization Service
Washington, D.C.

ACTION: PRIORITY
DATE: December 8, 1986
TO: All Regional Commissioners
All Regional Legalization Officers
All Chief Patrol Agents
All Officers in Charge
COTF GLYNCO

REFERENCE: Unclassified Telegraphic Message CO 1588 P (Wire #6) From COEAC
Legalization Wire #6 (Retransmission of Corrected Wire)

Referenced COEAC Wire was issued to effect selected revisions to unclassified telegraphic message CO 1588.P (Wire #1) from Commr Nelson Dated Nov. 14, 1986. However, foregoing wire cited incorrect "page numbers" and is being replaced/corrected by the provisions of this wire.

The following changes in telegraphic message CO 1588.P (Wire #1), Nov. 14, 1986, are results of discussions/decisions made during Commissioners Conference Nov. 18-21, 1986. The major thrust of these revisions is to provide for specified "A" files to be retained or forwarded to the appropriate file control office having jurisdiction over the aliens intended place or residence in lieu of sending such files to regional service centers. These new instructions are keyed to the referenced telegram.

Section 02.

Second paragraph (page 2 of Section 02) beginning with "aliens who establish a non frivolous claim" and ending with "Southern Region SRC;" change line 17 & 18 to read "on line 21 of the I-94 insert the three letter code of the appropriate file control office having jurisdiction over" in lieu of "the appropriate regional service center." Also delete lines 19 & 23 beginning with "the codes are as follows;" and ending with "Southern Region SRC."

Section 03.

12-8-86

LEGALIZATION WIRE #6

Second paragraph (page 2 of Section 03) beginning with "on line 21 of the I-94" and ending with "Southern Region SRC" change line 19 to read "of the appropriate file control office having jurisdiction" in lieu of "the appropriate regional service center." Also delete lines 20-25 of this paragraph beginning with "The codes are as follows:" and ending with "Southern Region SRC."

Fourth paragraph item (1) (A) line 5 revised - insert between "exists" and "open": "but is located in another FCO." Seventh paragraph (page 3) change "Regional Service Center" (lines 2 & 3) to read "File Control Office." Also delete eighth paragraph beginning "The Regional Service Center addresses are:" and ending "Lincoln, Nebraska 65808".

Section 04.

Delete paragraphs one thru three (page 1 of Section 04) beginning "Eastern Region Service Center" and ending "Southern Region Service Center," and insert in lieu thereof following: "A" files used and/or created as a result of referenced telegram are to be stored separately from the existing "A" files on the shelves of the file rooms to facilitate location/retrieval of these files during registration process.

Third paragraph (page 3) revised item (3) seventh line beginning "the file will be forwarded to the RAC" to read "The file will be forwarded to the FCO.

BENED all rooms; All Regional Legalization Officers; All CPAs; All OICS; COTF GLYNCO

COMMR (COINF)

App-28

12-17-86
LEGALIZATION WIRE #8*

[Facsimile Copy - Retyped from original]

FROM: Immigration and Naturalization Service/DOJ
ACTION: PRIORITY
DATE: December 17, 1986
TO: ROCOM, ROCOU, DIDIR, SHCAP, OIC
RE: Implementation Wire #8

All field officers should be thoroughly familiar with the 11/14/86 CO Telegram. As additional guidance all field offices are reminded that:

1. Any alien requesting advance parole in order to make a brief departure from the United States for a legitimate emergency or humanitarian purpose such as that occasioned by a family obligation involving an occurrence such as the illness or death of a close relative or other family need should have his/her request favorably considered if they are prima facie eligible for legalization or have a nonfrivolous claim to "SAW" status and submit an affidavit to that effect. Grants of advance parole must be recorded in the aliens A-File. Each office should maintain a list with the name and A# of each alien granted advance parole in accordance with paragraph 1 of this telegram. In these instances where such an alien is granted advance parole and is under a final order of deportation, steps should be taken to vacate the order of deportation.

2. Reasonable efforts should be made to publicize the fact that aliens who are currently under an order of voluntary departure or deportation are not required to depart the United States if they have a prima facie claim of eligibility for Legalization or have a nonfrivolous claim to "SAW" status. INS should take the opportunity to publicize and communicate this information when meeting with VOLAGS, press and other public interest groups.

3. An alien who requests admission at a port of entry and who executes an affidavit that establishes a prima facie claim to Legalization or a nonfrivolous claim to "SAW" status, shall be paroled into the United States in order to apply for temporary residence status under the appropriate provision if:

   A. The alien submits documentation establishing that he/she was removed from the United States on or after 11/06/86 in violation of the 11/14/86

*Portions amended by Wire #13.

---

telegram

or

   B. The alien unknowingly (without knowledge of such departure) departed the United States on or after 11/06/86.

4. An alien who meets prima facie eligibility for legalization and who meets the requirements of paragraph 3 above, shall be granted parole status until May 5, 1988. An alien who makes a nonfrivolous application for "SAW" status and who meets the requirements of paragraph 3 above, shall be granted parole status until December 5, 1988.

5. All ports of entry are encouraged to verify the alien's documentation described in paragraph 3(A) of this telegram, through existing service indices before granting the alien's request for parole.

6. Aliens who intend to apply for legalization or SAW status should by advised not to leave the country unless they have obtained advance authorization to travel from the INS.

App-29

12-30-86

LEGALIZATION WIRE #9*

TO: All Regional Commissioners, All Regional Legalization Officers, All District Directors, All Officers-In-Charge, All Chief Patrol Agents
FROM: Alan C. Nelson, Commissioner, INS
DATE: December 30, 1986
RE: Legalization Wire #9 (Modified)

The following guidelines and definitions are provided in response to questions and requests for guidance following the wire of November 14, 1986 relating to reform act implementation, hereafter referred to as Legalization Wire No. 1. These guidelines are to be used in determining whether aliens have established prima facie eligibility for legalization as that term is used in new Section 245A or a nonfrivolous claim to Special Agricultural Worker (SAW) eligibility as that term is used in new Section 210. The determination of whether an alien presents a prima facie case for legalization or makes a nonfrivolous claim to SAW eligibility must be made on a case-by-case basis.

Nonfrivolous Claim to SAW Eligibility. Section 210(d) provides that apprehended aliens who establish a nonfrivolous claim to SAW eligibility cannot be excluded or deported. Guidance has been sought with respect to what constitutes a nonfrivolous claim to eligibility as a Special Agricultural Worker.

The House-Senate Managers' Report on this section states their intention that the service do no more than secure the alien's attestation under penalty of perjury to basic facts concerning the alien's employment and the type of documentation the alien intends to produce during the application period to support his/her claim. Legalization Wire No. 1 set forth the information to be obtained in support of an alien's claim to eligibility. It is not necessary for the alien to provide with certainty and specificity every item of information relating to his/her claim. However, the following are minimum requirements:

1) At least 90 days of qualifying employment must be claimed;

2) Specific and plausible information with respect to the work activity and crop for all qualifying employment must be provided;

3) The alien should identify the type and nature of the documentation he/she intends to produce during the application period to verify the claimed employment;

* Portions amended by Wire #12

LEGALIZATION WIRE #9

4) Regardless of any showing concerning agricultural employment under these guidelines, aliens who indicate that they are excludable under Sections 212(a)(9), (10), (23) except as it relates to a single offense of simple possession of 30 grams or less of marijuana, (27), (28), (29) and (33) cannot establish a nonfrivolous claim to SAW eligibility;

The information provided must be accepted as true on its face unless the officer has contrary information. If the claim is denied the officer must state the basis of the denial on Form I-213.

A special affidavit form has been developed and will be available for use in the near future. Until then continue to use affidavit Forms I-215B or I-215W.

Follow the procedures described in Legalization Wire No. 1 and advise aliens who have established a nonfrivolous claim to eligibility that they must submit an application for SAW status between June 1 and June 30, 1987.

Other Perishable Commodities. The following interim definition of the term "other perishable commodities" as used in Section 210(h) is provided for use in determining nonfrivolous claims to SAW eligibility. This definition is subject to change by Department of Agriculture rulemaking pursuant to Section 210(h) but is to be used in the interim. This definition is derived from the language of Section 210(h) and is intended to exclude from classification as perishable commodities those products which are not produced by the types of labor listed in Section 210(h) which refers to "...field work related to planting, cultural practices, cultivating, growing and harvesting of fruits and vegetables of every kind and other perishable commodities...." This language indicates strongly that only plant products are contemplated to the exclusion of livestock and related products, wood, and processed products. The interim definition reads as follows: "The term 'other perishable commodities' means plant products which require planting, cultural practices, cultivating, growing and harvesting by agricultural field workers. Livestock, meat and meat products, dairy products, poultry and eggs, wood, and processed products are not perishable commodities for the purposes of determining a nonfrivolous claim to eligibility under Section 210(d)."

Prima Facie Eligibility for Legalization. Under Section 245A(e) aliens who are apprehended or in custody during the pre-application period who establish prima facie eligibility for legalization may not be deported. Prima facie eligibility is established if an alien states under

App-30

12-30-86
LEGALIZATION WIRE #9*

penalty of perjury that he meets the eligibility criteria for legalization and that he is not excludable under paragraphs (9), (10), (15), (23) except as it relates to a single offense of simple possession of 30 grams or less of marijuana, (27), (28), (29), and (33) of Section 212. The alien must provide facts and information sufficient to demonstrate eligibility. The information provided must be accepted as true on its face unless the officer has contrary information. If the claim is denied the officer must state the basis of the denial on Form I-213. For the purposes of Section 245A and alien is not excludable under Section 212(a)(15) if he demonstrates a history of employment in the United States which provided self-support without reliance on public cash assistance. The affidavit procedure set forth in Legalization Wire No. 1 is to be employed for this purpose. A special affidavit form is being developed for this purpose but Forms I-215B or I-215W may be used until the new form is available. Advise aliens who have established a prima facie case for eligibility that they must submit an application for legalization between May 5 and June 3, 1987.

Apprehensions at Entry. Clarification has been requested concerning the difference in meaning between the terms "interior" and "at entry" for the purposes of reform act implementation. The need for clarification arises from the fact that aliens who are in the United States and who are apprehended by the Service are entitled, under the express provisions of the reform act, to establish eligibility for legalization or SAW status and to avoid exclusion or deportation on that basis. Aliens apprehended at entry, however, are ineligible to apply for SAW status in the United States and are ineligible to apply for legalization.

Aliens apprehended in the act of effecting an illegal entry or aliens denied admission are therefore ineligible to apply for any SAW or legalization benefit in the United States. In other cases, aliens are to be regarded as having been apprehended at entry where the apprehending officer has probable cause to believe that the individual has just crossed the border. Apprehensions determined to be at entry based on probable cause cannot be defined in terms of distance from the border or other set factors. An alien found concealed in a vehicle or located in a remote border area would normally be considered a border apprehension regardless that his actual entry was not witnessed. An alien found in employment in a border city such as El Paso or Detroit would normally not be

*Portions amended by Wire #12

LEGALIZATION WIRE #9*

considered a border apprehension. The range of possibilities between these examples includes facts which would support or not support a determination based on probable cause that an arrested alien has been apprehended at entry. In each case the determination of whether an alien has been apprehended "at entry" or "in the interior" must rest on the statement of the apprehended alien and/or the judgment of the arresting officer and his supervisor.

Selective Service Registration. Guidance has been requested concerning the obligation of enforcement officers to determine whether or not apprehended aliens who are prospective legalization or SAW applicants have registered with Selective Service. Aliens apprehended during the pre-application period do not have to comply with Selective Service registration requirements. Selective Service registration procedures and information will be incorporated in the application process.

Criminal Excludability Under Section 210. Guidance has been requested concerning criminal excludability under Section 210. Section 245A contains specific language concerning the effect of misdemeanor and felony convictions on legalization eligibility. Section 210 does not contain parallel language. However, aliens claiming SAW eligibility are excludable under Sections 212(a)(9), (10), (23) except for a single offense of simple possession of 30 grams of marijuana, (27), (28), (29), and (33) and are ineligible for SAW status. No waiver of these grounds of excludability is available to SAW applicants.

App-31

1-9-87
DOS

[Facsimile Copy – Retyped from original]

Subject: Immigration Reform and Control Act of 1986, (P.L. 99-603)
Ref: Section 101(A)(15)(N) and 101(A)(27)(I)

1. One of the many changes made by the Simpson-Rodino Bill, S. 1200, the Immigration Reform and Control Act of 1986, concerns the granting of special immigrant status to certain G visa holders. The IRCA added sections 101(a)(27)(i) and 101(a)(15)(n) to accomplish that. The two sections read as follows:

(I)(1) An immigrant who is the unmarried son or daughter of an officer or employee or a former officer or employee of an international organization as described in Section 101(a)(15)(G)(i) of the act and who (I) while maintaining the status of a nonimmigrant under (a)(15)(G)(iv) or (a)(15)(n), has resided and been physically present in the United States for periods totaling 3 1/2 of the 7 years immediately preceding the application for an immigrant visa or adjustment of status under this subparagraph, and for periods totaling at least seven years between the ages of five and 21 years, and (II) applies for admission under this paragraph no later than his or her 25th birthday or by May 6, 1987 whichever is later;

(II) An immigrant who is a surviving spouse of a deceased officer or employee of such an international organization and who (I) while maintaining status of a nonimmigrant under 101(a)(15)(G)(iv) or (a)(15)(n), has resided and been physically present in the United States for periods totaling at least 3 1/2 years immediately preceding the application for immigrant visa or adjustment of status under this subparagraph, and for periods totaling at least 15 years before the death of the officer or employee, and (II) Applies for admission under this paragraph no later than 6 months after the death of such officer or employee or by May 6, 1987, whichever is later;

(III) An immigrant who is a retired officer or employee of such an international organization, and who (I) while maintaining status of a nonimmigrant under 101(a)(15)(G)(iv), has resided and been physically present in the United States for periods totaling at least 3 1/2 of the 7 years immediately preceding the application for an immigrant visa or adjustment of status under this subparagraph, and for periods totaling at least 15 years before the officer or employee's retirement from any such international organization and (II) applies for admission under this subparagraph before January 1, 1993, and no later than 6 months after the date of retirement or by May 6, 1987, whichever is later; or

(IV) An immigrant who is the spouse of a retired officer or employee of an international organization accorded special immigrant status under clause (III) and is accompanying or following to join such retired officer or employee as a member of his or her immediate family.

(N)(I) The parent of an alien child accorded the status of special immigrant under paragraph (27)(I)(1), but only if and while the alien is a child, or (II) a child of such parent or of an alien accorded the status of a special immigrant under clause (II), (III), or (IV) of paragraph (27)(I).

2. Special immigrant status under section 101(A)(27)(I) of the Act is available to four classes of aliens. The first class encompasses unmarried sons or daughters of a present or former officer or employer of a G International Organization, if the applicant while maintaining the status of a G or an "N" NIV classification has been physically present in the U.S. for three and a half years of the seven year period immediately preceding the date of the application for a visa (or adjustment of status). Furthermore, the applicant must have resided or been physically present in the U.S. for an aggregate period of at least seven years between the ages of five and twenty one years. The otherwise qualifying alien must apply for admission no later than his twenty-fifth birthday or six months after 11/6/86, the effective date of this law.

3. The second class listed in the section concerns an alien who is the surviving spouse of a deceased officer or employee of a G International Organization. While in G or N status the applicant must have resided and been physically present in the United States for an aggregate period of at least half of the seven years immediately preceding the date of application (or adjustment of status) and for an aggregate period of at least fifteen years preceding the death of a G employee. The alien must apply for admission no later than six months after either the death of the employee or the date of enactment (11/6/86), whichever is later.

4. The third class involves retired officers or employees of such G organizations. Similar to the other two classes, these aliens must have maintained G status for at least and have resided and been physically present in the U.S. for three and one half of the seven years immediately

App-32

preceding the date of application (Adjustment of status). The applicant must have resided and been physically present in the United States for at least fifteen years prior to his retirement. The alien must apply for admission before 1/1/93 and no later than six months after the date of retirement or six months after 11/6/86 whichever is later.

5. The last class is limited to the spouse (section 101(a)(35) of the Act) of the alien accorded special immigrant status in the third class mentioned above only. The spouse may accompany or follow to join the principal special immigrant. (See 22 CFR 42.1)

6. The application must submit evidence to meet each of the requirements listed below in order to establish entitlement to special immigrant status under section 101(a)(27)(I) of the Act.

-A. Employment with a G Organization:

It is necessary for the applicant to submit verification from the G organization(s) verifying the employment (1) as an official or employee and (2) the length of such employment of the alien in question, which in the case of I(I) is the parent, I(II) is the deceased spouse, and I(III) is the applicant himself. The verification of such employment should take the form of a certified letter from the chief personnel official of that organization.

-B. Relationship to the G Employee:

The usual documentation, such as verifiable civil documents, should be submitted to verify that the requisite relationship exists. In I(I) the applicant must establish that he or she is the unmarried son or daughter by submitting birth certificates or accepted secondary evidence in the absence of the birth document. In I(II) the alien must submit marriage and death certificates to establish the marital relationship with the now deceased employee.

-C. Residence is a statutorily defined term. Section 101(a)(33) of the Act states that "the term residence means the place of general abode; the place of general abode of a person means his principal, actual dwelling place in fact, without regard to intent. Residence shall be considered continuous for the purpose of sections 350 and 352 of Title III where there is continuity of stay but not necessarily an uninterrupted physical presence in a foreign state or states outside of the United States." Residence as defined by the statute constitutes the primary dwelling place of the individual. This definition provides latitude for temporary (even extended) periods of absence from the primary dwelling place and still be considered residence. Physical presence is the state of being in one place at a given moment; the statute requires the applicant to have resided in and have been physically present in the United States for certain periods.

The residence requirement should be met by verification of G status. As the G visa classification contemplates residence in the U.S., establishment of such status should be sufficient to meet the residence requirement. The law, however, adds an additional requirement of physical presence. Not only must the alien in question have been in G status, he must be maintaining or have maintained residence in the U.S., and he must have been physically present in the U.S. for a designated period. Consequently, the applicant must prove that while maintaining G status, and during or within the period of "residence" in the U.S. the alien was physically present in the Department as to how physical presence is to be computed. It is anticipated that the consular officer must compute the time period in the same fashion to the physical presence requirement for U.S. citizenship purposes. Consequently, the applicant must account for the years, months, weeks and days of physical presence in the U.S. It is possible to meet the residence requirement but not satisfy the physical presence requirement. If such cases arise, submit them for advisory opinion pending resolution of this issue of interpretation of physical presence as soon as it is resolved. The posts will be notified.

7. The statute requires that the alien meet the designated time periods of status, residence, and physical presence before the "date of application." These cases shall be processed just like other special immigrants. As no special forms are utilized, the submission of all the necessary documents to the consular post is essential to establish the alien's entitlement to status. The date of submission triggers the application process. This receipt of the evidence which the consular officer reasonably believes is sufficient to entitle the alien to this special immigrant status constitutes the "date of application" for purposes of this section. This does not mean that upon subsequent review that the officer might not require the submission of additional evidence deemed necessary to resolve any question in regard to the alien's entitlement to status. Any request for additional

evidence does not move the "date of application," as long as the consul was satisfied that on the face of the original document the alien was indeed qualified for this status.

8. The language of section 101(a)(15)(N) of the Act is self-explanatory. The key in adjudicating these applications concerns the verification of the employment with the International Organization and the establishment of the requisite relationship. INS is considering the issue of work authorization and admission periods. Consular posts will be informed of their decision as soon as the Department receives such.

9. The symbols for the visas are:

101(a)(27)(I)(iii)	SK1	Adjustment SK6
101(a)(27)(I)(iv)	SK2	SK7
101(a)(27)(I)(ii)	SK4	SK9
101(a)(27)(I)(i)	SK3	SK8
101(a)(15)(N)(i)	N-8	
101(a)(15)(N)(ii)	N-9	

10. As additional instructions and guidelines are developed or received from INS, they will be transmitted to consular posts.

1-14-87

LEGALIZATION WIRE #10

[Facsimile Copy - Retyped from Original]

FROM: Alan C. Nelson, Commissioner USINS
ACTION: Routine
DATE: January 14, 1987
FILE: CO 101-P, CO 214-P
TO: All ROCOMS, All DIDIRS (Including Foreign), All RAC Directors

CO 101-P, CO 214-P, Wire #10. P.L. 99-603, The Reform and Control Act of 1986, Section 312, created special immigrant and nonimmigrant classifications effective November 7, 1986.

(A.) The new Special Immigrant Provisions Section 101(A)(27)(I) establishes four groups of eligible applicants:

(I)(I) An immigrant who is the unmarried son or daughter of an officer or employee or an international organization as described in Section 101(A)(15)(G)(I) of the act and who

(1) While maintaining status as a nonimmigrant under (a)(15)(G)(iv) or (A)(15)(N), has resided and been physically present in the United States for periods totaling 3 1/2 of the 7 years immediately preceding the application for an immigrant visa or adjustment of status under this subparagraph, and for periods totaling at least 7 years between the ages of five and 21 years, and

(2) applies for admission under this paragraph no later than his or her 25th birthday or by May 6, 1987 whichever is later.

(I)(II) An immigrant who is a surviving spouse of a deceased officer or employee of such an international organization and who

(1) While maintaining status of a nonimmigrant under 101(a)(15)(G)(iv) or (a)(15)(N), has resided and been physically present in the United States for periods totaling at least 3 1/2 of the 7 years immediately preceding the application for immigrant visa or adjustment of status under this subparagraph, and for periods totaling at least 15 years before the death of the officer or employee, and

1-14-87

LEGALIZATION WIRE #10

(2) Applies for admission under this paragraph no later than 6 months after the death of such officer or employee or by May 6, 1987, whichever is later.

(I)(III) An immigrant who is a retired officer or employee of such an international organization, and who
(1) While maintaining status of a nonimmigrant under 101(A)(15)(G)(IV), has resided and been physically present in the United States for periods totaling at least 3 1/2 of the 7 years immediately preceding the application for an immigrant visa or adjustment of status under this subparagraph, and for periods totaling at least 15 years before the officer or employee's retirement from any such International organization and

(2) Applies for admission under this subparagraph before January 1, 1993, and no later than 6 months after the date of retirement or by May 6, 1987, whichever is later.

(I)(IV) An immigrant who is the spouse of a retired officer or employee of an international organization accorded special immigrant status under 101(A)(27)(I)(III) and is accompanying or following to join such retired officer or employee as a member of his or her immediate family.

(B.) The new nonimmigrant classification created by P.L. 99-603 is Section 101(A)(15)(N).

(N)(I) Provides nonimmigrant status for the parent of an alien child accorded special immigrant status under 101(a)(27)(I)(i).

(N)(II) Provides nonimmigrant status for an alien child of such a parent, or a child of an alien accorded special immigrant status under Section 101(A)(27)(I)(II), (III) or (IV) of the act.

(C.) The term "residence" will be applied as defined in Section 101(a)(33), the principle actual dwelling place without regard to intent. This definition provides some latitude for temporary periods of absence from the United States. However, the act adds an additional requirement of physical presence for certain designated periods. The application of physical presence has raised several issues, and has been referred to general counsel for an advisory opinion. At this time physical presence in the U.S., in fact, may be counted. However official leave outside the U.S. should not be counted until further notice.

App-35

1-14-87
LEGALIZATION WIRE #10

(D.) The applicant must comply with current adjustment application procedures as defined on Form I-485. A certified letter from the international organization employer may be accepted as evidence of employment and residence. Because the terms "resided and been physically present in the United States", as reflected in Section 312 of the IRCA, and "resided continuously in the United States" as used in IRCA sections relating to Legalization are similar in meaning, and since the act requires consultation with the Senate and House Judiciary Committees on the definition of the latter term, definitive instructions on the physical presence aspect are not included herein. Decisions in cases where clear evidence is not presented to establish continuous physical presence of applicants are to be held in abeyance pending resolution of the definition of "resided continuously", and issuance of clarifying instructions. The applicant must submit originals or certified copies of civil documents to establish the requisite family relationships.

(E.) The 101(A)(15)(N)(I) parent may apply for and remain in such status as long the 101(a)(27)(I)(i) child for whom eligibility was derived remains unmarried and under 21 years of age.

101(A)(15)(N)(II) children may apply for and remain in such status as long as they are under 21 years of age and remain unmarried.

Periods of residence and physical presence while in (N) nonimmigrant status may be counted towards fulfilling the requirements of Section 101(a)(27)(I).

(F.) The (N) nonimmigrant shall be given a three-year initial admission, with extensions in increments of three years, but not exceeding the date of the 21st birthday or marriage of the (I)(i) or (N)(ii), (I)(iii) or (iv) special immigrant parent. The service is consulting with the Department of State on ways to identify applicable birth date of the (I)(i) child from which the (N)(i) parent derived status to assist the service in determination of the appropriate length of stay.

(G.) The service is currently preparing regulations which will further explain this provision. If there is any question as to whether or not these provisions affect an applicant for adjustment, the application should be accepted and held in abeyance until the regulation appears in the Federal Register.

1-14-87
LEGALIZATION WIRE #10

The New Immigrant and Nonimmigrant Codes are:

Classification	Visas	Adjustments
101(a)(27)(I)(iii)	SK1	SK6
101(a)(27)(I)(iv)	SK2	SK7
101(a)(27)(I)(ii)	SK4	SK9
101(a)(27)(I)(i)	SK3	SK8
101(a)(15)(N)(i)	N-8	
101(a)(15)(N)(ii)	N-9	

Alan C. Nelson
Commissioner

App-36

1-16-87

[Facsimile Copy-Retyped From Original]

FROM: Office of General Counsel
DATE: January 16, 1987
TO: All Regional Counsels, All District Counsels
SUBJECT: Administrative closure of cases for legalization application

The Immigration Reform and Control Act of 1986 provides in part that an alien who is the subject of an Order to Show Cause must apply for legalization during the 30-day period after the Attorney General designates the application period.

Immigration Court Policy and Procedures

On November 7, 1986 the Chief Immigration Judge issued a Policy and Procedure Memorandum to all Immigration Judges advising them that the following alternatives were available for handling cases in which the question of legalization is raised:

(1) If the Service moves to terminate the Order to Show Cause, you may, of course, grant the motion. (Please keep in mind that there is no current authority for any conditional termination of an Order to Show Cause, i.e., until the legalization application is adjudicated).

(2) If both parties request that the case be administratively closed, you may grant the motion. If the motion is granted, the following language must be included in the Immigration Judge's order:

As both parties have so requested, it is hereby ordered that the case be administratively closed and is to be considered no longer pending before the Immigration Judge. No further action will be taken in this matter until such time as the case is presented for recalendaring and further proceedings.

(3) If the attorneys/representatives/applicants move to withdraw other applications for relief (without prejudice to the filing of a motion to reopen to reapply for the withdrawn relief if legalization is denied) and seek voluntary departure instead, and the Service agrees, you may grant a reasonable period of voluntary departure that will allow the alien to apply for legalization during or after

1-16-87

that period (when the stay provisions apply). This option will eliminate the need for any hearing or decision by the Immigration Judge on prima facie eligibility for legalization because the Service's agreement will presume that they have reviewed any necessary evidence.

(4) Proceed as usual and render a decision in the normal manner.

Service Attorney Policy and Procedures

In light of the above-outlined alternatives established by the Chief Immigration Judge, the following procedures shall be followed by all Service attorneys:

1. If an alien presents evidence of filing for legalization, the Service attorney will stipulate to administrative closing of the case.

2. If an alien is scheduled for a hearing before the period during which he/she may file an application for legalization, and such alien makes a prima facie case of eligibility for legalization to the satisfaction of the Service attorney and requests his/her case be closed administratively, the Service attorney will join in the motion to administratively close the case either at the scheduled hearing or prior thereto provided that the alien or his/her representative stipulates to provide the Service attorney evidence of filing for legalization within 30 days after the period during which the alien must file such application.

3. District Counsels will ensure that all administratively closed cases are entered immediately on 3x5 index cards with name, A-number, and date of closure.

4. If the alien/representative does not provide the Service attorney evidence of filing for legalization within the above-mentioned 30 day period, then the Service attorney will make a motion to the immigration court to recalendar the case.

5. If the alien/representative provides the Service attorney evidence of filing for legalization within the above-mentioned 30 day period, then the District Counsel will forward the A-file to the file room through the Deportation Branch. The index cards of all such cases shall be maintained separately in the litigation and legal advice office.

6. If the proceedings are closed administratively and the alien/representative has provided the Service attorney evidence of filing for legalization, no Service action

App-37

1-16-87

will be taken until after a _final_ determination on eligibility for legalization. If legalization is denied, Service attorneys will verify this from INS computers or other available data, with assistance from operations units, and submit a motion to recalendar the case for further proceedings.

PAUL W. SCHMIDT
Acting General Counsel

1-17-87

FROM: Immigration and Naturalization Service
DATE: January 17, 1987
TO: Field Investigative Units

By Memorandum dated 1/6/87, Commissioner Nelson expressed his concern about recent media articles regarding unscrupulous individuals taking advantage of undocumented aliens through offers of "guaranteed amnesty" for exorbitant costs. He has indicated his desire that the Service aggressively investigate such activities. Effective immediately therefore, field investigative units will observe the following guidelines:

(A) All leads and complaints containing such allegations will be referred within 48 hours for review by a supervisory special agent;

(B) Those determined to merit further investigation will be classified as Impact Level I, Line 513.2 Fraud Cases Under Case Management, and immediately assigned for follow-up by an agent. Investigations should be conducted with an eye toward

(1) Prosecution Under any Applicable Statutes. Possibilities might include 18 USC 1422 (Fraudulently collecting fees for registry of aliens), 18 USC 1341 (mail fraud), 18 USC 1343 (fraud by wire, radio or television), or 18 USC 1001 (fraud or false statements, generally).

(2) Civil Action Under any Available Statutes or Remedies. Possibilities might include 18 USC 1345 (injunctive relief for mail or wire frauds), or other applications for restraining orders by the District Court, or filing of complaints with the Federal Communications Commission and/or the United States Postal Service, for false advertising.

(3) Appropriate Administrative Relief. Possibilities include filing of complaints with the Bar Association for violations of the Canon of Ethics, if an attorney, or for the practice of law without a license, if a paralegal, consultant, notary or other non attorney. Also, for attorney practitioners or representatives authorized to practice before the Service, the Immigration courts or the BIA, disbarment proceedings should be considered, if violations of the Rules of Practice under 8 CFR 292 are revealed by investigation. Lastly, be advised that all investigations conducted under the terms of this wire are to be considered COINV reportable. District offices should immediately advise suboffices of the contents of this wire, to ensure servicewide compliance by investigations special agents.

1-17-87

App-39

1-19-87
LEGALIZATION WIRE #12

[Facsimile Copy - Retyped from Original]

FROM: United States Immigration and Naturalization Service
ACTION: Priority
DATE: January 19, 1987
TO: All ROCOMs, All DIDIRs, All OICs, All BPSHs, All District Counsel

Paragraph 4 of Legalization Wire Number 9, issued on December 30, 1986, and the revision of that paragraph, issued on January 2, 1987, should be disregarded. The following instructions should be used in determining whether apprehended aliens should be questioned regarding eligibility for Legalization and SAW status, and whether such aliens should be given an opportunity to establish a prima facie or nonfrivolous case of eligibility for the respective status, in accordance with the procedures set forth in Legalization Wire Number 1, dated November 14, 1986.

Any alien apprehended in the United States whose last entry was prior to November 6, 1986, (including such alien who has departed and returned to the United States since November 6, 1986 under a grant of advance parole from the INS) should have an inquiry made as to his or her eligibility for Legalization or SAW status in accordance with the procedures set forth in Telegram Number 1.

If there is no probable cause to believe that the alien's last entry occurred after November 6, 1986, the alien should be considered to have been in the United States since prior to November 6, 1986, for the purposes of processing under these instructions.

Any alien apprehended in the United States whose last entry was after November 6, 1986, will be considered ineligible to apply for legalization, or for SAW status in the United States, and will therefore not be queried as to eligibility for legalization or SAW status. Although an alien who entered after November 6, 1986 will not be allowed to remain in the United States to pursue a SAW application, such application may be made through a consular office abroad once the SAW application period begins. There is no such application process outside the United States for legalization applicants. An apprehended alien who entered after November 6, 1986, who meets the requirements for SAW eligibility, does not lose such eligibility by making an entry after November 6, 1986, but

1-19-87
LEGALIZATION WIRE #12

will be required to pursue his or her application from abroad.

Any questions relating to the interpretation of these instructions should be directed to the District Counsel, Regional Counsel, or General Counsel as appropriate.

Mark Everson, Executive Associate Commissioner

3-24-87
LEGALIZATION WIRE #13*

[Facsimile Copy - Retyped from Original]

FROM: Commissioner Alan C. Nelson
Immigration and Naturalization Service
Washington, DC 20536

ACTION: Routine
DATE: March 24, 1987
FILE: CO-245-C
RE: Legalization Wire #13

This wire discusses additional procedures involving the granting of advance parole to certain individuals who are prima-facie eligible for Legalization or have a nonfrivolous claim to SAW status. All field officers should re-read Legalization Wires #1 and #8 regarding this subject.

Effective immediately, all applicants for parole status in accordance with the first paragraph of Wire #8 will be required to submit a written request for parole in duplicate. In cases which are approved, authorization for parole (Form I-512) shall be prepared in the original and at least 3 copies. The original and one copy shall be given to the applicant, the second copy shall be kept in the applicant's A-file, and the third copy shall be attached to the duplicate written request for parole and then attached to the list of aliens granted advance parole, which is required in the first paragraph of the Wire #8.

On a monthly basis beginning April 1, 1987, a xeroxed copy of the list of aliens (and A-numbers) granted advance parole, and the attached requests for parole and relating I-512's shall be forwarded by each office to:

Office of General Counsel
425 I Street, N.W.
Suite 7048
Washington, D.C. 20536
Attn: Lori Scialabba

The report symbol will be CCOU 1.

In addition, each office shall make xeroxed copies of the parole request and Form I-512 of each alien whose name already appears on the list of those granted parole. These copies must be forwarded to the same address by April 1, 1987. These procedures will continue in effect indefinitely for all advance paroles granted to those

*Portions amended by Wire #29.

prima facie eligible for Legalization or who have a nonfrivolous claim to SAW status.

Alan C. Nelson, Commissioner

App-41

4-30-87
LEGALIZATION WIRE #14

[Facsimile Copy - Retyped from Original]

FROM: Alan C. Nelson, Commissioner
Immigration and Naturalization Service
Washington, D.C.

ACTION: Priority
FILE: CO 1588-P (Wire #14)
TO: All Regional Commissioners
All Regional Legalization Officers
All District Directors
All Chief Patrol Agents
All Officers in Charge
ODTF GLYNCO

Priority BEJEK Legalization Wire #1 dated 11/14/86, corrected Wire #9 dated 1/2/87 and Wire #12 dated 1/12/87.

Final IRCA regulations became effective on May 1, 1987. The following instructions should be used in determining whether apprehended aliens should be questioned regarding eligibility for legalization and SAW status, and whether such aliens should be given an opportunity to establish a prima facie or nonfrivolous case of eligibility to establish benefits under IRCA.

Effective immediately any alien apprehended or in service custody who was in the United States prior to May 1, 1987 should have an inquiry made as to his or her eligibility for legalization or SAW status. Those aliens who appear prima facie eligible for legalization must meet the continuous residence requirement.

"Resided continuously" means that the alien shall be regarded as having resided continuously in the United States if, at the time of filing of the application for temporary resident status: (1) no single absence from the United States has exceeded forty-five (45) days, and the aggregate of all absences has not exceeded one hundred and eighty (180) days between January 1, 1982 through the date the application for temporary resident status is filed, unless the alien can establish that due to emergent reasons, his or her return to the United States could not be accomplished within the time period allowed; (ii) the alien was maintaining residence in the United States; and (iii) the alien's departure from the United States was not based on an order of deportation.

Aliens who establish the aforementioned eligibility requirements shall continue to be processed in accordance

LEGALIZATION WIRE #14

with Wire #1 dated November 14, 1986 and shall be permitted to remain in the United States to pursue benefits under IRCA. The following procedures shall be implemented as of May 5, 1987 for legalization procedures and as of June 1, 1987 for SAW applicants.

1. Prepare I-213 with alien's claim to Legalization/SAW eligibility in the narrative.
2. Create an "A" file (forward to appropriate FCO with I-213 and photo of alien).
3. Fingerprint alien on FD-249 (FBI card) and forward to FBI.
4. Photograph alien.
5. Detach I-94 from I-213 and give to alien; endorse back of I-94 with the following: "Referred to Legalization Office."
6. In addition for cases in which eligibility claim is not established and the alien is to be removed from the United States (I-274) or scheduled for a deportation hearing (OSC) prepare affidavit (I-215 B).

For the purpose of processing under these instructions, the burden of proof is on the alien to establish to the satisfaction of the processing officer that he or she entered prior to 5/1/87.

Any alien apprehended in the United States whose last entry was after May 1, 1987 will be considered ineligible to apply for Legalization, or for SAW status in the United States, and will not be queried as to eligibility for Legalization or SAW status. Although an alien who entered after May 1, 1987 will not be allowed to remain in the United States to pursue a SAW application, such application may be made through a consular office abroad once the SAW application period begins on June 1, 1987. There is no such application time outside the United States for legalization applicants. An apprehended alien who entered after May 1, 1987, who meets the requirements for SAW eligibility, does not lose such eligibility by making and entry after May 1, 1987, but will be required to pursue his or her application from abroad.

BENED All Addresses.

Any questions relating to the interpretation of these instructions should be directed to District Counsel, Regional Counsel, or General Counsel as appropriate.

Alan C. Nelson
Commissioner

Official file
Division log

4-30-87
LEGALIZATION WIRE #15

TO: All INS Field Offices
FROM: INS Commissioner Alan C. Nelson
DATE: April 30, 1987
RE: Legalization Wire #15 (file CO 1588)

Due to changes in 8 CFR 210 and 8 CFR 245A between their proposed rule and final rule versions, certain instructions and items on Form I-687 (Legalization Application) and Form I-700 (SAW Application) are obsolete and incorrect. Addenda to these forms are under development for use until the forms can be revised in future printings. The following changes will be included in the addenda:

Form I-687 and Form I-700:

1. Instruction 9 - "Documents--General". Delete. Under the final rule original documents must be submitted "wherever possible" at the time of interview. Aliens who are scheduled for interview may retain originals until their interview and may attach certified copies of documents to applications filed before the interview date by mail or in person. For SAW applications, certified copies of third party records such as those of employers will be acceptable in lieu of originals.

2. Item 42, I-687; Item 25, I-700. Delete Parenthetical Instruction. Add "(check the first block if you or a member of your family has received such assistance and explain; including the name(s) of recipient(s) and Social Security number(s) used)."

Form I-700

1. Instruction page 1, Item 2, paragraph after (b)". Add after (November 6, 1986): "Absences that are brief, casual, and innocent will not break the physical presence requirement if made before May 1, 1987. Aliens who were outside of the United States on the date of enactment or departed the United States after enactment may apply for legalization if they reentered prior to May 1, 1987, provided they meet the continuous residence requirement and are otherwise eligible for Legalization."

2. Instruction 4, paragraph"(a)". Delete.

4-30-87
LEGALIZATION WIRE #15

1. Instruction 1, paragraph 2, line 2. Change "November 6, 1986" to "May 1, 1987".
2. Instruction 4, paragraph"(a)". Delete.
3. Instruction 7, lines 7-9. Delete beginning with "Applicants outside" and through "consulate".
4. Item 24. Delete.

App-43

5-5-87
SSA

FROM: Social Security Administration
TO: SSA Field Offices
DATE: May 5, 1987
SUBJECT: Processing SS-5's for Aliens who Want to Clarify Their Status Under the Immigration Reform and Control Act of 1986

On May 5, 1987, the Immigration and Naturalization Service (INS) will begin processing legalization applications from aliens who want to clarify their U.S. resident status. In most situations, INS will certify SS-5's for these individuals and forward them to designated SSA FO's for keying. In other situations, INS will refer the alien to an SSA FO to apply for an SSN. We will issue POMS instructions with exhibits of INS forms as soon as possible. In the meantime, we are issuing these emergency instructions.

INS will issue three different forms (I-689, I-688A, and I-688) which will allow aliens to work. Follow these instructions when an individual presents one of these forms to apply for an SSN.

I-689 (Fee Receipt Form)

INS personnel will issue these forms when they schedule the legalization interview at some future date. If the interview is scheduled more than 30 days from the filing date, INS will add an Employment Authorization Statement on the I-689 and refer these individuals to SSA FO's if they need an SSN. Process SS-5's for these individuals if they present this form with the Employment Authorization Statement and evidence of age and identity. If an individual presents this form without the Employment Authorization Statement, do not process an SS-5. Refer to INS individuals who question this decision.

Acceptable I-689's will contain at least the following information:

1. Form name and number
2. INS seal
3. Agency name
4. Alien's name
5. Filing date
6. "A" number
7. INS office name and address
8. Time and Date of scheduled interview
9. INS 3-digit alpha office code

10. Employment Authorization which expires on the scheduled interview date.

Complete SS-5's for these individuals according to current instructions except for the following items:

1. Citizenship Block - Check block B
2. NPN Block - Enter the "A" Number followed by the INS 3-digit alpha office code; e.g., A12345678XBU
3. Evidence Block - Enter "I-689, Employment Authorized" plus the evidence submitted for age and identity.
4. IDN Block - Enter an "A" code.

I-688A (Employment Authorization Form)

INS personnel will issue this form during the interview process, prior to forwarding the legalization application to another INS facility for a final determination. INS will recover old SSN cards. INS will certify SS-5's for the individuals to whom they issue this form but only when the alien goes to the INS office with a completed SS-5. INS will forward these SS-5"s to designated SSA FO's for keying. SSA will forward the SSN cards to INS and the alien will receive a separate notice of the SSN assigned (see explanation of process below). If an individual presents an I-688A and wants to apply for the original or replacement SSN card, proceed as follows:

1. If the individual states he/she already completed an SS-5 at the INS office, do not process another SS-5. Explain that SSA will forward the card to INS and that, shortly thereafter, he/she will receive a separate notice of the number assigned. Also, explain that INS will release the SSN card when the legalization application is approved. Refer to INS any individuals who question this arrangement.

2. If the individual states he/she did not complete an SS-5 at the INS office (or does not remember), process the SS-5 if he/she presents the I-688A (see explanation of process below).

Complete SS-5's for these individuals according to current instructions except for the following item:

1. Citizenship Block - Check Block B.
2. NPN Block - Enter the "A" number followed by the INS 3-digit alpha office code; e.g.; A12345678XBU.
3. Evidence Block - Enter "I-688A"
4. IDN Block - Enter an "A" code.

Acceptable Forms I-688A will be laminated and will contain at least the following information:

App-44

1. Form number and date prepared (on right edge of card)
2. Agency name with yellow background
3. "A" number
4. Applicant's name
5. Applicant's signature
6. Issue date
7. Date of birth
8. Country of birth
9. Explanation date with yellow background (6 months from issue date)
10. Fingerprint
11. Photograph
12. The words "Employment Authorization" at the top of the card with red background
13. INS 3-digit alpha office code beginning with "X" (on right side of photograph)
14. Agency seal(s) on the plastic cover
15. U.S. map outlined in red on the back

Explanation of Process

When you process an SS-5 using an I-689 or I-688A, recover any old SSN cards the individual has and dispose of them per RM 00201.035. The new SSN cards for individuals who previously obtained SSN cards in their own correct names will contain the same SSNs. Tell I-689 and I-688A applicants that SSA will forward the new SSN card to INS and that, shortly thereafter, they will receive a separate notice of the number assigned. Also, explain that INS will release the card to them when INS approves their legalization application. Refer to INS any individuals who question this arrangement.

I-688 (Temporary Resident Form)

INS personnel will issue this form when they approve an alien's legalization application and grant temporary lawful resident status. If INS previously issued an I-688A, they will recover the I-688A and issue the I-688, plus the SSN card. Some of these individuals will eventually apply for replacement SSN cards. If INS did not previously issue an I-688A, they will refer the individual to an SSA FO to apply for an original SSN card. [If] an individual submits an I-688, process the SS-5 for an original or replacement SSN card as you do when an I-551 is submitted; i.e., enter the form number followed by the "A" number in the evidence block (plus age evidence for an original SSN) and enter a "C" code in the IDN block. In these cases, SSA will mail the SSN card to the alien.

The I-688 will contain the same information as on the I-688A except for the following items:

1. The form number is different.
2. The expiration date is 31 months from the issue date.
3. The words "Temporary Resident" appear at the top of the card with a green background.
4. The U.S. map is outlined in green on the back.

When you process an SS-5 using an I-688, recover any old SSN cards the individual has and dispose of them per RM 00201.035.

App-45

LEGALIZATION WIRE #19

[Facsimile Copy - Retyped from Original]

FROM: INS Commissioner Alan C. Nelson
Immigration and Naturalization Service
Washington, D.C.

ACTION: Priority
DATE: May 8, 1987
TO: All Regional Commissioners
All Regional Legalization Officers
All District Directors
All Chief Patrol Agents
All Officers in Charge

On May 4, 1987 the United States District Court for the Eastern District of California, Judge Karlton, issued an injunction in Catholic Social Services v. Edwin Meese, III, No. Civ. S-86-1343 LKK. The court has enjoined the service from "excluding any alien apprehended during the period from November 6, 1986 to June 1, 1987, who can present a nonfrivolous claim for adjustment of status with the meaning of Section 210(A) of IRCA, regardless of the date of last attempted entry into the United States." This injunction applies to aliens apprehended by INS who have a nonfrivolous claim to SAW status. It does not apply to aliens who request admission at a port of entry, for the purpose of filing a SAW application, unless INS has apprehended the alien and placed him or her in exclusion proceedings. All other aliens not processed for exclusion will be treated according to Telegram #1 as modified by Telegram #14.

BENED All Addresses.

This injunction becomes effective May 9, 1987. As of that date all service personnel are to comply with the above quoted order of the District Court. Any questions should be directed to the Regional Counsel.

Alan C. Nelson
Commissioner

LEGALIZATION WIRE #19

5-11-87
LEGALIZATION WIRE #17

[Facsimile Copy - Retyped from Original]

FROM: Immigration and Naturalization Service
DATE: May 11, 1987
TO: All ROCOMS, All ROLEGS, All DIDIRS (Except Foreign), All OICS (Except Foreign)
SUBJECT: Legalization Wire #17
Information concerning the purchase of Legalization/SAW Forms through the U.S. Government Printing Office (GPO).

Recently, COLEG has received numerous inquiries relative to the purchase of Legalization/SAW forms through the U.S. Government Printing Office. In light of those inquiries, the following information is provided.

Forms I-687, I-690, I-693, I-700, and I-705 can be purchased by the public through the Superintendent of Documents, U.S. Government Printing Office and through the twenty-four Government Book Stores. The telephone number to be used by the public to purchase forms through GPO is (202)783-3238. Forms may only be purchased through GPO in packets of 100. Some Legalization/SAW forms have been sold out at the Government Book Stores. However, the book stores will be resupplied by GPO subsequent to receipt of outstanding requisition orders.

The following chart relates to the GPO stock number, cost per packet, packets on hand, pending requisition order, and the delivery date of GPO's outstanding requisition.

FORM	STOCK NO.	COST PER PACKET	PACKETS ON HAND GPO MAIN OFFICE	GPO PENDING REQUISITION PACKET	GUARANTEED DELIVERY DATE (AT GPO)
I-687	027-022-00336-5	$27	2,126	25,000	05/15/87
I-700	027-002-00337-3	$27	1,880	18,000	05/11/87
I-693	027-002-00340-3	$27	1,000	50,000	05/11/87
I-705	027-002-00339-0	$13	1,509	18,000	05/11/87
I-690	027-002-00344-6	$27	59	10,000	05/11/87

5-11-87
LEGALIZATION WIRE #17

Individuals or firms who request significant numbers of Legalization/SAW forms should be referred to either the 24 Government Book Stores or the Superintendent of Documents, U.S. Government Printing Office, Washington, D.C. 20401, Telephone: (202)783-3238. Meanwhile, reasonable numbers of such forms on hand should be given to attorneys and other legitimate individuals upon request.

Requests for additional Legalization forms needed at Legalization offices shall be reported through districts who in turn shall consolidate these requirements to the Central Office via Telefax or wire in accordance with outstanding instructions.

cc: INS: COLEG:PG Heinauer:633-5309:doc:05/06/87:DFRWIRE
COFAC

5-19-87
LEGALIZATION WIRE #20

TO: All INS Field Offices
FROM: INS' Office of Legalization
DATE: May 19, 1987
RE: Legalization Wire #20 (file CO 1588)

The Legalization Procedures Manual at pages IV-23 and IV-24 describes procedures to be followed when returning legalization or SAW applications to applicants. Presently the manual says that only a copy of Form I-72 is to be placed in the applicant's A90M file jacket. Effective immediately, a photocopy or duplicate Form I-687 or Form I-700 is also to be placed in the file jacket when an application is returned. This is necessary because Form I-72 contains insufficient data for a laps entry. Please advise all Legalization offices under your jurisdiction of this change as soon as possible. The procedures manual will be amended accordingly.

[Facsimile Copy-Retyped from original]

FROM: Richard E. Norton, Associate Commissioner
DATE: May 19, 1987
FILE: CO 249-P
TO: All Regional Commissioners:
    Eastern, Northern, Western, Southern
SUBJECT: Adjustment of Status Under Section 249 of the Act.

A number of inquiries have been received at this office concerning eligibility requirements under Section 249 of the Immigration and Nationality Act, in light of the updating of the registry date from June 30, 1948 to January 1, 1972 by Section 203 of the Immigration Reform and Control Act. This memorandum contains guidelines regarding Section 249, and is meant to supplement the Operations Instructions.

An applicant under Section 249 may have entered the country in a legal or illegal status, and may be in a legal or illegal status at the time of application. The applicant must also establish that he or she:

(1) entered the United States prior to January 1, 1972;

(2) has had his or her residence in the United States continuously since entry;

(3) is a person of good moral character; and

(4) is not ineligible to citizenship (paragraph (22) of section 212(a) of the Act).

The requirement of good moral character should be treated in a similar manner to the treatment of the requirement in the naturalization process. In addition, six Service decisions should be reviewed in this regard: Matter of P, (8 I&N Dec. 167); Matter of DeLucia, (11 I&N Dec. 565); Matter of Locicero, (11 I&N Dec. 805); Matter of Carbajal, (17 I&N Dec. 272); Matter of Seda, (17 I&N Dec. 550); and Matter of Piroglu, (17 I&N Dec. 578).

The requirement that the applicant establish that he or she has had a residence continuously in the United States since entry is discussed in Chapter II-52 of the Examinations Handbook. In addition, published decisions on this topic as listed in Chapter II-59 should be reviewed.

An applicant must also establish that he or she is not inadmissible under section 212(a) of the Act as it relates to criminals (paragraphs (9), (10), and (33)), procurers and other immoral persons (paragraphs (12) and (13), subversives (paragraphs (27), (28), and (29)), violators of narcotics laws (paragraph (23)) and smugglers of aliens (paragraph (31)). Other paragraphs of section 212(a) do not relate to registry cases. Thus, an applicant need not submit a medical examination with his or her application, or an affidavit of support, since none of the medical grounds, or public charge grounds of exclusion need be overcome.

It should be noted that, since the last revision of section 249 of the Act, two additional classes of ineligible aliens have been added to the exclusion provisions of section 212(a) in paragraphs (32) and (33). An individual who is deemed to have "ordered, incited, assisted or otherwise participated in the persecution of any person because of race, religion, national origin, or political opinion" can be classified as "criminal". In addition, due to the abhorrent nature of the acts described in section 212(a)(33), an individual ineligible for admission under that section is not to be considered an individual who is of good moral character. Therefore, any person ineligible for admission under section 212(a)(33) of the Act is statutorily ineligible for the benefits of section 249 of the Act. While Congress has not yet indicated an intention to again amend section 249, the Service views excludability under 212(a)(32) as it relates to certain graduates of foreign medical schools as a serious negative factor. Ineligibility under section 212(a)(32) should be given great weight in a discretionary decision under section 249. Any decision for the benefits of section 249 from an applicant ineligible under section 212(a)(32) will therefore be certified to the Associate Commissioner, Examinations.

It should also be noted that the requirements of section 212(e) must be met by any applicant who applies for the benefits of section 249 and was either admitted in, or changed to, a J nonimmigrant status. Therefore, any applicant who is subject to the foreign residency requirement must be eligible for and obtain a waiver of the two-year foreign residence requirement, as completion of the requirement would break the applicant's continuous residence after entry prior to January 1, 1972.

A Memorandum of Creation of Record (Form I-181) should be completed in each case which is approved. Copy 3 of the Form I-181, along with Form I-89, should be forwarded to the IMDAC facility upon approval. The class of admission for all applicants who establish entry prior to July 1,

5-19-87

1924 remains Z3-3. The class of admission for all applicants who establish entry on or after July 1, 1924 but prior to January 1, 1972 will be Z6-6.

Richard E. Norton
Associate Commissioner
cc: CONGR
cc: AILA
cc: Interpreter Releases

[Facsimile Copy-Retyped from original]

FROM: Department of State
DATE: May 27, 1987
TO: All Diplomatic and Consular Posts
State 144 377
SUBJECT: Immigration Control and Reform Act of 1986, Section 210: Special Agricultural Workers (SAW) Processing Procedures

1. Summary

The Department of State through its foreign service posts abroad will begin on June 1 to administer a new program providing temporary resident status for individuals who have worked in the past in seasonal agriculture in the United States.

Outlined below are definitions and operating procedures to be followed in implementing the Special Agricultural Worker (SAW) provisions of the Immigration Reform and Control Act of 1986. The overseas SAW application process will substantially follow immigrant visa procedures. However, Special Agricultural Workers whose applications are recommended for approval at overseas processing posts (OPP) will enter the United States with a SAW entry document rather than a visa.

INS forms referred to in this cable will be forwarded to those posts which have indicated that they may receive SAW applications (Mexico City, Kingston, Bridgetown, Ottawa, Port-Au-Prince, Santo Domingo, Nassau, Guatemala, San Salvador and Tegucigalpa). Other posts requiring forms should submit requests to the Department (CA/VO/F/P: Attn: Tony Perkins).

All procedural or policy questions relating to the SAW program should be directed to the Department (CA/VO/F/P) rather than to the Immigration and Naturalization Service.

End Summary.

2. Definitions

A. Application Period

Applications for temporary resident status as a Special Agricultural Worker will be accepted during an 18-month application period from June 1, 1987 through November 30, 1988. (An application is considered to have been accepted when the filing fee has been paid.)

B. Eligibility - Group 1 SAW.

Special Agricultural Workers who have performed qualifying agricultural employment in the United States for at least 90 man-days in the aggregate in each of the twelve-month periods ending on May 1, 1984, 1985, and 1986, and who have resided in the United States for six months in the aggregate in each of those twelve-month periods. The status of a Group 1 Temporary Resident will be adjusted to that of an Alien Lawfully Admitted for Permanent Residence as of December 1, 1989, or as of one year from the date of the alien's date of entry, whichever is later.

C. Eligibility - Group 2 SAW.

Special Agricultural Workers who during the twelve-month period ending on May 1, 1986 have performed at least 90 man-days in the aggregate of qualifying agricultural employment in the United States. The status of a Group 2 Temporary Resident will be adjusted to that of an Alien Lawfully Admitted for Permanent Residence as of December 1, 1990, or as of 2 years from the date of the alien's date of entry, whichever is later.

D. Family Members

There is no derivative status for family members under the Special Agricultural Worker program. Each member of a family must apply based on his/her qualifying employment.

E. FBI Namechecks

A 60-day no-response procedure does not apply to SAW cases. Posts will initiate the FBI clearance letter, but will not await a response prior to scheduling an appointment. If a HIT is received after issuance of the entry document, the OPP will forward the response to the Regional Processing Facility (RPF) having jurisdiction over the applicant's place of destination in the United States (see Paragraph 15.).

F. Ineligible Classes

Certain grounds of ineligibility will not apply to SAW applicants: Sections 212(A)(14), (20), (21), (25), and (32). The following sections of the Act may not RPT not be waived: 212(A) (9), (15), (23) except as it relates to a single offense of simple possession of 30 grams or less of marijuana, (27), (28), (29), and (33). Section 212(A) (15), however, shall not apply where the alien has a history of employment in the United States evidencing self-support without reliance on public cash assistance. Waivers on all other grounds are available for humanitarian purposes, to assure family unity, or when the granting of such waiver is found to be in the public interest.

G. Man-Day.

The term "Man-Day" means the performance during any day of qualifying agricultural employment for wages paid. If employment records relating to an alien applicant show only piece rate units completed, then any day in which piece rate work was performed shall be counted as a man-day. Work for more than one employer in a single day shall be counted as no more than one man-day.

H. Numerical limitations

The numerical limitations of Sections 201 and 202 of the INA do not apply to the adjustment of aliens to lawful temporary resident status under Section 210 of the Act. No more than 350,000 aliens may be granted temporary resident status in the Group I classification. If more than 350,000 aliens are determined to be eligible for Group I classification, the first 350,000 aliens who file applications for that classification shall be accorded that status upon approval of their applications. Other applicants who may be eligible for Group I classification shall be classified as Group 2 aliens. There is no limitation on the number of aliens whose resident status may be adjusted from temporary to permanent in Group 2 classification.

I. Overseas Processing Posts.

The Immigration and Naturalization Service and the Department (CA) have agreed that certain posts will serve as overseas processing posts (OPP) at which applications for admission as a Special Agricultural Worker are received, processed, adjudicated, and recommended for approval or denial. In Mexico, the embassy will initially process SAW applications. In all other countries, the immigrant visa issuing post in that country to which the alien, if an applicant for an immigrant visa, would make such application will process SAW applicants. Consular officers assigned to these posts are authorized to

recommend for approval an application for Special Agricultural Worker status if the alien establishes eligibility for approval, and to deny such an application if the alien fails to meet statutory requirements or admits fraud or misrepresentation in the application process.

J. Qualifying Agricultural Employment.

Qualifying Agricultural Employment is seasonal field work related to planting, cultural practices, cultivating, growing and harvesting of fruits, vegetables, and other perishable commodities as defined by the Secretary of Agriculture by regulation. Field work related to products other than fruits, vegetables, or other perishable commodities is not qualifying employment for the purpose of such eligibility. The requisite period of qualifying agricultural employment depends on whether the alien is applying for Group I or Group II status. (Further guidelines on perishable commodities will be provided SEPTEL. Final Department of Agriculture regulations will be published no later than May 29.)

K. Proof of Eligibility

An alien may establish eligibility through government employment records (e.g., State Unemployment records), records maintained by employers, pay receipts, and other reliable evidence. The applicant has the burden of proving the requisite employment by a preponderance of the evidence. Personal testimony by an applicant not supported by corroborating evidence will not meet the applicant's burden of proof.

3. Filing Application

A. General

All consular posts abroad will handle inquiries, provide instructions, and distribute forms to prospective SAW applicants. Only OPP's are authorized to receive applications, accept fees for, and have full authority to recommend approval or deny applications for SAW benefits under these procedures and in accordance with the burdens of proof and evidence and other requirements as set forth in 8 CFR 210. Although OPP denials will be subject to INS appellate oversight, there will be no INS regional review or confirmation of denials of SAW applications by consular officers. Jurisdiction over applications recommended for approval will be assumed by INS upon the applicant's entry into the U.S. Such applications may be reviewed by INS Regional Processing Facilities (RPF) on a random basis, or may receive no further review.

The processing of SAW applications, from receipt of the application through the collection and review of documentation and denial or recommendation of approval, will substantially follow the same pattern as established procedures for the processing of immigrant visas. Wherever possible, the OPP will utilize resources already dedicated to IV processing (computers and software, trained foreign service officers and foreign service national staff.) A new version of IVACS, which contains software specially designed for the SAW program, will be sent to IVACS posts. A memorandum describing IVACS SAW procedures will accompany the software release tape.

B. Information Sheet

At the earliest possible date, but in any case prior to June 1, 1987, consular posts will make available to the public an information sheet prepared by the Department of State on how to apply for the SAW program overseas (see State 144377). This information material will stress eligibility criteria and documentary requirements and include an abbreviated biographic data sheet that the applicant will be required to complete and mail to a designated OPP in order to request an application and related forms. Applicants will be instructed to apply by mail.

C. Record Creation

Upon receipt of the completed abbreviated biographic data sheet and application request, posts will create an OF-224B control card or enter the information into IVACS. The applicant's name, date and place of birth, and "visa symbol" (SAW category) will be noted on the OF-224B or in IVACS. S1W is the symbol for SAW Group 1 applicants, and S2W the symbol for SAW Group 2 applicants. Pending receipt of further information from the applicant, posts should provisionally indicate S2W in the visa symbol field. If more than one family member is applying as a SAW, a separate cross-reference card should be created for each case. Do not RPT not enter a registration/priority date until a completed I-700 (application form) is received.

D. Packet 3-S

The applicant will be sent a Packet 3-S which will include a cover letter, the I-700, I-705 (Affidavit of Employment), a biographic sheet (Form OF-179), and a check list containing instructions on requirements for a birth certificate, passport, photographs, police clearances, work and residence documentation, and fee. The covering letter should also advise applicants to retain duplicate copies of all RPT all documents submitted to the OPP with their I-700 application form. The sending date will be entered in the Packet 3 field. (For IVACS posts: The new version of IVACS will permit entry of S1W and S2W as visa symbols. It will also automatically generate for SAW cases a special Packet 3-S cover letter during the end-of-day process.)

E. Receipt of Application Form (I-700)

An applicant will indicate that he or she is ready to be interviewed by returning the Packet 3-S documents (I-700 with work and residence documentation attached, I-705 if required, and OF-179) and check list. Indicate the date of receipt in the remarks field on the reverse side of the OF-224B or in the "OF-179 Received" field in IVACS.

When a preliminary screening of the employment and relevant residence documentation indicates that the applicant may be eligible for SAW benefits, the OF-179 will be accepted (and retained for inclusion in the "Has Docs" field, and assign a registration date based on the date the I-700 is received. Enter that date in the "Priority Date" field. The registration date is the date recorded for purposes of identifying the first 350,000 Group 1 applications filed. The registration date should also be noted on the application form (I-700) in the upper right hand corner.

Check the I-700 to determine the SAW category (S1W or S2W) for which the person is applying, and modify the visa symbol if necessary. Detach the blue copy of the OF-224B and file it in chronological order by priority/registration date for S1W cases.

If the physical quantity of evidence submitted is so large as to make transmittal and storage prohibitive, the post will retain the most pertinent evidence with the application package. Other evidence should be summarized on the reverse of the examinations worksheet (Form I-696) and returned to the applicant. The applicant should be advised that in the event his/her application is denied and he/she appeals that decision, the applicant may submit the returned evidence to the OPP with the appeal.

App-53

F. FBI Clearance

At this point the FBI and post clearances will be initiated. Make the usual entries in the background investigation field. When the FBI clearance request letter is produced, type or stamp "SAW Applicant" across the top of the letter. (For IVACS posts: IVACS will print this automatically.) The 60-day no-response procedure is not RPT not applicable for SAW cases. FBI HITS received after issuance of the entry document should be forwarded to the RPF having jurisdiction over the applicant's destination in the U.S. (See Section 15). The remarks field of the OF-224B or IVACS should be annotated to indicate the applicant's U.S. destination and the responsible RPF.

G. Applications Rejected as Incomplete

Should the post determine that the I-700 is incomplete or that it does not satisfy the requirements of the law, the Packet 3-S documents, along with a cover letter (Form OF-194) indicating the reasons why they are being returned. The applicant should be informed that if he/she fails to resubmit the application within 90 days, it will be rejected for lack of action. Note the date of return in the remarks area of the OF-224B or in IVACS. Do not enter a registration date.

H. Packet 4-S

Once all documents and clearances have been received, the applicant will be sent a Packet 4-S containing an interview appointment date and information on the medical examination procedure. (For IVACS posts: The new version of IVACS will automatically generate for SAW cases a special Packet 4-S cover letter during the end-of-day process.)

The Packet 4-S will inform the applicant that on the date of the appointment, he/she will be expected to pay the required fee; present a passport, birth certificate, completed medical examination form, photographs, police certificate(s); be prepared to discuss employment experience and, for Group 1 applicants, residence in the United States. Male applicants over the age of 17 and under the age of 26 will be given a Selective Service form (SSS Form 1) to be completed and included in the SAW packet.

5-27-87
DOS

5-27-87
DOS

4. Evidence

In evaluating the evidence of residence and employment submitted by SAW applicants, OPPS must apply the "Just and Reasonable Inference" standard mandated by Section 210(b)(3)(iii) of the Act. Under this standard, an applicant cannot be denied temporary residence for failure to establish a complete documentary record of the full periods of required employment and residence if it is reasonable to conclude, from the evidence presented and the interview, the likelihood that the applicant meets the eligibility requirements. If the applicant has presented evidence which on its face established eligibility or from which eligibility may be reasonably inferred, the application must be recommended for approval, or the OPP must disprove the evidence.

The following points bear consideration in the analysis of documentary evidence:

A. Evidence will frequently relate to piece-rate work and will show volume of product picked or harvested rather than hours or days worked over a period of time. Productivity may vary significantly from day to day based on number of hours worked, weather, or assignment to other tasks.

B. Records of employment may be in the form of informal tallies of boxes, bushels, etc. of product. Such records may not be dated and may identify the worker only by a first name or nickname or not at all. Such evidence is of extremely limited probative value if not supported by a Form I-705 affidavit or by other information permitting verification.

C. Piece-rate work performed by an entire family is sometimes credited to a single principal member of the family. Information relative to the average productivity of individual workers will be useful in weighing claims that piece-rate evidence relates to more than one individual.

D. Individuals who worked as crew members for a farm labor contractor may only have vague information concerning the names of producers or farmers for whom the crew worked or concerning the names and specific locations of the farms on which they worked. However, in all cases, experienced farm workers can readily provide information concerning the crops on which they worked, the methods of cultivation or harvesting employed for specific crops, and the general geographic areas where specific products are grown.

App-54

Additionally, workers who claim to have harvested products which require field-sorting or selective harvesting should be able to describe selection criteria. The plausibility of documentary evidence is enhanced by an applicant's demonstration of familiarity with routine occupational information. Adjudicators should develop such information and test claims to eligibility against it in applicant interviews. However, an applicant's familiarity with particular agricultural operations, standing alone, does not serve to establish qualifying employment during the required period(s).

5. Adjudication

Cases in which eligibility is fully documented by employment records and other evidence shall be recommended for approval by the OPP. The specific evidence which establishes eligibility shall be noted on the worksheet (Form I-696).

Cases in which eligibility is not fully documented, but may be reasonably inferred from the evidence provided and the personal testimony of the applicant at the interview, shall be recommended for approval by the OPP. The specific evidence from which the inference was drawn and the basis for the inference shall be noted on the worksheet (Form I-696). If the interviewing officer believes that supporting documentation is insufficient, but that the information provided may be reasonably verified by the applicant through contact with an employer or by some other means which would establish or infer eligibility, the examinations worksheet should be clearly annotated, and the applicant instructed to provide the OPP with a completed Form I-705 or other evidence of his/her eligibility.

Cases in which eligibility is not fully documented, and may not be reasonably inferred from the evidence provided and the personal testimony of the applicant at the interview, shall be denied by the OPP. The basis for finding that the alien has not met his or her burden of proof shall be noted on the worksheet (Form I-696).

6. Fraud

INS document analysis units (DAU) will issue periodic bulletins as an aid to detection of fraud. These bulletins will be distributed to the OPP's.

Evidence must by reviewed to determine whether it fits fraud profiles or fraudulent document characteristics developed by the DAUS at the RPFS. Cases involving admitted fraud are to be denied by the OPP. In such cases, a sworn statement regarding the details of the fraud committed, including the alien's admission of fraud, is to be taken and included in the file. The worksheet (I-696) and refusal letter (OF-194) will be annotated with the reason(s) for denial.

Cases in which fraud or willful misrepresentation of a material fact is suspected, but not admitted to by the applicant, may be denied by the OPP if the evidence submitted, or the inconsistencies noted, form a basis for determination that the alien has not established eligibility for SAW status. The specific evidence and grounds for the suspicion of fraud shall be noted on the worksheet (Form I-696) and refusal letter (Form OF-194).

Fraud cases should be reported to the Department (CA/VO/L/A) for a rule of probability finding (also slugged for CA/FPP), entered in AVLOS, and a Category I File established.

7. Recommendation for Approval

If the case is recommended for approval, the consular officer will prepare a SAW package and entry document on a revised Form OF-155A. The SAW package will contain the following documents: An approved I-700 (on which the upper right-hand corner), proof of labor experience and relevant residence (for Group 1 SAWS), I-705 if submitted, OF-179 biographic form, two photos, a completed medical examination, a birth certificate, receipt of fee payment, police clearance certificate(s), and a completed Selective Service Form 1 if applicable. These documents will be grommeted.

Form OF-155A will be completed as usual, except for the following:

(1) Delete the line reading "Immigrant Visa and Alien Registration".

(2) Directly above the deleted line type or stamp the following two lines: "Special Agricultural Worker Document" (line 1), and "Immigrant/Visa References are Inoperative" (line 2). (For IVACS posts: The new version of IVACS will perform the above modifications on the OF-155A for SAW cases automatically.) In Visa Classification block,

App-55

enter "S1W" or "S2W", to denote whether the alien is a Group 1 or Group 2 applicant. If an ineligibility is waived under Section 210(c), post must make a manual notation to that effect in the "Ineligibility for Visa waived under Section" field on Form OF-155A. For SAW applicants who have a previous "A" file number, that number should appear on the OF-155A.

The SAW packet issued to an applicant recommended for approval must be presented by the applicant at the port of entry (POE) within the period of validity of the document (120 days from date of issuance.) Upon application for admission at a POE, the SAW OF-155A will be endorsed with an admission stamp showing the date and port of entry. The SAW packet will be returned to the applicant who will be directed to proceed within thirty (30) days to the Legalization Office (LO) nearest his/her proposed place of employment in the United States for further processing.

Upon presentation of the SAW package, the LO will "construct" an A90M file, issue the applicant a Form I-688A (Employment Authorization), and forward the A90M file to the document processing contractor (DPC) where interagency (including FBI) security checks will be performed. The DPC will then forward the A90M file to the regional processing facility (RPF) having jurisdiction over the LO that issued the applicant's Form I-688A.

In the event that DPC systems checks indicate the existence of derogatory information, a relating "A" file, lookout, or similar INS record, the application will be reviewed by the RPF to ensure that the applicant is admissible. Where a previously created "A" file exists, the DPC will also initiate a file transfer request (FTR). If it is decided upon review at the RPF that denial is warranted, appropriate action will be taken, and the OPP will be notified of that action. Information contained in the Legalization Adjudication Processing System (LAPS) will be updated.

8. Denials

When an OPP denies an application, the applicant will be formally notified of the reasons for denial (Form OF-194) and advised of his/her right to appeal. In Section 210 Denial Cases, post must ensure that the applicant understands what additional documents are required and must advise him/her that any additional information must be resubmitted within the application period. Appropriate forms (I-690 - "Application for Waiver of Grounds of Excludability", and/or I-694 - "Notice of Appeal of Decision") and filing instructions will be enclosed with the denial notice.

If a SAW application is denied because it does not meet SAW criteria as stipulated in Section 210 of the Act, indicate on the OF-224B that it is a Section 210 refusal. Section 210 refusals are not RPT not being entered into AVLOS. Applicable 212(A) ineligibilities should, of course, be indicated on the card, entered into AVLOS, and a Category I File created. (For IVACS posts: The new version of IVACS will permit entry in the RCA transaction of the heretofore unused Refusal Code 49 to indicate Section 210 refusals.)

9. Waivers

Applicants who are inadmissible under a ground of excludability which may be waived under Section 210(C) of the Act should be advised to file a waiver application accompanied by the correct fee (DOLS 50) receipt. The waiver application is to be filed at the OPP, and approved or denied by the senior consular officer. If an applicant indicates that he/she is inadmissible under a ground of excludability for which no waiver is available under Section 210(C) of the Act, his/her application is to be denied by the OPP, a Category I File created, and the alien's name entered in AVLOS. OPP's may return the personal documents to applicants ineligible to apply for a waiver, or whose waiver applications is denied. Waivers of Section 212(A) (9) or (10) of the Act previously obtained under Section 212(H) are not valid for the purpose of an issuance.

10. Appeals

An OPP may "sua sponte" (on its own initiative) reopen and reconsider its own adverse decision. In cases where the OPP issues a new decision that will grant SAW status, the aforementioned approval procedures will be followed, i.e., the applicant will be given a SAW package for presentation at a POE where he/she is directed to an LO for I-688A issuance.

When an application for SAW status is denied, the alien is given written notice setting forth the specific reasons for the denial on Form OF-194. Form OF-194 should contain advice to the applicant that he/she may appeal the decision and that an appeal must be accompanied by any additional new evidence and supporting brief, if desired. Additionally, Form OF-194 should provide a notice to the alien that if he/she fails to file an appeal from the decision, Form OF-194 will serve as a final notice of ineligibility. Included as part of the denial letter, the applicant is to be given Form I-694, Notice of Appeal, in triplicate.

While the appeal time for stateside cases is a period of 30 days, because of postal problems in many overseas countries, the appeal period has been extended to 60 days for OPP-processed applications. If no appeal is filed in the period of time allotted, the OPP may return to the applicant his/her personal documents submitted in support of the application. If an appeal is filed in triplicate, accompanied by the denied application package and fee (DOLS 50) receipt directly to:

Administrative Appeals Unit, Room 400
Immigration and Naturalization Service
1121 Vermont Avenue, N.W.
Washington, D.C. 20536

If an appeal is dismissed, the Administrative Appeals Unit (AAU) will notify the applicant and return the application package, with a copy of the AAU decision attached, to the OPP for return to the applicant. No further appeal lies from this decision. If an appeal is sustained or remanded, the AAU will notify the applicant and return the application package, with a copy of the AAU decision attached, to the OPP for appropriate action.

11. Fees and Accounting

INS has established fees of DOLS 185 for each adult and DOLS 50 for each child under the age of 18 for filing for temporary residence status as a seasonal agricultural worker. The maximum amount payable by a family shall be DOLS 420. For purposes of SAW fees, the family is defined as parents and children under the age of 18 years of age or older, even though members of the household, will not RPT not be considered family members for the family fee rate. SAW fees are payable at the time of the interview and are not refundable. Fees are payable in cash--either local or U.S. currency.

Because of the DOLS 420 limit on fees paid per family, there can be variations in the fees charged to members of the same family. For example, if a parent and two children apply together, the filing fees will total DOLS 285 (DOLS 185 for the parent and DOLS 50 for each child). If the other parent applies later and can furnish proof of relationship and of fees previously paid by the family, he/she will pay the difference between what the family has already paid and the DOLS 420 per family limit, in this case DOLS 135. If a third child of the same family applies at a later date, he will pay no application fee because the DOLS 420 limit for his family has already been reached.

The processing of I-700 applications by OPP constitutes a service for INS, and fees collected from SAW applicants should be reported to the Class B Cashier as part of INS fee collections in accordance with existing fee collection procedures. Additionally, the consular cashier should inform the Class B Cashier of the exact amount of money collected from SAW applicants each day. The Class B cashier should then indicate in the comment section of the OF-158 General Receipt form how much of the INS total for that day is for SAW fees. This will enable INS to keep track of the amount of money collected by OPP's for SAW applications. The accountable consular officer should ensure that the Class B cashier is aware of the need to provide a SAW subtotal on the OF-158.

ECR posts: Because of the small number of posts expected to process SAW applications, the Department has no plans to alter the electronic cash register software to record SAW fees. The Department is in touch with those posts that are expected to handle the bulk of SAW applications abroad to discuss ways to utilize the ECR in SAW processing. Posts not contacted by the Department should plan to use OF-233 cash receipts if called upon to process SAW applications. On those occasions when SAW fees are collected, the consular cashier at an ECR post should amend, and the accountable consular officer should initial, the ECR daily register report to include the SAW subtotal in the INS total.

If questions arise concerning SAW fees, posts should request guidance from the Department (CA/EX).

12. Loss of SAW Entry Package

In the event a SAW applicant loses his/her SAW entry package prior to entry into the United States, he/she should be instructed to reconstruct the file before a replacement can be issued. No additional fee will be charged.

13. Reports

The INS will periodically request information on the number of SAW Group 1 applicants registered at post. Specific reporting requirements have yet to be determined by the Service. The Department will advise posts once they are established. In anticipation of these reports, posts should use the blue copies of the OF-2246's to create a file of SAW Group 1 applicants, arranging them in chronological order by registration/priority date. (For IVACS posts: The new version of IVACS will produce an end-of-day report selectable from the query reports transaction that provides statistics on SAW applicants on file whose priority/registration dates are between user-specified date parameters.)

14. Record Purge

Destroy control cards for issued SAW cases one year after issuance. Instructions for purging of cards and files for denied applications and applications not processed to completion will be provided at a later date. (For IVACS posts: The new version of IVACS will purge SAW issuances one year from date of issuance. IVACS will for the time being treat Section 210 refusals in the same manner as 212(A) refusals, i.e., with a distant purge date. At an appropriate time, the Department will release a special software program to be run against the IVACS database to purge those SAW refusals and SAW cases not processed to completion that should be deleted.)

15. Regional Processing Facilities:
Addresses/Jurisdictions

The names and telephone numbers of the following regional legalization officers are for consular use only, and are not for public dissemination.

Regional Processing Facility (XPW)
U.S Immigration and Naturalization Service
Chet Holifield Federal Building
24000 Avila Road
Laguna Niguel, CA 92677

Bill King, Regional Legalization Officer
FTS: 8-795-6603
Commercial: 213-514-6603

(California, Nevada, Arizona, Hawaii, Guam)

Regional Processing Facility (XPS)
U.S. Immigration and Naturalization Service
1825 Market Center Boulevard
Dallas, TX 75207

William Zimmer, Regional Legalization Officer
FTS: 8/729-6005
Commercial: 214-767-6107

(New Mexico, Texas, Oklahoma, Arkansas, Louisiana, Kentucky, Tennessee, Mississippi, Alabama, Florida, Georgia, South Carolina, North Carolina)

Regional Processing Facility (XPM)
U.S. Immigration and Naturalization Service
Federal Building and U.S. Courthouse
100 Centennial Mall - Room B-25
Lincoln, NE 68508

James Bailey, Regional Legalization Officer
FTS: 8-725-3882
Commercial: 612-725-3882

(Washington, Oregon, Idaho, Montana, Wyoming, Utah, Colorado, North Dakota, South Dakota, Nebraska, Kansas, Minnesota, Iowa, Missouri, Wisconsin, Illinois, Michigan, Indiana, Ohio, Alaska)

Regional Processing Facility (XPE)
U.S. Immigration and Naturalization Service
P.O. Box 590
Williston, VT

Ed Wildblood, Regional Legalization Officer
FTS: 8-832-6587
Commercial: 802-951-6265/6239

(Maine, Vermont, New Hampshire, Massachusetts, Rhode Island, Connecticut, New York, New Jersey, Pennsylvania, Delaware, Maryland, West Virginia, Virginia, Puerto Rico, Virgin Islands, District of Columbia)

5-27-87
DOS

16. **Filing in 9 FAM**

Department will be forwarding a transmittal letter containing the preceding information. Meanwhile, it is suggested that posts file this case in 9 FAM, Appendix D, Under "Services for INS".

Shultz

Note: POUCH addresses protected by OC/T

6-3-87

FROM: COMMR (COLEG) JINS WASHINGTON DC
TO: ALL INS REGIONAL OFFICES (except foreign)
ALL INS DISTRICT DIRECTOR (except foreign)
ALL INS OFFICERS IN CHARGE (except foreign)
DATE: June 3, 1987
SUBJECT: Acceptance of facsimile copies of legalization special agricultural worker application forms.

In an effort to increase proficiency and quality of service, certain qualified designated entities have requested, permission from the Service to laser print facsimile copies of Form I-687, "Application for status as a temporary resident" (under section 245A of the Immigration and Nationality Act) and Form I-700, "Application for temporary resident status as a special agricultural worker" (under section 210 of the Immigration and Nationality Act).

Title 8 code of federal regulations, part 299.4 states in pertinent part, "...all forms required for compliance with the Immigration and nationality regulations which have been made available for purchase by the superintendent of documents may be printed or otherwise reproduced by an appropriate duplication process by private parties at their own expense. Forms printed or reproduced by private parties shall conform to the officially printed forms currently in use with respect to size, wording and language, arrangement, style and size of type, and paper specifications..."

In accordance with the foregoing, the service found facsimile copies acceptable and in compliance with the regulations. Consequently, legalization offices should expect to receive and should accept reproductions of Form I-687 and Form I-700.

App-60

LEGALIZATION WIRE #23

[Facsimile Copy - Retyped from Original]

FROM: INS Central Office
DATE: June 5, 1987
FILE: CO 1588
TO: All ROCOMS, All ROLEGS, All DDS, All OICs, All CPAS, COTP, GLYNCO

The following guidelines are provided in response to questions and requests for guidance following USDA's issuance of its final regulations for implementation of the Special Agricultural Worker (SAW) provisions of IRCA.

The following products not expressly listed in the USDA regulations are included under the USDA definitions of "fruits," "vegetables," and "other perishable commodities": Wheat, rice, oats, barley, rye, and other grains produced primarily for human consumption; all corn, sweet and other; beans, including soybeans, berries, and melons grown for human consumption; grapes; potatoes; tree nuts and ground nuts grown for human consumption, including peanuts; and mushrooms. In its press release upon publication of its final rule, USDA stated as follows: "Together, the definitions of fruits and vegetables include all plant crops grown for human food." With the exception of sugar cane, this statement may be used as general guidance with respect to questionable crops.

The following products not expressly listed in the USDA regulations are excluded from classification as "fruits," "vegetables," or "other perishable commodities": Sorghum, milo, millet, alfalfa, clover, timothy, and other grains and grasses grown primarily for forage and other uses aside from human consumption; gourds; seeds; and flax.

The USDA definition of "agricultural lands" expressly excludes "packing houses and canneries." Webster's New World Dictionary defines "packing Houses" as "a place where meats, and sometimes fruits and vegetables, etc. are prepared for future sale, by processing, canning, packaging, etc." Such processing facilities as freezing plants, processing plants, packaging plants, etc. are included under the term "packing Houses" and are not considered "agricultural lands" regardless of proximity to field production sites. Work performed in such facilities is not "field work" within the meaning of 7 CFR 1 d.4. However, stripping, grading, drying, or packing performed in or adjacent to the field where the produce is grown is

6-5-87
LEGALIZATION WIRE #23

"field work" if performed as an integral part of the picking and harvesting operation on that farm.

The guidelines provided above are not exhaustive. Generally, the USDA rule, including its preamble, and this telex should cover most questions. However, questions which do arise concerning the application of the USDA definitions to certain specific products and activities should be referred to COLEG through the appropriate regional Legalization officers. Field offices should not contact USDA directly for information.

District directors should distribute copies of this wire to Legalization offices within their jurisdiction immediately.

CODEP

6-9-87

FROM: Michael H. Landon, Special Assistant to INS Assistant Commissioner for Legalization William S. Slattery
DATE: June 9, 1987
TO: All INS Field Offices

Social Security Form SS-5 is not required to be submitted by applicants applying for benefits under the provisions of Sec 245A or Sec 210 of IRCA.

Please notify all legalization offices within your jurisdiction that applications shall not be rejected solely because Form SS-5 is not included in the package.

6-9-87

[Facsimile Copy - Retyped from Original]

FROM: Immigration and Naturalization Service
DATE: June 9, 1987
FILE: CO 1588-C
TO: All INS Regional Legalization Offices

It is the opinion of the General Counsel that cases involving expungements of criminal records should be recommended for approval by legalization offices and certified to the Regional Processing Facility via the document processing center.

The worksheet (Form I-696) shall be noted that the case involves an expungement of criminal record(s) of the applicant.

All files containing expungement documentation shall be referred to the adjudications section at the Regional Processing Facility for review by that section.

The Regional Processing Facility will, until further notice, certify all such cases with an appropriate decision. Certification shall be made in accordance with existing regulations.

This procedure is being instituted in order that case law regarding expungement of criminal records for legalization and SAW applicants will be established.

App-63

6-15-87

TO: ALL ROCOM'S
ALL DD'S
FROM: Kathy Sheehan
DATE: June 15, 1987

Please instruct all personnel performing inspections under your jurisdiction of the following:

1) Special agricultural workers (SAWS) - SAWS who were not in the U.S. before May 1, 1987 must apply for SAW status outside the U.S. at an overseas processing office (OPO). If recommended for approval, the OPO will issue to the SAW applicant an optional Form 155A, similar to an immigrant visa, grommeted to a packet containing Form I-700 SAW application and supporting documentation. Inspectors should leave the envelope sealed, place the admission stamp on the OF-155A and in the passport, writing in the SIW or S2W class symbol and an authorized period of stay 30 days from the date of admission. As SAW overseas applicants have submitted applications determined to be nonfrivolous by an OPO, they may not be excluded according to the provisions of section 210(D)(20) of the Act. Therefore, they may be placed in exclusion proceedings only if the inspector has reason to question the identity of the applicant or has reason to believe the applicant is ineligible in which case the envelope may be opened to obtain additional information. Inspectors must be aware that the exclusion provisions of 212(a)(14), (20), (21), (25), and (32) do not apply to SAWS. A waiver approved by the OPO for the other exclusion grounds will be noted on the OF-155A. Upon admission, the inspector must: 1) execute and mail to NIS an arrival form I-94. No departure I-94 is prepared or issued to the SAW; 2) return the stamped OF-155A and attached packet to the SAW and 3) direct the SAW to present the packet to the legalization office nearest his destination in the U.S. The legalization office will be provided with a list of the ports of entry will be provided with a list of legalization offices. The legalization office will issue to all SAWS (both those processed initially overseas and those processed in the U.S.) employment authorization form I-688A in the form of a plastic picture ID with the notation "210" on the bottom center portion. All SAW applicants are permitted to travel outside the U.S. and reenter upon the presentation of Form I-688A with a valid passport if coming from other than the Western hemisphere or adjacent islands. No I-94's (neither arrival nor departure) need to be executed for SAWS presenting form I-688A to the inspector. Upon approval of temporary resident status (approximately 2-6 months). The I-688A's will be replaced by temporary resident card Form I-688

which will also be utilized as a travel document.

2) Legalization applicants - legalization applicants must be physically present in the U.S. while their applications for temporary residence are pending. They may not travel abroad unless in possession of service advance parole Form I-512 in which case they should be paroled "until completion of 245A proceedings." Legalization applicants will be issued employment authorization form I-688A-if it states at the section of law printed on Form I-688A-if it states "245A", it pertains to a legalization applicant who must be in possession of Form I-512. Although legalization applicants will be readvised of the travel restrictions during the interview process, inspectors may encounter applicants not in possession of Form I-512. The district director must then exercise his or her discretion to either parole the applicant into the United States, initiate exclusion proceedings, refuse admission or allow the applicant to withdraw his application for admission. The concurrence of the regional commissioner must be obtained prior to any refusal or withdrawal in these cases. A deferral of inspection is not recommended as the district offices have no access to the "A" files of Reform Act applicants. The I-688A's will be replaced by temporary resident card form I-686 in which case travel abroad as a temporary resident is permitted provided the applicant: 1) has not been absent from the U.S. more than 30 days on the date application for admission is made, 2) has not been absent from the U.S. for an aggregate period of more than 90 days since the date the alien was granted lawful temporary resident status, 3) is not under deportation proceedings, 4) presents from I-688 with a valid passport if coming from other than the Western hemisphere or adjacent island, and 5) is otherwise admissible. The 30 and 90 day time restrictions in time 1 and 2 above may be waived at the discretion of the Attorney General in cases where the absence from the U.S. was due merely to a brief temporary trip abroad required due to emergent or extenuating circumstances beyond the alien's control. In these cases, a passport and visa waiver may be granted at the port of entry utilizing from authority of INS". The applicants "A" number must be placed on the I-193 which should then be routed to the regional processing facility (RPF) for inclusion in the applicant's "A" file. The $15.00 fee should be collected. A district director's denial of the waiver will result in either a refusal, a withdrawal or the initiation of exclusion proceedings with the regional commissioner's concurrence prior to any refusal or withdrawal. Form I-193 will be revised in the near future. COMMR (COLEG)

App-64

6-16-87

[Facsimile Copy - Retyped from Original]

FROM: ROCOM (ROLEG), JINS, Dallas, TX
DATE: June 16, 1987
TO: DISTRICT DIRECTOR, JINS, ATLANTA, GA
DISTRICT DIRECTOR, JINS, DALLAS, TX
DISTRICT DIRECTOR, JINS, EL PASO, TX
DISTRICT DIRECTOR, JINS, HARLINGEN, TX
DISTRICT DIRECTOR, JINS, HOUSTON, TX
DISTRICT DIRECTOR, JINS, MIAMI, FL
DISTRICT DIRECTOR, JINS, NEW ORLEANS, LA
DISTRICT DIRECTOR, JINS, SAN ANTONIO, TX

SUBJECT: Policy and information concerning DWI convictions in Texas.

There has been considerable confusion regarding the proper procedure to be followed in adjudicating those applications where in the applicant has been convicted under Texas Law of Driving while Intoxicated (DWI).

Under IRCA, section 245A, an applicant is ineligible to make application if the has been convicted of a Felony, and 8 CFR section 245A.1(B) defines "Felony" as a crime committed in the United States punishable by imprisonment for a term of more than one year. Regardless of the term such alien actually served, if any.

Although classified as a misdemeanor in Texas, the Texas statute, ART.670L-1, since its 1923 enactment and subsequent amendments, has always provided that a first offense DWI conviction may be punishable by confinement it jail for up to two years thereby meeting the standard of our federal definition of a felony.

Therefore, a DWI conviction under Texas Law presents a unique situation, and the proper adjudication procedure to be followed when the application to the regional processing facility for a final determination. (We anticipate that such cases will be certified to the AAU for a decision).

In cases where an application is received showing three or more DWI convictions in Texas this would be an example where an applicant clearly does not meet the statutory requirements (statutorily ineligible if convicted of three or more misdemeanors) and the procedure to be followed is to recommend denial and forward to the regional processing facility. Refer to CO wire of June 1, 1987, which amended present procedure.

6-16-87

BENED: District Directors Dallas, El Paso, Houston, Harlingen, San Antonio.

BETIL: District Directors Atlanta, New Orleans, Miami.

6-16-87

[Facsimile Copy - Retyped from original]

FROM: Richard E. Norton, Associate Commissioner, INS
DATE: June 16, 1987
TO: All QDEs

Ladies and gentlemen:

As part of an organization selected by the Immigration and Naturalization Service (INS) to serve as a Qualified Designated Entity in the Legalization Program for undocumented aliens, many of you were instrumental in assisting INS in the planning and development of that program. The program has now been in full operation for more than a month. I am extremely pleased to be able to advise you that the program's start-up phase has been completely successful. Only very minor technical or procedural problems have been encountered and those have been quickly and effectively rectified. However, some of you have advised INS officials with whom you have been in contact that QDE representatives engaged in assisting prospective legalization applicants require additional familiarization with the legalization process which cannot be obtained through formal training.

With the initial portion of the start-up phase behind us, we can now begin to address this and similar concerns. Under the terms of its cooperative agreement with you, INS is required to provide you members or employees with the training they require to provide to competent assistance to those aliens who utilize your services. INS acknowledges that training is an on-going process which does not end with the completion of a classroom program or the reading of law and regulations. Given that legalization is a completely new process unfamiliar even to persons acquainted with other INS programs, INS desires to respond as completely and flexibly as possible to your training needs.

The area of concern most frequently noted to INS has been that of documentary requirements for legalization. Some QDE representatives have advised us that the formal legalization training program and the language of the statute and regulations do not provide a clear sense as to what extent of documentation will suffice for an applicant to demonstrate eligibility. Clearly the most effective way for QDE representatives to familiarize themselves with the documentary evidence requirements is to submit cases to INS for adjudication. Understandably, some representatives are reluctant to submit cases without overwhelming evidence of eligibility for fear of endangering the interests of their legalization and SAW clients through inexperience with this new process.

To eliminate this problem, INS will adopt the following procedure. In any case in which an application for legalization filed with INS through a Qualified Designated Entity within thirty (30) days from the date of this letter is denied for lack of sufficient documentation of eligibility, the QDE involved will be permitted to submit additional documentation of eligibility within sixty (60) days from the date of denial. Such documentation should be submitted to the Regional Processing Facility (RPF) which denied the application. Regional Processing Facility directors will reopen those cases in which additional documentation is submitted and the RPF will review the new evidence and reconsider the application in light of it. No additional fee will be charged to the applicant.

Through this cooperative process, your employees will obtain valuable experience and feedback information and INS can fully discharge its training responsibilities under the cooperative agreement.

Sincerely,

RICHARD E. NORTON
Associate Commissioner
Examinations

6-16-87

6-17-87

[Facsimile Copy - Retyped from original]

FROM: INS
DATE: June 17, 1987
ACTION: Routine
TO: All INS Field Offices

This telex discusses two rules published in the Federal Register on 6-8-87 regarding acquired immune deficiency syndrome (AIDS) and human immune deficiency virus (HIV) infection, and the issue of ineligibility under 212(a)(6).

On June 8, 1987, Center for Disease Control, Public Health Service published a final rule at 52 FR 21532\33, amending 42 CFR part 43.2(B) by adding AIDS to the list of dangerous contagious diseases. This final regulation does not require the testing of any individuals for AIDS. In the preamble, it is stated that all medical examiners (PHS Physicians, INS designated civil surgeons, and state department designated panel physicians) will be required to establish a diagnosis and report the finding to the consular or immigration (inspections) officer "if there is clinical suspicion of AIDS." A clinical suspicion will be followed by an AIDS Test (Western Blot Test) confirming the diagnosis. The preamble also states that instruction will be provided to the medical examiners regarding obtaining the medical history and clinical signs to look for and how to diagnose AIDS.

Actions required of all DIDIRS and OIC's regarding this change at this time are as follows:

1) Forward current list of designated civil surgeons to ROCOMS by 6-22-87. ROCOMS will forward collated lists to COEXXM, ATTN:JDC by 6-26-87. This will be provided by PHS to provide instructional material to the designated physicians.

2) Advise all service personnel involved with medical examinations given to aliens of these regulatory changes. Aliens diagnosed a having AIDS should be place in exclusion proceedings. Applications for adjustment of status should be denied.

3) Aliens encountered who are suspected of having AIDS but have not been formally diagnosed by PHS must be referred to PHS for formal diagnosis before further action is taken.

Action by Central Office at this time will include:

1) Obtaining copies of instructions put out by PHS to medical examiners, when available, for distribution to ROCOMS, DIDIRS, and OIC'S.

2) Revising of 8 CFR 209.1(B) to require a second medical examination in the processing of refugee adjustment of status applications.

3) Determining a policy on pipeline applications for adjustment, refugee, and legalization applicants.

Also, on the same date at 52 FR 21607/08, PHS published proposed rule amending 42 CFR part 43.2(B) by deleting AIDS from the list of dangerous contagious diseases and adding HIV infection to the list. It should be noted that all persons who have AIDS have the HIV infection. This proposed comment period would until August 7, 1987. The proposed rule also would amend 42 CFR part 34.4 to require a serologic test for HIV infection in the country of origin a part of the medical examination. The regulation proposes that this test be "a sensitive and specific test, confirmed when positive by a test such as the Western Blot Blood Test or an equally reliable test."

Additional information concerning these issues will be forwarded as it becomes available.

COEXM

6-19-87
LEGALIZATION WIRE #16

[Facsimile Copy - Retyped from Original]

FROM: INS
TO: All Regional Offices
SUBJECT: Requests for employment records from agricultural producers, farm labor contractors or collective bargaining organizations.

8 CFR Part 210.3(b)(3) states in pertinent part..."the service may solicit from agricultural producers, farm labor contractors, collective bargaining organizations and other groups and organizations which maintain records of employment, lists of workers against which evidence of qualifying employment can be checked...".

COLEG recommends that with ROLEG oversight, districts and/or Legalization offices initiate requests for employment records or other pertinent records from local farms that are likely employers of SAW applicants, local farmworker unions and other farmworker assistance groups, local and state agencies that maintain employment records or other information that could be of assistance in verifying a SAW's employment history. Farmworker oriented QDE's could be of assistance in helping to identify sources of such records.

COLEG requests ROLEG to monitor the quantity and quality of the information received with the view of disseminating applicable records/lists to the various regional processing facilities.

Please provide Aaron Bodin, Deputy Assistant Commissioner, SAW, with a progress report relative to this effort no later than 6/19/87.

CODEP (COLEG)

6-19-87
LEGALIZATION WIRE #16

6-29-87

Statement of INS Commissioner Alan C. Nelson on Immigration Reform and Agricultural Labor

The Immigration Reform Act is working. The best evidence is the sharp decline in the number of people attempting illegal entry across our Southern border. INS Border Patrol apprehensions on the border are down nearly 40 per cent since the bill became law in November 1986.

Recently there have been concerns in the Western United States that there have been and may be a shortage of agricultural workers in the harvest months ahead. We all recognize and appreciate the vital role agriculture plays in our nation's economy. No one wants crop losses due to worker shortages. The evidence is mixed on the extent of the actual or potential labor shortage, but U.S. Government representatives have met with growers, Congressional representatives and others to explore ways to assure an adequate agricultural workforce.

Contained in the new Immigration Reform and Control Act are special provisions for agricultural workers, which the nation's growers worked very hard to achieve. By effectively using these provisions, the labor needs of agriculture can be met without undercutting the new immigration law.

Following are approaches the Federal Government is taking and further actions that will be initiated to ensure an adequate supply of agricultural labor. These have been discussed in detail with a group of Senators and Congressmen in several recent meetings on Capitol Hill.

I. **Existing Procedures in Place**

A. **Processing in United States**

Currently there are 107 legalization offices which accept Special Agricultural Workers (SAW) applicants. These offices were staffed and opened on June 1, 1987, to accept up to 16,650 applications per day. INS has designated 157 agricultural oriented Qualified Designated Entities (QDE's) to assist SAW applicants in applying for legalization status. Qualified applicants can receive temporary work authorization on the day they file their applications. Through June 24, 1987, 10,300 SAW applications have been filed in the United States.

B. **H-2A Processing**

The Immigration Reform and Control Act of 1986 (IRCA) established a new streamlined temporary agricultural program - H2A. This program is available to growers. To date no H-2A applications have been filed in the Western states.

1. **Emergency H-2A Processing**

In areas which may suffer emergency agricultural labor shortages during periods of peak labor demand, the Department of Labor and INS are prepare to process employer applications and petitions for temporary agricultural labor certification and petitions for H-2A classification on an expedited basis, provided that such employers can meet all labor standards and protections required under the H-2A program, such as wages and housing. In such instances the entire stateside H-2A process can be completed in one week.

2. **INS Emergency Utilization of H-2A**

Where the Department of Labor may deny a Section 216(e)(2) redetermination application based on its finding that American labor is available, an employer can file an appeal along with its H-2A petition to INS. The petition can be approved if the employer establishes to INS' satisfaction that domestic labor is not available.

C. **Processing in Mexico**

Currently SAW applicants who are in Mexico must apply at the Overseas Processing Post established at the U.S. Embassy of Mexico City. The applicants are notified of their interview appointment, and if found eligible, they proceed tho the United States and are given the six-month work authorization card. The procedure then follows the normal processing used for applicants in the U.S.A. As of June 24, 4,000 SAW applications have been distributed by the Embassy of Mexico City.

II. **New Procedure to be Implemented by the Government**

The Administration, in cooperation with key members of Congress and agricultural organizations, will pursue the following additional steps to avoid any potential crop losses in the 1987 growing season:

A. **SAW Processing in United States**

1. **Legalization offices**

To maximize SAW applications, legalization offices are prepared to open evenings and weekends to accommodate the scheduling of agricultural workers.

6-29-87

App-69

2. Rural Processing

To assist SAW applicants in remote areas, processing will be conducted by utilizing 40 INS mobile vans. This is in addition to the 107 Legalization Offices noted above.

3. Public Information

INS is expanding its existing public information campaign in agricultural areas, informing potential SAW applicants about the legalization program. INS will spend nearly $1 million on advertising and publicity to increase awareness of the SAW and H-2A programs in both the U.S. and Mexico to publicize the program. In addition written flyers will be distributed to encourage SAW participation among eligible workers and to encourage grower associations and others to actively pursue their responsibilities to identify, locate and assist eligible workers to apply.

4. Qualified Designated Entities

INS will work with agricultural QDE's to expedite their review process in order that SAW applications may be filed in a timely manner. Such QDE's must significantly increase their efforts with growers and workers to file applications.

5. Grower Associations

INS will work with grower associations to help them assist workers to document their eligibility and complete applications. Grower associations and labor organizations must significantly increase their efforts with growers and workers to file applications.

6. Interagency Clearing House

USDA, DOD, and INS will coordinate efforts to assist growers facing labor shortages. Grower associations and others will be assisted in carrying out their responsibilities in identifying eligible worker, preparing SAW applications for former workers, contacting former worker abroad through grower associations operations overseas and expediting the processing of H-2A applications. USDA Agricultural Extension Agents will head interagency teams in various rural areas starting in June 1987.

7. May 1 Cutoff Date

The date before which a SAW must have entered the United States in order to be eligible to file an application in the United States will be moved from May 1, 1987 to the date on which border processing at Calexico was initiated (June 26, 1987). This will permit SAW eligibles in the United States to remain here to file applications while those outside the United States will be able to avail themselves of expedited processing at overseas processing posts and the Calexico border port. By retaining a cutoff date there will be no inducement to prospective overseas applicants to enter the United States illegally.

II. Processing of SAW Applicants from Mexico

1. Processing in the Interior of Mexico

A SAW border processing center opened on June 26, 1987, at Calexico, California, as described below.

Application forms and accompanying instructions will be available at all consulates and at the nine consular agencies in Mexico by July 1. SAW processing under the temporary emergency procedures will be expanded in the interior of Mexico to include the acceptance and processing of applications at the consulates in Monterrey and Hermosillo in addition to the consular section at the Embassy of Mexico City. Possible expansion to the remaining non-border consulates, i.e., Guadalajara, Mazatlan, and Merida will be considered depending on the volume of applicants in the interior.

Any staffing difficulties encountered by the Department of State will be communicated to the INS, which will make available Spanish speaking staff. Such officers will be available within 10 days of notification.

2. Physicals

During this period of expedited processing, SAW applicants will be accepted without required physicals. The physical exam will be deferred, not waived. Work authorizations will be granted and the application will be placed in normal processing as the record of medical examination is received.

3. Border Processing

SAW eligibles residing in Mexican border states only will temporarily be permitted to present applications for SAW status at a border port of entry. INS legalization staff will be detailed to Calexico, California, to initiate

App-70

border processing which started June 26, 1987. Other ports may be designated to conduct border processing dependent on grower/applicant response. During the first 30 days, the success of this program will be monitored and such expansion or termination will be considered. Such additional locations, if any, will be opened within 10 days of decision.

4. **Admission Standards**

For the 1987 growing season, in order to assure an adequate agricultural workforce, Special Agricultural Worker (S.A.W.) applicants will be able to gain admission to the United States immediately by filing an application and fee at an American Consulate or INS border processing site. As long as the application clearly indicates the details of their qualifying employment, the workers will be given 90 days to collect supporting documentation in the United States. These procedures will be effective July 1, 1987.

These applicants will be given permission to work during this interim period while they are assembling this additional evidence of eligibility. By the end of this period the applicant will be required to be interviewed and otherwise comply with the requirements of this program such as provision of full supportive documentation and the medical examination in order to receive S.A.W. status under the law. The cooperation of growers, associations and others is required and expected in providing workers with the necessary documentation to complete the application.

The Federal Government is taking this significant step as a practical and flexible solution to allow persons who are apparently qualified for S.A.W. status to be admitted on a temporary basis for this growing season only. This action should not be perceived as a change in our legal analysis of the S.A.W. worker program which was developed over the extensive and open regulatory process culminating in final regulations published on May 1, 1987. Rather, this is a practical solution made in conjunction with Members of Congress to facilitate a smoother transition from widespread use of illegal workers in Western Agriculture to legal employment practices as provided in the Immigration Reform and Control Act of 1986.

5. **Processing of H-2A Applications Dissemination of Information of Successful H-2A Programs**

INS Northern Regional Commissioner James Buck is assisting Northwest Growers Association representatives obtain information on successful Idaho and Florida H-2A programs. Such information will be available to all growers nationwide. Similar efforts will be pursued in California and other areas.

III. **Actions for Growers to Pursue**

A. **Assistance in Mexico from Growers' Representatives**

It is desirable that a limited number of representatives from U.S. growers travel to Mexico to assist in the application process for those agricultural laborers who have worked for growers in the 12-month period ending May 1, 1986. The purpose of their presence will be to provide documentation concerning the applicant's employment and to assist in the preparation of the application at the port of entry processing facility as well as at interior consulates.

The presence of such grower's representatives in Mexico and any limitations on the types of activities they may pursue is to be discussed by the State Department with the Government of Mexico. Additionally, such representatives, prior to traveling to Mexico, should coordinate with consular officials at the U.S. Consulate in Mexico to which they are destined. Such coordination should ensure maximum orderliness in the processing procedures for targeted workers.

B. **Efforts to Identify Eligible Workers**

Extensive additional efforts by grower associations are necessary to locate eligible workers in the U.S. and overseas and assist with completing and filing applications. Only the growers and workers have the applications.

IV. **Other Available Sources of Agricultural Labor**

In addition to the special treatment Congress afforded agriculture in the Immigration Reform Act, other untapped labor sources have been successful in past situations and should be fully explored by growers and government officials. These include persons currently unemployed and/or on welfare, referrals from community groups and day workers who often gather at designated locations awaiting summer break, college and high school students on job offers.

The strong public and bi-partisan support for welfare reform, together with the need for additional workers in agriculture, provides a unique opportunity to develop both long term and short term programs. Among the approaches

App-71

that could be considered would be the development of child care centers to give welfare recipients and others the opportunity for productive employment in agriculture.

CONCLUSION

The Government has taken a number of special steps to ensure an orderly transition to the new Immigration Reform and Control Act and to avoid the prospect of crop losses due to labor shortages. The workers who qualify and the growers who alone can provide the necessary information to the workers must energetically act now.

The new immigration law is working, as is being currently demonstrated. We urge growers and others to support America by utilizing the legal labor sources provided under the new immigration law and by making a transition from previous practices of employing illegal labor.

6-29-87

FROM: INS Regional Legalization Offices
TO: All Consular Posts in Central and Latin America
DATE: June 29, 1987

Please notify all Legalization Offices under your jurisdiction to inform each applicant issued form I-688A (Employment Authorization) under Section 245A of IRCA that the document is not valid for travel outside the U.S. or reentry into the U.S.

In addition, each such applicant should be provided printed material, duplicated locally, stating in essence "please be advised that the attached document (form I-688A) is not valid for travel outside the U.S. or reentry into the U.S."

Each LO may wish to have signs printed locally and posted near the photo processing area setting forth a similar message.

App-73

FROM: State Department
TO: Consular Posts in Central and Latin America
DATE: July 1, 1987
SUBJECT: Transitional SAW Admission Procedures
REF: State 200485 (NOTAL)

1. Septel will explain revised INS transitional SAW admission standards. Following are guidelines to be used in processing applicants applying at all designated overseas SAW-Processing posts during the four-month transitional period (July 1 to November 1, 1987).

2. Effective July 1, applicants need only submit a fully executed Form I-700 SAW application and three (3) photographs (size and type normally used for immigrant visas). Qualifying employment will be claimed with the specificity required in the form. Applicants will be interviewed concerning their eligibility. An applicant who is presumed eligible and who meets standard admission requirements, including possession of a valid passport, will be admitted with work authorization for a period of 90 RPT 90 days during which time he/she can collect supporting documents and apply for SAW status at any legalization office. FBI clearances and medical examinations have been deferred, not waived. AVLOS checks are necessary. Subsequent to a determination that the applicant meets the transitional admission standards, posts will collect the dollars 185 RPT 185 FEE, issue a receipt and document him/her for entry into the United States. If an applicant is found ineligible under a waiverable ground, posts should take the waiver application. If it is approved, the alien can be documented under the transitional SAW admission standards. Findings of ineligibility for lack of credible qualifying employment should be made under section 210 of the Immigration Reform and Control Act (IRCA). But not RPT not entered in AVLOS.

3. Entry document: Posts will place a regular NIV stamp in the passport with the following modifications. Line through the words Nonimmigrant Visa at the top of the stamp. Insert the term S9 RPT S9 (no dash or space) in the classification space. The entry document will be issued for one entry, valid for 30 RPT 30 days from date of issuance.

4. A stamp reading "fee paid and date" should be place in the upper right hand corner of the I-700, and two photographs attached to the upper left corner. A sealed envelope containing the original I-700 should be stapled to the applicant's passport for presentation at the port of entry.

5. For record keeping purposes, posts should make a photocopy of all issued and refused I-700's, attach one photograph, and file them alphabetically. Form OF-186SAW, listing S9 issuances and refusals by nationality in the remarks section, should be submitted to the department monthly.

7-1-87

LEGALIZATION WIRE # 27

[Facsimile Copy - Retyped from original]

FROM: Immigration and Naturalization Service
ACTION: Priority
DATE: July 1, 1987
FILE: CO-1588
TO: All ROCOMS, All ROLEGS, All DDS, All OICS, All CPAS, ODTF, GLYNCO
SUBJECT: SAW processing under the Temporary Transitional Admission Standards

Beginning July 1, 1987, and until November 1, 1987, a Temporary Transitional Admission Standard will be in effect for overseas SAW applicants. Because the lack of ready access to documentary evidence of eligibility may limit the number of overseas applicants who can perfect their applications in time to work in the United States during the 1987 harvest season, the requirement to submit such evidence will be deferred during this temporary transitional period until after the applicant has had the opportunity to work in the United States.

Transitional Admission Standard: Under the Transitional Standard SAW applicants at designated ports of entry (POE) and all overseas processing offices (OPO) will present a fully executed Form I-700 SAW application with photographs, and the required fee. Qualifying employment and the documentary evidence of such employment to be submitted later will be described with the specificity required by the form. All applications presented under this standard are considered group 2 applications. Applicants will be interviewed to determine the credibility of their claimed eligibility. Examining officers will determine at the interview whether an applicant is excludable on medical grounds. An applicant who is credibly eligible and who meets standard admission requirements including possession of a valid passport will be admitted with work authorization for a period of 90 days. The application will be returned to the applicant for submission of a complete application including the required report of medical examination, fingerprint card, and documentation of eligibility at any Legalization office in the United States during the 90 day period. With the exception of the standard lookout system checks at entry, the initiation of applicant security checks will be deferred until after the complete application has been accepted at a Legalization office. Applicants who are excludable from the United States under a ground of

7-1-87
LEGALIZATION WIRE # 27

exclusion which may be waived in accordance with the provisions of 8 CFR 210.3 (e)(2) shall not be deemed to meet the transitional admission standard unless they submit an application for waiver of grounds of excludability on Form I-690 and such application is approved.

Border processing: Only residents of the six Mexican border states, (Baja California Norte, Sonora, Chihuahua, Coahuila, Nuevo Leon, and Tamaulipas) may apply for border processing at designated border POE's.

Calexico, California is the sole POE currently designated to conduct border processing. Other POE's may be so designated by the Commissioner dependent upon applicant response. Legalization staff will process SAW applications at designated POE'S.

Subsequent to a finding that the applicant meets the Transitional Admission Standard, the Service will collect the application fee (in U.S. currency only), will issue stamp the I-94, and will issue standard fee receipt Form F-21I. The applicant shall be issued a regular I-94 form with the applicable POE stamp noting the class of admission as S9 for a period of ninety days. The employment authorization stamp shall be noted on both copies of the I-94 below the I-94 arrival record on the front side of the I-94. The POE stamp shall also be placed in the upper left hand corner on page 1 of Form I-700. A copy of the annotated I-700 will be made and retained by the POE. The original I-700 application and supporting documentation shall be returned to the applicant. The applicant shall then be furnished such additional forms as are necessary for a complete application. The following information shall be stamped in both English and Spanish on the reverse of page 3 of the I-700. "You have been admitted to the United States and granted employment authorization for a period of 90 days. You must submit a complete application package including the required report of medical examination, fingerprint card and documentation of eligibility to any Legalization office in the United States during this 90-day period. Failure to do so may result in denial of your application for lack of prosecution. You are not authorized to work or remain in the United States beyond the 90-day period. If you leave the United States, you will not be readmitted unless you have obtained prior approval from the Immigration and Naturalization Service." An A-file shall not be created under the Transitional Admission Standard. Instead a manila folder shall be used to house the service's copy of the application and one photograph of the applicant which shall be attached to it. Applications shall be filed by date of entry in alphabetical order.

App-75

LEGALIZATION WIRE # 27

The Service copies of Form I-94 shall be batched on a daily basis covered with Form G-808 (white copy) secured by criss-crossing the rubberbands and forwarded to: ACS/NIIS, Box 150, London, KY 40741. Forwarding shall be accomplished on an overnight delivery basis.

Ineligible applicants: Applicants whose claimed employment on the I-700 does not meet the statutory requirement, or whose personal testimony at the interview in support of the claimed employment is not credible shall not be admitted, the fee shall not be taken and all documents presented shall be returned. The applicant shall be advised of the basis for the refused admission. Applicants shall be advised that, if they can overcome the basis for the refused admission they may reapply under the Transitional Admission Standard or submit a complete application at an OPO or designated POE.

Complete application processing at border POE's: SAW applicants may submit a complete application at a border processing POE. If the application meets the regulatory definition of a "nonfrivolous application," it shall be processed in accordance with the provisions at 8 CFR 210 pertaining to nonfrivolous applications filed in the United States. If the application does not meet the conditions of a "nonfrivolous application" as defined in the regulations, the application shall be processed under the Transitional Admission Standard described above. The determination as to whether an application shall be considered to be a "nonfrivolous application" shall be made before the fee is taken.

Overseas applicants: Applicants determined by OPO's to meet the Transitional Admission Standard will be issued an entry document similar to a nonimmigrant visa. The entry document stamp classification S9 will be placed in the applicant's passport. The applicant may apply for admission to the United States at any port of entry. The POE shall stamp the applicant's passport noting the class of admission as S9 for a period of ninety days. Employment authorization shall be noted on both copies of the I-94 below the "I-94 Arrival Record" and "I-94 Departure Record" on the front side of the I-94. The I-94 admission number shall also be noted on the top page of the I-700 application.

I-94 copies should be batched and forwarded to London, KY in accordance with the instructions as outlined above

LEGALIZATION WIRE # 27

under border processing.

Complete application processing at OPO's:

SAW applicants residing outside of the United States may continue to submit complete applications, which include a fully executed Form I-700, a report of medical examination, photographs, and documentary evidence of eligibility to any OPO. Such applications will be processed in accordance with existing standards and procedures set forth in 8 CFR 210 and in accordance with inspection instructions as identified in CO 235-C wire dated June 15, 1987.

Family members of SAW applicants who are admissible under existing standards or under the Transitional Admission Standard may not be admitted to the United States unless they are eligible in their own right for admission.

District directors should distribute copies of this instruction to all ports of entry within their jurisdiction.

CODEP (COLEG)

App-76

[Facsimile Copy - Retyped from Original]

FROM: Justice
ACTION: Priority
DATE: 07-06-87

This is a follow up to my June 17, 1987 telegram regarding the Public Health Service's (PHS) final rule on acquired immune deficiency syndrome (AIDS) and the issue of ineligibility under 212(A)(6) of the INA. The final rule, published in 523 Federal Register 109, pp. 21532/33 on June 8, 1987, amends 42 CFR 43.2(B) by adding AIDS to the list of dangerous contagious diseases. The rule become effective July 8, 1987. The instructions provided in this telex are to be followed by all service officers, including those cross-designated from other agencies, beginning July 8, 1987.

PHS, through the Centers for Disease Control (CDC), has provided all PHS physicians with instructional materials for medical examiners to follow in examining aliens for AIDS. All medical examinations completed on July 8, 1987 or later shall be presumed to conform to PHS guidelines regarding examination for AIDS. If a clinical observation of AIDS is conclusively supported by confirmatory testing, Form OF-157 or Form I-693 will be noted "Class A: AIDS". This final regulation does not require routine serologic testing by medical examiners for the Human Immunodeficiency Virus (HIV) infection. All offices are being provided a copy of the PHS guidelines by separate memorandum. The following instructions relate to the specific situations given:

IMMIGRANT AND FIANCE(E) VISA APPLICANTS AND REFUGEES:

The Department of State has advised that all panel and ICM contract physicians have been provided with the PHS guidelines regarding clinical examination for AIDS. Any individual who receives a report of a medical exam signed on or after July 8, 1987, will therefore be presumed to have been examined regarding AIDS. Applicants for Immigrant or Fiance(e) visas and refugee status who currently have pending applications and have already received medical exams will not be referred for an updated medical exam solely to obtain an AIDS observation. However, consular officers and service officers retain the authority to refer an applicant for re-examination if the applicant exhibits symptoms of AIDS or any other dangerous contagious disease. This should be done if the applicant exhibits the symptoms outlined in the PHS guidelines.

Service employees overseas are expected to process few, if any, AIDS cases. Referrals to panel or ICM physicians should therefore rarely be necessary.

ADJUSTMENT APPLICANTS AND LEGALIZATION APPLICANTS:
Service designated physicians have been provided the PHS guidelines regarding the clinical examination for AIDS. Any adjustment or legalization applicant who is medically examined on or after July 8, 1987 will therefore be presumed to have been clinically examined for AIDS. Applicants for adjustment of status or legalization who were medically examined before July 8, 1987 must properly file their applications (either with a service office or a qualified designated entity) before August 8, 1987 must either properly file an application prior to August 8, 1987 or return to the designated physician to get an update of the medical examination showing a clinical observation was made concerning AIDS.

Examiners adjudication applications for adjustment of status and legalization benefits have the authority to refer applicants back to the designated physician who performed the examination if an applicant exhibits the physical symptoms of the AIDS as with the symptoms of any other dangerous contagious disease.

INSPECTIONS:
Those individuals applying for admission on or after July 8, 1987, whose valid medical examinations were conducted prior to July 8, 1987 shall be inspected without a clinical observation of AIDS having been made. Inspectors at ports of entry who observe individuals exhibiting the clinical signs of AIDS have the authority to refer the applicant for admission to PHS in accordance with current procedures. Applicants for admission at International airports in Chicago, Honolulu, Los Angeles, Miami, New York, San Francisco, and Seattle are to be referred to the quarantine office posted at the inspector's port of entry. It is emphasized that the inspector's observation is one that can be done within the normal course of inspection for ineligibility under signs of the existence of any of the other dangerous contagious diseases. The inspector's observation should therefore not increase the time of inspection.

WAIVERS
There is no statutory authority to accept an application for a waiver of 212(A)(6) because of AIDS in Immigrant and Fiance(e) visa cases. Although there is statutory authority to waive section 212(A)(6) in refugee, legalization, and nonimmigrant cases. The discretionary authority of the Attorney General will not be used unless the applicant can establish that (1) The danger to the public health of the United States created by the aliens

7-6-87

admission to the U.S. in minimal, (2) the possibility of spread of the disease created by the alien's admission to the U.S. in minimal, and (3) there will be no cost incurred by any level of government agency of the U.S. without prior consent of that agency. All decisions on waiver applications regarding AIDS will be certified to the associate commissioner, examinations until further notice.

(CODEP)

TO: SR, ROCOM, STEPHEN MARTIN
WR, ROCOM, HARLOD EZELL
NR, ROCOM, JAMES BUCK
ER, ROCOM, STANLEY MCKINLEY
FROM: Richard E. Norton
DATE: July 7, 1987

At a recent meeting between representatives of Central Office and the National QDEs, several concerns and issues of importance necessary for the success of both the legalization program and QDE assistance were discussed.

Specifically,

1. For purposes of the legalization program, a qualified designated entity may present a cover sheet certification of all attached documents indicating that original documents have been seen and returned. The cover sheet must indicate a listing of all documents attached.

2. All cases prepared by a qualified designated entity should not be reviewed by a legalization assistant. The understanding of the cooperative agreement is that all cases prepared by a QDE will be complete and ready for interview. Duplication of effort occurs if this policy is not followed. Qualified designated entities are aware of the fact that if they submit unprepared cases, they are subject to loss of their QDE status.

3. An alien consent form submitted with a case prepared by a qualified designated entity becomes part of the alien's application and record. This form must accompany a QDE case. The application is not to be considered unless the consent form is attached.

4. Large, voluminous submissions of documents are not necessary. It is not necessary to document each day in the life of an alien. Although the burden of proof rests with the applicant, the preponderance of the evidence standard must apply. The inference to be drawn from the documentation provided shall depend not on quantity alone, but also on the credibility and amenability to verification. Sufficiency of all evidence submitted will be judged according to the probative value and credibility. Interviewers should apply their discretion in the quantities of documents requested.

If any alien submits large quantities of documentation, only those documents necessary to sufficiently establish their case for eligibility should be retained. Any documentation that is returned to the alien should be so noted on the examiner's worksheet.

All service officers are again reminded that the purpose of the origination of the qualified designated entity for the legalization program was, and continues to be assistance in the expedient and efficient processing of all applicants.

7-14-87
LEGALIZATION WIRE #25

[Facsimile Copy - Retyped from Original]

FROM: Mark W. Everson INS Deputy Commissioner
ACTION: Priority
DATE: July 14, 1987
TO: All ROLEGS. SRO. NRO. WRO. ERO.
RE: Legalization Wire #25 (file CO 1588-C)

Because of previous agreements reached between the State Department and the Canadian Government in "Stateside Criteria" petitions and in direct reference to OI 212.11 which stated in pertinent part:

"...an alien who was not granted an immigrant visa after entering Canada with this appointment letter shall be paroled into the United States if a properly endorsed letter is presented to the inspecting officer. The endorsement will include the reason for not issuing the visa to the applicant."

With regard to this "Stateside Criteria" agreement and the continuous residence requirements of legalization, the following guidance is provided:

An alien who has departed the United States to appear at a "Stateside Criteria" American Consulate in Canada for an immigrant visa interview but who subsequently is not issued an immigrant visa, and who is paroled back into the United States, shall not be considered as having interrupted his or her continuous residence as required at the time of filing as application for legalization purposes. Please process all cases accordingly.

COMMR (CODEP)

7-14-87
LEGALIZATION WIRE #25

7-14-87
LEGALIZATION WIRE #26

[Facsimile Copy - Retyped from Original]

FROM: Mark W. Everson, INS Deputy Commissioner
ACTION: Priority
DATE: July 14, 1987
FILE: CO 1588-C
TO: ROCOM, WRO, SRO, ERO, NRO
RE: Legalization Wire #26

For purposes of the Legalization Program, non-immigrant F-1 students who were granted duration of status (D/S) but who completed their full courses of studies and whose time period of thirty (30) days to depart the United States after completion of studies expired prior to January 1, 1982, shall be considered as aliens whose period of authorized admission expired through the passage of time and therefore eligible for Legalization. All other requirements of the Legalization Program apply. The date of completion of studies as well as entry into the workforce (if any) must be established through documentary evidence. Students who completed their bachelor degree program but continued in a graduate or advanced program and/or students who were engaged in periods of practical training on January 1, 1982 are not to be considered as having completed their full course of studies and thus are not eligible. On-campus employment pursuant to a scholarship, fellowship, assistantship, or postdoctoral appointment performed in conjunction with or after the student's course of study is considered to be part of the student's academic program, thereby also deeming the student ineligible for legalization benefits.

COMR (CODEP)

7-17-87
LEGALIZATION WIRE #30

[Facsimile Copy - Retyped from Original]

FROM: United States Immigration and Naturalization
Service
Central Office
ACTION: Priority
DATE: July 17, 1987
TO: All Regions
All PCO's Except Foreign
SUBJECT: Misuse of Form G-641 for Employment
Authorization/Identification Purposes.
(Legalization Wire #30)

Several of our offices advise that the usage of Form G-641 has increased because applicants are seeking proof of employment eligibility.

This message provides further guidance in the use of Forms G-641 and G-845 by aliens seeking documentations for employment and/or identification purposes.

Form G-641 and G-845 are not to be used as documentation to establish employment eligibility; additionally, they are not acceptable to establish an applicant's identity.

When the replacement of alien registration cards or I-94's are needed for demonstrating employability/establishing identity, aliens are to be advised to file Form I-90 or I-102 respectively. Form G-641 or save program Form G-845 are not to be used in lieu of filing for replacement of documentation.

Illegal alien applicants for Legalization, Special Agricultural Workers (SAW) or Cuban/Haitian adjustment benefits, who file G-641 or G-845 forms to seek verification of their presence in the United States prior to 1982 through official record should be advised that:

1. They are authorized to work in the U.S. until September 1, 1987, and they will not be required to present documents to prospective employers establishing employment eligibility until September 1, 1987 if the following special procedures, set forth in 8 C.F.R. Section 274a.11 are followed:

A. The individual must claim to be eligible and state his/her intent to apply or has applied for temporary residence status, (Section 245A); Cuban/Haitian adjustment benefits (Section 202) or Special

---

7-17-87
LEGALIZATION WIRE #30

Agricultural Worker status under (Section 210) of the Act.

B. The individual must attest that he/she qualifies for such benefits, in paragraph A above, by checking on the Form I-9, the third box of Section 1 ("Employee Information and Verification") and noting "Special Rule" in the space after "Alien Number A_____" and "September 1, 1987" in the space after "Expiration of Employment Authorization";

C. The individual must also provide a document listed in 8 C.F.R. Section 274a.2(b)(1)(V)(B) that establishes identity;

D. The employer shall follow all of the employment verification requirements, except the employer shall note on the Form I-9 that the individual has stated his/her intention to seek the above mentioned benefits by writing on the Form I-9 in Section 2 - ("Documents that Review and Verification") under List C ("Documents that Establish Employment Eligibility") in the space after "Document Identification" the words "Special Rule" and in the space after "Expiration Date, September 1, 1987".

E. That after September 1, 1987, they will be required to produce an employment authorization document and their employer will be required to examine this document to ascertain if the individual is authorized to work in the United States. Both parties must then update their part of Form I-9 so that it will reflect that the individual and the employer have fully complied with the employment verification requirements, set forth in 8 C.F.R. Section 274a.2(b).

Requesters seeking a copy of documents from INS records must submit a Freedom of Information Act or Privacy Act (FOIA/PA) request (letter or Form G-639) in accordance with Paragraph 18, AM 2751.

BENED, ROCOM, ER, SR, NR, WR, BETII ALL DIDIRS, OICS Except foreign.

Mark Everson
Acting Deputy Commissioner
(CODEP)

App-82

7-31-87
LEGALIZATION WIRE #29

FROM: Lori Scialabba
DATE: July 31, 1987
TO: All Regional Commissioners
All Regional Legalization Officers
All Regional Counsel
All District Directors
All Officers in Charge
RE: Instructions to Maintain List of Aliens Granted Advance Parole

Priority BEJEK Legalization Wire #13 dated March 24, 1987. It is no longer necessary to send xeroxed copies of the list of aliens granted advance parole, or copies of the requests for parole and relating I-512's, as requested in Wire #13. Please note that this is the only portion of Wire #13 that is no longer in effect. Continue to maintain a list of aliens granted advance parole, as required in the first paragraph of Wire #8. All other procedures concerning advance parole remain in effect. Those procedures are set out in Legalization Wires #1, #8 and #13.

7-31-87
LEGALIZATION WIRE #29

App-83

[Facsimile Copy - Retyped from Original]

FROM: Office of Legalization
SUBJECT: Waivers of grounds of excludability
DATE: August 6, 1987
TO: Regional Commissioners (ATTN: ROLEGS)
Regional Processing Facilities
District Directors
Chief Legalization Officers

Guidance has been requested concerning application of the waiver provision of the Immigration Reform and Control Act of 1986 (IRCA) relative to legalization and special agricultural worker (SAW) applicants.

Several offices have inquired whether the family relationship requirements of section 212(h) and (i) of the Immigration and Nationality Act must be met by legalization and SAW applicants seeking waivers of excludability under section 212(a)(19) and (23) of the Act. (Excludability under section 212(a)(23) may be waived only in instance involving a single offense of simple possession of 30 grams or less of marijuana.) Sections 212(h) and (i) of the Act and the family relationships required under those waivers of sections are not applicable to legalization and SAW applicants seeking waiver of section 212(a)(19) or (23) in connection with applicants for legalization or SAW status. Sections 210(c)(2)(B)(ii) and 245A(d)(2)(B)(ii) of the Act, which were established by IRCA, provide that legalization and SAW applicants may be granted waivers of certain grounds of excludability "...for humanitarian purposes, to assure family unity, or when it is otherwise in the public interest". These IRCA provisions are the sole authorities under which waiver of grounds of excludability may be granted to legalization or SAW applicants and the criteria set by these provisions are the sole criteria for administration of such waivers.

Several offices have also requested that guidelines be set for application of the criteria of "humanitarian purposes", "family unity", and "public interest". The term "family unity" is defined identically in 8 CFR 210 and 8 CFR 245A for the purpose of application of the waiver criteria of IRCA. It is clearly less restrictive than the family relationships required by sections 212(h) and (i) because there is no requirement that any member of the "family group" described in the cited regulations be a United States citizen or permanent resident. However, the remaining two criteria lend themselves far less readily to

any "bright line" test of applicability. Determinations must be based on the merits of each case and equities presented balanced against the weight of the facts which cause the alien's excludability or other adverse factors. In this regard, the case law relating to applications for waivers under section 212 of the Act remains instructive for the purpose of adjudication of waivers under the IRCA waiver criteria. Factors identified in the case law as heavily weighted adverse factors for the purposes of section 212 remain so for the purposes of IRCA. Such factors, unless outweighed by the equities presented, will continue to be a correct basis for denial of a waiver.

Given the difference between the terminology used for the IRCA waiver criteria and that employed in section 212(h), it is clear that Congress intended to establish a distinct standard for implementation of the waiver provisions of IRCA. Generally, the term "humanitarian purposes" sets a less stringent or restrictive standard than the "extreme hardship" requirement of section 212(h).

The "public interest" criterion, though not new to Immigration law, is set for the first time by IRCA as a standard for approval of a waiver of grounds of excludability. The interpretation at 8 CFR 212.5(a)(2) of the "public interest" standard for authorization of parole, is relatively specific and restrictive and is directed to the issue of detention of alien applicants for admission. The IRCA "public interest" criterion for waivers should be interpreted in broader fashion in the sense of a particular alien's admission to the United States somehow serving the public interest, e.g., because an alien is particularly eminent in his or her field or endeavor; because an alien has performed noteworthy charitable or public service; because an alien is employed in an occupation in which there is a shortage of workers; because an alien's admission would be beneficial to the national welfare or security or to the welfare of the locality in which he or she resides; or because an alien's admission would serve the interests of the government. These examples are not exhaustive.

The process of adjudicating applications for waivers of grounds of excludability under the IRCA criteria remains identical to the process for adjudicating section 212 waiver applications. The equities demonstrated by the alien which meet the applicable criteria are to be balanced against adverse factors which under case law or as a matter of public interest indicate that the application should not be approved. If the equities presented are determined to outweigh the identified adverse factors, the application should be approved; if not, it should be denied.

Finally, some offices have inquired whether previously obtained section 212(h) waivers of excludability under section 212(a)(9) or (10) are applicable to proceedings under sections 210 and 245A. They are not. As noted above, the sole statutory authorities for waivers in connection with legalization or SAW applications are the provisions of sections 210(c) and 245A(d) of the Act. Because, under those provisions, sections 212(a)(9) and (10) cannot be waived, a previously obtained waiver of those ground of excludability under the provisions of section 212(h) is without effect for the purpose of a legalization or SAW application. Prospective SAW or legalization applicants who are excludable under section 212(a)(9) or (10) cannot circumvent the provision of section 210(c) or 245(d) by obtaining a section 212(h) waiver prior to submitting a legalization or SAW application.

Similarly, because it is well settled that eligibility for a waiver of grounds of excludability is fundamentally based on eligibility for a lawful immigration status, district offices which receive application under section 212(h) for waiver of section 212(a)(9) or (10) from applicants who identify themselves solely as prospective SAW or legalization applicants should deny such applications based on the applicant's clear statutory ineligibility for legalization or for SAW status.

However, a waiver previously obtained under section 212(h) of excludability under section 212(a)(23) as it relates to a single offense of simple possession of 30 grams or less of marijuana may be effective for the purposes of an application for adjustment of status under section 210 or 245A if the family relationship on which the waiver was based continues to exit and meets the regulatory definition of "family unity", or if the likelihood of extreme hardship on which approval of the waiver was based continues to exist. Similarly, a waiver previously obtained under section 212(i) of excludability under section 212(a)(19) may be effective in SAW or legalization proceedings of the family relationship on which approval of the waiver was based continues to exit and meets the regulatory definition of "family unity". In such cases the SAW or legalization application may be accepted for adjudication without requiring the applicant to submit a new application for a waiver of grounds of excludability.

A copy of this memorandum has been provided under separate cover to the Visa Office for distribution to overseas processing offices.

WILLIAM S. SLATTERY
Assistant Commissioner

8-10-87

[Facsimile Copy - Retyped from Original]

SUBJECT: L.O. Consistency
DATE: August 10, 1987
TO: District Directors, Western Region
FROM: Office of Immigration Reform, Western Region

1. Legalization/SAW fees for a family may be accepted by the L.O. on a single cashier's check/money order. Individual cashier's checks/money orders may not be required for each person if the family elects to consolidate payment of fees for a family unit.

2. The following documents prepared by Attorney/QDE's constitute the minimum acceptable documentation at the time Legalization/SAW applications are initially filed with a legalization office.
    a. Completed and signed I-687 or I-700
    b. Fee cashier's check/money order
    c. Copy of identify document showing name and birth date
    d. Finger print card with correct ORI code
    e. Itemized list of documents to be submitted at interview or actual supporting documentation of admissability and financial responsibility
    f. Photographs
    g. Waiver application (if applicable)

3. Identity documents are not required to have a photo (see instruction Item 10)

4. Block 4 must be completed in entirety

5. A. When a waiverable exclusion is known prior to the filing of the application, the waiver will accompany the application. At the interview the appropriate recommendation will be made on the application.

   B. When the waiverable exclusion is discovered at the interview the applicant will be advised of the availability to the waiver, given the waiver application and instructed to file the waiver at the RPF (P.O. Box 30040, Laguna Niguel CA 92677). The officer's worksheet will be noted with the comment: "Advice on waiver given and waiver form provided to applicant". The application will then be recommended for denial and forwarded in the usual manner.

   C. If a waiverable exclusion comes to the attention of the Legalization Office after the interview (during supervisory review) the applicant shall be advised of the waiver availability on Form I-72. Along with the I-72, the applicant shall be provided with a waiver application. The I-72 shall also indicate that the waiver should be filed with the RPF (address above). A copy of the I-72 shall be placed in the 90 million file, and the file forwarded to the Document Processing Center (DPC).

6. Complete medicals are required at interview, not at filing. The medical is not complete if the Civil Surgeon indicates that additional treatment is required.

7. It is important that the adjudicator remember that Public Charge is a prospective vs. a retrospective determination. It is sufficient for an applicant to show a history of employment and self support. If an applicant is currently receiving public cash assistance and deemed likely to become public charge, a waiver may be filed nd the application (I-690) should be provided. If Item 42 on the I-687 is answered "yes", it is imperative that a complete explanation be provided. The applicant should also be advised that continued receipt will render him/her ineligible for permanent residency.

8. The adjudicator worksheet in relating family files should specially identify the pertinent documents in the principal alien's file. An I-134 is not mandatory; however, documentation is needed to show proof of financial support for every family member. This may be accomplished by supplying a copy of the applicant's employment letter, front page of Form 1040 or an I-134, affidavit of support.

9. Earning can be established in a variety of ways including, but not limited to, W-2 forms, earnings statements and E.D.D. statements. However, if copies of tax returns are submitted, it is not necessary to have every page in the return package copied. Only the front and back of the Form 1040 are necessary. This does not supercede previous policy regarding original of all documents suspected of being altered or fraudulent.

10. Residence shall be established by a reasonable presentation of documentation evidencing required presence. It is essential to establish an atmosphere of credibility at the beginning of the interview. To strictly require a piece of

documentation per a particular time period (i.e. 30 days, 45 day, 3 months) sets up an artificial threshold to approval. An alien applying for legalization should submit at least one document from each qualifying year. However one document might conceivably account for several years. There should not be any years that are not covered. If any document is questionable, supplemental proof may be required.

Additional documents are needed to cover both sides of an absence. The key factor is the credibility of the applicant as it is established by the evidence submitted and the supporting interview. When these two factors indicate no clear reason that an application would be recommended for denial, it should be approved.

11. Suggested documentation may be found in M-210 handbook, Section XIII B on Registry (a copy is attached).

12. Applications should not be adjudicated prior to fee in. They should be reviewed for prima facie eligibility. If, during prima facie eligibility review, it becomes apparent that additional documents are necessary, the review should itemize all deficiencies to the applicant on Form I-72. The entire legalization package should then be returned to the applicant.

13. When the need for additional documentation becomes apparent during the interview, the applicant should be given I-72 itemizing the deficiencies, and a period of time, not to exceed 30 days, should be granted to supplement the application. Application pending additional documentation shall be centrally stored in a manner that facilitates CLO monitoring and ready retrieval.

14. All Spanish surnames will be dealt with pursuant to the ADIT instructions previously provided.

15. Any changes made on an application must be made in red and initialed by the applicant. Any change that is material to the adjudication or the application must be thoroughly explained on the adjudicator's worksheet, failure to do so will result in the return of the application by the RPF.

16. Item #16 on the I-687 relates to the last entry into the United States (not necessarily the qualifying entry.) Items #22-30 relate to Item #16.

17. Place a red checkmark next to any of the Items A-R in question #43 which are specially addressed during the interview.

18. As the regulations did not specifically address the document to be used by a child to confirm support of a parent, an I-134 will serve to meet the criteria, as will an affidavit.

19. In the spirit of cooperation, representatives of QDE's will be allowed to accompany aliens in the interview process; however, unless they are also accredited representatives they will not be allowed to represent the alien. They can, however, serve as translators and/or observers. Any attorney or accredited representative must submit a G-28 in order to represent an alien at interview.

Dona L. Coultice
Associate Director, Legalization

8-14-87
LEGALIZATION WIRE #32

[Facsimile Copy - Retyped from Original]

DATE: August 14, 1987
TO: All Regional Associate Commissioners
All PCOs Except Foreign
REFERENCE: (Legalization Wire #32)
Unclassified Telegraphic Message CO 1588-P (Wire #1) Dated 11/14/86; Unclassified Telegraphic Message CO 1588-P (Wire #6) Dated 12/8/86.

Referenced wires detailed procedures to be followed when creating "A" files on apprehended aliens who establish a prima facie or nonfrivolous case of eligibility for benefits under IRCA. Some offices have requested further guidance on the handling of these files.

Information regarding "A" files created on apprehended aliens was entered into the Central Index System from an exchange of tapes from NIIS to CIS.

All PCOs should continue to segregate referenced "A" files from other "A" files on the shelves of the file rooms until request for transfer of the "A" file through the CIS file transfer request sub-system.

BENED, COMGM, ER, SR, NR, WR, BETIL All DIDIRS, OICS Except Foreign.

Irvin Klavan
Assistant Commissioner
(CORSD)

8-14-87
LEGALIZATION WIRE #32

8-14-87
LEGALIZATION WIRE #33

[Facsimile Copy - Retyped form Original]

FROM: INS
DATE: August 14, 1987
FILE: CO 1588
TO: All ROCOMS
All ROLEGS
All DDS
All OICS
All CPAS
ODTF, GLYNCO

The following guidelines are provided in response to questions and requests for guidance on qualifying employment for SAWS.

The question has been posed as to whether beekeeping for pollination, as opposed to honey production, would qualify as seasonal agricultural services for SAW purposes. Some crops require or are benefited by insect pollination and some producers of these crops keep bees near their fields or orchards as a cultural practice for crop production purposes. If beekeeping is conducted for the primary purpose of pollination of a perishable commodity, this is a cultural practice which constitutes field work, regardless that honey or queen bee production may be carried on as a peripheral activity. Some producers of perishable crops rent hives from apiarists for the purpose of pollination rather than keeping their own. If employees of producers of perishable crops transport, place, and maintain rented hives for the purpose of pollination, this constitutes field work. Employees of apiarists performing similar duties are not deemed to be performing field work because, although hives may be rented for pollination, the primary enterprise of the apiarist is honey production and hive maintenance rather than production of perishable crops.

2. In Legalization Wire #23 it was stated that "stripping, grading, drying, or packing performed in or adjacent to the field where the produce is grown is 'field work' if performed as an integral part of the picking or harvesting operation on that farm." Since distribution of that wire some Legalization offices have encountered cases where producers locate packing sheds at highways, railheads, or similar transportation points, or at central locations in cases of farms with separate, remote fields. Stripping, sorting, grading, drying, packing and similar harvest-related activities performed at such sites are field work

8-14-87
LEGALIZATION WIRE #33

if 85% or more of the produce packed has been produced by the grower/employer. This determination follows labor case law precedent under which packing is considered agricultural employment if performed "by a farmer or on a farm." Employment by an agricultural cooperative or commercial packinghouse does not constitute employment "by a farmer or on a farm" and is not field work. Work performed in a packinghouse, cannery, or similar facility where produce is processed (i.e., canned, frozen,, or otherwise prepared for consumption) is not field work. The distinction between a packing shed type operation and a packinghouse is that the activities performed in a packing shed are performed by the farmer or grower who produced the crop and are activities which can be and sometimes are performed in the field where the produce is grown as part of normal harvest operations.

App-89

8-14-87

[Facsimile Copy - Retyped from original]

FROM: INS
ACTION: Priority
DATE: August 14, 1987
TO: ALL ROCOMS, ALL ROLEGS
SUBJECT: Affidavits of support in legalization cases.

Section 245A.2(D)(4)(iii) states:

(iii) Form I-134, Affidavit of support, completed by a spouse in behalf of the applicant and/or children which guarantees complete or partial financial support of the applicant.

Acceptance of the affidavit of support shall be extended to other family members in unusual family circumstances. An example of an acceptable affidavit of support would be one filed by an aunt on behalf of a minor who has resided in her household since entry into the United States.

Richard E. Norton
Associate Commissioner
Examinations

8-14-87

[Facsimile Copy - Retyped from Original]

FROM: INS
ACTION: Priority
DATE: August 14, 198
TO: ALL ROCOMS, ALL ROLEGS
SUBJECT: Proof of financial responsibility in legalization under Section 245A.

Minors files should not contain proof of financial responsibility if the application is filed jointly with the parent(s). When an "A" file of a minor contains no evidence of financial responsibility, there must be a worksheet indicating that proof of financial responsibility was established and that the evidence submitted is contained within the parent's file with reference "A" number. It is noted, however, that each minor's file must contain evidence of the minor's residence in the United States prior to January 1, 1982. Applications lacking this documentation shall not be considered complete.

Richard E. Norton
Associate Commissioner
Examinations

8-19-87
LEGALIZATION WIRE #35

[Facsimile Copy - Retyped from Original]

FROM: U.S. Immigration and Naturalization Service
ACTION: Priority
DATE: August 19, 1987
TO: All ROLEGs: ERO, STO, NRO, WRO
All ROCOMs: ERO, STO, NRO, WRO

Legalization Wire #35

Legalization applicants who filed asylum applications prior to January 1, 1982, and who were subsequently denied, or whose cases have not yet been decided are to be considered in an unlawful status known to the government and thus, eligible for legalization benefits. A legalization applicant who previously had an asylum application granted should be advised to file for adjustment under Section 209 instead.

Mark W. Everson
Deputy Commissioner

cc: CODEP   COPDI   COEXM   COLEG
    C. Boothe   T. O'Reilly C. Lechner
INS: COLEG: C. Lechner:MLS: 8/10/87 Revised: REN:MLS:
8/18/87

8-19-87
LEGALIZATION WIRE #35

App-92

LEGALIZATION WIRE #34

[Facsimile Copy - Retyped from Original]

FROM: Immigration and Naturalization Service
ACTION: Routine
DATE: August 25, 1987
TO: All ROCOMS
　　　All ROLEGS
　　　All DDS
　　　All OICS
　　　All CPAS
　　　ODTF, GLYNCO
　　　All RPFS
SUBJECT: Legalization Wire No. 34
　　　　　Travel Authorization for SAW Applicants
REFERENCE: 8 CFR 210.4(b)(2) CO 235-C Wire Dated 06/15/87.

The purpose of this wire is to correct apparent misunderstandings and confirm that Special Agricultural Workers SAWS in possession of valid employment authorization Form I-688A are authorized to travel abroad. The above-referenced wire provides that all SAW applicants are permitted to travel outside the U.S. and reenter upon the presentation of Form I-688A. Persons coming from other than the western hemisphere or adjacent islands must also present a valid passport in addition to Form I-688A.

It should be emphasized that blanket travel authorization prior to the granting of temporary resident status extends only to SAW applicants and not to legalization applicants. SAW applicants are identified on Form I-688A by the notation "210" on the bottom center of the card. Legalization applicants are identified by the notation "245A".

CODEP

cc: INS:COLEG:GPaz:633-5309:dsc:08/07/87:DWIRE#34
　　　CODEP
　　　COEAC
　　　COEXM
　　　COPDI
　　　COINS
　　　SAW

8-25-87
LEGALIZATION WIRE #34

App-93

8-25-87
LEGALIZATION WIRE #36

[Facsimile Copy - Retyped from Original]

FROM: US INS
ACTION: Priority
DATE: August 25, 1987
TO: ROCOMS, ROLEGS, DIDIRS, OICS

For purposes of the Legalization Program, A and G nonimmigrants as defined in Sectin 101(a)(15)(a) and (g) who were granted duration of status (D/S) but whose qualifying employment terminated or who otherwise ceased to be recognized by the Department of State as entitled to such classification prior to January 1, 1982 and have thereafter continued to reside in the United States in an unlawful status shall be considered as aliens whose prior period of authorized admission expired through the passage of time and are therefore eligible to apply for legalization. All other provisions (statutory and/or regulatory) of the legalization program apply. The date as of which the alien ceased to qualify for classification as an A or G must be clearly established by the alien through documentary evidence.

Mark W. Everson
Deputy Commissioner

8-25-87
LEGALIZATION WIRE #36

FROM: INS-CO
TO: All INS Field Offices
DATE: 9-10-87

In determining whether or not an alien may be excludable under the provision of 212(a)(15), field offices are not to use the federal poverty income guidelines as a standard.

The provisions of 8 CFR 245a.2(K) apply:

An alien who has a consistent employment history which shows the ability to support himself and his or her family, even though his income may be below the poverty level, may be admissible under paragraph (K)(2) of this section. The aliens's employment history need not be continuous in that it is interrupted. It should be continuous in the sense that the alien shall be regularly attached to the workforce, has an income over a substantial period of the applicable time, and has demonstrated the capacity to exist on his or her income and maintain his or her family without recourse to public cash assistance.

This regulation is prospective in that the service shall determine, based on the alien's history, whether he or she is likely to become a public charge. Past acceptance of public cash assistance within a history of consistent employment will enter into this decision. The weight given in considering applicability of the public charge provisions will depend on many factors, but the length of time an applicant has received public cash assistance will constitute a significant factor.

An individual who was deported on or after January 1, 1982, is not eligible for legalization benefits under the provisions of the Immigration Reform and Control Act of 1986 (IRCA). If any applicant under IRCA was deported or removed prior to January 1, 1982, and did not spend five successive years outside of the United States, the exclusion charge of 212(A)(17) applies and a waiver is required.

The provisions of 8 CFR 212.2(A) consent to reapply for admission after deportation, removal, or departure at government expense shall extend to the legalization program. 8 CFR 212.2(a) states:

Any alien who has been deported or removed from the United States, who is applying for a visa, admission to the United States, or adjustment of status, must present proof to the satisfaction of the consular or Immigration Officer that the alien has remained outside the United States for more than five successive years following the last deportation which is satisfactory to the Consular or Immigration Officer, or who has not remained outside the United States for the requisite period, must apply for permission to reapply as provided under this part. A temporary stay in the United States with approval of the Attorney General, under section 212(D)(3) of the act does not interrupt the five-year absence requirement.

Furthermore, the provisions of 8 CFR 212.2(i) shall also be extended to the Legalization program, in which the approval of the waiver for 212(a)(17) filed in conjunction with an application for legalization retroactive to the date on which the alien embarked or reembarked at a place outside the United States or attempted to be admitted from foreign contiguous territory.

9-23-87

[Facsimile Copy - Retyped from Original]

FROM: Office of Examinations (COEXM)
DATE: September 23, 1987
TO: Regional Commissioner: Eastern, Western, Northern, Southern
RE: Guidelines for Determining Public Charge Issues under the Legalization provisions of the Immigration Reform and Control Act of 1986 (IRCA)

The following guidelines are provided to clarify the standards for determining whether or not a legalization applicant is likely to become a public charge under section 212(a)(15) of the Immigration and Nationality Act (INA) as it applies to 8 CFR 245a.2(d)(4), proof of financial responsibility.

Proof of financial responsibility under 8 CFR 245a.2(d)(4) is to be established by examining the totality of the alien's circumstances at the time of his or her application for legalization. The existence or absence of a particular factor should never be the sole criteria for determining if an alien is likely to become a public charge. The determination of financial responsibility should be a prospective evaluation based on the alien's age, health, income, and vocation.

The special rule for determination of public charge under 8 CFR 245a.2(d)(15) is to be applied only in cases in which the alien is considered inadmissible under the provisions of 8 CFR 245a.2(d)(15) regarding proof of financial responsibility. No waiver application is necessary to apply the special rule for determination of public charge.

Public cash assistance, as defined in 8 CFR 245a.1(i) includes only needs-based monetary assistance from federal, state or local programs designed to meet subsistence needs. Supplemental Security Income (SSI) is a program of monetary assistance to persons who are both very poor and are aged, blind or disabled. It is not a program of general assistance to the families of SSI recipients.

Public cash assistance does not include assistance in kind, such as food stamps, public housing, or other non-cash benefits, nor does it include work-related compensation or certain types of medical assistance. The list of medical programs noted in this definition is an illustrative, not an exhaustive, list of programs which are not to be considered public cash assistance.

Educational assistance programs are not to be considered public cash assistance as long as the funds provided are designated specifically to meet educational needs such as tuition and books. However, if the educational program also provides for subsistence needs, it should then be considered as public cash assistance.

Foster care payments from state or federal programs are not to be considered public cash assistance to the foster parent(s). Foster parents perform a service. Monies paid are for the benefit of the child and to cover expenses involved in taking care of the child.

Waivers of the public charge exclusion are necessary only in those cases in which the alien does not meet either the "proof of financial responsibility" standards or the "special rule" for determination of public charge. If a waiver of the public charge exclusion ground is required, it may be granted in accordance with 8 CFR 245.2(k)(2); that is, for humanitarian purposes to assure family unity, or in the public interest.

These guidelines should be relayed to the field as soon as possible to ensure that the regulations relating to the public charge issues are interpreted and applied in a correct and consistent manner Servicewide.

Richard E. Norton
Associate Commissioner

cc: COEXM COLEG T.O'TEILLY B.MATOS
INS: COLEG:BMATOS:MLS: 9/15/87

LEGALIZATION WIRE #43
9-25-87

TO: ALL INS FIELD OFFICES
FROM: MARK W. EVERSON, DEPUTY INS COMMISSIONER
DATE: SEPTEMBER 25, 1987
SUBJECT: Transfer of files for Legalization/SAW applications.
         Legalization Wire No. 43

At the recent Records Conference in St. Louis, MO, the Legalization RPF Directors reported a severe problem in FOs not transferring requested files to the RPFs. In particular, this problem related to files in the operating units, such as detention and deportation, investigations and trial attorneys.

Priority treatment is to be given to transferring files requested for Legalization/SAW to the RPFs. Including files located in operating units for the following reasons:

1. Any cases under docket control, whether under deportation proceedings, prehearings or pertaining to an alien in custody.

2. Alien has placed a bond with INS.

3. Alien's case is under active investigation.

4. Alien has a private bill.

If an operating unit requires a copy of the file requested for transfer, they may make such a copy and place the copied materials in a workfolder. Under no circumstances is a file to be withheld from transfer action to the requesting RPF.

If you have any questions on this matter, please contact Mary Ann Cathopoulis, Director, Records Reform Act Office at FTS 786-4768

[Facsimile Copy - Retyped from Original]

FROM: INS
ACTION: Routine
DATE: September 26, 1987
SUBJECT: Screening I-700 applications for the entry date prior to accepting the fee.

Several cases have recently been brought to our attention where the I-700 application and fee were accepted although the applicant's entry date as recorded on item #15 of the application was after the June 26, 1987 cutoff date.

The screening process that occurs upon receipt of the application should include a quick review of the applicant's entry date. If the entry date is after June 26, 1987, the application should be rejected and returned to the applicant instructing him/her to file abroad.

SAW applications with an entry date after June 26, 1987, should only be accepted after the applicant has been informed of the entry cutoff date requirement yet still insists upon filing his/her application.

COLEG

To: Western Region Field Offices
From: William S. King, Director, Immigration Reform
Date: September 30, 1987

A number of SAW applications have been received at the Regional Processing Facility accompanied only by Form I-705 (Affidavit confirming Seasonal Agricultural Employment) as evidence of qualifying employment. In view of increased reports by the RPF DAU indicating widespread submission of fraudulent SAW packages, the importance of submission of corroborative evidence in support of SAW applications must be emphasized.

While one may infer that an I-705 "confirms" or establishes the applicant's claim, as is suggested by the title it carries, it presents no persuasive satisfaction on the requirements of the regulations until item #15 of the Form I-705 is completely supported or explained and until Service verification is completed as set forth by 8CFR 210.3(b)(3). Further, the regulation is silent on its requirements of an I-705 as part of a complete application. Title 8, CFR, Section 210.1 states that:

"....A complete application consists of an executed Form I-700, Application for Temporary Resident Status as a Special Agricultural Worker, evidence of qualifying agricultural employment and residence, and the prescribed number of photographs."

An I-705 is not required to constitute a "complete application" nor does it alone establish a "just and reasonable inference" that the applicant indeed have performed "special agricultural services". Guided by 8 CFR 210.3(3) (Proof of Employment) please note that the affiant "must provide a certified copy of corroborating records or state the affiant's willingness to personally verify the information provided." It is acknowledged that if the latter case was opted by the affiant, the Service would be subjected to a wide latitude of fraud if the information was somehow not verified. Thus, it is suggested that a closer examination of item 15 of Form I-705 be conducted when received at a Legalization Office.

In the absence of Form I-705, 1 CFR 210.3(3) ... "Affidavits" may be submitted under oath, by agricultural producers..." but also asks of the applicant to provide pertinent information. See 210.3(3) under Proof of Employment. The affidavit must contain the same information sought by Form I-705. The required information is the following:

1. The affiant must be identified by name and address.
2. The name of the applicant and the relationship of the affiant to the applicant must be stated.
3. The source of the information in the affidavit (e.g., personal knowledge, reliance on information provided by other, etc.) must be indicated.
4. The exact number of man-days worked in each of the twelve-month periods ending May 1, 1984, 1985 and 1986 must be stated.
5. The type of crop must be identified.
6. The type of field work performed.

In either case, it is abundantly clear the SAW applications are to provide corroborative evidence or personal verification.

LEGALIZATION WIRE #42
9-87

FROM: Mark Everson, INS Deputy Commissioner
TO: INS Regional Offices
DATE: September, 1987
RE: LEGALIZATION WIRE #42

As previously discussed, production at the Regional Processing Facilities (RPFs) continues to be a major concern.

In order to clearly establish to the public, press, and Congress that the Legalization Program is successful, a dramatic increase must be seen in the number of final adjudicative decisions. This need is no greater now than ever, as we are coming up to the expiration of the Employment Authorization Cards (Forms I-688A).

A number of issues have been identified both technical and operational, that need resolution to ensure a proper workflow. The following steps should be implemented immediately upon receipt of this wire.

All cases relating to minors which are being held in abeyance pending final adjudicative decision of the parents(s) Legalization/SAW case will be adjudicated if the minor's file contains proof of residence and identity of the minor. The minor's file should reflect that financial responsibility for the minor has been established through evidence contained in the parent(s) file.

Cases that have been identified as deniable should be completed and denials issued by the end of September. Cases identified as deniable due to specific regulatory issues (NIV Reentry, etc.) should be held pending expected regulatory change.

Cases receipted during the months of May and June should be identified and where possible that adjudicative decision should be rendered by the end of September.

Problems with the Legalization Application Processing System (LAPS) that have been previously identified are being addressed by COINF. If improvement is not seen in the immediate future (by October 1) please inform this office.

It is expected that progress toward achievement of the production at the RPFs will be seen immediately to stem potential problems that will exist if we do not become

LEGALIZATION WIRE #42
9-87

more responsive.

10-02-87

FROM: Immigration & Naturalization Service
ACTION: Priority
DATE: October 2, 1987

The following samples of the more common reasons that may be used in I-700 denials are telefaxed for you consideration dissemination to the RPF directors.

COLEG

Department of Justice Notice Of Decision Refer to File No. A9
U.S. Immigration and Naturalization Service
Address

Decision

Upon consideration, it is ordered that your Application for Temporary Resident Status as a Special Agricultural Worker filed under Section 210 of the Immigration and Nationality Act (INA) be denied for the following reason(s):

(INSERT STANDARD DENIAL)

Example:

You are ineligible for temporary residence status under Section 210 of the INA because you are excludable from the United States because you have been convicted of a violation of a law or regulation relating to narcotic drugs or marijuana (Section 212(a)(23) of the INA). Additionally, 8 CFR Part 210.3(e)(3) specifically states that excludability under Section 212 (a)(23) may not be waived.

(INSERT SPECIFIC REASONS FOR DENIAL INCLUDING FACTS)

Example:

On June 2, 1986, in London, Kentucky you were convicted of narcotics trafficking. Because of that conviction, you are ineligible for temporary residence status and your application is denied.

You may appeal this decision to the Administrative Appeals Unit by completing the enclosed Form I-694 (NOTICE OF APPEAL) and filing it with this office together with a $50.00 fee in the form of money order, cashier's check, or

10-02-87

bank draft. Your NOTICE OF APPEAL must be filed within 30 days of this notice. Additional evidence, a brief, or the written statement in support of your appeal may be submitted with the NOTICE OF APPEAL. If no appeal is filed within the time allowed, this decision is final.

If a timely appeal is not submitted, all employment authorization previously granted by this Service will automatically be revoked.

Any questions which you have will be answered by the local Legalization Office or the Regional Processing Facility shown in the heading of this letter.

Sincerely,

Chief Legalization Officer (or Regional Processing Facility Director)

SAW DENIALS

You are ineligible for adjustment of status to that of a temporary resident under Section 210 of the INA because:

I. You have failed to establish that you were physically present in the United States before June 26, 1987.

8 CFR Part 210.(c)(1) states in pertinent part ..."Only aliens who were physically present in the United States before June 26, 1987, must file an application at the overseas processing office having jurisdiction over their current foreign residence or, if they are currently in the United States, at the overseas processing office having jurisdiction over the place of their last foreign residence prior to coming to the United States".

(Insert specifics)

Your application is therefore denied.

II. You have failed to fulfill the two-year foreign residence requirement.

8 CFR Part 21.3(d)(1) include the following class of aliens as ineligible for temporary residence. "An alien who at any time was a nonimmigrant exchange visitor under Section 101(a)(15)(J) of the Act who is subject to the two-year foreign residence requirement unless the alien has complied with that requirement or the requirement has been waived pursuant to the provisions of Section 212(e) of the Act."

(Insert specifics)

App-102

10-02-87

III. You have failed to establish by a preponderance of the evidence that you performed at least 90 man-days of employment in qualifying seasonal agricultural services during the twelve-month period from May 1, 1985 through May 1, 1986.

(a) 8 CFR Part 210.3 provides that the applicant has the burden of providing the requisite employment by a preponderance of the evidence. The evidence you have provided is not sufficient to support a just and reasonable inference that you have in fact performed the requisite employment.

(Insert specifics)

Your application is therefore denied.

(b) 8 CFR Part 210.3(b)(3) states in pertinent part...

"Affidavit and other personal testimony by an applicant which are not corroborated, in whole or in part, by other credible evidence (including testimony of persons other than the applicant) will not serve to meet an applicant's burden of proof"...

(Insert specifics)

Your application is therefore denied.

The documentation that you have submitted to establish the requisite employment is insufficient.

Your application is therefore denied.

IV. You are excludable from the United States because you have committed or have been convicted of a crime involving moral turpitude (Section 210(c) and 212(a)(9) of the INA).

(Insert specifics)

Your application is therefore denied.

V. You are excludable from the United States because you have been convicted of two or more offenses for which the aggregate sentences to confinement actually imposed were five years or more. (Section 210(c) and 212(a)(10) of the INA).

(Insert specifics)

Your application is therefore denied.

10-02-87

VI. You are excludable from the United States because of the likelihood of your becoming a public charge. You have failed to demonstrate a consistent employment history and ability to support yourself without reliance on public cash assistance. (Sections 210(c) and 212(a)(15) of the INA).

(Insert specifics)

Your application is therefore denied.

VII. You are excludable from the United States because you have been convicted of a violation of a law or regulation relating to narcotic drugs or marijuana. (Section 210(c) and 212(a)(23) of the INA).

(Insert specifics)

Your application is therefore denied.

VIII. The agricultural employment in which you were engaged is not qualifying employment in seasonal agricultural services.

In order to be eligible for temporary resident status under Section 210 of the Immigration and Nationality Act (INA), an applicant must demonstrate that he or she has engaged in seasonal agricultural employment in the United States for at least 90 man-days during the twelve-month period ending on May 1, 1986. Seasonal agricultural services is defined at section 210(h) of the INA as: "the performance of field work related to planting, cultural practices, cultivating, growing and harvesting of fruits and vegetables of every kind and other perishable commodities, as defined in regulations by the Secretary of Agriculture."

Under U.S. Department of Agriculture regulations at 7 CFR 1d.___

(a) is not considered to be a fruit, vegetable, or perishable commodity.

(b) is not considered to be field work.

(Insert specifics)

Your application is therefore denied.

App-103

10-05-87

[Facsimile Copy-Retyped from Original]

SUBJECT: Revision of forms - medical examination of aliens
DATE: October 5, 1987
FROM: Adjudications (COADN)
TO: All Regional Commissioners
    All District Directors
    All Officers in Charge

Recently, From I-693 revision date September 1, 1987, was distributed to all district offices, suboffices, and legalization offices. This form was designed to replace two forms - Form I-486, revision date December 29, 1979, and Form I-693, revision date February 14, 1987. Therefore, upon receipt of the September 1, 1987, revision of Form I-693, all current stock of the February 14, 1987 revision of Form I-693 and all stock of Form I-486 shall be destroyed.

No new I-486 forms will be printed. The new I-693 will be used both for legalization applicants and regular adjustment applicants from this time on.

Although old forms will no longer be distributed by the Service, they will be accepted for their proper use if:

1) The medical exam is conducted prior to December 1, 1987, and

2) The form is presented with a properly filed application (either to a Service Officer or a QDE) prior to January 1, 1988.

MEDICAL GIVEN ON OR AFTER DECEMBER 1, 1987
The results of any medical examination given on or after December 1, 1987 must be recorded on a new Form I-693. Any applicant who attempts to file an application after January 1, 1988 with an old medical form will be given a new medical from and instructed to return to the designated physician, have the results of the medical transferred to the new form, and have recorded the results of the HIV test. The applicant should be advised the physician may require an additional fee to conduct the HIV test.

MEDICALS GIVEN BEFORE DECEMBER 1, 1987
The results of a medical exam given before December 1, 1987 and submitted prior to January 1, 1988 may be submitted on the appropriate old form or on the newly revised I-693, it is not required that the HIV test be given or recorded. The applicant may, of course, request the physician to conduct an HIV test and, if so, the results will be recorded.

SUMMARY
If an applicant properly files an application for adjustment before January 1, 1988, he or she may submit any of the following:

1) Form I-486 (Rev. December 29, 1979) reporting the results of a medical taken prior to December 2, 1987.

2) Form I-693 (Rev. February 14, 1987) reporting the results of a medical taken prior to December 1 1987.

3) Form I-693 (Rev. September 1, 1987) reporting the results of a medical taken before December 1, 1987. In this instance, an HIV test is not required, but if given at the request of the applicant, will be recorded.

4) Form I-693 (Rev. September 1, 1987) reporting a medical examination given on or after December 1,1987. These exams must include the HIV test results.

All applications filed after January 1, 1988 must include Form I-693 (Rev. September 1, 1987), which includes the results of an HIV test.

R. Michael Miller
Deputy Assistant Commissioner

TO: All Regional Commissioners
All Regional Legalizations
All DDS (except foreign)
All OICS (except foreign)
All CPAS

FROM: COMMR (COEXM) JINS Washington DC
DATE: October 6, 1987

Section 210(A)(4) of the Immigration Reform and Control Act of 1986 (IRCA) provides that special agricultural workers (SAWS) who have been granted lawful temporary resident status have the right to travel abroad (including commutation from a residence abroad)... In the same manner as for aliens lawfully admitted for permanent residence. Accordingly, SAW commuters fall within the purview of 8 CFR 211.5.

Upon issuance of the temporary residence card, Form I-688, the legalization offices will present each SAW with a "notice to special agricultural workers" which states in pertinent part "To register for commuter status, you must present a current employment letter or payroll slip to the Immigration inspector at the port of entry upon your next application for admission into the United States. If you are not yet employed in the United States, you can still register for commuter status at the port of entry and enter the United States to seek employment." A copy of the notice to special agricultural workers will be forthcoming upon completion of format design.

If commuter status is granted, the port of entry should, being guided by OI 211.4 issue form I-176 commuter status (illegible) to the SAW and punch the symbol "S" horizontally in the upper right portion on form I-688 on the green and yellow lines.

[Facsimile Copy-Retyped from Original]

10-08-87

FROM: INS
TO: Designated Physicians
DATE: October 8, 1987

The Immigration and Naturalization Service has revised its medical forms to develop more consistency and to allow for the reporting of HIV test results.

Currently, individuals who are requesting medical examinations present Service Form I-693 with a revision date of February 14, 1987 to you if they intend to apply for the legalization benefits of the Immigration Reform and Control Act (IRCA) if 1986. Individuals requesting examination for application under the routine adjustment of status provisions of the Immigration Act present Form I-486, revised December 29, 1979. The form number and revision date are printed on the lower left-hand corner of the form.

In early October, Service offices stopped distributing these two forms and began distributing one consolidated form, I-693, revised September 1, 1987. The new I-693 form will be distributed to all applicants. You will note that the major difference in the new form is that the instruction sheet contains information about the HIV testing procedure and the form itself contains a block for you to record the results of any HIV test performed. In addition, all applicants (not just legalization applicants) are now requested to bring immunization records to the medical examination. You are asked to review the records presented to determine if immunizations are current, and encourage the applicant to obtain appropriate immunization if they are not current. The difference in requirements upon the two groups regarding tuberculosis testing remains.

INS offices will continue to accept the old forms if:

1) the medical exam is conducted prior to December 1, 1987 and
2) the entire application is submitted to INS before January 1, 1988.

In the period from now until December 1, 1987, you may therefore encounter the following situations:

A) An applicant for adjustment of status may present a Form I-486. If the applicant does not request an HIV

10-08-87

test, or says he or she intends to file before January 1, 1988, you may conduct the examination and record the results on the I-486.

If the applicant requests an HIV test, or intends to file after January 1, 1988, the applicant must first obtain a new I-693 (revised September 1, 1987) from INS. Record the examination results, including the HIV results, on the new form.

B) A legalization applicant may present an "old" I-693, (revised February 14, 1987. If the applicant does not request an HIV test, or says he or she intends to file before January 1, 1988, conduct the medical examination and record the results on the February 14, 1987 I-693. No HIV test is required.

If the applicant requests an HIV test, or intends to file after January 1, 1988, the applicant must first obtain a new I-693, (revised September 1, 1987) from INS. Record the examination results (including the HIV test) and record the results on the form.

C) A legalization or adjustment applicant requests an HIV test, or intends to file after January 1, 1988, conduct the examination (including the HIV test) and record the results on the form.

If the applicant states he or she does not want an HIV test conducted, and states he or she intends to file before January 1, 1988 you may still want to conduct the examination and fill out the new form I-693. In the space designated to record HIV test results, print "not conducted per applicant request".

On or after December 1, 1987 all medical exams conducted must include an HIV test and the results of the examinations must be recorded on the newly revised I-693 (revised September 1, 1987). You should not record the results of any medical exam given after December 1, 1987 on any form other than an I-693, September 1, 1987 revision date.

After January 1, 1988, you may also have applicants return to you who had medical exams conducted prior to December 1, 1987 and despite their original intentions, did not file with INS prior to January 1, 1988. Instruct these applicants to obtain a newly-revised I-693. You may then transfer the medical test results from the old I-693 or I-486 to the new I-693, conduct and record the results of the HIV test, and sign the new I-693. These applicants will be advised by the Service that designated physicians may charge an additional fee at this time for the HIV

App-106

test.

In addition you may wish to obtain a small number of newly revised I-693's to keep in your office. These forms are available through the Superintendent of Documents, Government Printing Office, Washington, DC 20401, and throughout the twenty-four GPO bookstores through the country. The form number is Form I-693 (revised September 1, 1987) and the stock number is 027-002-00355-1. Forms are available in packets of 100 at $27.00 per packet. You may also purchase forms through the Government Printing Office by calling (202) 783-3238.

James A. Puleo
Assistant Commissioner

FROM: Richard E. Norton, Associate Commissioner, INS
Office of Examinations (COEXM)
FILE: CO 1588-C
DATE: October 9, 1987
RE: Documentary Requirements to Establish Eligibility Under Section 245A of the Immigration Reform and Control Act
TO: All ROCOMS, ROLEGS, DDS (Except Foreign), OICS (Except Foreign)

Since the legalization program became fully operational on May 5, 1987, the area of concern most frequently noted to INS, especially by the representatives of Qualified Designated Entities (QDEs), has been that of the documentary requirements for legalization. Several experienced sources have advised us that the language of the regulations is unclear as to what extent of documentation is sufficient for an applicant to demonstrate eligibility.

While the broad language was intended to maximize case-by-case discretion, it has led to inconsistent documentary requirement practices at legalization offices establishing super regulatory guidelines and rules of thumb that impose unintended impediments.

In order to ensure a fair and equitable administration of the legalization provisions of the IRCA Servicewide, such local standards are to be avoided. Instead a balanced and flexible approach should be taken in evaluating an applicant's testimony and the overall sufficiency and probative value of the evidence he or she has provided to support his or her claim to eligibility. Discretion should also be applied in the types and quantities of documents requested. The submission of voluminous amounts of documents provided should depend not on quantity alone, but on the reliability, credibility and amenability to verification.

In addition, in order to eliminate any existing confusion with respect to documentary requirements, Central Office Legalization (COLEG) has developed an information sheet that may be used as a handout to assist QDEs and prospective applicants in gathering the types of documents the INS will consider as evidence to establish identity, continuous residence in the United States, and financial responsibility. The enclosed form should be reproduced locally and distributed to all QDEs and Service Legalization Offices.

Richard E. Norton
Associate Commissioner

App-108

10-15-87

FROM: Richard E. Norton, INS Associate Commissioner for Examinations
FILE: CO-1588-P
TO: All ROCOMS
DATE: October 15, 1987
RE: Minimizing G-641 Requests Relevant to Legalization Applicants

The current backlogs in processing both Freedom of Information Act and Privacy Act requests (Forms G-641 and G-639) partially can be attributed to local legalization offices requiring that documents establishing eligibility be requested from Service records prior to the submission of a legalization application.

In order to eliminate this problem, legalization office managers are to accept legalization applications that depend on information from an existing "A" file whether or not such information has been submitted with the application. This procedure will reduce the aforementioned backlogs without eroding the quality of adjudications, in that both files must be reviewed at a Regional Processing Facility (RPF).

To ensure proper review at the RPF, the Adjudicator's Worksheet should be noted as to the documents that are to be reviewed in the alien's previous file, and number 5 in section "B" of the worksheet should be checked.

[Facsimile Copy-Retyped form original]

ALAN C. NELSON
COMMISSIONER
IMMIGRATION AND NATURALIZATION SERVICE

SUPPLEMENTARY INFORMATION
FOR
THE APPEARANCE BEFORE THE HOUSE SUBCOMMITTEE ON
IMMIGRATION, REFUGEES AND INTERNATIONAL LAW
IMMIGRATION REFORM AND CONTROL ACT
OVERSIGHT HEARING
Wednesday, October 21, 1987
9:00 a.m.
Rayburn Office Building
Room 2237

TABLE OF CONTENTS

Item	Page
Family Fairness.	1
Training.	7
User Fees.	8
Liaison with Mexico.	10
HIV/AIDS Policy.	11

I. LEGALIZATION AND FAMILY FAIRNESS - AN ANALYSIS

GENERAL PURPOSE OF THE UNITED STATES IMMIGRATION LAWS AND THE IMMIGRATION REFORM AND CONTROL ACT OF 1986 (IRCA)

On November 6, 1986, President Reagan signed the Immigration Reform and Control Act of 1986 (IRCA) into law. This legislation, the most comprehensive reform of our Immigration laws since 1952, makes great strides to control illegal immigration while preserving our heritage of legal immigration.

While the theme of this legislation is focused on gaining control of our borders and eliminating the illegal alien problem through firm yet fair enforcement, it also reflects the nation's concerns for aliens who have been long-time illegal residents of the United States.

This is accomplished through a generous legalization program that is based on the same concepts of fairness that underlie the lawful immigration system. Both paths offer an orderly transition to permanent residence for those who have established their eligibility and provide an opportunity for family members to immigrate under a process that does not reward people who have circumvented

10-21-87

the law by entering illegally.

Immigration by close relatives of permanent residents and citizens of the United States forms the core of a lawful system centered on the reunification of families; the overwhelming majority of some six hundred thousand people who immigrate each year are such immediate family members. By legalizing their status, aliens who have been in this country since 1982 gain access to our family-oriented immigration policy, and ensure that their spouses and children may enter lawfully.

II. CONCEPT OF LEGALIZATION UNDER IRCA

IRCA is an enforcement law; its primary purpose is to stop illegal immigration. The legalization program is one part of a package that includes employer sanctions, enhanced border enforcement, the Systematic Alien Verification for Entitlements (SAVE) program, and a provision for removal of criminal aliens.

Legalization was the balance--a one-time program to legalize certain aliens, even though they were illegal, and allow them to become part of the American mainstream. This delicate balance was achieved through a statute that was carefully constructed to make passage of the bill possible. Even as crafted, legalization was still so controversial that the margin in favor of the provision in the House of Representatives was only seven votes.

The Congress accomplished the legalization balance by limiting the program to aliens with substantial equities in the United States. It did not intend to place all illegal aliens within a legal status. January 1, 1982, was set as the eligibility date for legalization, thus setting forth clear boundaries for establishing ties to this country. Those illegal aliens who arrived in the United States after January 1, 1982, remain illegal and are subject to deportation.

This Congressional intent as it applies to each alien is evidence in the plain meaning of the statute. This intent is further magnified by the legislative history of the bill, including the House Report, the State Report, and the Conference Report, and the Congressional floor debates (1986). There is nothing in these documents that would indicate Congress wanted to provide immigration benefits to others who didn't meet the basic criteria, including families of legalized aliens. To the contrary, the Senate Judiciary Committee stated in its report that:

It is the intent of the Committee that the families of legalized aliens will obtain no special petitioning right by virtue of the legalization. They will be

App-110

required to "wait in line" in the same manner as immediate family members of other new resident aliens. S. Rep. No. 99-131, 99th Cong., 1 Sess. 343 (1985).

With the legislative history so clear, the authority of the Attorney General to grant resident status must extend only to aliens who qualify on the merits of their own case, and not through a broad, extralegal derivative basis.

III. HOW LEGALIZATION HAS WORKED

In the six months allowed to prepare for implementation of the program, the INS engaged in an unprecedented action which opened the full regulatory process to the public. Comments were solicited at the earliest stage, and the thousands of responses were carefully considered in developing the final product. Meanwhile, INS undertook an implementation effort never matched in the agency's history. By May 5, 1987, one hundred and seven (107) new offices were opened with 2,000 people hired to staff these offices; a major automated data system was developed and installed; the public information campaign was begun; and training was provided to all that were to work in the legalization program.

As of October 16, 1987, roughly 5 1/2 months after opening, we have accepted over 865,000 applications. Over 85% of these applications were filed directly with the INS, indicating that there is no "fear factor" -- the alien population that has come forward exhibits trust in the Immigration Service. With this participation rate already doubling the results of all other legalization programs throughout the world in modern-day history, expectations are that 2 million illegal aliens will be processed by May 4, 1988.

IV. HOW LEGALIZATION SUPPORTS THE DUAL THEMES OF LEGAL IMMIGRATION AND FAMILY UNIFICATION

Through the legalization program made possible by IRCA, several million people will be able to shift from an illegal to a legal status. They will be able to come "out of the shadows", and eventually become full active participants in our society, and eventually become United States citizens. Many of these millions are in family units which have filed as a unit and have been found eligible for legalization. Many parents of United States citizen children have qualified on the merits of their own cases under IRCA.

The INS is exercising the Attorney General's discretion by allowing minor children to remain in the United States even though they do not qualify on their own, but whose parents (or single parent in the case of divorce or death of spouse) have qualified under the provisions of IRCA. The same discretion is to be exercised as well in other cases which have specific humanitarian considerations.

Many family members who would have otherwise been judged ineligible for legalization may now qualify due to recent policy decisions. Applicants who resided illegally in the United States prior to January 1, 1982, but who subsequently departed and then used legal nonimmigrant documents to re-enter the United States to resume their illegal residence, are now considered eligible for legalization benefits with the filing of a waiver to overcome the fraud at entry.

Upon being approved for permanent resident status, the legalized alien will be eligible to bring in immediate relatives under the current provisions of the Immigration and Nationality Act. Therefore, families of legalized aliens will be unified in the same manner as other immigrant families who have been waiting outside of the United States. (See the following chart for comparisons).

Legal Immigration

1. Married couple with wife in U.S. and husband in foreign country
2. Lawful resident wife files petition for husband
3. Petition approved; husband gains right to immigrate under preference system
4. Husband must wait for visa; cannot wait in U.S.
5. If husband comes to U.S. illegally, he is subject to deportation if routinely encountered
6. Husband must return to home country to obtain visa when it is available

Legalization

1. Married couple apply for legalization
2. Wife approved; husband denied
3. No effort to deport husband
4. Later INS contact (i.e., at place of work) could result in deportation proceedings against husband
5. Wife gains permanent resident status; files petition for husband

10-21-87

V. FAMILY FAIRNESS

6. See steps 3-6 under Legal Immigration

Congress, as well as the INS, recognized that there is a basic issue of fairness involved in the enactment of IRCA. Fairness dictates that illegal alien family members of persons eligible for legalization not be treated more favorably than the family members of legal permanent residents who may have to wait years to come to the United States due to the backlog of a demand for visas. To grant a derivative legalization benefit to unqualified aliens who are merely related to a qualified applicant, and attempt to gain benefits. This would create a second legalization program contrary to the intent of Congress and upset the delicate balance of IRCA.

Legalization is a unique act. Basic equity between those legal immigrants who patiently wait in foreign countries for legal visas and those who entered illegally, but have contributed to America and are being forgiven, should be maintained. However, unqualified family members will be in no worse a position than they were prior to the enactment of IRCA. In fact, as noted above, it is to the benefit of the unqualified to have their eligible relative apply for legalization in that it may qualify the in the future for permanent residence.

VI. UNFOUNDED BELIEF THAT UNLESS LEGALIZATION LAW BE EXPANDED, FAMILIES WILL BE BROKEN UP

As previously noted, legalization allows many families to stay in this country legally. Without legalization, individuals who are in the United States illegally have no right to any benefits of the immigration law and may not petition for relatives.

To the extent that there is a family separation, the separation was usually accomplished by the alien who left his or her family behind in the home country to seek an illegal life in the United States. If the family is separated because of legalization and decides not to wait for a legal means to bring the family unit together again in the United States, the option is always available for the family unit to return to the home country.

VII. INS PROCEDURES TO HANDLE FAMILY FAIRNESS ISSUES

Under the law no information from the legalization application will be used against any applicant or their

10-21-87

family. Once family members are recorded on the application, there cannot be subsequent modifications. Thus it is in the ineligible alien's best interest to be recorded as a family member now.

The confidentiality factor of the application, which Congress included in the legislation, prevents INS from taking any action as a result of information provided in the application. The only way family members of a legalization applicant would come under deportation proceedings is if they are apprehended during a routine INS operation at a workplace.

INS district directors may exercise the Attorney General's authority to indefinitely defer deportation of anyone for specific humanitarian reasons. They will continue to examine any case that involves an immediate relative of a successful legalization applicant. The district directors are instructed to review all evidence submitted, make a recommended finding, and make available all such cases for review and concurrence. This unusual step is being taken to ensure the consistency of decisions throughout the Service.

Guidelines for INS officials regarding the basis for issuing voluntary departure are as follows:

1. Voluntary departure shall generally not be granted to the ineligible spouses of legalized aliens whose only claim to such discretionary relief is by virtue of the marriage itself. Likewise, such relief is not available to the ineligible parents of either legalized applicants or United States citizen children.

2. Instead, certain compelling or humanitarian factors must exist in addition to the family relationship and hardships caused by separation.

3. In general, indefinite voluntary departure shall be granted to unmarried children under the age of eighteen (18) years who can establish that they were in an unlawful status prior to November 6, 1986. Such children should be residing with their parents and the granting of voluntary departure should be conditioned on the fact that both parents (or, in the case of a single parent house hold, the parent the child live with) have achieved lawful temporary resident status.

IX. CONCLUSION

The United States is now nearly half way through the largest program in world history to allow many illegal aliens to become legal. Legalization is a balance to enforcement efforts to deter and control illegal

App-112

immigration through border enforcement, job market and entitlement enforcement to deny jobs and entitlements to illegal aliens and stronger efforts against criminal aliens. By May 1988, the United States will legalize an estimated million people, five times those legalized by all other countries in the world.

Many of these 2 million being legalized are families. Additional exercise of the Attorney General's discretion assures that minor children living with their parents will be covered. Spouse not directly eligible for legalization will be reviewed on a case-by-case basis and can be granted permission to remain if special humanitarian factors present. Other ineligible spouses of legalized aliens are placed in the exact same position as spouses of legal immigrants -- they can become legal residents through the petition process.

Therefore, legalization itself is the most significant effort of the Congress and the Administration to pursue the goal of U.S. immigration laws -- family unification. Out of fairness to our legal system, to legal immigrants waiting patiently in line, and to adhere to Congressional intent, there is no basis to "blanket in" all ineligible spouses. They, like all American immigrants, must follow the laws nd fundamental principle of fairness.

It is extremely important, however, that persons who believe they re eligible for legalization apply because of the unique protection the law offers through the confidentiality provision. They should appear at an INS Legalization Office or pursue their case through a church or other organization (Qualified Designated Entity) whether or not other family members qualify, in order to ensure that their family situation is resolved through the lawful immigration process.

Alan C. Nelson
Commissioner, U.S. Immigration & Naturalization Service

10-27-87

[Facsimile Copy-Retyped from Original]

FROM: INS
FILE: CO1588
DATE: October 7, 1987
TO: ALL ROCOMS
ALL ROLEGS
ALL DDS
ALL OICS

SUBJECTS: 1. Inspection procedures for special agricultural workers (SAWS) who depart the United States prior to issuance of the temporary resident card (Form I-688) and who seek readmission with an expired employment authorization card (Form I-688A).

2. Issuance of a new Form I-688 by any legalization office (LO) to SAWS who after applying for temporary residence move to another area prior to receipt of Form I-688.

Because of their employment and migration patterns, many SAWS will no longer be residing near the LO where they submitted their application at the time temporary residence is granted. In some instance SAWS will have left the United States and returned to their foreign residence abroad.

#1. In cases where a SAW seeks readmission into the United States with an expired I-688A, the port of entry shall determine the status of the SAW's application for temporary residence. This can be accomplished by a check of the Central Index System (CIS) or direct contact with the Regional Processing Facility. Subsequent to verification of identity and verification that temporary residence was granted or is pending, the SAW shall be admitted into the United States. The I-688A shall be returned to the applicant who shall be instructed to proceed to any LO for issuance of Form I-688. It is not necessary to furnish the SAW with an I-94 or other documentation. In cases where the application for temporary residence has been denied, Form I-688A shall be confiscated and destroyed. The District Director can then exercise his or her discretion to initiate exclusion proceedings or allow the applicant to withdraw his or her application for admission.

#2. SAWS who relocate after applying for temporary residence but prior to receipt of Form I-688 may be issued a new I-688 at any LO. To receive a new I-688, the SAW must complete Form I-695, application for replacement of Form I-688. The application shall be clearly noted to reflect that a replacement is requested because the SAW has moved away from the LO where he or she applied for temporary residence status. The applicant must submit his or her application in person along with Form I-688S and the required photographs and fee.

If an applicant is not in possession of his or her I-688A or if the application is mailed to the LO, the I-695 shall be sent to the RPF for adjudication in accordance with existing instructions. The LO after verifying that temporary residence was granted shall issue the SAW a new I-688, and collect and destroy the I-688A camera-ready photo card and the I-688 located at that office. Form I-695 shall be sent by the LO to the regional processing facility for placement in the SAWS A90 million file and to update the LAPS system.

Please ensure that this wire is disseminated to all legalization offices and all personnel performing inspections under your jurisdiction.

10-27-87

FROM: COMMR (COLEG) JINS Washington DC
DATE: October 27, 1987
ATTN: RPFS, ROLEGS

In reference to COLEG Wire Co 1588 dated October 6, 1987, regarding the annotation of Form I-688 temporary resident cards for SAW commuters. Those affected ports of entry not in possession of an "S" perforator may, instead, grommet the I-688 in the upper right portion on the green and yellow lines. All commuter ports of entry should be in possession of the grommet equipment as this procedure is currently utilized pursuant to OI 211.4. Therefore, SAW commuters will be in possession of Form I-688 either bearing an "S" perforation or a grommett in the upper right portion, as well as Form I-178 commuter status card.

App-115

10-27-87

To: All INS Field Offices
From: INS CO
Date: October 27, 1987

The purpose of this wire is to correct apparent misunderstandings and confirm that Special Agricultural Workers may file an I-700 Application at any Legalization office without regard to jurisdictional boundaries. Only Legalization applicants within the purview of 8 CFR 245A are restricted to filing at a Legalization Office within the jurisdiction of the distriHouses" and are not considered "agricultural lands" regardless of proximity to field production sites. Work performed in such facilities is not "f

10-27-88

FROM: INS Central Office
TO: All INS Field Offices
         (File CO 1588)
DATE: October 27, 1987
SUBJECT: Inspection of Special Agricultural Workers
         (SAW) at Ports of Entry (POE)

Recently, two SAWs who were processed at the Overseas Processing Office (OPO) at Mexico City sought admission at two different POEs. In both instances the POEs took possession of the SAWs entry packets and sent them to the IMDAC facility as if they were immigrant visa cases. IMDAC then sent the packets to COLEG/SAW. One of the SAWs was located and his packet was sent to the respective legalization office. (LO) to complete processing. The other SAW was not located, consequently processing. appears at an LO for issuance of form I-688A, he will not have with him his entry packet which is required to complete processing and for issuance of the employment authorization card (Form I-688A).

COLEG/SAW is in possession of the entry packet and will hold it until such time that the applicant appears at an LO and the LO requests transfer of the packet.

Name and other pertinent data relating to the SAW follows:

ZAVALA, VALLE ANGEL: DOB 10/06/52, Mexico: DOE 08/07/87:
POE El Paso: Destination in the U.S.: 1249 W. 10th Avenue,
Denver, Colorado 80204

Existing inspection instructions are as follows:

In cases in which the SAW has submitted a complete application and the OPO has recommended approval, the OPO will issue the SAW a Form OF-155A, Immigrant visa amended as a "Special Agricultural Worker Document." The OF-155A is grommeted to a packet containing form I-700 and supporting documentation. Inspectors should place the admission stamp on the OF-155A and in the passport, writing in the S2W class symbol and an authorized period of stay 30 days from the date of admission. Upon admission, the inspector must: 1) execute and mail to NIIS an arrival form I-94, no departure I-94 prepared or issued to the SAW; 2) return the stamped OF-155A and attached packet to the SAW; and, 3) direct the SAW to present his/her packet to the legalization office nearest his/her destination in the U.S.

10-27-88

Please ensure that all LOs and all personnel performing inspections under your jurisdiction are familiar with these instructions.

LEGALIZATION WIRE #46

[Facsimile Copy - Retyped from Original]

FROM: Michael Landon
DATE: October 28, 1987
FILE: CO-I-588-C
TO: All ROCOMS
    All ROLEGS
RE: Legalization Wire #46

At the Commissioner's press conference on October 8, 1987, the reentry policy was announced.

A general statement of the reentry policy follows:

The eligibility requirements for Legalization are expanded to include the individuals who were present in the United States in an unlawful status known to the government, or whose authorized stay expired through the passage of time, prior to January 1, 1982, and who, subsequent to a brief, casual, and innocent departure from the United States, reentered the United States as a nonimmigrant in order to return to an unrelinquished unlawful residence.

Any applicant for Legalization under this rule change is required to file a waiver in order to have the Legalization application considered. Waivers are to be filed to overcome the excludability charge of 212(a)(19) through an applicant's statement that fraud was committed at the time of reentry to return to the unrelinquished unlawful residence. Each applicant must file an individual waiver. There will be no family units for fees on waivers.

Prior to the granting of a waiver, the applicant must establish that he or she had been in an unlawful status known to the government or that his or her stay had expired through the passage of time prior to January 1, 1982. The applicant must also establish that he or she was returning to an unrelinquished, unlawful residence after a brief, casual and innocent departure from the United States.

As previously stated in legalization waiver requirements memorandum of August 7, 1987, if all of the evidence is present, the waiver shall be granted for humanitarian purposes, to assure family unity, or when the granting of such a waiver is in the public interest.

The following guidelines are provided for your

LEGALIZATION WIRE #46

information:

Cases at the RPF with waivers already filed--
Those cases that are being held at the RPF's because waivers of 212(a)(19) had already been filed shall be reviewed. If the case fits within the new reentry guidelines it shall be adjudicated immediately. This includes the waiver as well as of the I-687.

Cases which have been denied--
If a case has already been denied based solely on the reentry issue, the service shall identify these cases and reopen on a service motion. Upon reopening, the applicant will be requested to submit a waiver of 212(a)(19) with the appropriate fee to the RPF. Upon receipt of the waiver the RPF will adjudicate the I-687 and waiver.

Cases pending without waivers having been filed--
In cases that are being held in abeyance at the RPF's without waivers awaiting this rule change the RPF's should issue an I-72 notice stating the reasons for the waiver issue and such notice will be mailed to the last address indicated on the application.

Cases being filed for the first time--
If an application indicates that he or she would be eligible for a waiver under the 212(a)(19) reentry issue, a waiver shall be filed with the application. The case shall be treated in the normal manner with recommendation for denial -waiver attached forwarded to the RPF (to overcome the automatic approval override for review in the system). Notations should also be made at the LOS as to whether or not the case should be actually approved or denied. The RPF shall review the case and adjudicate appropriately.

App-118

11-2-87

FROM: INS Central Office
DATE: November 2, 1987

This wire corrects and replaces COLEG Wire CO 1588 dated 11/02/87 regarding travel documentation for legalization applicants. Please destroy the previous wire.

It has recently been brought to COLEG's attention that not all ports of entry are complying with CO 235-C dated June 15, 1987, regarding the reentry processing of section 245A legalization for admission into the U.S., all section 245A legalization applicants must be in possession of advance parole Form I-512. The inspecting officer must place the parole stamp on the I-512 paroling the applicant "until completion of 245A proceedings." The I-512 should then be mailed to the appropriate regional processing facility (RPF) where the A-Files are housed. As the legalization offices do not retain A-Files, No I-512 should be mailed to any legalization office.

Note that this procedure does not apply to section 210 SAW applicants who may use the I-688A employment authorization card as a travel document and are not required to obtain advance parole. Inspectors encountering Form I-688A must therefore look at section of law printed on Form I-688A- if it states "210", it pertains to a SAW and travel is permitted; if it states "245A", it pertains to a legalization applicant who must be in possession of Form I-512.

11-03-87
LEGALIZATION WIRE #37

[Facsimile Copy - Retyped from Original]

FROM: INS-CO
ACTION: Routine
DATE: November 3, 1987
TO: All ROCOMS
All ROLEGS
All DDS (Including Foreign)
All RPFS
RE: Legalization Wire #37
SAW status eligibility for aliens who lawfully enter the United States after the June 26, 1987 cutoff date.

The purpose of this wire is to clarify that SAW applicants who lawfully enter the United States during the application period may apply for SAW status in the United States regardless of the date of entry.

The intent of the service in establishing a cutoff date was to avert a potential flow of illegal immigrants and to eliminate any inducement to unlawful entry.

It was not the intent of the service to prevent aliens who enter the United States lawfully from later applying for SAW status in the United States if they are otherwise eligible for that status.

Aliens who enter the United States lawfully may apply for SAW status in the United States regardless of their date of entry. However, aliens who enter the United States as nonimmigrants with the intent to obtain SAW status may be held to have circumvented consular SAW procedures and to be subject to exclusion under the provisions of Section 212(a)(19).

Applicants who apply for SAW status in the United States who currently have work authorization incident to status as identified at 247a.12(b) shall be granted work authorization by INS effective the date the alien's prior work authorization expires.

Form I-688A shall be prepared by Legalization offices at the time of interview and shall be retained along with the I-688A camera-ready photo card and Form I-688. Applicants shall be instructed to return to the Legalization office upon expiration of their work authorization.

The office of Legalization is preparing a regulation change on this issue.

CODEP (COLEG)

11-03-87
LEGALIZATION WIRE #37

11-03-87
LEGALIZATION WIRE #45

[Facsimile Copy - Retyped from Original]

TO: All ROCOMS, All ROLEGS, All DDS, All OICS, All OPAS, All RPFS, ODTE, GLYNCO
FROM: Jerry Heinauer
DATE: November 3, 1987
RE: Legalization Wire #45

This wire authorizes district directors to deny at the LO any clearly fraudulent application for temporary residence under the Legalization or SAW Program.

Under both Legalization and the Special Agricultural Worker Program, the applicant has the burden of proving eligibility by a preponderance of the evidence. To meet this burden the alien must establish that he or she has in fact performed the qualifying employment (Section 210) or meets the continuous residence requirement (Section 245A). If the application contains material inconsistencies or contradictory information, or if there are serious discrepancies between the information in the application and that provided during the interview, the alien has not met the requisite burden of proof. Fraud profiles and other information available to the examiner which may be relevant to the veracity of the applicant's claims should be considered. Examiners should carefully review applications and probe the credibility of the applicant's claim during the interview. If specific information is developed to discredit the applicant's claim, the applicant should not be credited with the employment or residence in question. Applicants who thus clearly fail to establish their eligibility should have their applications denied at the LO. The basis for denial should be set forth on Form I-292 using language such as the following: "You have failed to establish your eligibility for temporary resident status under (Section 210 or 245A) of the INA. You have not proved that you performed at least 90 man-days of seasonal agricultural services during the period May 1, 1985 to May 1, 1986, or if it is a 245A application, you have not proved that you entered the United States before January 1, 1982, (or cite other eligibility requirement which has not been met). Specifically, it has been determined that:"---(Here, set forth the specific reasons for disallowing the claimed employment or entry date). The applicant must be advised of the right to appeal and provided with the Notice of Appeal Form I-694.

The denial should take place after fee receipt and the

11-03-87
LEGALIZATION WIRE #45

application should under no circumstances be returned to the applicant.

Although district directors may at their discretion forward such cases to the RPF for denial there, they are urged to deny these fraudulent applications (and applications involving admitted fraud and clear statutory ineligibility) at Legalization offices. The workload should not be significantly greater if cases are denied at LO's. I-292's may be prepared in advance, with the specific grounds for denial entered following the interview. This same information must be entered on the worksheet in any event.

District directors should carefully consider which cases to refer for prosecution or to the DAU for further investigation which may lead to the prosecution of others involved in fraud. Worksheets on all applications involving fraud should be noted for further review at the DAU.

App-121

11-10-87

FROM: Office of the Deputy Commissioner
DATE: November 10, 1987
SUBJECT: Modifications in the Legalization Process and Extension Requests for Six (6) Month Employment Authorization (I-688A)
TO: Regional Commissioners: Eastern
                        Southern
                        Northern
                        Western

As we approach the sixth month anniversary of the legalization program, a need for mid-course modifications of the legalization process have been identified. This memorandum outlines potential problem areas that may arise and the recommended solutions to each. These modifications are being made to ensure a consistent and efficient processing of all legalization applications.

In the original planning of the legalization program, a six month processing window was established to ensure that sufficient information was available for the proper adjudication of the applications. It was anticipated that this window would allow enough time for completion of all actions. The overwhelming majority of cases are being handled promptly. However, with nearly a million applications in the system it is inevitable that some will be delayed awaiting the location of a relating file, the completion of security checks or the resolution of an investigation.

As can be seen, two of the three key reasons for delay in processing of applications are matters the Service can control: The retrieval of relating Service files, and the completion of investigations.

In order to alleviate these potential problem areas the following actions have been taken. The Office of Information Systems has been directed to place top priority on the retrieval and forwarding of relating Service records to the appropriate Regional Processing Facility (RPF). A diligent search standard similar to that utilized in the processing of naturalization applications has been established. LAPS will continue to request related records for a period of 3 months; if after 90 days the file has not been received at the RPF, a case review worksheet will be cenerated to allow adjudication of the case. The related records will be placed on the Servicewide circular until located. LAPS will be modified to reflect the continued on-going search and the case will be flagged for further review at a later date.

Furthermore, one month prior to the expiration of a I-688A (Employment Authorization) applicants will be automatically notified to return to the legalization office where they were interviewed to have their employment authorization extended. With regard to fraud it is clear that decisions to prosecute violators must be made expeditiously. The application period is short and the deterrent affect on applicants contemplating fraud will be lost unless action is taken. Regional Commissioners are responsible for making enforcement components under their jurisdiction aware that cases referred to them should be acted upon as expeditiously as possible. With decisions being made expeditiously, the desired deterrent effect will be realized and requests for extension of employment authorization will be reduced.

I have directed the Associate Commissioner, Examinations to develop a detailed operational and procedure plan on the extension of Employment Authorization Cards (I-688A). This detailed plan is being forwarded under separate cover.

The Immigration Reform and Control Act of 1986 (IRCA) has provided the Service with high public visibility and we have experienced extensive media coverage in all areas of the legalization program. Therefore, ensure the above-stated actions are implemented immediately in your jurisdictions.

MARK W. EVERSON
Deputy Commissioner

App-122

11-10-87

[Facsimile Copy - Retyped From Original]

TO: William Slattery, Assistant Commissioner, Legalization
FROM: Raymond M. Momboisse, General Counsel
DATE: November 10, 1987
SUBJECT: Opinion as to Whether Foster Children who are Legalization Applicants are Subject to Section 212(a)(15) of the INA

This is in response to your request for our opinion regarding the issue of whether foster children who are legalization applicants are subject to section 212(a)(15) of the INA during the application process for permanent residence.

We have reviewed this issue and conclude that federal foster care payments made pursuant to Title IV, Part E of the Social Security Act constitute "public cash assistance" for purposes of the special rule for determining public charge.

The statutory term "public cash assistance" as used in section 210(c) and 245A(d) is clear and unambiguous. We read the term to include all assistance in the form of cash paid from public funds and to exclude "in-kind" assistance. It is clear to us that benefits paid under the AFDC-FC program are cash assistance. It is also clear, on review of Title IV Part E of the Social Security Act, 42 U.S.C. Section 608, that AFDC-FC payments are made to foster care home on behalf of the child. See 42 U.S.C. Section 608 (b). It is the need of the "dependent child" which is considered in determining eligibility, 42 U.S.C. 606(a), 608(a), not the need of the foster parent. In fact, the financial condition of the foster care home is irrelevant to the eligibility of the child for AFDC-FC benefits.[1]

Despite the fact that we have determined that payments to, or on behalf of, foster children constitute public cash assistance, receipt of such payments is not the sole determinant of "public charge." We would suggest that the Service look at the totality of the child's circumstances, including affidavits of support from the foster parents. Obviously an unemancipated child will be unable to provide a history of employment. Therefore, the review of the public charge ground with respect to minor children should be much more flexible than that of an able bodied adult.

If you require further assistance regarding this matter please contact Lori Scialabba at 633-3197.

---

[1] Some states have authorized special supplemental payments for related foster care assistance based on the needs of the related foster care parents. See Youakim v. Miller, 44 U.S. 125, 131 n. 12 (1979). That aid does not, however, affect eligibility of the child for AFDC-FC.

11-10-87

App-123

11-13-87

From: Office of the Commissioner
To: All Regional Commissioners, District Directors, Officers-In-Charge
Date: November 13, 1987
Subject: Family Fairness: Guidelines for Voluntary Departures under 8 CFR 242.5 for the Ineligible Spouses and Children of Legalized Aliens

The following guidelines are provided to implement the family fairness policy set forth on page five (5) of the enclosed legalization and family fairness analysis dated October 21, 1987.

A request for voluntary departure by an ineligible spouse or child of a legalized alien is to be made in writing to the district director in whose jurisdiction the ineligible spouse or child resides. The request must include the name, address, and A90M number of the principal alien; the relationship to the legalized alien (proof required); the names, addresses, and immigration status of ineligible spouse's minor children, if any; and the grounds for requesting voluntary departure. Form I-213, "Record of Deportable Alien," shall be prepared for each ineligible spouse or child making such a request.

In order to ensure the consistency of decisions throughout the Service in the adjudication of requests for voluntary departure for these family members, the following instructions are to be followed:

Upon submission of a request the applicant will be given the I-94 portion of the I-213 (which in and of itself will not convey employment authorization), and which will be clearly marked "Application Pending" - Valid to (fill in date - not to exceed 120 days from date of action). District directors will forward all requests received during the first forty-five (45) days after implementation to their regional commissioner. The submission will be accompanied by an opinion from the district director setting out the reasons for granting or denying the request. The narrative is to include the A90 file number and relationship of the legalized alien.

The regions will establish a panel to review all requests submitted during the initial 45-day period. All documentation submitted by the district director will be reviewed. The panel will advise the district director as to whether the opinion does or does not meet with Central office guidelines. The case will then be returned to the district director for appropriate action.

COLEG will send a staff representative to be a member of the regional panel in order to assist in the implementation of the Commissioner's guidelines.

These guidelines shall not preclude the granting of voluntary departure under any other provision of 8 CFR 242.5 to the ineligible family members of legalized aliens who are statutorily entitled to such discretionary relief.

Once a determination has been made to grant or deny voluntary departure to ineligible family members of legalized aliens, they should be placed under docket control. Detention and Deportation shall thereafter be responsible for controlling the case. For those cases placed under docket control, the criteria utilized under 8 CFR 274a.12 shall be employed in considering requests for employment authorization.

This guidance/analysis package should be promptly reviewed with field office managers. The legalization and family fairness analysis should also be utilized in briefing local government officials, the local media and special interest groups on the position the Service has taken in this matter.

ALAN C. NELSON
Commissioner

11-13-87

App-124

Date: November 18, 1987
From: INS Central Office
File: CO 1588

Pursuant to the order in the case of Jose Rosario Romero-Romero, et al, decided November 4, 1987, by U.S. District Judge Robert C. Broomfield, in Phoenix, AZ, the following procedures shall be immediately implemented by Legalization Offices in the states of Arizona and Nevada.

These procedures only apply to LOs in Arizona and Nevada:

All I-700 (SAW) applications are to be reviewed prior to being receipted in. If the necessary supporting documentation to establish eligibility for SAW status does not accompany the application you are to ask the alien if he or she was apprehended since the enactment of IRCA (November 6, 1986) and if he or she entered the U.S. before June 26, 1987. If the alien replies in the affirmative to these two questions, the fee and the I-700 application will be taken and an A90 million file shall be created.

In these cases where the supporting documentation is not submitted with the I-700 and the alien answers the questions in the affirmative, the LO shall prepare Form I-72 and on it indicate what supporting documentation is lacking for the application. The Form I-72 shall indicate that these supporting documents must be submitted within 30 days or else the I-700 application will be denied for lack of prosecution.

The alien will be given the fee receipt with the following notation "I-700 application submitted at (LO code) on (Date filed at LO). Employment authorized for 30 days valid until (30 days from date of filing I-700)." The LO will retain the A-file along with the I-700 and any supporting documentation. The I-700 application will be held by the LO for 30 days.

When the alien returns to the LO within the thirty-day period, he or she will be granted employment and travel authorization on Form I-688A after an interview has been conducted in connection with a nonfrivolous application.

In cases where the alien does not return to the LO within 30 days with the requested documentation, the I-700 will be denied by the LO for lack of prosecution. The I-700 application and denial will then be forwarded to the RPF through the DPC.

This procedure only applies to LOs in the states of Arizona and Nevada.

App-125

11-20-87

To: All INS Field Offices
From: INS CO
Date: November 20, 1987

This wire corrects and replaces COLEG wire CO 1588 dated 11/02/87 regarding travel documentation for Legalization applicants. Please destroy the previous wire.

It has been recently brought to the COLEG's attention that not all ports of entry are complying with CO 235-C dated June 15, 1987 regarding the reentry processing of section 245A Legalization applicants. Upon application for admission into the U.S., all section 245A Legalization applicants must be in possession of advance parole form I-512. The inspecting officer must place the parole stamp on the I-512 paroling the applicant "until completion of 245A proceedings." The I-512 should then be mailed to the appropriate Regional Processing Facility (RPF) where the A-files are housed. As the Legalization Offices do not retain A-files, no I-512 should be mailed to any Legalization Office.

Note that this procedure does not apply to section 210 SAW applicants who may use the I-688A Employment Authorization card as a travel document and are not required to obtain advance parole. Inspectors encountering form I-688A must therefore look at section of law printed on form I-688A-if it states "210", it pertains to a SAW and travel is permitted; if it states "245A", it pertains to a Legalization applicant who must be in possession of Form I-512.

11-20-87

To: All INS Field Offices
From: INS Co
Date: November 20, 1987

Effective immediately, an Order to Show Cause against an alien, who has applied for Legalization or SAW status and whose prosecution for fraud has been declined by the U.S. Attorney in lieu of deportation, is to be held in abeyance and not served or filed pending further instructions from CO.

FROM: Office of Examinations
DATE: November 23, 1987
TO: Regional Commissioners: Eastern
Southern
Northern
Western

SUBJECT: Public charge issues under the legalization provisions of the Immigration Reform and Control Act of 1986 (IRCA): Receipt of Supplement Security Income (SSI)

REFERENCE: CO 1588-P, dated September 23, 1987- Guidelines for determining public charge issues under the legalization provisions of the Immigration Reform and Control Act of 1986 (IRCA).

The purpose of this memorandum is to further clarify the definition of "public cash assistance" under 8 CFR 245a.1(i) relative to the receipt of Supplemental Security Income (SSI).

SSI is a Federal program of financial assistance for persons who meet certain financial eligibility requirements and are aged, blind or disabled. The amount of an SSI award is not conditioned upon the size of the SSI recipient's family.

For purposes of evaluating proof of financial responsibility under 8 CFR 245a.2(d)(4), SSI should be considered as public cash assistance only with regard to the person who receives it. SSI should not be attributed as public cash assistance to the immediate family members who reside with the recipient, but who themselves are non recipients.

RICHARD E. NORTON
Associate Commissioner

12-1-87

FROM: Office of Legalization (COLEG)
DATE: December 1, 1987
TO: William King, Jr.
Director for Reform Western Region
SUBJECT: Legalization Eligibility County Dependent Children

This office recently requested an opinion from the office of the General Counsel (COGOU) as to whether foster children who are legalization applicants are subject to section 212(a)(15) of the Immigration and Nationality Act.

In a response dated November 10, 1987, the General Counsel concludes that federal foster care payments made pursuant to Title IV, Part E of the Social Security Act constitute "public cash assistance" for purposes of the special rule for determining public charge.

However, despite this finding that payments to, or on behalf of foster care children, constitute public cash assistance, receipt of such payments should not be the sole determinant of "public charge". Rather, the totality of the child's circumstances, including affidavits of support from the foster parents should be examined and considered. A flexible approach should, therefore, be taken in reviewing public charge issues with respect to minor children.

A copy of the General Counsel's opinion is enclosed for your information and use.

William S. Slattery
Assistant Commissioner
Legalization

Enclosure

12-3-87
LEGALIZATION WIRE #50

DATE: December 3, 1987
TO: CO 1588
ALL ROCOMS
SUBJECT: LEGALIZATION WIRE #50
Legalization and Special Agricultural Worker (SAW) Fraud

More than 1,000,000 applications have been submitted in the first six months of the legalization and SAW programs. In most aspects the programs are well coordinated and operating efficiently. However, an area that continues to be of concern is that of fraudulent applications.

Congress' concerns over fraud in the application process is clearly demonstrated in the statute. The amount of fraud being uncovered servicewide dictates that all regions must have in place a program that identifies, tracks, refers, and follows up on fraud and suspect fraud applications. We must make it perfectly clear to the public and fraud perpetrators that we mean business and that we have the ability to and are in fact detecting fraud and prosecuting fraud perpetrators.

The Eastern and Western regions have submitted detailed documents concerning the status and operational procedures of the Document Analysis Unit (DAU) and the fraud enforcement program that is in place within their regions. Regional Commissioners for the Northern and Southern Regions are requested to furnish this office with a similar document that outlines the status and operational procedures of the DAU and the regional fraud enforcement program. All regions are requested to provide this office with a summary update identifying areas of particular concern as well as regional accomplishments with respect to the detection of fraud, I.E., the number of cases that have been: denied because of fraud or suspect fraud, referred for investigations at district offices, the number of indictments, prosecutions, etc. All requested information should be submitted to this office no later than December 28, 1987.

CODEP

cc: INS, COLEG, FGHeinauer, dsc, 11/23/87: DROCOM18
CODEP COCCO COEXM COENE COPDI
CODOP COINS SAW

12-3-87
LEGALIZATION WIRE #50

12-23-87
LEGALIZATION WIRE #51

[Facsimile Copy - Retyped from Original]

FROM: Central INS Legalization Office
DATE: December 23, 1987
TO: ROCOMS, ROLEGS, DDS (including foreign), OICS, RPFS, ODIF
RE: Legalization Wire #51
ACTION: Routine Provisional Implementation of amendment to Section 210(d) of the INA

On December 22, 1987, the President signed into law a bill containing an amendment to the provisions of Section 210 of the INA which governs the Special Agricultural Worker (SAW) Program.

The following provisions were added to Section 210(d):

(1) A credible SAW applicant may be admitted into the United States and issued employment authorization at a designated port of entry upon presentation of an I-700 SAW application without the normally required evidence of the performance of qualifying employment. (The ports of Calexico, Otay Mesa, and Laredo have been designated to receive such applicants.);

(2) An alien who does not enter through a port of entry or is otherwise amenable to deportation is subject to deportation and removal;

(3) Any alien who has filed a "nonfrivolous application" as that term is defined by the service is entitled to a stay of deportation and work authorization until a final determination has been made on the application.

Elimination of the June 26, 1987, cutoff date.

This amendment effectively eliminates the June 26, 1987 cut-off date by which an alien must have been present in the United States to be eligible to file a SAW application in the United States. Therefore, effective immediately and until December 1, 1988, any alien may submit a complete application to a Legalization office notwithstanding the alien's last date of entry was subsequent to June 26, 1987.

Preliminary applicant admission standard at designated ports.

Effective immediately and until December 1, 1988, a SAW applicant may be admitted to the United States at a designated port for 90 days with authorization to accept employment if he or she:

(1) Presents proof of identity in the form of a valid passport, a "cartilla" (Mexican military service registration booklet), a Form 13 ("Forma Trece"-- Mexican lieu passport identity document), or a certified copy of a birth certificate accompanied by additional evidence of identity bearing a photograph and/or fingerprint of the applicant.

(2) Presents a fully completed and signed Form I-700, application with fee and photographs. The application must contain specific information concerning the performance of qualifying employment in the United States and identify the documentary evidence the applicant intends to submit to a Legalization office within 90 days as proof of such employment.

(3) Is otherwise admissible to the United States under the provisions of Section 210.3(e). Applicants who are excludable from the United States under a ground of exclusion which may be waived in accordance with the provisions of 8 CFR 210.3(e)(2) shall not be deemed to meet the preliminary admission standard unless they submit an application for waiver of grounds of excludability on Form I-690 and such application is approved at the port of entry. Examining officers will determine at the interview whether a physical examination is needed to determine whether an applicant is excludable on medical grounds.

(4) Establishes to the satisfaction of the examining officer during an interview that his or her claim to eligibility for Special Agricultural Worker status is credible.

An applicant who does not satisfy these requirements shall be refused admission to the United States.

12-30-87

TO: All INS Field Offices
FROM: Richard E. Norton, INS Associate Commissioner for Examinations
DATE: December 30, 1987

On December 23, 1987, the Department of State Authorization Bill, public law 100-204, was signed into law. Section 901 of that bill, also known as the Moynihan-Frank Amendment, affects the exclusion provisions of Sections 212 (a)(27), (28), and (29) of the Immigration and Nationality Act to the extent that no alien may be denied a visa or excluded from the United States based on any beliefs, statements, or associations which would be constitutionally protected if engaged in by a United States citizen. Under the express provisions of the amendment, terrorists, Nazi war criminals, and certain other categories of aliens remain excludable. The amendment becomes effective on January 1, 1988, and is to be implemented on that date.

Aliens listed as excludable under section 212(a)(27), (28), or (29) of the Act or aliens who Inspectors have reason to believe are excludable under those grounds should be examined, and relating record material reviewed, to determine if the alien remains excludable under the terms of the Moynihan-Frank Amendment. More detailed interpretation of the amendment, instructions for implementation, and specific case guidance will be provided as they are developed.

1-13-88
LEGALIZATION WIRE #48

[Facsimile Copy - Retyped from Original]

FROM: Immigration and Naturalization Service
          Central Office
DATE: January 13, 1988
FILE: CO 1588
TO: All Field Offices
SUBJECT: SAW Applicants Who Worked Non-Qualifying
          Crops.

District Directors are granted discretionary authority to deny an I-700 application at a Legalization Office when the applicant is clearly ineligible for SAW status.

I-700 applicants who have worked in crops other than those included in USDA Regulations 7 CFR Part 1d which are not considered to be fruits, vegetables or other perishable commodities are clearly ineligible for SAW status. Such applicants should be so advised before the fee is taken. If in spite of this advisement, they wish to file they may do so. District directors have the discretion to deny such applications at the Legalization Office, or forward it to the RPF with a recommendation for denial. District directors are encouraged to deny such applications locally, notwithstanding whether inclusion of a particular crop in the USDA regulations is at issue in litigation.

In cases where a final denial is issued at a Legalization office, the applicant shall not be granted employment authorization. The applicant shall be given written notice of the denial on Form I-692, advised of the right to appeal, and provided with Form I-694, notice of appeal.

1-13-88
LEGALIZATION WIRE #48

App-133

LEGALIZATION WIRE #53
1-19-88

TO: ALL FIELD OFFICES
FROM: INS CENTRAL OFFICE
DATE: JANUARY 19, 1988
SUBJECT: Post-Admission procedures for "Preliminary Applicants" under the SAW program.

Legalization Wire #51 addressed in part the admission procedures to be followed at the designated ports of entry for "preliminary applicants." This wire concerns itself with post admission procedures for "preliminary applicants under the SAW program.

1. On a daily basis designated POEs will mail the A-files to the DPC for temporary storage. The DPC will supply the POE with special mailing boxes and labels.

2. Upon receipt of a preliminary applicant's complete I-700 application, the LO will remove the barcode with backing stapled to the original I-700 and place it on an empty workfolder jacket. The original I-700, supporting documentation, and the alien's departure I-94 should be placed in the workfolder to the DPC to be matched with the original A-file and forwarded to the RPF.

It is to be expected that preliminary applicants may not accurately remember the facts of their qualifying employment and that some of the information on the supporting documentation may be different from that originally shown on the I-700 application (names of growers and foremen, date of employment, etc.). The interviewing officer will therefore need to amend the I-700 application accordingly, as the applicants were instructed at the port of entry not to make any subsequent changes on the application. The officer should initial each change and indicate the blocks changed on the worksheet. However, if the interviewing officer at the LO suspects that the applicant has altered the original I-700 application subsequent to admission, the officer should annotate the worksheet requesting that the RPF compare the original I-700 with the copy housed in the A-file. If major discrepancies are encountered, the RPF should deny the applicant or require a second interviewer at the LO.

3. During the adjudications process, the RPF examiner should compare as often as possible the original I-700 with the copy made at the port to detect potential fraud.

4. Upon completion of the adjudication process, the RPF will remove the applicant's departure I-94 from the A-file, write "adjusted" or "denied" on the reverse of the I-94 in the departure information portion and forward it to ACS/NIIS.

5. At the end of the application period, the DPC will forward the remaining A-file to the approivate RPF for their preparation and forwarding of a notice of denial for lack of prosecution to the applicant.

LEGALIZATION WIRE #53
1-19-88

LEGALIZATION WIRE #54

[Facsimile Copy - Retyped from Original]

FROM: Immigration and Naturalization Service
Commissioner Alan C. Nelson
DATE: January 21, 1988
FILE: CO 1588
TO: All INS Field Offices
SUBJECT: Fraud Prosecution in Legalization and SAW cases.

1. The implementing regulations to Section 245A and Section 210 of the INA provide that an alien may be criminally prosecuted if the alien commits fraud in the application process. The regulations also provide that if the U.S. Attorney declines prosecution in lieu of deportation, INS may place the alien in deportation proceedings. See 8 CFR 210.2(E)(4) and 8 CFR 245A.2(T)(4).

2. Effective immediately you are directed not to issue an Order to Show Cause in cases where prosecution for fraud has been declined by the U.S. Attorney, if the basis for the OSC is the fraud in the application. Any information obtained through the application or the investigation of the information in the application cannot be used as the basis for an OSC.

3. The confidentiality provision does not apply to information that INS has obtained independent of the application process. Deportation proceedings may be commenced based on that information.

4. Any OSCs that have been issued against an alien who committed fraud in the application process are to be terminated as improvidently begun if the issuance of the OSC was based on information obtained in the application process.

5. The use of information obtained from the application process in connection with deportation proceedings would subject INS officials to criminal penalties.

6. Field officers should seek the assistance of the INS District Counsel in presenting cases to the U.S. Attorney for prosecution. In the event a U.S. Attorney consistently fails to prosecute Legalization and SAW fraud cases, you are to contact the Regional Counsel who will take whatever measures are appropriate.

1-21-88
LEGALIZATION WIRE #54

1-22-88
LEGALIZATION WIRE #52

To: INS Field Offices
From: INS CO
Date: January 22, 1988
SUBJECT: Procedures relating to apprehension of SAW-eligible aliens pursuant to amendment to Section 210(d) of the INA.

On December 22, 1987, the President signed into law a bill containing an amendment to the provision of Section 210 of the INA which governs the Special Agricultural Worker (SAW) Program.

1. The following provisions were added to section 210(d):

   A) A credible SAW applicant may be admitted into the United States and issued Employment Authorization at a designated port of entry upon presentation of an I-700 SAW application without the normally required evidence of the performance of qualifying employment. The ports of Calexico, Otay Mesa and Laredo have been designated to receive such applicants; B) An alien who does not enter through a port of entry is subject to deportation and removal; and C) Any alien who has filed a "nonfrivolous application" as that term is defined at 8 CFR 210.1(j) is entitled to a stay of deportation and work authorization until final determination has been made on the application.

2. This amendment effectively eliminates the June 26, 1987, cut-off date by which an alien must have been present in the United States. Therefore, any alien amenable to deportation regardless of date of entry is subject to deportation and removal unless such alien has filed a nonfrivolous application.

3. It is expected that during the course of normal operations SAW-eligible aliens will be encountered who have not yet filed an application. Officers should take into consideration an alien's credible claim to SAW eligibility and/or the fact that an alien may have already initiated the SAW application process by visiting a Legalization Office or QDE when making a custodial determination with respect to an apprehended alien.

4. Officers shall take into consideration the location of apprehension in determining the likelihood of an alien to abscond. An alien who has entered without inspection shortly before apprehension is less likely

1-22-88
LEGALIZATION WIRE #52

to possess equities within the United States and may be considered more likely to abscond. Such alien, even if he asserts a credible claim to SAW eligibility, may like any other alien in the United States illegally, be offered voluntary return or issued an Order to Show Cause. SAW-eligible aliens apprehended along the border shall be informed of their potential eligibility for the SAW program and of the opportunity to obtain legal entry through a designated port of entry.

5. An alien who is considered unlikely to abscond, and has a credible claim to SAW eligibility, shall be released from custody and afforded an opportunity to file a nonfrivolous SAW application at a legalization office. The Procedures for release of a SAW-eligible alien set forth in Legalization Wire #14 shall be followed.

LEGALIZATION WIRE #58

TO: ALL ROCOMS
       ALL ROLEGS
       ALL DDS INCLUDING FOREIGN
       ALL OICS INCLUDING FOREIGN
       ALL CPAS
       ALL RPFS
       ODFF, GLYNCO
FROM: CODEP (COLEG)
DATE: FEBRUARY 24, 1988
       LEGALIZATION WIRE NO. 58

SUBJECT: SUMMARY JUDGEMENT FROM THE COURT THAT COTTON
           IS A FRUIT

On February 8, 1988, the United States District Court for the Northern District of Texas entered a Summary Judgement in the case of National Cotton Council of America v. Richard E. Lyng, Secretary of Agriculture.

It was the determination of the Court that "cotton is a fruit and thus within that ambit of the term 'fruits and vegetables of every kind' as used in a 8 USC Section 1160(h) and also within the ambit of the Defendant's regulatory definition of the term "fruits" as used in said statute, codified at 7 CFR Part]d.5".

The Department of Agriculture and the Solicitor General are considering whether to appeal this decision. Therefore, effective immediately and until further notice, a SAW application claiming field work in cotton as qualifying agricultural employment shall be considered a nonfrivolous application if otherwise acceptable. Applications involving qualifying agricultural employment in cotton are to be recommended for approval by the legalization office (LO) and the applicant is to be issued Form I-688A.

Regional Processing Facilities (RPFs) are to hold such cases in abeyance until further notice. Cases involving employment in cotton which have been denied by the LO or the RPF should be reopened on Service Motion and held in abeyance. Applicants in such cases shall be notified that their applications have been reopened and that they are eligible for the issuance/extension of their I-688A.

CODEP (COLEG)

Legalization Wire #55

Date: February 17, 1988
Legalization Wire: No. 55
From: INS Central Office
To: All Service Field Offices
File: CO 1588
Subject: Stateside verification of overseas Special Agricultural Worker (SAW) applications.

1. Effective immediately, with the exception of OPOS in Mexico, all SAW applications submitted at OPOS will be referred to INS prior to issuance of the SAW entry packet.

2. After receipt of a complete application, and an initial interview, the OPO will forward the original I-700 application and all supporting documentation to the Director of the Regional Processing Facility (RPF) that has jurisdiction over the area where most of the alleged employment occurred.

3. Upon receipt, RPF directors shall: examine the application and supporting documentation for veracity, compare the application package against fraud profiles and other intelligence information, and shall attempt to verify the alleged employment.

4. In cases where the RPF director believes an investigation is warranted, the case shall be forwarded to the appropriate district office. These cases shall be expeditiously investigated by field offices.

5. Upon conclusion of the investigation or upon verification or failure to verify the employment, the application, supporting documentation, and a brief memorandum that addresses the verification results or investigative report shall be sent back to the OPO for completion of the interview and a determination to deny or recommend approval of the application.

To: ALL ROCOMS, ALL ROLEGS, ALL DDS INCLUDING FOREIGN, ALL OICS INCLUDING FOREIGN, ALL OPAS, ALL RPFS, ODTF, GLYNCO
From: Jerry Heinauer
Date: February 24, 1988
Re: SUMMARY JUDGEMENT FROM THE COURT THAT COTTON IS A FRUIT

On February 8, 1988, the United States District Court for the Northern District of Texas entered a summary judgement in the case of National Cotton Council of America v. Richard E. Lyng, Secretary of Agriculture.

It was the determination of the court that "cotton is a fruit and thus within the ambit of the term 'fruits and vegetables of every kind' as used in 8 USC Section 1160(h) and also within the ambit of the defendant's regulatory definition of the term "fruits" as used in said statute, codified at 7 CFR Part 1d.5."

The Department of Agriculture and the Solicitor General are considering whether to appeal this decision. Therefore, effective immediately and until further notice, a SAW application claiming field work in cotton as qualifying agricultural employment shall be considered a nonfrivolous application if otherwise acceptable. Applications involving qualifying agricultural employment in cotton are to be recommended for approval by the Legalization Office (LO) and the applicant is to be issued Form I-688A.

Regional Processing Facilities (RPFs) are to hold such cases in abeyance until further notice. Cases involving employment in cotton which have been denied by the LO or the RPF should be reopened on service motion and held in abeyance. Applicants in such cases shall be notified that their applications have been reopened and that they are eligible for the issuance/extension of their I-688A.

Date: March 2, 1988
From: James A. Puleo, INS Assistant Commissioner for Examinations
To: All INS field offices

This is to restate the service's position regarding statutory ineligibility for admission because of HIV infection and waivers of those statutory provisions. This basis position was first stated in a Central Office telegram of July 6, 1987 regarding the Public Health Service's final rule of June 8, 1987 adding AIDS to the list of dangerous contagious diseases.

There is no statutory authority to accept an application for waiver of 212(a)(6) because of HIV infection in immigrant and fiance(e) visa cases. Although there is statutory authority to waive §212(a)(6) in refugee, legalization, and nonimmigrant cases, the discretionary authority of the Attorney General will not be used unless the applicant can establish that (1) the danger to the public health of the United States created by the alien's admission to the U.S. is minimal, (2) the possibility of the spread of the infection created by the alien's admission to the U.S. is minimal, and (3) there will be no cost incurred by any level of government agency of the U.S. without prior consent of that agency. All written decisions on waiver applications regarding HIV infection will be certified to the Deputy Commissioner, Attn: Associate Commissioner, Examinations, in accordance with 8 CFR §103.4. All decisions with regard to nonimmigrant visa waivers under 212(d)(3) of the Act will be made after consultation with the Office of the Associate Commissioner Examinations (Attn: COINS).

3-7-88

Date: March 7, 1988
From: INS Central Office
To: All INS Regional Commissioners and Regional Processing Facilities
File: CO 1588-C
RE: COPIES OF DENIALS TO Q.D.E.s

Effective immediately copies of denial notices shall be sent to Q.D.E.s when the A.D.E. number appears on the application. This includes denials issued at legalization offices.

Date: March 23, 1988
From: Office of Examinations
To: Regional Commissioners
Subject: Eligibility of Foster Children for Legalization Benefits
ATTENTION: Regional Legalization Officers

On November 10, 1987, the Service issued a policy memorandum addressing the eligibility of foster children for legalization benefits. Since issuance of the guidance, the Service has received numerous inquiries concerning the equity of the policy.

The Service has reviewed the entire foster care issue including current Service policy, legal precedents relating t public charge issues, and the concerns raised by the public. After a complete review it has been determined that a modification of the November 10, 1987 policy is in the best interest of all parties involved.

The Office of General Counsel has readdressed this issue in a legal opinion issued on March 23, 1988 (Copy attached). In summary, the legal opinion states that due to the fact that no monetary payment is made to the child or the child's family in a foster care environment and that the benefit received by the child from the program is a result of judicial order, the services received should be considered in-kind-assistance. This type of income or means-based assistance does not come within the purview of IRCA's definition of public cash assistance.

Although children in foster care programs will not be considered to have received public cash assistance, the absence of support from relatives or friends renders them excludable under section 212(a)(15) of the Act. In order to overcome this exclusion ground, foster children should be considered under the special rule for determination of the public charge provisions.

Under the special rule for determination of public charge, presumption of the likelihood to become a public charge may be overcome if the applicant can demonstrate a history of employment without receipt of public cash assistance. A child who has not had yet reached an "employable age", cannot be reasonably expected to meet this burden. Therefore, a child who is in a foster care program and otherwise eligible for legalization, will be considered to have met the special rule for public charge for purposes of excludability under section 212(a)(916) of the Act, if

documentary evidence of the judicial order placing the child in the foster care program or some evidence of the state's responsibility to provide foster care to the child is presented as part of the legalization application.

This policy modification is effective immediately and all field legalization operations should be notified of this change as soon as possible.

RICHARD E. NORTON
Associate Commissioner

Attachment

3-24-88
Internal Revenue Service

PRESS RELEASE

Washington -- The Internal Revenue Service today advised illegal aliens who have not applied or will not be qualified for Amnesty to write "SSA 205(c)" in the spaces for Social Security numbers for themselves, their spouses and dependents on their federal income tax returns. This statement will allow these taxpayers' returns to be processed at IRS service centers. The procedure is for IRS processing purposes only and does not give any legal residence status or other rights to these taxpayers, IRS said.

The same advice applies to illegal alien dependents of Amnesty applicants, but the IRS urged all Amnesty applicants who have obtained Social Security numbers to use those numbers on their tax returns.

Social Security law Section 205(c) does not allow the Social Security Administration to assign numbers to illegal aliens unless they have applied for Amnesty and have obtained permission to work from Immigration Service. Illegal aliens who do not qualify for Amnesty are expected to pay federal tax on their earnings in the United States, regardless of their legal status in this country, just as all other aliens pay tax on their U.S. income, the IRS said.

The IRS emphasized that no information from any taxpayer's federal income tax return can be shared with other persons or government agencies without the taxpayer's consent.

3-24-88
Internal Revenue Service

Date: April 11, 1988
From: Richard E. Norton, INS Associate Commissioner for Examinations
To: All INS Field Offices
File: CO 1588-P
RE: LEGALIZATION APPLICATIONS INVOLVING "KNOWN TO THE GOVERNMENT"

This references the April 1, 1988 wire pertaining to the "known to the government" issue and the case of Ayuda, Inc. v. Meese No. 88-0625SS (March 30, 1988).

On April 7, 1988, Judge Stanley Sporkin of the U.S. District Court for the District of Columbia issued a summary judgement in favor of the plaintiffs. The entire court order is being transmitted under separate cover.

A determination whether to appeal the decision is under consideration.

The following steps must be taken immediately by District Directors:

1. Accept and adjudicate all "known to the government" applications, following the court's standard. The court has ordered that a nonimmigrant alien must establish that prior to January 1, 1982, documentation existed in one or more government agencies so that when such documentation is taken as a whole it would warrant the finding (i.e., shows) that the nonimmigrant alien's status in the United States was unlawful. Said documentation must be in the files of the government prior to January 1, 1982, or such other time as may be permitted by INS regulations. The burden is on the nonimmigrant alien to meet his standard;

2. Until further notice, permit such applications to be filed without fee. The fee will be deferred for collection at a later date, depending on the outcome of the appeal;

3. Encourage all individuals who may believe they are eligible under the Court's order to apply by May 4, 1988;

4. Allow applicants to participate in "simplified filing" program;

5. Check #5 in Block B (Verification Requested) of the Examiner's Worksheet in all cases affected by this court order;

6. Issue all applicants an Employment Authorization card (I-688A) unless the application is clearly fraudulent; and

7. Forward all such cases through normal channels to the Regional Processing Facilities (RPFs). RPF Directors should hold final decisions in abeyance until further guidance is provided by Central Office.

Further information concerning this lawsuit will be disseminated as it comes available.

App-144

Date: April 11, 1988
From: Office of Examinations (COEXM)
To: Regional Commissioners, Regional Legalization
Officers
All District Directors, Administrative
Appeals Unit
Subject: Denial and Appeal Procedures in the Legalization
Process
ATTENTION: Legalization Appeals Unit

After discussions concerning the denial and appeal procedures between Central Office and several groups, (including the American Immigration Lawyers Association, the American Bar Association, the AFL-CIO, and several NCAs), new procedures were developed to better assist the field offices and the Regional Processing Facility in the processing of applications, denials, and appeals.

NOTICE ON I-72-TYPE NOTICE WHEN ADVERSE INFORMATION ENCOUNTERED

Section 103.2(b)(2) of the regulations states that if a decision will be adverse to an applicant on the basis of derogatory evidence considered by the Service and of which the applicant is unaware, he or she shall be advised thereof and offered an opportunity to rebut it and present evidence in his or her behalf before the decision is rendered, except that classified evidence shall not be made available to him or her.

It was brought to the Service's attention that in some instances denials were being issued without first making adverse information available to the applicant and allowing the applicant an opportunity to rebut the evidence.

Effective immediately, an I-72-type notice should be sent to an alien and to his or her legal representative if a case is being denied based upon adverse information not previously furnished to the Service by the alien. The notice should include a statement referencing the derogatory information obtained and included in the Record of Proceeding (ROP). The alien should also be offered thirty (30) days within which to rebut the derogatory information and to present evidence in his or her behalf before the final denial decision is rendered.

In the case of a denial which was previously issued based upon a finding of derogatory information without a previous I-72-type notice or review of derogatory information provided to an alien, the alien and his or her legal representative shall be allowed to file a motion to reopen in order to review the information.

REVIEW OF RECORD OF PROCEEDING

It has been determined that the original thirty (30) days within which to file an appeal is often not sufficient time to request and obtain a review of the record of proceedings.

If a review of the ROP is requested by the alien or his or her legal representative and an appeal has been properly filed, an additional thirty (30) days, shall be submitted directly to the Legalization Appeals Unit, Washington, D.C.

NOTICES OF DENIAL

Contrary to section 103.3(a) of the regulations, specific reasons for denial have not been included in some denial notices issued to date. Denial notices should contain clear and precise information concerning the appeal process available to the applicant. All denials should also clearly and specifically state the reason for denial. Those denials that already have been issued with material flaws or omissions will not be reissued.

Attached are examples of correct and incorrect denial format.

SERVICE OF DENIAL AND APPEAL PERIOD

An inconsistency in policy appears to exist between regions as to when the 30 days begins to toll for the filing of an appeal.

Notices of denial are to be sent by regular mail. In accordance with Section 103.5a(b), if service is presented by regular mail, the 30-day time period for submitting an appeal begins three days after the notice of denial is mailed.

REQUESTS FOR ADDITIONAL INFORMATION

Due to the fact that Qualified Designated Entities (QDEs) are an integral part in the successful completion of many applicant's documentations, QDEs shall be notified of all requests for applicants' additional documentation if a QDE participated in the original filing.

If a waiver or additional information is requested and a Qualified Designated Entity (QDE) assisted in the completion of the original application, in addition to the copy of

4-11-88

request mailed to the applicant, one copy of the request should also be mailed to the QDE.

MAILING OF NOTICES OF DENIAL

Again, because of the necessity to work closely with applicants who submitted applications through a QDE, the Service will provide QDEs with copies of denial notices in instances where a case has been filed through a QDE representative.

Any questions in reference to this memorandum may be directed to Mr. Terrance M. O'Reilly, Deputy Assistant Commissioner, Legalization, FTS 633-5309.

RICHARD E. NORTON
Associate Commissioner

4-11-88

Date: April 21, 1988
From: Office of Examinations
To: Regional Commissioners
Subject: THE EFFECT OF THE RECEIPT OF AFDC BENEFITS ON ELIGIBILITY FOR LEGALIZATION

The Service has received a number of inquiries regarding the effect that receipt of AFDC benefits by a legalization applicant or a member of the applicant's immediate family has on eligibility for legalization. The purpose of this memorandum is to reiterate the policy with regard to this issue and its relationship to the public charge determination.

As a general rule, the receipt of AFDC benefits by a member of the legalization applicant's family is not attributed to the applicant for purposes of determining the likelihood that the applicant will become a public charge. For example, if a family of three applied for AFDC and the parents were both ineligible aliens, the benefit would still be granted to the United States citizen child and the situation would not be considered to have received public cash assistance for purposes of the determination of likelihood to become a public charge. If, however, the family is reliant on the AFDC benefits as its sole means of support, the legalization applicant may be considered to have received public cash assistance. This determination must be made on a case-by-case basis and upon consideration of the totality of the applicant's circumstances.

I. Public Charge Determination

Section 245A(d)(2)(B)(ii)(II) of the Immigration and Nationality Act, as amended (INA), relating to aliens likely to become a public charge, may not be waived insofar as it relates to an application for adjustment to permanent residence by a lawful temporary resident. Section 212(a)(15) of the Immigration and Nationality Act provides for the exclusion of aliens "who, in the opinion of the consular officer at the time of application for a visa, or in the opinion of the Attorney General at the time of application for admission, are likely to become public charges". It is well settled that an applicant for adjustment of status is in the same posture as though he were an applicant before an American consular officer abroad seeking issuance of an immigrant visa.

State Department regulations regarding the public charge determination provide, in pertinent part, as follows:

(iii) An alien relying solely on the personal income he will be receiving to establish eligibility under section 212(a)(15) of the Act who does not establish that he will have an income above the income poverty guidelines published annually (or any shorter interval deemed feasible and desirable) by the Office of the Assistant Secretary for Planning and Evaluation, Department of Health and Human Services, and who is without other adequate financial resources, shall be presumed ineligible under that section of the Act.

22 C.F.R. §42.91(a)(15)(iii). The Foreign Affairs Manual (FAM) provides guidance regarding the family-size to be considered in the determination of public charge as follows:

3.5 An alien who is relying solely on personal income family members after admission should be presumed ineligible for an immigrant visa under section 212(a)(15) unless his prospective income, including that to be derived from an offer of prearranged employment, will equal or exceed the income poverty guideline level for his family-size as shown in the most recent income poverty guideline table published by the Community Services Administration (exhibit I to this section). When considering the applicant's family-size as shown in the most recent income poverty guideline table published by the Community Services Administration (exhibit I to this section). When considering the applicant's family-size for purposes of evaluating his prospective income in light of the income poverty guideline levels, prime consideration should be given to the circumstances which indicates that the applicant will probably become a charge upon the public after entry into the United States. Normally all accompanying dependent family members and all dependent family members already in the United States should be deemed to be within the family for purposes of applying the income poverty guidelines. However, unique circumstances might justify a finding of eligibility in some cases in which the applicant does not have a prospective income equal to that shown in the applicable table. For example, an applicant seeking an immigrant wife and two citizen children already in the United States and already receiving permanent resident wife and two citizen children public assistance may be determined eligible receiving the

App-147

public charge provisions even though his prospective income will be below that of four. In such a situation there would be no question about issuance of a visa to an alien likely to become a public charge provided the alien father established that his prospective income in the United States will exceed that shown on the income poverty guideline table for an individual and in all probability the public assistance benefits to his family will diminish after he has joined the family.

FAM, Part III, Vol. 9, note 3.5 to 22 C.F.R. 42.919a)(15).

The FAM also discusses the factors pertinent to the determination as follows:

In evaluating evidence of support in immigrant cases the consular officer should be flexible in his requirements, predicating his decision on facts relating to the applicant's age, physical condition, vocation, and existing conditions in the United States coupled with their probable effect on the applicant's likelihood of becoming a public charge after admission into the United States...The consular officer's assessment of the likelihood of the alien's becoming a public charge 'at any time' should always be based upon a reasonable projection of present circumstances rather than upon possible consequences which are contingent upon speculative eventualities. (Amended)

FAM, Part III, Vol. 9, note 1 to 22 C.F.R. 42.91(a)(15). The foregoing factors have been applied by the Service, the BIA, and the Attorney General in various contexts involving excludability under Section 2129a)(15). See Matter of Vindman, 16 I&N Dec. 131 (R.C. 1977), (aged SSI recipients found ineligible); Matter of Perez, 15 I&N Dec. 136 (1974), (28 year old welfare recipient, in Matter of Harutunian, 14 I&N Dec. 583 (R.C. 1974), (70 year old welfare recipient with no other means of support ineligible); Matter of Martinez-Lopez, 10 I&N Dec. 409, 421-423 (A.G. 1964), (promise of employment not required).

II. Special Rule

Even if an applicant would be inadmissible as likely to become a public charge under the foregoing analysis, he may be admissible under the terms of the "special rule". Section 245A(d)(2)(B)(iii) of IRCA provides the following special rule for the determination of public charge:

Special Rule for Determination of Public Charge. -An alien is not ineligible for adjustment of status under this section due to being inadmissible under section 212(a)(15) if the alien demonstrates a history of employment in the United States evidencing self-support without receipt of public cash assistance.

(Emphasis added). The regulations define "public cash assistance" as follows:

"public cash assistance" means income or means-based monetary assistance, to include but not limited to supplemental security income, received by the alien or his or her immediate family members through federal, state, or local programs designed to meet subsistence levels. It does not include assistance in kind, such as food stamps, public housing, or other non-cash benefits, nor does it include work-related compensation or certain types of medical assistance (Medicare, Medicaid, emergency treatment, services to pregnant women or children under 18 years of age, or treatment in the interest of public health).

8 C.F.R. §245a.1(i).

In summary, the special rule requires: 1) establishment of a history of employment evidencing self support; and 2) no receipt of public cash assistance. Both of these requirements must be met for the special rule to apply. The requirements regarding proof of financial responsibility and history of employment are set forth at 8 C.F.R. 245a.2(d)(4).

III. Treatment of AFDC Benefits

AFDC benefits are means-based monetary assistance designed to meet subsistence levels and are thus considered "public cash assistance". However, for purposes of applying the special rule, AFDC benefits are to be attributed only to the recipient of those benefits. For example, when AFDC benefits are granted to an eligible U.S. citizen child of ineligible alien parents, only the child's need is considered in determining the amount of benefits paid and the child is considered by the administering agency to be the recipient. Normally, in that situation, receipt of AFDC

---

[1] An exception has been created to the "history of employment" requirement with respect to foster children receiving foster care benefits. See memorandum CO 1588-P, dated (?).

4-21-88

benefits to the child provide the sole means of support for a family, the other family members will be considered to have received public cash assistance. Of course in that case the applicant would not have been able to establish the first part of the special rule equation, i.e., a history of employment evidencing self support.

Because circumstances will differ in each case, it is important to remember that the public charge determination must be based on an examination of the totality of the individual applicant's circumstances on a case by case basis. Accordingly, the existence or absence of a particular factor should never be used as the sole criterion in determining the likelihood of an applicant to become a public charge.

IV. Waiver of Section 212(a)(15)

Finally, you should remember that a waiver of inadmissibility is available under Section 245A(d)(2)(B)(i) for those individuals not aided by application of the special rule. See 8 C.F.R. §245a.1(i). If there is any indication that the applicant may be inadmissible, the applicant should be advised to apply for such a waiver. The waiver applies only to the application for temporary residence and not for the subsequent application for permanent residence. You should note, however, that a temporary resident has a period of thirty-one (31) months within which to apply for permanent residence and thus, within which to render himself admissible.

Richard E. Norton
Associate Commissioner

Date: April 22, 1988
From: Office of Examinations
To: All Regional Commissioners
Subject: WHAT CONSTITUTES A CONVICTION FOR PURPOSES OF LEGALIZATION

In order to be eligible for legalization under Section 245A of the Immigration and Nationality Act (INA), an applicant must establish that he or she is admissible to the United States as an immigrant, and has not been convicted of any felony or three or more misdemeanors committed in the United States. See 245A(a)(4)(A) and (B) of the INA.

Section 245A(d)(B)(ii) lists the grounds of exclusion which may not be waived by the Attorney General for purposes of legalization. This lists includes sections 212(a)(9), (10) and (23), which preclude the admission to the United States of any alien who (1) has committed a crime involving moral turpitude; (2) has been convicted of two or more offenses for which the aggregate sentence to confinement actually imposed was five years or more; and (3) has been convicted of violating any law relating to a controlled substance; or (4) is reasonably believed to have been a trafficker in controlled substances. There is already in existence extensive case law relating to the application of these grounds of exclusions. This case law is applicable in determining whether an alien is inadmissible under one of these grounds of exclusion and therefore ineligible for legalization.

Neither the statute nor the legislative history clearly states what constitutes a conviction for purposes of determining whether an applicant has been convicted of a felony or three or more misdemeanors, thereby rendering the applicant ineligible for legalization. Neither indicates whether the interpretation of "conviction" in this context is meant to be the same as or different from the interpretation that has been developed in the context of the above exclusion grounds. Since the statute is relatively new there is no existing case law which addresses this issue, which becomes particularly unclear when a conviction has been expunged, or the adjudication of guilt has been deferred.

After careful consideration it has been determined that the existing case law that applies to determinations of what constitutes a conviction for purposes of deportation or exclusions, will be applied when determining whether an applicant has been convicted of a felony or misdemeanor for purposes of legalization eligibility.

The Board of Immigration Appeals (BIA) has recently issued a decision, In Re Ozkok, Interim Decision 3044 (BIA January 26, 1988), in which the Board addressed the question of what state action constitutes a conviction with sufficient finality for purposes of the immigration laws. This decision shall be the basis for determining whether an alien has been convicted for purposes of legalization eligibility. In order to assist the Regional Processing Facilities (RPFs) in determining whether a conviction exists for purposes of legalization the following summaries have been prepared.

EXPUNGEMENTS

Expungement of a non-drug conviction eliminates the conviction as a bar to legalization eligibility. An expungement of a drug-related conviction will not eliminate the conviction as a bar to legalization eligibility. The court ordered expungement must be final at the time the applicant is interviewed. It is sometimes difficult to determine whether a conviction has actually been expunged. Therefore, these types of cases should be referred to the RPF attorney for review. The alien must provide evidence that the conviction has been expunged. For BIA precedent regarding this issue refer to Matter of G-, 9 I&N Dec. 159 (BIA 1960; A.G. 1961), Matter of Ibarra-Obando, 12 I&N Dec. 576 (BIA 1966; A.G. 1967), Matter of Gutnick, 13 I&N Dec. 672 (BIA 1971).

DEFERRED ADJUDICATION OF GUILT

If an adjudication of guilt has been withheld, the state authority under which the court acted must be reviewed, and the test enunciated in Ozkok, supra, must be applied. The BIA has stated in Ozkok that

...a conviction will be found for immigration purposes where all of the following elements are present:

(1) a judge or jury has found the alien guilty or he has entered a plea of guilty or nolo contendere or has admitted sufficient facts to warrant a finding of guilty;

2) the judge has ordered some form of punishment, penalty, or restraint on the person's liberty to be imposes (including but not limited to incarceration, probation, a fine or restitution, or community-based sanctions such as a

App-150

rehabilitation program, a work-release or study-release program, revocation or suspension of a driver's license, deprivation of nonessential activities or privileges, or community service); and

(3) a judgement or adjudication of guilt may be entered if the person violates the terms of his probation or fails to comply with the requirements of the court's order, without further availability of further proceedings regarding the person's guilt or innocence of the original charge.

It is recommended that these cases also be reviewed by the RPF attorneys before decisions are issued.

PARDONS

If an alien has been granted a full and unconditional pardon by the President of the United States or by the Governor of any state, he or she has not been convicted for purposes of legalization eligibility. This does not, however, apply to a narcotics conviction, since section 241(b) of the INA specifically precludes narcotics convictions.

WRIT OF CORAM NOBIS

The continuing inherent power of a court to modify an order is exercised through the writ of coram nobis. The writ vacates or corrects a judgment where no other remedy exists. Where a conviction has been vacated, no conviction exists upon which to base deportability. Matter of Sirhan, 13 I&N Dec. 592 (BIA 1970).

Similarly, it has been held in Matter of O'Sullivan, 10 I&N Dec. 320 (BIA 1963; reconsidered on Service motion and affirmed, BIA 1963) that the order of a trial judge, granting a motion for a new trial, after conviction and sentence, and dismissing the case nolle prosequi, for all purposes sets aside the convictions under state law.

Since these writs vacate convictions, no conviction exists. Thus the conviction will not count for purposes of legalization eligibility.

JUDICIAL RECOMMENDATION AGAINST DEPORTATION (JRAD)

JRADs differ from expungements and pardons, which have a purpose beyond the immigration laws. Expungements and pardons affect non-immigration benefits and privileges of

4-22-88

the recipient, but JRADs do not. JRADs simply prevent the conviction from forming the basis for deportability pursuant to section 241(a)(4). There is no application of JRADs to a benefit such as legalization. Therefore, a JRAD will not nullify a conviction for purposes of legalization eligibility.

JUVENILE OFFENSES

It is well settled that an act of juvenile delinquency is not a crime in the United States and that an adjudication of delinquency is not a conviction within the meaning of the immigration laws. Matter of O'N, 2 I&N Dec. 319 (C.O. 1945; A.G. 1945); Matter of F, 2 I&N Dec. 517 (C.O. 1945; BIA 1946). Therefore, applicants for legalization are not to be found ineligible based upon juvenile offenses unless the applicant was tried as an adult. See Matter of Espinoza, 15 I&N Dec. 328 (BIA 1975).

FEDERAL FIRST OFFENDER PROVISIONS OF THE CONTROLLED SUBSTANCES ACT AND STATE COUNTERPARTS

If an applicant is convicted under the federal first offender provisions of the Controlled Substances Act, the applicant shall be considered eligible for legalization if the conviction took place before November 1, 1987. This also applies if the applicant was convicted under a state equivalent of the federal first offenders provisions. Matter of Kaneda, 16 I&N Dec. 677 (BIA 1979); Matter of Werk, 16 I&N Dec. 234 BIA 1977). The reason for the November 1, 1987 cutoff is that the federal first offender provisions of the Controlled Substance Act were repealed by the Comprehensive Crime Control Act of 1984, which became effective on November 1, 1987. The BIA in Ozkok held it is no longer appropriate to permit an exception from the conviction of offenses under the state equivalents of the federal statute subsequent to the date the statute was repealed. Therefore, any conviction under the state equivalent of the federal first offenders statute that takes place after November 1, 1987 will be considered a conviction for purposes of legalization.

FEDERAL YOUTH CORRECTIONS ACT

If an applicant was convicted before October 12, 1984 under Federal Youth Corrections Act the applicant shall be considered eligible for legalization. This also applied if the applicant was convicted under a state equivalent of Federal Youth Corrections Act. The Federal Youth Corrections Act was also repealed by the Comprehensive Crime

4-22-88

App-151

4-22-88

Control Act of 1984. Therefore, an applicant convicted under the state equivalent of the Federal Youth Corrections Act after October 12, 1984 will be considered convicted for purposes of legalization eligibility.

What constitutes a conviction for purposes of legalization is a difficult question that may require a legal analysis of the state statute under which the alien was convicted. If you have any questions or require assistance, consult the attorney or attorneys who have been assigned to the RPF.

RICHARD NORTON
Associate Commissioner
Examinations

Date: May 4, 1988
From: Richard E. Norton, INS Associate Commissioner for Examinations
To: All INS Field Offices
File: CO 1588-C

The Centers for Disease Control (CDC) recently requested that the U.S. Public Health service be informed of all SAW applicants admitted into the United States who have a class A or B medical illness.

In accordance with existing instructions, in cases where the SAW applicant has been processed at an overseas processing office and the inspector has reason to believe the applicant may be ineligible for admission to the United States, the SAW packet should be opened to obtain additional information.

This clearly includes opening the envelope when the packet contains a medical notation of a class A or B illness.

Wherever a class A or B SAW applicant is encountered, the inspector must make a copy of: (1) the OF-157, (2) the front and back of the I-690 waiver application, and (3) the I-700 application, and forward the copies to the U.S. Health Service Quarantine Division, having jurisdiction over the port of entry.

Date: May 12, 1988
From: INS Central Office
To: All Field Offices
File: CO 1588-C
Subject: SERVICE CONFISCATION OF THE TEMPORARY RESIDENT CARD (FORM I-688)

The following information is provided in response to a recent request from the field for guidance concerning confiscation of form I-688 and I-688A.

Prior to confiscation of the I-688 or I-688A and/or any other enforcement action, the service must insure that the alien has been afforded due process. Legalization and SAW procedures are separated due to the variances of those programs.

Special Agricultural Workers (SAWS)-Section 210

When a service officer at a port of entry determines that an alien is not admissible to the United States or was not eligible for issuance of form I-688, the district director should initiate exclusion proceedings, form I-688 and I-688A shall not be confiscated from a SAW granted temporary residence until an immigration judge has ordered the applicant excluded and deported from the United States. Any SAW presenting form I-688A may be given the choice of an exclusion and deportation hearing before and immigration judge or voluntarily withdrawing his application for admission to the United States. The I-688A will be lifted if the alien voluntarily withdraws for admission and form I-275 will be completed. The I-275 and I-688A will be forwarded to the appropriate RPF for action.

SAW Applicants or Temporary Residents Encountered in the Interior of the United States

Aliens who are encountered within the United States who are determined to have been ineligible for issuance of form I-688 and/or who have become deportable under Section 241 of the Act are subject to issuance of an Order to Show Cause and warrant of arrest, however, the SAW I-688 holder must be ordered deported by an Immigration Judge prior to confiscation of the I-688. See 8 CFR Part 210.4(D)91) and (2).

Legalization-Section 245A

Applicants for Admission to the United States

Applicants for admission with form I-688 issued under Section 245A will be treated the same as SAW applicants for admission, i.e., when a service officer at a port of entry determines that an alien is not admissible to the United States or was not eligible for issuance of form I-688, District Directors should initiate exclusion proceedings.

Temporary Residents in the Interior of the United States

Unlike Section 210 application whose status can only be terminated by an immigration judge, temporary residence for 245A applicants may be terminated by the service upon occurrence of the following:

(I) It is determined that the alien was ineligible for temporary residence under 245A of the Act;

(II) The alien commits an act which renders him or her inadmissible as an immigrant;

(III) The aliens is convicted of any felony or 3 or more misdemeanors; or

(IV) The alien fails to file for adjustment of status from temporary resident to permanent resident within 31 months of the date he/she was granted status as a temporary resident.

245A.2(U) sets forth in the pertinent part, the termination procedures for 245A temporary residents.."If the alien's status is terminated, the Director of the RPF shall notify the alien of the decision and the reasons for the termination. Any From I-688 previously issued will be declared void by the Directory of the RPF within 30 days if no appeal of the termination decision is filed within that period. If no appeal is filed the I-688 shall be deemed void and must be surrendered without delay to an immigration officer or the issuing office of the Service."

App-154

5-26-88

Date: May 26, 1988
From: Terrance M. O'Reilly, INS Deputy Assistant Commissioner for Legalization
To: All INS Field Offices

COLEG has received word that certain legalization offices are refusing to accept legalization applications from qualified designated entities (QDEs).

All Legalization Offices are reminded that 8 CFR 245a.2(f) allows QDEs to submit a complete legalization application (I-687, medical, supporting documents, and fee) to the Service within 60 days of receipt. All such applications should be supported by a consent to forward form signed by the applicant and a representative of the QDE dated no later than May 4, 1988.

Cases filed by applicants with a QDE on May 4, 1988, must be submitted to the Service no later than July 5, 1988.

Date: June 1, 1988
From: INS Central Office in Washington, DC
To: All Service Field Offices
File: CO 1588-C

The Service has been enjoined from applying its regulatory definition in 8 CFR 245a.1(g) of "brief, casual, and innocent" under an order issued by the United States District Court for the Eastern District of California in the case of Catholic Social Services, Inc. (Centro de Guadalupe Immigration Center), et. al. v. Edwin Meese. The following class of legalization applicants are covered under the order of the court:

"All persons prima facie eligible for legalization under INA Section 245A who departed and reentered the United States without INS authorization (i.e., "advance parole") after the enactment of IRCA following what they assert to have been a brief, casual, and innocent absence from the United States."

All applications by aliens with or without advanced authorization should be adjudicated on a case-by-case basis, as ordered by the court. Any application that was denied based the "brief, casual, and innocent" regulation should be reopened and reconsidered. The applicant should be contacted for work authorization and any needed additional information.

Further information concerning this issue will be supplied as it becomes known.

Date: June 2, 1988
From: INS Central Office
To: All INS Field Offices
File: CO 1588-C

This is to once again reemphasize proper procedures for the acceptance of forms I-772, Declaration of Intending Citizen. Please review my previous cable of November 17, 1987 (File CO 274A-P) and May 19, 1988 on this subject. In addition, please review the Commissioner's memorandum of April 18, 1988 concerning this subject.

Form I-772 may be filed with any INS officer at any service facility. The service officer must simply verify the applicant's eligibility to file, then complete and sign the "received and filed by" section of the form.

Those eligible to file are listed in question #5 of the form. The form may be submitted in person or by mail. The verification by the service officer may be done by seeing documents presented by the applicant, or by verifying eligibility through the Central Index System (CIS).

Once completed by the service office, the copy of the form is returned to the applicant, and the original is sent to the applicant's A-file. Note that to be eligible to submit the form, the applicant only needs to be a member of one of the classes of aliens listed in question #5. The applicant does not need to meet any of the requirements of the naturalization sections of the Act to be eligible to file form I-772.

Please ensure tha all personnel are familiar with the filing procedures of form I-772.

Date: June 10, 1988
From: Office of the General Counsel
To: Raymond Penn
    Assistant Commissioner
    Office of Legalization
Subject: LEGAL OPINION: IMPACT OF RECEIPT OF EDUCATIONAL ASSISTANCE BY TEMPORARY RESIDENT ON ADMISSIBILITY UNDER §212.5(A)(15)

I. Question Presented

The question presented is whether receipt of educational assistance by lawful temporary residents will impact on the determination of admissibility under §212(a)(15) of the Immigration and Nationality Act (I&NA) at the time of adjustment to permanent residence.

II. Summary Conclusion

The receipt of educational assistance by a temporary resident will not impact on his admissibility under §212(a)(15).

III. Discussion

A. The Typical Student Will Probably Not Be Considered Likely to Become a Public Charge

Section 212(a)(15) of the Immigration and Nationality Act provides for the exclusion of aliens "who, in the opinion of the consular officer at the time of application for a visa, or in the opinion of the Attorney General at the time of application for admission, are likely to become public charges." It is well settled that an applicant for adjustment of status is in the same posture as though her were an applicant before an American consular officer abroad seeking issuance of an immigrant visa.

State Department regulations regarding the public charge determination provide, in pertinent part, as follows:

(iii) An alien relying solely on the personal income he will be receiving to establish eligibility under section 212(a)(15) of the Act who does not establish that he will have an income above the income poverty guidelines published annually (or any shorter interval the Secretary of Health and Human Services deems feasible and desirable) by the Office of the Assistant Secretary for Planning and Evaluation, Department of Health and Human Services, and who is without other adequate financial resources, shall be presumed ineligible under that section of the Act.

22 C.F.R. §42.91(a)(15). The Foreign Affairs Manual (FAM) provides further guidance as follows:

In evaluating evidence of support in immigrant cases the consular officer should be flexible in his requirements, predicating his decision on facts relating to the applicant's age, physical condition, vocation, and existing conditions in the United States coupled with their probable effect on the applicant's likelihood of becoming a public charge after admission into the United States....The consular officer's assessment of the likelihood of the alien's becoming a public charge 'at any time' should always be based upon a reasonable projection of present circumstances rather than upon possible consequences which are contingent upon speculative eventualities. (Amended).

FAM, Part III, Vol. 9, note 1 to 22 C.F.R. §42.91(a)(15). The foregoing factors have been applied by the Service, the BIA, and the Attorney General in various contexts involving excludability under section 212(a)(15). See Matter of Vindman, 16 I&N Dec. 131 (R.C. 1977) (aged SSI recipients found ineligible); Matter of Perez, 15 I&N Dec. 136 (1974) (28-year-old welfare recipient, in good health, capable of finding employment not ineligible); Matter of Harutunian, 14 I&N Dec. 583 (R.C. 1974) (70-year-old welfare recipient with no other means of support ineligible); Matter of Martinez-Lopez, 10 I&N Dec. 409, 421-423 (A.G. 1964) (promise of employment not required).

In applying this analysis to the typical student who is receiving education assistance, the student's age, physical condition and education weigh in the student's favor. It is unlikely, therefore, that the typical young, healthy student whose future is being enhanced by an education would be found likely to become a public charge, even if his income is below the income poverty guidelines.

B. A Student Who May Be Inadmissible As Likely To Become a Public Charge May Be Admissible Under the "Special Rule" if He Has a History of Self-Support and Has Not Received Public Cash Assistance

Even if an applicant would be inadmissible as likely to become a public charge under the foregoing analysis, he may be admissible under the terms of the "special rule." Section 245A(d)(2)(B)(iii) of IRCA provides the following

App-158

special rule for the determination of public charge:

Special Rule for Determination of Public Charge.- An alien is not ineligible for adjustment of status under this section due to being inadmissible under section 212(a)(15) if the alien demonstrates a history of employment in the United States evidencing self-support without receipt of *public cash assistance*.

(Emphasis added.) The regulations define "public cash assistance" as follows:

"Public cash assistance" means income or means-based monetary assistance, to include but not limited to supplemental security income, received by the alien or his or her immediate family members through federal, state, or local programs designed to meet subsistence levels. It does not include assistance in kind, such as food stamps, public housing, or other non-cash benefits, nor does it include work-related compensation or certain types of medical assistance (Medicare, Medicaid, emergency treatment, services to pregnant women or children under 18 years of age, or treatment in the interest of public health).

8 C.F.R. §245a.1(i).

In summary, the special rule requires: 1) establishment of a history of employment evidencing self support, and 2) no receipt of public cash assistance. Both of these requirements must be met for the special rule to apply. The requirements regarding proof of financial responsibility and history of employment are set forth at 8 C.F.R. 245a.2(d)(4). The pertinent inquiry here is whether education assistance is considered public cash assistance for purposes of applying the special rule.

  c. Education Benefits under Title IV of the Higher Education Act of 1965 Should Not Be Considered Public Cash Assistance

Title IV of the Higher Education Act of 1965, as amended, 20 U.S.C. 1070-1099, 42 U.S.C. 2751-2756, provides for needs-based educational assistance in the form of grants, loans, and work study programs.[1] In our opinion, loans and work study programs clearly do not fit within the definition of public cash assistance contained in the regulation. Accordingly, the only relevant inquiry is with regard to grants. Grants are awards that are not repaid by the student. Within this category are the Opportunity Grants (SEOG), 20 U.S.C. 1070b.

Both the Pell Grant and SEOG are awarded on the basis of financial need. Each provides for at least a portion of the money to be paid directly to the student for subsistence purposes. The definition of public cash assistance contained in 8 C.F.R. §245a.1(i) includes those programs "designed" to meet subsistence levels.

A review of the two programs at issue indicates that the program goal for both is the provision of educational opportunity to those students in financial need. Under both programs financial need is based on the difference between the student's cost of education (e.g. tuition, fees, room, board, books, supplies, and other related expenses) and the amount the student and the student's family are expected to contribute toward the education. Pell Grants are limited to undergraduate students enrolled at least half-time and to five full years of study. SEOG's are limited to undergraduates and to availability of funds at a given school. The amount of the award is relatively small. Maximum awards for the 197-88 academic year were $2100 for Pell Grants and $4000 for SEOG'S. It appears, therefore, that while subsistence is necessarily a cost of education, for most grantees, it is only incidental to the program goals of Title IV grants.

V. Conclusion

The regulatory definition of public cash assistance is designed to encompass those programs aimed at providing subsistence. An analysis of Title IV grants indicates that

---

[1] Section 245A(h)(1)(A) of the I&NA provides that lawful temporary residents are ineligible for a period of five years for certain programs of financial assistance furnished under Federal law. Assistance furnished pursuant to Title IV of the Higher Education Act of 1965 is specifically exempted from being construed as one of those programs of "financial assistance." Thus, newly legalized students are not precluded from receiving Title IV benefits. However, this provision regarding "financial assistance" has no bearing on the determination of what constitutes "public cash assistance" for purposes of applying the special rule.

App-159

6-10-88

subsistence is only incidental to the program goal of providing educational opportunity. Accordingly it is our opinion that financial assistance provided pursuant to Title IV of the Higher Education Act of 1965 or similar programs that may be administered by the States should not be construed as public cash assistance for purposes of applying the special rule for determination of public charge. If you have any questions or require further information, please contact Paul W. Virtue, Associate General Counsel, at 633-2656.

RAYMOND M. MOMBOISSE
General Counsel

6-10-88

Date: June 17, 1988
From: INS CO
To: All INS Field Offices
File: CO 1588-C

This is in reference to COLEG's June 1, 1988 wire pertaining to section 245A cases in which the service was enjoined from using its definition of "brief, casual, and innocent" ("B, C & I") by Chief Judge Lawrence K. Karlton of the United States District Court for the Eastern District of California in the case of Catholic Social Services Inc. (Centro de Guadalupe Immigration Center), et al. v. Edwin Meese.

To reinforce our June 1, 1988 wire, the following class of legalization applicants (subclass 1) are covered under the court's order:

"All persons prima facie eligible for legalization under INA section 245A who departed and reentered the United States without INS authorization (i.e., "advance parole") after the enactment of IRCA following what they assert to have been a brief, casual, and innocent absence from the United States."

On June 10, 1988, Chief Judge Karlton issued the following order:

1. Legalization applications shall be accepted immediately at Los through November 30, 1988, (as ordered by the Court) from those applicants who fit within the subclass 1 definition established by the Court. These subclass 1 cases shall be held at the LOS until further instructions from central office are issued.

2. The definition of subclass 1 has been extended to include those individuals who failed to file an application within 30 days of receipt of an order to show cause, and those who applied for and were denied advance parole under 8 CFR 245a.1(g).

3. The terms of the Court order apply only to members of subclass 1. INS has 15 days from the date of issuance of the order within which to impose procedures and guidelines setting forth the evidentiary requirements and standards of proof to be imposed on this subclass.

4. In the interim, applications accepted from subclass 1 members shall be accompanied by the applicant's sworn declaration stating:

(a) that the applicant was absent from the U.S. for a brief period on or after May 1, 1987, and returned other than pursuant to INS advance parole,

(b) how the applicant was aware of the INS regulations, 8 CFR 245a.1(g), or the agency policy pursuant thereto and therefore reached the conclusion of ineligibility for legalization, and

(c) based upon such belief of ineligibility, did not file an application on or before May 4, 1988.

5. INS shall process all applications filed by legalization applicants on or before May 4, 1988, pursuant to the Court's definition of "B, C & I."

6. INS shall reopen and reconsider all cases that were denied or recommended for denial on the previous INS definition of "brief, casual, and innocent". Central Office has requested a specific report from LAPS that will assist the RPFs in identifying such cases. Additional information should be requested from applicants as to how they meet the court's standard. Final decisions on these cases should be held in abeyance pending further guidance from C.O. This includes those cases that have been appealed to the LAU.

7. Those within the subclass who have a prima facie claim to legalization, "shall be provided a stay of deportation and temporary employment authorization pending final adjudication of their applications."

The decision as to whether or not the INS will seek an emergency stay and/or an appeal are pending.

COLEG will inform all offices as soon as further information becomes available.

App-161

Date: June 30, 1988
From: INS Central Office
To: All INS Field Offices

Pursuant to a U.S. District Court Order issued by Judge Hogan on June 29, 1988, effective immediately, INS shall accept and hold in abeyance skeletal I-700 applications without fee, medical report of examination or documentary evidence of employment filed by individuals in the United States who declare they have 90 days of employment in sugar cane during each of the 12 month periods ending on May 1, 1984, 1985, and 1986 (Group I) or during the 12 month period ending on May 1, 1986 (Group II). The employment must conform to the existing USDA definition of "seasonal agricultural services" as defined at 7 CFR Part 1d. Applicants shall be issued an I-688A employment authorization card and granted a stay of deportation. In addition, upon any applicant's request, INS shall reopen and hold in abeyance any I-700 application previously denied or rejected upon the basis of employment in sugar cane without requiring a new I-700 application. The application shall be held until further notice.

Date: July 12, 1988
From: INS Central Office
To: All INS Field Offices
File: CO 1588-C

This is in reference to CO wire CO 1588-C dated July 1, 1988 regarding I-700 applications for sugar cane workers. INS will accept skeletal applications without fee, medical, or supporting documentation from any alien who declares 90 man-days of field work in sugar cane between May 1, 1985 and May 1, 1986. The alien will be scheduled for interview 30 days or more from the filing date, depending upon LO workload, and issued employment authorization valid from the filing date until the date of interview. Pursuant to 8 CFR 210.4(b)(2), applicants who currently have work authorization incident to nonimmigrant status will be granted employment authorization on the date the applicant's prior employment authroization expires. At the time of the interview, it is expected that a determination will be made as to whether or not the application is based on a fraudulent claim. Following anticipated modifications to the order by the District Court, the service will specify procedures for verifying employment as a sugar cane worker.

In order to preserve the right of application ordered by the court, all cases will be held in abeyance at the LOs pending further instructions from COLEG. Further instructions will be issued within the 30 day period.

Date: July 29, 1988
From: INS Central Office
To: All INS Field Offices
File: CO 1588-C

This is to reiterate service policy on applicants for legalization whose I-693s indicate infection with the HIV virus or the AIDS disease. All such applicants are statutorily eligible to apply for a waiver of section 212(a)(6) on I-690.

Under the discretionary authority of the Attorney General, waivers may be granted if the applicant can establish that: (1) the danger to the public health of the United States created by the alien's admission to the United States is minimal, (2) the possibility of the spread of the infection created by the alien's admission to the United States is minimal, and (3) there will be no cost incurred by any government agency without prior consent of that agency. Also note that waivers are to be granted only for humanitarian purposes, to assure family unity, or when the granting of such a waiver is in the public interest in accordance with 245a.2(k)(2) of the regulations.

Waivers are to be submitted to the Regional Processing Facility; all written decisions on waiver applications based upon the HIV virus or AIDS disease will be certified to the Deputy Commissioner, Examinations, in accordance with 8 CFR 103.4 until further notice.

Date: August 10, 1988
From: INS Central Office
To: All INS Field Offices
File: CO 1588-C

On August 10, 1988, the District Court modified its order of June 29, 1988, to allow INS to verify the claims of sugar cane SAW applicants. Effective immediately, the following procedures supersede the procedures set forth in wires of June 30, 1988, July 1, 1988, and July 12, 1988.

Pursuant to the court order, no I-700 filing fee or supporting documentation is required until further notice. The LOs in Florida have obtained lists of former H-2 Florida sugar cane workers from the sugar cane associations. Either upon the applicant's appearance at the LO for a previously scheduled interview or for an initial filing:

(1) LOs in Florida will check the H-2 lists and issue the I-688A employment authorization card to an applicant whose name appears on the list. No interview will be scheduled for an applicant whose name is on the list. LOs outside Florida will phone the LO at Okeechobee, Florida, (813-763-3078), who will check the H-2 list. If the Okeechobee LO cannot be reached, LOs outside of Florida should contact the RPF. If Okeechobee verifies that the name appears on the list, the applicant will be issued I-688A without a scheduled interview. If the Okeechobee LO or the RPF can be contacted for verification, the applicant shall be issued the I-688A without a scheduled interview.

(2) An applicant's whose name does not appear on the list may be issued the I-688A, at the discretion of the LO, if the applicant presents reliable documentation as proof of the qualifying employment.

(3) If an applicant's name does not appear on the lists and the LO does not exercise its discretion to rely on documentation presented by the applicant, the LO will schedule the applicant to reappear 31 days from the date of filing for an interview and will issue the applicant form I-689 with employment authorization valid from the filing date to the date of interview. The applicant is not required to bring any supporting employment or medical documentation or pay the I-700 filing fee when he/she returns for interview. The sentence, "Please bring any original documents which support your application," will be blocked out on the I-689. During the 31 day period, the LO will attempt

to verify the employment by contacting the employer. If the alleged employment was in Florida, verification may be obtained through the Okeechobee LO. Upon the applicant's return to the LO, an I-688A shall be issued without a scheduled interview (a) if the employer verifies the employment; (b) if the LO was unable to contact the employer; or (c) if the employer failed to respond.

If the employer is contacted and disavows the alleged employment, the applicant will be interviewed upon his/her return to the LO and afforded an opportunity to rebut the employer's disavowal. Following this interview, if the applicant's claim still does not appear credible, the I-688A work authorization will not be issued.

If, at the time of filing the skeletal application, the applicant already has work authorization incident to H-2A or other nonimmigrant status, employment authorization will not be issued until after the expiration of the previous work authorization. However, if the H-2A employment terminated prior to the expiration of the applicant's authorization for reasons other than the applicant's voluntary termination of employment, form I-688A shall be issued.

Form I-696 worksheets will be prepared for each case specifying the results of the employment verification and how the verification was obtained. No adjudicatory recommendation will be made or annotated on the I-700 or I-696. In order to preserve the right of application ordered by the Court, all cases (including those in which employment authorization has not been granted) will be stored at the LOs pending further notification from COLEG.

The Judge's order and the procedures outlined herein also pertain to SAW applicants whose qualifying agricultural employment is comprised, at least in part, of field work in sugar cane.

App-165

Date: September 26, 1988
From: INS Central Office
To: INS Field Offices
File: CO 1588-C

The Social Security Administration (SSA) has recently brought to SSA COLEG's attention that some Legalization Offices who are scheduling interviews have been placing on the reverse side of Form I-689 fee receipt the alien's photo and a stamp over the photo that states the I-689 is a document that establishes employment eligibility for Form I-9 purposes. This procedure conflicts with SSA field processing instructions, and may further confuse employers by adding another variation of official proof of employment authorization. Therefore, effective immediately, all Los should cease placing photos and/or stamps on Form I-689.

The issue of employers who are not recognizing Form I-689 with "Employment Authorization" for I-9 purposes was resolved via COLEG Memorandum (CO 1588-C) dated July 14, 1988 to all Regional Legalization Officers which attached a sample employer letter to be signed in behalf of the District Director and given to applicants experiencing this problem. This procedure is the recommended resolution.

10-17-88

Date: October 17, 1988
From: INS Central Office
To: All Field Offices
File: CO 1588-C
REFERENCE: CO 1588-P November 13, 1987 from Commissioner to all Regional Commissioners, all District Directors, all Officers-in-Charge
SUBJECT: Family Fairness: Guidelines for voluntary departures under 8 CFR 245.5 for the ineligible spouses and children of legalized aliens

This wire is to clarify that the referenced family fairness guidelines are applicable to all aliens legalized under Sections 245A and 210 of IRCA.

Date: October 24, 1988
From: INS Central Office
To: INS Field Offices
File: CO 1588-C

It has recently been brought to COLEG's attention that fraud cases are being presented for prosecution based upon document analyses conducted exclusively by the Document Analysis Unit (DAU) without being forwarded to the forensic document lab (FDL) in Tysons Corner, Virginia. In the Legalization Fraud Procedures Manual, the section entitled "Structure of the Document Analysis Unit", it states that in cases that are to be presented for prosecution which may require expert testimony, the document analyst will forward the questioned documents to the FDL. It further states that it is imperative that all document examinations requiring expert testimony in a court of law be conducted by qualified forensic document analysts certified by forensic document analysts certified by the American Board of Forensic Document Examiners. RPF Directors should ensure that the procedures in the manual are followed by the DAU. In addition, District Directors should ensure that in fraud cases that are to be presented for prosecution whcih may require expert testimony, the special agent forwards the questioned documents to the FDL if the DAU failed to do so.

In addition, the FDL has advised that they will accept select cases, other than prosecution cases, that cannot be resolved by other means (e.g. field investigation, telephone employment verification, etc.). However, prior to submission to the FDL, the DAU should contact the chief document analyst at the FDL, FTS 285-2482, providing chief document analyst at the FDL, the DAU should contact the him with specific information such as the number of pieces of evidence to be examined and the type of examination requested so that a decision can be made whether the FDL will be able to accept the case and respond in a timely manner.

Date: October 26, 1988
From: INS Assistant Commissioner for Adjudications James A. Puleo
To: All Field Offices
File: CO 245-C
SUBJECT: APPLICATIONS FOR ADJUSTMENT OF STATUS UNDER THE CUBAN-HAITIAN PROVISIONS OF IRCA.

Section 202 of IRCA allows for the filing of adjustment applications by certain Cuban or Haitian nationals. One of the filing requirements is that the applicant must apply for adjustment within two years after the date of enactment of IRCA. IRCA was enacted on November 5, 1986. Therefore, under the language of the statute the last date an application for adjustment can be filed is Saturday, November 5, 1988.

In accordance with the rules of civil procedure, when the last day of a period falls on a Saturday, Sunday, or legal holiday, the period shall be extended to the next business day. Accordingly, applications received on Monday November 7, 1988 either in person or in the mail room, will be accepted. Applications received either in person or in the mail room on or after Tuesday November 9, 1988, will not be accepted.

The reference to Tuesday as November 9 is obviously a typographical error. Tuesday is November 8, and in this context it is clear that November 8 was the date intended.

10-27-88

Date: October 27, 1988
File: CO 1588-C
To: All INS field offices
From: INS Central Office

This wire is a reminder that the application period for receipt of I-700 applications from Special Agricultural Workers will terminate November 30, 1988.

QDEs may file completed SAW applications at an LO in the United States until January 30, 1989, if the applications were filed with the QDE in the United States by November 30, 1988.

After November 30, 1988, neither the American Embassy in Mexico City nor the three ports of entry (Otay Mesa, Calexico and Laredo) which are now accepting preliminary applications will accept any SAW applications. There are no QDEs operation in Mexico with whom applications are filed within the purview of 8 CFR 210.2(b)(1). Preliminary (S-9) SAW applicants whose 90 day employment authorization has not expired by November 30, 1988 must file complete applications with a Legalization Office before March 1, 1989.

In order for LOs to accurately gauge their workloads, QDEs will be instructed to complete and submit to the LO a survey form (similar to the form utilized at the end of the Legalization application period) which indicates the total number of SAW applications filed with the QDE by November 30, 1988 which will be submitted within the 60 day period. QDEs will be directed to submit the survey form to the LOs by December 9, 1988.

App-170

10-31-88

Date: October 31, 1988
From: James A. Puleo, INS Assistant Commissioner for Adjudications
To: All Field Offices
File: CO 245-C

The Technical Corrections Act of 1988 was signed by the President on October 25, 1988. Section 1.(small I) of that Act amended Section 202 of the Immigration Reform and Control Act of 1986 (IRCA) relating to adjustment of status of certain Cuban and Haitian nationals. The amendment provides that the Attorney General may, in his discretion, waive the grounds for exclusion under Section 212(a)(19) in Cuban-Haitian adjustment cases. The effective date of this amendment is retroactively applied as if it was included in the enactment of IRCA and thus applies to the entire application period which ends November 7, 1988 (REFTEL MY 245-C of 10/26/88, applications for adjustment of status under the Cuban-Haitian Provisions of IRCA).

Because of the extremely short time period left in the application period relative to the date of passage of this amendment, the Service has agreed to accept skeleton applications for benefits under the Cuban-Haitian provisions from now until the end of the application period from those individuals who have not yet filed for benefits.

Individuals who are eligible but have not yet filed for Cuban-Haitian adjustment are to be advised to file Form I-485 only on or before 11/7/88. All supporting forms must be submitted by the time the applicant is interviewed.

If an individual filed an application but was denied the benefits because of ineligibility under Section 212(a)(19), that individual is not required to submit anything else to the Service prior to 11/7/88 to preserve eligibility under the amendment of the Technical Corrections Act.

In the near future, you will receive further instructions on how to reopen and decide those cases which have previously been denied.

App-171

Date: November 1, 1988
File: CO 1588-C
To: All INS field offices
From: INS Central Offices

On November 30, 1988, the SAW application period terminates. In order to handle the predictable surge of SAW filings on November 30, 1988, as well as ensure that every opportunity is afforded eligible aliens to apply for SAW benefits on the last day of the application period, the following procedures are to be implemented on November 30, 1988.

(1) All LOs will remain open until at least midnight on November 30, 1988. Any office which has people waiting in line to file SAW applications at the midnight deadline will remain open until all such persons have been accommodated. Applications that cannot be processed upon submission will be placed in an envelope, sealed, and kept at the LO to be processed the following workday(s).

(2) The applications of all SAW applicants who come to a Legalization Office on November 30, 1988 shall be considered filed as of the date even though long lines may prevent acceptance of the application prior to midnight on November 30, 1988. I-700 applications submitted by mail should be postmarked on or before midnight November 30, 198, in order to be considered filed within the prescribed application period.

(3) At the District Director's discretion, Legalization Offices with substantial I-700 receipts can be open on the Sunday before November 30, 1988.

(4) The Service will not encourage the filing of "simplified" applications (those without supporting documentation or medical report) as it did at the end of the legalization application period.

(5) If possible, the LOs will immediately screen the application for eligibility and completeness. If the application is incomplete, the case will be feed in and returned to the applicant with Form I-72 and fee receipt, Form I-689, without Employment Authorization. The I-72 will instruct the applicant to submit the requested documentation to the LO within 30 days, at which time the applicant will either be interviewed or scheduled for interview. Applicants will be issued Employment Authorization on Form I-689 if the interview cannot be scheduled within 30 days of receipt of the complete application.

(6) The employment verification process outlined in the Deputy Commissioner's wire of September 14, 1988 should be conducted prior to the interview.

App-172

11-4-88

Date: November 4, 1988
From: INS Central Office
To: All INS field offices

The positions of the INS regarding the granting of employment authorization to class denied at LOs is outlines below:

Denials at LOs should only take place in two situations:

1. Where fraud is clearly established; and/
2. Where the applicant is clearly statutorily ineligible.

When one or both of these situations are established, the following rule should be applied concerning employment authorization:

It is required that before employment authori can be granted to 245A applicants, that the applicant must be prima facie eligible for the benefit sought and in Section 210 cases the applicant must submit a nonfrivolous application.

Therefore, if #1 or #2 or both are done at LOs the applicants have failed to meet the prima facie or non frivolous standards established by IRCA and are not entitled to employment authorization.

11-7-88

Date: November 7, 1988
From: INS Central Office
To: Southern and Western Regional Legalization Offices

File: CO 1588-C

When an alien seeking admission as an S-9 at a port of entry is determined to be inadmissible, he must be processed for a refund of his application fee. The refund will be processing on form G-266 immediately after the alien withdraws his application for admission. If the alien requests an exclusion hearing, the refund should not be processed until a final exclusion order is issued.

Date: November 15, 1988
From: INS Central Office
File: CO 1588-C

This is in reference to COLEG wire dated 10/17/88 regarding the backlog in the interview of SAW cases. Option #3 allows the applicant to return to Mexico and have his case transferred to the port of entry at Calexico or Otay Mesa upon return. Applicants must be warned that if their application is denied, they will not be allowed to reenter the United States. Notices must be given to each applicant in English and Spanish. The file should be noted that the warning has been given. For purposes of uniformity, the following wording should be used:

Upon your request, your scheduled interview at the _____ legalization Office is being cancelled and you be interviewed at the _____ Calexico _____ Otay Mesa port of entry regarding your application for temporary resident status. You are advised that if at the time of your interview at the port of entry, your application is denied, you will not be allowed to return to the United States.

In referencia a su solicitud, su entrevista en la oficina de legalizacion en _____, ha sido cancelada. Usted va a hacer entrevistado en el puerto de entrada en _____ Calexico _____ Otay Mesa con referencia a su aplicacion para residente temporal. Usted esta avisado que al tiempo de entrevista en el puerto de entrada. Si su aplicacion es negada no se va a permitir su entrada a los Estados Unidos.

12-13-88

Date: December 13, 1988
From: Central INS Legalization Office in Washington, DC
To: Four Regional Legalization Offices
File: CO 1588-C
SUBJECT: DISTRIBUTION OF M-306 HANDBOOK

COLEG is receiving complaints that field offices are not distributing M-306s (with amendment notice and adhesive label). COLEG previously (9/8/88) advised that M-306s should be provided to applicants if the applicants state that they have not received the M-306 in the mail and their eligibility to file date has been reached. Attorneys and other accredited representatives can also be furnished with M-306 and their eligibility to file date has been reached. The Service has printed 5.4 million M-306 handbooks so field locations should distribute the handbooks to eligible applicants and attorneys or other accredited representative of those applicants. Field offices should also be advised that I-698 applications will be available for direct purchases from the Government Printing Office. Projected availability is late December.

PLEASE ADVISE ALL FIELD LOCATIONS ACCORDINGLY.

Date: December 16, 1988
From: INS Central Office in Washington, DC
To: All Service Field Offices
File: CO 1588-P

The Legalization/SAW application receipt form I-689 is not a travel document. However, there are three circumstances in which I-689 holders are allowed to travel. First, are SAW applicants subject to COLEG wire of 10/17/88, allowing residents of Mexico to return to Mexico and schedule their interview at Calexico or Otay Mesa upon their return to the United States. Other nationalities need an advanced parole to travel.

If a Mexican resident departed the United States without having his file transferred to a border port, he should be refused admission and referred to one of the border processing ports. The processing port will make arrangements to obtain the file and schedule an interview. Upon a determination by a legalization officer that the application is nonfrivolous, Form I-688A will be issued and the applicant admitted.

The second exception relates to SAW applicants who had work authorization incident to status as identified in Section 2741.12(b) when they applied. Such applicants are not issued an I-688A until their nonimmigrant employment authorization expires. Nonetheless, some of these individuals have filed non-frivolous applications and have the right to travel outside the United States. The third exception is for a SAW alien who was issued, but has lost form I-688A.

SAW applicants for admission representing an I-689 should be asked: (1) if they had been issued an I-688A/I-688, or (2) if they had applied for SAW status when they were in H-2A or other nonimmigrant status. If the response to both is negative, follow the procedure described above. If the response to either is positive, it must be determined if a nonfrivolous application was filed and if that application was subsequently denied. A check of the Central Index System or direct contact with the Regional Processing Facility should be done to determine the status of the case. If there is no record, verification must be made with the LO issuing the I-689. If the determination is made that the SAW application is not nonfrivolous, the alien should be refused admission. The SAW applicant should be admitted if status is verified and identification established. Legalization applicants cannot travel while their applications are pending, except with advanced parole.

Therefore, legalization applicants must establish identification and must have had their case approved before being admitted.

Officers should refer to 8 CFR 210.1(j) for the definition of a nonfrivolous application. Skeletal applications filed pursuant to court orders in sod and sugar cane should be considered as nonfrivolous. Refer to CO wire dated 10/18/87 for information concerning expired I-688As. That directive can also be used for guidance in cases of lost I-688As and I-688s.

Date: December 22, 1988
From: INS Central Office in Washington, DC
To: All Field Offices
File: CO 1588-P

Offices are reminded that S-9 applicants will be filing completed applications up until March 1, 1989. They are not required to pay the application fee a second time when submitting the complete application. 8 CFR 210.2(c)(4)(iii) provides that S-9s are required to submit evidence of eligibility within their 90 day admission period. A District Director may, for good cause, extend the ninety-day period and grant further authorization to accept employment in the United States. An I-689 with a scheduled appointment can be used to extend the authorized stay and employment. Directors may also, for good cause, decide to accept completed applications from S-9 applicants where the authorized stay has already expired.

The document processing center (DPC) will be instructed to forward cases where the authorized stay has expired and no completed application has been received, to the Western RPF (XPW) for denial. Denials will be for lack of prosecution. In order to avoid denying cases in the pipeline, the DPC will only send cases where 120 days or more has lapsed since entry. When an LO decides to accept a completed application from an alien whose authorized stay has expired by thirty days or more, they should advise the alien to contact the LO if he receives a denial. The LO can then determine if an appeal is necessary. If the LO refuses to accept a completed application, it will not be necessary to take any action, except to advise the alien he will receive a denial in the mail. Change of address cards in these type cases should be forwarded to XPW to facilitate delivery of denials.

LO's should review all S-9 cases that cannot be immediately forwarded, to determine if the authorized stay is about to or has expired. In these cases, a copy of the I-689 generated at the LO should be sent to the DPC by December 31, 1988. The DPC will begin forwarding cases to XPW after that date. Subsequent cases that cannot be forwarded within 120 days after entry should also have a copy of the I-689 sent to the DPC as soon as possible after receipt.

Date: January 9, 1989
From: Richard E. Norton, INS Associate Commissioner for Examinations, and Clarence M. Coster, Associate Commissioner for Enforcement
To: All Service field offices
File: CO 1588-C
Subject: SERVICE CONFISCATION OF THE EMPLOYMENT AUTHORIZATION CARD (FORM I-688A) AND THE TEMPORARY RESIDENT CARD (FORM I-688); COMMENCEMENT OF EXCLUSION OR DEPORTATION PROCEEDINGS
Reference: RESCINDS CO-1588-C DATED JUNE 20, 1988, CONCERNING THE SAME SUBJECT. REPLACES COLEG WIRE OF DECEMBER 27, 1988 TO INCLUDE THE LAST PARAGRAPH INADVERTENTLY OMITTED FROM THE ORIGINAL.

The purpose of this wire is to correct previous instructions on confiscation of forms I-688A and I-688 and to provide instructions on commencement of exclusion or deportation proceedings for aliens holding such forms. Legalization and SAW confiscation procedures are separated due to the variances of those programs. This wire applies to applicants for legalization or SAW status who are in possession of their own genuine documents. Aliens presenting counterfeit or altered documents or an otherwise valid document belonging to another person are not protected from deportation or exclusion by IRCA.

Special Agricultural Workers (SAWs)-Section 210.

1. Aliens with an I-688A (Section 210 Work Authorization) who present themselves at a port of entry and appear to have obtained the I-688A through fraud in their SAW application or who appear excludable may not be excluded or deported until a final determination on their SAW application has been made. The I-688A may not be confiscated until a final determination on the application is made. Any adverse information obtained at the port of entry should be forwarded to the Regional Processing Facility having jurisdiction over the Legalization Office where the alien filed the SAW application and presented to the United States Attorney for possible prosecution for fraud. Pending a final determination on the SAW application, such aliens with an I-688A at the port of entry should be released on parole, except that such aliens may be detained if they appear excludable under grounds of exclusion that may not be waived under IRCA (8 CFR 210.3(E)(3)). Exclusion charges against such aliens may not be based on information obtained from the SAW application. Because of the difficulties of proving fraud on a SAW application without submitting the application into evidence (which is prohibited by the confidentiality provisions of IRCA), exclusion charges should be based on grounds other than 212(a)(19) with relation to the SAW application. See Legalization Wire #54, dated January 4, 1988.

However, should an alien present a counterfeit or altered I-688A or should the alien be an imposter presenting an otherwise valid I-688A belonging to another person, the alien should be processed for an exclusion hearing pursuant to standard service operation procedure.

2. An alien in possession of an I-688A (Section 245A temporary resident status) who is within the United States, may have that status terminated on the grounds provided in 8 CFR 245A.2(U)(1)(I-III). The I-688 may be confiscated upon completion of the termination proceedings. An alien whose status has been terminated shall not be referred to examination or enforcement for exclusion or deportation proceedings. Such an alien encountered independently by an investigatory or border patrol agent may be placed in deportation proceedings. However, deportation charges may not be based on information from the 245A application. Information relating to fraud detected on that application or of the Phase II application and presented to the United States Attorney for prosecution. The I-68 of a Section 245A alien in deportation proceedings may not be confiscated until there is a final administrative order of deportation.

S-9 Aliens with I-94s and I-700s (Preliminary SAW applicants)

1. An alien who presents an S-9 preliminary application may be deemed inadmissible by a legalization officer of by an immigration inspector upon a finding that the alien has not presented a credible application or upon a finding that the alien is excludable under the INA. If such an alien requests an exclusion hearing, the alien should be charged in the same manner as may other alien seeking admission without a visa. However, the exclusion charge may not be based on any information from the preliminary application or on any detected fraud in that application.

2. S-9s with I-94s who are encountered within the interior of the United States are treated in the same manner as aliens encountered within the interior of the United States with I-688As. See #2 and #3 on SAWs, above.

App-179

1-16-89

Date: January 16, 1989
From: INS Central Office's Legalization Division
To: All INS field offices
File: CO 1588-C

S-9 entrants are not covered under the agreement between INS and the Social Security Administration (SSA) for delayed issuance of social security cards to SAW applicants. Therefore, they are issued a social security card immediately, as [is] any other alien with work authorization on an I-94, without having to wait for their case to be approved. The SSA has experienced a problem with receiving duplicate social security applications (SS-5's) from S-9 applicants. To eliminate the possibility of duplicate issuance of social security cards, LO's should question S-9 applicants to determine if they have already applied for an SSA number. SS-5's should not be accepted for applicants who previously applied with the SSA.

1-18-89

Date: January 18, 1989
From: INS Central Office
To: All Field Offices
File: CO 1588-C
RE: STANDARD 100 U.S. HISTORY AND GOVERNMENT QUESTIONS/ANSWERS

Effective January 20, 1989, the correct answers to questions number (14), "Who is the President of the United States today?", and number (15), "Who is the Vice-President of the United States today?" will be "George Bush", and "Dan Quayle", respectively. Please take appropriate action to change these answers on the list of 100 standard U.S. History and Government Questions/Answers.

In response to questions from the field concerning distribution of the list of 100 standard U.S. history and government questions/answers, this list should be made available to the public for use as a study guide at local service offices involved in Phase II Legalization processing.

1-18-89

Date: January 18, 1989 cable
From: INS Central Office, Legalization Division
To: INS Southern Regional Office
File: CO 1588-C):

Under the Court's Order of August 22, 1988, in HRC v. Nelson, INS is required "in those cases in which the INS considered evidence adverse to the applicant of which the applicant was unaware, contrary to 8 C.F.R. 103.2(b)(2), the INS shall vacate the denials, afford the applicant an opportunity to examine the adverse evidence, to rebut it, and to offer additional evidence before rendering a decision."

The INS must comply with this order, while at the same time keeping the confidentiality provisions of IRCA in mind. The following guidelines should assist you in determining how information may be provided to the alien.

1. Any information gathered by INS, independently of an individual application, may be examined by a SAW applicant (if such information contained adverse evidence used to deny the applicant SAW status). Examples of such information are contractor lists, intelligence bulletins, or lists of farm labor contractor licenses obtained from state offices. However, whenever possible, such information should be segregated so that the applicant sees only that information relating to his own application.

2. Any information that was obtained from an application of another alien may not be examined by an applicant. An example would be the signature from the alien's own application may be examined by that alien.

App-182

1-26-89

Date: January 26, 1989
From: INS Central Office
To: All INS Regional Offices
File: CO 1588-C
Re: Catholic Social Service v. Meese

COLEG's previous telefax of October 4, 1988 remains in effect. All legalization personnel should be advised accordingly.

From: State Department
Cable No. 89-State-051207
To: All diplomatic and consular posts
Date: February 17, 1989
SUBJECT: TRAVEL LETTERS FOR CONDITIONAL RESIDENTS AND LEGALIZATION BENEFICIARIES

1. Department has received a number of questions from posts concerning procedures for dealing with holders of lost or expires I-688/I-688A cards seeking to return to the U.S. INS has sent guidance to INS domestic and overseas offices on SAW/legalization applicants travelling overseas whose documentation has expired or been lost. In order to clarify procedures and remove inconsistencies the INS guidance is repeated for posts' use:

BEGIN TEXT:

1. Special Agricultural Workers (SAWs) - Section 210 of the Immigration Reform and Control Act of 1986 (IRCA).

A. Form I-688-A (Employment Authorization Card): Although I-688As are issued to both SAW and legalization applicants, it is an authorized travel document for SAWs only. To differentiate, the bottom center portion of the I-688A will either state "210" (SAW) or "245A" (Legalization). Due to adjudications backlogs, legalization offices (LOs) placed one or more red or white 90-day extension stickers on many of the I-688As.

A SAW who filed a nonfrivolous application cannot be excluded or deported until a final determination has been made on his/her I-700 application. A final determination is: (A) a grant by the Regional Processing Facility (RPF) or a denial by the RPF that is not timely appealed, or (B) a grant or denial by the Legalization Appeals Unit (LAU). An I-700 denied at the LO is one that was not nonfrivolous at the time of filing and thus the stay of exclusion/deportation does not apply. Accordingly, if the office abroad encounters a SAW in possession of an expires I-688A or who has lost it, a cable must be sent to INS, COREC (Central Office Records) requesting verification of status. If the verification reveals that temporary residence either is pending, was granted, or was denied by the RPF and an appeal is pending, than a transportation letter should be issued to the alien directing the port of entry to admit the SAWs into the United States as either a temporary resident or an applicant for temporary resident status (whichever is appropriate). The office abroad should also advise the applicant to appear at the LO following admission into the U.S. to either extend the I-688A or file form I-695 for replacement. However, if temporary residence either was denied by the RPF and no appeal is pending or was denied by the LO irrespective of a pending appeal, the alien will not be issued a transportation letter and his/her I-688A will be lifted and forwarded to the RPF Director via a memorandum to the file.

If the office abroad suspects or establishes that the SAW's application is based on fraud and the verification reveals that temporary residence is pending or was granted, a transportation letter will be issued directing the port to admit the SAW as either a temporary resident or an applicant for temporary residence (whichever is appropriate); and a memorandum addressing the fraud will be forwarded to the RPF Director for appropriate action.

B. Form I-688 (Temporary Resident Card): Form I-688 is issued to both SAW and Legalization applicants granted temporary residence and, if valid, is an authorized travel document for both SAW and legalization temporary residents. It also is annotated "210" or "245A" on the bottom center portion of the card. Legalization offices placed a one-year extension sticker on SAW I-688s that expired 1/1/91. The stickers have a black background and the legend color shifts from the green to orange. If the office abroad encounters a SAW with an expired I-688 or who has lost it, a cable must be sent to INS, COREC, requesting verification of status. If the verification reveals that temporary residence was granted, a transportation letter will be issued directing the port to admit the alien as a temporary resident. However, if the verification reveals that temporary resident status has been terminated, a transportation letter will not be issued and the alien's I-688 should be lifted and forwarded to the RPF Director via a memorandum to the file.

2. Legalization Applicants-Section 245A of IRCA

A. Form I-688A: Legalization applicants are not authorized to travel with form I-688A. They must obtain advance parole from I-512 prior to departing the United States. IRCA precludes the deportation of legalization applicants until a final determination has been made on their I-687 application. Exclusion is not stayed. If the office abroad encounters a legalization applicants in possession of an expired I-512 or who failed to obtain an

App-184

I-512 prior to departing the U.S., a cable must be sent to COREC requesting verification of status. If the verification reveals that temporary residence is pending or was granted, a request for parole must be made to the District Director who issued the original I-512 or to INS CORAP (Central Office Refugee, Asylum and Parole) if the alien failed to obtain an I-512 prior to departing the U.S. However, if the verification reveals that temporary residence has been denied and no appeal is pending, parole should not be considered. Instead, Form I-688A should be lifted along with the I-512, if any, and forwarded to the RPF Director via a memorandum to the file. However, if an appeal is pending, form I-688A cannot be lifted until a final decision has been rendered.

B. Form I-688: Temporary residents who have their status adjusted to permanent resident will receive a sticker of the back of their I-688 that extends the validity of the I-688 and accords it temporary evidence of permanent residence and employment authorization. The stickers have a blue background and the legend color shifts from green to orange in normal light. If an office abroad encounters a legalization alien with an expired I-688 or who has lost it, a cable must be sent to INS, COREC requesting verification of status. If the verification reveals that temporary residence was granted, a transportation letter will be issued directing the port to admit the alien as a temporary resident. However, if the verification reveals that temporary resident status has been terminated, a transportation letter will not be issued and the alien's I-688 should be lifted and forwarded to the RPF Director via a memorandum to the file. End Text.

3. Following is INS guidance regarding legalization (Section 245A) beneficiaries traveling overseas seeking to return to the U.S. after thirty day limit has expired:

BEGIN TEXT. Section 245A Temporary Residents are permitted "brief and casual absences" from the United States. 8 CFR 245A.1(H) defines brief and casual absences as temporary trips abroad as long as the alien establishes a continuing intention to adjust to lawful permanent residence. The length of the absences, however, must comply with 8 CFR 245A.3(B)(2) in that no single absence has exceeded 90 days, unless the alien can establish that due to emergent reasons or circumstances beyond the alien's control, the return t the U.S. could not be accomplished within the time period(s) allowed.

8 CFR 245A.3(B)(2) also states that a single absence of more than 30 days, and aggregate absences of more than 90 days shall break the continuity of such residence, unless the temporary resident can establish to the satisfaction of the INS District Director that he or she did not, in fact, abandon residence in the U.S. during such period.

It is reasonable to assume that aliens have a continuing intention to adjust to lawful permanent residence since they are desiring to return to the U.S. This being the case, a transportation letter should be issued but noted to reflect the length of absence. Upon arrival at a port of entry in the U.S., the temporary resident alien will have to establish to the satisfaction of INS that he or she did not in fact abandon residence in the U.S. (END TEXT)a

App-185

2-25-89

Date: February 25, 1988
File: CO 1588-C
From: INS Central Office
To: All INS field offices
SUBJECT: **LEGALIZATION WIRE #58 DATED FEB. 24, 1988; IDENTIFICATION OF "COTTON" SAW APPLICATIONS BY LEGALIZATION OFFICES**

SAW applications involving fieldwork in cotton must be clearly identified by the LO before forwarding the application through the DPC to the RPF. LO's are instructed to check Block #B, 5. "Verification Requested" on the examinations worksheet. This action is necessary to ensure that such cases are identified and held in abeyance at the RPF.

DATE: December 23, 1988

TO: All QDEs and Provider Organizations

FROM: E.B. Duarte, Jr.
          Director/Government Project Manager
          Outreach Program/Cooperative Agreements

SUBJECT: Q & A for 312 Requirements of IRCA

Attached is the official INS list of 100 questions and answers, some of which INS examiners may ask IRCA temporary resident applicants wishing to be tested at the time of their interviews on the Section 312 requirements of a minimal understanding of ordinary English and a knowledge and understanding of the history and government of the United States. The INS examiner may ask the applicant to reply to any of the questions.

The list of questions/answers was compiled by the INS Central Office Legalization Unit and is based on the Level I series of the Federal Citizenship Texts.

The list is being disseminated as a study tool to IRCA applicants, authorized course providers, qualified designated entities, community and ethnic organizations and the general public.

For further information please contact Nydia Cope, INS Outreach Deputy Director, Room 2108, 425 I Street, N.W., Washington, DC 20536; phone 202/633-4123.

1. What are the colors of our flag?
2. How many stars are there in our flag?
3. What color are the stars on our flag?
4. What do the stars on our flag mean?
5. How many stripes are there in the flag?
6. What color are the stripes?
7. What do the stripes on the flag mean?
8. How many states are there in the Union?
9. What is the 4th of July?
10. What is the date of Independence Day?
11. Independence from whom?
12. What country did we fight during the Revolutionary War?
13. Who was the first President of the United States?
14. Who is the President of the United States today?
15. Who is the Vice-President of the United States today?
16. Who elects the President of the United States?
17. Who becomes President of the United States if the President should die?
18. For how long do we elect the President?
19. What is the Constitution?
20. Can the Constitution be changed?
21. What do we call a change to the Constitution?
22. How many changes or amendments are there to the Constitution?
23. How many branches are there in our government?
24. What are the three branches of our government?
25. What is the legislative branch of our government?
26. Who makes the laws in the United States?
27. What is Congress?

28. What are the duties of Congress?
29. Who elects Congress?
30. How many senators are there in Congress?
31. Can you name the two senators from your state?
32. For how long do we elect each senator?
33. How many representatives are there in Congress?
34. For how long do we elect the representatives?
35. What is the executive branch of our government?
36. What is the judiciary branch of our government?
37. What are the duties of the Supreme Court?
38. What is the supreme law of the United States?
39. What is the Bill of Rights?
40. What is the capital of the state?
41. Who is the current governor of your state?
42. Who becomes President of the United States if the President and the Vice President should die?
43. Who is the Chief Justice of the Supreme Court?
44. Can you name the thirteen original states?
45. Who said, "Give me liberty or give me death."?
46. Which countries were our enemies during World War II?
47. What are the 49th and 50th states of the Union?
48. How many terms can a President serve?
49. Who was Martin Luther King, Jr.?
50. Who is the head of your local government?
51. According to the Constitution, a person must meet certain requirements in order to be eligible to become President. Name one of these requirements.
52. Why are there 100 Senators in the Senate?

53. Who selects the Supreme Court justices?

54. How many Supreme Court justices are there?

55. Why did the Pilgrims come to America?

56. What is the head executive of a state government called?

57. What is the head executive of a city government called?

58. What holiday was celebrated for the first time by the American colonists?

59. Who was the main writer of the Declaration of Independence?

60. When was the Declaration of Independence adopted?

61. What is the basic relief of the Declaration of Independence?

62. What is the national anthem of the United States?

63. Who wrote the Star-Spangled Banner?

64. Where does freedom of speech come from?

65. What is the minimum voting age in the United States?

66. Who signs bills into law?

67. What is the highest court in the United States?

68. Who was President during the Civil War?

69. What did the Emancipation Proclamation do?

70. What special group advises the President?

71. Which President is called the "Father of our country"?

72. What Immigration and Naturalization Service form is used to apply to become a naturalized citizen?

73. Who helped the Pilgrims in America?

74. What is the name of the ship that brought the Pilgrims to America?

75. What were the 13 original states of the U.S. called?

76. Name 3 rights or freedoms guaranteed by the Bill of Rights.

77. Who has the power to declare war?

78. What kind of government does the United States have?

79. Which President freed the slaves?
80. In what year was the Constitution written?
81. What are the first 10 amendments to the Constitution called?
82. Name one purpose of the United Nations.
83. Where does Congress meet?
84. Whose rights are guaranteed by the Constitution and Bill of Rights?
85. What is the introduction to the Constitution called?
86. Name one benefit of being a citizen of the United States?
87. What is the most important right granted to U.S. citizens?
88. What is the United States Capitol?
89. What is the White House?
90. Where is the White House located?
91. What is name of the President's official home?
92. Name one right guaranteed by the first amendment.
93. Who is the Commander in Chief of the U.S. military?
94. Which President was the first Commander in Chief of the U.S. military?
95. In what month de we vote for the President?
96. In what month is the new President inaugurated?
97. How many times may a Senator be re-elected?
98. How many times may a Congressman be re-elected?
99. What are the 2 major political parties in the U.S. today?
100. How many states are there in the United States?

ANSWER SHEET

1. Red, White, and Blue
2. 50
3. White
4. One for each state in the Union
5. 13
6. Red and White
7. They represent the original 13 states
8. 50
9. Independence Day
10. July 4th
11. England
12. England
13. George Washington
14. George Bush
15. Dan Quayle
16. The electoral college
17. Vice-President
18. four years
19. The supreme law of the land
20. Yes
21. Amendments
22. 26
23. 3
24. Legislative, Executive, and Judiciary
25. Congress
26. Congress

App-192

27. The Senate and the House of Representatives
28. To make laws
29. The people
30. 100
31. (insert local information)
32. 6 years
33. 435
34. 2 years
35. The President, cabinet, and departments under the cabinet members
36. The Supreme Court
37. To interpret laws
38. The Constitution
39. The first 10 amendments of the Constitution
40. (insert local information)
41. (insert local information)
42. Speaker of the House of Representatives
43. (William Rehnquist)*
44. Connecticut, New Hampshire, New York, New Jersey, Massachusetts, Pennsylvania, Delaware, Virginia, North Carolina, South Carolina, Georgia, Rhode Island, and Maryland
45. Patrick Henry
46. Germany, Italy, and Japan
47. Hawaii and Alaska
48. 2
49. A civil rights leader
50. (insert local information)

51. Must be a natural born citizen of the United States; Must be at least 35 years old by the time he/she will serve; Must have live in the United States for at least 14 years
52. Two (2) from each state
53. Appointed by the President
54. Nine (9)
55. For religious freedom
56. Governor
57. Mayor
58. Thanksgiving
59. Thomas Jefferson
60. July 4, 1776
61. That all men are created equal
62. The Star-Spangled Banner
63. Francis Scott Key
64. The Bill of Rights
65. Eighteen (18)
66. The President
67. The Supreme Court
68. Abraham Lincoln
69. Freed many slaves
70. The Cabinet
71. George Washington
72. Form N-400, "Application to File Petition for Naturalization"
73. The American Indians (Native Americans)
74. The Mayflower
75. Colonies

76.
1. The right of freedom of speech, press, religion, peaceable assembly and requesting change of government.

2. The right to bear arms (the right to have weapons or own a gun, though subject to certain regulations).

3. The government may not quarter, or house, soldiers in the people's homes during peacetime without the people's consent.

4. The government may not search or take a person's property without a warrant.

5. A person may not be tried twice for the same crime and does not have to testify against him/herself.

6. A person charged with a crime still has some rights, such as the right to a trial and to have a lawyer.

7. The right to trail by jury in most cases.

8. Protects people against excessive or unreasonable fines or cruel and unusual punishment.

9. The people have rights other than those mentioned in the Constitution.

10. Any power not given to the federal government by the Constitution is a power of either the state or the people.

77. The Congress

78. Republican

79. Abraham Lincoln

80. 1787

81. The Bill of Rights

82. For countries to discuss and try to resolve world problems;

to provide economic aid to many countries.

83. In the Capitol in Washington, D.C.
84. Everyone (citizens and non-citizens living in the U.S.)
85. The Preamble
86. Obtain federal government jobs; travel with a U.S. passport; petition for close relatives to come to the U.S. to live
87. The right to vote
88. The place where Congress meets
89. The President's official home
90. Washington, D.C. (1600 Pennsylvania Avenue, N.W.)
91. The White House
92. Freedom of: speech, press, religion, peaceable assembly, and, requesting change of government
93. The President
94. George Washington
95. November
96. January
97. There is no limit
98. There is no limit
99. Democratic and Republican
100. Fifty (50)

EXCLUSION GROUNDS INA Sec. 212 (a) 8 USC Sec. 1l8.2 (a) Note: All grounds are waivable via parole 212(a)(5)	IMMIGRANTS	REFUGEES	LEGALIZATION (PRE-1982 ENTRANTS) AND EVD NATIONALS	SEASONAL AGRICULTURAL WORKERS	CUBANS & HAITIANS	PRE-1972 ENTRANTS (REGISTRY)
(1) Mentally retarded	Waivable 212 (g) [1-601] 212 (c) [1-191] Cf 234	Waivable 207 (c) (3) [Form 1-602]	Waivable 245A (d) (2) [Form 1-690]	Waivable 210 (c) (2) [1-690]	Waivable 212 (g) [1-601] Cf 234	Inapplicable
(2) Insane	Waivable 212 (c) Cf 234	Waivable 207 (c) (3)	Waivable 245A (d) (2)	Waivable 210 (c) (2)	Cf 234	Inapplicable
(3) Attack(s) of Insanity	Waivable 212 (c) 212 (g) Cf 234	Waivable 207 (c) (3)	Waivable 245A (d) (2)	Waivable 210 (c) (2)	Waivable 212(g) Cf 234	Inapplicable
(4) Psychopath, sex deviant, mental defect	Waivable 212 (c) Cf 234	Waivable 207 (c)(3)	Waivable 245A (d)(2)	Waivable 210 (c) (2)	Cf 234	Inapplicable
(5) Drug Addict alcoholic	Waivable 212 (c) Cf 234	Waivable 207 (c) (3)	Waivable 245A (d) (2)	Waivable 210 (c) (2)	Cf 234	Inapplicable
(6) Dangerous contagious disease	Waivable 212 (c) 212 (g)	Waivable 207 (c) (3)	Waivable 245A (d)(2)	Waivable 210 (c) (2)	Waivable 212(g)	Inapplicable
(7) Physical defect or disability effecting ability to earn a living	Waivable 213[1-352] 212 (c)	Waivable 207 (c) (3)	Waivable 245A (d) (2)	Waivable 210 (c) (2)	Waivable 213[1-352]	Inapplicable

EXCLUSION GROUNDS INA Sec. 212 (a) 8 USC Sec. 118.2 (a) Note: All grounds are waivable via parole 212(a)(5)	IMMIGRANTS	REFUGEES	LEGALIZATION (PRE-1982 ENTRANTS) AND EVD NATIONALS	SEASONAL AGRICULTURAL WORKERS	CUBANS & HAITIANS	PRE-1972 ENTRANTS (REGISTRY)
(8) Pauper, beggar, vagrant	Waivable 212 (c)	Waivable 207 (c)(3)	Waivable 245A (d) (2)	Waivable 210 (c) (2)		Inapplicable
(9) Convicted or admits crime of moral turpitude	Waivable 212 (h) [1-601] 212 (c)	Waivable 207 (c) (3)	NOT WAIVABLE under 245A (d) (2); 212 (h)?	NOT WAIVABLE under 210 (c) (2); 212 (h)?	Waivable 212 (h) [1-601]	Waivable under 212 (h) [1-601]
(10) Convicted of 2 offenses & sentenced to 5 years	Waivable 212 (h) 212 (c)	Waivable 207 (c) (3)	NOT WAIVABLE under 245A (d) (2); 212 (h)?	NOT WAIVABLE under 210 (c) (2); 212 (h)?	Waivable 212 (h)	Waivable under 212 (h)
(11) Polygamist	Waivable 212 (c)	Waivable 207 (c)(3)	Waivable 245A (d)(2)	Waivable 210 (c) (2)		
(12) Prostitute, Procurer	Waivable 212 (c) 212 (h)	Waivable 207 (c) (3)	Waivable 245A (d)(2)	Waivable 210 (c) (2)	Waivable 212 (h)	Waivable under 212 (h)
(13) Entry to engage in immoral sex act	Waivable 212 (c)	Waivable 207 (c) (3)	Waivable 245A (d)(2)	Waivable 210 (c) (2)		
(14) Entry to perform skilled/ unskilled work without Labor Certification	Waivable 212 (c) 212 (k) [1-193]	Inapplicable	Inapplicable	Inapplicable	Inapplicable	Inapplicable

App-198

EXCLUSION GROUNDS INA Sec. 212 (a) 8 USC Sec. 118.2 (a) Note: All grounds are waivable via parole 212(a)(5)	IMMIGRANTS	REFUGEES	LEGALIZATION (PRE-1982 ENTRANTS) AND EVD NATIONALS	SEASONAL AGRICULTURAL WORKERS	CUBANS & HAITIANS	PRE-1972 ENTRANTS (REGISTRY)
(15) Likely to become a public charge	Waivable 212 (c) 213	Inapplicable	Special Rule 245A (d)(2)(B); Waivable under 245A(d)(2), as to Temp. Res. Not Waivable as to Perm. Res. Cf 213	Special Rule 210 (c)(2); Not Waivable under 210 (c) (2) See 213	Inapplicable	Inapplicable
(16) Excluded within previous year, no permission to re-apply	Must seek permission to re-enter 8 CFR 212.2 [Form I-212] 212 (c)	Waivable 207 (c) (3)	Waivable under 245A (d) (2)	Waivable 210(c)(2)	Inapplicable	Inapplicable
(17) Deported or removed at Gov't expense within previous 5 yrs., no permission to re-apply	Must seek permission to re-enter 8 CFR 212.2 212 (c)	Waivable 207 (c) (3)	Waivable 245A (d) (2)	Waivable 210 (c) (2)	Inapplicable	Inapplicable
(18) Stowaway	Waivable 211 (b) [I-193] 212 (c)	Waivable 207 (c) (3)	Waivable 245A (d)(2)	Waivable 210 (c) (2)	Waivable 211(b) [I-193]	Inapplicable
(19) Seeks or procures visa or other doc. by fraud or willful misrep. of material fact	Waivable 212 (i) [I-601] 212 (c)	Waivable 207 (c) (3)	Waivable 245A (d)(2)	Waivable 210 (c) (2)	Waivable 212i [I-601]	Inapplicable

EXCLUSION GROUNDS INA Sec. 212 (a) 8 USC Sec. 118.2 (a) Note: All grounds are waivable via parole 212(a)(5)	IMMIGRANTS	REFUGEES	LEGALIZATION (PRE-1982 ENTRANTS) AND EVD NATIONALS	SEASONAL AGRICULTURAL WORKERS	CUBANS & HAITIANS	PRE-1972 ENTRANTS (REGISTRY)
(20) Not in possession of valid entry doc. and passport	Waivable 211 (b) 212 (c) 212 (k)	Inapplicable	Inapplicable	Inapplicable	Inapplicable	Inapplicable
(21) Visa not issued in compliance with numberical limitations	Waivable 212 (c) 211 (b) 212 (k)	Inapplicable	Inapplicable	Inapplicable	Inapplicable	Inapplicable
(22) Ineligible to citizenship	Waivable 212 (c)	Waivable 207 (c) (3)	Waivable 245A (d)(2)	Waivable 210 (c) (2)		Inapplicable
(23) Drug-related conviction	Waivable 212 (c)	Waivable 207 (c) (3) except trafficking	NOT WAIVABLE under 245A (d)(2) unless marijuana- less than 30 grams	NOT WAIVABLE under 210 (c)(2) unless marijuana- less than 30 grams		Waivable under 212 (h) if less than 30 grams of marijuana
(24) Arrived on non-signatory line	Waivable 212 (c)	Waivable 207 (c) (3)	Waivable 245A (d)(2)	Waivable 210 (c)(2)		Inapplicable
(25) Illiterate over age 16	Waivable 212 (b) 212 (c)	Inapplicable	Inapplicable	Inapplicable	Inapplicable	Inapplicable
(26) Not in possession of a valid passport or visa at entry	Waivable 211 (b)	Waivable 207 (c) (3)	Waivable 245A (d) (2)	Waivable 210 (c)(2)	Waivable 211 (b)	Inapplicable

EXCLUSION GROUNDS INA Sec. 212 (a) 8 USC Sec. 118.2 (a) Note: All grounds are waivable via parole 212(a)(5)	IMMIGRANTS	REFUGEES	LEGALIZATION (PRE-1982 ENTRANTS) AND EVD NATIONALS	SEASONAL AGRICULTURAL WORKERS	CUBANS & HAITIANS	PRE-1972 ENTRANTS (REGISTRY)
(27) Likely to engage in activities prejudicial to the public interest	Inapplicable 1-1-88 to 2-28-89 If Constitutionally Protected activity					
(28) Anarchist, Communist, Subversive, advocate overthrow of U.S. Distributor, writer etc. of subversive material * Unless involuntary or actively opposed for 5 years	Inapplicable 1-1-88 to 2-28-89 If Constitutionally protected activity	Waivable 207 (c) (3)				
(29) Spy, sabateur, national security threat	Inapplicable 1-1-88 to 2-28-89 If Constitutionally protected activity					
(30) Accompanying excluded alien	Waivable 212 (c)	Waivable 207 (c) (3)	Waivable 245A (d) (2)	Waivable 210 (c) (2)		Inapplicable
(31) Aided alien smuggling for gain	Waivable 212 (c)	Waivable 207 (c) (3)	Waivable 245A (d) (2)	Waivable 210 (c) (2)		Inapplicable

EXCLUSION GROUNDS INA Sec. 212 (a) 8 USC Sec. 118.2 (a) Note: All grounds are waivable via parole 212(a)(5)	IMMIGRANTS	REFUGEES	LEGALIZATION (PRE-1982 ENTRANTS) AND EVD NATIONALS	SEASONAL AGRICULTURAL WORKERS	CUBANS & HAITIANS	PRE-1972 ENTRANTS (REGISTRY)
(32) Foreign med. school grad who hasn't passed NBME exam		Inapplicable	Inapplicable	Inapplicable	Inapplicable	Inapplicable But see INS Memo 5-19-87
(33) Associated with the Nazis			NOT WAIVABLE	NOT WAIVABLE		Inapplicable But see INS Memo 5-19-87
212 (e) Exchange-visitor- 2 years foreign resid. requirement	Waivable 212 (e) [I-612]		Legalization: Waivable 212(e) [I-612] EVD Nationals: Not Applicable	Waivable 212 (e) [I-612]	Waivable 212 (e)?	Applicability unclear See INS Memo 5-19-87

LIBRARY USE ONLY
DOES NOT CIRCULATE